The Widening Gulf

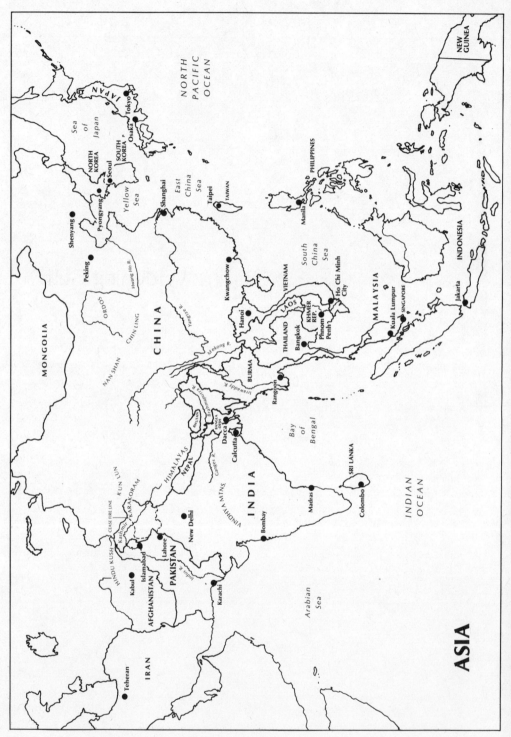

ASIA

The Widening Gulf

Asian Nationalism and American Policy

Selig S. Harrison

THE FREE PRESS
A Division of Macmillan Publishing Co., Inc.
NEW YORK

Collier Macmillan Publishers
LONDON

To Barbara, Cole, and Kit

The Free Press
A Division of Macmillan Publishing Co., Inc.
866 Third Avenue, New York, N.Y. 10022

Collier Macmillan Canada, Ltd.

Library of Congress Catalog Card Number: 76-57881

Printed in the United States of America

printing number

1   2   3   4   5   6   7   8   9   10

Library of Congress Cataloging in Publication Data

Harrison, Selig S
   The widening gulf.

   Includes bibliographical references and index.
   1.   Asia--Foreign relations--United States.
2.   United States--Foreign relations--Asia.
3.   Nationalism--Asia.   I.   Title.
DS33.4.U6H35   327.73'05   76-57881
ISBN 0-02-914080-3

Contents

Preface   ix

I NATIONALISM AND POWER

1. The Meaning of Nationalism   3

    The Drive to Catch Up
    Nationalism or Subnationalism?
    The Dimensions of Identity
    Nationalism and Growth
    The Two Faces of Nationalism

II NATIONALISM AND COMMUNISM

2. The Limits of Asian Communism   45

    India: The Costs of Subnationalism
    In-Groups and Out-Groups
    Indonesia: The Legacy of Madiun
    The Poverty Factor in Perspective

3. Nationalism and Maoism   69

    The Anti-Japanese Banner
    The "Peasant Nationalism" Debate
    Country in Danger

4. Vietnam: Nationalism Ascendant   87

    The Land Question and the United Front Strategy
    Ethnicity and Elitism: The Noncommunist Alternative
    The Gold Sword of Legitimacy
    The Taint of Collaboration
    Catholics and Buddhists

Unification: The Built-In Disability
The "Southern Solution"
The American Label
Flies in Amber

5. Korea: Nationalism Neutralized   131

Rule or Ruin
The Northern Base of North Korean Communism
The Making of a National Legend
Puppet Liberated
The Communist Dilemma in the South

III NATIONALISM AND THE AMERICAN EXPERIENCE

6. After Vietnam: Asia Alienated   159

Japan: The Lessons of North China
The Constraints of Dependence
"Support" Reappraised
Allies and Mercenaries
The Vulnerable Dominoes

7. After Korea: The Stresses of Division   209

Nationalism Goes Underground
Containing the Unification Issue
"Development First"
Peaceful, Yes; Coexistence, No
The American Role and the Korean Image

8. Nationalism and the American Military Presence   253

On Balancing Power
The Pakistan Alliance: Case History of a Mistake
Burden-Sharing and a Nuclear Japan

9. Nationalism and the American Economic Presence   311

Nationalism and Foreign Investment
Nationalism and Public Enterprise
Has India Failed?
Japan, China, and the United States

IV NATIONALISM AND AMERICAN POLICY

10. The Future of U.S. Military Policy in Asia   361

The Case for an Indigenous Balance of Power
The Case for a Detached U.S. Posture
Bases, Military Aid, and Arms Control

The idea for this book was first suggested to me by Walter Lippmann in 1966 following my return from an assignment in South Asia and the publication of an article* in which I surveyed the wreckage of American policy in India and Pakistan in the aftermath of the 1965 war. It was possible to pursue the task seriously, however, only when I was invited by the Brookings Institution to serve as senior fellow in charge of Asian studies during 1967 and 1968. This appointment enabled me to conduct extensive field research in parts of Asia in which I had not lived and stimulated a new interest in East Asia. Immediately thereafter, four years as a correspondent based in Tokyo greatly enlarged the original concept of the book, and an appointment as a senior fellow at the East-West Center in Honolulu in 1972-1973 gave me the opportunity to begin the writing.

I would like to record my gratitude to Brookings and to the East-West Center for their support and interest. In particular, I would like to thank H. Field Haviland, Jr., former director of foreign policy studies at Brookings, and Henry Owen, his successor; Lyle Webster and Michio Nagai, who served as directors of the East-West Communication Institute at the East-West Center during the period of my work there; and Everett Kleinjans and John Brownell, chancellor and vice-chancellor, respectively, of the East-West Center. Above all, I am indebted to Philip Foisie, assistant managing editor of the *Washington Post*, in charge of its foreign coverage, whose confidence enabled me to live and work for ten memorable years in a wide range of Asian countries as a foreign correspondent. The commitment of the *Post* to the serious reporting of foreign affairs made it possible for me to explore the Asian environment in a manner not normally possible for newspapermen confronted with deadline pressures.

Among the many colleagues who have helped with research, editing, and translation at various stages of this enterprise, I should mention Judith Davison, Ann Overby Kay, and Sallie Mitchell, formerly of Brookings; Seiji Yamaoka, formerly of the *Washington* bureau in Tokyo; Patricia Loui, of the East-West Center; Sian Fisher, of the Carnegie Endowment for International have profited greatly from comments on early drafts of the text by A. Doak Barnett, John K. Fairbank, George McT. Leslie Embree, Rupert Emerson, and Richard L. Park. However, of these colleagues should be held responsible in any the views or interpretations presented herein.

I like to express a special word of thanks to Brookings East-West Center for supporting the translation of primary

son, "America, India, and Pakistan: A Chance for a Fresh Start," 1966, pp. 56-68.

11. The Future of U.S. Economic Policy in Asia   395

    The Challenge of Public Enterprise
    New Approaches to Asian Industrialization

    V NATIONALISM, "ASIANISM," AND THE COLOR LINE

12. The Meaning of Regionalism   421

    Nationalism Writ Large
    Beyond the Balance of Power?
    Hiroshima, Vietnam, and the Taint of Racism
    "The Eastern Three"
    The Impact of U.S. Policy

Bibliography   450

Index   460

Preface

This is a book about the American encounter with nati
Asia, past and present, and about some of the ways in v
American policy could be more sensitive to nationalism
cover a lot of territory, the reader should recognize at t
I do not intend this to be a comprehensive work on
such. Nor do I seek to pay equal or symmetrical a
gamut of policy issues confronting the United State
full range of factors that would have to be add
encompassing all of the external relationships c
This volume is deliberately selective. Thus, I
develop a broad conceptual framework applica
nationalism in Asia as a whole but have focuse
a detailed examination of nationalism in tho
most relevant for an understanding of the
Given the special American preoccupation y
I have made an intensive effort to analy
nationalism and communism, utilizing
proach that was not necessary in dealin
American experience. Similarly, in discu
the United States, I have made no e
placing this discussion alongside a p
attitudes toward the Soviet Union an

In its methodology, this work r
investigative techniques of journal
achieve a richer result than eit
basic approach has been determir
countries as a journalist over a
time, this volume is not an
Rather, I have used my expe
complementary academic rese

11. The Future of U.S. Economic Policy in Asia   395

The Challenge of Public Enterprise
New Approaches to Asian Industrialization

V NATIONALISM, "ASIANISM," AND THE COLOR LINE

12. The Meaning of Regionalism   421

Nationalism Writ Large
Beyond the Balance of Power?
Hiroshima, Vietnam, and the Taint of Racism
"The Eastern Three"
The Impact of U.S. Policy

Bibliography   450

Index   460

Preface

This is a book about the American encounter with nationalism in Asia, past and present, and about some of the ways in which future American policy could be more sensitive to nationalism. Although I cover a lot of territory, the reader should recognize at the outset that I do not intend this to be a comprehensive work on nationalism as such. Nor do I seek to pay equal or symmetrical attention to the gamut of policy issues confronting the United States in Asia and the full range of factors that would have to be addressed in a book encompassing all of the external relationships of Asian countries. This volume is deliberately selective. Thus, I have attempted to develop a broad conceptual framework applicable to the study of nationalism in Asia as a whole but have focused for the most part on a detailed examination of nationalism in those countries and cases most relevant for an understanding of the American experience. Given the special American preoccupation with communism in Asia, I have made an intensive effort to analyze the interplay between nationalism and communism, utilizing a country-by-country approach that was not necessary in dealing with other aspects of the American experience. Similarly, in discussing Asian attitudes toward the United States, I have made no effort to sweeten the pill by placing this discussion alongside a parallel consideration of Asian attitudes toward the Soviet Union and other non-Asian powers.

In its methodology, this work represents an attempt to unite the investigative techniques of journalism and scholarship and thus to achieve a richer result than either would separately permit. Its basic approach has been determined by my direct contact with Asian countries as a journalist over a twenty-six-year period. At the same time, this volume is not an impressionistic, first-person report. Rather, I have used my experience as the point of departure for a complementary academic research effort.

The idea for this book was first suggested to me by Walter Lippmann in 1966 following my return from an assignment in South Asia and the publication of an article* in which I surveyed the wreckage of American policy in India and Pakistan in the aftermath of the 1965 war. It was possible to pursue the task seriously, however, only when I was invited by the Brookings Institution to serve as senior fellow in charge of Asian studies during 1967 and 1968. This appointment enabled me to conduct extensive field research in parts of Asia in which I had not lived and stimulated a new interest in East Asia. Immediately thereafter, four years as a correspondent based in Tokyo greatly enlarged the original concept of the book, and an appointment as a senior fellow at the East-West Center in Honolulu in 1972-1973 gave me the opportunity to begin the writing.

I would like to record my gratitude to Brookings and to the East-West Center for their support and interest. In particular, I would like to thank H. Field Haviland, Jr., former director of foreign policy studies at Brookings, and Henry Owen, his successor; Lyle Webster and Michio Nagai, who served as directors of the East-West Communication Institute at the East-West Center during the period of my work there; and Everett Kleinjans and John Brownell, chancellor and vice-chancellor, respectively, of the East-West Center. Above all, I am indebted to Philip Foisie, assistant managing editor of the *Washington Post*, in charge of its foreign coverage, whose confidence enabled me to live and work for ten memorable years in a wide range of Asian countries as a foreign correspondent. The commitment of the *Post* to the serious reporting of foreign affairs made it possible for me to explore the Asian environment in a manner not normally possible for newspapermen confronted with deadline pressures.

Among the many colleagues who have helped with research, typing, and translation at various stages of this enterprise, I should like to mention Judith Davison, Ann Overby Kay, and Sallie Mitchell, formerly of Brookings; Seiji Yamaoka, formerly of the *Washington Post* bureau in Tokyo; Patricia Loui, of the East-West Center; and Susan Fisher, of the Carnegie Endowment for International Peace. I have profited greatly from comments on early drafts of the manuscript by A. Doak Barnett, John K. Fairbank, George McT. Kahin, Ainslie Embree, Rupert Emerson, and Richard L. Park. However, none of these colleagues should be held responsible in any degree for the views or interpretations presented herein.

I should like to express a special word of thanks to Brookings and the East-West Center for supporting the translation of primary

*Selig S. Harrison, "America, India, and Pakistan: A Chance for a Fresh Start," *Harper's*, July 1966, pp. 56-68.

source materials in Asian languages, especially Japanese, Korean, Chinese, Vietnamese, Indonesian, Thai, and Lao. In transliterations from these languages, I have used the Wade-Giles system for Chinese, the Hepburn system for Japanese, and the Reischauer-McCune system for Korean. However, exceptions have been made in certain cases in which a political figure or author is known abroad under a name transliterated differently. In these cases the standard system is modified to make the name comprehensible to Western readers (e.g. Park Chong-hui, Rhee Syngman, and Kim Il-sung) or, in the case of authors, abandoned entirely in favor of the form used by the author. I should like to express my thanks to Gari Ledyard, Suh Dae-sook, and Millidge Walker, among others, for their assistance in reviewing the transliterations used by the many translators who have assisted me at various stages of this work, but the responsibility for any errors is solely my own. Regrettably, the orthographic complexities of Vietnamese and certain other languages have made it typographically impracticable to include the appropriate diacritical markings, and the use of a sharp, rather than a curved, diacritical in the case of Korean is also dictated by typographical limitations.

Access to Asian language materials greatly strengthened my confidence in my assessments of Asian attitudes and greatly enriched my analysis. Indeed, if this book enhances understanding between Asia and the United States, it will be largely because it gives Asian voices the attention and respect all too often lacking in U.S.-centered appraisals of the Asian scene.

I
NATIONALISM
AND POWER

1. The Meaning of Nationalism

The necessary first step in seeking to understand the American experience in Asia and in charting a future approach to American policy is to place the contemporary Asian scene in its correct historical time frame. For behind all the mini-debates on transitory, specific issues of policy lies a larger and more fundamental debate over where Asia stands in its passage through the age of nationalism. In its broadest sense, this is a debate over what the concept of "nationalism" means today in the Asian context. The nature of American interests in Asia and proposals concerning the future American presence can be meaningfully discussed only in the light of this overarching issue. This book begins, accordingly, at the Asian end of the telescope, defining the Asian context as it molds and limits policy choices—in contrast to others that have started at the American end, first identifying American objectives and only then giving incidental attention to the limitations imposed by the Asian environment.

THE DRIVE TO CATCH UP

By and large, American policy since World War II has rested on the implicit assumption that nationalism in Asia is a passing phenomenon destined to wane in strength as the colonial past recedes and as modern technology releases ever more powerful "transnational" forces. Zbigniew Brzezinski has been a representative spokesman of this view, contending that in the "technetronic era" of satellite communication and jet aircraft, nationalism remains "a principal object, but no longer the vital subject, of dynamic processes" and is progressively "diluted" as it becomes increasingly anachronistic.[1]

3

This "nationalism" is seen implicitly in European terms. It is loosely equated with the concept of self-determination and identified, in particular, with the search for linguistic and ethnic self-determination that came to its climax in Europe during the nineteenth century. Nationalism has already passed its zenith, in these terms, wherever self-determination has been achieved in Asia through the expulsion of colonial powers. Where the postcolonial state contains multiple linguistic and ethnic groups, the subnationalism of these groups is perceived as an expression of arrested self-determination, and the subnational identity is seen, accordingly, as a more authentic embodiment of nationalism than the larger identity resulting from the accidents of colonial cartography. In this perspective, the need for "nation-building" in socially heterogeneous Asian states is a measure of the obsolescence of nationalism in twentieth-century terms. Where "nation-building" succeeds in these states, the result will be an artificial monument to a contrived nationalist ideal; where Balkanization triumphs, the product will often be an entity too small to be economically viable. Sooner or later, in this view, all of the new states of Asia, regardless of size and social composition, will be overlain or superseded by regional institutions that will reach out, in turn, to the Western world, facilitating the infusion of "transnational" influences into Asia. Nationalism and regionalism are juxtaposed as opposites, representing basically different urges, just as subnationalism and nationalism are viewed as mutually contradictory.

It is the premise of this book that a concept of nationalism restricted by the narrow confines of European experience is only superficially relevant to the developing countries today and is peculiarly blind to the character and power of nationalism in Asia. To be sure, the experience of Europe has not been uniform. In France, Germany, and Italy, self-determination was achieved through a process of unification; whereas in the Balkans self-determination came with the disintegration of the multilingual Austro-Hungarian empire. Still, in both cases, nationalism arose within a relatively limited political universe in which European peoples were seeking to redefine their identities in relation to each other. By contrast, nationalism in Asia has emerged in a complex global environment. It comes as a response to inequities of wealth and power that not only are more severe and more pervasive than those of Europe in earlier centuries but also are reinforced by basic racial divisions. The continuing strength of nationalism in Asia cannot be adequately understood, therefore, solely in terms of the desire to assert linguistic, cultural, or ethnic identity as such. This desire goes together with an urge to find political foci of identity and self-respect that can provide relief from the inferiority feelings generated by white, Western dominance. In the first stages of this search, language, culture, or ethnicity may define the horizons of identity, but nationalism frequently finds more satisfactory realization in a larger unity. Subnationalism, nationalism, and regionalism are all expressions of the same hunger for a reordering of world power relationships.

It should be noted that one must distinguish sharply between the narrow popular usage of "nationalism" (interchangeably with "patriotism" or "chauvinism") to denote national pride, or the belief that one's own country is best, and the usage of "nationalism" here in a larger sense to describe the motive force that impels societies to define and assert their identity in relation to a particular historical environment. In Asia, as we shall see, nationalism in this historical sense can best be understood as the aspiration for greater equity in relation to the West, reflected in a search for the most appropriate and workable vehicles of the Asian response to Western dominance. In many ways, this nationalism offers parallels to the European model, but it also has specifically Asian aspects.

The surface resemblance between the European experience and the contemporary scene is that the breakdown of traditional societies under the impact of industrialization led to the rise of new social identities in Europe and to a consequent crystallization of new nation-states in a process broadly similar to the convulsion of social change now taking place in the developing countries. Compared with the tumultuous character of the postcolonial upheaval in Asia, Africa, and Latin America, however, the passing of traditional societies in Europe was a relatively tame affair in which the number of people embraced in expanding networks of "social mobilization"[2] grew by slow stages. In most cases, it was the middle class that spearheaded national revolt since an exclusive national preserve offered this new class the most promising arena for the pursuit of its economic, cultural, and political ambitions. Now history is "syncopated,"[3] and a process that unfolded over centuries in the past is telescoped into decades. Entire societies, suddenly exposed to wholesale appeals for social and political justice, are rapidly acquiring a generalized recognition of their rights and their collective strength. New communications and transportation technologies offer new opportunities to transcend social diversity and organize vast populations. Far from signaling the death knell of nationalism, the global reach of the multinational corporations and other "transnational" economic forces only steps up the syncopation, continually churning up new layers of social consciousness at an intensifying rate.

As newly activated millions look to new horizons, they gravitate initially to caste, tribal, linguistic, or other primary social identities in a seeming repetition of the European pattern. But something new has been added. Today, this newly aroused social awareness arises for the most part against the backdrop of a deeply humiliating common experience of foreign incursions or direct colonial rule less than a generation ago, followed by a sharp, continuing divide between the "have-not" continents and the North American–European–Soviet "West." In contrast to the narrow middle-class dynamic of nationalism in Europe at a time when the rest of the populace lagged behind in social awareness, in the developing countries nationalism is a more broadly based, multiclass response to Western dominance. The cry for justice is directed not only against rivals and oppressors close to home but also against the entire prevailing structure of global power. As John Fairbank has noted in the case of China, even if a country really has itself mainly to blame for its failure to modernize, this does little to alter its sense of victimization in the face of the present lopsided world order.[4]

Often, the anti-Western attitudes characteristically found in Asian countries are dismissed as a mere hangover of colonialism; in time, it is assumed, they will be dispelled by adequate doses of economic growth, competent administration, and cosmopolitanizing influences not present in the past. This assumption goes naturally with a myopic historical perspective in which the expulsion of the colonial power is regarded as the final fulfillment of nationalism. Viewed in a more meaningful perspective, however, the end of colonial rule marks the birth of nationalism, not its zenith, for it is only with the attainment of independence that the drive to catch up with the West can begin.

Seeking to define nationalism, John Kautsky has said that "anti-colonialism must be understood as opposition not merely to colonialism narrowly defined but also to a colonial economic status. It is opposition to colonialism so defined and to those nationals who benefit from the colonial relationship that constitutes nationalism in underdeveloped countries."[5] In itself, the advent of independence does not guarantee that nationalism will find effective political expression because nationalist objectives are often sacrificed by opportunistic leaders for personal or factional gain. For a variety of other reasons to be explored in this book, nationalism may be poorly mobilized in one country at a time when it is full blown in another. But independence heightens nationalist consciousness by bringing Asian countries face to face with global inequities and awakens an ever-growing desire for greater strength and adequacy in relation to the West. Nationalism thus becomes a visceral compulsion and is likely to assert and reassert itself for at least as long as Asia continues to feel a sense of subordination in world affairs.

Since the color line coincides with the global economic gap, the effort to catch up is a drive for a world of racial as well as economic equity. Asia has yielded the most virulent and deeply rooted expressions of this new nationalism because the colonial contact has been most intensive there[6] and because the major Asian cultural identities have an older, prouder, more continuous lineage than their less highly developed counterparts in Africa or Latin America. Even Japan, for all of its economic progress, is still propelled by an unsatisfied hunger for a position of full parity in world power relationships more than a century after Meiji, and even Japan has an Asian racial self-image in confronting the West despite its nouveau-riche condescension toward other Asian countries.

The fact that Japanese nationalism arose without the stimulus of colonial oppression underscores the essential character of nationalism in Asia as a broad response to Western dominance rather than as a reaction to the colonial experience narrowly viewed. At the very moment when nationalism was emerging with one meaning in the nineteenth-century European context, Japan was giving it a very different significance in its Asian expression as an instrument for warding off the newly perceived threat of Western domination and for organizing to attain equality of status with the Western powers. The nation-state model was not a compelling one for Asia at that point in history apart from its utility as a means of coping with the West. Each of the major Asian cultures was individually comparable to the all-embracing cultural framework of Christendom within which the separate Western nation-states arose. The concept of self-determination had little meaning where cultures were so self-contained and where each had produced such a strong sense of identity in its own terms. It eventually became necessary to define these identities anew not in relation to challenges felt within the Asian context but as part of a general Asian response to the Western intrusion.

When Japan set the pace in the Meiji period, the rest of Asia was not yet alert to the Western challenge and balked at abandoning traditional values until the full force of the colonial impact and the advancing industrial age had been felt. India had managed well enough with a "Universal Society whose common name is Hinduism," Rabindranath Tagore warned after a trip to Japan, and would lose what was distinctive in its nature if it sought to replace this with the "Universal Empire" represented by Western-style nationalism.[7] China struggled for decades between the claims of a "culturalism"[8] rooted in its image of itself as a self-sufficient "Middle Kingdom" and the political nationalism launched by Sun Yat-sen. In the end, nationalism took hold everywhere in Asia, stimulated by the parallel influx of Western political thought and the anti-imperialist message of Leninism, in addition to the direct shock of colonialism itself. No sooner had the colonial period ended than a new and even more intensive Western intrusion began in the postwar decades of American involvement. The American presence at one and the same time meant a massive penetration of modernizing influences on an unprecedented scale and brought a powerful but often slow-burning nationalist response.

Paradoxically, as contact with the West increases, the spirit of nationalism grows "but is less discernible because Western culture has been incorporated in indigenous culture."[9] This spirit is not to be confused with nativist resistance to all things foreign, for nativism is not the same thing as nationalism. Rather, nationalism in the sense discussed here is to be found in the urge for modernization itself. The modernizer who disdains obsolete tradition and embraces Western mores is most often motivated, behind it all, by a desire to make the nation stronger in relation to the West. He does not want to abandon his own national identity but to redefine and adapt it in order to confront the West as effectively as possible. Consciously or not, he tends to pick and choose taking those things from the West that fit most comfortably into his indigenous value system and social structure, sometimes at the cost of the modernization objective, sometimes not, depending on the nature of the indigenous institutions. It has thus become a truism that modernization does not necessarily mean westernization, and Japan is the prime case in point most often cited. But it is not enough to say that Japan remains "exceedingly Japanese" in the limited sense that it prefers to remain "culturally distinctive."[10] More than a sentimental attachment to old ways lies behind the "Japaneseness" that persists after the century of selective borrowing from the West initiated by the Meiji leaders. Modernization has not become westernization in Japan because the very reason for becoming modern in the first place was to stand up to the West both psychologically and politically.

As Edward Seidensticker has observed, the wisdom of the West was not seen as a challenge to tradition because "foreign learning was hardly thought of as wisdom at all, but rather as a mass of techniques. Japan was the repository of wisdom, and the techniques were but to shore it up."[11] A similar desire to copy from the West in order to compete with it underlies the drive for modernization in most developing countries today and thus constitutes a psychological common denominator found throughout Asia, in varying measure, despite the many conflicts of interest dividing Asian countries and the many internal social divisions complicating their response to the

West. This pervasive climate of nationalism embraces not only countries that were colonized but semicolonized China as well. In a more complex form, it now embraces Thailand, which escaped colonialism completely, and Korea, a victim of Asian colonialism at the hands of Japan. It is basically the same phenomenon in homogeneous Japan and in multilingual, heterogeneous India or Indonesia; in countries that won their freedom only through a bitter, sustained struggle and in others, like the Philippines and Malaysia, that emerged from colonialism under different circumstances and developed their nationalist consciousness after independence.

The frustrated aspiration of socially heterogeneous or socially stratified countries to assert coherent identities deserves the label of nationalism side by side with the more successfully mobilized nationalism of countries at later stages of social mobilization, "nation-building," and economic development. It is the aspiration itself that defines non-Western nationalism in a syncopated period of history in which the horizons of identity open up in such rapidly widening panoramas. With new layers of political consciousness continually unfolding, it is artificial to draw a tight distinction between dormant, "prenationalist" rural masses and the "nationalist fervor . . . of a relatively small portion of the population found mostly among the elite and urban-dwellers."[12] This distinction is blurred as the external pressures imposed by a shrinking world environment sharpen an expanding collective awareness of nascent identity. The circumstances in which nationalism is now emerging compel countries to defend their image of what they hope to become long before they actually get there. This is why Indian or Indonesian nationalism rests on powerful reserves of domestic support in the face of external challenges even though it lacks the internal vitality shown by Japanese or Chinese nationalism as models of more complete social mobilization and social change. This is why peoples weary of the old anticolonial slogans and impatient for tangible economic progress are nonetheless dedicated to achieving this progress on terms consistent with their new identities.

To say that nationalism is a psychological common denominator throughout Asia is not to suggest a monolithic Asian nationalism expressive of an "Asian mind." It is self-evident that "there is no Asia"[13] in cultural or racial terms. For purposes of this analysis, "Asia" is a meaningful reference group in the critical but limited sense that Asian countries find themselves, historically, in more or less the same boat vis-à-vis the West. This sensitizes their awareness of the kindred elements in disparate Asian cultural legacies. It gives Asians a feeling of racial community and of identification with other non-Western regions, similarly placed, notwithstanding the significant racial divisions within Asia. Asian consciousness of a shared historical destiny in relation to the West has produced broadly similar reflexes in responding to post-World War II American policies, and these policies, as it happens, have tended to treat the arc from Korea to Pakistan as a loosely related strategic and geopolitical category.

As a common response to Western dominance, nationalism generates an overall Asian effort to catch up economically; yet at the same time its primary vehicle, the nation-state, defines an internecine competition within Asia over the limited spoils of incremental progress. This seeming contradiction often overshadows the meaning of nationalism as a psychological common denominator in Asia. Envy and the competitive impulse are mingled with vicarious satisfaction when one Asian power scores points against a Western rival in the economic, political, or military sphere. This was true in 1905 when Japan won the Russo-Japanese War, and it is still true in the response of other Asian countries to the Japanese economic resurgence.

As we shall see in later chapters, Japan provokes widespread resentment when it seeks to dominate other Asian economies but wins applause from its neighbors when it stands up to the United States or the European Economic Community in economic disputes. China inspires more admiration than fear in Asia with its nuclear program; and Vietnam emerged as a symbol of Asian bravery and determination in resisting superior Western strength. When one Asian power makes progress or is able to hold its ground in a confrontation with a Western power, other Asian states find at least a temporary sense of relief from their inferiority feelings as well as enhanced hope for a general reordering of East-West relationships in which all Asian states are likely to fare more equitably. For this reason, it is just as misleading to focus solely on the differences dividing Asia as it is to overrate the potential for regional cooperation. Similarly, as we shall elaborate in Chapter 8, even Asian countries without already developed petroleum resources have had mixed feelings in the face of the price increases enforced by the Organization of Petroleum Exporting Countries (OPEC). Despite the immediate hardships involved, most Asian countries have identified their own long-term interests with OPEC efforts to drive a harder bargain with the West and to "index" world trade in raw materials, food, and industrial goods.

NATIONALISM OR SUBNATIONALISM?

The missing dimension in Western thinking about nationalism was highlighted in a comment by Henry A. Kissinger in the course of a discussion on developing countries. It is a "curious" nationalism, he said, "which defines itself not, as in Europe, by common language or culture but often primarily by the common experience of foreign rule."14 The most striking deficiency in this observation is that Kissinger failed to distinguish the receding legacy of colonialism from the ongoing challenge of Western dominance and thereby inherently underrated the continuing power of nationalism in Asia. But equally important, Kissinger viewed the linguistic and cultural component of nationalism in isolation, without reference to the drive for a balance of power with the West. On the one hand, he was peculiarly insensitive to the strength of nationalism in a homogeneous country such as Japan, where it not only represents a response to Western dominance but also has the added cohesion and force provided by a common linguistic, cultural, and ethnic identity. On the other, he implicitly underestimated the potential of nationalism as a unifying force in socially heterogeneous Asian states, where the divisive pull of subnational identities is moderated by the desire for a strong posture in world affairs.

By seeking to apply the European model to Asia, the non-Asian observer loses sight of the critically important interdependence between nationalism and subnationalism. What this missing dimension implies can best be appreciated by pondering for a moment the postcolonial map of Asia. The homogeneity of Japan and Korea are striking exceptions to a general pattern of states notable for their internal cultural, linguistic, religious, and ethnic differences, often overlapping and often reinforced by economic disparities. India is the most dramatic case, with nine major language territories arrayed around the Hindi-speaking Gangetic plain and regional caste identities that are normally defined by linguistic boundaries. Indonesia and the Philippines, as archipelagoes, exemplify the special problems arising when variations of language or dialect coincide with territorial fragmentation. West Pakistan remains a cauldron of conflict between four distinct linguistic groups following the separation of Bangladesh. Sri Lanka is the scene of a continuing struggle between a dominant majority and a significant minority separated by mutually reinforcing cultural, religious, and linguistic differences. Burma, Thailand, and Laos are all polyglots with substantial tribal minorities. Even China is far from homogeneous. On top of the significant ethnic minorities along its periphery, the vast Han heartland encompasses eight separate spoken languages, providing the basis, in part, for distinct and ancient provincial identities that have recurrently defined the boundaries of warlordism during periods of a weak central authority. In all of these instances, internal social differences provide a persistent basis for subnational movements, and an automatic transposition of the European model could lead to the simplistic conclusion that Asia is inevitably in for a rerun of Balkanization.

Up to a point, the European model has a certain limited validity if only because many of the incongruous cartographic legacies of the colonial period are still intact. One such legacy was the creation of a geographically bifurcated state lumping Moslem Bengalis in the east together with Moslem Punjabis, Sindhis, Baluchis, and Pathans in the west solely on the basis of religion despite 1,000 miles of intervening Indian territory. This was patently "extraordinary" and "unnatural," as former prime minister Sato of Japan later exclaimed;[15] and in the absence of a shift to a looser, confederate relationship, the separation of Bangladesh from West Pakistan unfolded like a Greek tragedy, corresponding broadly to the nationalist protest movements of oppressed linguistic minorities in Europe. The case of Pakistan is an unusual one, however, since its separating eastern wing had a larger population than the "parent" western wing. By contrast, in other socially heterogeneous Asian states, there is a more stable power relationship between majority and minority groups. In Indonesia, the Javanese constitute 58 percent of the national population, and the next largest group, the Sundanese, do not equal Javanese strength even when combined with the lesser Madurese and Balinese.

In Sri Lanka, the Sinhalese command a 67 percent majority, and even in India, where the Hindi bloc claims only 37 percent of the population and falls short of unchallengeable dominance, non-Hindi language groups are each so much smaller than the Hindi population that an uneasy equilibrium has been achieved. In Burma, where tribal disaffection has taken unusually stubborn form, the Shans, Karens, and Kachins each claim only 6 percent, 7 percent, and 7 percent of the population, respectively; in Laos, the non-Lao tribes total only 31 percent of the population. Most separatist movements in Asia reflect the aspirations of minorities using the threat of separation to maximize local autonomy and achieve a more equitable relationship with dominant majorities. In this characteristic pattern of multilingual, multiethnic states in Asia, "nationalists" and "subnationalists" are seldom clearly distinguishable because subnationalism and nationalism are both expressions of a common Asian awakening in relation to the West.

India offers both the most obvious parallel with the European model and the most dramatic illustration of a promising attempt to reconcile nationalism and subnationalism. Regional business groups were prime movers in the successful campaign for the redemarcation of state boundaries in India along linguistic lines. They were seeking a stronger political position in order to compete more effectively in the economic sphere with pan-Indian Marwari business monopolies, a competition strikingly similar to the rivalry between the rising

Balkan middle classes and the Viennese financiers in the Austro-Hungarian empire. As I have suggested in an earlier work, however, the two situations are radically different because centrifugal forces in India today are operating side by side with "the quite contradictory urge for unified national power in the face of the power of others," and this urge "to confront other world powers on equal terms is an elemental urge common to all Indians."[16] The tempestuous interplay between centrifugal and centripetal forces molds Indian political institutions and has a critical impact on economic development. But it will not necessarily break up the Indian union because an Indian identity based on a harmonization of subnational identities gives a greater sense of relief from the inferiority feelings produced by Western dominance than would an exclusively Tamil or Marathi or Malayali identity. The underlying spirit of Indian nationalism was reflected on the eve of independence by Rajendra Prasad, later India's first president. Seeking to rebut advocates of a separate Pakistan who argued that the new Moslem-majority state would be bigger than some of the smaller European nations, Prasad exclaimed: "Why should we be content to be bigger than the smallest of the smaller ones of Europe? Why should we not aim at an India that will be bigger than the biggest of Europe, bigger than the biggest of America, very nearly as big as the biggest of Asia? Is not that an ambition worth living and dying for?"[17]

The horizons of social consciousness in Asia can be likened to a series of concentric circles. Newly activated social awareness is defined initially by the inner circle of one's identity, but a narrow clan, caste, tribal or regional focus is gradually extended to encompass the national state as rising economic expectations merge with a sharpening perception of the competitive challenge posed by other states. In an age of bigness, the larger unit generally offers both a greater sense of security against predatory neighbors and greater hope for economic progress. The larger unit has intrinsically greater attractive power, however, only to the extent that it coincides with horizons of identity meaningful in social, historical, or cultural terms as a source of psychological support in the contemporary world setting. It is "the linguistic core of human identity"[18] that most readily defines these horizons except in special circumstances. The meaning of being Japanese or Vietnamese or Filipino is not essentially a matter of ethnicity or of fondness for traditions and customs that may have to be radically reshaped to suit changing needs. Rather, it lies in a sense of membership in a communication universe with shared emotional patterns setting this universe apart from others.

When an interlocking cultural, religious, and social unity subsumes linguistic identities, as in the case of the Sanskritic heritage in Hindu society, a political unity transcending linguistic differences can be constructed. Such a unity suffers from inherent stresses, but Indian nationalism has nonetheless shown great durability and resilience. Where religion alone is involved and the sociocultural cement is weaker, as in the case of Pakistan, a multilingual state is not necessarily viable. This was illustrated with special force in the separation of Bangladesh, when linguistic divisions were aggravated by the problem of geographic distance and by gross economic inequalities. The built-in dilemmas that bedeviled Pakistan were apparent long before the Bangladesh secession in the intractable constitutional stalemate over what it means to be an "Islamic state." Where kindred linguistic groups were given a common political umbrella for the first time by a colonial ruler, as in Indonesia, the colonial unit served as a natural receptacle for nationalism, though it remains to be seen whether an even larger "Maphilindo" identity will ultimately link more of the Malayo-Polynesian linguistic family. Conversely, where colonial boundaries reflected a divide-and-rule approach, as in Vietnam, the nationalist response was to brush aside subnational colonial units of administration and treat the outer circle of linguistic identity as the natural framework for a modern nationalism.

The lack of a continuous historical tradition of political unity in Vietnam was often cited during the war years as a rationale for separate North and South Vietnamese states. This argument totally ignored both the "syncopation factor" already noted and the vast historical time lag between Asia and the West despite the compression of centuries into decades. To place Asian countries in their correct historical time frame, one must think of them as passing through stages of national emergence comparable to those that characterized the rise of European states between the sixteenth and nineteenth centuries. Since the impact of the industrial revolution and the disruption of traditional societies have come to Asia so late, Asian countries are late starters in the search for identity. The moment of their social mobilization and national awakening has only now arrived, as it did for European states at earlier points in time, and the absence of a continuous political unity in the past under inauspicious historical circumstances is therefore beside the point. Not only is the global context different today, as we have seen, making the compulsion to find and assert an identity greater, but the tempo of national emergence is also greatly accelerated, and this increase in tempo means a much more concentrated focus on nationalist objectives at any one time than would otherwise be the case. The issue now is whether the bonds of language, culture, and historical memory are strong enough to provide the basis for a modern nationalism capable of harmonizing subnational differences, and in Vietnam the nationalist answer has been a categorical "yes."

Historians are not yet able to explain completely why the Vietnamese proved to be the only people who were incorporated as a Chinese province for an extended period and yet escaped permanent sinification. It is generally agreed, however, that the origins of Vietnamese identity can be clearly traced to the tenth-century collapse of the T'ang empire, with the recurrent impact of Chinese invasions in the eleventh, thirteenth, fifteenth, and eighteenth centuries gradually reinforcing a latent national consciousness rooted in common social institutions. The peasants who migrated southward from the Tonkin Delta to Annam and Cochin China went in large village groups, carrying their social structure and patterns of life with them, so that "wherever they settled, there was Vietnam, because Vietnam, as a totality and continuity of human existence, was the Vietnamese village."[19] Sociologically, Vietnam slowly acquired "the unity of a chain"[20] as migration followed migration. The Vietnamese Chu Nom script began to emerge alongside Chinese as early as the fourteenth century. In literary imagery, the ideal of a unified Vietnam gradually found expression in the concept of the *tram ho* (100 clans) and the triumph of the mandate of heaven principle despite continuing dynastic turmoil and feudal rivalries. When rival mandarin factions struggled over the succession to Emperor Le The Tung in the sixteenth century and the country was partitioned, both the Nguyen rulers in the south and their Trinh rivals in the north claimed power in the name of the prestigious Le dynasty. This appears more significant, in retrospect, than the often cited fact that for 150 years a wall separated north and south along the seventeenth parallel.

The Tay Son revolt in 1771 was explicitly dedicated to the reestablishment of unity, partly reflecting the aspirations of rising Vietnamese merchants who saw that an end to north-south barriers would open up bigger markets and improve their competitive position against local Chinese financiers. Here were the first faint stirrings of nationalism, spurred by elements of middle-class support similar in kind, if not in degree, to the middle-class drive behind the budding nationalisms of Europe at the same period. The short-lived Tay Son regime set up after a fifteen-year civil war officially encouraged the Chu Nom script for the first time. Both the torment and hope of the Tay Son period were mirrored in the first major literary work written in Chu Nom, *Kim Van Kieu*, a national epic treasured today throughout Vietnam.[21] A tenuous structure of unity had been reconstructed when a Nguyen descendant, Emperor Gia Long, unseated the Tay Son rulers in 1802 and restored the continuity of the imperial tradition interrupted by the Le collapse. It was this tradition that the last of the Nguyen line, Bao Dai, represented when he handed over the imperial seal to the Ho Chi Minh regime at the time of his abdication in 1946. Despite mounting foreign pressures on the loose structure of unity during the nineteenth century, Vietnam nominally held together until France partitioned the country in 1884, conducting diplomatic relations with foreign powers as a single entity. The colonial regime thereafter played systematically on conflicts of interest between rice-rich Cochin China and the rest of Vietnam in order to maintain the division of the country and to reestablish a South Vietnamese state after World War II. But the historical and cultural foundations were solidly established for the achievement of a modern Vietnamese identity superseding and reconciling subnational loyalties.

As islands, Okinawa and Taiwan provide unusually suggestive illustrations of the interaction between nationalism and subnationalism because subnational identity has been reinforced in both cases by the factor of territorial separation. Both have evolved distinctive local linguistic forms, spoken and written, falling short of the status of completely separate languages but going beyond mere dialect differences.[22] At the same time, both derive their ethnic and cultural identity as part of larger ethnic and cultural entities, and their search for a focus of political loyalty relevant in twentieth-century terms has gradually drawn them to these larger identities. The postwar American presence in Asia affected the timetable governing the search in both cases but has not fundamentally altered this broad historical trend.

During the postwar American occupation of Okinawa, a movement for independence developed in parallel with the drive for reversion to Japan, reflecting widespread fears that the island would once again be a neglected and exploited outpost of Tokyo as it had been in the prewar years. The heavy casualties suffered during the American invasion of 1945 were directly blamed on the fact that Japan had used the island as a defense buffer and stationed its troops there, thus inviting American attack. The Okinawan businessmen and American *colons* who promoted the independence movement argued that a continued U.S. military and investment presence would assure the economic vitality of the island. Still, despite the limited resource potential of Okinawa and the strength of the economic argument, the independence idea never gained serious momentum because Okinawans placed a higher value on their Japanese identity. This identity was basically perceived as a source of strength and security at a time when Japanese power was rising and a Sino-U.S. conflict was widely feared in Asia. Two decades of American military occupation had accentuated Okinawan feelings of "Asian" solidarity with Japan, and American bases, especially nuclear bases, were increasingly viewed not as an economic bonanza or a security guarantee but as a magnet likely to attract military trouble. Nationalism acquired its meaning for Okinawans as part of a newly reassertive Japanese nationalism animated by a world view almost identical with their own.

The position of Taiwan in relation to China differs significantly from that of Okinawa in relation to Japan for substantial historical reasons. After four decades of Japanese colonialism had blocked its links with the mother country, the island suddenly experienced unprecedented repression at the hands of its new refugee rulers from the mainland, first in the March 1947 massacre and later in the form of a refugee-dominated authoritarian regime granting only token representation to the island-born majority. This gave rise to the demand for a sovereign Taiwan, based on a "Taiwanese nationalism" that sought to distinguish the newly arrived mainlanders from the Taiwan-born Chinese who had immigrated during the seventeenth and eighteenth centuries. Fears of Communist economic controls on the part of Taiwan-born peasant proprietors and businessmen strengthened the desire for freedom from mainlander domination in any form. By its nature, however, the "Taiwan independence movement" was largely an offshoot of the cold war, resting as it did on hopes for special patronage from the United States or Japan or both.

In concrete terms, the "independence" demand proved to be more a symbol of opposition to Kuomintang rule than a serious objective in its own right as the cold war subsided. The concept of a sovereign Taiwan was also undermined by the rise of a resurgent Japan and the parallel emergence of a nuclear-armed China speaking more and more in the accents of Chinese nationalism. The growing Japanese economic hold over Taiwan established under the aegis of the Kuomintang regime reawakened the underlying sense of Chinese identity among the Taiwan-born Chinese and made it progressively more difficult for them to accept the prospect of a permanent dependence on Japan as the major source of sustenance for Taiwanese independence.[23] Significantly, the idea of a Taiwanese nationalism separate from Chinese nationalism had never been very strongly rooted on the island even during the colonial period. The "Taiwan National Movement" organized by local political and cultural leaders to combat the excesses of Japanese rule was not inspired by any clear vision of the future. To the extent that the movement had a long-term perspective, it was a Chinese perspective in which a strong, unified regime was expected to emerge on the mainland at some unspecified future time and to liberate the island. Historical studies recently published in Taiwan have described vividly the excitement generated by Sun Yat-sen's 1911 revolution among Taiwan Chinese on the island and abroad. Discussing the impact of Sun's rise on

Taiwanese students in Japan, a book of memoirs coauthored by five prominent veterans of the Taiwan movement observed that

> Before the 1911 Revolution, the fatherland was nothing but a disappointment to Taiwanese. The three words which Japanese commonly used to insult them were 'Ch'ing-kuo nu' (slaves of the Ch'ing Dynasty), and on this account, some Taiwanese students in Tokyo always had a sense of inferiority and tried to conceal their identity. But the success of the 1911 Revolution struck a ray of hope in the hearts of overseas students. Their national consciousness was stimulated, their sense of inferiority vanished, and they increasingly gravitated toward their fatherland. At the same time, they developed great confidence in their fatherland and put their hopes for freedom and the liberation of the Taiwanese in the future of their fatherland.[24]

One group of overseas students known as the 'tsu-kuo p'ai' (ancestors' country faction) "wanted to go back to the mainland and help to build the fatherland in order to hasten the day of liberation," the book recalled. In a similar vein, a Japanese intelligence report in 1930 said that the political activists on Taiwan

> can be divided into two groups. One group puts a lot of hope in the future of China; they think that in the near future China's situation will become more normal and that China will be a world power, at which point, naturally, it could recover Taiwan. Therefore, for the present, they seek only to preserve their national characteristics, nurture their strength, and wait for the time to come. With such a national consciousness, they long for China. Every time they open their mouths, they emphasize the 4,000 years of China's history to bolster their national confidence. . . . The other group doesn't have wild hopes about China; they emphasize Taiwan's own independence and existence. Their theory is that it is pointless for Taiwan to return to the fatherland, only to suffer the same despotic rule it is now suffering. . . . The source of this attitude, however, is disappointment with the present chaotic situation in China; they feel they have no alternative but to think this way. One day, when China becomes strong, it is inevitable that they will have the same point of view as the other group.[25]

Many observers have pointed out that the Japanese did not face the degree of resistance from the Taiwan Chinese that they did from the Koreans when the Japanese established their colonial rule in Korea, and have sought to explain this phenomenon by suggesting that the Taiwan Chinese were able to assimilate Japanese culture and mores more readily than the Koreans. It is argued often that the Taiwan Chinese were relatively content with Japanese rule. This explanation is partly valid in that there is a cultural basis for the congenital friction between Japanese and Koreans that does not exist between Japanese and Chinese. To suggest that Japanese colonialism sat lightly on Taiwan, however, is to ignore the latent feelings of political identification with the mainland that were stirring in Taiwan during the colonial period. Japanese rule came at a point in history when an effective central power had yet to emerge on the mainland and the Taiwan Chinese were only beginning to feel the gravitational pull of Chinese nationalism. By contrast, the postcolonial Japanese economic offensive that began after the Kuomintang takeover of the island in 1949 aroused a sharpened sense of Chinese identity because it came at a time when a well-established mainland regime was winning increasing international respect.

Emphasizing the psychological importance of Peking's emergence as a nuclear power, a Japanese visitor in 1970 found that "the native Taiwanese feel great pride as Chinese when Peking launches its satellites and missiles." The Kuomintang, he noted, has fostered a feeling of "Chineseness" that could ultimately backfire by emphasizing Chinese culture and the return to the mainland in school curricula.[26] With their distaste for Tokyo and their admiration for Peking growing apace, the Taiwan-born Chinese had lost interest in Japanese support for the independence objective even before the restoration of Japanese diplomatic ties with China in 1972. There was still widespread distrust of the Communist regime on the island in 1977, but there was also a new note of ambivalence marked by a growing hope that it might be possible, in time, to work out a "One China" accommodation with the mainland that would permit Taiwan to retain much of its economic autonomy. The result of this reappraisal was a reversal of the situation prevailing during the early postwar decades, when a Kuomintang rapprochement with Peking was regarded as the contingency most likely to bring a change in the status of Taiwan. Given the newly ambivalent attitude of the Taiwan-born majority, the Kuomintang was now cast as the foremost defender of the status quo and sought to disarm its critics by making limited concessions to the Taiwan Chinese. No longer able to claim the mantle of a mainland regime as a result of its ouster from the United Nations, it was forced to take on Taiwanese colors, to some extent, in order to justify its continued separate existence.

The complexities of the search for identity on the part of the Taiwan-born Chinese reminds us that nationalism in Asia involves something more than merely tidying up the map to make political boundaries correspond to ethnic and cultural realities. To be sure, the ethnic identity of the Taiwanese with other Chinese is incontestable, whether one views their migration from Fukien and other coastal provinces as the rebellious flight of "hardy pioneers" to a new frontier[27] or, instead, as part of a nationalist crusade to displace Dutch rule on the island and set up a springboard for liberating the mainland from Manchu rule.[28] Viewed purely in terms of ethnic and ancestral origin, however, the Taiwanese are not necessarily "more Chinese than . . . the early Americans were British."[29] What matters most to the Taiwanese in contemporary terms is not where they came from but where they are going. One vision of the future as a small island republic surrounded by giants, its economic life largely controlled from the outside, is weighed against the alternative of identification with an ambitious regime seeking to stake out a meaningful role in the world power game. To the extent that China has a gravitational pull, it lies in Peking's ability to give a more self-respecting identity to the Taiwan-born Chinese than they would have on their own. This depends, in turn, on whether China remains an economically viable, politically integrated state sufficiently sure of itself to combine autonomy for self-conscious subnational units with a unified military and diplomatic posture in relation to the non-Chinese world.

THE DIMENSIONS OF IDENTITY

The relationship between individual and group identity is a central element in the study of nationalism throughout the world but merits special emphasis in a study of nationalism in the special social and cultural circumstances of Asia. Increasingly, psychiatry and social psychology have recognized the importance of this relationship, going far beyond Freud's "ritual acknowledgment" of the "social factors" in individual personality development.[30] In contrast to Freud, who alluded vaguely to man as "a member" of a race, nation, caste, or profession,[31] Erich Fromm went on to state flatly that "the average man obtains his sense of identity from belonging to a nation, rather than from his being a 'son of man,' "[32] and Erik H. Erikson spoke of "the mutual complementation of ethos and ego, of group identity and ego identity."[33] Erikson's concept of "psychosocial" as distinct from "psychosexual" development stresses that "true identity . . . depends upon the support which the young individual receives from the collective sense of identity characterizing the social groups significant to him: his class, his nation, his culture."[34] Identity must rest on the foundations of a secure maternal relationship in the first of the "eight ages of man," Erikson argued, but at the critical stages of identity formation in later years a social identity must "confirm individual identity."[35] The ultimate discovery of identity where it exists in its "most central ethnic sense" involves feelings of "deep communality known only to those who share in it, and only expressible in words more mythical than conceptual . . . a process 'located' *in the core of the individual* and yet also *in the core of his communal culture*, a process which establishes, in fact, the identity of these two identities."[36]

As Lucian W. Pye has observed, Erikson's pioneering attempts to explain the interdependence between individual and group identity "can serve as a powerful intellectual tool for understanding the process of nationbuilding in transitional societies."[37] Erikson's central concern, however, was the leader-follower relationship as a factor in shaping identity,[38] and he thus stopped short of defining which group identity matters most and why. A more explicit attempt to probe the interplay between individual and group identities as a tool for political analysis is found in the writings of Harold R. Isaacs, who stresses that a group identity heightens or diminishes an individual's "sense of belongingness and the quality of his self-esteem" in accordance with "the *political* conditions in which his group identity is held, the relative measure of power or powerlessness with which it is endowed." Secondary sources of belongingness and self-esteem in social, educational, and occupational life are determinative in shaping individual personality, Isaacs contends, "only where the conditions created by the basic group identity do not get in the way." At bottom, the issue is one of "relative power," of "how dominant or how dominated is the group to which this new individual belongs? How static or how shifting is this condition, and how, therefore is he going to be able to see and to bear himself in relation to others?"[39] It is the "need for self-esteem, the need to acquire it, feel it, assert it," Isaacs concludes, "that has in our time become one of the major drives behind all our volcanic politics. The drive to self-assertion, to group pride, has fueled all the nationalist movements that broke the rule of the empires."[40]

The psychological factors discussed by Erikson, Isaacs, and others in universal terms have a special meaning in an Asian social and cultural milieu marked by a traditional emphasis on the place of the individual as part of larger collective personalities. The observations of two American psychiatrists after research in South Vietnam could be applied to most cases in Asia. According to Walter Slote, "The sense of a unique self in essential mastery over one's own destiny has been a severely limited concept for the Vietnamese [for he] regards himself as a component within a far greater totality . . . not one's family alone . . . a broader collective ego structure." In another view, for the Vietnamese "the 'me' is an illusion, not a reality. One fits into the totality of a family or a societal unity."[41] As a state of mind, this emphasis on the collectivity is expressed in the belief that a consensus rather than a majority is necessary to legitimize group action, a belief typified in the Indian *panchayat* tradition ("God Speaks in Five"), the Indonesian *mufakat* idea, and the Sino-Japanese *jen* ideal, measuring individual behavior by social yardsticks. As a sociological phenomenon, it leads to social structures that institutionalize the relationship between individual and group identity in unusually rigid and explicit form. In each Asian country, the nature of the social structure sets the primary boundaries of social identity and determines the degree of difficulty involved in forming a viable national unit. Thus Hindu society, at one extreme, poses peculiar problems for the architects of Indian nationalism quite apart from the problem of integrating a large Moslem minority, since caste identities delimited primarily by language boundaries have never been part of a pan-Indian structure of political unity with a single legitimate ruler at its apex. It is necessary to go from caste identity to regional identity to an Indian national identity in deliberate psychological leaps. In China and Vietnam, both falling somewhere in the middle of the spectrum, subnational identities are not similarly congruent with rigidly structured social groups. Fukienese or Annamite loyalties reflect a more soluble and loosely defined "provincialism" rooted in dialect variations and nuances of custom but tempered by the larger tradition of a Confucian order symbolized historically in one legitimate emperor.

By far the most striking case of a social structure suited to the needs of nationalism is that of Japan. One level of identity leads upward to the next in a hierarchy of integrated loyalties linking individual identity to a group identity bounded only by the horizons of the national state itself. The "conscious social engineers" of the early Tokugawa period neutralized the power of *daimyo* and *shogun* and made family loyalties inseparable from higher allegiances in an interlocking feudal hierarchy culminating in the emperor.[42] Korea and China lacked nonkinship intermediary allegiances connecting the bottom with the top of the social pyramid, and in the Korean case the monarchy descended into the political arena, thus becoming the symbol of a corrupt order in a role quite unlike that of the Japanese emperor. Francis L. K. Hsu has pointed out that their social institutions literally compel Japanese to find "permanent circles of intimacy" beyond the bounds of the family, in marked contrast to the Chinese case. Primogeniture in Japan means that all of the sons except the eldest, inheriting son have to go outside their original kinship group to seek their fortune, and the Japanese ethos quickly draws them into hierarchical group relationships. The key to this cohesion of the Japanese social structure lies in the spirit of the master-disciple relationship known as *iemoto*. Originally identified with the relationship between the potter or calligrapher and his followers, the *iemoto* principle now pervades Japanese group psychology in office and factory even where *iemoto* in the old form no longer exists, an "all-inclusive and nearly unbreakable command-obedience, succoring-dependence relationship between the old and the young, the senior and the junior, the superior and the subordinate."[43] In Hsu's interpretation, Japan is "one huge *iemoto*," and Japan's "*iemoto*-like companies and other social organizations may be described as greatly-expanded versions of Chinese kinship organizations, including links with deceased ancestors. In the widest extension of the *iemoto*, the Japanese emperor is comparable to the Chinese head of the living clan."[44]

China, not to mention India and many other Asian countries, must endure a social revolution in order to achieve what Japan already has achieved by doing what comes naturally. The "vertical structural principle"[45] underlying Japanese institutions goes hand in hand with psychological conditioning for dependence on the group beginning in infancy. William L. Caudill's penetrating studies of sleeping patterns in Japanese homes show that crowded housing is not the only reason for the persistence of the traditional practice of children sleeping beside parents. Even where space permitted separate bedrooms, Caudill discovered, most children in the families studied slept with one or both of their parents until the age of ten, and half until age fifteen.[46] Caudill concluded that conjugal intimacy between husband and wife takes second place to the goal of "a more general family cohesion" because sleeping patterns are "part of the gradual process of building into the child a distinctively Japanese way of relating to other people. The Japanese consciously search for interdependent relationships throughout their later lives and shun individuality even though some hunger for it intellectually."[47]

What Caudill calls a propensity for "leaning up against each other" is the same thing others have detailed in an elaborate specialized literature as the *amae* phenomenon.[48] It is what Isaiah Ben-Dasan calls "Nihonism," a "national religion of human nature and human relations" deifying the sense of comfortable community provided by sharing in Japanese identity.[49] This basic social and psychological linkage has been greatly reinforced by the unusually intensive communication network consciously built up from the start of the Meiji period through programs of language standardization and mass education. But the underlying factor explaining the strength of Japanese nationalism is the social-psychological linkage itself, the happy marriage of vertically structured social institutions and vertically ascending horizons of identity focusing on the national state. With their peculiarly strong sense of hierarchy and their peculiarly complete merger of individual and national identity, Japanese are peculiarly dependent for their self-esteem, as Herbert Passin has noted, on their estimation of the "success" and international rank order achieved by Japan.[50]

The merger of individual and group identity characteristic in varying degrees of many non-Western societies provides an antidote to the pervasive psychological malaise of an age that exalts bigness for its own sake. Isaiah Berlin sees all mankind as caught up in a chain reaction of protest against Burke's "sophisters, calculators and economists," indeed against "the central doctrines of nineteenth century liberal rationalism itself." In industrial or postindustrial societies, the protest is often that of "individuals or groups whose members do not wish to be dragged along by the chariot wheels of scientific progress." In poor or excolonial countries, it is the hunger for equality in relation to the rich countries and for elbow room in the face of "the 'global' calculations . . . which guide the policy planners and executives in the gigantic operations in which governments, corporations and interlocking elites of various kinds are engaged."[51] Harold D. Lasswell suggests in similar terms that the "revolution of rising expectations" is now directed against what is seen as a "unified transnational oligarchy."[52] This spirit of protest is essentially the same phenomenon whether it comes in the form of the "craving for 'natural units' of human size" shown by the Welsh or the Basques or of efforts by the poor countries to counter bigness with bigness by enlarging their political units. In both cases, Berlin observes, the "original impulse appears to be the same sense of outraged human dignity . . . resistant to dilution, assimilation, depersonalization." "Nationalism" in this broadest sense is "still in its early beginnings" everywhere, he believes, and should no longer be a bad word, reflecting as it does "a profound and natural need," especially where it is the vehicle for non-Western countries hungering for recognition and respect.

The recrudescence of ethnic loyalties in an American society "not as melted as many thought it to be"[53] is part of the universal phenomenon described by Berlin. It also illustrates the fact that the United States is passing through a protracted national "identity crisis" of its own, which makes it more difficult than ever for Americans to get in tune with nationalism in Asia. For most Americans, the "American" component of identity has been derived from association with a state unparalleled in power and symbolizing political ideals presumed to be universally valid as well as an economic system setting the pace for the world in science and technology. Now, as the universal relevance of the American political system is called into question, as American technological supremacy wanes, and as the limits of American power become apparent, this identity has provided diminishing psychological support, leading to self-doubt, swaggering displays of military strength, and a resurgence of older subidentities in a search for reassurance. The torment of the Vietnam years was reflected in a White House comment during the crucial stage of the peace negotiations in 1973 that the war had to be ended "in a way that the country can preserve its confidence in itself."[54]

Americans, like others, derive their individual identity partly from larger group identities, but the social foundations of American nationalism differ fundamentally from the social bases of nationalism in Asian countries. This poses an obstacle to understanding quite as fundamental as other societal differences that are often given greater attention, notably the fact that the United States, "born free" as it was, did not have a feudal system and thus has not known the anguish of a social revolution. As a federal system bound by an idea, its constituent parts defined by historical accident rather than ethnic or cultural identity, the United States differs both from Asia's federal states, made up of distinct social and cultural groups, and Asia's homogeneous states such as Japan and Korea. In both cases, nationalism in Asia rests on territorially based "total identities."[55] These identities remain the bedrock units of power and political energy whether or not they are joined with others in larger political entities. They cannot themselves be severed without payment of a heavy psychological price. Given their own willingness to fight a civil war for the preservation of a union established on quite different foundations, many Americans were jarred by a Bangladesh secession movement that subordinated the unity of Pakistan to the claims of Bengali identity, and given the absence of culture-centered identity in the American ethos, they have been equally unable to understand the psychological impact of the division of their countries on politically conscious Vietnamese and Koreans.

For many Vietnamese and Koreans I have known over the past twenty years, the division of their countries has been a persistent psychic bruise, as gross and artificial an incongruity in their eyes as it has been a matter of indifference to many Americans. Discussing the Vietnamese case, Bernard B. Fall observed that "depending on an individual's identification with his national group and area," the partition of his territory may have a psychological impact "as drastic as the amputation of his own limbs."[56] American policy was based, however, on an image of a separate South Vietnam as "an embryonic nation."[57] This image was shared by prowar political scientists, who frequently spoke of a "nation-building" process in Saigon, rejecting the view that a Vietnamese national identity, by definition, presupposed some form of territorial unification giving Vietnam a single personality in the world context.

NATIONALISM AND GROWTH

An analysis of nationalism in Asia stressing the political and psychological evolution through which Asian countries are passing collides squarely with other interpretations viewing nationalism in relation to stages of economic growth. By explaining nationalism as a search for identity and self-respect in a world of economically and racially lopsided power relationships, this analysis places primary emphasis on the impact of these shifting power relationships in stimulating cycles of nationalist awareness. It focuses not on "past humiliations,"[58] as Walt W. Rostow did, but on continuing power imbalances; not on struggles between "transitional leadership groups" over economic versus noneconomic priorities but on the recurring internal adjustments between social groups necessary for viable national structures. It thus treats the remainder of the twentieth century as a relatively early phase in a long historical process of nationalist consolidation and self-assertion in Asia that has no definable end in sight. It consciously brackets together countries at varying stages of growth, economically, calling into question the very assumption that economic growth as such is the principal preoccupation of Asian countries.

What most people in most Asian countries are seeking, in a variety of ways and under a variety of differing national circumstances, is not growth as an end in itself but growth consistent with their nationalist purposes. In the domestic context, this means growth with social justice, since national solidarity is undermined to the extent that one group or another feels cheated out of its share of the fruits of development. In the world context, it means growth with a maximum of national control leading to as much nationally controlled economic power as their particular bargaining position makes possible. Both the domestic and international perspectives of nationalism define goals that are not necessarily measurable by the rate of increase in the gross national product.

The domestic challenge of nation-building may dictate slower growth, more equitably shared, when rapid growth can be achieved only at the cost of widening social disparities and threatening the fabric of national unity. It is one thing for a country to give an ever rising GNP explicit priority over social equities[59] when it has a business community wedded to national goals as Japan does and a homogeneous population largely identifying its interests with the success of business. It is quite another matter in other Asian countries with different social environments. In most Asian countries, with their wide gap between rich and poor, mercantile and entrepreneurial groups are not regarded as custodians of national progress as they are in Japan. In addition to the overseas Chinese factor, grossly disproportionate economic power in both industrial and agricultural life is held by certain indigenous social minorities as an inheritance from the preindependence period. Regional and linguistic differences often coincide with economic disparities, so that development pursued as an end in itself only aggravates federal imbalances. The maintenance of equilibrium between contending regional economic claims has been an overriding problem for all Asian countries from continent-sized China to the insular Philippines, a far more sensitive challenge to nation-builders in impoverished developing countries with limited resources than comparable internal adjustments in the West.

The appeal for limits to growth made by the Club of Rome and others, largely from a Western, environmentalist perspective, has its Asian variant in a growing recognition that growth at the expense of social equities is a time bomb. Two leading regional economic organizations, the U.N. Economic Commission for Asia and the Far East[60] and the Colombo Plan,[61] have formally challenged the premise of many Western development economists that distributive justice must be sacrificed in order to achieve growth. More and more observers echo the view that the political underpinnings of growth are endangered when "large portions of the population do not benefit much or at all" from development processes that have basically served to widen the urban-rural gap or to concentrate wealth in the hands of a small group of businessmen.[62] Even the "green revolution" has been increasingly perceived as a mixed blessing, with its characteristic tendency to widen the gap between peasant proprietors and landless laborers.

While Western aid agencies were still applauding Pakistan as a model of development, a former Pakistani planning official observed, "the system in Pakistan exploded, not only for political but for economic reasons."[63] Real wages in the industrial sector were declining by one-third during a period in which the concentration of industrial wealth was growing and disparities in per capita income between East and West Pakistan were doubling. The Moslem League leaders responsible for the creation of Pakistan in the first place had based their appeal almost exclusively on religion because they represented narrow feudal economic interests. It thus followed naturally that successive regimes largely ignored social equities until Zulfiqar Ali Bhutto made his effort to salvage something from the ruins in the wake of the Bangladesh war. Pakistan's Twenty Families in the Ayub Khan period have had their counterpart in the Hundred Families of South Korean political symbolism during the Park Chong-hui regime, the sugar barons in the Philippines, and the "Tju-kong" alliance of military figures and Chinese financiers in Indonesia. As these cases suggest, the concentration of wealth is not only anathema, as such, in poor countries but its impact is also magnified, politically, because it so often goes together with official corruption.

In a climate of poverty and social tensions, corruption is a faithful barometer revealing the strength of nationalism. The visceral impulse in a setting of scarcity is one of "every man for himself" unless there is strong countervailing social pressure. Corruption, in this context, is not so much a breach of abstract moral or ethical standards as it is a betrayal of the national effort to rise up from deprivation. The petty graft of the underpaid bureaucrat is tolerated as a lubricant that sustains the system and serves the common interest. Corruption becomes unacceptable when it signifies a system diverted from national goals to large-scale private aggrandizement. Governments may be "nationalistic" in the chauvinistic sense whether or not they are sensitive to social·equities, but nationalism acquires its power as a dynamic, constructive mass force only to the extent that leaders are believed to represent the aspiration for social and economic justice, if not the reality, and to personify self-sacrificing dedication to the national cause. This is the critical test of legitimacy in Asia. It is an elusive test that is often difficult to apply, transcending as it does the structural distinction generally drawn between authoritarian governments and governments chosen through Western-style electoral processes.

Where a military leader has been free from the taint of personal or family corruption and has helped to fight for his country's independence, as in the case of Ziaur Rahman in Bangladesh, his regime can have valid nationalist credentials notwithstanding its authoritarian character. By the same token, where military leaders are regarded as corrupt and have collaborated with the colonial ruler, as was the case in South Vietnam, they are more vulnerable than other authoritarian leaders whose skirts are no cleaner but who have fought against colonial rule, such as Suharto in Indonesia and Ferdinand Marcos in the Philippines. In South Korea, it is Park Chonghui's reputation for spartan probity that has given his embattled regime a measure of nationalist acceptability, though Park's legitimacy is inherently weakened by other significant factors discussed in Chapter 7, notably his record as an officer in the Japanese colonial army. Similarly, in Pakistan, Ayub Khan was tolerated for more than a decade despite his heavy-handed authoritarian style, but his downfall came quickly after his son Gohar became a millionaire overnight through government truck contracts.

Even in India, where parliamentary institutions had been more firmly established than elsewhere in Asia, Indira Gandhi was initially given the benefit of the doubt when she assumed authoritarian powers because she wore the colors of the freedom movement and presided over a Congress party government that had been relatively free from large-scale corruption at the top. She lost her charisma when her son and his confidants appeared to be profiting financially in a big way from her monopoly of power. This is the principal reason why the opposition was able to exploit the excesses of the emergency period as effectively as it did in the 1977 elections. The corruption issue struck directly at Mrs. Gandhi's moral authority as the personification of nationalism and undermined the credibility of her efforts to defend emergency rule in nationalist terms by arguing that it was necessary to make the country stronger in the face of external challenges. By contrast, the opposition had an untarnished rallying symbol in Jayaprakash Narayan, who was able to claim the nationalist mantle from Mrs. Gandhi as the only remaining giant of the freedom movement still active in public life. Significantly, the opposition implicitly recognized that the Congress party's nominal commitment to socialism had more to do with nationalist symbolism than with ideology. Instead of repudiating the socialist objective, the Janata party platform contended that the Congress brand of socialism had become a cover, in practice, for the unfettered concentration of wealth by a "new class" and pledged that its own economic policies would assure more equitably shared progress.

The case of China underlines the fact that the nationalist bonafides of a regime are not necessarily determined by its dedication to Western parliamentary values. In China, the Communist commitment to social equity has been far more authentic and credible than that of the postindependence leadership in India and provides the psychological lubricant necessary to make a stern totalitarianism viable. As Chapter 3 elaborates, the Chinese Communists acquired their nationalist legitimacy initially as the most effective leaders of the struggle against Japan, but they have kept nationalist élan alive by living up to the egalitarianism inherent in the communist ideology. Viewed in long-range historical terms, the strength of Chinese nationalism is basically explained by its deep roots in an unusually self-contained culture. What has made the Chinese Communists peculiarly effective as nationalist leaders since 1949, however, has been their ability to reconcile the claims of equity with the claims of growth. The manner in which the post-Mao leadership handles the growth-with-equity issue is likely to be a critical factor determining the continuing vitality of Chinese nationalism as the unifying struggle against Japan grows more distant.

All Asian countries face a common dilemma: they must somehow partake of a steadily expanding fund of new technology or fall increasingly behind in the economic race; yet their underlying objective is to establish broad-based, independent economic power fortifying their nationalist identity. When their development becomes a mere extension of an externally controlled investment nexus or aid dependency, as we shall see in later chapters, this negates one of the central objectives of development and breeds xenophobic reactions making it that much more difficult to establish cooperative world economic patterns. "By industrialization we do not merely mean the industrialization of the Philippines in a territorial sense," said Filipino nationalist Claro Recto. "It is not factories we want, as such, or higher G.N.P. for the Philippines as a geographic unit, but factories that belong to us and national wealth that we control as a nation."[64] In this perspective, as we shall see, public ownership of industrial enterprises takes on a new meaning in many cases as a function of nationalism rather than socialism, and the countries Americans might think of as "success stories" are not necessarily so regarded in Asia without considerable qualification.

Japan, for example, is a success story in the eyes of other Asian countries to the extent that it has maximized its economic sovereignty by mobilizing domestic savings and limiting foreign equity holdings to areas of the economy in which these have served Japanese objectives. It is resented to the extent that its position of regional economic dominance has been stimulated by American technological largesse, given for cold war reasons, or by trade expansion linked to the Korean and Vietnam wars. Thailand comes off better than Burma by the growth yardstick, but a representative Japanese observer found little to choose between them. Burma had its ration lines and maladministration, but it also had green streets and self-reliant austerity; while post-Vietnam Thailand, by contrast, had high rises, a foreign exchange deficit, conspicuous consumption side by side with slums, and a growing urban-rural gap symbolized by legions of unemployed migrants. "Who are the happier people," he asked rhetorically, "the Burmese or the Thais?"[65] China is ridiculed in the American press for boasting of its debt-free status and its lack of dependence on world trade, "as if that self-imposed piece of hobbling were a great achievement";[66] but the Asian perspective, as American intelligence analysts have noted, is one of admiration for Peking's ability to develop while "skillfully avoiding the primrose path of large-scale foreign borrowing which has left India, Pakistan, Indonesia and others with a crushing burden."[67] For American aid officials, South Korea is a prize exhibit, but for Singapore prime minister Lee Kuan Yew it is a sorry example of an economy mortgaged to Japan.[68] As a Council on Foreign Relations study has observed, South Korea and Taiwan have received per capita U.S. aid inputs far bigger than those given to other Asian aid recipients, a factor not unrelated to their growth rates.[69] The ultimate test of "success" in the eyes of most Asian observers, in any case, is not only GNP, export volume, and the degree of utilization of industrial capacity in a given year but what these statistics represent in terms of progress equitably shared, nationally controlled, and harnessed to political goals.

The nature of the relationship between growth and nationalism is graphically illustrated in the course of an examination of the two Koreas in Chapter 7. North Korea exemplifies the virtues and limitations involved in maximizing self-reliance and achieving egalitarian living standards at a low consumption level. The South offers higher living standards for some in a consumer economy erected on a structure of heavy indebtedness to Japan and the United States. The North gets the greater psychological satisfaction from progress achieved with minimal dependency but is unable to present itself convincingly as the custodian of Korean identity for ineradicable historical reasons discussed in Chapter 5. Both Korean states think of themselves as building one-half of a house without relation to the work in progress on the other half, and both are aware that their bargaining power in economic dealings with other countries is weakened by their division. So long as their country remains severed, in short, most Koreans in North and South alike acquire little sense of nationalist identity from their economic achievements because these achievements do not yet go to support a posture of maximum Korean self-respect in relation to the outside world.

THE TWO FACES OF NATIONALISM

Nationalism has two faces, one turned inward on the task of marshaling national strength, another looking vigilantly outward. Both aspects are part of the same historical continuum, inseparably linked in a close cyclical interaction. At times nationalism may seemingly "go underground,"[70] but this is deceptive. Once born, it has an indefinite life span, recurrently emerging into clear view in a variety of manifestations under external stress. It is not something that comes "only once in the life of a race, and no more."[71]

The state of national consolidation in a country at a given time is the principal determinant of its confidence in confronting the external world and thus of its response to external pressure. The response may be defensive, with the cry of "Country in Danger" used in time-honored fashion as the cement for holding together the social fabric. Alternatively, a country may feel sure of its internal solidarity but insecure internationally, which can lead to the aggressive outward reach typified in its most extreme form by homogeneous Japan during the prewar period. Often, both of these responses are covered loosely by the pejorative usage of "nationalist." As Chapters 7-9 seek to show, however, this indiscriminate approach only helps to push nationalism into defensive or aggressive extremes at the expense of its essentially constructive drive.

The case of China exemplifies the meaning and importance of this interplay. Confronted with deep provincialism aggravating its inherent economic problems, Peking was internally preoccupied during the early postwar decades and disposed of much less effective power for expansionist adventures than American official estimates suggested. Precisely because of this internal weakness, however, the specter of American and later Soviet pressure evoked a powerful nationalist response providing much of the motive power behind nation-building. The cry of "Country in Danger" was consciously utilized to harness national energies, producing the very opposite of the result intended in a containment policy designed to weaken Peking. This mitigated but by no means removed the stresses inherent in Chinese nationalism during its formative period, and the Cultural Revolution, for all of its complexities, clearly mirrored these stresses. As an ideological adventure, the Cultural Revolution not only represented Mao's search for a "new man," as often suggested, but also his desire as a nationalist leader to rekindle patriotic élan by stressing absolute social equality. As a power struggle, it corresponded closely to the lines of regionally based factionalism linked with continuing federal tensions. The reassertion of central authority in the aftermath of the Cultural Revolution reflected a new federal equilibrium sufficiently stable at that point in time to give Peking the confidence needed for a turn outward and a new foreign policy.

The American response to Indian neutralism has provided another striking demonstration of insensitivity to the special significance of the domestic mainsprings of foreign policy in developing countries. In its deepest sense, neutralism is not outer directed but is rather a symbolic posture serving to remind heterogeneous countries of their new collective personality in world affairs. By projecting New Delhi onto the world stage as an independent, freewheeling entity pursuing its own national interests, Nehru and his successors have held out before Punjabis and Tamils and Bengalis a mirror image of themselves as Indians. Nehru believed that alignment with either side in the cold war would engender a basic lack of confidence, a psychological reversion to past feelings of dependence and inferiority still lurking just beneath the surface of political consciousness in all excolonial peoples.[72] Once having lost their newly found sense of national destiny, he feared, Indians would soon drift back to their past patterns of fratricide.

Nehru knew all too well that he was posturing and that India did not have the strength in being to match its pretensions as a world power. Still, he consciously sought to exploit the bargaining opportunity conferred by the cold war to strengthen the foundations of Indian pride. This inner-directed nationalism was not motivated by an animus toward particular foreign powers. It exemplified the difference between the xenophobic chauvinism often mislabeled as nationalism and nationalism as a projection of a constructive nation-building process based on some form of popularly accepted political order permitting the accommodation of divergent views and interests. In Indonesia and South Korea, by contrast, as Japan has discovered, popular discontent against authoritarian regimes that cannot be vented on domestic targets has been easily diverted toward foreign scapegoats, magnifying what might otherwise have been more limited protective reactions against economic inroads.

The psychological damage suffered by India during the Chinese border clashes of 1962 gradually led to a new self-image as a regional power, accompanied by a new determination to assert regional primacy reflected in the 1965 Indo-Pakistan war and in the support given by India to the Bangladesh independence struggle. As Chapter 9 shows, however, the United States has been equally insensitive to the dynamics of Indian nationalism in its early stages of development, when Nehru played a world role, and later, when his successors scaled down their ambitions to the regional level. American economic aid, often producing constructive results in economic terms, has been all but nullified as a political plus in Indo-U.S. relations because Washington has been so oblivious to the mainsprings of Indian policy, above all to the legacy of partition, the unresolved controversy over the "two-nation" theory, and the interstitial relationship linking domestic political life in India and Pakistan. Except for brief interludes, the United States has not treated the Indian subcontinent as a factor in its own right but rather as a subsidiary element in policy equations focused primarily on the communist powers.

This disregard for the specific characteristics and personality of nationalism in China and India has typified the American encounter with Asia generally and results naturally from an egocentric approach in which other societies are bracketed together and compared in accordance with American-defined universal categories. A cultural conditioning based on a view of non-Western societies as uniformly "strange, backward and essentially 'barbaric' " by American standards[73] intrinsically downgrades the importance of distinctions between one species of primitivism and another. Richard Lambert pointed to this egocentricity when he pleaded the case for "uniquists" as against "comparativists" in American scholarship relating to Asia. As Lambert argued, it is only by studying at least one non-Western culture thoroughly in its own terms, plumbing its unique aspects and its emotive wellsprings, that one is lifted "out of his own cultural bind" as an American and discovers the capacity "to empathize universally."[74] Correspondingly, it is the failure to treat each Asian nationalism separately in its own terms that has been at the bottom of most major errors of American policy, leading to the overestimation or underestimation of what countries could or would do and of how they would react in given situations.

Over time, the motive power of nationalism in a given country can only be as great as the degree of its social integration, its social mobilization, and its social equity. Power relationships in Asia will ultimately be governed by these domestic dynamics of nationalism. Thus, by glossing over the internal challenges to Indian nationalism, the United States fell into its futile effort to cast India as a counterweight to China, dismissing India's own ambitions, in the bargain, for a South Asian regional preeminence more in line with its potential. By overrating Pakistan, out of a similar insensitivity to internal factors, the United States embarked upon the futile policy of attempting to build it up as an offset to India, four times its size. In both of these newly launched countries, facing difficult challenges of internal social adjustment, grossly inflated expectations of economic progress disregarding these handicaps set the stage for correspondingly premature U.S. disillusion when progress came more slowly than aid lobbyists had promised.

The most extensively discussed and pervasive errors of overestimation have come in cases such as South Vietnam and Laos, where there was little or no nationalist dynamic at all. By viewing "power" narrowly in military or economic terms, apart from its political, social, and psychological components, the United States easily succumbed to the costly conclusion that artificially induced infusions of outside resources could compensate for what was lacking internally. This simplistic view of power also made it difficult to recognize strength where it did exist, blurring the distinctions between client or quasi-client relationships with dependent regimes and very different relationships in which governments propelled by their own steam were using U.S. help for their own purposes.

In the most important cases discussed in this book, the United States has underrated the strength of nationalism, injecting extra increments of strength where indigenous momentum already existed or seeking to contain countries too strong to be contained. Chapter 9 discusses Japan, the example par excellence of overkill resulting from this miscalculation. Despite its own unparalleled internal dynamism rooted in a uniquely cohesive social structure, Japan was buttressed by the United States as a cold war bastion and was systematically encouraged to become involved in the weak, vulnerable economies of neighboring countries not yet cohesive enough themselves as national entities to defend their interests effectively. This reflected something more than the temporary priorities of the cold war period. As we shall see, it rested basically on a patronizing view of Japan, a view emphasizing the physical destruction inflicted during the war while minimizing, conversely, both the strength of the Japanese social structure and the enduring psychological strength of the Meiji tradition as the basis for a new expression of nationalism adapted to a new historical situation. At various times, the United States sought to make Japan its surrogate in dealing with other Asian countries and in so doing it revealed a still more patronizing view of the other countries concerned, notably neighboring South Korea. Even when a revived Japanese nationalism became increasingly visible, the United States continued to underrate its potential, coupling a newly tough stance on economic issues with an abrupt, unilateral shift in China policy.

By underestimating nationalism, the United States failed to see the potential for division between China and the USSR and thus based its entire approach to Asia on oversimplified premises. Moreover, in the Asian context itself, as the next four chapters demonstrate, the United States fundamentally underestimated the staying power of the Peking and Hanoi regimes because it failed to see that in China and Vietnam, alone in Asia, nationalism and communism were fused into a combined force of extra potency. By the same token, the United States overestimated the communist expansionist potential in other parts of Asia where communist parties have failed to achieve the leadership of nationalism. In the instance in which the United States intervened most effectively to forestall communist expansionism, Korea, this was possible, as Chapter 5 shows, because nationalism had been neutralized, giving the Korean and Vietnamese cases their fundamentally different character.

The record of postwar American policy in Asia has been explained variously by the myopia of all-consuming security and economic perspectives that have alternately blocked out other aspects of Asian reality; the plans of oil companies; the juggernaut of ever changing military technology; and the new "liberal imperialism."[75] All of these factors and others have been involved, but the critical common ingredient of failure has been insensitivity to the power of nationalism, a factor quite as "real" in the equation of realpolitik as military or economic power. Similarly, where real or apparent successes have been scored, these have generally come through fortuitous accidents in which the "right" or workable thing has been done for reasons unrelated to an empathetic valuation of what nationalism means in Asia.

Chapter 6 discusses the deep psychological gulf between the United States and Asia created by this insensitivity, with special reference to Asian perceptions of the Vietnam conflict. Examining relevant case histories of American experience, Chapters 10 and 11 set the stage for a discussion of future policies capable of bridging this gulf and of making the American military and economic presence more compatible with nationalism than it has been in the past. Chapter 12 suggests detailed guidelines for such policies and shows that nationalism and regionalism are merely differing stages in the same Asian search for identity and for a new world constellation of power.

The conclusion suggested by this book points to a series of profound ironies. While thinking of itself as the defender of nationalism, the United States has in actuality misunderstood what nationalism is in the Asian context and has more often than not been its enemy. Similarly, while historically dedicated to maintaining a balance of power in Asia, the United States has inadvertently warped and distorted the evolution of power relationships in Asia since the end of World War II, strengthening power imbalances and posing the unprecedented danger of a regional consolidation hostile to American interests. Having thrown history temporarily out of joint, as it were, the United States now faces the difficult task of reassessing the Asian landscape with more finely sensitized antennae, recognizing, albeit belatedly, that nationalism will ultimately "keep cropping out of whatever is laid over it, like trees forcing their way through rocky mountainsides a mile high."[76]

NOTES

1. Zbigniew Brzezinski, *Between Two Ages: America's Role in the Technetronic Era* (New York: Viking, 1970), pp. 4-5, 54.

2. This useful concept is elaborated in the works of Karl W. Deutsch, especially *Nationalism and Social Communication*, 2d ed. (Cambridge: MIT Press, 1966).

3. Gunnar Myrdal, "A Comparison of European and Asian Nationalism," in *Asian Drama: An Inquiry into the Poverty of Nations* (New York: Twentieth Century Fund and Pantheon), 3:2119.

4. John K. Fairbank, *China: The People's Middle Kingdom and the U.S.A.* (Cambridge: Harvard University Press, Belknap, 1967), p. 95.

5. John H. Kautsky, ed., *Political Change in Underdeveloped Countries: Nationalism and Communism* (New York: Wiley, 1962), p. 39. For a well-argued similar interpretation see also the discussion of "sovereignty" and "authority" in George Lichtheim, *Imperialism* (London: Allen & Unwin, 1971), pp. 8-9; Herbert S. Dinerstein, *Intervention against Communism* (Baltimore: Johns Hopkins Press, 1967), p. 36; and Tibor Mende, *Southeast Asia between Two Worlds* (London: Turnstile, 1955), p. 291.

6. Rupert Emerson, *From Empire to Nation* (Cambridge: Harvard University Press, 1960), pp. 205-206.

7. Rabindranath Tagore, *Nationalism* (New York: Macmillan, 1917), pp. 135-36; see also Stephen N. Hay, *Asian Ideas of East and West: Tagore and His Critics in Japan, China, and India* (Cambridge: Harvard University Press, 1970).

8. Joseph R. Levenson, *Liang Ch'i-ch'ao and the Mind of Modern China* (Cambridge: Harvard University Press, 1953), pp. 109-112; see also S. Y. Teng and John K. Fairbank, *China's Response to the West* (Cambridge: Harvard University Press, 1954), esp. chap. 7.

9. John K. Fairbank, "China's Response to the West," *Journal of World History*, July 1956, pp. 404-405, cited in Mary Matossian, "Ideologies of Delayed Industrialization," *Economic Development and Cultural Change*, April 1958, p. 10.

10. Edwin O. Reischauer, *Beyond Vietnam: The United States and Asia* (New York: Knopf, 1967), p. 110.

11. Edward Seidensticker, *The United States and Japan* (Englewood Cliffs: Prentice-Hall, 1966), pp. 5-6.

12. Werner Levi, *The Challenge of World Politics in South and Southeast Asia* (Englewood Cliffs: Prentice-Hall, 1968), p. 47; chap. 2, "The Problem of Nationalism," develops this view in detail.

13. Dwight Cooke, *There Is No Asia* (Garden City: Doubleday, 1954), p. 1.

14. Henry A. Kissinger, "Central Issues of American Foreign Policy," in *Agenda for the Nation*, ed. Kermit Gordon (Washington: Brookings Institution, 1968), p. 603.

15. Interview with C. L. Sulzberger, *New York Times*, 10 March 1972, p. 5.

16. Selig S. Harrison, *India: The Most Dangerous Decades* (Princeton: Princeton University Press, 1960), pp. 5, 7, 337.

17. Rajendra Prasad, *India Divided* (Bombay: Hind Kitabs, 1946), p. 391.

18. George Steiner, *Extraterritorial: Papers on Literature and the Language Revolution* (New York: Atheneum, 1971), p. xi; see also pp. 60-61, 81, 88.

19. Joseph Buttinger, *The Smaller Dragon: A Political History of Vietnam* (New York: Praeger, 1958), p. 173; see also Le Thanh Khoi, *Vietnam: Histoire et civilisation* (Paris: Editions du Minuit, 1955), p. 497.

20. Paul Mus, *Vietnam: Sociologie d'une guerre* (Paris: Editions du Seuil, 1952), p. 236.

21. Nguyen Du, *Kim Van Kieu*, trans. Le Xuan Thuy, 2d ed. (Saigon: Khai-tri, 1965). *Kim Van Kieu* is discussed and commemorated in "Nguyen Du and

'Kieu' " a special issue of *Vietnamese Studies*, no. 4 (Hanoi: Xunhabasa, 1965); and Maurice Durand, *Mélanges sur Nguyen Du*, L'Ecole française d'extrême-orient, vol. 59 (Paris: Adrien-Maison-neuve, 1966). See also Tran Van Dinh, "Astounding Captured Document Reveals Mind of Enemy," *Washingtonian*, April 1968, pp. 40–47.

22. Basil Hall Chamberlain stressed the separateness of Okinawan in "Essay in Aid of a Grammar and Dictionary of the Luchuan Language," *Transactions of the Asiatic Society of Japan*, vol. 23 (supp.) (Tokyo, 1895). For a contemporary Japanese view treating Okinawan as a dialect of standard Japanese see Shirō Hattori, *Nihongo no Keitō* [Lineage of the Japanese language] (Tokyo: Iwanami Shoten, 1959). Masanori Higa, "Notes on the Social and Psychological Aspects of Metrics," *Kwansei Gakuin University Annual Studies*, vol. 16 (Nishinomiya Center, Tokyo, November 1967), pp. 90–91, refers to Okinawan as "the only sister language of Japanese, so similar that it is often treated as a Japanese dialect."

23. Selig S. Harrison, "Taiwanese Hope for Gains from Nixon Trip to China," *Washington Post*, 27 July 1971, p. A15; and idem, "Japan, China Agree on Taiwan Dealings," second in a series of eight articles on "Japan in Asia," *Washington Post*, 26 February 1973, p. 1. This conclusion is based on five extended visits to Taiwan in 1967, 1968, 1971, and 1972, during which I interviewed Taiwanese underground independence movement leaders and a representative spectrum of Taiwan-born Chinese of other persuasions.

24. Ts'ai P'ei-huo, Lin Po-shou, Ch'en Feng-yuan, Wu San-lien, Yeh Jung-chung, *Taiwan Min-Tsu Yün-Tung Shih* [A History of Taiwan's National Movement] (Taipei: Independent Evening News Publication Series, 1971), p. 76.

25. Ibid., p. 161.

26. Kikuo Shimura, "The Taiwan That Japanese Travelers Fail to See," *Shokun* (Tokyo), December 1970, pp. 2, 5, 12–14.

27. George Kerr, *Formosa Betrayed* (Boston: Houghton Mifflin, 1965), p. 3.

28. William G. Goddard, *Formosa* (London: Macmillan, 1966), pp. 68–69, 156, 201.

29. Lau Tabin, "Who Are the Formosans?" *Independent Formosa* (New York), March 1968, pp. 17–19. For a more comprehensive analysis seeking to establish the validity of a separate Taiwanese nationalism see Peng Ming-min, *A Taste of Freedom* (New York: Holt, Rinehart & Winston, 1972).

30. Harold R. Isaacs, "Group Identity and Political Change" (Paper presented to the Psycho-History Group, American Academy of Arts and Sciences, Philadelphia, 16 October 1971), p. 29.

31. James Strachey, trans., *Group Psychology and the Analysis of the Ego* (New York: Liveright, 1922), pp. 169–70.

32. Erich Fromm, *The Sane Society* (New York: Rinehart, 1955), p. 58.

33. Cited in Isaacs, "Group Identity and Political Change," p. 31.

34. Erik H. Erikson, *Insight and Responsibility* (New York: Norton, 1964), p. 91; see also idem, *Identity: Youth and Crisis* (New York: Norton, 1968), esp. "Race and the Wider Identity," pp. 295–320; idem, "The Problem of

Ego Identity," *Journal of the American Psychoanalytical Association*, January 1956, pp. 56-121; and idem, "Ego Development and Historical Change," in *The Psychoanalytical Study of the Child* (New York: International Universities Press, 1946). I am indebted to Judith K. Davison for a research paper providing a detailed analysis of Erikson's writings on the relationship between individual and group identity.

35. Erik H. Erikson, *Childhood and Society*, 2d ed. (New York: Norton, 1963), esp. pp. 247, 258, 261-262, 269; see also idem, *Identity: Youth and Crisis*; and idem, "Psychoanalysis and Ongoing History: Problems of Identity, Hatred, and Non-Violence," *American Journal of Psychiatry*, September 1965, esp. p. 246.

36. Erikson, *Identity: Youth and Crisis*, pp. 21-22.

37. Lucian W. Pye, *Politics, Personality, and Nation-Building: Burma's Search for Identity* (New Haven: Yale University Press, 1962), p. 52; see also pp. 4-5, 53, 187, 290.

38. For example, Erik H. Erikson, *Young Man Luther: A Study in Psychoanalysis and History* (New York: Norton, 1958); and idem, *Gandhi's Truth* (New York: Norton, 1969).

39. Isaacs, "Group Identity and Political Change," pp. 41-42.

40. Harold R. Isaacs, *Idols of the Tribe: Group Identity and Political Change*, (New York: Harper and Row, 1975), p. 44. See also pp. 38-42 and an earlier unpublished paper, "Basic Group Identity."

41. Walter H. Slote, "Psychodynamic Structures in Vietnamese Personality," in *Transcultural Research in Mental Health*, ed. William P. Lebra (Honolulu: East-West Center, 1972), p. 116. Slote also quotes Erich Wulff.

42. Marion J. Levy, "Contrasting Factors in the Modernization of China and Japan," in *Economic Growth: Brazil, India, Japan*, ed. Simon Kuznets, W. E. Moore, and J. J. Spengler (Durham: Duke University Press, 1955), esp. pp. 523-532.

43. Francis L. K. Hsu, "Psychological Homeostasis and *Jen:* Conceptual Tools for Advancing Psychological Anthropology," *American Anthropologist*, February 1971, pp. 37-38.

44. Francis L. K. Hsu, *Iemoto: The Heart of Japan* (Cambridge: Schenkman, 1973), chap. 13, pp. 31, 34-36; see also chap. 10, pp. 25-26; chap. 11, pp. 6, 10, 15; and chap. 12, p. 28.

45. Chie Nakane, *Japanese Society* (London: Weidenfeld & Nicolson, 1970), esp. pp. 141-151.

46. William L. Caudill and David Plath, "Who Sleeps by Whom?" *Psychiatry*, 29 April 1966, pp. 344-366; see also William L. Caudill and L. Takeo Doi, "Interrelations of Psychiatry, Culture, and Emotion in Japan," in *Man's Image in Medicine and Anthropology* (New York: International Universities Press, 1963).

47. Selig S. Harrison, "Mama-san Moves Up Front," *Washington Post*, 31 May 1970, p. B5.

48. Takeo Doi, *Amae no Kōzō* [The structure of *amae*] (Tokyo: Kōbundo, 1971); idem, "A Japanese Interpretation of 'Love Story' " mimeographed

(Tokyo, 1972); and Minami Hiroshi, *Nihonjin no Shinri* [The psychology of the Japanese] (Tokyo: Iwanami, 1953).

49. Isaiah Ben-Dasan, *The Japanese and the Jews* (New York: Weatherhill, 1970), esp. pp. 99, 105–131; see also articles by Ben-Dasan on "Nihonism" in *Shokun* (Tokyo), May, July, August, September, October, and November 1971.

50. Herbert Passin, "Socio-cultural Factors in the Japanese Perception of International Order," *Annual Review* (Tokyo: Japanese Institute of International Affairs, 1970), esp. p. 53.

51. Isaiah Berlin, "The Bent Twig: A Note on Nationalism," *Foreign Affairs*, October 1972, esp. pp. 24–30.

52. Harold D. Lasswell, "The Future of World Communication" (Address presented at the East-West Center, Honolulu, 29 September 1972), p. 22.

53. Isaacs, "Group Identity and Political Change," pp. 16–19.

54. Interview with Henry A. Kissinger, *Life*, 6 February 1972, p. 19.

55. Ali A. Mazrui, "Pluralism and National Integration," in *Pluralism in Africa*, ed. C. A. Kuper (Berkeley: University of California Press, 1969), cited in Isaacs, "Group Identity and Political Change," p. 20.

56. Bernard B. Fall, "Sociological and Psychological Aspects of Vietnam's Partition," *Journal of International Affairs*, July 1964, pp. 179–180.

57. William P. Bundy, "Reflections," *Preuves* (Paris), May 1971, cited by Milt Freudenheim, *Chicago Daily News*, 26 June 1971, p. 1.

58. W. W. Rostow, *Politics and the Stages of Growth* (Cambridge: At the University Press, 1970), esp. p. 29; see also idem, *The Stages of Economic Growth* (Cambridge: At the University Press, 1960).

59. This is discussed with particular reference to industrial location policies in *Industrial Location in Japan* (Tokyo: Ministry of International Trade and Industry, 1962).

60. United Nations, Economic Commission for Asia and the Far East, *Annual Survey*, (report of the 27th meeting, Manila, 20–30 April 1971), p. 34.

61. "Socially Just Economic Programs for Southeast Asia," *Mainichi* (Tokyo), 20 February 1971, p. 2.

62. Dwight Perkins, "The United States and Japan in Asia" (Paper delivered at the conference on "Peace in Asia," Kyoto, 10 June 1972), pp. 19–20; see also "New Concepts for Old," *Insight* (Hong Kong), September 1972, p. 14.

63. Mahbub ul Haq, "Let Us Stand Economic Theory on Its Head: Joining the G.N.P. Rat Race Won't Wipe Out Poverty," *Insight*, January 1972, p. 18.

64. Renato Constantine, ed., *The Recto Reader: Excerpts from the Speeches of Claro M. Recto* (Manila: Recto Memorial Foundation, 1965), p. 50.

65. Minoru Kōryu, "Evaluating the Overseas Deployment of Industry" (Symposium report compiled for the Japanese Ministry of International Trade and Industry by the Mitsubishi Economic Research Institute, Tokyo, June 1972), cited in "Aid Founders on Inequality in Poor Lands," *Asahi Shimbun* (Tokyo), 14 July 1972, p. 4.

66. Joseph Kraft, "China's Great Problem," *Washington Post*, 23 March 1972, p. 24.

67. Arthur G. Ashbrook, Jr., "China: Economic Policy and Economic Result, 1949–71," in *People's Republic of China: An Economic Assessment* (Compendium of papers submitted to the Joint Economic Committee, U.S. Congress, 18 May 1972), p. 7.

68. Maynard Parker, "I Am Not Playing Dominoes" (interview with Lee Kuan Yew), *Newsweek*, 24 July 1972, p. 52.

69. Kenneth M. Kaufmann and Helena Stalson, "U.S. Assistance to Less-Developed Countries, 1956–65," *Foreign Affairs*, July 1967, pp. 715–725.

70. Rupert Emerson, "Post-Independence Nationalism in South and Southeast Asia: A Reconsideration," *Pacific Affairs*, Summer 1971, p. 192.

71. Takeo Kuwabara, "Acculturation, Modernization and Nationalism: The Case of Modern Japan" (Address presented at the East-West Center, Honolulu, 12 February 1973), p. 26. Michio Nagai rebuts this view in a symposium with Kuwabara, "Nihon no Shōrai" [The future of Japan], in a special issue of *Ushio* (Tokyo), November 1971, pp. 160–169.

72. This is a distillate of conversations with Nehru from 1951 to 1964, in particular an unpublished conversation on February 1, 1961, and interviews on March 2 and October 16, 1963. See also Selig S. Harrison, "The Splendid Pretender," *Washington Post*, 31 May 1964, p. E1; and O. Mannoni, *Prospero and Caliban* (New York: Praeger, 1956), esp. pp. 11, 32, 39–49, 77, 97, 102–106.

73. Reischauer, *Beyond Vietnam*, p. 235.

74. Richard D. Lambert, "Comment: Comparativists and Uniquists," in *Approaches to Asian Civilizations*, ed. William de Bary and Ainslee Embree (New York: Columbia University Press, 1964), esp. pp. 240–242.

75. These and other Vietnam-focused postmortems on U.S. Asia policy are discussed in Leslie Gelb, "The Pentagon Papers and the Vantage Point," *Foreign Policy*, Spring 1972, pp. 25–41; George A. Kelly, "A Strange Death for Liberal America?" ibid., esp. pp. 16, 18, 22; and R. M. Pfeffer, ed., *No More Vietnams* (New York: Harper & Row, 1967).

76. Isaacs, "Group Identity and Political Change," p. 23.

II

NATIONALISM
AND COMMUNISM

2. The Limits of Asian Communism

The American collision with nationalism in Asia has resulted in large part from an undifferentiated assessment of the nature and potential of Asian communism. In Korea, the United States made one appraisal of the communist challenge, concluding that future expansive thrusts elsewhere would repeat the pattern of conventional aggression. In Vietnam, this assumption was revised to make way for a new strategic doctrine emphasizing the threat of "people's wars." But the same underlying assessment governed U.S. policy in both of these theaters of major U.S. engagement in Asia. Communism has been treated as a monolithic challenge that should be stopped, at any cost, everywhere, since victory in one country will inevitably lead to eventual communist control of the entire area. This image of a monolithic threat has been reinforced by the companion belief that in Asia, with its overpopulation and its poverty, communism is a peculiarly irresistible and ubiquitous danger.

Ironically, at the very time when the United States was becoming most deeply committed in Vietnam, the familiar stereotypes of the cold war were increasingly being called into question by the Sino-Soviet conflict and the acceleration of a worldwide national communist trend. The intellectual confusion of the Vietnam years was clearly apparent in the ambiguity surrounding official attempts to define the enemy. At times it was purely and simply China.[1] More characteristically, the Johnson administration stopped short of defining the Vietnam conflict in terms of a monolithic international communism or even of a Peking-Hanoi axis. It was altogether consistent with the rationale of U.S. policy to declare that Hanoi's intervention in the South "proceeded from impulses which were substantially independent of Communist China."[2] American support for Saigon would serve its greatest historic purpose, in this view, by

45

deterring other Asian revolutionaries who might similarly seek to apply the Chinese "people's war" model on their own. Having left the image of a monolithic challenge behind, Washington then went on its way in a continuing search for new policy moorings, still inclined to believe that communism inherently menaces U.S. interests but no longer quite as certain why. Shortly before assuming office, former president Nixon wrote that national communism is still communism, posing a threat that "by being subtler . . . is in some ways more dangerous than the old-style international Communism."[3] Yet it was Nixon who institutionalized the confusion and ambivalence in the American perception of communism in Asia by initiating the U.S. détente with Communist China while continuing to treat Hanoi as an enemy.

The pendulum swings during the Vietnam period from one oversimplified image to another were exemplified when former ambassador Reischauer denied that communism in Asia was ever really communism at all, describing it as "but one of nationalism's vehicles."[4] This aptly characterized the reality in some cases, as we shall see, but overlooked the wide variations in the tactics pursued by communist parties in diverse parts of Asia and the resulting differences in the patterns of interaction between nationalism and communism. Surveying Asian communist experience from country to country, one finds that the degree of communist identification with nationalism has invariably been the critical determinant of past success or failure and offers the surest contemporary barometer of future prospects. Moscow was singularly insensitive to the importance of this relationship in the Asian setting, leading most parties in the area astray at the formative period in the political evolution of their countries. The success of Asian communist parties was also conditioned, in varying degree, by a wide range of local factors that affected their ability to compete for the leadership of nationalism.

Where a strong noncommunist leadership arose in the independence struggle, as in India or Indonesia, communist fortunes would have suffered even if party strategy had been in tune with nationalist objectives, especially since Nehru and Sukarno consciously stole the thunder of the Communists with socialist programs. Where the armed forces played a nationalist role, as in Burma, the communists were denied the favorable political opportunity to create their own military machine provided by the presence of the French colonial army in Vietnam. In favorable economic terrain, communist parties have often established localized foundations of strength whether or not there were other issues to exploit. Allowing for such variations, however, one finds a clear common denominator cutting across the experience of every Asian communist party. Communist strength in

Asia is greatest in the two countries in which the leadership of nationalism has been added to other appeals in the communist armory, China and Vietnam, and it is deeply rooted elsewhere only where party leaders have had a base in subnational minority groups that have been seeking to define their identity in relation to the nationalist upsurge.

The political battle cry of "No More Vietnams" clearly bears little relation to an Asian scene in which there are, quite literally, no more Vietnams left. China and Vietnam emerge in our analysis as completely exceptional cases defying comparison with other Asian communist experience. The success of the Chinese and Vietnamese parties in appropriating nationalism stands in remarkable contrast to the record of communist movements in the rest of Asia, which not only failed in one degree or another to gain nationalist leadership but also were at times actually ranged against the nationalist cause. To some extent the explanation for their success lies, as we shall see, in fortuitous historical circumstance and in ruthless opportunism practiced at the expense of their noncommunist rivals. But this was something more than a case of being in the right place at the right time, with the appropriate tools of organization and discipline. The Communist leadership in these two isolated instances made what was a conscious and purposeful attempt to harmonize the pursuit of nationalist and communist objectives. They were not merely manipulating nationalist symbols for communist ends. They became communist nationalists quite as much as national communists, playing a role broadly parallel in long-term historical perspective to that played by noncommunist nationalists elsewhere in Asia. This was initially a role of national mobilization against foreign rule, but Mao Tse-tung and Ho Chi Minh, like Nehru and Sukarno, gave expression to the larger meaning of nationalism as an ongoing search for national identity and self-respect. Marxist-Leninist ideology, in their hands, was exalted not only for its own sake but also, inseparably, as a key to the rapid achievement of national strength through an equitably shared process of economic modernization.

A comparative examination of the interplay between communism and nationalism in each of the countries of Asia is essential to understand why the roots of Vietnamese communism have been so peculiarly stubborn and deep and why the political environment confronting the United States in Korea has been so very different. Such an examination underlines the need for a differentiated American approach to "Asian communism" and turns our attention, in so doing, to the wide range of hopeful policy choices open to the United States in communist and noncommunist capitals alike.

INDIA: THE COSTS OF SUBNATIONALISM

In the immediate aftermath of the Russian Revolution, the new international communist movement faced a receptive audience in Asia and a unique opportunity. Appealing for justice not only between man and man but between nation and nation, the communist message seemed to be directly addressed to the new nationalist elites. Lenin's theory of imperialism, in particular, acquired an overnight vogue among intellectuals throughout the colonial countries, providing both a systematic explanation for their economic plight and a catchall foreign scapegoat in the concept of an industrial capitalism increasingly dependent on the "superprofits" milked from low-wage colonial labor. After the first flush of idealism, however, the disparate demands of a worldwide revolutionary movement gradually led to a confused and ambivalent stance toward nationalism in Asia. The Comintern rocked back and forth in indecision during the critical period of the twenties, leaving local communist parties largely to their own devices while noncommunist nationalists were rapidly preempting political leadership in their societies.[5]

Lenin and Stalin alike assigned an implicitly Europe-centered role to Asian communist parties. Initially their task was to harass the colonial rulers through militant subversion, thus weakening them at home. Noncommunist nationalists were to be denounced to keep in step with the party line in Europe irrespective of the impact this would have on the long-term development of local communist strength. By the time of the Popular Front in 1935, when Asian communist parties were free for a brief period to adopt more flexible tactics, they were already isolated from the nationalist mainstream in most Asian countries. Their nationalist bona fides were deeply suspect long before the flip-flops of the communist line during World War II. After the war, the insurrectionist Zhdanov line completed the process of alienation, and post-Stalin Soviet policy implicitly recognized what had happened by shifting to a new and benign approach toward noncommunist neutralism.

The fate of the Indian Communists offers perhaps the classic illustration of the constrictive effects of Soviet policy on the growth of an Asian communist party. After initial approval by the Sixth Congress, tactical collaboration with "bourgeois" nationalists in India was totally barred in 1929. Even the left wing of the Congress party, led by Jawaharlal Nehru, was not exempted from this blanket prohibition, and the doctrinaire leadership of the Indian party, once described by Nehru as "the stupidest of the Communist parties of the world,"[6] embraced the Moscow directive with exaggerated zeal.

The advent of the Popular Front in France and the subsequent worldwide relaxation of the united front taboo found the Communist Party of India (CPI) one of the last in the entire international movement to adapt to the new climate.

The initiative in establishing a left-nationalist coalition in 1936 was taken not by the Communists but by the Congress Socialist Party (CSP), the principal left-wing group within the nationalist fold. Communist leaders were extremely chary of the softened Comintern line. As partners in a united front with the Socialists until their expulsion from the CSP three years later, the Indian Communists concentrated singlemindedly on strengthening their party machinery at the expense of the Socialists. They acted unabashedly and exclusively as communists, not even paying lip service to the notion that group interests should be subordinated in the common cause against the foreigner.

When Nazi Germany invaded the Soviet Union in June 1941, signaling an abrupt change from Comintern disdain for an "imperialist war" to support of what was now a "people's war," Congress leaders gave the Communists their last chance. The willingness of the CPI to get into step with the new line, dictating as it did collaboration with the British raj, appeared to the nationalist camp as unimaginable betrayal, especially since the Communists were reaping the benefits of legal status at a time when Congress leaders languished in British jails.

The impact of the pro-British stand maintained by the Communists throughout the war was aggravated when the CPI coupled the "people's war" line with a still more far-reaching departure from nationalist assumptions. The leaders of the Congress movement had articulated the goal of a strong independent India uniting Hindus and Moslems under the banner of a single sovereignty. While respecting the need for a measure of autonomy on the part of diverse religions and regional particularisms within Indian society, Nehru insisted that decisive power remain in the hands of the central authority. The Congress image of a united India as a potential great power was thus directly and frontally assaulted when the Communists set forth a broad theoretical rationale on the "national question" in India that defined the fourteen linguistic identities in the subcontinent as separate nationalities, each endowed with the ultimate right to accept or reject membership at any given moment in a future free Indian federation. Superimposed on top of this was a corollary analysis stressing the geographical concentration of Indian Moslems in certain contiguous linguistic areas and the consequent validity of the Moslem League demand for the creation of a sovereign Moslem-majority state of Pakistan.7

The Communist stand inevitably won sympathizers in Moslem League ranks and gave the party what was to be an enduring identification with the grievances of Andhra, Kerala, Bengal, and other disaffected regions. By the same token, the CPI had now totally outraged most of the Congress leadership as well as the nationalist elite in all parts of the country. Both Hindu chauvinists and Nehru-style secularists, whose opposition to the creation of Pakistan stemmed from totally opposite motivations, were united in their distaste for the Communist position. Nationalists of all stripes were appalled at the contention that India was not one nation. Nehru attacked "the treacherous attitude of the Indian Communists, who want to create a dozen or more divisions of India. . . . The Communist Party by its treacherous policy has isolated itself from the masses."[8]

The Communist accent on the distinctive linguistic identities encompassed in the new states of India and Pakistan was carried over after independence in the form of a systematic campaign to dismantle multilingual provincial units created at the whim of British mapmakers. Indian Communist sponsorship of the regionalist demand for the demarcation of new state boundaries along language lines proved to be a potent weapon against the new Nehru government and became the centerpiece of Communist strategy. This posture was soon reversed, however, when Stalin's passing led to the establishment of cordial ties between Moscow and New Delhi and a redefinition of Communist nationality policy. Assertions of the right of disaffected regions to secede from the union. were severely muted,[9] as a by-product of the new policy, and the Communist Party of India dedicated itself to forging unity with "progressive" Congress forces. It seemed that Indian communism had finally made its peace with Indian nationalism until the intensification of conflict between India and China and the sharpening of Sino-Soviet hostility split Indian communism down the middle. The division of the CPI into separate Left and Right parties corresponded with deep differences not only over the 1962 Chinese border incursions but also over the proper balance between regional and national claims.

In addition to its equivocal stand on Chinese incursions, the Left Communists took a clear turn back toward the pre-1953 party line on nationality policy. The draft program adopted by the first Left Communist convention at Tenali in 1964, while not explicitly reaffirming the right of secession, pleaded for "full autonomy" for all states and charged that New Delhi was seeking to impose the north Indian Hindi language on unwilling non-Hindi regions. "Growing contradictions" between the states and the central government could be resolved, the draft program declared, only by reducing central powers, including the powers of the president.[10] Since 1964, the Left Communists, known as the Communist party of India (Marxist), have consistently stressed regional grievances against New Delhi, if only because their principal centers of strength are in non-Hindi Andhra, Kerala, and West Bengal, where they substantially outnumber the Right group, still calling itself the "Communist Party of India."

The post-Stalin rapprochement between New Delhi and Moscow signified a new Soviet estimate of the strength of Indian nationalism as well as a general revision of earlier assumptions concerning "bourgeois" nationalist regimes in developing countries. Similarly, China and the Left Communists turned to the disruption of Indian unity when relations between New Delhi and Peking deteriorated. But it is not as if separatism has been a mere tactical gambit contrived to suit short-term international communist interests. The Indian Communists embraced it in response to powerful indigenous social pressures, and the most immediate beneficiaries of this policy were, after all, the Kerala, Andhra, and Bengal party leaders, who were consciously seeking to make their Communist commitment consistent with their role as champions of regional interest.

The persistence of Communist strength in Kerala, Andhra, and Bengal during years in which Communist strength elsewhere in India has steadily dwindled serves as a reminder that one man's poison is indeed another's meat. By solidly identifying themselves with regional aspirations, the Communist units in these regions have struck deep local roots, but they have necessarily done so at a cost to Communist growth elsewhere. It is noteworthy that the separatist policy pursued by the party after 1942 had long been actively promoted by Communist organizations in non-Hindi southern and coastal states. These have been disproportionately powerful units in the overall party power balance from the earliest days of Indian communism. Responding to local sentiment in their own constituencies and anxious to enhance their own local popularity, Communist leaders in the non-Hindi areas pressed for a national party line that would conform to their purposes. Their perception of their own immediate social environment was accurate in its own terms and led to effective local Communist strategies. It was for the Soviet Union, China, and the national Indian Communist leadership to impose a nationalist perspective, and in the absence of this, the regionalists in Communist ranks ran away with the game. Nehru and Gandhi, by contrast, sought to accommodate particularist loyalties within the broader framework of a pan-Indian nationalism, succeeding to a remarkable extent despite their notable failure in the case of the Moslem League and the Pakistan movement.

IN-GROUPS AND OUT-GROUPS

The characteristic dilemmas of Asian communist parties have been how to relate to independence movements and how to choose after independence between the irreconcilable alternatives of national and parochial roles. In most cases, as in India, Soviet ambivalence immobilized or completely misguided Asian communists and gave noncommunist nationalist movements a decisive head start. Where a communist party has gained a firm foothold, in spite of its failure to capture the leadership of nationalism, the source of its strength is almost invariably found in a subnational or parochial coloration roughly comparable to the Kerala, Andhra, and Bengal Communists. There has been no middle ground between nationalism and subnationalist or separatist commitment. Economic factors alone have failed to provide a solid basis on which to build a broad-based communist allegiance in an Asian environment.

Communism in Malaysia began as the expression of a Chinese "out-group" and never lost its exclusively Chinese-minority character. Favored by British colonial administrators and predisposed by tradition and religion to distrust Marxism-Leninism, the Malay majority responded coolly to international communist organizing efforts from 1920 to 1930. The early Indian immigrants to Malaysia also were proving to be relatively poor revolutionary material at a time when the Chinese were responding readily to communist appeals. While the Tamil Indian laborer came to Malaysia through officially sponsored group recruiting channels, the restless Chinese arrived in helter-skelter fashion as indentured laborers under the control of labor contractors. Like the overseas Chinese elsewhere in Southeast Asia, they faced discrimination in allotments of land and jobs, as well as in the political arena. The Communist party became a natural forum for disgruntled Chinese youth, and once it had acquired a Chinese stamp, it became automatically suspect in Malay and Indian eyes.

Although other factors obviously contributed to the defeat of the Malaysian Communist insurgency, the Chinese identity of the guerrillas was in itself critically disabling. The Malay peasantry followed the noncommunist Malay leadership of Tungku Abdul Rahman and Tun Razak even though the Malay nationalist movement was then relatively new and untested. More recently, since the defeat of the insurgency, the underground Communists in Malaysia have made desultory attempts to establish a Malay base but continue to be overwhelmingly Chinese. The principal opposition group with Communist links operating openly in Malaysian politics, the Labor party, led by a respected noncommunist intellectual, Tan Chee-khoon, is

y nationalism has been firmly
ional Organization (UMNO),
g coalitions. To the extent
olitical temper among the
ectively in recent years
aders of the UMNO or
nationalist group es-

ghout its early history,
the same endemic disabil-
ew ethnic Thais in Communist
d structurally apart in an uneasy
considerably stronger group of Chinese
nal progress of Thai communism prior to
attributed in large part to its alien image, which
y the extraterritorial procommunist propensities
mese émigrés in northeast Thailand loyal to Ho Chi

avid Wilson has taken issue with the widespread interpreta-
ion[11] that the Chinese and Vietnamese face of communism in
Thailand was the one and only determining factor in its early
repudiation by the ethnic Thai majority. His basic argument is that
Marxist methods do not go easily with the individualistic Thai
political style and tradition. Moreover, Thai intellectuals have in
Buddhism "a Weltanschauung which is both satisfactory and comfortable"; they did not experience colonialism, and such favorable
economic factors as low population density and a land surplus have
also weakened the communist appeal. Nevertheless, having registered
this caveat with respect to the reasons for the ethnic Thai rejection,
Wilson concurs in the estimate that communism has been "almost a
complete monopoly of Chinese and Vietnamese. . . . At the same
time, the anti-Communism of the Thai government has been linked
and confused with the national policy of restriction and control of
these alien minority groups."[12]

Given their alienation from the core of Thai society, the Communists in Thailand found that the manipulation of regional separatism
in two key ethnic-minority areas was the only role open in the
country following World War II. Although Communist support for
the grievances of Meo, Lahu, and Lissu tribal groups in northwest
Thailand could conceivably acquire future importance, the most
significant Communist efforts to capitalize on regional protest have
been in the four Moslem-majority provinces of southern Thailand,
largely Malay, and in the impoverished, primarily Lao-speaking
northeast. In both of these cases the Communists were quick to ally

themselves with indigenous noncommunist
Ironically, however, the American presence
years, accompanied by rising Japanese economic
such an intense nationalist reaction in Thailand tha
have been able to add ethnic Thais to their ranks.
ethnic Thai support for the Communist movement ha
cally accelerated by the continuing struggle betwee
opposition groups and a coalition of military and right
widely regarded in Thailand as American supported.

In the Thai case, most of the Lao northeast and the
Moslem provinces, for all of their sense of grievance, have g
remained under the effective authority of Bangkok. In Burn
tribally based loyalties of the Karen, Kachin, and Shan rebels
posed a challenge of a deadlier order to the very existence of
Rangoon regime, and this has made the intermittent identification
Burmese Communist groups with the insurgents a peculiarly un
settling affront to Burmese nationalists.

Initially, both Than Tun, leader of the postindependence White
Flag Communists, and Thakin Soe of the smaller Red Flags, were an
integral part of the nationalist movement in Burma. Than Tun, in
particular, was closely linked in the popular mind with the preeminent leader of the Burmese independence cause, Aung San. As one of
the Thirty Comrades in Aung San's Thakin movement and as secretary-general of Burma's nationalist united front, the Anti-Fascist
People's Freedom League (AFPFL), during the decisive last phase of
the anti-Japanese resistance, Than Tun enjoyed a patriotic aura
paralleled by few Asian communist leaders at the end of World War
II. His short-lived nationalist role appears to have been incidental to
what was basically a narrowly conceived communist commitment,
however, reflecting the temporary identity of interest between the
Comintern "people's war" line and the anti-Japanese requirements of
the Burmese situation.

In India, the image of the Communists was tainted by their stand
on Pakistan and by a policy of support for the war, which was
viewed in its pro-British rather than its anti-Japanese colors. In
Burma and in other Southeast Asian countries in which the Japanese
had actually arrived on the scene, the communists could join in the
nationalist front against the invader and yet remain true to the
Comintern line. They were able to have it both ways. Once the war
ended and the Comintern adopted its "hard" Zhdanov line in Southeast Asia, the communist parties in the area faced a direct choice
between nationalist and communist priorities, and at this point Than
Tun went all the way with the Comintern. The break between the

Burmese Communist leadership and the dominant Socialist faction of the AFPFL in February 1948, soon after independence, coincided directly with the final adoption of the Zhdanov line at the Calcutta communist conference. It was thus viewed not only as an act of betrayal by the precariously established nationalist regime, facing as it did the tribal separatist challenge, but also as a betrayal dictated by foreign interests. The subsequent dependence of both Burmese Communist groups on their on-again, off-again alliances with the tribal insurgents for the maintenance of significant striking power against Rangoon has antagonized nationalist opinion of all shades. To the extent that the White Flags and allied paramilitary Kachin groups in the north have appeared to be in collusion with Peking, the gulf between nationalists and Communists has widened.

The patterns of communist success and failure are strikingly consistent throughout Asia. Thus, Cambodia under Sihanouk offered an uncomplicated, archetypal case of an ethnic majority of 85 percent led by an effective nationalist leader who faced separatist insurgencies identified with Vietnamese and Chinese Communist minorities. It was only after American military intervention following the ouster of Sihanouk that the Communists and allied groups were able to play a credible nationalist role despite their Vietnamese patronage and to acquire their mass base. The Vietnamese and Chinese minorities in Cambodia had conspicuously lacked a localized territorial homeland comparable to the northeast mountain provinces in which the Pathet Lao made its home base during struggle.

In the case of Laos, while Souphanouvong himself is a lowlander, he has delegated effective power to Kha tribal chieftains, and the Pathet Lao has acquired solidity as a coalition of the four leading Lao Teung tribal groups of the Boloven Plateau. By contrast, the Nepal Communists have been dominated by a high-caste leadership centered primarily in Khatmandu and have rarely reached out to the tribal hill areas. The Nepal party also lacked a compensating link with nationalism until 1962, when it embraced its anti-Indian and proroyalist policy. The Ceylon Communists have similarly failed to establish a solid social identification with either the majority Sinhalese community or with the Tamil minority, building their major strength on a class rather than on an ethnic or linguistic basis in coastal labor areas. In some countries, as we shall see, the specific geographical patterns of communist strength and failure require a more detailed discussion than these eminently tidy cases, but in every instance the common denominator characterizing unsuccessful communist parties is to be found in their inability to add nationalism or subnationalism to their armory.

INDONESIA: THE LEGACY OF MADIUN

The complex and tempestuous history of Indonesian communism offers an unusual example of an Asian communist movement that managed to recover from the doctrinaire mistakes of its early years and to achieve a remarkable degree of nationalist identification in the postindependence setting. As Johnny-come-latelies in the critical period of competition for nationalist leadership, however, the Indonesian Communists found themselves arrayed against an overpowering balance of hostile established forces. They were never entirely able to wipe out the stigma of their past. In the implacable opposition of the orthodox Islamic *santri* forces, in particular, they faced the characteristic dilemma of a communist party in the rigidly stratified Asian social setting, for *santri* opposition was a response to their own corresponding base in the rival, pre-Islamic *abangan* tradition of rural Java.

Soviet ambivalence about the proper relationship between communist parties and nationalist forces in the twenties left the way open for dogmatist elements in the Indonesian leadership to take the party on a course of reckless self-destruction in the name of the Comintern scriptures. On the critical issue of relations with the Sarekat Islam, a powerful quasi-nationalist organization of 2.5 million with strong religious moorings, Moscow "attempted to blow and swallow simultaneously,"[13] and when the Communists failed to gain control of the Sarekat Islam machinery, the dominant party faction pursued a vindictive rule-or-ruin policy.

By June 1926, the Indonesian party had embarked on the madcap adventure of an armed insurrection against Dutch rule. Foredoomed from the start by the weakness of the new party and actively undermined by factional bickering, the 1926 revolt was a fiasco that was to lead to the elimination of the Communists as a significant force in Indonesia until the end of World War II. As the first national martyrs at the hands of Dutch colonialism, the Indonesian Communists might justifiably be credited today with a pioneering nationalist role. But at the time, the abortive and narrowly based 1926 uprising had only a fleeting impact on a population just beginning to acquire political consciousness. The most important practical consequences of the revolt were that it fostered uncompromising anticommunist attitudes in the emerging leadership of Indonesian Moslems and, equally important, placed the organizational custody of Indonesian nationalism in the noncommunist hands of Sukarno and the moderate Islamic leader Mohammed Hatta. Sukarno's "Marhaenism" gave his new Nationalist movement a proletarian flavor that significantly undercut the Communist economic appeal. Despite some success by their underground cadres in infiltrating noncommunist nationalist groups during the Popular Front period, the Communists remained fragmented and demoralized throughout the decisive years of rapid political transition marking the Japanese occupation and early postwar period. Their wartime guerrilla activities were generally less effective than those of Socialist leader Sutan Sjahrir and other underground leaders. They were thus unable to acquire the nationalist luster gained through an anti-Japanese role by communist parties in Indochina, Burma, the Philippines, and, to some extent, Malaya. At the same time, they were not in a position to reap the fruits of legal status.

Having established a claim of their own to preeminent leadership, Sukarno and Hatta were the natural beneficiaries of Japanese efforts to win Indonesian collaboration in the war effort. By giving the appearance of collaboration and accepting a nominal place in the political structure set up under the Japanese occupation, they preserved a limited legal scope for aboveground nationalist activity. It was Sukarno and Hatta, with their skillfully contrived freedom of maneuver, who proclaimed Indonesian independence under the very noses of the Japanese on August 17, 1945, and it was Sukarno and Hatta who assumed national leadership during the confused four-year struggle thereafter against British and Dutch troops seeking to overturn the new republic. Isolated and frustrated, the Communists resorted once again to an insurrectionary adventure in 1948, egged on this time by a Comintern policy directive to all parties in Asia calling for revolutionary action.

Whether or not the so-called Madiun revolt of September 1948 was directly inspired by Moscow or grew out of local factors is still the subject of debate. In any case, the involvement of the hard-line faction leader, Musso, who had just made a dramatic, secret return to the country after more than a decade as a political fugitive in the Soviet Union, gave a made-in-Moscow image to the rebel "National Front Government" proclaimed at Madiun. The Communist move came at a moment when popular anxieties were focused on the danger of an imminent Dutch attack. As George McT. Kahin has observed, "The Communists were attacking leaders who had become the very symbol of nationalism and of Indonesian independence. Sukarno, in particular, had for an undoubted majority of the Indonesian rank and file come to symbolize the Republic."[14] The damaging legacy of Madiun in later years stemmed not only from this generalized odium of national betrayal but also, quite specifically, from the hatreds engendered in the ranks of loyalist army units and the deepened alienation of the orthodox Moslem leadership. In the tension and abandon of hit-and-run warfare with government troops during their month-long retreat from Madiun, the embattled Communist forces committed atrocities upon anticommunist elements in the countryside, singling out adherents of militant Moslem political groups in the orthodox *santri* tradition, who responded with their own paramilitary counterattack on Communist supporters throughout central Java.

The partial recovery of the Indonesian Communists from the Madiun debacle and their subsequent progress to the very brink of power in 1965 were the result of a skillful and deliberate effort by a new leadership to reestablish nationalist bona fides. Herbert Feith draws a sharp contrast between the "older, foreign-trained leaders," who had taken the party in such hapless directions, and the new post-1951 group led by D. N. Aidit, "all of them children of the Indonesian Revolution, who emphasized rather its loyalty to nationalism."[15] Aidit fundamentally reshaped party strategy "to subordinate the class struggle to the national struggle." Although the Dutch were gone, their residual presence in West Irian remained as a lingering symbol of colonial rule. In addition, the Communists were able to find a focus for their united front appeal in the carefully nurtured image of a new Western "imperialist" threat spearheaded by the United States.

The first opportunity to use the United States as a nationalist target came in May 1952, with the disclosure of a secret Indonesian-U.S. mutual security pact that had been signed by the foreign minister of the moderate Masjumi regime then in power without the knowledge of the prime minister or the cabinet. This marked an abrupt departure from the country's popular neutralist foreign policy and led to the resignation of the cabinet. More important, the ensuing political turmoil offered Aidit an occasion to drive a wedge between Sukarno and Hatta, the Masjumi leader, thus setting the stage for a major political realignment based on a Communist liaison with Sukarno and his Nationalist party. Another target of special utility for the Communists came in the anti-Sukarno, anti-Java revolt staged by dissident elements in the outer islands. As early as December 1956 the Communists had sensed the cold war propaganda potentialities of the revolt, declaring that the establishment of regional councils by the insurgent generals in Sumatra "divides and stabs the Indonesian republic from within; in this way we directly benefit the Dutch and American imperialists."[16] Later, with the dramatic evidence of American support for the rebels provided by the capture of pilot Allan Pope in early 1958, the Communists acquired an anti-American weapon that was to retain its potency for many years.

The manipulation of nationalist symbolism continued to be a dominant element in Communist strategy until the party suffered its disastrous setback in 1965. Justus van der Kroef has vividly detailed the agile Communist performance in preempting the issue of "confrontation" with Malaysia. In this case, the Communists were able to place themselves at the head of the nationalist procession, setting the pace, at times, even for Sukarno.[17] Yet the 1965 debacle made it abundantly clear that it is not enough for a communist party to manipulate the symbols of nationalism if it has not, in reality, played a consistent nationalist role and if it has failed to reach a plateau of leadership transcending basic social divisions within the national body politic.

The timely action of General Suharto and the unified response of dominant elements in the armed forces underlined the determined anticommunist commitment of the Indonesian military. Rooted in memories of Madiun and in the persistent image of the Communists as a creature of foreign interests, an image powerfully reinforced by the close Peking links of the Aidit leadership, this anticommunism has been more than anything else an assertion of deep nationalist distrust of Communist motives. The Indonesian military grew up with the nationalist movement, in marked contrast to the experience of some Asian armies that were instruments of the colonial ruler. Although originally created under the aegis of the Japanese occupation authorities, the armed forces were molded as a nationalist force and imbued with a nationalist ethos by Sukarno and Hatta, who persuaded the Japanese that only an army with a strong patriotic fervor could effectively defend the country. In the early battles to safeguard Indonesian independence from 1945 to 1947, at Madiun in 1948, and most important in the recurring struggle to subdue separatist challenges to the new republic, the army has developed a strong self-image as the principal defender of Indonesian nationalism.

For all of its importance in the immediate Indonesian context, the response of the army may not be as relevant for our general understanding of the relationship between communism and nationalism as the bitter vengeance wrought by the *santri* Moslem forces following the coup. The institutional opposition of the armed forces to the Communists could not by itself have brought about the decimation of Communist cadres achieved at the village level in Java with such assiduous grass-roots cooperation during the spring of 1966. This convulsive process of repression and the political polarization accompanying it depended, clearly, on organized Moslem support and corresponded directly to the long established social rivalry in rural Java between adherents of *santri* Moslem orthodoxy and the populist *abangan* tradition. Religious conviction, as such, is only the nominal basis of this rivalry. *Santri-abangan* tension centers around a "religious" conflict, but it has grown into a broader communal clash between kin groups and village factions in many parts of Java where adherents of the two traditions coexist within the same villages.

The roots of this phenomenon can be traced to the golden age of Javanese tradition during the Modjopahit dynasty (A.D. 1292–1518). When coastal rulers in the seventeenth century embraced the newly implanted Islamic faith, inland dynasties, harking back to Modjopahit, fought to preserve the traditional, pre-Islamic Javanese tradition. The inland kings recruited socially exclusive bureaucracies drawn consciously from families with "pure" Javanese lineage. The Dutch then utilized this existing bureaucratic structure and gave other direct and indirect institutional recognition to what had become a firmly established distinction between *santri* and *abangan* traditions. The unbending militance of the Islamic crusade offered a total contrast to the tolerant, syncretistic temper of *abangan* religiosity with its semimystical style and its many marks of early Hindu influence. Explicitly substituting Arabic borrowings for Javanese esthetic and religious lore, the *santri* creed provoked a nativist reaction dedicated to the defense of distinctively Javanese elements in religious practice and precept. Inescapably, the two traditions became the focus of contemporary political competition when Moslem-oriented parties vied for popular support with the Communists and Sukarno's Nationalists. To the *santri* faithful in many areas, all local *abangan* organizations came to be lumped together as "communist" during the fifties as the process of polarization proceeded between the Communist-Nationalist alliance and Moslem parties led by the Masjumi.[18]

In retrospect, it is clear that the odds were stacked heavily against Communist success in Indonesia once the party became irrevocably committed to one side of the *santri-abangan* division. Powerful *abangan* support gave the Communists 27.4 percent of the total vote in Java in the 1957-1958 elections and led to exaggerated estimates of their potential. But as Donald Hindley has pointed out, the Communists faced an "effective block" to further expansion in the unremitting hostility of the 38 percent of the Javanese electorate that voted *santri*.[19] The fact that the *abangan* tradition was restricted to Java automatically consigned the Communists to the status of a regional party and acted as a fundamental barrier across their path to power. Nevertheless, it was their failure to transcend the major social division within Java itself, in addition to their restricted regional character as a Java-based party, that explains the depth of the Communist failure.

THE POVERTY FACTOR IN PERSPECTIVE

To emphasize the importance of nationalism without reference to local economic variations or to the special historical circumstances conditioning certain major cases in Asia would greatly oversimplify and distort our analysis. The economic topography of Asia bears an obvious and direct relationship to the patterns of communist strength, a relationship reinforcing and complementing the patterns revealed by a study of political and social factors.

Donald Zagoria has pointed out that many parts of Asia in which communist strength is centered are fertile deltaic or low-lying coastal areas with dense concentrations of sharecroppers and landless laborers raising labor-intensive crops such as rice or sugar. This description would fit central Luzon in the Philippines, where the Huks are strongest; south-central China, where the Chinese Communists got started; the Irrawady River Delta in Burma; central and east Java; and the Krishna-Godavari and Tanjore deltas of south India.[20] The existence of a poor-peasant foundation does not by itself enable a communist movement to capture power, however, as each of these examples indicates, not only because areas such as these are geographically delimited but also because even in impoverished Asia the support of the dispossessed does not by itself provide an adequate foundation for political authority.

Given the extremely rigid social stratification of Asian countries, most of them still largely feudal, the structure of village and local power is such that the mobilization of lower income groups is often dependent on the partial support or at least the toleration of peasant proprietor and other upper income elements. The experience of regional communist movements within India underlines this factor and confirms in microcosm the limitations of a strictly economic appeal. The Tamil Communists in the Tanjore Delta have failed because local patriotism in the Tamil language area was captured by the Dravidian movement, with its advocacy of Tamil separatism. In the Godavari Delta, the Andhra Communists were able to parlay their strength among landless laborers into a regionwide appeal when they could transcend class and caste identification by leading the broader fight for the recognition of an Andhra regional identity in the demarcation of state boundaries. China and Vietnam offer the most powerful case histories in which Communist leaders have successfully built upon poor-peasant foundations by seeking a multiclass nationalist appeal, and these will be considered separately later.

In the Philippines, the experience of the Hukbalahap movement has been one of notable frustration despite the deep poverty prevailing in its central Luzon strongholds and the consistent failure of the

Manila government to alleviate the problems of tenancy and rural indebtedness. The reasons for this include an endemic factionalism and other organizational failings. But the underlying dilemma of the Huk movement has been its inability to add nationalism to its other appeals for more than a passing period of its history. The very name of the movement testifies to its original nationalist motivation: in its wartime form it was Hukbo ng Bayan Laban sa Hapa Hapon (National Anti-Japanese Army). Gaining rapidly in strength during the war years, when they possessed the aura of guerrilla fighters, the Huks have since proved unable to translate this patriotic image into political terms relevant to the postwar Philippine environment. During the war, the Huks and other guerrilla groups had an uncomplicated target in wealthy Filipinos who collaborated with the Japanese. After the war, political alignments became more diffused as many prominent citizens who had not collaborated gravitated to the new conservative Roxas regime. The Huks had never monopolized anti-Japanese guerrilla activity, in the first place, and many leaders of noncommunist guerrilla bands, among them Ramón Magsaysay and Ferdinand Marcos, took the conservative side.

The strong support given by the United States in the early postwar years to all anticommunist elements, ex-collaborators included, provoked an effort by the Huks to convert their wartime anti-Japanese nationalism into a new anti-American nationalist appeal. But this was frustrated by a powerful legacy of Filipino-U.S. goodwill, much of it established during the shared anti-Japanese resistance. William Pomeroy, an American sympathizer who fought with the Huks and served a prison sentence in Manila, has offered an interesting analysis of the reasons for their inability to use the United States as an effective nationalist target. According to Pomeroy, part of the explanation lies in the fact that the United States did give the country its independence and that the new Manila government included popular veterans of the "American-influenced" guerrilla forces. Still more important, he added, was the legacy of wartime cooperation itself: "The nature of the anti-fascist alliance in the country created illusions, even among the Huk masses, and a tendency to regard the American Army as an ally."21

Even during the war years, some Filipino Communist leaders saw the limitations of a narrowly Japanese-focused nationalist appeal that failed to encompass the Americans,22 and a later vehicle of Communist activity, the Bagong Hukbo ng Bayan (New People's Army), founded in 1969, addressed itself more expansively to the American military presence and to the growing economic penetration of the Philippines by the United States and Japan alike. Echoing Mao Tse-tung, the new Huk leaders mixed insurrectionist tactics with calls for a united front embracing the "national bourgeoisie." This reflected, in large part, their recognition of significant changes in popular attitudes toward the United States. Gradually, the sublimated psychological aftereffects of American colonial rule have been felt in the growth of a potent economic nationalism, accompanied by a progressively increasing clamor for the removal of U.S. bases that was accelerated by the Vietnam war. The new Huk movement was sensitive to this transformation, but starting from scratch as it was, in organizational terms, it made erratic progress.

Communism in the Philippines was fundamentally handicapped by the historical inheritance of a Filipino colonial experience that differed in many important respects from other cases in Asia. The fact that the United States gave in to Filipino pressures for independence without the bitter, last-ditch resistance shown by other colonial powers not only delayed the emergence of Filipino nationalism but inevitably conditioned its intensity and character. For somewhat different reasons, as we shall see, Korea is also one of Asia's special cases in an analysis of the relationship between communism and nationalism. The Korean experience of colonialism at the hands of Japan, a non-Western power, gives Korean nationalism a unique perspective. And in Japan itself the absence of a colonial experience created distinctive historical circumstances that have made the task of the Communist movement peculiarly difficult.

In Japan, as in most of Asia, the Communist movement in its early years betrayed a strong urban bias and spent its energies in doctrinal debates over the character and degree of development of Japanese capitalism. Even if a more astute leadership had made an attempt to capture nationalism, however, the Japanese Communists would still have confronted a barren path. Japan offers the one case in Asia in which the Communists never really had the opportunity to make a bid for nationalist leadership. Thailand and Korea, like Japan, escaped Western colonialism. But the distinguishing feature of the Japanese experience was the strong nationalist response of the Meiji leadership to Western contact, notwithstanding the absence of colonial rule, and the consequent head start enjoyed by Japan in modernization. When the Communist party was formed in 1922, a conservative elite had already set in motion the process of transition from an agrarian to an industrial society—and had done so under the banner of a traditionally sanctioned nationalism enshrined in the emperor.

Viewed in terms of classical Marxist-Leninist categories, as Robert A. Scalapino has pointed out in his study of Japanese communism, Japan seemingly contained the essential ingredient necessary for rapid Communist growth. In contrast to many other

Asian countries at that time, Japan had a large intellectual community and one culturally equipped to absorb and embrace Marxism. The restless, newly emergent industrial labor force was "no lumpen proletariat." Fresh from the village, most Japanese workers, like the deprived tenant farmers they left behind, were at least semiliterate as a consequence of the mass literacy programs of the Meiji period. They were well within the range of mass communication and propaganda. Yet communism made notably little progress. The explanation would appear to lie in the "enormously significant" fact that the Japanese Communists "were unable to capture and use nationalism, but instead were forced to fight it because it was a deadly weapon in the hands of their opponents . . . and because its primary symbol was the Emperor system."23

If the conservative nationalist elite had become corrupt or had failed to carry modernization forward in its own way, the Japanese Communists could conceivably have attempted to take over the nationalist edifice erected by their rivals. But this was not the case. They were left instead with the thankless task of opposing their own national imperialism until the postwar environment of Japanese-American relations gave them a meaningful antiforeign target.

Beginning with salvos against the U.S. occupation in 1946, the Japanese Communists competed consciously with their Socialist rivals for the leadership of nationalist protest against the U.S. military presence, culminating in their effort to make Washington, rather than the Kishi government, the focus of the 1960 riots against continuance of the Japan-United States security treaty. The protracted antitreaty agitation gave the Communists an unprecedented emotional fillip and paid off handsomely in a dramatic rise in party membership from 40,000 in 1958 to 90,000 in 1961 and 140,000 in 1964. Nevertheless, while sentiment for a modification of the Japan-United States defense relationship remained widespread and deeply rooted during subsequent years, the Communists were not in a position to corner this sentiment for themselves. They were forced to compete for nationalist popularity with the socialist parties; with the Kōmeito, political arm of the Buddhist Sōka Gakkai movement, and at times with powerful elements of the ruling Liberal Democratic party. They nurtured their continuing growth in membership and electoral appeal, accordingly, by turning their fire on the Soviet Union and China, as well as the United States. Ideologically, the Japanese Communist party vied with the North Korean Workers party for the strongest articulation of a national communist line within the international communist world. Politically, the Communist demand for the Soviet return of the entire Kuril island chain went beyond the demands of all other major parties in Japan and included suggestions, on occasion, that southern Sakhalin should also be restored to Japan. But the Communists still found themselves confined to the status of an influential minority, struggling against great odds to overcome the disabilities imposed by history.

The Japanese case demonstrates that the manipulation of nationalist symbolism can work its ultimate magic only when it is part and parcel of the actual process of nationalist awakening in a country. In Japan, this process was largely completed before the Communists came on the scene, and now the Japanese Communists face what is in many respects a "post-Marxist society."[24] By contrast, China and Vietnam began their adaptation to a world of nation-states at a later point in time that broadly coincided with the rise of communist parties in Asia. In these two distinctive cases, as we shall now see, communist movements were able to shape the national response to a foreign military challenge, thus legitimizing and energizing other claims to national leadership that were powerful in themselves.

NOTES

1. See especially the address by Hubert H. Humphrey at the National Shrine of Our Lady of Czestochowa, Doylestown, 15 October 1967.
2. Walt W. Rostow, Sir Montague Burton Lecture, University of Leeds, 23 February 1967, in *U.S. Department of State Bulletin*, 27 March 1967, p. 494.
3. Richard M. Nixon, "Asia after Vietnam," *Foreign Affairs*, October 1967, p. 115.
4. Edwin O. Reischauer, *Beyond Vietnam: The United States and Asia* (New York: Knopf, 1967), p. 64.
5. For useful general surveys of this period see Charles B. McLane, *Soviet Strategies in Southeast Asia* (Princeton: Princeton University Press, 1966), esp. pp. 73–79; and John P. Haithcox, *Communism and Nationalism in India* (New York: Research Institute on Communist Affairs, Columbia University, 1964), chaps. 1–3.
6. Quoted in John H. Kautsky, *Moscow and the Communist Party of India* (Cambridge: Technology Press; New York: Wiley, 1956), p. 2.
7. For a full treatment of the Indian Communist line on nationality policy see Selig S. Harrison, *India: The Most Dangerous Decades* (Princeton: Princeton University Press, 1960), chap. 5; and Gene D. Overstreet and Marshall Windmiller, *Communism in India* (Berkeley: University of California Press, 1959), esp. pp. 212–217. For the text of the Communist proposal for the transfer of power from Great Britain to fourteen Indian entities see "Declaration of Independence—Communist Resolution for the Constituent Assembly," Resolution of the Central Committee of the Communist Party of India, published in *People's Age* (Bombay), 15 December 1946, p. 1.

8. *National Herald* (Lucknow), 9 March 1946, p. 1.

9. "Nationalities and the Right of Secession," *Crossroads* (Indian Communist weekly), 6 September 1953, p. 10.

10. Communist Party of India, *Draft Program* (Calcutta: Ganashakti, 1964), pp. 16–18, 21, 30.

11. For example, Virginia Thompson and Richard Adloff, *The Left Wing in Southeast Asia* (New York: Institute of Pacific Relations and Sloane, 1950), p. 52.

12. David A. Wilson, "Thailand and Marxism," in *Marxism in Southeast Asia*, ed. Frank Trager (Stanford: Stanford University Press, 1959), p. 86; see also idem, *Politics in Thailand* (Ithaca: Cornell University Press, 1962).

13. Arnold Brackman, *Indonesian Communism* (New York: Praeger, 1963), p. 11. The most authoritative accounts of the early history of Indonesian communism are found in George McT. Kahin, *Nationalism and Revolution in Indonesia* (Ithaca: Cornell University Press, 1952); and Ruth T. McVey, *The Rise of Indonesian Communism* (Ithaca: Cornell University Press, 1965).

14. Kahin, *Nationalism and Revolution in Indonesia*, p. 301.

15. Herbert Feith, *The Decline of Constitutional Democracy in Indonesia* (Ithaca: Cornell University Press, 1962), p. 241.

16. Cited in Donald Hindley, *The Communist Party of Indonesia: 1951–1963* (Berkeley: University of California Press, 1966), p. 260.

17. Justus van der Kroef, *The Communist Party of Indonesia* (Vancouver: University of British Columbia Publications Center, 1965), esp. pp. 273, 294; see also Hindley, *Communist Party of Indonesia*, p. 291; and Hindley, "Indonesia's Confrontation with Malaysia: A Search for Motives," *Asian Survey*, June 1964, pp. 904–913.

18. Robert R. Jay, "Santri and Abangan: Religious Schism in Rural Central Java" (Ph.D. diss., Harvard University, June 1957), p. 201; see also idem, *Religion and Politics in Rural Central Java* (New Haven: Yale University Press, 1965); Clifford Geertz, *The Social Context of Economic Change: An Indonesian Case Study* (Cambridge: Center for International Studies, MIT, 1956); and Deliar Noer, "Masjumi: Its Organization, Ideology, and Political Role in Indonesia" (M.A. thesis, Cornell University, February 1960).

19. Hindley, *Communist Party of Indonesia*, p. 225.

20. Donald S. Zagoria, "Who's Afraid of the Domino Theory?" *New York Times Magazine*, 21 April 1968, esp. p. 64.

21. William J. Pomeroy, *Guerrilla Warfare: Liberation and Suppression in the Present Period* (New York: International Publishers, 1964), pp. 60–72.

22. For a detailed analysis of the Huk movement that demonstrates its reliance on anti-Japanese symbolism in building popular support and the lack of an anti-American appeal during the war years see Benedict Kerkvliet, "Peasant Rebellion in the Philippines: The Origins and Growth of the H.M.B." (Ph.D. diss., University of Wisconsin, 1972), esp. pp. 205–207, 377, 393–394. Kerkvliet shows that Communist leaders such as José Lava foresaw the

future ineffectuality likely to result from such a narrowly focused nationalist appeal (pp. 226–229).

23. Robert A. Scalapino, *The Japanese Communist Movement, 1920-1966* (Berkeley: University of California Press, 1967), pp. 44, 328–333.

24. Ibid., p. 354. For a challenge to Scalapino's view see J. A. A. Stockwin, "Is Japan a Post-Marxist Society?" *Pacific Affairs*, Summer 1968, pp. 184–198.

3. Nationalism and Maoism

In seeking to explain the rise of the Communists to power in China, scholars were fundamentally influenced for more than a decade by the lingering perspectives of the civil war and the companion American domestic debate over the merits of Chiang Kai-shek. The tendency in most early assessments of the sources of Communist success was to focus myopically on the two antagonists without adequate reference to the extraordinary wartime circumstances in which they struggled. Our attention was addressed primarily to the relative strengths and weaknesses of the Kuomintang and the Communists in their contest with each other: to such factors as KMT corruption, Communist identification with rural discontent, and, above all, to the contrast between disciplined, ideologically motivated Maoist cadres and factionalized Nationalists. Almost no emphasis was given to the fact that both the Nationalists and the Communists had faced a common Japanese enemy for nine wartime years before the climactic phase of civil strife from 1945 to 1949. The Japanese invasion was treated as little more than a macabre backdrop for the KMT-Communist struggle rather than as a central conditioning factor in its own right. To the extent that observers stressed the war, they did so most often in the narrow context of its disruptive effects on the economy and the administrative structure, citing this to explain why the Nationalists failed to carry out economic reforms or to account for the sudden success of the Communists in consolidating their north China "base areas" from 1937 to 1945.

With the benefit of a longer historical overview and an expanding body of relevant scholarship, it is now increasingly apparent that the Japanese invasion was not merely a backdrop but a dominant and pervasive factor defining the essential character of the KMT-Communist struggle in its definitive stages. Clearly, a wide range of military, economic, and political ingredients combined to bring about the ultimate Communist victory. But it was only when nationalism was added to all the rest that the Communists found their formula for success. The continuing Japanese challenge, beginning with the Manchurian crisis in 1931, overshadowed the Chinese scene and made the internal struggle above all else a competition for the leadership of Chinese nationalism. Mao Tse-tung perceived this clearly from the outset. He grabbed the banner of anti-Japanese resistance early and set the nationalist pace throughout the war years, forcing Chiang Kai-shek to follow his lead in the establishment of a united front. Moreover, the Communists made a more effective appeal than the KMT to the leadership of nationalism in its more comprehensive sense. With its unusually powerful, historically based sense of identity, China had clung complacently to a self-centered "culturalism" and had been slow to accept the proposition that it was but one among many nation-states, confronted by growing power rivalries that made it necessary to mobilize its own latent power. It was the Japanese invasion that first aroused a mass nationalist consciousness, and it was the Communists who offered the most effective response to the Japanese challenge.

THE ANTI-JAPANESE BANNER

Prior to 1931, the Kuomintang enjoyed an effective monopoly on nationalism, for Chiang had risen to power, after all, primarily on the strength of a militantly "anti-imperialist" appeal; he had forced a reduction in the extraterritorial concessions enjoyed by foreign powers and he had won unprecedented diplomatic status for China. Nationalism in the twenties was basically anti-Western, and the KMT was the principal custodian of this nationalism as the immediate heir to the mantle of Sun Yat-sen. The Manchurian crisis radically altered the situation, however, confronting Chiang with an unprecedented external military challenge and a profound tactical dilemma.

If he failed to stand up to the Japanese, he risked abdicating nationalist leadership to the Communists. At the same time, powerful arguments for seeking an accommodation were insistently advanced by important elements within the Kuomintang. China's only hope, some argued, was to gain time in which to build military strength. Abortive efforts to resist by inferior, poorly equipped forces would prove suicidal. Others openly advocated accommodation in the name of pan-Asian solidarity, insisting that Japan could be appeased at a tolerable price and that Tokyo and Chungking should cooperate in a partnership independent of Western influence. Still others stressed the tasks of internal development facing China and warned that war would set the country back a generation. Chiang himself was guided by his determination to exterminate the Communists and the warlords before turning to Japan. In the end, this was primarily responsible for his choice of the policy of "internal pacification before resistance to external attack."

As Japan rapidly spread her control over Manchuria and steadily infiltrated Inner Mongolia and large areas of north China, it became increasingly unfashionable among educated Chinese to support the Kuomintang. An American journalist then in China found that "great numbers" of students and intellectuals were disenchanted by Chiang's failure to respond to Japanese incursions and were heartened when the Chinese Soviet Republic in Kiangsi declared war against Japan in April 1932.[1] At first, the atmosphere was one of repressed outrage, but student patriotism finally flared in the face of continuing Japanese efforts to create an "autonomous" north China. On December 9, 1935, Peking University students ignited a nationwide protest against the Chiang policy. The December 9 movement began as a series of spontaneous, self-generating, and poorly coordinated outbursts by scattered local student groups. Later, as John Israel has demonstrated, "Communist techniques shaped raw nationalism into a purposeful political force."[2]

The precise degree of Communist control over the student movement during the mid-thirties became a subject of considerable controversy when the KMT used charges of Communist penetration to justify severe repressive measures. Even if it is true that the movement did fall substantially under Communist domination in early 1936, however, this does not impugn its character as a deeply rooted and authentic expression of student sentiment. The reality as reflected in careful studies of this period[3] is not that masterful Communists manipulated and molded pliant students. Rather it is that a powerful student upsurge helped to propel Chinese communism in a nationalist direction. A two-way process of interpenetration occurred. While Communist leaders gave organizational focus and a measure of national coordination to disparate student efforts, student activists poured en masse into Communist ranks, giving the party at a critical stage in its development a new layer of dynamic young leadership motivated primarily by nationalism. In addition to its impact on the internal evolution of the Communist party, the student upsurge also had far-reaching repercussions affecting the relationship between the KMT and the Communists. Both the December 9 movement and the parallel National Salvation movement were a response to the spectacle of internecine division in the nation at a time of external danger, and both groups consistently harped on the need for national solidarity against the Japanese. For the Communists, who had the most to gain from a united front, this offered a golden opportunity to put the KMT on the defensive. The crystallization of nationalist sentiment resulting from the student protests made it possible for the Communists to cast the KMT ever more irrevocably in the role of a reluctant partner in the national cause.

Throughout the war, the KMT and the Communists were as busy jockeying for position in their developing civil war as they were in fighting the Japanese. Chiang was especially anxious to make certain that Communist troops were cordoned off in north China and thus prevented from exploiting wartime chaos to establish strongholds in the Yangtze Valley. With an eye to the coming postwar struggle, the Communists took advantage of every opening they could find to bolster their own position vis-à-vis Chiang, but they also attached overriding importance to the united front. They proved to be more sensitive to the psychological significance of the united front in the competition for the loyalty of uncommitted Chinese than Chiang with his driving anticommunist animus.

"The government was *legally* within its rights in denouncing the activities of the Communists and in attacking their armies or their newspapers," Chalmers Johnson has observed, "but in so doing it jeopardized its own reputation with the masses, whose predominant political concern was 'national salvation' and 'resistance to Japan.' The Communists could violate Nationalist military directives with impunity so long as they appeared more anti-Japanese than the government, and they knew it."4 Unwittingly, the Japanese lent support to Communist claims of nationalist legitimacy by singling out the Communists for unusually venomous attacks in their propaganda and by treating them as their most consequential enemy. The Nanking puppet regime set up by Japan appealed incessantly to Chungking for unity in the anticommunist cause. Chiang was characteristically depicted, by implication, as a dupe of the Communists who was not really anti-Japanese and had joined with the Communists in a united front less out of genuine patriotic motives than for reasons of mere political opportunism.

THE "PEASANT NATIONALISM" DEBATE

The importance of nationalism as the key to Communist success in winning the support of students and intellectuals prior to 1945 has gained relatively wide recognition in analyses of the Communist rise to power. Often, however, there has been a tendency to treat student nationalism as an isolated, self-contained phenomenon restricted to urban centers and to stress economic discontent as the major source of Communist peasant support. Primarily as a result of the contribution made by Chalmers Johnson, one now finds wide scholarly acceptance of the view first advanced by most on-the-scene observers during the period of the Communist rise: that nationalism was a factor cutting across the urban-rural barrier. Johnson's findings in Japanese army archives and the expert discussion that these have provoked leave little doubt that in north China, at any rate, the Communists consolidated their hold over the countryside by mobilizing a broad-based nationalist resistance against the Japanese invader. There, as in other areas, revolutionary economic appeals were a central and compelling part of Communist symbolism. But the war provided a rationale for a multiclass strategy in which revolutionary objectives could be selectively pursued to suit the exigencies of a crisis situation. Specific class appeals were successfully fused in an overarching nationalist appeal, and this is what gave the Communists a solid territorial springboard for their ultimate victory.

Briefly summarized, Johnson's analysis shows that by deliberately soft-pedaling the class struggle in their wartime united front strategy, the Communists were able to neutralize the opposition of rural vested interests and to spread their control over progressively expanding areas of the north China countryside during their 1937-1945 guerrilla operations. The Kiangsi soviet had failed largely because the party could not reconcile its radical agrarian reform objectives with the need to secure the collaboration of upper and middle peasants during Communist military campaigns. During the war against the Japanese, the Communists avoided major land reform drives, limiting their efforts in areas under their control to rent reduction and debt rationalization. Despite this sublimation of their revolutionary economic appeal, they were able to rally their greatest popular following in north China during the war years, and the reason lay in the extraordinary rapacity of the Japanese. It was this that aroused the latent nationalist consciousness in the hitherto quiescent peasantry.

Prior to 1937, "nationalism in China was a powerful sentiment among many leadership groups, but the social milieu in which they acted was not nationalistic."[5] When the war changed this situation, especially in north China, where the Japanese onslaught was most directly felt, the Communists alone had a strategy explicitly designed to exploit the vacuum of leadership and administration created by the invasion. They also had an organizational capability and discipline that had been perfected in the trial and error of their futile earlier experience. In Shansi province, dominated by the warlord Yen Hsi-shan, the KMT had never ruled in the first place, offering a relatively clear field for Communist operations. Johnson traces the steady expansion of Communist enclaves in Shansi, Shensi, Hopei, and Shantung provinces after 1937, illuminating the interplay between the doggedly resistant peasantry and frustrated Japanese attackers who multiplied their brutality and terror in direct proportion to the resistance they encountered, only to provoke still more determined resistance. The Communist Army grew tenfold in numbers during the guerrilla struggles from 1937 to 1945. Johnson points to the "scorched earth" tactics used by the Japanese in 1941 and 1942 as peculiarly important in solidifying peasant resistance and in completely dislocating the old rural administrative structure. Moving into the vacuum, the Communists proved to be the most competent organizers of resistance, systematically putting into effect a well-developed program of rural administration calculated to win the loyalty of specific functional groups. The mere fact that the Japanese had driven the KMT out of large areas, opening the way for the Communists, would not by itself have meant much in the absence of a coherent Communist strategy and an effective Communist organizational capability for exploiting this opportunity.

Ironically, the KMT forces bore as much or more of the fighting against the Japanese as the Communists in China as a whole, if one considers the entire war period and the overall quantitative disposition of forces. But the psychological impact of this was to some extent swallowed up in the din of Communist united front propaganda, and in north China, as Johnson shows, central government troops rarely remained in an area after waging a battle. It was because the Communists provided sustained, on-the-scene leadership to the peasantry, establishing a new form of local governmental machinery to suit the new setting of guerrilla war, that they were able to establish enduring control in areas in which they waged the anti-Japanese struggle. Out of their shared sacrifices, the Communists and the peasants forged bonds of mutual confidence that gave the new Communist regime its legitimate basis of authority in 1949.

The Johnson thesis finds consistent support in on-the-scene accounts of the war period by a wide range of observers. George E. Taylor first used the phrase "peasant nationalism" to describe the phenomenon he found in Communist-ruled areas of north China.[6] In view of his later role as secretary of state, it is noteworthy that John Foster Dulles returned from a tour of China in late 1938 struck by the contrast between KMT and Communist postures toward the Japanese. Dulles wrote in an unpublished letter to Raymond B. Fosdick of the Rockefeller Foundation that

> outside of a few Chinese, who have been touched by missionary and educational influences from the Western powers, the only real resistance comes from the so-called Red Army group of the Northwest. The resistance elsewhere is mostly professional, highly mercenary and very ineffective. The

Kuomintang element, which we seem disposed to support, has until now represented this latter group.7

Looking back on his experiences in China, Jack Belden, a meticulous journalistic chronicler of the war years, stressed Communist success in winning over local administrative personnel in many areas of north China, attributing their success mainly to the partisan attitude of the KMT toward the united front and the divisive effects this had on anti-Japanese activities.8 Theodore White and Annalee Jacoby underlined the nationalist emphasis of Communist united front strategy in its approach to the landlords. Although rents were cut, landlords were assured of payment; and although interest rates were reduced, moneylenders could count on repayment of their loans. There was no expropriation except in cases of landlords who collaborated with the Japanese, and in general "the landlords and the well-to-do of north China hated the Japanese as much as the peasantry did. They, too, died and suffered; they, too, were fired with patriotism. . . . The black nature of Japanese conquest was common foe to every man, rich or poor, learned or ignorant."9

Although the scholarly discussion provoked by the Johnson study has not produced unanimity among academic specialists on China, there has been a growing consensus emphasizing the nationalist component in the Communist rise to power, and the factual analysis underpinning the Johnson thesis remains unchallenged. Thus, Benjamin I. Schwartz, while also citing other factors, believes that the invasion was a "necessary condition" of the Communist victory and strongly emphasizes the fact that the war enabled the Communists to "make a strong appeal to nationalistic sentiment, which they undoubtedly shared. . . . As a result of the Japanese aggression, the Chinese Communists were able to wed their rural strategy to a genuine national appeal."10 C. P. Fitzgerald joins Johnson in the view that Chinese communism should be "understood as a species of nationalist movement," stressing the crucial importance of the nationalist leadership attained by the Communists during the war but adding that afterward economic factors were decisive in "inducing the peasantry to give continuing support to the new regime, once they felt assured that it had come to stay."11 Stuart Schram praises Johnson for "substantiating . . . by solid historical evidence" what had hitherto been a mere impressionistic assumption of many scholars. But he adds a sharp reminder that Chinese nationalism is 2,000 years old and did not begin in 1937.12 Franz Michael, while arguing that the Communists simply put their communist goals "in cold storage" during the war years and have always been Communists, first and last, appears to agree that they did successfully exploit a nationalistic appeal during the war.13

The only critic who has attempted to challenge Johnson by demonstrating that the basis of wartime Communist support lay in economic appeals, rather than in nationalism, is Donald G. Gillin, author of a study of the Shansi warlord Yen Hsi-shan.[14] Gillin provides new evidence serving to support the Johnson contention that the Communists used nationalism to rally the support of aristocratic elements in Shansi.[15] As for the peasantry, however, he seeks to show that the Communists had gained strong peasant support on an economic basis prior to the Japanese invasion. He cites the writings of Yen Hsi-shan to show the Shansi warlord's sensitivity to Communist propaganda on economic issues as early as 1935 and attempts to establish the existence of a high degree of peasant support for Communist troops in clashes with those of Yen Hsi-shan in early 1936, attributing this to the Communist economic appeal.[16] Gillin's analysis conflicts with the preponderance of scholarly evidence indicating that Communist strength in Shansi was confined almost entirely to the capital of Taiyuan prior to the Japanese invasion. As Mark Selden has demonstrated, even in adjacent Shensi province Communist strength was concentrated largely in areas of Shensi bordering on Kansu province, not on the eastern border adjacent to Shansi, and the one significant Communist foray into Shansi in early 1936 was a mere foraging expedition to gather foodstuffs, which did not lead to significant peasant mobilization.[17]

Confronting Gillin's argument on a more fundamental plane, Johnson has observed that the support obtained by the Shansi Communists through the utilization of economic appeals in 1935 and 1936 only becomes meaningful when it is compared with the degree of support obtained after the start of full-scale hostilities with the Japanese both in Shansi and elsewhere. The issue is not whether economic appeals evoke support, he points out, a fact that he himself affirms, but rather whether such appeals were effective enough in Shansi prior to the Japanese invasion there to produce the broad momentum achieved by the Communists after 1937. Prior to the invasion, it was possible for the Communists to make simultaneous use of land reform and anti-Japanese slogans, for there was no contradiction between the demands of the agrarian front and the military front. Whatever success was achieved by the party under these circumstances, Johnson agrees, might well have been attributable to economic appeals. This was not enough to command "militarily significant" support from the peasants, however, and it was not until the full force of the Japanese onslaught that the peasantry as a whole was effectively mobilized, even though the shift to a broadened united front strategy meant softened policies toward rich and middle peasants.[18]

A more pertinent contribution by Gillin that should be taken into account is his reminder that noncommunist forces played a significant role in the early stages of the anti-Japanese fighting in north China. He points specifically to the resistance offered by KMT and Yen Hsi-shan units at the Nan-k'ou pass in the first major Shansi engagement in August 1937, as well as in other battles shortly thereafter in the Hsin-k'ou mountains and at Yuan-p'ing. His attempt to depict the Communists as having played a "secondary" role against the Japanese is extremely far-fetched, however, ignoring as it does the main period of the war after early 1938. Gillin glosses over the fact that the major battles in north China were fought in the later years of the war and that the military involvement of the KMT in north China steadily diminished after 1938. It was during these post-1938 years that Japanese depredations were greatest and that Communist-led guerrilla resistance saved the day. As Gillin himself acknowledges,[19] the mobile Communist guerrilla tactics employed during the last years of the war were eminently more appropriate to the Japanese challenge than the "suicidal" earlier insistence of Yen Hsi-shan on fighting a positional war.

In Gillin's case, his emphasis on economic appeals is but one aspect of a broadly unsympathetic treatment of the Communist wartime role and was accompanied by insinuations that Johnson was a dupe of Peking propaganda. Significantly, a later wave of scholars, writing from a frankly sympathetic perspective, criticized Johnson because his accent on nationalism was regarded as a denial that China had built a Maoist "new society." Thus, Selden, in his valuable analysis of the Yenan period, oscillates between admiration for the spirited "new nationalism"[20] that enabled China to resist Japan and insistence that this was not the principal factor giving the Communists their powerful bond with the peasantry. Selden cites a land reform program in a township of the Shen-Kan-Ning Soviet in Shensi province to establish that "agrarian revolution, not nationalistic rhetoric, paved the way for the increasingly effective military and political participation of the rural population."[21] His argument is basically weakened, however, by the fact that the Shen-Kan-Ning area was not itself invaded by the Japanese and was thus an atypical enclave in wartime north China. He does not provide evidence to rebut Johnson's basic contention that united front tactics during the war period led to a postponement of major land reform in most embattled areas; even if he were to do so, this would not necessarily alter the importance of the role played by the Japanese as a unifying threat in areas in which their presence was felt. To say this, though, is not to dispute Selden's pertinent reminder that the Communist bond with the peasantry would have proved less enduring if it had rested on anti-Japanese sentiment alone. While softening their tactics toward rich and middle peasants, as a temporary expedient, the Communists were able to preserve their bedrock support in the ranks of poor peasants and tenant farmers because their bona fides were periodically demonstrated by rent reductions and debt rescheduling. The analyses of Johnson and Selden are complementary. As Johnson maintains, it was the war and its dislocations, activating nationalist consciousness on a narrow, antiforeign basis, that accelerated Communist mass mobilization during the 1937-1945 period. Nevertheless, as Selden contends, it was a programmatic commitment to egalitarian economic reform dating back to the war years that reinforced the legitimacy of Communist rule during the initial postwar decades. Such a commitment epitomizes the broader horizons of nationalism as a shared "national" drive for strength and self-respect.

Another important refinement of Johnson's analysis has been suggested by Jeffrey Race, who points out that Communist propaganda against the Japanese had a comparatively limited impact in rural areas of south and central China, where Japanese forces utilized velvet glove methods contrasting markedly with their tactics in north China. Japanese domination, as such, was not enough to enlist support for the Communist guerrillas in the absence of a direct threat to the physical security of the peasantry, thus demonstrating, in Race's view, that " 'nationalism,' understood as opposition to invading foreigners, is neither necessary nor sufficient to motivate a revolutionary movement."

Race points to "self-protection" as the crucial motive; this is equally operative when an entire population faces a foreign invader, as in north China, or when a village or other group is caught up in a civil struggle within the same society, as in Vietnam.[22] What enabled communist movements to win peasant support in both of these cases was not their appeal for loyalty to "an abstract national community" but rather their ability, underlined by Johnson, to organize a secure local social and economic order amidst the tumult of war. This was strengthened, in turn, by a "ladderlike progression of loyalties" that gave local Communist leaders a channel of "continuous vertical promotion" within the party hierarchies concerned,[23] a theme developed earlier by John McAlister.[24] Race helps to put the Johnson thesis in perspective by stressing that a peasant populace, long politically quiescent, may not have a clearly defined concept of national identity and may be most responsive to political stimuli at a more immediate level. At the same time, he makes no distinction between politically activated leadership elements and their mass following. He thus fails to acknowledge that nationalism, in its most comprehensive sense, was the psychological cement binding together the "ladderlike progression of loyalties" within both Chinese communism and, as we shall see, Vietnamese communism. For many party leaders down to the local level, nationalism, "understood as opposition to invading foreigners," was part of a larger social vision characterized by the merger of personal and national identity discussed in Chapter 1.

It was their emergence as leaders of nationalism in this broadest dimension that impelled the Chinese Communists to make their fundamental doctrinal break with Moscow by subordinating the class struggle to the multiclass united front strategy described as "Maoism." In contrast to Lenin's manipulative attitude toward nationalism, as Van Slyke emphasizes, "nationalism was—and is—an ultimate value" for the Chinese party.[25] An assessment of communism and nationalism in Asia must rest on acceptance of this central fact, while recognizing, at the same time, that nationalism need not be "the" ultimate value[26] for a communist movement and that communism and nationalism are not likely to be "synonymous."[27] The ideological torment of the Chinese party over the proper formulation of united front doctrine was a measure of the subtlety of the Communist-nationalist symbiosis. Chinese and Vietnamese communism are best described, accordingly, in C. P. Fitzgerald's phrase, as "a species of nationalist movement," no less legitimate than other species by virtue of their distinctive communist identity and clearly no less formidable.

COUNTRY IN DANGER

Reviewing the record of the period 1931-1945, one is left with little doubt that the Communists captured the leadership of anti-Japanese nationalism and that their success in north China set the stage for their ultimate triumph. It would be an overstatement, however, to say that they came to power as the recognized heirs to the entire tradition of twentieth-century Chinese nationalism. It would be more precise to say that the KMT had defaulted in carrying forward the Revolution of 1911; that this increasingly left a vacuum of leadership; and that the Communists, secure in their north China base areas and riding a wave of war-born popularity, found themselves with a beckoning opportunity in 1945 to prove themselves more effective custodians of the revolution.

The specific failures of the Kuomintang may all be viewed as part of a broad failure to fulfill the mission of national regeneration initiated by Sun Yat-sen. Thus, the supreme test for a nationalist leadership committed to making China strong was in the field of economic modernization. Here the KMT defaulted not only in the general sense that its achievements were relatively limited but also in the deeper sense that its economic policy increasingly came to be regarded as an instrument of special interests. As if ineffectuality were not bad enough, Chiang added insult to injury in nationalist eyes by pursuing policies that operated primarily for the benefit of a privileged minority of upper income speculators and profiteers and "a few relatively advanced provinces."[28] The wealth and power of the Four Families epitomized a corrupt regime dedicated to the pursuit of group interest rather than the national welfare. To the extent that KMT economic policies favored foreign as against domestic investors, they also enhanced the belief that Chiang was becoming unduly dependent on foreign support and was abandoning all pretense of devotion to the "anti-imperialism" enshrined in Sun's *Three Principles of the People.* The fact that the KMT was frankly attempting to build progress atop a traditional Confucian social structure intrinsically hampered the modernization program. Finally, in the cultural sphere, the emphasis on Confucian values implicit in the "New Life" movement basically compromised the KMT as a contender for the leadership of a modern nationalism. For as Joseph R. Levenson has shown, to confuse "culturalism" with "nationalism" was, in effect, to abdicate nationalist leadership[29] at a time when the country faced the rising challenge of the peculiarly disciplined Japanese national state.

Chiang plainly failed in a wide range of ways to realize the promise of 1911, and yet one cannot be sure what would have happened in China if the war had not intervened. Despite its weaknesses, the KMT did continue to dispose of great military power in its contest with the warlords and the Communists. The military performance of the KMT in the internal power struggle prior to 1937 suggests that Chiang might conceivably have held his own by sheer weight of numbers and might have bought a considerable period of time for his regime. On the very eve of 1937, it should be remembered, Kuomintang forces scored a significant success by pushing the Communists out of the areas they had occupied in southeastern China. To be sure, Mao Tse-tung blamed the prewar Communist failure on the fact that he was not in control of the party at the time and that his "people's war" strategy had not yet been followed. But the critical issue is why this was so. Maoism was not meaningfully developed or successfully applied in the internal Communist power struggle because it was molded in response to a foreign invasion and acquired its raison d'être in the face of the mounting Japanese onslaught. While it is possible that the Communist party would have triumphed eventually, war or no war, this is far from clearly supported by the record. What we do know is simply that the Communists were able to gain nationalist legitimacy and their first reliable territorial base as a result of the distinctive circumstances created by the Japanese invasion. Mao repeatedly pointed to the "gigantic national mobilization" made possible by the Japanese invasion as the key to the Communist victory.[30] Twice Mao told Edgar Snow that "it was the Japanese militarists who taught revolution to the Chinese people."[31]

Since winning power, the Communists themselves have consistently attempted to establish their claim as the true inheritors of the entire 1911 tradition. This has been clearly exemplified in the place of honor accorded to the Five Elders—among them Madame Sun—who give the regime an explicit symbolic linkage to 1911 and even to the turn-of-the-century Reform movement. Communist imagery stresses the identification of the older generation of party leaders with the early, "good" KMT tradition, and painstaking efforts have been made to establish the participation of the party in the Northern Expedition of 1926-1927 as a milestone in national unification.

Peking has made extensive use of anti-Japanese propaganda,[32] recalling the shared suffering of the 1937-1945 period, but this has been overshadowed by a dominant emphasis on the original, Western-focused rationale of the Sun Yat-sen tradition. Chinese nationalism as set forth by Sun was a broad summons to national regeneration addressed primarily to the challenge posed by Western dominance; as we shall elaborate in Chapter 10, Sun even made a serious attempt to forge an anti-Western alliance with premilitarist Japan. The Communist objective was to link the Sun tradition with Marxist-Leninist ideology in an integrated nationalist commitment dedicated to uncompromising self-reliance. The enemy was not any one country but rather all forms of foreign domination and dependence. Thus, Peking was careful not to single out the defeat of Japan in such a way as to depict the Japanese as inherently evil. The normalization of Chinese relations with Japan in 1972 was justified with little difficulty because Japanese militarism, together with its alleged post-war "vestiges," had been presented to the Chinese public as an aberration in a larger historical pattern of Sino-Japanese friendship. The defeat of Japan was treated as a memorable but transitory episode in a continuing struggle to restore Chinese self-respect after centuries of humiliation.

Despite the passage of years and the declining force of wartime memories, the Chinese Communists have found it relatively easy to retain the aura of a nationalist leadership by pointing to a continuing external menace, first in the form of the United States and later in the twin Western challenges of a Soviet "social imperialism" and a less menacing but nonetheless suspect American capitalist imperialism. The United States began to take its place in this nationalist symbolism, following in the footsteps of the departing Japanese, even before Chiang had been driven from the mainland. "In the eyes of millions of Chinese," White and Jacoby reported, "their civil war was made in America. We were the architects of its strategy; we flew government troops into Communist territory, we transported and supplied Kuomintang armies marching into the Communists' Yellow River Basin and into the no man's land of Manchuria."[33] Against the background of a symbolism reaching directly into the civil war itself, the specter of the United States looming behind the Chiang regime in Taiwan was thus a real and forbidding one to most Chinese from the start.

The decision of the Chinese Communist leadership to intervene in Korea appeared to reflect a considered and genuine belief that the United States intended to attack China from footholds in Korea, Taiwan, and Indochina in an effort to reinstall Chiang. Allen S. Whiting has powerfully demonstrated the defensive state of mind underlying Chinese intervention in Korea as well as the intimate relationship between Korea and Taiwan in Chinese thinking.[34] The advance of American forces toward the Chinese frontier made it appear to the Chinese public that the United States did indeed intend conquest and cast the Communists, once again, in the role of leaders of a patriotic struggle. This time the struggle was against a non-Asian power, the world's military colossus, making the internal political impact of a successful resistance effort greater than ever. Peking was enabled at a stroke to unite the pan-Asian nationalist sentiment discussed in Chapter 10 with Chinese nationalism and to give China its new self-image as the vanguard of Afro-Asia. For two decades thereafter, Chinese leaders could utilize the cry of "Country in Danger" in the face of a U.S.-supported force on Taiwan of more than 600,000 men and a ring of American bases around China in Thailand, Vietnam, the Philippines, Okinawa, and South Korea. The Indochina war, in particular, gave credibility to the imagery of a persistent external threat and assured an enduring place for the United States as a bête noire of Chinese political symbolism.

In terms of its historical experience, China has even greater reason to harbor suspicions toward the Soviet Union than toward the United States, given the record of Russian territorial acquisitions in central Asia and Siberia through unilaterally imposed "unequal treaties." Moscow makes a tempting nationalist target, and it was natural for Peking to focus on the Soviet Union after the United States withdrew from Vietnam. By 1968, Sino-Soviet ideological exchanges had begun to take on clear racial overtones. The presence of large-scale Soviet forces along the border posed a direct military threat to the oil fields and nuclear installations located in or near border areas. In certain ethnic-minority regions adjacent to the Soviet Union, Moscow has perennially sought to stimulate separatist activity. Still, it is not easy to establish the extent to which Peking believes that it faces an authentic Soviet military threat and the extent to which it has been manipulating anti-Soviet sentiment for domestic political purposes. A U.S. government analyst has argued that the Ussuri River clashes in 1969 were deliberately provoked by Mao in order to discredit Lin Piao supporters who maintained that China did not face a Soviet military challenge.[35] On the one hand, it is evident that Peking has been seriously preparing for a possible military conflict with Moscow. On the other, it should be remembered that the cry of "Country in Danger" is likely to be extremely useful for the leaders of a large and diverse country seeking to contain the pulls of warlordism, especially in the unsettled post-Mao period.

To be understood in a meaningful, long-term perspective, Chinese communism should be viewed not as a revolution grown to maturity but as a nationalist movement striving to retain its original patriotic élan. Like other nationalist movements forged in common struggle against a foreign foe, the Chinese Communist party has inevitably lost some of its unifying discipline as the struggle has receded into the past. To some extent, as suggested in Chapter 1, the Cultural Revolution can be interpreted as a distinctively Maoist expression of nationalist leadership. By attempting to block the emergence of a bureaucratic "new class" and to instill anew a spirit of selfless egalitarianism, Mao was seeking to ensure that China would not slide back into its age-old internecine divisions following his demise. Similarly, a post-Mao leadership is likely to feel an even greater need to reassert and redefine Chinese nationalism. The compelling question is not whether future Chinese leaders will seek to sustain a nationalist mystique but how they will seek to do so.

A common post-Vietnam assumption was that the Soviet Union would completely replace the United States as a rallying symbol. In this view, Peking and Washington have a new community of interest in their shared fear of Moscow, a geopolitical bond powerful enough to cancel out Chinese memories of the cold war decades. An alternative assessment stressed the power potential of Japan and assumed an inexorable Sino-Japanese rivalry rooted, psychologically, in the traumatic 1937–1945 experience. As Chapter 10 suggests, however, both of these projections fail to take into account the central historic thrust of Chinese nationalism as a response to Western dominance.

As laid down by Sun Yat-sen, China's overriding goal was to build countervailing Asian power; the United States and the Soviet Union alike would be "Western" in a contemporary Chinese nationalism actuated by this vision. Japan, by the same token, would stand on a different footing. One must reserve judgment, in short, with respect to the ultimate historical meaning of the wartime Sino-Japanese collision, while recognizing clearly how crucial it was in giving definition to Chinese nationalism at a formative stage and how instructive it is in assessing the overall communist experience in Asia.

NOTES

1. Relman Morin, *East Wind Rising* (New York: Knopf, 1960), p. 194.

2. John Israel, *Student Nationalism in China, 1927-1937* (Stanford: Hoover Institution, 1966), p. 152.

3. Lyman van Slyke, *Enemies and Friends: The United Front in Chinese Communist History* (Stanford: Stanford University Press, 1967), esp. pp. 65-69; see also Israel, *Student Nationalism in China*, esp. pp. 153-156, 188-194.

4. Chalmers Johnson, *Peasant Nationalism and Communist Power* (Stanford: Stanford University Press, 1962), pp. 139-140; see also Van Slyke, *Enemies and Friends*, p. 130. Tetsuya Kataoka stresses that the united front strategy forced Chiang to relax his offensive against the Communists (*Resistance and Revolution in China* [Berkeley: University of California Press, 1974]). Barbara Tuchman has shown that Chiang saw American forces as "a surrogate to fight Japan," permitting him to concentrate on the civil war (*Stilwell and the American Experience in China, 1941-1945* [New York: Macmillan, 1970], esp. pp. 103-106, 118-119, 131-138, 142-149, 166-173).

5. Johnson, *Peasant Nationalism and Communist Power*, p. 24.

6. George E. Taylor, *The Struggle for North China*, Institute of Pacific Relations Inquiry Series (New York: Institute of Pacific Relations, 1940), pp. 96-117, esp. p. 101.

7. Dulles to Fosdick, 4 January 1939, John Foster Dulles Papers, Princeton University Library.

8. Jack Belden, *China Shakes the World* (London: Gollancz, 1950), p. 72; see also pp. 161-163.

9. Theodore H. White and Annalee Jacoby, *Thunder Out of China* (New York: Sloane, 1946), pp. 204-205.

10. Benjamin I. Schwartz, "Peasant Nationalism," *China Quarterly*, July-September 1963, pp. 168, 170-71; see also his statement before the Senate Committee on Foreign Relations, 16 March 1966, esp. pp. 6-7.

11. C. P. Fitzgerald, "Peasant Nationalism and Communist Power," *Pacific Affairs*, Fall 1963, p. 302.

12. Stuart Schram, *Mao Tse-tung* (New York: Simon and Schuster, 1966), p. 186.

13. Franz Michael, "Chalmers Johnson: Peasant Nationalism and Communist Power," in *Annals of the American Academy of Political and Social Sciences*, September 1963, pp. 211-212. A noncommittal reaction praising Johnson's "objective" analysis but questioning some of his conclusions may be found in a review by George E. Taylor, "Peasant Nationalism and Communist Power," in *American Historical Review*, October 1963, pp. 228-229.

14. Donald G. Gillin, *Warlord Yen Hsi-shan in Shansi Province, 1911-1949* (Princeton: Princeton University Press, 1967).

15. Donald G. Gillin, " 'Peasant Nationalism' in the History of Chinese Communism," *Journal of Asian Studies*, February 1964, pp. 274-277.

16. Ibid., pp. 269-272.

17. See Mark Selden's two-part article "The Guerrilla Movement in Northwest China: The Origins of the Shensi-Kansu-Ninghsia Border Region," *China Quarterly*, October-December 1966, esp. pp. 67-69; and ibid., January-March 1967, esp. pp. 65, 67, 70.

18. Johnson has discussed the response to *Peasant Nationalism and Communist Power* at length in an unpublished critique entitled " 'Maximum Feasible Misunderstanding': A Sinological Instance," mimeographed (Berkeley, 1972). See esp. pp. 27-30, for a response to Gillin's criticism.

19. Gillin, *Yen Hsi-shan*, pp. 297-298.

20. Mark Selden, *The Yenan Way in Revolutionary China* (Cambridge: Harvard University Press, 1973), p. 277.

21. Ibid., p. 79.

22. Jeffrey Race, "Toward an Exchange Theory of Revolution," in *Peasant Rebellion and Communist Revolution in Asia*, ed. John W. Lewis (Stanford: Stanford University Press, 1974), pp. 199-200.

23. Jeffrey Race, *War Comes to Long Ân: Revolutionary Conflict in a Vietnamese Province* (Berkeley: University of California Press, 1972), pp. 179-180, 206-208.

24. John McAlister, *Vietnam: The Origins of the Revolution* (New York: Knopf, 1969).

25. Van Slyke, *Enemies and Friends*, p. 100; see also pp. 114, 256; and see Kataoka, *Resistance and Revolution in China*.

26. Schwartz, "Peasant Nationalism," p. 167.

27. Johnson, *Peasant Nationalism and Communist Power*, p. 176.

28. Douglas S. Paauw, "The Kuomintang and Economic Stagnation, 1928-1937," in *Modern China*, ed. Albert Feuerwerker (Englewood Cliffs: Prentice-Hall, 1964), pp. 127, 130-135.

29. Joseph R. Levenson, *Liang Ch'i-ch'ao and the Mind of Modern China* (Cambridge: Harvard University Press, 1953), pp. 109-122; see also S. Y. Teng and John K. Fairbank, *China's Response to the West* (Cambridge: Harvard University Press, 1954), esp. chap. 7.

30. Mao Tse-tung, "On the Protracted War," in *The Political Thought of Mao Tse-tung*, ed. Stuart R. Schram (New York: Praeger, 1963), pp. 208–209.

31. Edgar Snow, *The Long Revolution* (New York: Random House, 1972), pp. 173, 179.

32. In June 1972, shortly before the normalization of Sino-Japanese relations, I found on a tour of China that pictorial accounts of the anti-Japanese resistance were popular items in bookstores. Reaching at random to a shelf at the main bookstore of the Kwantung People's Publishing House, I selected *Jih-pen Chün-kuo Chu-i Pi Chang Tsai Tse Shih Pai* [Japanese militarism is bound to fail] (Kwantung: Kwantung Publishing House, August 1971); *Ti Tao Chan* [Tunnel warfare] (Kwantung: Kwantung Publishing House, May 1971); *Sha Chia Ping* (Shanghai: Shanghai Publishing House, June 1971) (Sha Chia Ping is a market town near Chiangnan); *Ho Pei Min Ping Ke Ming Tao Chung Ku Shih* [Stories of the revolutionary struggles of the People's Militia in Hopei province] (Tientsin: Hopei Publishing House, September 1970 [vol. 1]; May 1971 [vol. 3]); and an annotated collection of songs from *The Red Lantern*, an operatic saga concerning a guerrilla detachment in the Cypress Mountains (reproduced in English as a supplement to *China Pictorial* (Peking), no. 5 [1972]).

33. White and Jacoby, *Thunder Out of China*, p. 318.

34. Allen S. Whiting, *China Crosses the Yalu* (New York: Macmillan, 1960), esp. pp. 151–162.

35. Roger Glenn Brown, "Chinese Politics and American Policy: A New Look at the Triangle," *Foreign Policy*, Summer 1976, pp. 4–6.

4. Vietnam: Nationalism Ascendant

Looking back on the triumph of the Vietnamese Communists, historians will long debate precisely when the issue was irrevocably decided and whether there was ever an opportunity for effective American intervention after the isolation of noncommunist nationalist leaders during the struggle against the French. Would it have made any real difference if the United States had not supported France? If American support had been extended after 1954 with greater political sophistication? If the American profile had been lower, and American military forces had not directly intervened? Or if, on the contrary, American forces had taken the battle directly to Hanoi?

The search for answers to these and related questions embraces a wide range of factors beyond the scope of this book but it is governed, at bottom, by how one perceives and evaluates the internal competition that set the course of Vietnamese nationalism. It is the nature of this competition that we shall consider here, partly through the use of hitherto untranslated or unpublished documents, in seeking to explain the intractable character of the environment confronted by the United States in Vietnam. This will enable the reader, in turn, to understand the radically different U.S. experience in Korea considered in Chapter 5. As we shall see, both Communist and noncommunist contenders for the leadership of nationalism in Vietnam were exceptions to the general pattern in Asia. Like the Chinese Communists, the Vietnamese Communists gave nationalism primacy over the class struggle and thus achieved a momentum unrivaled by communist parties elsewhere in Asia. Their message was broadly addressed not only to the urge for national freedom but also to the companion urge for rapid modernization. The early noncommunist nationalist groups in Vietnam, for their part, were peculiarly narrow in their appeal, conspicuously deficient in the programmatic vision of egalitarian national development that enabled Nehru and Sukarno to compete successfully with their Communist rivals. Dedicated to xenophobic antiforeignism for its own sake during the anti-French struggle, the ultra-elitist, ideologically vacuous Greater Vietnam, or Dai Viet, party later went to the other extreme and became an appendage of the American presence in its single-minded anticommunism. The contest in Vietnam was an unequal one from the start, and this indigenous struggle between unevenly matched claimants to Vietnamese nationalist leadership fundamentally conditioned the American role.

The case of Vietnam underlines the necessity to distinguish between the popular usage of the term "nationalism" as patriotic or chauvinistic feeling (which may actuate "nationalists" of varying political hues within a society in differing ways) and nationalism in the larger, impersonal sense (as the effort of a society to find the most appropriate vehicle for defining and asserting its national identity). Measured with this distinction in mind, the noncommunist nationalists who competed unsuccessfully for the leadership of nationalism in Vietnam were not necessarily less patriotic or "nationalistic" than their Communist rivals. Ngo Dinh Diem, in particular, as we reveal here, had a personal brand of nationalism that led him to resist the introduction of American forces in Vietnam as well as related plans for the construction of major bases, notably Cam Ranh Bay. For a variety of reasons that we shall explore, however, the noncommunist Vietnamese nationalists were uniformly ineffectual, and their already precarious position was intrinsically weakened following the Geneva partition of 1954.

The rationale underlying American involvement after 1954 critically handicapped Saigon as a contender for the leadership of nationalism in the larger historical sense. Conceived as it was in the limited perspective of the containment policy, American intervention in Vietnam was addressed to the preservation of a separate South as an objective sufficient unto itself. South Vietnamese advocates of a "march to the North" were viewed as troublesome extremists. By contrast, from the Vietnamese perspective discussed in Chapter 1, the Geneva partition was a psychological dead-end street, a new interruption in the three-century-old effort to consolidate national identity and strength. For Saigon regimes, a defensive commitment to the indefinite division of Vietnam meant that the Communists could monopolize the issue of unification and national identity. This is not to suggest that an American-supported "march to the North" would in itself have settled the future of Vietnam, given the ineffectuality of nationalist political leadership in the South. Rather, it is to emphasize the inherent tension that existed between short-term American objectives and the historically deep-rooted forces that were

operating in Vietnam. In analyzing the American clash with nationalism, we will also take incidental note of the related failure to
compensate for this by exploiting subnationalism as the French had
done. Nationalism had largely eclipsed subnationalism by the time
Washington came onto the scene, but it was a measure of American
clumsiness, nonetheless, that the United States gave its major support
to Northern refugee elements and their Saigon allies instead of
promoting a "Southern" South Vietnam. The containment perspective made the United States equally insensitive to both dimensions of
the Vietnamese search for identity.

As our discussion of China has made clear, there is a striking
parallel between the role of the Japanese invasion in the development
of Chinese nationalism and the French-American impact in Vietnam.
During most of the Vietnam years, however, this similarity was
obscured by a widespread view of the war as an externally instigated
Chinese creation calling for a corresponding external response. When
Marshal Lin Piao proclaimed his widely discussed manifesto on
"people's war" in September 1965, commemorating the twentieth
anniversary of the Japanese capitulation in China, the debate in the
West surrounding this compelling document completely disregarded
its emphasis on the anti-Japanese struggle. One view characterized
the Lin Piao treatise as the *Mein Kampf* of a Berchtesgaden preparing
to sponsor overt Chinese invasions throughout the world. Another
saw it as the "do-it-yourself" manual of a Vatican relying on the
revolutionaries of other countries to carry the banner of the true
faith. But both of these interpretations missed the central fact that
the key element in the Lin Piao victory formula was the presence of
a foreign invader.[1]

Despite its formulation in universalistic terms purportedly applicable to all developing countries, the Lin Piao manifesto was clearly
inspired by the Vietnam war and addressed primarily to the Vietnamese Communists. There is no doubt a symbolic continuing importance in the generalized Chinese threat of a global revolution in
which the industrialized "cities" of the world are encircled by an
aroused "countryside." But the threat loses force in military terms if
the "people's war" model is viewed apart from its central assumption
of a national resistance struggle. What emerges most sharply from a
study of Asian communist experience is a sense of how very far
removed China and Vietnam were in this respect from the rest of
what was happening in Asia. Enclosed in their own historical recep-
tacles, as it were, the Communist parties in these two neighboring
countries responded to the distinctive opportunities confronting
them with a nationalist sixth sense that other Asian communist
parties lacked. When we study Lin Piao or Vo Nguyen Giap, there-

fore, it is not to project a future of ever victorious insurgencies. It is to see the past in a meaningful perspective and to understand why Vietnam, like China, produced such a tenacious Communist movement.

THE LAND QUESTION AND THE UNITED FRONT STRATEGY

Communism in Vietnam developed from its earliest years with the same conscious emphasis on the mobilization of nationalism found in Chinese communism. Both the Chinese and Vietnamese Communist parties, alone in Asia, have more or less consistently formulated their appeal in nationalist rather than exclusively class terms. If anything, the development of a nationalist, multiclass "united front" strategy by Vietnamese Communist leaders predated the development of Maoism. In China, Maoism provoked bitter intraparty warfare when it was first formulated and acquired its clear doctrinal justification only with the Japanese invasion. In Vietnam, it was never necessary for the Communist movement to experience the shattering inner conflicts that marked the prewar period of Chinese communism. The oppressive weight of a colonial regime more uncompromising than any Western colonialism in Asia gave the initial communist response in Vietnam an unambiguous nationalist motivation.

In one of the more careful discussions of this little-studied early period, Milton Sacks has emphasized the impact of Ho's experience at the Versailles conference as the spokesman of a group of Vietnamese émigrés who petitioned Clemenceau for Vietnamese freedom. It was the brusque rejection of the Vietnamese demand by the peace conference that propelled Ho and other young Vietnamese in France into Communist ranks; yet from the start he was a rebellious gadfly who made no secret of his dissatisfaction with the policy of the French Communist party on colonial matters.[2] At the same time that Ho Chi Minh was enlisting his early recruits for his new Communist-cum-nationalist movement in Paris, another young intellectual then in Vietnam who was later to join forces with the nascent Communist movement, Dao Duy Anh, was developing an independent rationale for a nationalist revolutionary party in his *Study of the Vietnamese Revolution*. Dao stressed the limited industrial development of Indochina and thus the "precapitalist stage" of Vietnamese social development. The absence of a "true" Vietnamese capitalist class and the limited size and class consciousness of the

Vietnamese proletariat, together with the predominance of small peasant proprietorships in agriculture, defied conventional Marxist-Leninist analysis. Dao contended that a revolutionary party would have to "recruit its supporters among the advanced elements of all the social classes" and that as a consequence its program "must be nationalist and not combat the interests of any one of the diverse social elements which would form the revolutionary front."[3]

Although Dao Duy Anh concluded from his analysis that a communist party was inappropriate for Indochina, Ho Chi Minh, like Mao in China, was proceeding on the implicit assumption of Leninist theory that the communist party itself could speak in the name of the proletariat, irrespective of the actual class origin of party members and of the stage of proletarian development in the country. Ho ultimately converted both Dao Duy Anh and his close associate in the New Vietnam Revolutionary party, Vo Nguyen Giap, who led a group of their nationalist partisans into Communist ranks following a party split in 1929. Like the impact of the student influx into the Chinese Communist movement after 1935, the acquisition of this left wing of the New Vietnam Revolutionary party and of another kindred group, the Nguyen An Ninh association, gave Vietnamese communism a hard core of nationalist leadership in its formative early stages. The Communist party that Ho brought together out of the pre-1930 amalgam of feuding Vietnamese revolutionary groups was notable not only for its well-defined nationalist commitment but also for a broad social base appropriate to its mission. Ho's own personal machine in the Tonkin areas of North Vietnam was dominated largely by the sons of "well-off peasants and small landlords."[4] It had a natural rural orientation that set it sharply apart from the urban-minded organizations then appearing in other parts of Asia. As for the New Vietnam Revolutionary party, the split that had developed in the group between 1926 and 1929 grew directly out of a clash between the snobbish social attitudes of the urbanized civil servants who formed its old-line membership and a group of younger populist revolutionaries, led by Anh and Giap, who were not afraid to dirty their hands in the villages.

Reflecting in part the social origins of so many of their leaders in the lesser landed gentry, the Vietnamese Communists were acutely sensitive to the nuances of the rural power structure and were confident from the start that they could rally powerful landed interests to their side in a struggle directed against foreign influence. Their land policy was the very foundation of their nationalist strategy, directly paralleling peasant-oriented Maoist appeals in China and in the Andhra area of India.[5] A sharp distinction has been drawn in

Vietnamese Communist literature between *dia-chu* (landlords), on the one hand, owning fifty or more hectares of land, and *phu-nong* (rich peasants), owning between five and fifty hectares; *trung-nong* (middle peasants), owning less than five hectares; and *banco-nong* (poor peasants), agricultural laborers or tenant farmers. Communist policy prior to 1954 was focused on rent reductions and the redistribution to poor peasants of French-owned land and the land of those Vietnamese landlords "identified with the French."[6] After 1954, the land redistributed to poor peasants came mainly from landlords and absentee owners. Rich and middle peasants were rarely dispossessed.[7] Only in three isolated cases were dissident party elements able to stage doctrinaire "antipeasant" adventures. In 1930, when the French levied punitive taxes at a time of mass starvation, local Communist groups organized rural soviets in Nghe An and Ha Tinh provinces, engaging in indiscriminate land confiscation and redistribution. Twenty-five years later, the party departed from the united front policy when Secretary-General Truong Chinh forced through the rigidly doctrinaire program of land reform and collective farming that led to the disastrous peasant uprisings of 1956 and to his ouster in disgrace. Finally, between 1960 and 1965, there were "certain bad deviations" in the South in which land was taken from middle peasants, but these brought a strong rebuke from the party high command.[8] In each of these cases, the party formally reaffirmed the place of rich peasants, middle peasants, and "patriotic" landlords in the "national united front."

Vietnamese Communist policy on the land question completely belies the conventional image of communism in poor countries as essentially an expression of economic discontent on the part of the have-nots. Successful as they have been in identifying themselves with the cause of the poor peasant, the Vietnamese Communists found the secret of their success not through class appeals but through the reconciliation of class conflict in the name of the common cause against the foreigner. Saigon belatedly proclaimed a meaningful land reform program in 1969 designed to win the support of tenant farmers. But apart from deficiencies in its implementation, the program did not strike at the roots of Communist strength in the countryside. A RAND Corporation study has provided strongly suggestive evidence indicating that NLF strongholds in the South Vietnamese countryside were areas dominated by the individual peasant proprietor, wedded to the plot of land he worked and strongly resistant to outside intrusion in the immemorial tradition of peasants the world over.[9] The clear picture arising from this study and innumerable impressionistic reports on Communist land policy is one of a broadly based movement that succeeded in organizing itself for a nationalist role by deliberately soft-pedaling the class war.

ETHNICITY AND ELITISM: THE NONCOMMUNIST ALTERNATIVE

The first clear opportunity to put their multiclass doctrine to the test and to apply their carefully developed organizational machinery in a national confrontation came to the Vietnamese Communists during the military phase of their effort to oust the French after 1946. As a leading noncommunist nationalist has observed, however, "by taking over the legitimate nationalist cause, the Vietnamese Communists won their greatest victory before the Resistance War began."[10] The necessary preliminary question in assessing Vietnamese Communist success is how it happened that the Communists, rather than their noncommunist nationalist rivals, were able to assume the vanguard role in the fight against the French.

First and foremost among the factors explaining Communist success is clearly the default of the noncommunist groups themselves during the critical formative period of the nationalist movement and the ruthless exploitation of this failure by Ho Chi Minh. By 1930, Ho had welded together a nationwide Communist party, but his initial rival, the Vietnam Nationalist party, generally known as the VNQDD (for Vietnam Quoc Dan Dang), a Tonkinese group, and the New Vietnam Revolutionary party, based in central Vietnam, were unable to unite. The VNQDD hastened its own demise by staging an abortive uprising in 1930 that gave the French an excuse for repressive measures and resulted in the execution of its leader, Nguyen Thai Hoc, one of Ho's few real rivals. Apart from this episode and the factionalism that ensued, however, the party's potential was inherently limited by its failure to offer programmatic leadership.

Except for a vague, general pledge to overthrow the "feudalist capitalist" colonial regime, the party made its bid for support with little or no doctrinal rationale,[11] concentrating almost entirely on anti-French terrorist adventures. Even the VNQDD's generalized sympathy for Sun Yat-sen's stand in favor of social revolution was rejected by the dissident faction that left the party in 1939 to form the Dai Viet. With its uncompromising opposition to class struggle ideas in any form, the Dai Viet objected to Sun's "weak" ideology as an "invitation to Communism."[12] In its place, the Dai Viet offered its "Dan Toc Sinh Ton," or "National Survival," doctrine,[13] depicting man as actuated by a primordial selfishness that expresses itself in "disruptive" class conflict and personal aggrandizement necessitating a rigidly totalitarian regime. In contrast to the Communists, with their detailed prescription for national modernization after the attainment of independence, the Dai Viet spoke more diffusely of *phuc duc*, a Vietnamese variant of the Confucian ethic, justifying its brand of totalitarianism in the name of "racial consciousness, the strongest, most constant and most innate of man's impulses."[14] Ethnicity was elevated to the status of an ideology. The party looked for inspiration to militarist Japan and received financial support from Tokyo as part of the Japanese effort to supplant wartime French power in Indochina. "We were also very much impressed with Germany at that time," recalled Dang Van Sung, an early Dai Viet leader, "and greatly inspired by the Nazi system."[15]

For the VNQDD and the Dai Viet, the movement was an end in itself, and their leaders were more interested in perfecting the model elitist organizational machinery that would administer a free Vietnam than in the program that would be administered. Thus, one of the reasons for the Dai Viet split off from the VNQDD was the size of its cells (twelve members). The Dai Viet decided instead to have four-member cells, a move originally designed to prevent detection by the French police but one that gradually served to crystallize the ingrown character of the party as a secret brotherhood largely isolated from mass support. Semiofficial histories of both groups recount this isolation in candid detail and offer frequently conflicting alibis to explain why the Communists had a charisma that they lacked[16] and were able to outmaneuver them at nearly every turn.[17] One explanation is that the coherent Communist program for the modernization of Vietnam confounded the major noncommunist groups with their limited conception of a negative, xenophobic nationalism. Looking back on this two decades later, Dang Van Sung explained that in 1945 "the world seemed to become smaller"; for the first time it was not enough for a nationalist

> merely to be opposed to foreign rule. We had to have a clear-cut political and social viewpoint, and a knowledge of internal and international conditions, which we did not have. The various nationalist groups ... became disoriented in the face of too complicated a situation. Out of sheer irresolution, they let the Communists assume the initiative of the Resistance Movement.[18]

Above all, what emerges from these accounts is a sense of the ever recurring factiousness produced by the combination of a doctrinal vacuum and the lack of a commanding leadership personality. The assassination of Dai Viet leader Truong Tu Anh in 1947, presumably at Communist hands, accelerated a process of fragmentation in Dai Viet ranks that culminated in a series of bitter disputes over the terms for collaboration with the French following Ho's successful installation of a Communist-led Vietnamese regime.

Ho took full advantage of the weaknesses of his divided rivals during the formative years of the nationalist competition, even to the extent of collaborating with the French police to help along the process of their destruction. It is not as if the Vietnamese Communists established a special claim to nationalist purity in the confused and tortured early skirmishes between rival nationalist groups. In 1926, when Phan Boi Chau's New Vietnam Revolutionary party was just beginning to gain momentum, Ho passed on the information that enabled French police to make Phan's arrest in Shanghai, allegedly using the payoff received from the French to finance Communist activities. Later, according to firsthand accounts, Vietnamese Communists in China kept an eye on Revolutionary party recruits sent for training to the Whampoa Military Academy and tipped off the French police with photographs obtained through an espionage network in the academy.[19] Ironically, in view of their later struggle, the French authorities proved ready to collaborate with the Communists throughout the years leading up to the 1946 breach because they saw them as less of a threat than the more xenophobic and uncompromising noncommunist nationalists. This readiness of the French to cooperate with Ho Chi Minh at the expense of the noncommunist parties proved to be of incalculable value to Ho in consolidating his power during the critical months of early 1946.

THE GOLD SWORD OF LEGITIMACY

While one is struck by the clarity of purpose that guided Ho at home and abroad, it should be noted that the events leading up to his actual seizure of power following V-J Day were marked by a series of highly fortuitous circumstances. Ho's first stroke of luck was the fact that the wartime French regime in Indochina happened to be pro-Vichy in its sympathies and therefore willing to collaborate with the Japanese. In most of Southeast Asia, Tokyo saw native elites as more suitable vehicles for their rule than Western colonial bureaucrats. In Vietnam, the pro-Vichy French regime was permitted to operate intact, and with the independence movement driven underground, the Communists, as the best organized national party, became the principal focus of sentiment against both the French and the Japanese. Having made the most of the opportunity presented by French-Japanese collaboration, the Vietnamese Communists were once again fortunately situated when a Gaullist shift within the ranks of French civil service and military personnel in Indochina led to the French-

Japanese rupture of early 1945. The French regime in Indochina was totally disabled by a Japanese coup that resulted in the mass imprisonment of French military and civilian personnel. This created an administrative hiatus at a time when the Japanese were too preoccupied with defensive preparations in the face of the Allied advance to establish an effective substitute occupation authority. Even Japanese granaries had been left unguarded, offering the Communists an opportunity to win prestige by distributing food to famine-stricken peasants. The field was left completely clear for a bold initiative by the well-organized Communists, who found public buildings in Hanoi undefended when they set up their free Vietnamese regime in August.

With their nationalist credentials widely accepted as a result of their opposition to the French and the Japanese during the wartime years, the Communists had moved quickly during the five months between March and V-J Day to identify themselves with the ascendant Allied forces. Ho saw the importance of winning recognition by the victors as the legitimate authority in an independent postwar Vietnam and of using this international recognition as a weapon for consolidating his domestic position. It was thus an added dividend that he was able to make a convincing claim to American support as a result of his ties with the OSS. This identification with the Allies as the likely victors was probably a more important factor in Ho's accession to power than the small but much publicized amounts of weaponry provided by the OSS in return for his espionage on Japanese troop movements and his help in rescuing American pilots.

Precisely because he was identified with the losing side in the conflict, Emperor Bao Dai had failed to rally popular support following his installation as head of a Japanese-sponsored nationalist regime in March 1945. But the emperor was still the unquestioned and preeminent symbol of Vietnamese identity. His abdication on August 26 had decisive importance for the Viet Minh, and the psychological impact of his dramatic gesture was heightened when he was followed into the Viet Minh camp by the head of the Council of the Imperial Family, Prince Ung Uy, a great-grandson of the Emperor Minh Mang, who did not repudiate the Viet Minh later as Bao Dai did. In turning over the imperial seal and the emperor's traditional gold sword, Bao Dai signaled to the tradition-minded Vietnamese people that a momentous historical transfer of power had occurred. He gave formal and irrevocable recognition to Ho's nationalist bona fides and to the preeminent position achieved by the Communists in the competition for nationalist leadership. The full significance of this action can be appreciated only if one gives due importance to "the Confucian spirit"[20] in Vietnam and to Vietnamese identification with the Chinese political principle that one and only one political order at a time can have the Mandate of Heaven. Once having acquired "the mantle of legitimacy," as Douglas Pike observes, the Viet Minh enjoyed "a momentum it never lost and that its nationalist opponents could never match. It put Ho Chi Minh and his fellow Communists firmly at the helm of the anti-colonialist struggle."[21]

The impact of independence was greatest in Hanoi, where the Viet Minh had its strongest and oldest organizational network, and in the old capital of Hue, where a triumphal Viet Minh procession had received the imperial seal and sword from Bao Dai. But Ho Chi Minh also won immediate, broad national acceptance of his regime in the south as well. On the day of Bao Dai's abdication, the Viet Minh established a southern branch of the Hanoi-Hue regime in Saigon, taking over the government palace, the city hall, and the police force. In the greatest mass demonstration in the history of the city, the streets were filled throughout the day with hundreds of thousands who "marched in perfect order past their new leaders, obviously content that in Saigon, too, the revolution was now being led by the Viet Minh."[22] When the Viet Minh set up its governing Southern National Bloc Committee, representative nationalists of all stripes from Hoa Hoa potentate Huynh Phu to leading Trotskyists joined in the new grouping. The authority of the Viet Minh and its allies within the Vietnamese context was largely established when British troops arrived on the scene in late September and added a new external dimension of power. Authorized by the Potsdam agreement to disarm the Japanese, the British enlarged on their mandate by overthrowing the month-old regime to prepare ground for the reassertion of French control.

The ability of the Viet Minh to maintain nationalist solidarity in the south was vitiated by bitter factional battles with Trotskyist groups and other noncommunist nationalist forces resulting in part from the heavy-handed tactics of an old-line Stalinist, Tran Van Giau, who had never fully conformed to the united front approach of Ho Chi Minh and the dominant northern faction of Vietnamese communism. After he was replaced by the more supple Nguyen Binh, the Viet Minh was able to create another southern nationalist coalition, the National Union Front, in a historic conference on April 20 at Ba Queo. The front maintained its unity in the face of powerful French pressures until July 13, 1946. Nguyen Binh won wide support with the argument that Ho Chi Minh and other representatives of the new Democratic Republic of Vietnam, then about to enter into the Fontainebleau negotiations with France, would be strengthened by the existence of a unified nationalist coalition in the south.

Binh also argued prophetically that the front would lay the ground-work for a strengthened resistance movement if the negotiations should fail. Milton Sacks writes that "the Ho Chi Minh government might have managed to maintain this precarious unity, and even gotten a temporary truce underway in South Vietnam, if the French had not torpedoed these efforts by undertaking a policy of stimu-lating separatist political tendencies."[23]

In viewing the later development of the Vietnam conflict, it is important to remember that Vietnam was intermittently united under an effective national leadership throughout 1945 and 1946 and that France had given recognition to this unity in the March 1946 agreement between Ho and Jean Sainteny. By recognizing Vietnam as a "free state," France had accepted the principle of one Vietnam and had given the Hanoi regime de facto recognition as the only legitimate Vietnamese authority for the entire country. The provision in the agreement for a referendum to determine the status of Cochin China was clearly regarded at the time as a French concession since "the positive outcome of such a referendum was a foregone conclusion. . . . Everybody knew what the outcome of such a referendum would be."[24] On the strength of his agreement with Sainteny, Ho moved to consolidate Vietnam's newly won unity at the Fontainebleau conference, but during the very week of his departure for Fontainebleau, the ultra-rightist French proconsul in Saigon, acting without authorization from Paris, took the fateful step that was to lead France and Vietnam into their long and bloody struggle. In direct contravention of the Ho-Sainteny agreement, Adm. Thierry d'Argenlieu proclaimed a separate and sovereign Republic of Cochin China in the south.

A State Department intelligence report at the time declared that the political leaders who gave a facade of Vietnamese support to the new republic "comprised mainly middle class and wealthy Vietnam-ese, the bulk of whom were French citizens. Their popular influence was negligible."[25] D'Argenlieu's effort to split the nationalist move-ment by carving out his new southern entity thus had the opposite effect of hardening nationalist resistance and strengthening the posi-tion of the Communists as the already entrenched leaders of the only existent united front. In north and south alike, the separatist chal-lenge became an overriding symbolic issue, giving an indelible colo-nialist stamp to all post-1946 Saigon regimes established on the foundations of the southern "republic."

Hoang Van Chi, a sharp critic of the Communists, stressed the importance of their achievement of a unified Vietnam during 1945 and 1946 in distinguishing between the partitions of Germany and Korea, and that of Vietnam. While communist governments in East

Germany and North Korea were set up by Soviet occupying forces, he observed, in Vietnam

> the Communists seized power by their own means—and throughout the country. It was the French intervention which later reduced their area of control, and ultimately limited their domination to the present territory of North Vietnam. Thus, while the German and Korean Communists feel "lucky" for having obtained "free" half of their respective countries, the Vietnamese Communists . . . feel deeply frustrated because, in their view, "the imperialists have grabbed from their own hands half of their former domain." . . . "Our people is one, our country is one," said Ho Chi Minh, not Walter Ulbricht.26

Once the Communists had succeeded in placing themselves at the head of an independent, nationwide Vietnamese regime opposed to the French, noncommunists could not become anticommunists without also becoming identified to some extent as antinationalist. It has been argued that the Bao Dai restoration movement would have been more successful as a rival to Hanoi if it had been credibly anti-French as well as anticommunist. But the Communists were so widely viewed in a nationalist light by 1947 that their exclusion from nationalist political evolution would have been virtually impossible. When he echoed the French propaganda line that the Viet Minh was not a bona fide nationalist spokesman, Bao Dai polarized Vietnamese politics and drove many noncommunist nationalists into Communist arms. Thereafter, as Joseph Buttinger concludes, the transformation of nationalists into Communists or Communist sympathizers became "the dominant trend of Vietnam's political evolution."27

To be sure, there were bona fide noncommunist nationalists in the Restoration movement who thought they were pursuing the best interests of Vietnam. They reasoned that the colonial era in Asia was coming to an end and that France would be unable to retain her colonial possessions indefinitely. Recognizing that the Communists would never share control with them for long in a broad-based nationalist coalition, they hoped to use their influence in a Bao Dai regime to dislodge the French in gradual stages. This was a plausible rationale until France made clear in its Ha Long declaration of September 10, 1947, that it was not willing to give a Bao Dai regime even nominal self-rule. By the time Bao Dai returned to Vietnam in July 1949 to establish his government, it was difficult for noncommunist nationalists who were not supporting the new regime in Hanoi to justify their support for what was so blatantly a French puppet regime. Some sought to do so by pointing to the Chinese and Russian support then being given to the Ho regime. But as Takashi Oka has observed, the Ho regime was very much its own master, and most Vietnamese recognized this. The contrast between a Communist regime making its own decisions, while accepting advice and limited material help from outside, and a so-called nationalist Bao Dai regime completely dependent on the French for its very existence, led many Vietnamese nationalists at this period to choose the Communists, on the ground that at least they were fighting for national independence.[28]

The dilemma confronting noncommunists in Vietnam after 1947 was a poignant one. If they continued to seek a compromise with the French, their nationalism became suspect. Yet many of them were not prepared to undergo the physical rigors and personal sacrifice involved in fighting with the resistance in the countryside, and some, especially the influential Catholic minority, saw communism as a threat to Vietnam even more despicable than French rule. This led to the emergence of a large middle group of *attentistes*, among them Ngo Dinh Diem, who waited in France, in the United States, and in the French-controlled cities of Vietnam for a more opportune moment to act. The *attentistes* kept their personal credentials unsullied, but they failed to contribute to the growth of a rival force during a critical period in which the Viet Minh was solidifying its position and broadening its nationalist acceptance.

THE TAINT OF COLLABORATION

In much American discussion of Vietnam, Ngo Dinh Diem and 1954 have marked an implicit starting point. It is almost as if the nine preceding years did not exist. If Diem had been less of an autocrat, it is said, less of a mandarin and less responsive to the pressures of nepotism, the story in Saigon might have been very different. For all of this preoccupation with Diem's failings, however, the critical factor in an overall historical assessment is that the Saigon regime established in 1954 was on the defensive from the start. Even if Diem had made better use of his opportunity to rally uncommitted nationalist elements, he would still have been greatly inhibited by the political legacy of the years 1946 to 1954.

It is often said that Diem was a nationalist. This is valid in the limited negative sense that he had scrupulously shunned collaboration with the French. Despite Viet Minh propaganda to the contrary, his reputation was not tarnished by his associations with the Japanese during the war, which were comparable to those of Sukarno and could be defended as having been motivated by long-term nationalist aims. At the same time, Diem came to power in 1954 with no positive nationalist identity. The most that can be said is that he was not rejected out of hand by public opinion for prior collaborationist activity.

The fact that the victory over the French had been won by the Hanoi regime made the shadow of Ho Chi Minh a long one in the South and meant a corresponding reduction in the stature of each noncommunist Saigon leader beginning with Diem. To denounce the Viet Minh on the ground that it was Communist was even more self-defeating for noncommunist nationalists in 1954 than it had been in 1947. Soon after its formal inaugural in 1956, the Diem regime revealed its apologetic posture on the nationalist issue in an official history that attributed the victory over the French to noncommunist support of the Viet Minh. "Most of the nationalists preferred to side with their Communist countrymen to fight a colonialist army," said the brochure, "rather than to side with a colonial army to fight their countrymen."[29] The same theme was echoed in Diem's 1962 "Surrender Plan," designed to attract noncommunists away from the NLF, which claimed that "the success of the Resistance War was due not to the leadership of the Communists but to the work of nationalist members of the Resistance."

Perhaps the greatest problem faced by Diem in projecting a nationalist image was that his regime was necessarily built on the foundations of the civil service and army structure inherited from French colonialism and its successor puppet regimes in the South.[30] Few new entrants had gone into the Saigon bureaucracy during the war years, when those who could afford it went abroad rather than work for the French or fight in the villages. The reluctance of those who stayed behind to associate themselves with the Bao Dai government was so pronounced that recruitment came to a virtual standstill in June 1950, forcing the emperor to issue a decree requisitioning technicians for specialized posts.[31] Bao Dai had given virtually all of his key appointments to men actively identified with the separatist Republic of Cochin China, and the Diem regime, constituting in turn "the final outgrowth of the Bao Dai movement,"[32] was bracketed in the popular mind with the whole collaborationist-tainted machinery over which the new ruling group presided.

"Collaboration" is a concept that has its full emotional significance only for those within a society who have had to choose between the easy way of accommodation to a foreign presence and the harder path of the resistance fighter or of the *attentiste*. In the case of Vietnam, with its unusually oppressive brand of colonialism, the emotional gulf between the tiny urban minority who profited from colonial patronage and the remaining majority of the population was wide and unbridgeable. Among traditional elite families particularly, tensions between those who adapted to the French and those who refused to do so date back to the late nineteenth century, and to this day intermarriage between these contending families and their descendants has been described as "inconceivable."[33] It should be noted that the mere fact of government employment under the French was not in itself a source of opprobrium. Lower level clerical posts and even high-ranking appointments in professional and technical spheres such as medicine and engineering were regarded as patriotically acceptable. To be able to win admission and promotion in higher administrative echelons, however, connoted a dubious political intimacy with the colonial rulers.

When he disassociated himself from the Bao Dai government in 1949, Diem gave explicit recognition to the schism between nationalists and collaborators, declaring that "the best positions in the new Vietnam should be reserved for those who have earned the gratitude of the fatherland. I refer to the Resistance elements."[34] But once in power, he relentlessly persecuted most noncommunist nationalists with a Viet Minh background unless they gave unquestioning support to his autocratic rule, branding them as Communists to justify his repression. At the same time that he was shutting out noncommunist Viet Minh elements from his regime, Diem took over almost completely intact the Vietnamese component of the Bao Dai regime's civil service machinery and replaced departing French officialdom in the higher administrative posts largely with northern refugees who had served the colonial regime in Hanoi and Haiphong.[35]

Diem inherited an army that was crucial to the consolidation of his power but was even more suspect in the public mind than the civil service. Most of its officers had only a few short years earlier accepted sharply subordinated status under the French in a war against their own countrymen. Their uniforms were the same as the uniforms used by the French Union forces in Vietnam, with only the epaulettes changed. The new army had its origins after the French defeats at Caobang and Langson in the fall of 1950. Beginning as a unit of six battalions and expanding to 205,000 by the end of 1953, it marked a belated effort by the French to confront the Viet Minh with a nominally Vietnamese opponent. But more than two-thirds of this armed force consisted of units transferred intact from what were known as "yellowfied" regiments of the French Union forces. As the former U.S. chargé d'affaires in Saigon, Edmund A. Gullion, observed, there were few Vietnamese volunteers for an army "whose officers and non-coms were primarily white Frenchmen."[36] Even conscription proved to be difficult. Phan Quang Dan recalls that when general mobilization was decreed in September 1951, military trucks were sent to French-controlled villages to pick up all male adults between eighteen and thirty years of age; yet most of the unwilling recruits succeeded in escaping from conscription camps en masse within a week. Bao Dai told Dan that he thought it would be dangerous to expand the army because it might defect en masse to the Viet Minh.[37]

To supplement the "yellowfied" Vietnamese officers co-opted from the colonial forces, the French also opened officer training schools at Nam Dinh in the north and Thu Duc in the south, giving control over recruitment to Dai Viet ministers in the Bao Dai government trusted for their anticommunism. Dai Viet ministers also organized paramilitary training programs of their own that added to the hard core of officers later used in setting up the post-1954 Saigon military establishment. Dai Viet leader Nguyen Ton Hoan, who served as secretary of state for youth affairs, recalled in a privately circulated 1963 memoir that he had been uncertain as to whether the Dai Viet should serve under the French in view of their refusal to accept party demands for a greater degree of power to noncommunist nationalist elements. His doubts had been resolved, he wrote, by a representative of the newly established American legation in Saigon who had urged participation in the Bao Dai regime.[38] Hoan made little effort to disguise the early U.S. contacts established by the Dai Viet, recalling that its leaders "decided to move the party into the camp of liberty" in 1947 following Ho Chi Minh's assumption of power and their realization that "if liberal democracy had its weaknesses, they were much less serious than those that undermine authoritarian regimes."[39] As vocal anticommunists with paramilitary ambitions, Dai Viet members and sympathizers were automatically among those who attracted U.S. interest when the wartime Vietnam involvement of the OSS was converted into a continuing effort by the newly established CIA to help the French between 1947 and 1954.

American aid to the French included some support for Dai Viet military training programs in addition to the direct U.S. military aid given to the French forces and to the French effort to set up a "Vietnamese" army. An internal U.S. embassy blue book on Vietnamese political factions, cited earlier, gave details of one such program in Yen Bay that claimed among its alumni Gen. Pham Xuan Chieu, later secretary-general of the High Military Council in Saigon from 1965 to 1967.[40] A former OSS official who served in Vietnam told me that "our relationships with a number of people active since then go back to what we were doing in those days" and specifically mentioned U.S. contacts with Nguyen Van Thieu dating back to 1948.[41]

Against the background of the bloody years leading up to 1954, most of those who made up the new army were widely regarded as mercenaries, at worst, and at best as something less than lustrous patriots. The military regimes that followed Diem's assassination also suffered fundamentally from the fact that the bulk of the ruling officers had started their careers in the French army and had fought the Viet Minh under French command. A careful journalist surveyed the top officer corps of the army in mid-1967 and found only two officers holding the rank of lieutenant colonel or higher who had fought with the Viet Minh.[42] In some cases, notably those of Gen. Duong Van Minh and Gen. Nguyen Chanh Thi, leading military figures were able to rid themselves of some of the onus of their past by virtue of their anti-Diem political records, and for all of the alternating junta personalities, freedom from corruption became an increasingly important determinant of public esteem. Despite a rapidly changing political milieu, however, memories of the colonial antecedence of the armed forces lingered. To most Americans, the Saigon generals were generals; to most Vietnamese, they were former French lieutenants. This gap in perception was epitomized in a representative U.S. commentary on the disastrous retreat from Pleiku in 1975 that ultimately led to the collapse of the Thieu regime. It was puzzling to the writers to see such a disappointing performance from the Pleiku corps commander, Maj. Gen. Pham Van Phu, who had, after all, such a "long and valorous record as one of only two Vietnamese officers in the French Army at the fatal 1954 battle of Dien Bien Phu."[43]

Accompanying and reinforcing the tired image presented by his carry-over of pre-1954 bureaucratic and military elements was Diem's perpetuation of the entire colonial social order that these elements represented. An estimated 6,300 landholders, most of them absentee landlords, owned 45 percent of all rice land in the south at the time of the Diem takeover. Patronized by the colonial regime, these were the same families who became the backbone of the new order after 1954. Their sons were the best trained Vietnamese products of the French-patterned educational system then prevailing and continued to hold the top army and civil service posts. For the mass of the peasantry, physically and emotionally cut off from the "foreign city"[44] of Saigon, feudal land exploitation by this French-linked elite had been the central reality of colonialism. Thus, the often discussed failure of successive Saigon regimes to carry out effective land reform and other agrarian programs was not only important in its own right as a matter of social and economic justice. It was also a major factor explaining the inability of these regimes to acquire a nationalist coloration.[45]

CATHOLICS AND BUDDHISTS

One of the more complex issues encountered in examining the competition for nationalist leadership after 1954 is the degree to which the strongly Catholic tenor of Saigon regimes vitiated their nationalist character. History poses this issue sharply, since Catholicism was closely associated with colonialism in Vietnam and Catholic missionaries were the advance guard of French rule. Among the Vietnamese Buddhist majority in particular, Catholics have been traditionally regarded as "the claws which enabled the French crab to occupy Vietnam,"[46] and when politically awakened Buddhist groups began to play an activist role, the heavily disproportionate Catholic representation in the Saigon power structure[47] naturally became their principal rallying cry. Nevertheless, the fact that Catholicism is widely viewed by non-Catholics as an unwanted legacy of the colonial era hardly means that there were no Vietnamese Catholics in the resistance or that Catholicism, as such, has been regarded as incompatible with nationalism. In Vietnam as elsewhere, the church has played a multifaceted role, with Catholics dividing along a variety of regional and social lines in their political allegiance.

The focus of the anti-Catholic feeling directed toward Diem and most U.S.-backed Saigon regimes was not Catholic influence in a generalized sense but the strong position of a particular group of northern refugee Catholics who did have an ambivalent record in relation to the French. Out of a total of some 900,000 Vietnamese who came south after 1954, an estimated 750,000 were Catholics; of these, the great majority came from two bishoprics, Phat Diem and Bui Chu, which had organized an autonomous Vietnamese militia to oppose the Viet Minh. Initially, these two bishoprics had been given considerable autonomy by Ho Chi Minh, but the Viet Minh had gradually attempted to introduce its own men into the governments of even overwhelmingly Catholic villages. This had prompted the bishops of Phat Diem and Bui Chu to opt for Bao Dai, who was married to a devout Catholic and had received his strongest support throughout Vietnam from Catholics fearful of their future under a communist regime.[48]

When the Phat Diem and Bui Chu refugees streamed into Saigon after 1954, they settled in a ring of fortified villages around the city, set up their own private militias, and became the militantly anticommunist political shock troops of the new regime. Added to the image of the refugees as supporters of the French during the war was Diem's favoritism toward fellow Catholics from his native Hue and the fact that the church in the South had fallen heir to many former French properties. The disproportionate strength of Catholic influence in the Vietnamese-controlled sector of the economy, as well as in the police and the intelligence and military services, led to the suppression not only of the Communists but also of noncommunist elements regarded as rivals to Diem, including the militantly anticommunist Dai Viet party and leading Buddhist groups.

The experience of the Dai Viets during the Diem period illustrates the significance of the northern refugee character of Catholic influence. With their nativistic brand of nationalism, the Dai Viets were often die-hard anti-Catholics, and many of their key leaders were northern refugees themselves. In 1947 and 1948, during the same period of political confusion in which Catholic bishops ruled Phat Diem and Bui Chu, Dai Viet leaders had been given control over large areas of the Tonkin Delta by the embattled French, resulting in the alleged persecution of Catholics in many villages. The Diem period offered a chance to settle old scores, and most Dai Viets were jailed or went underground. Dai Viet-Catholic tensions subsequently became a continuing element in the factionalism of Saigon regimes, though the inherent failings of the Dai Viet, discussed earlier, make it unlikely that the party would have provided a focus for noncommunist leadership even in the absence of Catholic influence.

A more critical question is whether the harassment and political isolation of Buddhist groups at the hands of Catholic-backed leaders prevented their emergence as a competitor to the Communists for nationalist leadership in the South. Here it is necessary to recognize that Buddhist political activism, while triggered by Catholic ill-treatment, represented much more than a defense of sectarian religious interests. Initially sectarian in character, the political role of the Buddhists became increasingly broad-based after 1966 and was marked by frequent cooperation with like-minded Catholic elements who shared the feeling that Saigon had become a hapless pawn in great power rivalries. The assertion of Buddhist identity became, in effect, a vehicle for the assertion of Vietnamese identity. Thich Tri Quang and the An Quang Buddhists, in particular, gave voice to the broad sense of unease in the South over the continued division of the country, which we shall discuss in the next section of this analysis.[49] Nationalism, in this perspective, could not find fulfillment within the framework of indefinite division and indefinite confrontation between Communists and anticommunists. There were only two meaningful alternatives open to South Vietnam. Hypothetically, at least, there was the military unification of the country by the South, a course once suggested by some Buddhist leaders. In the absence of this, the Buddhist objective was to modify the uncompromising anticommunism of the Saigon regime, opening the way for the gradual realization of political symbiosis and the eventual emergence of more compatible regimes in the North and the South better able to reduce external influence. Unlike most Catholics, in short, the An Quang leaders saw themselves as competing with the Communists in the South only in the limited sense that they wanted noncommunist nationalist strength to be consolidated as the prelude to a coalition bargain. This is why the United States sought so consistently to limit their power and to prevent the largely Annam-based An Quang leadership from creating a united front with other, more conservative Buddhist elements with differing regional roots.[50]

As the majority social group in Vietnam, the Buddhists were doing what comes naturally in groping for a political expression of national identity, while religious and social minorities were preoccupied, by their nature, with how to preserve their autonomy and security within the larger context of Vietnamese society. Post-1954 Saigon regimes consequently fell easily into their reliance on cooperative minorities and their deepening estrangement from freewheeling Buddhist groups. Bedrock organized support of the government consistently came from refugee Catholics and important elements of the church in the South, the Hoa Hao and Cao Dai sects, the Khmer ethnic minority, and cooperative factions of the Montagnard, or hill, peoples. All of these were self-contained communal groups functioning as virtual states within a state. They existed as enclaves emotionally and politically insulated from the larger political currents in the country. In the case of the Hoa Hao and Cao Dai, when they had to choose between their sectarian interests and the nationalist cause during the Japanese and French occupations, many of their leaders opted for collaboration.

As Samuel P. Huntington has observed, the relationship between communalism and governmental authority in South Vietnam was the complete opposite of what it was in neighboring Southeast Asian countries, in which the central government was cast as the defender of nationalism against disaffected minorities. In Thailand, Burma, Cambodia, Laos, and Malaysia, as we have seen, ethnic, sectional, and religious minorities have provided the principal sources of opposition to the political system. But in South Vietnam, Huntington wrote in 1968, "the religious and ethnic minorities are centers of support for the system, and the relatively unorganized rural majority—the ethnic Vietnamese with Confucian, Buddhist and animist religious beliefs—is the principal source of alienation and disaffection."[51]

UNIFICATION: THE BUILT-IN DISABILITY

In addition to their neocolonial image and their narrow social base, post-1954 Saigon regimes inherited an even more critical, built-in disability inhibiting their efforts to establish a nationalist identity. The very nature of the situation resulting from Geneva gave the overriding issue of reunification to Hanoi and led to an ambivalent response on the part of Saigon. On the one hand, it was necessary to hold out the hope of reunification and to assert the unity of Vietnam. South Vietnamese representatives at Geneva pointedly refused to acknowledge the validity of the partition. The anniversary of the Geneva agreements, July 20, became Quoc Han (Day of National Shame), and the Constitution of October 26, 1956, proclaimed Vietnam to be "an independent, unified, territorially indivisible Republic." At the same time, however, once the date for the projected 1956 elections passed, Saigon was increasingly forced to justify the existence of a separate Southern regime.

In a 1956 information brochure, the Diem regime made no mention of the reunification objective, stressing instead in a list of historical milestones the "war between North and South Vietnam" from 1620 to 1674.[52] Thereafter, it was North Vietnam that put forward the most insistent proposals for reunifying Vietnam and for establishing normal trade and other relations in the interim. Consistently rejecting such overtures, the South was "maneuvered into the position of seeming to wish to perpetuate a divided country"[53] even though Saigon, too, made occasional ceremonial gestures of its own in the direction of reunification. The South was boxed in by its stand that unification had to come peacefully through a cease-fire and separate elections on both sides of the seventeenth parallel. Southern leaders found themselves trapped in a defensive posture when the North called for a type of peaceful unification process (e.g., neutralist or coalition rule) that was automatically ruled out by virtue of the Saigon-Washington alliance, quite apart from the South's lack of confidence in its own internal political strength. The Communists, by contrast, were able to treat unification as a supreme, overriding objective that properly merited military measures, if necessary, and they were able to get outside support for a unification-oriented policy that was not available to Saigon.

There were scattered occasions in the years after 1954 when a variety of influential figures in South Vietnam urged the United States to support an invasion of the North and encountered a predictable rebuff. These were most often military men. Significantly, however, militant Buddhist leaders also spoke hopefully of an American-backed reunification adventure in unreported private exchanges with U.S. representatives. The presence of American power was not abhorrent to them, as such, if it did not support Catholic interests and if it served the cause of Vietnamese nationalism—which is to say, national reunification; what they could not abide, said Thich Tri Quang, was the indefinite division of the country as an end in itself.

To some foreign observers, the blame for the division of Vietnam appeared to rest with Hanoi quite apart from the pros and cons of the post-Geneva controversy over the terms of unification. Ellen Hammer has suggested that Ho was only too willing to sacrifice or at least defer the goal of a unified Vietnam in order to pursue his communist goals within a state restricted to the North.[54] Frank N. Trager has argued that "Communism has been successful in splitting Vietnam at the Seventeenth Parallel."[55] To most Vietnamese, however, the partition was a by-product of the larger East-West conflict and could not be blamed exclusively on either Hanoi or Saigon, least of all on Hanoi. The Soviet interest in cementing relations with Paris in 1954 clearly made an accommodation in Vietnam desirable for the USSR, and if there was a Communist villain, it was not Hanoi but Moscow.

Given U.S. unwillingness to support a march on the North, South Vietnamese increasingly tended to see themselves as "pawns on the international chessboard,"[56] fighting a short-term holding action with the "American" objective of denying the South to the North and to communism. In a postmortem soon after Diem's assassination, one of his erstwhile supporters, a prominent Catholic professor at Saigon University, reflected that his basic error had been "treating anti-Communism as a self-contained objective, separated from the creation of conditions for the reunification of the country."[57] An interfaith group of influential Catholic and Buddhist leaders, established to promote greater civilian authority in the Ky regime, observed in its 1965 manifesto that whatever ideological basis the war might once have had no longer existed. In the light of "peaceful coexistence" and the decline of the "strict revolutionary character" of the Soviet regime, Soviet-U.S. differences now had to be judged "on the basis of Russian and American national interests rather than on the basis of bloc or ideology." It was no longer relevant to view the war in Vietnam as one "between 'Communist' and 'anti-Communist' Vietnamese. The partition of the country is losing its initial meaning. Should we die to protect the influence of the Soviet Union or Red China or the United States?"[58] As the war dragged on, this image of the conflict was more and more widely shared among politically conscious Vietnamese of all shadings, and the antigovernment manifestos and journals that mushroomed during the last years of the Thieu regime[59] talked not only of corruption and repression but also—and even more insistently—of the victimized position in which Vietnam found itself.

The underlying sense of malaise in the South resulting from the prospect of indefinite division found a partial outlet in a recurring preoccupation with Vietnamese identity in popular literature. At times, this was explicit, as in Thao Truong's imagery of a symbolic bridge upon which he stands, surveying the North-South breach,

> looking intently at the other side. It is as if by listening carefully I can hear the rhythm of the heartbeats of the people on the two banks. It is as if my blood vessels are linked to the blood vessels of those on the other side. . . . I reject the protests, demonstrations and resolutions, the banners, the slogans. . . . Everything which bears any trace of the concept of division, I want to cast it all away. In the conference rooms of those with authority, those with red pencils in their hands, drawing a line along a river is such a simple thing to do, but how can they draw such a terrible separation in our souls? There remains within me a hidden confidence that this division is merely a phase and there will come a day when people will no longer have to halt at this or that end of the bridge.[60]

More often, it found its way obliquely into poetry, as in Nguyen Vy's "Sounds of Gunfire on a Spring Night," asking whether

> Anyone can hear in the deep and boundless night
> The guns crack wildly and then fall silent.
> Each corpse is one soul of the Vietnamese nation,
> Each grave is a fragment of our heart.
> Each flower overflows with tears, forming dew.
> The entire motherland is one long spring of resentment.[61]

Anti-Americanism, literary or otherwise, was generally infused with an assertion of identity that encompassed Vietnam as a whole, as in Doan Quoc Sy's paean to Vietnamese virtues, originally published in 1957 in response to the first influx of American advisers. "Among the strangers coming to Vietnam," Doan wrote,

> there are those who are geniuses at organization, there are those who are master spies, there are those who can devise miraculous schemes. When we encounter these geniuses it is to us as if we enter an immense library where we can find all manner of books. And in return, we would like to present them with a book. This is not a book to be read with the eyes, nor heard with the ears, nor to be understood by the intellect alone, but to be comprehended by the entire human being. This is the book of a life of adversity and pain, of the glorious victories of an entire people who have struggled continuously to survive, intact, since the founding of our nation until the present time, we the people of Vietnam.[62]

Absorbed as it was with achieving its own political and military objectives in Vietnam, the United States was largely oblivious to the psychological strains inherent in continued division. Initially, Washington was content to pay lip service to the ideal of reunification while at the same time keeping a firm hand on Saigon "hawks." But as American involvement in Saigon grew, so did the importance of treating the North-South division as part of the natural scheme of things. The United States could no longer acknowledge the civil war aspects of the struggle even by implication without undermining the justification for the American military presence and later for the bombing of the North. Gradually, the United States placed an ever more insistent emphasis on the concept of a South Vietnamese "nationhood." American officials spoke increasingly of "the new nation"[63] and of "nation-building"[64] as the central objectives of American policy.

Even some academic studies arising out of the American presence tended to accept this frame of reference for discussions of Vietnamese nationalism. Douglas Pike fluctuated awkwardly between a central emphasis on "deeply ingrained regional differences," on the one hand, and passing bows to "the unity ingrained in Vietnamese bones."[65] Another scholar, Robert Scalapino, frequently echoed the theme that the United States has been "building a nation" in South Vietnam.[66] In the rhetoric of South Vietnamese officials, the concept of "nationhood" was not often handled so carelessly, but the American perception of the Vietnamese scene remained a semantic muddle to the very end. The *Washington Post* headlined its postmortem on the last days of Saigon "The Unraveling of a Nation."[67]

THE "SOUTHERN SOLUTION"

Compounding its failure to recognize the strength of nationalism and of the unification issue, in particular, the United States was also slow to perceive the importance of the subnational identities in Vietnam discussed in Chapter 1. France had consciously utilized divide-and-rule tactics during the colonial period by creating a separate Cochin China regime that played on Southern fears of Northern domination and gave preference in civil service jobs to Southerners. A losing game in the long run, given the power of nationalism, this approach was nonetheless useful in prolonging the French presence. The United States, by contrast, was a prisoner of its own rhetoric, treating Saigon governments as "national" despite their truncated territorial jurisdiction.

During the upheaval in Vietnam following the 1954 partition, the energetic performance of the Diem regime and American private relief agencies in resettling Tonkinese refugees from the North excited a natural admiration in the United States. In its impact on the Southern body politic, however, this infusion of a tightly knit refugee bloc proved to be a major liability. With their special access to the Diem family, the aggressive northern Catholics in particular were more than a match for the easygoing Cochin China southerners and rapidly moved into many of the most desirable positions in the government and the economy.[68] The South embraced parts of Annam, or central Vietnam, but two-thirds of its population was in Cochin China. The subordinate political position of the Cochin Chinese majority in the South was modified for a fleeting period in the immediate aftermath of the Diem assassination, reflecting in part the influence of southern generals and politicians in the anti-Diem movement. But when Gen. Nguyen Khanh took over from Gen. Duong Van Minh in early 1964, northern refugee elements quickly regrouped, with northern Dai Viet elements and northern Catholics equally dedicated to containing southern power despite their own mutual animosity. The complex power struggle that raged throughout 1964 was not only over military as against civilian authority as if often seemed to Washington at the time, but also over the contending claims of northerners and southerners. In the decisive phase of the struggle, Tran Van Huong, a southern conservative, gave a strongly Cochin Chinese cast to his short-lived civilian cabinet, triggering countermoves by a refugee-dominated military clique that ultimately resulted in the Nguyen Cao Ky regime.

Ky, closely identified with northern refugee elements, greatly increased the representation of northerners not only in the cabinet but in his governing military directorate as well. North-South tensions in the Ky regime finally came to a head on the eve of the Manila conference in October 1966, when his abrupt replacement of certain Cochin Chinese officials with northerners prompted a vocal southern protest. Ky retaliated by arresting the Cochin Chinese deputy health minister on charges of "separatist maneuvers," prompting the walkout of all five southern cabinet ministers. The charge of separatism underlined a significant division in noncommunist Cochin Chinese ranks between conservatives with a rigid anticommunist commitment, on the one hand, among them Catholics and old-line Buddhists such as Tran Van Huong, and others who put their regional loyalties above ideology or party. In many cases, the ministers ousted in 1966 were identified with Cochin Chinese sentiment for a "Southern solution" to the Vietnam conflict—a rapprochement between noncommunist Cochin Chinese excluded from the power structure in Saigon and Cochin Chinese members of the National Liberation Front (NLF) believed to be wary of Hanoi.

There were new substantial differences in view with respect to what such a rapprochement would mean in practical terms, ranging from outright advocacy of a coalition government to more characteristic proposals for a gradual, evolutionary process of accommodation in which some of the Communist-dominated areas of the South would be tacitly or explicitly surrendered to local NLF administrative control. Unlike other proposals for a "checkerboard" solution to the war, envisaging a continuation of the Ky-Thieu power structure, the "Southern solution" was predicated on the assumption of a genuinely southern-controlled Saigon regime able to woo fellow southerners in NLF ranks on a regionalist basis. Blood was thicker than ideology, it was argued, and substantial NLF elements could be detached from Communist discipline, creating a fluid situation in which a neutralist South could emerge.

Au Truong Thanh, a Cochin Chinese who resigned as Ky's economic minister in the 1966 walkout, was among those who argued privately [69] that a continuation of northern-dominated anticommunism in Saigon would directly set the stage for a northern-dominated communist structure later on; whereas a regionally based strategy would maximize the chances for prolonging a separate South either outside or inside the framework of a communist Vietnam. This view was shared by Tran Van Van, an aristocratic landowner and a leader of Cochin Chinese deputies in the National Assembly, who was assassinated in November 1966 at a critical phase of the north-south maneuvers in Saigon. It has never been clearly established whether Van was murdered by hard-core Communist elements or by northern Dai Viet elements dedicated to the perpetuation of refugee power in Saigon. Both were disturbed by signs that Van was making progress in his efforts to move toward a "southern solution." Three weeks before his murder, Van had recounted these efforts to the *Washington Star* correspondent in Saigon, declaring that "we have started a dialogue to create a schism in the National Liberation Front, to appeal to its middle class wing."[70] Van, who had been a major contender in the presidential election and one of the most effective foes of the Ky regime, denounced what he described as "a cabal of refugees" holding disproportionate governmental power in the South.[71]

The United States was deeply suspicious of Au Truong Thanh and Tran Van Van as witting or unwitting Hanoi agents and looked on the concept of a "southern solution" as inherently incompatible with its anticommunist objectives. Nevertheless, partly as a reaction to the shock of the Van assassination, the American embassy in Saigon made conscious efforts at the time of the 1967 elections to encourage noncommunist Cochin Chinese candidates for the National Assembly and later, in 1968, strongly urged the appointment of Tran Van Huong as prime minister under newly installed President Nguyen Van Thieu. An Annamite, Thieu had supplanted Ky largely by lining up with Cochin Chinese and Annamite generals against Ky's bloc of Tonkinese officers; out of twenty-three leading generals classified in the 1968 U.S. embassy critique cited earlier, twelve were in Thieu's camp, eight of these Cochin Chinese, including four division commanders, and two Annamites.[72] The foundations of the Saigon regime were thus more "southern" after 1968, but they were such narrowly military foundations that the Huong appointment and the subsequent choice of southern-dominated cabinets [73] had a relatively marginal political impact.

In contrast to the northern coloration of successive regimes in Saigon, the Communists put a southern best foot forward while making their appeal for southern support. The forty top leaders of the National Liberation Front were all native to areas embraced in South Vietnam. NLF chairman Nguyen Huu Tho, Trinh Dinh Thao, chairman of the Communist-sponsored Alliance of National and Democratic Peace Forces, and Huynh Than Phat, president of the Provisional Revolutionary Government set up in 1969 all had strong roots in "old" Cochin Chinese society. In Hanoi itself, the ruling Lao Dong party has long given pride of place to prominent Communists from areas south of the seventeenth parallel, such as Premier Pham Van Dong and Le Duan, party secretary-general, projecting the image not of a northern but of a national regime.

One of the keys to Communist strength during the war years was their manipulation of the delicate but integral relationship between nationalism and subnationalism. Hanoi spoke in the name of the national objective of a reunified Vietnam, invoking the Geneva accords and repudiating the U.S. contention that the 1954 partition line was a valid line between two sovereign entities. The Southern Communists thus had a stake in an all-Vietnamese movement. As Frances FitzGerald has observed, "One definition of a 'hard core' Viet Cong cadre is a man who understands his community to include not just the village or the district but Vietnam as a whole."[74] At the same time, Hanoi adapted itself to the desire of party cadres in the South for a separate identity within the overall structure of Vietnamese communism by creating the People's Revolutionary party (PRP), with a separate leadership hierarchy nominally parallel to the Lao Dong party structure.

Behind their Southern facade, the PRP and the NLF appeared to be subject to residual control on basic issues from Hanoi throughout the war years. This was certainly true after 1962, when the PRP was formed under the Lao Dong aegis, and it appears most unlikely that the unification of Communist-led military units in the South achieved in 1960 could have occurred without the strong guiding hand of the Northern regime. In a limited sense, the much discussed State Department white paper of 1965 was correct in describing the NLF as controlled by the North. Even apart from the fact that the

NLF never acknowledged the existence of two Vietnams, however, the Department greatly oversimplified the complex reality of Vietnamese communism. By attributing the existence of the NLF to the North's initiative and by flatly asserting that "it is neither independent nor southern,"[75] the white paper failed to take account of regional nuances within the national framework of Vietnamese communism that had been given direct recognition by the Communists themselves. Northern military muscle and the emotive power of the nationwide Viet Minh tradition were married in the NLF and PRP to what was an authentic and preexistent southern response to the repression of the Diem regime.

Ironically, in view of American objectives in Vietnam, the entrance of the United States as a direct participant in the conflict served to consolidate the ties between the Northern and Southern wings of Vietnamese communism. The NLF and the PRP were thrust into a necessarily greater operational military dependence on Hanoi than had existed in the initial guerrilla stages of the war. By the same token, as a result of their rapid growth during a decade of struggle against American-backed regimes, the Southern Communists and their allies became an asset of unprecedented importance to the North and acquired enhanced bargaining power in the overall Vietnamese Communist structure. In opposing the U.S. military presence, the Southern Communist leaders had a far more favorable opportunity to reap the harvest of a united front policy than they ever did during the original Viet Minh struggle. With notable exceptions, the most massive French forces had been concentrated in northern theaters of combat. The limitation of the ground war to the South by the United States and the introduction of air strikes on a greatly increased scale made the American presence more intensive and more visible than the French, offering a clear and dramatic target for a nationalist struggle.

THE AMERICAN LABEL

The failure of successive Saigon regimes to reclaim the nationalist mantle assumed by Ho Chi Minh in 1945 was to a great extent foreordained by the political realignment that had taken place in Vietnam during the years leading up to Dien Bien Phu and Geneva. This would have been true even if the United States had maintained a "low posture" in its efforts to bolster their power. With the American presence so highly visible and with Saigon ever more dependent on Washington, however, the Communists received an important dividend greatly adding to their nationalist appeal.

Even during the war against the French, the United States had been lumped together with the colonial power in the eyes of many Vietnamese nationalists as a result of its substantial aid to the anti- Viet Minh forces. Beginning with a $150 million per year program in 1950, American aid for the French military effort grew to $1.33 billion during the 1954- 1955 fiscal year. More than three-fourths of the cost of the war was borne by the United States at the time of the Dien Bien Phu disaster. Although the United States initially attempted to channel its aid to Bao Dai in the hope of enhancing his independence, the French effectively blocked these efforts, leaving the United States totally identified with the last-ditch stand of French colonialism. Communist propagandists found a ready audience when they sought to carry over the unfavorable image of the United States established during the war and to discredit post-1954 Saigon governments as "neocolonial" dependencies.

John Kennedy appropriately declared in an address on June 1, 1956, that "if we are not the parents of little Vietnam, then surely we are the godparents. We presided at its birth, we gave assistance to its life, we have helped to shape its future." Although Diem took office free of a pro-French taint, his regime was soon swathed in U.S. colors as the USIA conducted a vigorous campaign in the countryside to bolster his image. At a time when Saigon's dependence on U.S. aid was steadily growing, the proportion of foreign aid in the North Vietnamese budget was dropping from 65.3 percent in 1955 to 21 percent in 1960. Diem guarded his prerogatives against American encroachments as jealously as he did against those of domestic rivals, however, and for all of his unpopularity he was never regarded as a pure and simple American puppet to the extent that his successors were. The Buddhist crisis of 1963 offered one vivid example of his capacity for intransigence in dealings with Washington. Shortly before his murder, Diem related another little-known chapter of U.S.-Vietnamese relations to Father Cao Van Luan, a close friend and leading Catholic dignitary. Diem told Father Luan that he had rebuffed a series of American overtures in 1963 for permission to build the giant U.S. base at Cam Ranh Bay.

The authenticity of the story and its salient details are difficult to establish beyond all doubt, but it is chronologically clear that construction work on the base did not begin until November 1964, more than a year after Diem's death, as part of the overall intensification of the American commitment following the Tonkin Gulf incident. "He told the American Ambassador that this was not necessary for the war against the Viet Cong," recalled Father Luan, a ranking Jesuit educator in pre-1975 Saigon. "His view was that the United States wanted this base for its own use against China, rather than basically for the sake of Vietnam. The Americans did not like Diem because he tried to lessen the American presence. He never asked for U.S. troops."[76] In his 1971 memoirs, Father Luan stopped short of the specific mention of Cam Ranh Bay that he twice made in my interviews with him. However, he did state that Diem had been at odds with Washington over the introduction of U.S. forces during the period preceding his assassination. When Father Luan advised Diem to bend before American pressures for domestic reform, warning that "they will destroy you if you defy them," Diem retorted that

> if we make a concession now, then the Americans will demand more; how many concessions will we have to make to satisfy them? I want enough arms only for our own security forces, the civil guard and the combat youth. But the Americans don't agree. I want to strengthen the Army, but the Americans refuse to give arms and supplies. The Americans only want to bring their Army to Vietnam.[77]

The Pentagon Papers, indicating that Diem had consistently resisted a U.S. force presence in Vietnam from 1961 until his death,[78] brought him posthumous respect in the South "as a dedicated nationalist who was overthrown because he would not permit foreign troops in his country."[79]

The identification of Saigon regimes with the United States grew dramatically following the assassination of Diem and the advent of a series of military regimes lacking even the limited domestic base Diem had enjoyed in the Catholic community. Frustrated and impatient because of the South's increasing inability to cope with the war, the United States made a conscious decision in early 1964 to move into what was viewed as a power vacuum and to establish an expanded "shadow government" of U.S. advisers paralleling the top echelons of the Vietnamese administrative machinery. Little effort was made to disguise U.S. dissatisfaction with the slow-moving style of Diem's immediate successor, Gen. Duong Van Minh; firsthand accounts clearly indicate that top U.S. military aides, suspecting neutralist sympathies on the part of the general's key advisers, gave active encouragement to the coup staged by Nguyen Khanh. The Communists soon had an unprecedented symbol of the American presence in the hitherto unknown young premier. When Khanh and Secretary McNamara made their memorable tour of the countryside together, they hailed roadside crowds with their hands clasped together overhead, "all but telling them outright that 'This is our man.' "[80]

Directly wedded to the assumption of a more aggressive U.S. political role during the post-Diem period was the shift in the military arena from a nominal advisory role to a direct American presence. The most significant point of departure marking this shift came when the United States upgraded its military assistance advisory group to an operational military aid theater command in February 1962. The Pentagon's concern at this time was not to soft-pedal the increase in the American role but rather to emphasize it as a manifestation of U.S. resolve. General Paul D. Harkins was promoted from lieutenant general to four-star rank, thus outranking the chief-of-staff of the Army of the Republic of Vietnam (ARVN). Military aid was sharply increased to counter what was seen as growing Northern support for the Viet Cong and to compensate for continuing ineffectuality on the part of Saigon.

By 1963 the number of U.S. advisers in South Vietnam had reached 15,000. Soon an American officer took his place beside each Vietnamese division, regiment, and battalion commander, and in paratroop and ranger units, six American advisers were attached to each company. Yet as late as mid-1964, the State Department continued to stress the advisory character of the U.S. role, explicitly rejecting the option of sending U.S. troops.[81] As the U.S. presence grew to 25,000 in July 1964, 54,000 in June 1965, and 128,000 in September 1965, Gen. Nguyen Chanh Thi warned that the Communists were consciously contriving to transform the conflict into a Vietnamese nationalist war against a foreign "aggressor." General Thi, then the highly successful commander of the First Army Corps in the Hue-Danang area, was later exiled after a clash with Marshal Ky. In a confidential warning to Gen. Nguyen Van Thieu, then president of the military leadership committee, he pointed out that in battles at Pleime and Chu Prong,

> The Viet Cong seemed to avoid or deliberately reduce combat with the Vietnamese armed forces, instead using the whole of their forces against the allied troops and inviting casualties in their ranks. They would appear to have resorted to a new tactic, extremely dangerous if successful—a political tactic aimed at switching the fighting target from the Vietnamese armed forces to the allied forces. This would reduce our Army and people and the regime of South Vietnam to the rank of a by-product of an international power and would . . . turn the war of aggression and subversion started by the Communists into a war of liberation against foreigners.[82]

The Vietnamese army, declared General Thi, must "hold the main role. They are neither actors on a stage playing a role in the interests of outsiders, nor mercenaries. . . . They are not and cannot permit themselves to be regarded as 'legionnaires.' "[82]

It was in the Pleime- Chu Prong area that the United States first employed its "search and destroy" strategy in late 1965, only to find that Communist troops were spoiling for a direct confrontation with American forces. From October 20 to November 26, intermittent conflict raged. The climactic battle came on November 15, when troops of the First Cavalry, confronting the 304th North Vietnamese Army Division, were forced to form a defensive perimeter around a helicopter landing zone in the Iadrang Valley. Neil Sheehan wrote that the Pleime- Chu Prong struggle had "altered the character of the war" and that Communist offensive thrusts, marked by hour after hour of "vicious hand-to-hand combat," had led American officers to ask "who is the hunter and who the hunted."[83]

Communist policy statements indicate a deliberate decision in 1965 to engage the arriving U.S. forces directly and aggressively with the twofold objective of polarizing the war on a nationalist basis and accentuating antiwar sentiment in the United States. Pleime is specifically cited as a turning point marking the first major application of the new, U.S.-focused strategy.[84] While the accelerated American buildup beginning in 1965 created massive logistical problems for the Communist forces, the opportunity to place primary emphasis on a foreign threat gave them a potent psychological advantage over the ARVN. The staying power shown by the Communist side in the face of U.S. military might was carefully nurtured through appeals to a millennial tradition of successful Vietnamese resistance to foreign armies. Correspondents who visited Hanoi during the period 1965-1968 found the theme of the Vietnamese David resisting the American Goliath directly blended with anti-Chinese and anti-French imagery both in war propaganda and in historical tableaux at the State Revolutionary Museum.

Lacking a foreign enemy of its own, the ARVN made desultory and largely unsuccessful efforts to instill motivation and élan in its units through programs of anticommunist ideological indoctrination in which Hanoi's Soviet and Chinese links were emphasized. On a visit to Saigon in November 1965 I found Gen. Edward G. Lansdale, political troubleshooter for a succession of American ambassadors in Saigon, deeply preoccupied with the problem of infusing nationalist fervor in the army comparable to the spirit of the Viet Minh fight against the French. Lansdale and Gen. Nguyen Duc Thang, then minister of reconstruction, eventually enlisted the services of an erstwhile popular songwriter, Pham Duy, who had composed some of the rousing martial anthems used by the Viet Minh and had fallen on lean days in Saigon. Pham Duy was commissioned to write a series of patriotic songs that would give new inspiration to troops going into battle against the Viet Cong. But there was no magic way to put patriotic excitement into a struggle against a visible enemy consisting solely of fellow Vietnamese, and the project fell distinctly flat. The "Case of Pham Duy" was later advanced as an example of how the omnipresent Americans, "who have given up their advisory role to take control . . . go about buying over people and destroying their prestige."[85]

The progressive diminution of the ARVN role following the stepped up U.S. troop influx aggravated the sense of inferiority that had plagued the Saigon army since its inception and played into the hands of Communist propagandists. Formally enshrined in the Manila declaration of October 1966, the long developing U.S. decision to limit the ARVN role to "pacification" and "clear-and-hold" actions completed the Americanization process launched with the establishment of a theater command in 1962. By the time Defense Secretary Clifford recast this policy in May 1968, a popular conception of the ARVN as errand boys of the Americans had crystallized in wide areas of South Vietnamese public opinion. "What do these words mean?" asked an antigovernment Saigon student leader in a clandestinely circulated 1967 journal:

> We pledge to fight to the end. Who are 'we' here? How can we pledge to fight to the end when the decisions are not in 'our' hands? How can we build democracy, freedom, independence, dignity when foreigners are all over our country, when we have to line up monthly to receive salaries from them? . . .
>
> All these heroic songs praising 'soldier's life,' 'soldier's death,' 'soldier's love' have become so many empty words unable to deceive anybody. Serving the Army is patriotic, serving the Army is protecting one's Fatherland, but what Fatherland is there left to serve? The Fatherland already destroyed by bombs? The Saigon Fatherland of snack bars stinking with whisky; of slim girls in the embrace of hairy arms; of sumptuous buildings surrounded by barbed wire, reserved for foreign soldiers; of the debauching, smuggling, embezzling way of life of our fat bigwigs?[86]

Communist tactics in the political as well as the military arena were designed to make the most of the post-1965 escalation, consistently reflecting the assumption that "the more directly the American Army becomes engaged in the war, the more seriously will the conflict develop between the Vietnamese people and the American imperialists, and between the Americans themselves and their henchmen."[87] Leading South Vietnamese civilian political figures had perennially cautioned against "indiscriminate" military tactics that would drive uncommitted villagers into Communist arms,[88] but the rise of a military leadership in Saigon removed the last Vietnamese barriers to escalation. On top of an expanded troop commitment, the introduction of airpower on a large scale obviously created a dramatic and unavoidable awareness of the American presence throughout South Vietnam. The resulting dislocation of the countryside and "the politicization of much of rural Vietnam" under Communist leadership have been directly compared by John T. McAlister, Jr.,[89] to the impact of the Japanese invasion in north China as described by Chalmers Johnson in *Peasant Nationalism and Communist Power.* Johnson himself has made a similar comparison between Chinese and Vietnamese experience. In both cases, he observes, Communist success was based on nationalist appeals, in contrast to other countries in which "the revolutionaries could not establish a clear title to the mantle of nationalism."[90]

As Johnson has pointed out, the use of "selective terrorism" by the Vietnamese Communists was one of a number of distinct departures from Chinese tactical patterns[91] and undoubtedly led to an ambivalent attitude in rural areas where Communist brutality matched the American-ARVN impact. While taking this into account, however, one should not lose sight of the historical factors that explain Vietnamese variations in what is "the third generation of guerrilla warfare." In the absence of a rival Vietnamese nationalist force comparable in strength and leadership to the Kuomintang, the Vietnamese Communists, as the unchallenged leaders of the fight against the French, could concentrate on ousting the colonial ruler and strengthening their own party position. They did not have to engage in a domestic competition for peasant loyalty to the extent that the Chinese Communists did throughout the anti-Japanese war. Because they enjoyed greater logistical help from secure sanctuaries outside the country than the Chinese did, they were not as dependent for military support on the population in their base areas. The combined effect of these factors was a tendency to resort to terrorist tactics when it suited Communist purposes as a frankly opportunist departure from established doctrine. This was evident on a relatively small scale at first during the war against the French. During the Diem period, the assassination of village chiefs became a deliberate technique, and from 1962 to 1965, under the pressure of the expanding U.S. commitment, incidents of terrorism increased. But this was permissible only because the Communists felt so secure in their basic acceptance as the custodians of nationalism and in their competitive political position. They could risk the selective use of terror as an adjunct to an essentially political strategy because they faced factionalized and narrowly based opponents who relied on terror as a substitute for politics.

Where there were effective U.S. "clear-and-hold" operations, followed up by "pacification" teams, it might logically follow that the onus would then have been on the Communists for any disturbance to the status quo. This would have been true, however, only if the villages concerned had been politically untouched in the past and were antiseptically neutral. In actuality, if there ever were such areas in South Vietnam after nine years of war against the French, few remained following the intensification of the war in 1965. By May 1968, U.S. troops in Vietnam totaled 526,000, nearly eight times the number of white French troops in all of Indochina in 1954.[92] In addition to the troops and a U.S. civilian presence of 11,509 people in direct and indirect U.S. government employment, there were more than 110,000 Vietnamese employed by American government agencies and their contractors in South Vietnam.[93] The fact that these employees were Vietnamese did not remove the American identification of the programs they were carrying out. Notwithstanding its concrete achievements in welfare activities, the "pacification" program suffered fundamentally in its political impact from its American control as well as from its disproportionate recruitment among Vietnamese Catholics and among narrowly based anticommunist political factions, notably the Dai Viet and the VNQDD, regarded as uncritically "pro-American." Dai Viet leaders directed the National Institute of Administration, where deputy district chiefs were trained, as well as the Vung Tau School of Rural Development, the training center for most of the top officials in the Revolutionary Development program, the major component of the "pacification" effort.[94] Takashi Oka, a veteran observer of Vietnam, reported in a careful case study that the anti-Buddhist orientation of Dai Viet and VNQDD "pacification" teams in the First Corps area, a Buddhist stronghold,

> acts as a divisive rather than a healing element in the politics of these provinces. . . . Vietnamese and American observers alike are convinced that until the government makes pacification a program with real political content, it will not be able to give its cadres a motivation sufficient to compete effectively with the Vietcong. . . . Without this, the pacification cadre cannot be more than what he is already accused of being—an American mercenary.[95]

As we have indicated earlier, the Dai Viet and VNQDD had lost out to the Communists in the early years of the competition for nationalist leadership precisely because their elitist appeal did not have "real political content." Thereafter, anticommunism had become their only ideology, and they were no longer popularly viewed as leaders of a political movement but rather as part of the American-subsidized administrative machinery that was so visible everywhere in Vietnam. In the eyes of many Vietnamese, Saigon leaders as a whole from 1954 through 1975 were in the position of "contractors" who had been hired by the Americans to do the job of organizing U.S. operations in South Vietnam. Anticommunist author Hoang Van Chi often has used this analogy,[96] and Nguyen Van Trung, a leading Catholic intellectual, attributed the lack of motivation on the part of many South Vietnamese civil servants and military men to "the unfortunate policy of the foreigners in contracting with an individual here and giving their contractor a monopoly of leadership." In such a situation, Trung wrote, "the mentality of the Vietnamese is that of a hired hand who has lost sovereignty and nationality in his own country and works merely for the paycheck with no sense of patriotic involvement."[97]

FLIES IN AMBER

The psychological impact of an intensified American presence clearly reinforced Communist identification with nationalist feeling and to a great extent offset the severe additional military burden imposed on the Viet Cong by direct U.S. participation in the war. But it is a distortion to suggest that Americanization of the war basically changed the political environment within South Vietnam or to imply that until the aberration of 1965, a significant noncommunist nationalism had been developing in Saigon. The United States made a more limited and supplementary contribution than this to the Communist scenario in Vietnam. By the time the American role took on significant proportions in 1954, the issue had already been largely decided. The embattled years of the anti-French struggle were decisive years in which the pattern of Vietnamese political alignments was set for decades to come. Like flies caught in amber, politically conscious Vietnamese became committed irreversibly to postures and identities assumed in 1948 or 1950 or 1952. The resistance was a testing time of such traumatic significance in Vietnamese national life that what followed could only be anticlimactic.

To some dispassionate observers, Ho's elimination of his original nationalist rivals left little doubt about the ultimate outcome in Vietnam as early as 1930. This view has been typified in the work of a distinguished Vietnamese Catholic lawyer and intellectual, Tang Thi Thanh Trai, former dean of the Hue University Law School. At the very latest, this argument runs, the balance of forces in Vietnamese leadership strata had solidly crystallized by August 1945, when "the Vietnamese nation as a whole was well under Communist control."[98] A more conventional assessment, to which I would subscribe, focuses on the polarization process following Ho's rupture with the French in December 1946. Joseph Buttinger, as we have noted earlier, believes that throughout most of 1947 "there still existed a good chance to prevent the transformation of nationalists into Communists or Communist sympathizers from becoming the dominant trend of Vietnam's political evolution." But this required the creation of a noncommunist movement "as firmly nationalist, as consistently anti-colonial as the Viet Minh."[99] In this interpretation, the point of no return came in September 1947, when the French took their obdurate stand at Ha Long Bay and when so many noncommunist Vietnamese chose to collaborate or sit on the sidelines rather than challenge the Viet Minh monopoly of the national cause. Robert Shaplen, in his broadly parallel analysis, takes the more hopeful view that French concessions leading to a genuinely independent Bao Dai regime might still have led to a consolidation of noncommunist nationalism between 1948 and 1953.[100]

To make an assessment that the Communists captured the leadership of nationalism in Vietnam is not necessarily to say that they were the only "true" nationalists. This is a judgment that can appropriately be made only within Vietnamese society. As we have seen, however, the Communists were clearly "better" nationalists, offering more effective leadership not only in fighting the foreigner but also in pointing the way to equitably shared modernization. The leaders of noncommunist nationalism lost out largely by default. When history beckoned, they dithered, and when some did belatedly show a sense of purpose, their opportunity to play a nationalist role had passed. The Communists, for their part, proved to be extremely possessive guardians of the nationalist cause, successively liquidating their major rivals to make as certain as possible that patriotic virtue was never really put to a strict test. They also enjoyed extraordinarily good luck in the chain of circumstances leading up to their 1945 inheritance of the Mandate of Heaven. Whether they deserved to win or not will long be debated. But the fact remains that they did succeed in seizing the nationalist banner at the opportune moment and that their opponents were consistently unable to reclaim it despite ever accelerating infusions of foreign support.

NOTES

1. Lin Piao, "Long Live the Victory of the People's War" (New China News Agency, Peking, 2 September 1965), pp. 12, 16, 20-23, 25-27.

2. I. Milton Sacks, "Communism and Nationalism in Vietnam: 1918-1946" (Ph.D. diss., Yale University, 1960), pp. 38-42; see also Jean Lacouture, *Ho Chi Minh: A Political Biography* (New York: Random House, 1968), esp. pp. 28-32.

3. Cited in Sacks, "Communism and Nationalism in Vietnam," pp. 77-80.

4. Hoang Van Chi, *From Colonialism to Communism* (New York: Praeger, 1964), p. 56.

5. For an elaboration of Maoist united front strategy and its emulation in India see John H. Kautsky, *Moscow and the Communist Party of India* (Cambridge: Technology Press; New York: Wiley, 1956); and Selig S.

Harrison, *India: The Most Dangerous Decades* (Princeton: Princeton University Press, 1960), esp. pp. 148, 160–164.

6. See the review of Communist land policy in Stanford Research Institute, "Land Reform in Vietnam," Report prepared for the Republic of Vietnam and the U.S. Agency for International Development (Menlo Park, 1968), p. 24.

7. For samples of Communist land policy after 1954 see Vo Nguyen Giap, *People's War, People's Army* (New York: Praeger, 1962), p. 74; "Program of the National Liberation Front of South Vietnam," in *The Vietnam Reader*, ed. M. G. Raskin and Bernard B. Fall (New York: Random House, Vintage, 1965), p. 218; Douglas Pike, *Viet Cong: The Organization and Techniques of the National Liberation Front of South Vietnam* (Cambridge: MIT Press, 1966), pp. 277–278; and National Liberation Front of South Vietnam, *Political Program* (Hanoi, 1 September 1967), p. 9.

8. The captured Communist document containing this rebuke is cited in Joint United States Public Affairs Office, *The South Vietnamese Communists and Rural Vietnam* (Saigon, August 1966), p. 11.

9. Edward J. Mitchell, "Land Tenure and Rebellion: A Statistical Analysis of Factors Affecting Government Control in Vietnam," Memorandum RM-5181-ARPA (Santa Monica: RAND Corporation, June 1967), p. 31.

10. Dang Van Sung, "A Contribution to a Way Out of the Present Dilemma in Vietnam," mimeographed (Saigon, 25 January 1963), p. 13.

11. Hoang Van Dao, *Vietnam Quoc Dan Dang, 1927–54* (Saigon: Khai Tri, 1970), pp. 27–43, describes the intraparty discussions leading up to the VNQDD manifesto and reproduces the text of the declaration and the party constitution.

12. Nguyen Ton Hoan, a leader of the original Dai Viet who founded the New Dai Viet, or Tan Dai Viet, in South Vietnam, emphasized the VNQDD's attachment to Sun's ideas in "Le Dai-Viet Quoc-Dan Dang et son idéologie," mimeographed (Paris, 1963), pp. 1–2.

13. An updated version of the Truong Tu Anh doctrine was prepared by Hung Nguyen (pen name for Nguyen Ngoc Huy), *Chu-Nghia Dan-Toc Sinh-Ton* [Doctrine of national survival] (Saigon, 1964). This was a party tract with no publisher identified. The second volume (pp. 55–65) adds a discussion of man's social instincts to Truong Tu Anh's exclusive emphasis on man's selfishness.

14. Nguyen Ton Hoan, "Le Dai-Viet Quoc-Dan Dang et son idéologie," p. 8.

15. Interview, Saigon, 2 May 1971.

16. See especially Hoang Van Dao, *Vietnam Quoc Dan Dang*, pp. 247-252, 285-287, 434-435.

17. Nguyen Ton Hoan, "Le Dai-Viet Quoc-Dan Dang et son idéologie," esp. p. 2; see also Hoang Van Dao, *Vietnam Quoc Dan Dang*, esp. pp. 271-279.

18. Dang Van Sung, "A Contribution to a Way Out of the Present Dilemma in Vietnam," pp. 11-12.

19. Hoang Van Chi, *From Colonialism to Communism*, pp. 18-19.

20. Paul Mus, *Vietnam: Sociologie d'une guerre* (Paris: Editions du Seuil, 1952), pp. 26-28, 30-32.

21. Pike, *Viet Cong*, p. 28.

22. Joseph Buttinger, *Vietnam: A Dragon Embattled* (New York: Praeger, 1967), 1:312–313; see also 1:299.

23. Sacks, "Communism and Nationalism in Vietnam," p. 248; see also "Political Alignments of Vietnamese Nationalists," Report no. 3708 (Washington: Office of Intelligence and Research, Department of State, 1 October 1949), pp. 79–80; and Buttinger, *Vietnam*, 1:413.

24. Buttinger, *Vietnam*, 1:369, 381.

25. "Political Alignments of Vietnamese Nationalists," p. 134.

26. Hoang Van Chi, "Why No Peace in Vietnam," in *Vietnam Seen from East and West*, ed. S. N. Ray (New York: Praeger, 1966), pp. 35–36.

27. Buttinger, *Vietnam*, 2:702.

28. Takashi Oka, "Vietnam, 1968," Report no. TO-37 (New York: Institute of Current World Affairs, 12 February 1968), pp. 10–11.

29. *Vietnam* (Washington: Embassy of the Republic of Vietnam, 1956), p. 8.

30. For two Vietnamese images of the post-1954 civil service as linear successors to the colonial governing apparatus see Nguyen Van Trung, "Nhan Dinh va Tim Hieu Thoi Cuoc Hieu Tai a Mien Nam Vietnam" [Researches and views on the present situation in South Vietnam], *Tim Hieu* [Research] (organ of Saigon University), 1 November 1964, esp. p. 3; and Tran Van Hao, "Nhung Ao Tuong Cua Dan Anh" [The illusions of the older generation], *Sinh Vien* [Student] (organ of Saigon University Student Union), 1 August 1967, pp. 4–5.

31. Phan Quang Dan, *Volonté vietnamienne* [The will of Vietnam] (Dornach: Hutter, 1951), p. 32.

32. Sacks, "Communism and Nationalism in Vietnam," p. 260.

33. Hoang Van Chi, "A Solution for Vietnam," *Peace News* (London), 8 January 1965; see also Paul Isoart, *Le phénomène national vietnamien* (Paris: 1961), pp. 126–137.

34. Interviewed in *Echo du Vietnam* (Paris), 16 June 1949, p. 28.

35. David Wurfel, "The Saigon Political Elite: Focus on Four Cabinets," *Asian Survey*, August 1967, pp. 534–535; see also Robert Shaplen, *The Lost Revolution* (New York: Harper & Row, 1965), p. 189; and Jean Lacouture, *Vietnam: Between Two Truces* (New York: Random House, 1966), p. 125.

36. Cited in Shaplen, *Lost Revolution*, p. 82; see also Ellen Hammer, *The Struggle for Indochina* (Stanford: Stanford University Press, 1952), p. 288.

37. Phan Quang Dan, "The War in Indochina," mimeographed, Saigon (1954), p. 26; and Buttinger, *Vietnam*, 2:816.

38. Nguyen Ton Hoan, "Le Dai-Viet Quoc-Dan Dang et son idéologie," pp. 4–5. In exploring Dai Viet history, I have drawn on interviews with Dang Van Sung, Phan Huy Quat, and other Dai Viet figures as well as VNQDD leaders Phan Quang Dan and Tran Van Tuyen. A useful source of information on some aspects of Dai Viet history is Richard Critchfield, *The Long Charade* (New York: Harcourt, Brace, 1969), drawing as it does on certain U.S. State Department records and on biographies of Dai Viet leaders

obtained by Critchfield when he was a correspondent resident in Saigon. However, Critchfield utilizes his data on the Dai Viet as part of a polemical tract against the party, greatly exaggerating its importance and often making it difficult to separate solidly based fact from loosely employed argumentation.

39. Nguyen Ton Hoan, "Le Dai-Viet Quoc-Dan Dang et son idéologie," p. 3. Efforts to obtain American support as early as April 1945 by the kindred VNQDD are described in Hoang Van Dao, *Vietnam Quoc Dan Dang*, p. 222.

40. "Nationalist Politics in Vietnam" (Secret study by the Senior Liaison Office, American Embassy, Saigon, May 1968), p. E3.

41. Conversation with Archimedes Patti, Washington, 10 July 1968.

42. R. W. Apple, *New York Times*, 10 August 1967, p. 3; see also Neil Sheehan, "Not a Dove, But No Longer a Hawk," *New York Times Magazine*, 9 October 1966, pp. 27-81, for a perceptive discussion of the pre-1954 origins of army leaders.

43. Rowland Evans and Robert Novak, "Autopsy of a Collapse," *New York Post*, 16 April 1975, p. 43.

44. The gap that developed in Vietnamese society between Saigon as a foreign-dominated cosmopolitan center and an alienated peasantry cut adrift from traditional centers of control is thoughtfully analyzed in Frances Fitz-Gerald, "The Struggle and the War," *Atlantic*, August 1967, p. 77.

45. Ton That Thien, former editor of the *Saigon Guardian* and information minister in the 1968 Tran Van Huong cabinet, discussed this issue in his privately circulated paper "The Alienation of the Peasantry" (Saigon, September 1967). See also Tran Van Hao, "Nhung Ao Tuong Cua Dan Anh," p. 16, for a related analysis of peasant imagery.

46. Jerrold Schecter, *The New Face of Buddha* (New York: Coward-McCann, 1967), p. 169.

47. For a first-hand account of Catholic influence in Saigon regimes see Nguyen Chanh Thi, *Vietnam Tu-Do: Di Ve Dau?* [What future for free Vietnam?] (Saigon: privately published, 1964), esp. pp. 9–20. Bernard B. Fall, in "Vietnam in the Balance," *Foreign Affairs*, October 1966, p. 7, stated that more than half of South Vietnamese army officers then were Catholics.

48. Hammer, *Struggle for Indochina*, pp. 276, 285; see also Lacouture, *Vietnam*, pp. 104–105.

49. The views attributed here to the An Quang Buddhists are based on a three-hour conversation with Thich Tri Quang on November 12, 1967, and interviews with lay Buddhist leaders in Saigon on visits in 1964, 1967, 1971, and 1974.

No attempt is made in this context to discuss the significant differences over tactics within the ranks of An Quang Buddhist leaders or to compare An Quang views with those of Buddhist elements such as those identified with Thich Tham Chau or Mai Tho Truyen. However, on the strength of conversations with these leaders I believe that their differences with Tri Quang on the long-term future of Vietnam were not as great as often supposed. In characterizing Tri Quang's views with respect to a symbiosis of Communist and noncommunist elements, I wish to dissociate my analysis from that of Marguerite Higgins, *Our Vietnam Nightmare* (New York: Harper & Row, 1965), and of others who viewed Tri Quang as an agent of Communist interests.

50. The U.S. response to Buddhist political activism is best recorded in a six-part series by Takashi Oka, *Buddhism as a Political Force* (New York: Institute of Current World Affairs, 17 July, 21 July, 29 July, 4 August 1966; 29 May, 30 May 1967); see also Schecter, *New Face of Buddha*, esp. pp. 177–198, 212–220. A representative sample of Buddhist charges of U.S. tactics designed to "split" Buddhist ranks is found in *Bao Ve Tu Do* [Protecting Freedom] (Saigon), 15 December 1964, esp. pp. 2–6. American embassy officials outlined detailed plans to me for dividing Buddhist elements, regarded as anti-American, in background interviews in Saigon on November 13 and 14, 1964.

51. Samuel P. Huntington, "The Bases of Accommodation," *Foreign Affairs*, July 1968, pp. 646–647.

52. See the South Vietnamese embassy publication, *Vietnam*, p. 6.

53. Robert Scigliano, *South Vietnam: A Nation under Stress* (Boston: Houghton Mifflin, 1963), p. 158.

54. Hammer, *Struggle for Indochina*, p. 323.

55. Frank N. Trager, ed. *Marxism in Southeast Asia* (Stanford: Stanford University Press, 1959), p. 293; see also idem, *Why Vietnam?* (New York: Praeger, 1966), pp. 59, 118.

56. Maj. Gen. Nguyen Chanh Thi, commander of the First Army Corps, to Maj. Gen. Nguyen Van Thieu, president of the National Leadership Committee, 1 December 1965, pp. 7–8. This classified document was made available to me by General Thi and translated from the Vietnamese by Hoang Van Chi.

57. Nguyen Van Trung, "Nhan Dinh va Tim Hieu Thoi Cuoc Hieu Tai a Mien Nam Vietnam," p. 5.

58. *Cach Mang De Toi Hoa Binh* [A revolution to achieve peace] (Saigon: National Salvation Front 24 March 1965), pt. 1, pp. 2, 4–5.

59. For example, see *Doi Den* [New Light] (Saigon), Winter 1973, a special issue on "Vietnam 1945–73"; *Tin Sang* (Saigon), 27 August 1971; "Mattran Nhandan Vietnam Tranh Thu Hoa Binh" [Declaration of the Vietnamese People's Front struggling for peace] (Saigon, 7 November 1974); and "Lap Truong Hanh Dong Cho Cong Bang Xa Hoi Cua Tong Lien Doan Sinh Vien Cong Giao Vietnam" [Standpoint of the Vietnamese Catholic Students Association on the situation in Vietnam] (Saigon, 12 November 1974).

60. Thao Truong, *Mau Va Sac* [Color and hue] (Saigon: Tu Do, 1962); see also idem, *Thu Lua* [Boat along the river] (Saigon: Tu Do, 1962).

61. Nguyen Vy, "Tieng Sung Dem Xuan" [Sounds of gunfire on a spring night], in *Vietnam Thi-Nhan Tien-Chien*, ed. Nguyen Tan Long and Ng Huu Trong (Saigon: 1967), 1:452. This is an extract from a poem written

in Nhatrang in 1951. The translation was made available by Neil Jamieson from an unpublished anthology.

62. Doan Quoc Sy, "Nguoi Viet Dang Yeu" [The lovable Vietnamese people], *Nguoi Viet Dang Yeu* (Saigon: 1965), pp. 27-53. The translation of this passage was made available by Neil Jamieson from an unpublished anthology.

63. Address by George W. Ball, undersecretary of state, Detroit, 30 April 1962, p. 2.

64. Address by Roger Hilsman, director of intelligence and research, U.S. Department of State, Pomona College, 18 September 1962, p. 1.

65. Pike, *Viet Cong*, p. 3.

66. Robert Scalapino, "The United States and Vietnam," *New York Times Magazine*, 11 December 1966, p. 133.

67. *Washington Post*, 5 May 1975, p. 1.

68. Scigliano, *South Vietnam*, pp. 51-54.

69. Thanh set forth his views in a luncheon interview with me in Saigon on November 10, 1967. See also Au Truong Thanh and Vu Van Huyen, "Thu Tim Mot Giai Phap Lien-Ton De Cuu Nguy To-Quoc Va Xay-Dung Mot Xa-Hoi Viet-Nam Tu Do Va Thanh Binh" [Let us try a religious coalition as a solution for national salvation and construction of a free and peaceful Vietnamese society] (Saigon, 30 June 1967).

70. Critchfield, *Long Charade*, p. 16. Critchfield's overall treatment of Tran Van Van is given a distorted, anticommunist twist in order to fit his thesis that the northern Dai Viets were in league with Hanoi.

71. *Washington Star*, 5 December 1966, p. 3b.

72. "Nationalist Politics in Vietnam," pp. 9-10.

73. An analysis of the Thieu cabinet made in Saigon during a visit I made on November 28, 1974, showed ten Cochin Chinese, five Tonkinese, five Annamites, and one Montagnard.

74. FitzGerald, "The Struggle and the War," p. 75.

75. U.S. Department of State, *Aggression from the North: The Record of North Vietnam's Campaign to Conquer South Vietnam* (Washington: U.S. Government Printing Office, 1965), p. 20.

76. Interviews, Saigon, 11 November 1967 and 4 May 1971.

77. Cao Van Luan, *Ben Giong Lich Su* [Beside the stream of history] (Saigon: Tri Dung, 1972), p. 339. This book states that the meeting took place on June 24, 1963.

78. *The Pentagon Papers* (Boston: Beacon, 1971), 2:62-69.

79. Peter A. Jay, "Diem Death Haunts Viet Conscience," *Washington Post*, 4 November 1971, p. 3.

80. Takashi Oka, "Buddhism as a Political Force—III," Letter no. TO-26 (New York: Institute of Current World Affairs, 29 July 1966), p. 8. Mimeographed.

81. *Questions and Answers: Vietnam, the Struggle for Freedom*, Department of State Publication no. 7724 (Washington: Government Printing Office, August 1964), p. 21.

82. Nguyen Chanh Thi to Nguyen Van Thieu, pp. 7–8.

83. "U.S. Troops Renew Search for Enemy in Vietnam Valley," *New York Times*, 20 November 1965, p. 1.

84. Nguyen Van Vinh, *The Vietnamese People on the Road to Victory* (Hanoi: Foreign Languages Publishing House, 1966), pp. 4, 18.

85. Tran Van Hao, "Nhung Ao Tuong Cua Dan Anh," p. 24.

86. Ibid., pp. 19, 22–23.

87. "Resolution of the Central Office for South Vietnam" (Classified Viet Cong document captured by the 101st Airborne Division, U.S. Army, 21 April 1967; released by the U.S. Mission, Saigon, 18 August 1967), p. 19; see also pp. 17, 29, 50.

88. Phan Quang Dan, "The War in Indochina," pp. 34–35; see also Dang Van Sung, "A Contribution to a Way Out of the Present Dilemma in Vietnam," pp. 71–72.

89. J. T. McAlister, Jr., "The Possibilities for Diplomacy in Southeast Asia," *World Politics*, January 1967, p. 305.

90. Chalmers Johnson, *Revolution and the Social System* (Stanford: Hoover Institution, 1964), pp. 61–62; see also idem, *Revolutionary Change* (Boston: Little, Brown, 1966), pp. 161–162.

91. Chalmers Johnson, "The Third Generation of Guerrilla Warfare," *Asian Survey*, June 1968, esp. pp. 442, 445–446.

92. The majority of French troops in Indochina were Senegalese and Vietnamese. According to authoritative French estimates, French civilian administrative personnel for all of Indochina totaled 4,317 in 1947–1948. This number increased substantially during the war period.

93. Compiled from data supplied by U.S. agencies operating in Vietnam.

94. "Nationalist Politics in Vietnam," esp. pp. E5–E9. Dai Viet influence in the Central Intelligence Organization, the police, and the judiciary is also detailed in this U.S. embassy analysis.

95. Takashi Oka, "Pacification—Why It Doesn't Work" (New York: Institute of Current World Affairs, 24 April 1967), pp. 10, 12.

96. Interviews, Washington, 3 November 1966 and 2 February 1967; see also Hoang Van Chi, "A Solution for Vietnam."

97. Nguyen Van Trung, "Nhan Dinh Va Tim Hieu Thoi Cuoc Hieu a Mien Nam Vietnam," pp. 4-5; and ibid., 7 November 1964. A Japanese newspaper used a similar analogy, referring to "the hiring of Asians as soldiers" (*Asahi Shimbun* [Tokyo], 6 February 1971, p. 6).

98. Tang Thi Thanh Trai, "American Policy and the Vietnamese Revolution from 1940 to 1963" (Ph.D. diss., University of Chicago, 1967), pp. 93, 211.

99. Buttinger, *Vietnam*, 2:701–702.

100. Shaplen, *Lost Revolution*, pp. 385–387.

5. Korea: Nationalism Neutralized

In direct contrast to its frustrating experience in South Vietnam, the United States has maintained a continuous presence in South Korea since 1945, surviving a succession of military and political tests and successfully escaping a "neocolonialist" label despite the best efforts of Communist propagandists. This is only in a very limited sense attributable to the obvious differences in geography and physical terrain distinguishing the two cases. Viewed solely in operational military terms, Korea undoubtedly offers a more favorable environment than Vietnam. It is a peninsula accessible on all sides from the sea. It has no mountain jungles and no malarial swamps. Looking back on the Korean War, however, General Ridgway made little of these and related factors in discussing lessons applicable to Vietnam. His focus was instead on the fundamental political distinction that

> in South Korea, we had a workable government led by a patriotic and powerful civilian leader whose opposition to communism was widely known and who held the allegiance of the majority of his people.... United Nations personnel rode in open jeeps throughout our zones without ever drawing an assassin's fire. Our power easily contained guerrilla activity, even though our forces were neither as well-equipped nor as mobile as they were in Vietnam.[1]

What makes Korea a case apart from Vietnam has indeed been its very different political environment. But the underlying reason for the difference is not to be found in the degree of positive support commanded by the embattled authoritarian regimes of Rhee Syngman and Park Chong-hui. The determining factor in the Korean scene has rather been the essential political weakness of the Korean Communist movement, which has thus far failed to achieve the leadership of Korean nationalism. Despite continual political turbulence in the South, North Korea has been unable to exploit a persistent leadership vacuum there because history has robbed

131

Korean communism of the special claim to nationalist legitimacy found in the Vietnamese case.

From the special vantage point of Vietnam itself, this contrast between the two Communist movements has been only too painfully clear. The case of Korea was "absolutely different from ours," observed Dang Van Sung, the anticommunist Vietnamese nationalist, for the elemental reason that the North Korean regime was an external Soviet creation after the East European pattern. "The Korean Communists merely took advantage of the Russians to impose their control. They had done nothing to earn their power, and they could not hope to have as much of a grip on the mass psychology as the Vietnamese Communists did."2

While there were Communist factions in Korea prominently identified with the nationalist movement, their role was generally secondary to that of noncommunist nationalist leaders. To the extent that widely known Communist leaders with nationalist credentials did exist in 1945, they have since been systematically purged by Kim Il-sung. The essence of the difference between Korea and Vietnam is illuminated in this sharp breach dividing pre-1945 Korean communism and the altogether new implant personified by Kim. As a political newcomer initially dependent on the Soviet occupation forces, Kim felt compelled to make a clean break with the past to consolidate his personal power. But the result was to cripple the Korean Communist potential. The fact that Kim achieved his power without a preexisting base in Korea itself and without a leading place in the Korean nationalist tradition is of critical importance. It not only explains his inability to play the role of a Korean Ho Chi Minh in an all-Korean context but also accounts for an increasingly free-wheeling Pyongyang posture in the communist world designed to give his regime in North Korea nationalist legitimacy.

RULE OR RUIN

By the time a communist movement began to stir in the country following the Russian Revolution, Korea already had an established first generation of grass-roots nationalist leadership centered in the Ch'ŏndogyo (Teaching of the Way of Heaven), a populist, welfare-oriented religious movement preaching a distinctively Korean blend of Confucianism, Buddhism, Taoism, and shamanism. Like its predecessor, the Tonghak movement, sponsor of the Tonghak rebellion of 1894–1895, the Ch'ŏndogyo gave expression to the powerful xenophobic Korean reaction generated by Japanese and Western cultural incursions. Its political aims were only thinly camouflaged behind a facade of religious respectability.

Paralleling the growth of covert activity within the country, nationalist exile groups mushroomed under noncommunist leadership. They were faction ridden and geographically dispersed, but most of them found a commonly acceptable symbol of the nationalist cause in Rhee Syngman, who was not then the abrasive figure he was to become in later years. Rhee had pioneered in émigré nationalist activities from the earliest days of the Japanese regime and had first established the international identity of Korean nationalism when he presented the demand for Korean self-determination to Wilson in 1918. The assertive spirit of the independence movement was demonstrated in the abortive uprising of March 1, 1919, a traumatic episode in modern Korean history that provoked years of savage reprisals and gave Korean nationalists their Bastille Day. Only a handful of Communists were on the scene at the time of what became the most widely remembered symbolic event in Korean nationalist history, and Communist leaders were conspicuously missing among the March 1 martyrs.

In addition to their late start in the competition for nationalist leadership, the Korean Communists suffered even more than their noncommunist rivals during the successive waves of Japanese repression touched off by the 1919 revolt. There has been nothing in the annals of Western colonial rulers quite like the severity achieved by the Japanese in Korea. The Japanese police demanded notice of any gathering of three or more persons, even in private homes, and the slightest hint of hostile political activity meant years of imprisonment. Nationalist activity of every political coloration was necessarily a sometime thing, starting and stopping unpredictably as fugitive underground leaders shuttled back and forth between Seoul, Pyongyang, and assorted émigré centers in Japan, Manchuria, and China. In its pursuit of the Communist movement, however, the Japanese security apparatus was particularly assiduous and efficient as an extension of operations against the nascent Communist movement in Japan itself. The resultant dislocation and interruption of Communist organizing efforts served to aggravate the factionalism common during this formative period to all Korean political movements. Unlike the Vietnamese Communists, who made good use of their early years in recruiting peasant cadres, the warring Korean leaders carried their organizing efforts to the countryside only at sporadic intervals and built their major strength in cities and towns. No one Communist leader was able to pull together a united party leadership for more than a few years at a stretch or to retain continuing Comintern recognition as the unchallenged leader of Korean communism.

With two notable exceptions, the Korean Communists failed to employ the united front strategy so crucial to the success of the

Chinese and Vietnamese Communists. The first and most important of these came in a series of attempts to work with Ch'ŏndogyo and other noncommunist groups from 1927 to 1931 following the return of leading members of a nationalist-minded student communist faction from Tokyo.

For nearly five years, until its dissolution at the hands of the Communists in May 1931, Korean nationalists of all shades were united in the powerful Sin'ganhoe coalition. During a brief, nine-month interlude in 1929, the Communists captured the Sin'ganhoe leadership, but for the most part they were clearly relegated to a secondary role. Even when they controlled Sin'ganhoe, the Communists were unable to put forward a suitable chairman drawn from the party apparatus itself, selecting instead a fellow-traveling lawyer who had won his fame representing nationalist defendants in Japanese courts. Harassed by the Japanese, faction ridden, and lacking a popular national leader, the Communists had entered the coalition partly in the hope of using it to compensate for what was their own narrow organizational base. In the case of Korea, however, the noncommunist nationalists had access to an established mass organizational network in Ch'ŏndogyo to fortify their position, and it was the noncommunists who were able to use the Communists, rather than the other way around. Japanese divide-and-rule tactics deliberately played on the divisions in Sin'ganhoe ranks. This was acidly pointed out by the Comintern, which had first instructed the Korean Communists to capture Sin'ganhoe but later ordered its destruction as a useless "nationalist reformist" group. The Korean Communists suffered a series of internal crises over the united front issue as a result of the Comintern attitude. Even more important, their rule-or-ruin tactics in destroying what had been a uniquely promising move toward nationalist unity badly damaged their popular standing.

The Sin'ganhoe experience offers a striking case history illustrating the failure of the early Korean Communists to capture the leadership of nationalism. Another telling episode of shorter duration but in some respects even more revealing occurred on the eve of the American occupation in 1945. When a coalition of Communists and militant nationalists set up a Preparatory People's Republic, hoping to confront the arriving Americans with the fait accompli of an independent regime, the Communists once again found themselves in a secondary position. The principal organizer of the republic was noncommunist Yŏ Un-hyŏng, a leading publisher-politician with powerful mass platform appeal who had carried on underground resistance activity for many years and had begun organizing in secret to prepare for independence as early as 1944. His was the role in the Korean context most closely paralleling that of Ho Chi Minh during the immediate prelude to the Japanese surrender. At a historic "people's congress" of more than 1,000 delegates called to launch the new republic on September 6, 1945, Rhee Syngman was chosen in absentia as chairman and Yŏ Un-hyŏng as vice-chairman. The Communists had thrown up popular local and regional figures such as Pak Hŏn-yŏng in the South and O Ki-sŏp in the North in the years after the Sin'ganhoe fiasco. But they were still unable to claim a place in top leadership ranks at the critical moment of nationalist consolidation in 1945.

While the Communists wielded disproportionate power in the staff machinery directing the activities of the republic,[3] knowledgeable Korean observers contend that it was not initially Communist controlled.[4] As we shall see in a later chapter, only when it lost its character as an authentic coalition in the face of hostile pressures from the U.S. occupation regime did the republic movement fall into Communist hands in the South. Noncommunist nationalists gradually broke away when it became clear that the U.S. military government would not give recognition to the republic and was bent on fostering the growth of a conservative political force under the leadership of Rhee. Left on their own, the Communists in the South proved unable to make up for their earlier inability to build a powerful mass base despite remarkably rapid progress in some areas. They fled to the North in April 1948, a step ahead of the anticommunist offensive set in motion by Rhee with American blessings.

The willingness of many of the leading noncommunist militant nationalists in Korea to join hands with the Communists in 1945 reflected not only their confidence that they could keep control out of Communist hands but also their acceptance of the Communists as bona fide nationalists. Although they had failed to coalesce into an effective, unified force capable of claiming nationalist leadership, the pre-1945 Korean Communists were in many cases popular personalities in Seoul and other localities. They were among those who had kept underground resistance alive in the later years of Japanese rule at a time when many solid citizens with a less steadfast nationalist commitment were making adaptations to the colonial regime to advance their personal fortunes. Like militant noncommunist nationalists, they enjoyed greater popular trust than the moderates, landed gentry, and business leaders, identified in the main with the Korean Democratic party, who later provided the local base for Rhee and other returning conservative émigré leaders. If these "old" Communists had found their way into positions of real power in Pyongyang, the emerging North Korean regime might have acquired in much smaller measure a touch of the attractive power held from the start by the Viet Minh regime in Hanoi. While the "new" Communists were busy consolidating their position under the aegis of the Soviet occupation forces in the North, however, the "old" Communists made the fatal mistake of continuing to center their activities in Seoul. They took it for granted that an independent, unified Korea would emerge following the anticipated withdrawal of American and Soviet troops; by the time they recognized their mistake, Kim Il-sung and other lesser figures even more closely linked to Soviet patronage were firmly entrenched.

THE NORTHERN BASE OF NORTH KOREAN COMMUNISM

Kim was only thirty-three when he made his appearance with the Soviet occupation army in 1945 after more than a decade as an émigré guerrilla leader in Manchuria closely allied with the Chinese Communists. The details of his early career are a subject of continuing controversy and are still not clearly established. Most evidence indicates, however, that he spent the last three years of the war in the Soviet armed forces after taking refuge from an advancing Japanese column in Siberia with his guerrilla followers in 1941. Some sources state that Kim became a major.[5] Despite published denials,[6] his shift to Siberia was seemingly confirmed by a conspicuous hiatus in the exhibits at the newly opened National Revolutionary Museum, which I visited during a five-week 1972 tour[7] of North Korea. First one is shown a proclamation issued in August 1939, ordering Kim's guerrilla units to help defend the Soviet Union in the face of a Japanese attack along the Soviet-Mongolian border. Then, after viewing a photo taken with guerrilla comrades in 1940, labeled as "shortly before the Liberation," one next sees a smiling Kim in August 1945, side by side with Soviet troops arriving in North Korea.

Taking full advantage of his initial Soviet sponsorship, Kim and his coterie of close friends from Manchurian days proceeded to build their own exclusive power base after their arrival in Pyongyang, gradually purging every leading Communist figure popularly identified with the mainstream of pre-1945 political life in Korea. The principal southern Communist leader, Pak Hŏn-yŏng, arrived in Pyongyang confident that he would enjoy coequal status with Kim and that the rest of his fugitive southern Communist apparatus would be hospitably integrated into the Communist organization then being set up in the North under the Soviet aegis. Kim did go through the initial motions of hospitality by making Pak vice-chairman of his regime, while gradually taking steps, at the same time, to dismember and destroy southern party cadres. In 1953, following the Korean armistice, Pak and another key leader of the southern faction, Yi Sŭng-hwa, were blamed for falsely estimating Communist strength in the South during the Korean war and charged with insidious U.S. ties. The Chinese Communist military presence in Pyongyang helped Kim to strengthen his position at that time, and Pak, Yi, and twelve others eventually were executed. Kim's rivals from the few "old" Communist local organizations based in the northern provinces were eliminated with equal dispatch. Thus, O Ki-sŏp, who had acquired a considerable local reputation as an anti-Japanese guerrilla fighter in Hamgyŏng, was successively demoted, jailed, and finally purged in 1958, along with other leaders of the northern Pungno faction.8 Another venerable revolutionary with a nationalist image, Kim Tu-bong, leader of an important former exile group known as the Yenan faction, was also purged.

Preoccupied as he was with denying effective power to locally rooted Communist leaders who might constitute a potential opposition, Kim Il-sung relied, to some extent, on the preexisting civil service machinery taken over from the Japanese in North Korea, just as Rhee Syngman did in the South for his own expedient reasons. In its early stages, at least, the bureaucratic face of Kim's regime thus had a tired look, but far more important as a tarnishing factor was its made-in-Moscow stamp. Not only were Kim and his personal Kapsan faction from Manchuria viewed from the start as creatures of the Soviet occupation. The Russians had also brought with them a group of trusted "Soviet-Koreans" who held Soviet citizenship and had risen through the ranks of the Communist apparatus in the Soviet Union itself as representatives of a sizable Korean minority. When the Russians set up a Communist apparatus in Pyongyang, their choice to head the organization committee was Hŏ Kae, a veteran party functionary in Tashkent and one-time secretary of the Communist Central Committee in the Soviet Maritime Territories. In this key post Hŏ Kae had the power to screen, promote, and demote party members and to spot "Soviet-Koreans" where it counted most throughout the government apparatus. Another Soviet operative, Pang Hak-se, was installed by the NKVD as chief of the potent Political Security Bureau in Pyongyang. Given the great power wielded by the "Soviet-Koreans" in its formative years, Kim's regime suffered from the taint of foreign domination long after he had consolidated his personal position and had sent most of them back to the Soviet Union with Chinese help in 1956.

Kim has demonstrated a driving desire to remove this taint and to legitimize his regime in the emphasis of his domestic propaganda, as well as in his assertively nationalist posture within the communist world. While Ho Chi Minh's task was to sustain and prolong the patriotic élan generated by the Viet Minh during the fight against the

French, Kim's challenge as ruler of North Korea has been to acquire a charisma that he singularly lacked upon coming to power. He has gone to great lengths to create a national legend in which he is cast as the liberating hero who led a mighty guerrilla army to victory over the Japanese in Manchuria. This has made it necessary to invest relatively minor escapades with the aura of grand adventure and to play down or conceal many of the more inconvenient realities of his early life.

THE MAKING OF A NATIONAL LEGEND

Actually, Kim's life story does include a clear record as a guerrilla fighter against the Japanese, contrasting sharply, as we shall see in a later chapter, with Park Chong-hui's record as an officer in the Japanese forces in Manchuria. South Korean claims that this anti-Japanese record is a fabrication appear to be incorrect. Born near Pyongyang, Kim grew up on a farm in Manchuria, where his father had emigrated during the wave of political persecution following the March 1 uprising of 1919. Kim went to Chinese schools and became fluent in Chinese, a fact that was to prove of material importance in determining the character and sponsorship of his early guerrilla activity. According to the best available evidence, he became a protégé of the Chinese Communist military in Manchuria as a young man and led a detachment of 150–300 men in a Chinese Communist guerrilla force known as the Northeastern People's Revolutionary Army beginning in 1932. He can lay claim to a part in the Korean nationalist cause in the limited sense that the men under his command were Koreans primarily, drawn from the 600,000 Korean émigrés in Manchuria, and that they were engaged in fighting the Japanese, largely in Korean-majority areas. On one occasion, while battling Japanese police just inside the northern border of Korea at Poch'ŏnbo on June 4, 1937, Kim banded together with a noncommunist nationalist group, the Korean Fatherland Restoration Association. For all practical purposes, however, Kim spent most of his guerrilla years fighting as part of the Chinese Communist effort to rid Chinese territory of the Japanese, rather than as leader of a concerted Korean nationalist movement to liberate Korea. He was serving nationalist ends, but so were others who were much better known, especially in the south. As Suh Dae-sook observes, Kim's nationalist stature in the pre-1945 period was intrinsically diminished by the fact that he had been "educated and trained by the Chinese Communists as one of their own, not as a delegate or representative of Korean Communists among the Chinese."[9]

Kim Tu-bong and the Yenan faction enjoyed their nationalist image precisely because they had been in the center of Korean nationalist activity for many years before turning to the Chinese Communists for help and, even then, had been able to retain their separate identity in the Korean Independence League. Kim Il-sung and his men had no such independent identity. They were an integral part of the Chinese Communist movement. Kim rose in the ranks of the Chinese forces in Manchuria at a time when many less adaptable Koreans who had worked with the Chinese Communists there were being purged for their insubordination. He was not among the purged Korean comrades who had complained of domineering Chinese ways in mid-1933 and had appealed to the Comintern for the creation of a separate Manchurian communist movement detached from Chinese control. In an unusually acrimonious incident in 1934, climaxing a long period of Korean-Chinese tension in Manchuria, the Chinese Communists had charged certain Koreans with serving as informers for the Japanese and staged a mass execution of Korean party members. Kim was spared. From that point forward, a distinct odium attached to cooperation with the Chinese among Koreans in Manchuria, but Kim continued his association. Captured Japanese documents suggest, however, that he functioned as an autonomous coequal of the nominal local Chinese commander in his area.[10]

Like "a multitude"[11] of other guerrilla leaders who were active in Korea and Manchuria during the Japanese period, Kim Il-sung won a fleeting notoriety, especially after successful encounters such as the battle of Poch'ŏnbo. Many Koreans had never heard of him, however, when he turned up in Pyongyang in 1945. The guerrilla folklore coming out of Manchuria had centered largely on the Korean Revolutionary Army, a nationalist group that shunned cooperation with the Chinese Communists and refused to accept anyone in its ranks who had fought under Chinese leadership of any stripe. As for Kim's Northeastern People's Revolutionary Army (NPRA), it shared the limelight with a number of noncommunist Chinese guerrilla groups organized by warlord leaders, and many of these groups have been credited with a more important role than the NPRA in fighting the Japanese, even in official Chinese Communist accounts.[12] Lee Chong-sik made a detailed study of Korean newspapers and tabloids published during the heady political ferment of mid-1945 and found no mention of Kim Il-sung.[13] Kim's name was conspicuously missing from the long list of nationalist and Communist luminaries, among them many other exiles, drawn up by the Preparatory People's Republic in Seoul. The major claim to popular acceptance that Kim had when he emerged as the leader of the new, Soviet-sponsored regime was his cloudy identification in the minds of some older Koreans with the legend of a turn-of-the-century folk hero named Kim Il-sung. Many a young revolutionary had adopted the pseudonym of this vaguely remembered, possibly imaginary Korean Robin Hood, and this appears to have been the case with Kim, whose original name was Kim Sŏng-ju.

Those who had heard of a Kim Il-sung and who turned out to receive him at a public rally in Pyongyang on October 14, 1945, expected to see a grey-haired old patriot of Rhee's generation. Instead, they found a pudgy young man in his thirties who bore no resemblance to the legendary hero. One account suggesting the flavor of the popular response to Kim's first public appearance has been given by O Yŏng-jin, a leading noncommunist who was present on the dais. He relates in his memoirs that Kim

> wore a blue suit which was a bit too small for him, and he had a haircut like a Chinese waiter. He is a fake! All the people gathered in the athletic ground felt an electrifying disgust, disappointment, discontent and anger. But oblivious to the sudden change in the mass psychology, Kim Il-sung continued with his monotonous, plain and duck-like voice to praise the heroic liberating struggle of the Red Army. He particularly offered the greatest gratitude and glory to the Soviet Union and Marshal Stalin.[14]

Even if one allows for the animus pervading the writings of exiles from North Korea, it has become apparent from a wide variety of sources[15] that Kim Il-sung was relatively little known at the time of his initial appearance and deeply handicapped by his lack of a major nationalist reputation. His effort to overcome this and to establish himself as the liberator who vanquished the Japanese oppressor has proven a stubborn task even for a totalitarian regime, but this has only led Kim to intensify the ever more insistent nationalist refrain dominating North Korean internal propaganda. The origins of the struggle for Korean independence are traced back to an underground group said to have been established by Kim's father in 1917, and the day on which this group was founded is now commemorated as a national holiday. North Koreans also celebrate the anniversary of a 1936 gathering at the Manchurian town of Nan-hu-t'ou, where Kim claims to have enunciated a united front strategy for the anti-Japanese struggle. They are exhorted to study an unending succession of historical tracts on the minutiae of Kim's Manchurian years. In 1972, the two most popular long-running hit operas at the Pyongyang Opera House were "Sea of Blood" and "Speak, Ye Forest," both depicting anti-Japanese guerrilla exploits. Publications directed to Korean residents in Japan solemnly describe the inauguration of nationwide study classes in industrial installations, informing the reader that in the Pyongyang thermal power plant, "before adjusting the heat regulator of the Sixth Boiler, the chief boilerman never forgets to read the *Reminiscences of the Anti-Japanese Partisan Fighters.*"16

By far the most important focus of the Kim legend is the Poch'ŏnbo episode. A 126-foot-high monument showing Kim and a group of guerrillas locked in combat with the Japanese was unveiled there on the anniversary of the battle in 1967, and June 4 has now become a North Korean Fourth of July and Memorial Day rolled into one. The streets of Kaesŏng were alive with jubilant thousands staging a torchlight parade when I visited the North Korean city on Poch'ŏnbo Day. In the Revolutionary Museum, the most dramatic exhibit is an amphitheater with a life-sized reproduction of the Japanese stockade at Poch'ŏnbo under siege by Kim's forces. Hushed audiences sigh, weep, and cheer lustily as shifting photo montages are projected onto the stockade backdrop and patriotic songs blare, creating the illusion of a battle in progress followed by Kim's adoration on the shoulders of triumphant villagers. The special utility of Poch'ŏnbo lies not only in the fact that a clash did clearly take place there but also that it was the one encounter of any consequence between Kim and the Japanese that occurred in part, at least, on the Korean side of the Korean-Manchurian border. In this instance, as in the rest of the official legend, however, Kim has been presented as the leader of a *Korean* guerrilla army. The approved version of his career not only inflates his small guerrilla detachment into a thundering legion but speaks of it as the "Korean People's Revolutionary Army," never mentioning the Northeastern People's Revolutionary Army, which was widely known in Korea as Chinese. North Korean efforts to appropriate the tradition of noncommunist Korean nationalist groups such as the Korean Revolutionary Army and the Korean Fatherland Restoration Association have provoked powerful rebuttals from Korean exiles in Tokyo.17

The first indication that Kim has been on the defensive with respect to his early Chinese links came in a subtle change in the treatment of his early life during 1968. Rather than ignore completely his Chinese ties in earlier years, the official history of the partisan period praised Kim for exposing "left chauvinists" who had been guilty of "national prejudices . . . disruptive of the unity and cohesion of the revolutionary ranks. Comrade Kim Il-sung effected a general mobilization of all possible anti-imperialism forces for the annihilation of Japanese imperialism on a national and international scale . . . including the Communists and people of the neighboring country." It was Kim who had led the Chinese, however, and "the Korean people are proud that the Korean Communists under the personal leadership of Comrade Kim Il-sung honorably played the role of an international vanguard in the anti-imperialist united front movement."[18] By 1972, the Revolutionary Museum was more explicit, glorifying Kim for "bold, direct negotiations" with the Chinese that led to successful joint action under his command against the Japanese.

Kim seeks to neutralize attacks on his own past by waging a countercampaign to discredit his pre-1945 precursors in explicitly nationalist terms. Posing as the ideological father of Korean nationalism, he charges that "flunkeyism and dogmatism led the Communist movement in our country to blindly accept the doings of the Comintern or greater foreign powers without minding if they were right or not, if they suited the actual conditions of the country." The Soviet Union is given major blame for the failure of the "old" Communists in Korea to adopt a united front policy at a time when "Comrade Kim Il-sung, the iron-willed genius commander, flatly rejecting such flunkeyism," was giving a correct national lead in the Nan-hu-t'uo line.[19] In a major policy declaration in December 1955, marking the start of his intensified effort to "Koreanize" the image of his regime, Kim condemned the failure of the early Communists to join in the uprising of March 1, 1919. "The absence of leadership by the Communist Party was the principal cause of the failure of the March First Uprising," he declared. "But who can deny that the March First uprising was a nationwide resistance to Japanese imperialism?"[20]

PUPPET LIBERATED

It was in this 1955 statement that Kim first articulated the *Juche* (autonomy or organic integrity) policy, which has become the principal article of faith of his regime and the symbol of its increasingly freewheeling posture in relations with Moscow and Peking. "We are not engaged in the revolution of another country but in our Korean revolution," Kim declared. "By the establishment of *Juche* we mean solving all problems concerning the revolution independently; relying mainly on one's own efforts. If we mechanically copy from foreign experience it will lead to dogmatic errors."

When *Juche* was first proclaimed, it was addressed pointedly to the Russians; later it was broadened to embrace the Chinese as part of a total rejection of the concept of a monolithic communist movement. This has been a reflection in the ideological sphere of an overall process of change in the North Korean position within the communist world. Passing from a one-sided tutelage under Moscow to an additional dependence on Peking occasioned by the Korean War, North Korea has gradually won increasing independence from both Communist patrons. Kim gave ideological support to Peking in the early stages of the Sino-Soviet dispute even when this provoked a violent Soviet response, culminating in the cutoff of badly needed aid in 1962. But he carefully guarded against a repetition of his original unilateral dependence.

By 1964, North Korea had formally rejected the entire concept of a "leading party" in international communism, demanding in its place the concept of a communist commonwealth more far-reaching in its heretical implications than any other national communist deviation then on record. "All fraternal parties are equal and independent," declared an official Pyongyang pronouncement.[21] "There may be a large party and a small party but not a higher party and a lower party, nor a guided party and a guiding party. No majority principle and no centralized discipline is applicable to the relations among fraternal parties." In its much quoted manifesto of August 12, 1966, "Let Us Declare Our Independence," Kim's party organ summed up North Korean policy as one of "*Juche* in ideology, independence in politics, self-reliance in economy and self-defense in national defense."[22] "Perhaps more than any other nation in the Communist bloc," said President Nixon after the EC-121 episode in 1970, North Korea is "completely out of the control of the Soviet Union or Communist China."[23]

The atmosphere enveloping the visitor more than vindicates the judgment that North Korea is an example par excellence of "the triumph of nationalism over certain traditional Communist values."[24] Apart from the fact that past Soviet and Chinese help is only reluctantly mentioned, most often with pained allusions to "the dangers of depending on unreliable foreign friends," it soon becomes clear in casual as well as staged conversations that *Juche* has a vivid, intense meaning for a wide variety of people. This is apparent in the faces of workers showing off crude, domestically made machines in a Wŏnsan factory, explaining how "foreign friends" had refused to supply the blueprints; in the frequent choked up reactions of spectators at operas and films to patriotic themes; and in beaming crowds hovering over a simple refrigerator, unveiled for the first time in a Pyongyang department store amid purring loudspeaker reminders that none of the parts came from foreign countries.

The *Juche* policy has been both a useful handle for Kim in defending his personal power position as well as an authentic Korean nationalist response to Soviet and Chinese pressures. Quick to recognize that de-Stalinization could be converted by his domestic rivals into a rationale for opposing his one-man rule, Kim has consistently based his opposition to "revisionism" on the argument that it is an alien doctrine calculated to weaken and divide North Korea. First he liquidated domestic enemies who dared to question his ties with foreign communist parties. Now he castigates rivals for following foreign ideas and seeking foreign allies. Kim has skillfully appropriated *Juche* as his personal property while at the same time making it the basis of national pride. Sheathed in this ideological armor, he can claim to be the sole interpreter of what is "correct" for North Korea and to label all opponents as foreign tools.

To say that Kim achieved power without impeccable nationalist credentials and has been unable to play the role of a Ho Chi Minh, in Korea as a whole, is not to deny him the label of a nationalist, as we have seen, or to disqualify him permanently as a contender for the leadership of Korean nationalism. In explaining his determined posture toward Moscow and Peking, a case might be made that precisely because he spent so much of his early life as an exile, adapting to the whims of his mentors, he could be expected to react with a peculiarly strong assertiveness once given the chance. Cho Soon-sung stresses that Kim did, after all, endure great privation in order to fight the Japanese and that only the "Soviet-Koreans" ever really behaved as trained seals for Moscow. Cho demonstrates that the pattern of North Korean relations with Moscow and Peking has been dictated by nationalist rather than communist priorities and cannot be adequately explained as a mere function of the Sino-Soviet rivalry. North Korea today is not only national communist but also nationalist in a more general sense, he contends, motivated by assessments of Korean self-interest that have been "reinforced and encouraged" by specific developments in the Sino-Soviet rift but that would eventually have found expression even if the conflict had never occurred.[25]

From a Pyongyang perspective, Moscow and Peking have consistently betrayed an unabashed concern for their national power interests and a willingness to downgrade the objective of Korean reunification, which can only have had the effect of sharpening a strongly defensive sense of North Korean identity. The beginnings of disillusion with the Soviet Union date back to the mid-1951 impasse in the Korean War, when Moscow proved ready to sacrifice Korean interests rather than escalate the conflict. Moscow at least paid lip service to the unification goal, in contrast to Washington's negative, containment approach to Korea, but Soviet concurrence in the armistice was nonetheless seen as a betrayal. Later, when Khrushchev made his notable statement at the 1959 Supreme Soviet that the United States was not inclined toward aggressive action in Korea, North Korean fears of abandonment greatly increased. The Chinese also proved to be equally self-centered "great power chauvinists" in Korean eyes when they gave their own tactical objectives in the Sino-Soviet dispute priority over an effectively unified communist program of assistance for North Vietnam. In pressing for united action by the Russians and the Chinese to facilitate aid deliveries to Hanoi, Kim Il-sung was reminding them that Korea, too, is a partitioned country unreconciled to permanently truncated status and facing the danger of a potential explosion. This is a message he most insistently addressed to the Russians as their relations with the United States steadily moderated. Coexistence might have its rationale for great powers, he warned Moscow in 1966, but "socialist countries should be duly vigilant over the fact that the U.S. imperialists, while refraining as far as possible from worsening their relations with big countries, concentrate their aggression on a country like Vietnam, and intend to swallow up such divided or small countries as Korea, Cuba and East Germany one by one."[26]

The most significant concrete expression of the *Juche* policy and the major source of tension in Moscow-Pyongyang relations has been the North Korean effort to establish an independent economic base. As their distrust of their mentors has grown, so has their desire to gain greater maneuverability and to fortify themselves against the danger of a Soviet or Chinese diplomatic sellout. Tension began to develop over the terms of Soviet-North Korean aid relationships as early as 1956, when Moscow first pressed the COMECON concept of a blocwide "division of labor." Blatantly seeking to mold the North Korean economy to the pattern of Soviet raw material needs, Moscow did its best to frustrate Pyongyang's decision to emphasize heavy industry and to create its own machine-building capability. North Korean efforts to attract Chinese aid as an offset to Soviet dependence, accompanied by ideological gestures ·to Peking, eventually provoked a heavy-handed Soviet crackdown on Pyongyang in early 1962. Economic and military aid came to a virtual halt until a post-Khrushchev turnabout in Soviet policy in late 1965 brought a restoration of assistance at reduced levels.

Kim Il-sung made no apparent compromise of basic economic policy to obtain a renewal of aid and has continued to use the Soviet Union as a nationalist whipping boy. Even with the renewal of aid, Kim has attacked the Soviet Shylock, recalling that "the modern revisionists . . . brought economic pressure upon us, inflicting tremendous losses upon our socialist construction."[27] In its climactic proclamation of the *Juche* policy in August 1966, *Nodong Sinmun* stressed that "economic dependence inevitably entails political dependence" and declared that North Koreans were being taught "the habit of using homemade products, even though of inferior quality." On my visit to the North in 1972, I was told by a guide at the National Industrial Exhibition that "when we first wanted to produce tractors and trucks, foreign countries wouldn't provide the designs, so our Leader ordered us to make them for ourselves. The first tractors we made went backward, but we learned."

In 1972, North Korea was making not only its own tractors and other farm machinery but also twenty-five-ton trucks, buses, bulldozers, automated textile looms, generators, mining machinery, diesel engines, and electric locomotives. With twenty-seven major types of machine tools in its inventory and an estimated machine tool output of 30,000 machine tools annually, Pyongyang was producing enough lathes to export and was equipping its factories largely with domestically made machinery except for specialized high-technology items imported reluctantly and sparingly. The industrial center of Hamhŭng symbolizes the emphasis placed by the regime on heavy industry as the key to self-reliance. Nearly everyone in North Korea seemed to know that the vast Yŏngsang heavy machine plant, popularly known as the country's "mother factory," had made a high-precision boring machine capable of reaching one micron in accuracy; an automated lathe with a speed of 3,200 revolutions per minute; and some 70 percent of the equipment for the big Vinalon textile plant in Hamhŭng. The textile plant is a special source of pride because Vinalon, a cotton substitute, was reputedly invented by Korean scientist Li Sung-gi, who says that he received his first encouragement from Kim Il-Sung after rebuffs from U.S. occupation authorities. The process uses limestone and anthracite coal, both abundant in North Korea, and Vinalon is called "the symbol of *Juche.*"

In general, on the basis of available information, North Korea appears to have made substantial progress in maximizing self-sufficiency despite its continued dependence on imports of oil and petroleum products, rubber, and food grains. Building on the base of the industrial plant and skilled labor force inherited from the Japanese, Pyongyang claims to have expanded steel production from 144,000 tons in 1949 to 2.2 million tons in 1970. Self-reliance has its limits, however, and the North has increasingly recognized its need for foreign collaboration in some spheres of technology. One of the indirect blessings resulting from the Soviet aid squeeze has been a forced trade diversification which gave Pyongyang a new awareness of its options in attaining needed high-technology items for its industries. Instead of having to take what it can get from the Soviet Union and Eastern Europe, continually multiplying a one-sided dependence for spare parts, Pyongyang has gradually increased its trade with Japan and other noncommunist countries, and North Korean imports from Communist countries have declined from 83 percent of all imports in 1970 to 48 percent in 1974. Indeed, this shift has been attempted too rapidly, as the North discovered to its chagrin in 1976 when the prices received for its raw material exports did not go as high as anticipated and it was unable to meet nearly $600 million in scheduled debt payments abroad.

Paralleling the Pyongyang-Moscow rift over economic aid has been conflict stemming from the North Korean determination to maximize its military independence. To a great extent, the basic objective underlying Kim's drive for economic self-sufficiency has been a desire to create the base for an expanded arms industry and thus to work toward greater freedom of action in his military confrontation with South Korea. Fears that the Soviet Union could not be relied upon in a showdown were aroused by the Cuban missile crisis and were accentuated when Moscow cut off military aid as part of its effort to swing Pyongyang into line during its dispute with Peking. While still completely dependent on the Russians for sophisticated items such as Mig-21s, SAM missiles, and W-type submarines, and to a lesser extent on the Chinese for fighter aircraft, Pyongyang has made increasingly high budget allocations for its own defense production, especially in the infantry field. North Korea claims to have achieved self-sufficiency for all weapons below 120-millimeter caliber and can make most of the components for its "workhorse" model tanks and heavy artillery.

The achievement of increasing military self-reliance is a fundamental element in the North Korean effort to acquire nationalist legitimacy. Contrasting the U.S. presence in the South with the absence of foreign forces in the North since the departure of the last Chinese troops in 1959, Pyongyang can pose as the valorous defender of Korean self-respect against the might of "American imperialism." Memories of the Chinese advance across the Yalu have begun to recede in the South and must be periodically rekindled to sustain the vitality of nationalist imagery there. For the manipulator of public opinion in the North, however, it was still possible to point to American troops in the South in 1977, and this could be linked directly to the searing national experience of the Korean War.

The American visitor is reminded constantly that the scars left by the war are unusually deep in the North. The South suffered brutal but relatively brief anguish during the latter part of 1950, with Pyongyang using little close air support in its operations there. The North, by contrast, endured three years of heavy U.S. bombing in addition to the Yalu offensive. This left the North economically crippled and added to its short-run dependence on Moscow and Peking, but it also led to a new Korean self-image based on pride in having survived an encounter with the most technically advanced power in the world. A Japanese visitor, struck by the cocky nationalist spirit of the North, found the roots of this pride in the American defeat at Taejón and the capture of General Dean.[28] In North Korean imagery, the war was an American invasion designed to forestall a unified Korea for American strategic reasons, and in frustrating this design North Korea emerged not only as the victor but also as the proven champion of Korean nationalism. The *Pueblo* incident is used to reinforce this image of imperialism foiled and might well have been prompted mainly by the desire to keep alive the symbolism of a brave little Belgium unafraid to stand up to all comers.[29] For all of its anti-American coating, North Korean propaganda about the Korean War and the *Pueblo* via television and other media did not appear to play primarily upon xenophobic hatred at the time of my visit. The keynote was rather a glorification of Korean virtue in which the American imperialist had the role of the fall guy who proves the bravery and invincibility of Korean antagonists fortunate enough to be led by Kim Il-sung.

THE COMMUNIST DILEMMA IN THE SOUTH

Kim Il-sung pointedly defines the mission of his armed forces in terms of the American challenge precisely because in this way he hopes to direct an all-embracing nationalist appeal to the South as well as the North. By deliberately identifying the major threat as American rather than South Korean, he seeks to exploit the fact that the only visible enemies currently available to Seoul are fellow Koreans. The thrust of North Korean propaganda in the South is that Korean should not fight Korean and that all should join in a "broad anti-U.S. united front for national salvation." Addressing his own party cadres, Kim conceded that the revolution in the South has "a tortuous way to go" because the South, unlike the North, is still infected with "ideas of flunkeyism. . . . Today, not a few people in South Korea fail to see the aggressive nature of U.S. imperialism, and think as if they could not live on without U.S. 'aid.' The trend to worship and rely on the United States is a great obstacle to the struggle for national liberation and independence."[30] Nevertheless, difficult as the challenge is, its nature is unambiguous, for "Pak Jung Hi and his clique, trying to cover up their traitorous acts with the signboard of anti-communism, are disguising themselves as nationalists."[31] The inescapable task of Communists in the South is to capture the nationalist banner by exposing "the neocolonialist aspects of South Korean society" and by linking the specter of a contemporary American-Japanese axis with the history of Korean struggles against the Japanese.

Although accurate assessments of its strength are elusive, the underground Communist organization in the South appears to have been distinctly unsuccessful in its continuing effort to capture nationalist sentiment. Kim has gained greater legitimacy for his own regime by pursuing an independent line but has been consistently unable to extend his appeal beyond the thirty-eighth parallel. The basic reason for this lies in the secondary role claimed by Korean communism during the pre-1945 independence movement, as we have seen, and in Kim's failure to exploit even the marginal identification of the "old" Communists with the nationalist tradition. But there have clearly been important additional factors inherent in the post-1945 Korean drama that help explain why Kim has been unable to overcome his historical legacy.

It would be difficult to overestimate the traumatic impact of the Korean War in crystallizing attitudes in the South that were quite the reverse of those in the North. The shock of partition was only slowly and painfully being absorbed. Suddenly, the South found itself in the throes of a savage ordeal blamed upon a regime in the North widely assumed at that time to be a creature of Soviet influence. While the Rhee government had shown its authoritarian teeth by 1950 and was far from beloved, the president still enjoyed respect as a legitimate claimant to the nationalist mantle. The South thus saw itself as the victim of a foreign-inspired aggression carried out essentially to advance the global power drive of what was then regarded as a monolithic communist bloc. This belief was gradually tempered, as we shall see, by the realization that Pyongyang was throwing off its foreign yoke and by a corresponding recognition that nationalist as well as communist motives might have impelled the Northern role in the war. But the changing climate in the South and the political weaknesses of successive Seoul regimes have not been translated by the Pyongyang leadership into a stronger Communist political base in the South.

For all of its verbal dedication to the goal of a "broad national front," the North has never employed sustained united front tactics comparable to those of the Viet Minh and later the National Liberation Front, calculated to neutralize the emotions left by the war. The Vietnamese Communists appealed to noncommunist leadership elements primarily as nationalists, assuring them that they were not expected to embrace communism. For many years, North Korea said instead, in tones of stern dogmatism, that South Koreans would have to develop a "correct understanding" of the social system in the North and learn to accept Marxism-Leninism. Dominant factions in the North have continually rejected a "soft" line designed to broaden the base of the Communist movement in the South, and one of the few major party leaders favoring a united front line, Yi Hyo-sun, Central Committee secretary, lost out in a 1967 purge that reflected the increasing power of military leaders allied with Kim Il-sung. It was only in 1972 that the tone of the Northern line began to change as part of the broad shift in the Pyongyang approach to the South, culminating in the establishment of the North-South Coordinating Committee. An essential element in the new line was the reassurance that different economic systems in North and South could coexist under a confederal form of unification.

Given his lack of a charismatic position comparable to that of Ho Chi Minh, Kim rules in a rigid Stalinist style that inherently militates against an authentic united front strategy. He and his intimates of the Manchurian Kapsan faction are reluctant to share power even with potential rivals near at hand, let alone with Communist leaders seeking to build a separate power base in the South dependent on uncertain noncommunist alliances. One of the central reasons for Kim's failure in the South is simply that he has never been willing to risk the existence of a parallel Communist leadership there. His party is almost entirely northern. There is no deeply rooted Communist organization in the South able to participate in Pyongyang policymaking from a position of independent local strength and to argue for tactics realistically oriented to conditions in the South. Kim's systematic destruction of the men who built the original Communist movement in the south, notably Pak Hŏn-yŏng, has left the underground leadership there in the hands of minor personalities. Those who may have emerged in the post–Korean War period can have no compelling stake in a movement controlled by an exclusive faction of Communists rooted in the North.

This is in complete contrast to the pan-Vietnamese character of the Communist leadership in Vietnam. From the beginning Vietnamese communism has been a national movement in which power has been shared by Northern and Southern leaders, with Premier Pham Van Dong symbolizing the Southern stake in the party high command. It came into being with a nationalist mission in the liberation of all of Vietnam presupposing, by its nature, an integrated nationwide organization. Vietnam's division, first at the hands of the French in 1946 and later at Geneva, was artificially imposed on top of a political environment that in fact had a common denominator of unity in this national Communist movement with its anticolonial élan. Korea and Germany were vulnerable to division of a more thoroughgoing and enduring variety because they emerged under altogether different historical circumstances. North Korea and East Germany were the ad hoc products of a war's unplanned denouement, and their accidental leaders, put into power by Soviet armies, have had more than enough to do in building the local base to support their "lucky"[32] inheritance of power. Created at a time when Korean communism lacked a unified organization with an established national leadership, North Korea has since evolved as a politically self-sufficient sectional entity ruled by a sectionally based elite. It has yet to create the political infrastructure in the South necessary for a Vietnam-style reunification effort. As we shall see in a later chapter, however, this does not mean that the South is reconciled to the partition or that the situation in Korea is irrevocably frozen.

The task of building a viable political order has been made easier in South Korea than in South Vietnam by the fact that the refugee population from North Korea has been relatively easy to absorb. In Vietnam, the northern refugees, largely Catholics, were a deeply abrasive social group. In Korea, north-south regional differences are less intense than those of Vietnam, and there is no Catholic-Buddhist rivalry. To be sure, Korea has its own problems of family, clan, and provincial factionalism that frustrate efforts to consolidate noncommunist political unity in the South. But these are fissures within the framework of a broadly homogeneous society. There are no tribal enclaves comparable to the Montagnard areas of South Vietnam slicing up the geographic integrity of South Korea. Basically, the internecine divisions that have plagued South Korea have been uncomplicated struggles over the spoils of political and economic power. While the Communists can attack the entire order in Seoul as corrupt and authoritarian, they cannot manipulate deep social divisions comparable to those that have been available to the Communists in Vietnam.

The most frustrating fact of life confronting the North in its effort to mobilize nationalist sentiment in the South is the lack of an underlying anti-American or anti-Western animus rooted in the Korean colonial experience. The long postwar dependence of the South on Washington has created its own deep strains, and there are many noncommunist Koreans who feel strongly that the United States was partly or mainly to blame for the division of the country.[33] In its basic psychological response to the American presence, however, Korea is worlds apart from Vietnam and other parts of Asia that have shared the experience of Western colonial domination. The fact that Koreans suffered their colonial insults under Japanese rather than Western overlords would have made it difficult for the North to use "American imperialism" as an effective rallying symbol in the South even if it had not been for the American role in the Korean War. But the other side of the coin is that Koreans still retain bitter anti-Japanese feelings, and it is here, as we shall see, that the

North has found its greatest response. The Japan–South Korea normalization treaty has been a propaganda bonanza for Pyongyang. Each new license granted for a Japanese business venture in the South is cited as added proof that corrupt officials are selling the national birthright once again as they did in the prelude to Japanese rule. If Pyongyang should succeed in attaching a durable Japanese label to the Seoul regime, branding the United States as Tokyo's mentor in a new imperialism, then Kim may at last have the key to a winning nationalist appeal.

In addition to a continuing effort to bracket the United States with Japan in its propaganda, the North constantly plays on the many frictions that inevitably arise in a patron-client relationship, especially in matters relating to the U.S. military presence. The long controversy over a status of forces agreement left its clearly visible scars. Communist propagandists have also been able to exploit the widespread belief that U.S. economic aid gives insufficient emphasis to heavy industry and is unnecessarily perpetuating dependence on Washington. The United States has often been blamed for the authoritarian excesses of a series of regimes in Seoul that could not have survived without U.S. support. Important as these issues are in a short-term perspective, however, they have rarely generated enough steam to convert antigovernment and anti-American sentiment into pro-North sentiment. On the contrary, the major opposition forces in Seoul have shared in the anticommunist consensus and have shown restraint in their use of the United States as a political target. Most South Koreans have been only too painfully aware of their overwhelming dependence on the United States. They have been temporarily reconciled to the American presence despite all of its irritations and the deep unease accompanying their awareness that no end to the division of Korea is in sight.

Despite an unchanging propaganda refrain, the South has been no more successful in discrediting the Northern regime on a nationalist basis than the North has been in its efforts to tar Seoul with the American brush. Once, when Kim Il-sung's obeisance to the Russians was clearly apparent, he could be dismissed as the pliant instrument of a monolithic international communism. Now the monolith is no more, and the creator of the *Juche* policy cannot credibly be characterized, in any case, as a mere satrap of Moscow or Peking. North Korea has freed itself from the puppet status that provided such a clear rationale for American intervention in the Korean War. The import of this far-reaching development for a comparative analysis of Asian communism is that nationalism has now been neutralized as a factor in the Korean equation. In contrast to the case of Vietnam, where the Communist side had the political and military strength to pursue a successful unification strategy, neither the North nor the South is able to claim a position of preeminent national leadership in Korea. Yet nationalism simmers beneath the surface in both the North and the South, all the same, steadily growing in the dangerously explosive potential discussed in Chapter 7.

NOTES

1. Matthew B. Ridgway, "Pull-out, All-out, or Stand Fast in Vietnam?" *Look*, 4 May 1966, p. 82.

2. Dang Van Sung, "A Contribution to a Way Out of the Present Dilemma in Vietnam," mimeographed (Saigon, 25 January 1963), p. 13; see also Phan Quang Dan, "The War in Indochina," mimeographed (Saigon, March 1954), pp. 6, 15.

3. Harold Isaacs, *No Peace for Asia* (New York: Macmillan, 1947), pp. 98-100; see also Gregory Henderson, *Korea: The Politics of the Vortex* (Cambridge: Harvard University Press, 1968), pp. 115-119.

4. For example, see Suh Dae-sook, *The Korean Communist Movement, 1918-1948* (Princeton: Princeton University Press, 1967), pp. 299, 304; and Cho Soon-sung, *Korea in World Politics, 1940-1950: An Evaluation of American Responsibility* (Berkeley: University of California Press, 1967), pp. 68-69, 72-73. Suh Dae-sook specifically addresses his rebuttal to charges made by E. G. Meade, *American Military Government in Korea* (New York: King's Crown, 1951), pp. 62-63.

5. Suh Dae-sook, *Korean Communist Movement*, p. 289. Kim himself denies that he left Manchuria and joined the Russian army. However, despite the absence of conclusive documentation, most qualified observers consider the evidence establishing his presence in the USSR to be overwhelming.

6. Baik Bong, *Kim Il-sung* (Tokyo: Miraisha, 1970), 2:151.

7. For articles written by Selig S. Harrison from North Korea in 1972, see the *Washington Post* of the following dates: May 26, June 6, June 12, June 26, July 2, July 3, and July 4.

8. Kim Ch'ang-sun, *Pukhan sibonyŏnsa* [Fifteen years of North Korea] (Seoul: Chimun'gak, 1963), chap. 3, sec. 12, esp. pp. 57-60, discusses the purge trials of the southern leaders in detail. For an excellent analysis of the downfall of the "old" Communist factions see Suh Dae-sook, *Korean Communist Movement*, pp. 311-324. Kim Sam-gyu, *Konnichi no Chōsen* [Korea today] (Tokyo: Kawade Shobō, 1956), argues that Pak might well have inflated Communist strength in the South and even encouraged the Korean War in the hope of recouping his old power base. For propagandistic "official" accounts of North Korean factional struggles see *Pukkoe ŭi p'abŏl t'ujaeng'sa* [A history of struggles in the North Korean puppet regime] (Seoul: Center for the Study of Domestic and Foreign Problems, 1962); and *Third Congress of the Workers Party of Korea: Documents and Materials* (Pyongyang: Foreign Languages Publishing House, April 1956).

9. Suh Dae-sook, *Korean Communist Movement*, p. 293.

10. Lee Chong-sik, "Counterinsurgency in Manchuria: The Japanese Experience, 1931–40," Memorandum RM-5012-ARPA (Santa Monica: RAND Corporation, January 1967), p. 285.

11. Lee Chong-sik, "Kim Il-sŏng of North Korea," *Asian Survey*, June 1967, p. 377.

12. Cited in "Analysis of the Kim Il-sung Legend," *Koria Hyōron* (Tokyo) [Korea review], November 1967, pp. 7–8.

13. Lee Chong-sik, "Communism and Nationalism in Korea, 1945–48" (Research memorandum prepared for The Brookings Institution for the author's use, October 1967), p. 6.

14. O Yŏng-jin, *Hana ŭi chŭngŏn* [One witness account] (Pusan: Kungmin sasang chidowŏn, 1952), p. 141.

15. See especially the documentary sources cited by Suh Dae-sook, *Korean Communist Movement*, pp. 255, 294–324; and by Lee Chong-sik, "Kim Il-sŏng of North Korea," pp. 374–382. Kentarō Yamabe, in "A Note on the Korean Communist Movement by Suh Dae-sook," *The Developing Economies* (Tokyo: Institute of Asian Economic Affairs, June 1967), asserts that Kim did have a wide reputation but offers little substantiating evidence. Yamabe states that leaders of other Communist factions jailed by the Japanese "apostated their former faith while in jail. Therefore, they dared not challenge or criticize Kim Il-sung, a man who had fought with armed forces against Japanese imperialism" (p. 411).

16. *People's Korea* (Tokyo), 13 September 1967, p. 6.

17. See especially "Analysis of the Kim Il-sung Legend," pp. 8, 12–16.

18. "The Anti-Japanese Armed Struggle of the Korean People Organized and Waged under the Personal Leadership of Comrade Kim Il-sung," *People's Korea*, 22 March 1968, pp. 4–5.

19. Ibid., pp. 1, 4.

20. Kim Il-sung, "On Eliminating Dogmatism and Formalism and Establishing *Juche* in Ideological Work," in *Selected Works* (Pyongyang: Foreign Languages Publishing House, 1965), 1:315, 318; see also Suh Dae-sook, *Korean Communist Movement*, p. 55.

21. Radio Pyongyang, 31 August 1964.

22. *Nodong Sinmun* (Pyongyang), 12 August 1966, p. 1.

23. Nixon press conference, 18 April 1969.

24. Robert A. Scalapino and Lee Chong-sik, *Communism in Korea* (Berkeley: University of California Press, 1972), 1:684; see also 2:1298, 1303, 1312.

25. Cho Soon-sung, "North Korea and the Sino-Soviet Rift" (Paper delivered at the 20th Annual Convention of the Association for Asian Studies, Philadelphia, 23 March 1968), esp. pp. 2, 4.

26. Kim Il-sung, *The Present Situation and the Tasks of Our Party* (Pyongyang: Foreign Languages Publishing House, 1966), p. 7.

27. Kim Il-sung, *On the Occasion of the Twentieth Anniversary of the Workers Party of Korea* (Pyongyang: Foreign Languages Publishing House, 1965), p. 26.

28. Tokuma Utsonomiya, *Hankyō Ideologie Gaikō o Haisu* [I oppose anticommunist ideological diplomacy] (Tokyo: Iwanami Shoten, 1966), pp. 54, 48.

29. In a seminar presentation at the Washington Center for Foreign Policy Research, February 15, 1968, Paul Langer viewed the incident as a gesture of small power defiance occasioned by a tacit U.S.-Soviet agreement, made without North Korean concurrence, barring attacks on intelligence vessels.

30. Kim Il-sung, *The Present Situation*, p. 114.

31. Kim Il-sung, *Twentieth Anniversary of the Workers Party*, p. 37.

32. Hoang Van Chi, "Why No Peace in Vietnam," in *Vietnam Seen from East and West*, ed. S. N. Ray (New York: Praeger, 1966), pp. 35-36.

33. For example, see Cho Soon-sung, *Korea in World Politics*, pp. 73-74, 90-91; see also Kim Sam-gyu, *Konnichi no Chōsen*, pp. 136-137, 141, 156-158; and Ch'a Chi-ch'ŏl, *Uriga sewŏyahal chwap'yo* [The coordinates that we must build] (Seoul: Pŏmmunsa, 1966).

III

NATIONALISM AND THE AMERICAN EXPERIENCE

6. After Vietnam: Asia Alienated

The fusion of communism and nationalism in Vietnam and China has long been apparent to politically conscious elements throughout Asia if only because these two cases stand in such striking contrast to communist isolation from the nationalist mainstream in most parts of the region. As a consequence, American intervention in Vietnam on the side of Saigon was viewed widely as both a frontal attack on self-determination in Vietnam itself and, in a larger sense, the crowning symbol of a pervasive American insensitivity to nationalism. This is why the emotional gulf between the United States and Asia resulting from the Vietnam conflict is so wide and so deep. The war not only left a legacy of straightforward racial resentment generated by U.S. bombing and by the recurring application of preponderant American military power in other forms. By underlining American insensitivity to nationalism, it has also created a sense of psychological distance, a feeling that Asian and American perspectives may be too different to permit meaningful communication and basic trust.

Asian perceptions of the Vietnam war have reflected varying local perspectives, to be sure, and Asian leadership groups have adapted to the American role in accordance with short-range calculations of personal, factional, and national interest that have differed from situation to situation. In most cases, however, the expedient adaptations made by local elites have had little relation to their image of the Vietnam situation as such. American understanding of Asian attitudes toward the Vietnam issue has been clouded by a failure to distinguish between the expedient level of the Asian response and underlying public opinion. This confusion was aggravated, during the war years, by the single-minded intensity that marked the prosecution of the American commitment once it had been made. Most Asian governments were seldom asked for their views on Vietnam by the successive American administrations that pressed for their support. Thus spared the embarrassment of an answer, they were free to concentrate on making a profitable and politically viable adjustment to the American presence. For allies, there were special economic inducements, and for others dependent in numerous ways on American aid and trade there were also powerful reasons for wanting to keep relations with the United States on an even keel. The result was a gap between private assurances of sympathy, given to itinerant U.S. officials known for prowar views, and more ambiguous public positions on the war ranging from muted support to muted opposition, all characteristically excused with the argument that domestic political minorities made it difficult to give full and open support to the American position.[1]

JAPAN: THE LESSONS OF NORTH CHINA

The case of Japan graphically illustrates this dichotomy. As we shall see, the bitter Japanese experience in Manchuria and north China from 1931 to 1945 profoundly influenced the older generation, instilling a clear recognition that nationalism is not extinguishable with military force. On the one hand, the conservative establishment could see history repeating itself in Vietnam and rated the prospects for American success as marginal; on the other hand, from the standpoint of Japanese interests, it was advantageous to let the free-spending Americans make their own mistakes. In spirit if not in stridency, the older generation of conservative Japanese leaders shared the pervasive Japanese feeling of racial affinity with the embattled Vietnamese reflected in the overt antiwar stand taken by activist youth and leading intellectuals. Nevertheless, in the imagery of many American leaders during the Vietnam years, the resilient Japanese posture in adapting to U.S. policies was mistaken for the actual Japanese estimate of the war.

In the Dulles rationale, Japan needed a noncommunist Southeast Asia, and thus a noncommunist Indochina, in order to survive economically and escape absorption into the communist orbit.[2] More than a decade later, Henry Kissinger stressed that a Japanese perception of American failure in Vietnam would be costly in balance of power terms, seemingly oblivious to the fact that more direct damage to the Japanese-American relationship had already been done. "We have yet to see the foreign leader who tells us, 'For God's sake, get out of Vietnam, it isn't worth it,'" Kissinger declared in 1970, adding that

> Most of the foreign leaders, in fact I would say almost all, no matter what they say publicly, tell us exactly the opposite. If the United States utterly

fails in something that it has undertaken with so much effort, it is bound to affect the judgments of other countries as to the degree to which the United States can be significant in their area. Look at the history of Japan. Twice in a century it changed its domestic structure entirely, and with it its foreign policy orientation, not on the basis of abstract ideology, but because of a change in the balance of power as they perceived it. Who can say that if they become convinced that the United States has become irrelevant in Asia that they will stick on our side simply because of an abstract loyalty.[3]

Kissinger, in his own way, appeared to be as blind to the underlying Japanese appraisal of the American role as his predecessors had been in a cold war context. Given their experience in Manchuria and north China, Japanese leaders had viewed the deepening American embroilment in Vietnam as a damaging demonstration of reckless ineptitude fundamentally affecting their entire image of the United States. It was the Vietnam war more than any other single factor that aroused a Japanese sense of overcommitment to Washington and stimulated a search for more diversified economic and diplomatic ties.

For the most part, the Japanese government avoided both direct support of the war and direct criticism of the United States, keeping one eye cocked on Washington and another on domestic antiwar opinion. In 1967 and early 1968, however, Japan launched its diplomatic offensive to regain Okinawa with a series of unashamed pro-Saigon gestures for the benefit of the White House. This created an impression of Japanese support for the war that was to linger during subsequent years and explains, in part, why the American perception of Japanese attitudes toward the war was so wide of the mark.

Initially, the bombing of the North had prompted "a clearly discernible trend in Japan to disassociate our country from American foreign policy."[4] In the course of 1967, the White House made it increasingly clear that a more positive Japanese attitude would be helpful in opening up a dialogue on Okinawa, and on the eve of his visit to Washington in November 1967 Sato set the stage with a Southeast Asian tour designed to project a more sympathetic approach to the Vietnam conflict. Even when his White House meetings with Johnson brought no immediate progress on Okinawa, Sato joined the president in a statement indicating support for American policies. A correspondent accompanying Sato at the time wrote that "it was understood here that Sato's emphatic stand on Vietnam had been regarded as part of the inducement for what he hoped would be an American pledge on Okinawa."[5] The linkage between the prospective return of Okinawa and the Vietnam issue brought a series of even more strongly pro-United States statements in succeeding months by Japanese ambassador Takeso Shimoda in Washington.[6]

Once the United States was finally committed to a definite date for the reversion of Okinawa, however, Defense Minister Yasuhiro Naka-sone said candidly in a television interview that Japan could heave a sigh of relief and "begin to take a more independent approach toward Washington on Vietnam and other matters, since the Oki-nawa issue has been linked unavoidably with Vietnam and with economic issues. In a way, the United States has had the 1 million people of Okinawa as a hostage, and we have been in a very difficult bargaining position."[7]

Over and above the Okinawa issue, Japanese political and business leaders have had ample reason to adapt themselves gracefully to U.S. policies that increasingly have spelled substantial economic benefits for Japan. The enormity of the Vietnam bonanza enjoyed by Japan was undoubtedly the determining reason for the studied dissemblance marking the Japanese response to the war. Economists differ, but statistics provided by the U.S. Defense Department and an analysis of comprehensive expert studies by the Nomura Research Institute,[8] the Japan Economic Research Council,[9] the Sanwa and Kangyō banks,[10] and competent private scholars indicate a cumulative direct profit to Japan from the war of at least $11.5 billion between 1965 and 1972. This includes the Vietnam-related portion of U.S. military spending in Japan, PX purchases of Japanese goods in the Pacific, Japanese exports to the United States made possible by war-induced shortages, and, above all, more than $6 billion in a Japanese export upsurge to Asian countries over and above the natural export growth that might have been projected in the absence of the Vietnam conflict.[11] Antiwar elements in Japan have suggested even bigger figures, contending that Japan's dramatic post-1968 increase in foreign exchange reserves was attributable largely to the war; official Japanese estimates are substantially lower.[12]

Conservative Japanese economists have demonstrated, for their part, that the Vietnam boom came along at a time when the Japanese economy was already burgeoning for a wide variety of other reasons. They agree that the Korean War played a key role in Japan's meteoric rise, but they downgrade the importance of the economic stimulus provided by Vietnam. In global terms, most experts agree that Japanese economic expansion would clearly have been phenomenal even if there had never been a Vietnam war. In Asia, however, the war gave enormous extra purchasing power to countries that were suffering payments deficits before 1965 and have since been slipping back into the same morass. This enabled Japan to make its breakthrough in Asian markets under artificial optimum conditions, dominating key market areas in a relatively short span of years and building overnight popularity for Japanese brand names.

The importance of the Vietnam boom as a factor setting the tone of the Japanese posture toward the war during the sixties became clear, in retrospect, as the boom tapered off and the war lost its utility for Japan. In Asia, American-backed regimes were no longer able to finance their trade deficits with Japan out of U.S. aid inputs and military procurement dollars, and in Washington itself the cumulative economic impact of the war had a backlash that markedly affected Japanese-American relations. Abruptly, dissemblance came to an end. It was one thing to let the Americans make their own mistakes in Vietnam when it was profitable for Japan. It was quite another when a U.S. balance of payments deficit, rooted partly in a continuing outflow of Vietnam-related spending, precipitated U.S.-Japanese economic conflicts in which Japan became a major scapegoat for the American dilemma. As the international monetary crisis loomed in early 1971, Finance Minister Takeo Fukuda attributed the impending showdown directly to American economic problems that were aggravated by the continuance of the Vietnam struggle.[13] "Logically speaking, inequities in Japan-U.S. economic relations which American businessmen complain of are a problem quite separate from the Vietnam war," wrote the editor of the influential business daily *Nihon Keizai*. "But psychologically speaking, particularly from the Japanese point of view, it seems that the United States is demanding unilateral remedies from Japan to cure the economic curses which have been fundamentally caused by the Vietnam war."[14]

The skeptical attitude of the Japanese business community toward the Vietnam conflict came to the surface when the United States pressed for Japanese aid and investment in the South during the declining years of the American presence and later sought a major Japanese commitment to projected Saigon reconstruction efforts. To appease Washington and Saigon, Tokyo solemnly sent study missions and made token investments and aid contributions, but Japanese officials privately ridiculed the idea of making major outlays in a setting of such political and military uncertainty. Japanese doubts about Saigon dominated a report on reconstruction prospects by a delegation sent to the South in 1970 by Keidanren, the most powerful organizational spokesman of Japanese business.[15] The modest Japanese investment and aid role in Saigon had the limited objectives of protecting access for Japanese exports, preempting technological control over selected areas of the economy, and acquiring economic intelligence with an eye to the future. Even when oil prospects grew encouraging, Japan carefully limited its involvement. Tokyo was playing a waiting game, marking time in the expectation that a Saigon regime acceptable to Hanoi would eventually emerge and that this would provide the necessary basis for a compatible pattern of aid and investment to both the North and the South. Throughout the war, Japan had maintained a modest level of trade with the North, keeping the door open for future increases, and Tokyo lost no time in expanding its contacts with Hanoi following the Nixon visit to China.

The American failure to look behind the expedient Japanese adaptation to the Vietnam conflict was only one manifestation of a general tendency to view Japan in narrow cold war terms without regard for the historical and psychological roots of Japanese behavior. In the case of the Vietnam struggle, this cold-war myopia blocked out the conspicuous, overarching fact that Japan had gone through a similar experience of its own in Manchuria and north China within the relatively recent past. The older generation exemplified by the Keidanren leadership had been particularly influenced by the Imperial Army's ordeal, as we have suggested, but the attitudes of the younger generation also showed the imprint of a national trauma so recent and so profound. For nine years after the establishment of the Manchukuo regime in September 1931, Japanese forces had struggled to subdue some 360,000 guerrillas in Manchuria. When the conflict showed no signs of abating in 1934, the army felt compelled to start its massive collective hamlet program, herding some 5.5 million people into 10,600 fortified villages during the next six years. In Manchuria, the Japanese had enjoyed impressive assets prior to undertaking their counterinsurgency effort, especially the elaborate intelligence network built up by the South Manchurian Railway in the years prior to the direct establishment of the Manchukuo regime. In north China, by contrast, as we have seen in an earlier chapter, Japan started from scratch and experienced even greater frustration in its bloody encounter with a tenacious nationalist resistance between 1937 and 1945.

The most forceful reminder I have had of the importance of the Manchuria–north China experience in shaping Japanese attitudes toward Vietnam came in November 1970, shortly after Secretary Kissinger's Japan-focused defense of his Vietnam policies, cited earlier, and a major address by President Nixon on "Vietnamization." The late foreign minister Kiichi Aichi was asked at a private dinner meeting whether the president was justified in his anxiety that "our Asian allies would lose confidence in America" if the United States agreed to a settlement involving the replacement of the Thieu regime. "We are your friends," replied Aichi. "We don't want to add to your difficulties. We will not harass the United States with public criticism as some others do, but you should understand our attitudes. Most of us feel you should be working to salvage what you can of a bad bargain. The truth is that you have committed yourselves to unworthy people." The older Japanese of the World War II generation, he added, "know what it is to get into a bog like this. In North China we felt our honor was at stake, just as you do, and we too failed to understand the limitations of our military power. We know you will respect your commitments. In Vietnam, however, what we are concerned about is not good faith but rather good judgment."[16]

Aichi reflected conservative Japanese opinion in the governing Liberal Democratic party, and the impact of the Manchuria-north China experience was a disproportionately important element in shaping conservative attitudes toward the war. As former ambassador Reischauer has observed, however, most Japanese of all ages and persuasions tended to bracket U.S. intervention in Vietnam with the prewar and World War II period in their own history. When the bombing of the North began in 1965, Reischauer reported:

> The Japanese public responded explosively in fear and dismay. They thought that Washington had become dominated by unthinking militarists, as had Tokyo in the 1930s, and that we would inevitably go on to war with Communist China and that Japan would then become involved because of our bases there and in Okinawa. They felt that we had embarked on a hopeless war with Asian nationalism, as they had during the 1930s, and 1940s in China. . . . The government throughout has expressed its "understanding" of the American position but, in view of the strength of public feeling, has said no more.[17]

Responding to American intervention in Cambodia in 1970, a group of 110 members of the Liberal Democratic party in the Japanese Diet issued a statement that U.S. behavior in Indochina was

> very similar in nature to the mistakes made by the militarists of our country in the process leading from the China Incident to the outbreak of the Pacific War. . . . This endless expansion of hostilities finally led to the Pacific war and brought our country to the verge of extinction. Their greatest mistake lay in believing in the possibility of a military victory over nationalism.[18]

Hawks as well as doves implicitly endorsed this analysis, and a prominent veteran of the China front, Gen. Makoto Matsutani, retired commander of the Northern Region of the Self-Defense Forces, gave detailed emphasis to nationalism in a 173-page textbook on the war issued to officers attending the National Defense College in May 1973.

> The Americans have failed to grasp the strength of the Communist organization in Vietnam because they failed to take into account the power of national feelings. They were unable to grasp the strength of Ho Chi Minh and the Communist organization he established largely because they were so emotionally attached to the cause of anti-Communism. The Communist side

waged the war as a war of resistance against foreign invaders, which effectively helped to organize a united front among the Vietnamese people. But the Americans were excessively ideology-oriented.[19]

Hamstrung by their inability to use nuclear weapons and to invade North Vietnam directly, Matsutani said, the Americans faced an "endless" struggle and should have reformulated their war aims after the death of South Vietnamese president Ngo Dinh Diem in 1963. Instead, he lamented, U.S. policy was designed "to keep South Vietnam within the American camp by stopping the spread of Communist influence at the 17th parallel." General Matsutani warned that Japan should

> keep this example clearly in mind now that we stand on the threshold of great power status. Among the national characteristics of the Americans, we see that they are extremely quick-tempered and impulsive. Their guiding precepts appear to be unqualified faith in their power, a desire to American-ize other countries and an emphasis on the immediate rather than the long-range results of their actions. Even with this mighty military power, the United States could not defeat the Communists in Vietnam. The French discovered that scorched-earth tactics, meant to destroy Communist bases, only inflamed the spirit of popular resistance. But the Americans refused to learn the lessons of history.[20]

In general, the image in military writings of the Vietnam struggle struck a similar note. A historical study in the journal of the leading Japanese officer training school emphasized that

> North and South Vietnam are one and the same geographically and histori-cally, with a high degree of homogeneity in race, culture, and customs dating back to ancient times. [From the beginning] the driving power for the unification of the race has been found in the North. Although Vietnam is temporarily divided into North and South by a political demarcation line, the migration of the race, the permeation of culture and the flow of the independence movement have always been directed from North to South geographically and historically. We must not dismiss the desire for unifica-tion as a superficial one but should recognize that it is deep-seated and unyielding. Under the influence of Western culture and the development of communism, nationalism has been combined with communism and has become strengthened, especially since the victory of Ho Chi Minh over the French with Soviet and Chinese help.[21]

With its own historical experience as a basis for comparison, Japan had a clear perception of American intervention in Vietnam as a clash with nationalism and thus a solid intellectual basis for comprehending the futility of the war. This provided a pragmatic antiwar rationale that served, in turn, to fortify the visceral Japanese distaste for the war felt at the emotional level. As the war intensified, the phenomenon of a small Asian state seeking to defend itself against the greatest military power in the world aroused a strong and growing sense of racial affinity with North Vietnam. Oda Makoto, the popular Japanese novelist and antiwar leader, emphasized the racial aspect of the war in his writings, declaring that this factor made the antinationalist character of U.S. intervention "even more shameful."[22] As Lawrence Olson has observed, the war provoked the latent Japanese spirit of *minzoku-shugi*, or racial nationalism, as distinct from *kokka-shugi* nationalism, emphasizing the nation-state, an emotional undercurrent in which specifically Japanese and broader pan-Asian elements are intermixed.[23] The conservative newspaper *Sankei* reflected the expansive character of this emotion, urging that "it be conveyed to the United States that *minzoku-shugi* in Asia is racialism full of resistance, born under the control of a foreign race."[24] The *Asahi Shimbun* bluntly discussed the racial dimension of the war in replying to Westerners who asked why the Japanese public was so opposed to the war despite the fact that Japanese business profited so greatly from American procurement orders. "The answer," said *Asahi*,

> lies in racism. To the Japanese, the war in Vietnam presents the spectacle of strong whites bullying a weak yellow people. The Pentagon papers published by the American press revealed that the matter of primary concern to the United States in its involvement in Vietnam are American prestige and American casualties. Scarcely any thought was given by the Pentagon to the destruction of life and property suffered by the yellow people of Vietnam.[25]

Daniel I. Okimoto, an American scholar of Japanese ancestry who revisited Japan during the war years, stressed the racial element in antiwar feeling, with "some people even coming right out with interpretations of the war as an attempt by the whites to keep the yellows suppressed." After arriving in Japan with the "mistaken impression" that the Japanese public backed the United States on Vietnam, Okimoto wrote, he found that even right-wing students reacted to the war in racial terms, objecting to "the 'arrogance' of a global power like the United States thinking it had the right to 'push around' a country like South Vietnam." An eminent professor at Tokyo University remarked that as a result of the Vietnam war, the U.S. "use of the atomic bomb, which had been regarded as a tragic but inescapable consequence of war, was being reinterpreted by a growing number as a barbarous act of genocide against yellow people."[26]

It was the bombing of the North in 1965 that exacerbated latent Japanese racial consciousness and brought long simmering antiwar feelings to a boil. In earlier years, the war had not been a major issue in Japan, and opposition to the U.S. role in Saigon was only one facet of a broader uneasiness over the U.S. alliance that was neutralized by the economic rewards flowing from Japanese-U.S. ties. Once the bombing started, however, it became progressively more embarrassing to be a military staging area for American operations in Vietnam. The bombing produced a sudden popular realization that the United States was caught in a quagmire in which Japan, too, might become engulfed. The retiring Japanese ambassador to the United Kingdom, Shunichi Matsumoto, toured Indochina as a special envoy of the Japanese government from March 18 to April 1, 1965, sharply questioning U.S. assumptions in Vietnam in contrast to the tacit endorsement of U.S. policies by the Sato government. Testifying before the Foreign Affairs Committee of the lower house of the Japanese Diet, Matsumoto declared that "while the Vietcong is not unrelated to Communism and in fact receives North Vietnam aid, its core is nothing but the vehement nationalism within South Vietnam. I am doubtful of the effect of the U.S. air bombing of North Vietnam. Any further continuation of the bombing will excite China and the Soviet Union and corner the whole Vietnamese population into anti-American defiance."[27]

The strong Japanese reaction to the bombing produced a striking demonstration of the reflexive tendency to discount and resist antiwar criticism that progressively insulated the United States from an understanding of Asian attitudes toward the war. As the conflict escalated in early 1965, the Japanese press sought to capitalize on what was a growing *betonamu mūdo* (Vietnam mood) and began to publish unsparing coverage of the war from correspondents sent to the scene, evoking an American embassy effort to tone down criticism of the war through behind-the-scenes pressure on the newspapers and newsmen concerned. This came to a climax in a much publicized episode in October 1965, when the foreign editor of *Mainichi*, Minoru Omori, was forced out of his job after a controversial dispatch on the alleged U.S. bombing of a North Vietnamese leprosarium.[28]

For the most part, Japanese antipathy toward the war was dismissed in the United States as a deviant phenomenon reflecting the minority views of left-inclined intellectuals and opposition politicians. This explained, in part, why the American press generally failed to mirror the underlying climate in Japan. The *Newsweek* bureau chief in Tokyo reported in 1967 that a majority of the Japanese public "not only opposed the war but felt the U.S. responsible." Nevertheless, he complained, while this attitude was "completely apparent" as early as February 1965, "it was almost totally unreported in the United States."[29]

As we have observed, the Japanese government consciously sought to play down antiwar feeling during the period preceding the return of Okinawa, even encouraging the belief that antiwar demonstrations were unrepresentative. To the extent that the opposition was using the Vietnam issue effectively as a political weapon, the government found itself forced to make defensive gestures suggesting greater agreement with U.S. policy than actually existed, and all but a few leading Liberal Democrats avoided discussion of the subject where possible. Takeo Miki, then foreign minister and later prime minister, characterized the war as a "serious mistake" in a private 1967 interview[30] and implicitly questioned the U.S. Vietnam commitment in challenging Japan's China policy during his 1969 attempt to displace Eisaku Sato as prime minister.[31] But Miki upheld the Sato line in public during his tenure as a member of the Sato cabinet. Tied as Tokyo was to the American chariot by the Japan-United States security treaty, the ambivalence marking the Japanese posture toward the war was not entirely a matter of deliberate dissemblance. There were influential elements with a direct vested interest in American success, above all the ruling Liberal Democratic factions linked to Sato, closely identified with the United States, who could see their own future threatened by the overall changes in U.S. Asian policy that seemed likely to accompany disengagement from Vietnam. There was also a widespread tendency to mute antiwar criticism on the part of those who did not want to see Japanese opinion toward the United States polarized as a result of the war. Kinhide Mushakoji, a leading middle-of-the-road intellectual, reflected this attitude in his response to the 1967 "Tuxedo statement" rationalizing the war by a group of U.S. scholars:

> [The signatories of the statement] put their fingers on Japanese feeling when they contend that "any effort by the U.S. to press for more positive support at the present time could only evoke a crisis in Japanese politics." This view is sharply to the point because the Japanese public, including this writer, is torn between a feeling of friendship for the United States, on the one hand, and serious doubts about the overly involved U.S. policy in Vietnam and anxieties concerning the possibility of Japanese entanglement with it on the other.[32]

As the conflict proceeded, fears of Japanese involvement led to sharp outcries from scattered points on the political spectrum. In January 1968 Masamichi Inoki, a leading academician who later became superintendent of the National Military Academy, criticized the "arrogant bombing of North Vietnam" by the United States and argued that the Japan-United States security treaty was gradually losing its validity for Japan as "America's Asian policy toward China and Vietnam produced one failure after another."[33] The leader of the Buddhist Sōka Gakkai, Daisaku Ikeda, called for an immediate ceasefire in Vietnam and a withdrawal of American troops, warning that the war was "on the verge of bringing about another conflict between the United States and mainland China."[34] Significantly, Ikeda reflected the growing nationalist mood in Japan during the latter war years, equating "the problem of Czechoslovakia and that of Vietnam . . . as representing moves running counter to the current of history on the part of the super powers that are still clinging to the old authoritarianism."[35] In a significant essay foreshadowing his dramatic suicide two years later, novelist Yukio Mishima wrote in 1968 that antiwar sentiment acted as a catalytic agent in the growth of postwar Japanese nationalism and went hand in hand with the rise of sentiment against the American military presence in Japan. American bases in Japan "stimulated the sentiment for independence and imposed an intangible psychological burden on the people," Mishima declared, and these sentiments have "been cultivated for a long time by the Vietnam war" in view of the fact that most Japanese identify with those Vietnamese opposing the United States. This "act of substitution," he wrote, has been extended "to another nation's sentiment for independence, thereby crystallizing the frustration in one's own national sentiment for independence."[36]

The fact that U.S. bases in Japan and U.S. air bases in Okinawa were used for Vietnam logistical support and later for bombing operations, directly or indirectly, gave the war a direct and tangible meaning in everyday life. A *Sankei Shimbun* survey showed 73 percent opposition to the Vietnam-related use of U.S. base facilities.[37] In the wake of U.S. intervention in Laos and Cambodia, in particular, the symbolism provided by the Vietnam issue heightened long existent antibase campaigns focused on the proximity of many installations to major population centers. This culminated in a widely backed 1972 protest drive that blocked the movement of Vietnam-bound tanks and personnel carriers from the U.S. Army maintenance depot in Sagamihara to the Yokohama dock. Much of the equipment involved was South Vietnamese, not American, and Foreign Minister Ohira declared on the eve of the 1972 Honolulu summit meeting between President Nixon and Premier Kakuei Tanaka that Japan was not obligated under the Japan-United States security treaty to cooperate in the supply or transport of U.S. military equipment to be used by a third country.

By the time Nixon and Tanaka met at Honolulu, the breakthrough in Sino-U.S. relations had already brought into sharp relief the artificiality of the official Japanese posture of cooperation in the Vietnam effort as an obligation under the security treaty. The first Japanese overtures to North Vietnam came before the Shanghai communiqué, leading to a slow but steady expansion of trade in later years despite the continuance of U.S. military aid for Saigon. The turnabout in the Japanese posture was greatly eased by the publication of the Pentagon Papers and the resulting vindication of Japanese critics of the Vietnam war. Here was authoritative confirmation in American documents leaving little doubt that extensive damage had in fact been inflicted by the United States on nonmilitary targets in the North. Besides making it more difficult than ever for the Japanese government to support the war, the Pentagon Papers produced a flurry of sympathetic comment depicting the United States as a society capable of self-criticism and self-correction. "There are those who say that the prestige of the state may have been temporarily damaged by these disclosures," said the *Asahi*. "Yet what is 'prestige' that has been built up on lies? It seems as if we are hearing the voice of the conscience of the American people which will not permit lies. There is the feeling that the United States is still all right."[38] An underlying basis for a cooperative future relationship still remained, but the sense of alienation engendered during the war years placed a subtle and elusive psychological barrier between Japan and the United States that was to remain for years to come.

THE CONSTRAINTS OF DEPENDENCE

Even without the direct inducement of a war-born economic bonanza comparable to the Japanese case, other Asian countries with a trade, aid, or investment dependence on the United States also showed varying degrees of restraint in voicing their attitudes toward the war. Indonesia provides a striking example of this adaptive behavior, and even India, outspoken as it was, would have been more belligerently antiwar but for its dependence on American assistance.

Indonesian opinion was predominantly unsympathetic to American intervention in Vietnam even after the increase in the power of militantly anticommunist elements under the Suharto government established in 1966. This was obscured by an official posture of "cautious ambivalence"[39] attributable, above all, to the dependence of the new regime on Washington. An important secondary factor contributing to Indonesian reticence on the Vietnam issue was the existence of significant variations in the emotional response to the war within the post-Sukarno leadership. As we explained in Chapter 2, the adventurist early phase of Indonesian communism left deep wounds, and this anticommunist legacy strongly colored the attitudes toward the war held by a clearly defined but vocal minority centering in the military hierarchy as well as in certain Moslem and

Catholic factions. To assume that the anticommunist militants welcomed American intervention, however, would be to oversimplify what was a complex amalgam of conflicting feelings and to exaggerate the degree of division over the war within Indonesian ranks. The militants were torn between their desire to maintain an uncompromising anticommunist posture vis-à-vis their Indonesian political enemies and their postcolonial response to the Vietnam conflict as such. To a limited extent, they attempted to use the Vietnam issue as a rhetorical stick in the domestic struggle between "old order" and "new order" forces. At the same time, they made only token efforts to align Jakarta with Saigon and Washington at the foreign policy level because they shared the prevailing Indonesian imagery of the Vietnam struggle as one between embattled Asian nationalists and intrusive Western power.

The dominant Indonesian image of Vietnamese communism as a nationalist force grew directly out of the national experience of Indonesians as a whole. Indonesia proclaimed its independence from Dutch rule within weeks of Ho Chi Minh's proclamation of freedom from the French. The Vietnam war and the Indonesian independence struggle were bracketed together explicitly in a 1967 speech by Soedjatmoko, the prominent anti-Sukarno intellectual and Socialist leader, shortly before his appointment as ambassador to the United States, a post he held from 1968 through 1971. Likening the partition of Vietnam in 1954 to the separatist strategy pursued by the Dutch in Indonesia, Soedjatmoko pointed to

> the attempts of the Dutch to Balkanize Indonesia through the imposition of a federal system in which a majority of puppet states were to hedge in the barely tolerated Republic of Indonesia and thus render it powerless. The Dutch hoped that such a structure would soon deprive Indonesian nationalism of its military capacity and its political will. This abortive attempt thoroughly discredited the idea of federalism and engendered a continuing fear of Balkanization by an outside power, while also instilling a ready sympathy for all nations threatened by the imposition of such artificial divisions as part of a neo-colonial strategy. The case of post-Geneva Vietnam comes to mind in this connection. . . . There is a considerable sympathy for and identification with the Vietnamese people in Indonesia. . . . The fact that Vietnam's popular movement is Communist-dominated, or has become increasingly so, has not significantly reduced the awareness of Indonesians of the many similarities in the national experience of these two countries. But for the weakness of the Dutch as an adversary in the revolution for independence, and for the lack of a nearby strong Communist power, the similarities might even have been greater.[40]

In his carefully structured interviews with fifty-six Indonesian leaders of all shades in December 1969, Franklin Weinstein found that a perception of the Communists as the leading nationalist force in Vietnam was a common denominator cutting across Indonesian attitudes. As a consequence, 70 percent expected the Communist side to win and 68 percent saw no direct threat to Indonesia in a Communist victory, though 14 percent did see such a threat and 18 percent saw an indirect threat. Even Islamic and Catholic elements blamed the war on American intervention rather than on Communist aggression and felt that the war "symbolized the willingness of the big powers to pursue their own national ambitions at the expense of weaker countries."[41] Similar views were expressed to me in a variety of less systematic interviews with Indonesians on visits during the period 1967-1972. An unusually direct expression of the Indonesian response to the war as a Western intrusion in Asia was a series of articles in mid-1966 by former foreign minister Sunario. This came during an interlude of relatively open public discussion after the ouster of Sukarno but before the consolidation of the Suharto regime. A leading figure in the moderate founding group of the Nationalist party (PNI), as distinct from its later, Communist-allied leadership, Sunario was a representative voice of the Javanese civil servants and intellectuals who played such a central role in the independence movement and continued to dominate Indonesian bureaucratic and political life during the Sukarno period. He blamed the United States for the collapse of the Geneva agreement and attributed the war primarily to the massive influx of U.S. military aid and U.S. troops.

> A matter keenly felt by every Asian is the fact that in Vietnam the people's blood has been spilled for years on end, first when they faced the French colonial army and later on when they began to resist the military might of America, which they consider as an "aggressor," a label which acquires meaning from U.S. actions in Vietnam.... Those of us who have ever experienced bombardment by the Dutch and the Allied Forces can fully realize the suffering of the Vietnam people in the South and in the North as well as a result of U.S. air attacks.[42]

Pointing to Britain, France, and Holland, which made an "orderly retreat" from Asia after avoiding revolution on the part of the local peoples, Sunario found it "a strange thing that the United States, by contrast, is making an 'orderly advance' in these regions."[43]

The strength of the subsurface Indonesian reaction to the war was reflected in a brief phase of overt government criticism of the American bombing of North Vietnam in 1967, a time when the American aid commitment to Indonesia was still tentative. Noting the "very great risks to those not involved in the military operations," the Indonesian ambassador to the United States, Suwito Kusumowidagdo, declared that "it is difficult to understand why North Vietnam should be bombed without a declaration of war. We compare the size of the two countries involved and these are just two unequal countries. We wonder very often if there is not any other possibility."[44] Foreign Minister Adam Malik followed this remark at the U.N. General Assembly with the flat statement that "if a peaceful settlement at the conference table is to be reached promptly, the first step must be the immediate and unconditional end to the bombing of North Vietnam in order to promote conditions conducive to mutual agreement and settlement."[45] Malik later equated the Indonesian attitude toward the war with the French and depicted the Communists as leaders in a struggle for self-determination.[46]

Malik's stand in the United Nations provoked a dissent from the official newspaper of the Defense Ministry, *Angkatan Bersendjata*, describing the conflict in Vietnam as one "between Vietnamese patriots who are defending their freedom, on one side, and others seeking to impose Communist domination."[47] As a subsequent change in tone on the part of *Angkatan Bersendjata* showed, this was far from representative of the full range of views on Vietnam within the armed forces, including substantial support for the government position expressed by Malik. Franklin Weinstein found evidence suggesting that those responsible for the editorial were reprimanded.[48] By early 1968, the Defense Ministry newspaper spoke admiringly of the Viet Cong offensive against Khesanh and the storming of the American embassy premises for six hours in Saigon, suggesting that it was time for the South Vietnamese armed forces, rather than the American forces, to face the Communist onslaught.[49]

Despite its anticommunist orientation, the military leadership, especially its Javanese components, had a postcolonial world view marked by a suspicion of Western influence in Asia reminiscent of the Sukarno period. Soon after the Suharto takeover, the army conducted a six-day seminar of top military leaders at which the American presence in South Vietnam was viewed warily. A secret declaration adopted at the conclusion of the seminar said that "the war in Vietnam is disrupting the peace in Southeast Asia and affects Indonesia's defense and security."[50] At another early 1966 seminar bringing together military leaders and leaders of the student groups partly responsible for overthrowing Sukarno, Major General Suwarto, director of the Army Command and General Staff College, declared that "the war in Vietnam and the foreign military bases around it clearly increase the threat of attack against us. Similarly, the conflict of foreign interests in Southeast Asia has a direct impact on the political and economic situation in Indonesia."[51]

The Suharto regime was critically dependent on American aid, trade, and investment at its inception and showed deliberate restraint about Vietnam as part of an overall effort to win friends in Washington. At the same time, Jakarta resented what was regarded as a disproportionate American aid involvement in Vietnam, comparing the more than $20-billion annual influx of American resources into a country of 14 million people with the $65 million in U.S. aid given to Indonesia from 1965 to 1967. Even when Indonesian aid doubled and tripled, the disparity remained great between the enormous U.S. military expenditures in Vietnam and the carefully regulated assistance levels in Jakarta. It was only adding insult to injury when American journalists and officials, seeking to make a case for the Johnson policy on Vietnam, pointed to the overthrow of Sukarno by anticommunist Indonesians as a consequence of the American presence in Vietnam. Vice-President Humphrey had the misfortune to arrive in Jakarta on his 1967 visit in the angry aftermath of an article by columnist William S. White contending that the show of "purpose" by the United States in Vietnam had given Indonesian anticommunists the courage to act.[52] Even the strongly anticommunist Catholic newspaper *Kompas* declared flatly in its editorial of welcome to Humphrey that

> the crushing of the P.K.I. and Communism in Indonesia was totally unrelated to the escalation of the Vietnam war by the U.S. or to U.S. policies. This was a domestic problem. The elimination of Communism was the consequence of the rebellion against the Pantjasila ideology, and against the government, and was in the national interest of Indonesia. That the destruction of the P.K.I. and Communism in Indonesia was advantageous to U.S. global strategy is their own affair. Therefore, we do not expect any reward for it. We clarify this problem because on a clear basis we can cultivate a more durable cooperation.[53]

A prominent anticommunist columnist identified with the Moslem Masjumi party had complained earlier that American efforts to link the overthrow of Sukarno with Vietnam were leading to the isolation of Indonesia. In order to enlist nonaligned countries in Indonesian-sponsored regional initiatives, argued S. S. Tasrif, former editor of the Masjumi journal *Abadi*, "we must take a clear stand on Vietnam and avoid overidentification with the U.S." [54] *Angkatan Bersendjata*, the Defense Ministry organ, attacked "the rash statement of those U.S. officials who have stated that Indonesia's crushing of the Gestapu-P.K.I. was related to the presence of U.S. troops in South Vietnam. This superficial opinion is not only totally wrong but may also be easily exploited by the Communists at home and abroad to discredit the Suharto administration."[55]

Indonesian attitudes toward the Vietnam issue have been largely misunderstood in the United States, obscured as they were by the distorted use of the Indonesian case in prowar apologias and the reticence of Indonesian leaders anxious to avoid ruffling both Washington and their own domestic anticommunist militants. The sporadic character of American press coverage of Indonesia has been partly responsible for this communication failure. Indian attitudes, by contrast, were only too well understood by American administrations that more and more insistently sought to discourage criticism from New Delhi as the war intensified. Conscious of a dependence on U.S. food supplies even more critical than the Indonesian aid dependence, especially in the lean crop years immediately following the 1965 escalation in Vietnam, Indian leaders alternated between calculated restraint and occasional objections to U.S. policy in response to press and public opinion prodding. With its national political life conducted in English, much greater foreign press coverage than Indonesia, and a formal peacekeeping role as chairman of the International Control Commission (ICC), India was a known quantity on Vietnam from the start.

More explicitly than any other Asian leaders, Prime Minister Nehru and later Prime Minister Indira Gandhi have consistently given public recognition to the nationalist character of the Hanoi leadership and the resulting limitations imposed on foreign intervention in Vietnam.[56] Nehru's 1961 visit to the United States provided a conspicuous demonstration of the conflict between Indian disapproval of American intervention, on the one hand, and a tactical need to moderate criticism of Washington for the sake of what was then a substantial aid dependence. President-elect Kennedy's sympathetic interest in Indian development as a senator had aroused hopes in New Delhi that New Frontier Washington would reverse the American military aid commitment to Pakistan and greatly step up long-term development lending. Kennedy was preparing to move in both of these directions but wanted a quid pro quo in the form of a more positive Indian policy of "sharing the burden" in Vietnam. The president expressed his views on this matter to Nehru and found the prime minister "not very forthcoming." When Nehru finally did loosen up with Kennedy, he dwelt on the nationalistic character of the Viet Minh and pointed to Ho Chi Minh's pro-Moscow leanings in the Sino-Soviet rivalry to underscore the historic Vietnamese antipathy toward China. In working meetings, however, American participants reported, Indian officials had agreed to modify the Indian ICC role to suit the needs of a closer U.S. relationship by "looking the other way" when outsized contingents of U.S. military advisers or questionable U.S. military equipment turned up and to press charges against the Viet Cong more vigorously when specific information was provided by the Diem regime. In return, the United States agreed to press Diem to liberalize his regime and hinted at increases in U.S.

economic aid to India and corresponding decreases in military aid to Pakistan. Indian officials stressed that they had made a clear distinction between U.S. advisers and U.S. combat personnel in Vietnam.[57] The American-Indian honeymoon on Vietnam thus proved to be a brief one in the aftermath of the 1961 visit as the influx of U.S. personnel into Vietnam rapidly accelerated, gradually leading to the introduction of combat personnel and eventually to the bombing of the North in 1965.

Beginning in mid-1966, six months after she took office, Prime Minister Gandhi periodically advocated a halt to American bombing followed by a cessation of hostilities by all parties throughout Vietnam in keeping with the Geneva agreement. Except for the dissent of a few ultra-conservative leaders, notably C. R. Rajagopalachari, who advocated that India dispatch troops to Vietnam, most Indians wanted the government to take an even stronger line than it did and to condemn the United States directly for its air attacks on the North. The underlying Indian attitude toward Vietnam during this period was expressed by one of the leading pro-American voices in New Delhi, J. J. Singh, former president of the India League of America, who declared that

> most of the world believes that the Vietnamese who are fighting against the Americans are freedom fighters and are laying down their lives for the freedom of their country just as the Americans did in 1776. . . . Even if the Americans win militarily in Vietnam, and someday the sledge hammer is likely to get the gnat, in the eyes of the world, they will have become moral lepers.[58]

Attacking the "policy paralysis" in New Delhi and the failure of the Indian government "to mobilize the forces of restraint on the Vietnam issue," the *Times of India* declared that "a complete endorsement of America's Vietnam policy would be intellectually far more respectable than this sort of anemic dithering—making gestures of disapproval according to formula but avoiding any serious effort to prevent the avalanche towards disaster."[59] The government made little secret of its view that there would be "little to lose and probably much to gain" if the United States were to halt its bombing unilaterally.[60] Nevertheless, as a gesture to Washington, New Delhi unsuccessfully pressed Hanoi to give a pledge of a reciprocal concession in the event of a U.S. bombing halt. Public impatience over the restrained government approach to the Vietnam issue reached its peak when U.S. planes staged a bombing and missile attack near the center of Hanoi in November 1967, killing an Indian sergeant attached to the International Control Commission and wounding an Indian soldier. The government played down the incident despite a burst of anti-American feeling. To the White House, Indian refusal to support the war and increasingly close ties with the Soviet Union were exasperating at a time when U.S. aid to New Delhi was so substantial. But in the Indian context, Prime Minister Gandhi was leaning over backward to avoid offense to Washington.

The contention that Indian leaders privately welcomed U.S. intervention in Vietnam as a diversionary anti-China move was put forward periodically by U.S. officials but had little foundation in actual Indian attitudes. Antiwar gestures were necessary for domestic political reasons, it was said, concealing "pragmatic" Indian attitudes underneath. In reality, the reverse was true, and sympathetic gestures were made to pacify Washington despite a broad-based antiwar consensus embracing not only diverse sectors of Indian opinion but also diverse elite groups. Even military leaders saw U.S. intervention as self-defeating. General K. S. Kumaramangalam, army chief of staff, said in a 1967 interview that he felt "sympathy, as a military man, for what your people are being put through in Vietnam. But this is not essentially a military problem, and there is not likely to be a military solution or even a solution helped much by the use of military force." While the war might have a "very minor" utility in adding to the diversity of strains on Chinese resources, this was offset, in his view, by the opportunity for the Chinese to "fish in troubled waters" as a result of the continuing division of Vietnam. A united Vietnam, even under Communist control, would provide a better counterweight to Chinese power and would be more helpful to India.[61]

In a hitherto unpublished conversation in late 1967, Prime Minister Gandhi made clear that her own disdain for the "ineptitude and insensitivity" shown by the United States in its Vietnam involvement had not been fully reflected in her public utterances.

On the one hand, America tries to keep away Communism and on the other hand you create conditions which encourage intervention by the other side. A foreign presence encourages the Communists. They are nationalists. If Vietnam had been helped to get on its feet it would have resisted China on its own. All their racial memories are anti-Chinese.[62]

Recalling her visit to Hanoi in October 1954, when she accompanied her father on his North Vietnam stopover following the Geneva conference, the prime minister declared that

the older generation whom we met were clearly anti-Chinese. It is really quite absurd when Americans say that we want you to do what you are doing in Vietnam because of our own position in relation to China. How does this affect India? It does not prevent the Chinese from massing troops on our borders. It merely gives a greater opportunity to the Chinese to abuse us as running dogs of the American imperialists. It makes our position more difficult. Even more important, what really counts is that China's neighbors should be economically strong, and this war has made many of them weak and dependent, distorting their development.[63]

Mrs. Gandhi objected vigorously in a subsequent 1969 interview when I mentioned that former White House adviser Walt Rostow continued to justify American intervention in Vietnam as a contribution to India's long-term security against China.

It hasn't made any difference at all in strengthening our position with respect to China as far as we are concerned. If there had not been a war, both Vietnams would have been in a stronger position to resist China if China ever did wish to menace them. [President Johnson was] very impatient of criticism, and we were a favorite whipping boy for some time, whether it was Vietnam or the Middle East. In fairness, this impatience is perhaps not just his characteristic. It's an American characteristic. Mr. Nixon was here recently, and he also showed a similar impatience. In any case, the public attitude towards the Government's Vietnam policy has been changing gradually in the United States, and so fortunately the differences between us on the war have narrowed.[64]

"SUPPORT" REAPPRAISED

An analysis of the pronouncements of Singapore prime minister Lee Kuan Yew sharply underscores the characteristic discrepancy in Asia between what leaders thought of the Vietnam war and what they did to adapt to the situation created by unilateral American action. Often depicted as a supporter of the war, Lee made many statements calculated to give this impression, especially when he visited the United States in October 1967. On careful examination, however, his attitude turned out to be much more complicated, reflecting economic considerations and a fear of U.S. support of Indonesia at Singapore's expense. The United States was ill-advised to become involved in Vietnam, Lee believed, but having done so, was then obliged to secure the best bargain possible for the sake of nearby governments that had been forced to take sides as a result of U.S. intervention.

When the United States escalated the war in 1965, Singapore found itself with a sudden surge of procurement orders, and its exports to South Vietnam increased from $37.4 million in 1965 to $85.5 million in 1966. Eventually, one-third of its exports were Vietnam related. Singapore had a clear and growing economic stake in the war and was eyeing continued American patronage, especially in the form of business investment and customers for the shipping repair facility that would be built in the docks to be vacated by the retiring British naval force. This alone would have been enough to prompt Lee's 1967 visit to Washington, but he cited more far-reaching concerns.

In addition to wanting to hold his finger to the wind in order "to see which way the wind is going to blow next year" in U.S. Vietnam policy, Lee stressed that his reason for going to Washington was "to debunk what I know has been propaganda put out deliberately—that Singapore is a third China, and that this is a dangerous place." It was necessary to avoid criticism of Vietnam policy, he suggested, in order to get a sympathetic image for Singapore and head off any American plans for building up an Indonesian-Malaysian alliance on a Malay racial basis as a counterweight to China.[65] Citing Russian military aid to Indonesia during the Sukarno years, Lee added that "I want to know from the Americans whether they believe that Singapore has the right to survive as a nation, as a people. Or whether they also are going to start supplying aircraft, missiles and ships." When he expressed these anxieties to American leaders, Lee recalled, "they said no, no. That I have too vivid an imagination and that the regime in Indonesia is peace-loving, etc. But I asked them, can you guarantee me that we will always have in Indonesia a pragmatic, realistic, hard-headed, cooperative, peace-loving regime?" He warned specifically against surface-to-surface missiles to Indonesia as part of any U.S. military aid.[66]

Even in his American appearances, Lee carefully qualified his comments on the war, calling for "a great deal more caution, more selective exercise of your enormous range of weapons" and declaring that the bombing of North Vietnam "could be reduced and even stopped without any decisive changes in the course of the war." Whether or not the United States stopped the bombing, Lee added, Hanoi would not necessarily go to the conference table.[67] When asked if he agreed that "the American position of force and resistance to the 'east wind' is essential to give [Singapore] and other newly independent countries a bulwark behind which you can develop your independence," Lee demurred, recalling impatiently that when the United States became committed in Vietnam in 1954,

> you never asked the rest of Southeast Asia. We were not consulted again, in 1956, when you decided that Diem should not have free elections. . . . Or in 1961, when things got a little bit difficult for Diem and you decided to put in American advisors. And by 1963 you had your last chance when Diem got knocked down by a bus, or perhaps it was a tank, and you could have got out and said to the generals, "well, we will help you—guns, food, uniforms to pay for the troops"—but you have decided rightly or wrongly to go in, and this is 1967.[68]

Dennis Bloodworth, a British journalist based in Singapore who has observed Lee at close range for many years, wrote following the premier's Washington visit that his warnings against an abrupt American disengagement from Vietnam "do not imply approval of their involvement as some Americans think. For Lee and many like him, the Vietnam situation is the disastrous result of thirteen years of consistent error."[69] The United States had a series of "let-off points when they could have got off the hook" in Vietnam beginning in 1954, Lee believed, and could have "drawn the line west of the Mekong" as late as 1963.[70] In two conversations with Lee in 1967 and 1971, I asked him why he felt that the impact of a Communist Vietnam on Thailand would have been easier to defuse in earlier years than in the sixties.

> At earlier points in time they would have found it credible to believe that you would remain committed to Southeast Asia despite falling back. Dulles could and should have told this to Marshal Sarit. Dulles could have said that this line is indefensible and we are going to fight a rear guard action there, but the Mekong is the final line where we still stand.[71]

The first of these conversations came in the immediate aftermath of his American visit, and Lee spoke acidly of his encounters with President Johnson and Secretary of State Rusk. At one point he exploded: "I'd rather go Communist than be a client of the Americans—the monkey to your organ grinder. I told your Johnson and Rusk that and I got bugger all for it."[72]

Lee's comments on the Vietnam situation consistently betrayed his distaste for the pervasive American presence in Asia during the war period and an empathetic identification with embattled Asians demonstrating nationalist spirit in the face of superior Western power. He clearly viewed the Communists as the more dynamic Vietnamese political force. In the Middle East, Lee said, the United States had supported the Israelis against the Arabs, "but in Southeast Asia they are doing just the opposite. They are supporting the more . . . they have decided to support—this is a very broad comparison—the Muslim against the Israeli."[73] Lee explained: "The Americans should have fought west of the Mekong, not in Vietnam because in Vietnam, they are fighting a very tough people,"[74] an "intense" people in the East Asian cultural mold as distinct from "unintense" Southeast Asians.

> If you had decided to defend Thailand and had just fought a rear guard action in South Vietnam, then both the Vietnamese and the Chinese and the Russians would be training . . . Laos and Meos . . . nice, charming, delightful people with a leisurely graceful life. If you give them a sophisticated surface to air missile, you will have to have the instructor there until the end of

time. When sophisticated weapons were given to people who were not intense ... I am not saying that intense people are better than unintense people, I am just saying that some people are intense and their cultural patterns are different.[75]

ALLIES AND MERCENARIES

The artificiality of nominal Asian support for the war was demonstrated in the case of two allies with much touted troop commitments in Vietnam—the Philippines and South Korea—both bitterly divided internally over their involvement and both motivated in their support for the war primarily by the attendant economic rewards.

Filipino opinion was split on the war from the start: in a 1966 poll, 32 percent of those expressing a definite opinion favored a more conciliatory attitude on the part of the United States.[76] When Saigon pressed for combat engineers in April 1965, President Dios-dado Macapagal gave nominal support to the idea but let Ferdinand Marcos, then president of the Senate, kill the plan. After Marcos was elected president in November 1965, however, he soon realized that American loans and procurement spending needed to ease the deteri-orating Filipino economic situation would be jeopardized if he did not reassess the Filipino stand on Vietnam. Marcos not only decided to make an active bid for procurement dollars but also saw an opportunity to use a Vietnam commitment as leverage in overall Filipino-U.S. bargaining on base and economic issues. In February 1966, he requested an appropriation for a combat engineering battal-ion for Vietnam, underlining the common religious heritage of the predominantly Catholic Filipinos and the Catholic population of South Vietnam by stressing the Filipino moral obligation to sustain "peoples of kindred faith fighting in defense of their freedom."[77]

Marcos was on the defensive from the start and devoted a good portion of his television address announcing the request to justifying the modesty of the proposed commitment and stressing that it was a "symbolic," token gesture.[78] The Vietnam issue became a focus of controversy not only in its own right but also as a symbol of nationalist discontent with the Manila-Washington alliance that had already been growing before the war. It was only after four months of angry debate in and out of Congress that Marcos was able to push through the Vietnam appropriation. Washington agreed, in turn, to equip ten Filipino engineering battalions for rural reconstruction work in the islands; to pay the Filipino officers and enlisted men who volunteered for Vietnam duty the difference between their basic allotments and the salary levels established for overseas assignments;

to transport the troops to and from Vietnam; and to permit unlimited access to American PX facilities in Vietnam. Other unannounced U.S. concessions that figured in the Marcos decision were a relaxation of previous restrictions on the hiring of Filipinos in Vietnam; the procurement of Vietnam supplies from the Philippines; the continued use of marginal base facilities such as Mactan Airfield, regarded as expendable by the United States but economically advantageous for the Philippines; the continued purchase of ammunition and commercial consumables for the Filipino armed forces; and the retention of Filipinos on various American military and government payrolls in the islands. Washington blinked at the fact that the actual Filipino commitment was a force of only 2,000 men. Even more significant, the United States did not make an issue of the Filipino refusal to commit a specially trained SEATO battalion or to permit B-52 strikes against Indochina targets from Clark Field.

In a discussion with the commander of the Thirteenth Air Force at Clark Field in early 1967, I was told that the heavy buildup of Thai bases and the virtual prohibition on the use of Clark Field for combat missions reflected in part the "sensitive atmosphere" in the Philippines at that time on the Vietnam issue and the ambivalence of Filipino officials below the "very top level" on the wisdom of Filipino involvement in U.S. military engagements beyond the defense of the islands themselves. In the early stages of the bombing of North Vietnam, the Philippines sought an explicit reassurance that Manila would be consulted prior to the use of Clark Field for any direct operational missions and made it clear that such use would be regarded as undesirable. I was told that if pressed the Philippines would have yielded on the use of Clark and that there were other conspicuous factors in the decision to rely on the Thai bases, such as the proximity of Thai bases to Vietnam and the existence of airfields in Thailand that had already been established under the military aid program and needed only widening and improvement.[79] Whatever the factors favoring the Thai choice, however, it was clear in a conversation with Marcos[80] that he was cool to the U.S. role in Vietnam and would have found a combat role for Clark politically devastating.

Marcos made a state visit to Washington in September 1966, after the Filipino engineers had left for Vietnam. The White House meetings resulted in a reduction in the term of U.S. base rights from ninety-nine to twenty-five years, back pay for Filipino veterans, and an agreement that Marcos would play host at a Manila summit conference of "troop contributing nations" to be attended by President Johnson. In the United States, the Manila summit served as a useful symbol for the Johnson administration in selling its Vietnam policy. In the Philippines, however, the conference did not have the favorable impact that Marcos had apparently anticipated. Instead of flattering the national ego, the choice of Manila aggravated the growing controversy in the Philippines resulting from the Marcos commitment. The abrupt American dismissal of a motion drawn up at the conference by the Filipino ambassador to the United States, Salvador P. López, casting doubt on the bombing of North Vietnam, added fuel to this controversy.

Marcos paid a continuing price for the Vietnam commitment in punitive action by political opponents resulting in serious delays on urgent economic measures. Opposition to the Vietnam involvement grew so acute that Marcos was not able to go to Congress for another appropriation to support the engineering battalions. He avoided a congressional showdown initially by reallocating funds within the defense budget and utilizing aid from Washington that was not then visible to the Filipino public. By 1968, however, the money for the engineers had run out, and the continuing presence of Filipino troops in Vietnam without legislative sanction became an increasing embarrassment. Marcos began to make statements implicitly indicating acceptance of a coalition government in the South as a result of peace talks, declaring that "national leaders must discard their previously set ideas about the government of Vietnam and its future."[81] Feelings over the Vietnam issue, said Michael Onorato, "had become ugly, and were beginning to remind many Filipinos of the Philippine-American war."[82] As the 1969 presidential campaign approached, Marcos announced that he would remove the troops after the election, pointing to the fact that even President Nixon had begun withdrawing U.S. forces.

The end of the pretense that Manila was part of the war effort brought a new note of candor when Foreign Secretary Carlos P. Romulo told an American audience that there is "a very strong feeling in the Philippines against the Vietnam war."[83] Then came a U.S. Senate subcommittee's revelations of how much the United States had spent to obtain a show of Filipino support. As Ward Just wrote, reviewing these disclosures, the $38.8 million provided to support the Filipino role in Vietnam itself was "only the tip of the iceberg." In addition, the United States added sweeteners to its spending on bases in the Philippines, pushed military assistance for the Filipino armed forces to a $22.5 million per year level, and dispensed secret "general purpose" payments totaling at least $19.6 million.[84] Looking back on the war in 1973, Marcos reflected that "had the principles of self-determination and de-colonialization been observed by France and the United States, there would have been no war. Now the U.S.A. and the world have re-learned this lesson."[85]

Like the Philippines, South Korea was also able to use its troop commitment to Vietnam as a political and economic bargaining lever, but the special position of the South as a heavily militarized garrison state facing a Communist challenge of its own made possible both a bigger commitment and much bigger rewards. At their peak, South Korean forces in South Vietnam totaled 48,000. The most direct quid pro quo for this commitment came in the form of foreign exchange earnings that totaled $1.083 billion from 1965 through July 1972.[86] This included more than $232 million in construction and other service contracts, Vietnam-related exports,[87] $178 million in soldiers' pay, and $166 million in engineers' and laborers' salaries. Millionaires emerged overnight during the war years, a few of them multimillionaires like Cho Ch'ung-hun, president of Hanjin Transportation, which netted nearly $100 million from trucking and construction work in Vietnam. In addition, the United States pledged that American troop withdrawals from Korea would be deferred to compensate for the reduction in South Korean military strength caused by the Vietnam commitment or that other compensation would be made in the form of military assistance. The result was not only a continuation of an annual outlay for the U.S. force presence in the South approximating $700 million but also a five-year, $1.5 billion military aid "modernization" package accompanying the withdrawal of 20,000 troops in 1970. The so-called Brown memorandum signed by Ambassador Winthrop G. Brown on March 4, 1966, foreshadowing these arrangements, also suspended a commitment previously made by Seoul to assume a $193 million share of the operational and maintenance costs of the South Korean armed forces.[88]

Both in the United States and in South Korea itself, the most sensitive aspect of the Vietnam commitment was the level of payments to the Korean forces involved. Defenders of Seoul in Washington argued that the South Korean commitment demonstrated authentic support for the war not only because the South had an anticommunist orientation but also because participation in the Vietnam conflict relieved a sense of obligation to the United States resulting from the Korean War. Congressional skeptics pooh-poohed this contention by pointing to the fact that the South Korean private who normally earned $1.60 a month was paid an additional $37.50 a month in Vietnam. Generals who earned $300 a month at home got another $300 a month. In some classifications, the Vietnam pay scale represented twenty times the normal home front pay.[89] Columnist Marquis Childs concluded that the Korean soldiers involved were "essentially mercenaries. They may not have fought, in the dictionary definition of mercenary, solely for pay. But they would never have gone to Vietnam if their government had not exacted a high price for their commitment."90 Gregory Henderson styled them more charitably as "at best, mercenaries with convictions."91

As Chapter 7 elaborates, South Korea has complex emotions regarding its relationship with the United States, a blend of gratitude for U.S. help and a contradictory feeling that Washington, as one of those responsible for the division of the peninsula, has an obligation to subsidize Seoul until unification can be achieved. This ambivalence was strikingly reflected in the government rationale used to win support for the Vietnam commitment domestically. On the one hand, officials reassured the people that they were repaying a debt, only to reverse this argument by justifying the deal in monetary terms and stressing that Washington had assumed a new obligation of its own in foreclosing any troop reductions. The confusion in South Korean feelings and the degree of nationalist uneasiness over the "mercenary" label were underlined by the protracted public resistance to the Vietnam commitment. It took fifteen months of careful preparation of public opinion before the first commitment of 10,000 combat troops could be made in August 1965, and not until the Brown memorandum seven months later was the number of troops upgraded to division strength.

When the White House asked all allied countries to send units to Vietnam in May 1964, Seoul responded cautiously in July with a decision to send a 133-man medical unit and a team of karate instructors. By January 1965, the government had announced plans for a 2,000-man "logistical support unit" and stepped up pressure in the ruling Democratic Republican party (DRP) for a National Assembly vote of approval. At a tense caucus on January 30, a week before a scheduled floor vote, party leaders finally overpowered an influential opposition bloc led by Sŏ In-sŏk, later publisher of the *Korea Herald*, and party elder Chŏng Ku-yŏng, a respected jurist who served as first president of the DRP in 1963, prior to the assumption of the party presidency by Park Chong-hui. The independent *Chosŏn Ilbo* reported that one-third of the caucus had voted against the troop commitment despite leadership pressures and an open ballot, with "many of the assembly men in a deep agony of conscience" over the issue.92 Park's 1963 presidential rival, opposition leader Yun Po-son, came out against the troop commitment, and National Assembly spokesmen for the leading opposition party, then known as the Minjŏng, voiced doubts about the nationalist character of the Saigon regime in the ensuing floor debate. Deputy Kang Mun-dong declared that the Americans themselves "are wondering whether the war in Vietnam is one waged by the Vietnamese or the Americans. Not only that, the Vietnamese people themselves are against the war.

It is all too clearly a war by proxy. Why do we have to jump into such a war and share in the responsibility for it?" Yun Po-sŏn's leading factional opponent in the opposition party, Kim Dae-jung, who was later to make a strong challenge as Park's opponent in the April 1971 presidential election, branded the troop commitment unconstitutional in the absence of a mutual defense pact with South Vietnam. Asking the Assembly to "ponder the meaning of America paying the salary of Korean army men fighting in other lands," he pointed to the "strong opinion even in the U.S. for neutralizing Vietnam" and pondered "the doubtful prospects for the solution of the war." Defense Minister Kim Sŏng-ŭn made no effort to meet these charges, replying in essence that "sending our troops to Vietnam is the most expedient way to persuade the U.S. to keep its forces in Korea."[93] When the Assembly voted to authorize a troop commitment on January 26, 1965, 106 to 8, the sixty opposition members had left the floor as a gesture of protest. Later, when the government upgraded its commitment to a 10,000-man combat force, the opposition again was absent. The government pushed the measure through at a time when public attention was focused on the Japan-Korea normalization treaty then pending and the opposition was busy organizing a protest movement against the normalization pact. With student demonstrations against the treaty rocking Seoul, and martial law in force, the 10,000-man Vietnam commitment was approved in the absence of the opposition deputies on August 13, 1965.

By the time Vice-President Humphrey came to Seoul in February 1966, seeking an expanded troop commitment, Washington had greatly increased the economic inducements for participation in the war. Nevertheless, dissident elements of the ruling DRP joined the opposition Minjŏng in a last-ditch effort to block the move in Defense Committee hearings, focusing on the worldwide opposition to the Vietnam conflict and the diplomatic damage that Seoul would suffer as a result of its direct identification with the U.S. cause. Sŏ In-sŏk made a veiled attack on the American role, declaring that "any settlement of the Vietnam war should be based on the Geneva agreement. This is the drift of worldwide opinion. Our government has failed so far to clarify our position on this issue and the impact of our troop commitment on the Geneva agreement."[94] When the National Assembly voted on March 20, 1966, the opposition staged a filibuster lasting for two days and nights. Opposition leader Yun Po-sŏn attacked the Park regime for "making us all mercenaries in a war by proxy and trading the dear lives of our young men for a few despicable dollars." The final vote of 95–27 took place amid fisticuffs and confusion after the DRP Assembly chairman called a point of order and an opposition member cut the microphone to block a voice vote.

A strong undercurrent of uneasiness over the Vietnam commitment persisted in the wake of the National Assembly showdown despite a collapse of organized political opposition and a feeling of pride in the exploits of Korean forces. At bottom, this anxiety reflected a growing awareness among politically conscious elements that the cold war was ebbing. Kim Hong-ch'ŏl, a professor at the National War College, wrote that the Vietnam involvement unnecessarily antagonized a newly powerful China that had acquired nuclear arms and should be wooed by Seoul not only as an offset to Japanese economic power but also as part of a meaningful unification strategy.[95] This theme was frequently echoed in the hearings of the National Assembly Committee on Reunification, a brief interlude of partially unrestricted public discussion of foreign policy in late 1966, which will be discussed in a broader context in Chapter 7. In carefully oblique language, the committee's final white paper noted that Seoul had "played an active role in the Manila summit conference of Vietnam allies," observing that

> it is open to question to what extent this type of diplomacy is contributing to the real interests of Korea. By identifying itself with the military policies of the United States in Asia, there is a certain tendency for Korea to limit the scope of its diplomacy and, apart from certain bilateral questions involving Korea and the United States, such a tendency reduces our effectiveness and credibility. This is expected to be a heavy burden for Korean diplomacy in the future.[96]

During a discussion on Vietnam in the course of the hearings, Sŏl Kuk-hwan, a journalist and later president of Korean Greyhound Lines, spelled out this view more directly, arguing that "the war in South Vietnam must basically be viewed as part of the transition from a world of ideologies to a world of power struggles, and as such, it is basically a conflict between the desire of China for a greater place in Asia and the forces trying to check China." Peking will emerge from the war stronger, he hinted, and Seoul would be better off without such a total commitment to the U.S. effort in Vietnam since "it is when we have had peaceful relations with China that we Koreans have had peace, unity and independence."[97]

By 1970, when President Nixon decided to commit U.S. ground troops to Cambodia, South Korea had lost its tolerance for the war. Seoul served notice that the reception would be icy if the United States decided to approach Seoul for a further troop increase. Impatience with the continuance of the existing troop commitment in

South Vietnam was apparent in comments by Kim Chang-gŭn, official spokesman of the ruling Democratic Republican party, who told me that "we don't want to become the whipping boy of Asian nationalism." In a front-page editorial occasioned by the Cambodian move, Ch'oe Sŏkch'ae, editor of *Chosŏn Ilbo*, called for the return of Korean troops from Vietnam in company with the U.S. pullout then beginning to take place. Ch'oe pointed out that Australia, Thailand, and the Philippines had all started to withdraw their troops or had expressed the desire to do so, and "we are the only ones who stick to our stations. As time passes, the gratitude of the Vietnamese people toward us has begun to diminish and Korean troops are regarded as some sort of parasite." Now that the U.S. forces were beginning to depart, he reflected, the Vietnamese public realized that the Americans were not there as aggressors—but "in the past, the U.S. forces have been generally viewed by the nationalistic-minded Vietnamese people as nothing different from the colonial French forces."[98]

THE VULNERABLE DOMINOES

As the dominoes in the "domino theory," the countries nearest at hand were the most sensitive in Asia to the potential implications of a unified Vietnam and were thus peculiarly ambivalent about American intervention on the side of the South. Like the rest of Asia, they lacked faith in Saigon and recognized that Hanoi had captured the leadership of Vietnamese nationalism. Like the rest, they did not like the overpowering American presence in Asia that accompanied the war and the wanton use of American military power against fellow Asians. Unlike most Asian countries, however, they saw a unified Vietnam as a possible threat to their vital interests. In the eyes of Malaysia, Thailand, Laos, and Cambodia, the North appeared menacing not only as a Communist regime but, more fundamentally, as the standard-bearer of an emergent Vietnam seeking to come into its own for the first time in intraregional power relationships. To the extent that they supported American intervention, accordingly, this was not to defend Vietnamese self-determination, as the United States professed to be doing, but to frustrate its realization for as long as possible. Thailand, in any event, was the only country on the Southeast Asian mainland that gave clear-cut support to the war, and even Thailand, profiting as it did from war-related spending, grew increasingly uneasy over its involvement as the American presence burgeoned and as the human costs of the war became generally apparent. Laos and Cambodia, at the other extreme, were more directly in the line of fire and reacted more

cautiously from the start, seeking unsuccessfully to avoid embroilment in the holocaust.

The gradual transformation of Malaysia from a lukewarm sympathizer to a caustic critic typified the revulsion engendered by the war
in nearby countries. Prior to the bombing of the North, Malaysia
gave qualified support to Saigon, training more than 3,000 South
Vietnamese officers in antiguerrilla operations beginning in 1961.
The Malaysian experience in combating Communist-led guerrillas was
often cited during the early war years as a model for South Vietnam
to emulate, and a persistent border insurgency problem in the Thai-
Malaysian frontier area gave Malaysian officials an added sense of
affinity with South Vietnam. In economic terms, Malaysia had compelling reasons to cooperate with the United States, given its heavy
dependence on a stable American price for its tin and rubber. As
James Gould showed in a 1969 study, however, "the strong Malaysian support of the war effort in Vietnam does not mean that the
Malaysian population was unified behind the administration. There
was considerably more popular uneasiness about American involvement than the Malaysian or American governments would be willing
to admit."[99] The start of the bombing in 1965 brought the first
open attacks against the American role, including sporadic stoning of
the USIS library in Kuala Lumpur, mild criticism from Prime Minister Tungku Abdul Rahman, and stinging condemnation from the
influential Pan-Malayan Islamic party (PMIP).[100] Prominent intellectuals, led by Wang Gung-wu, chairman of the history department
at the University of Malaya, ridiculed the "domino theory."[101]

The gradual crystallization of antiwar feeling was closely linked
to a belated nationalist awakening on the part of the Malay majority
and a broadening of the narrow base of political activity that existed
in the immediate aftermath of British rule. Malaysia had received its
independence with only a token struggle. Britain had passed power
on to a group of conservative feudal leaders, led by Tungku Abdul
Rahman, who were not motivated by the intense anticolonialism
found in most other parts of Asia. It was only after independence
that a newly vigorous political life produced a heightened group
political consciousness on the part of an expanding Malay leadership.
This was focused primarily on achieving economic equity with the
dominant Chinese business community. But as mass political awareness grew, so did a sharpened nationalist perception of the external
environment. The Vietnam conflict provided the stimulus for a
coalescence of nationalist feeling that cut across the political spectrum from the Malay chauvinist PMIP on the far right to the Labor
party on the noncommunist left. In between, the ruling United

Malay National Organization (UMNO) responded to the new climate of mass expectations with a gradual movement away from the old-line conservatism represented by Rahman. In domestic affairs, this brought a more militantly Malay accent that was to come to a climax in a 1973 coalition with the PMIP, which advocated a frankly Malay-based nationalism rather than the multi-racial type espoused by UMNO. In foreign policy, it meant a growing sensitivity to nationalist currents in other parts of Asia that made identification with the U.S. role in Vietnam less and less comfortable. The subsurface tensions in Malaysia over the Vietnam issue were brought home to me forcefully in November 1967, when Ghazali Bin Shafie, permanent secretary for foreign affairs, sought to defend the government posture on the war at a dinner party in Kuala Lumpur. Ghazali was startled to find himself openly challenged in the presence of a foreign visitor by a leading UMNO political power, Ismail Bin Abdul Rahman, then party vice-president and a former home minister who was later to become deputy premier. Tun Ismail spoke passionately of the need for a neutralization of Southeast Asia in which China would inevitably have to be one of the guarantors. He criticized American intervention in Vietnam as an obstacle to the achievement of this objective,[102] foreshadowing the later Malaysian initiative for neutralization initiated by Prime Minister Tun Razak after Tun Ismail had rejoined the government.

By December 1968, Ghazali Bin Shafie was publicly declaring that the experience of the United States in Vietnam "showed so clearly how difficult it was for her military presence to be effective unless Vietnamese nationalism can be fully harnessed. . . ." Pondering the lessons of Vietnam, he delicately buried the idea that the Communist challenges in Malaysia and Vietnam were comparable, obliquely pointing to the distinction, examined in Chapter 2, between the narrow social roots of the Malaysian insurgency in the Chinese minority and the broader leadership of nationalism achieved by the Communists in Vietnam. Without naming Malaysia directly, he contrasted the relative homogeneity of Vietnam with a country "where the population is not homogeneous—or to put it more precisely, where a proportion of the population in a country are of the Chinese race and the Communist leadership and support come from this element." The significance of the Communists' victory in Vietnam would thus be basically different, he argued, from the triumph of the Malaysian Communists. Implicitly accepting the view that "a Vietnam, united but Communist, would be a counterweight to any Chinese expansionism," Ghazali Bin Shafie cautioned that "those who believe this must accept that this is only possible because of the homogeneity of her population"; whereas a communist victory in a country with a Chinese-dominated communist movement would inevitably mean Chinese hegemony.[103]

Even in the early stages of American intervention, prior to the bombing of the North, Malaysian sympathy for the Saigon cause was relatively tepid. Malaysian fears of a unified Vietnam were remote and vaguely defined. Thailand, by contrast, if only as a result of greater geographical proximity, found the prospect of a strong Vietnamese neighbor genuinely unsettling. Throughout the eighteenth and nineteenth centuries, as we saw in Chapter 1, Vietnam had been a weak and strife-torn country struggling to translate its inherent unity into lasting political form. The Thai monarchy had a centralized cohesion not yet achieved in Vietnam, and a unified Vietnamese state, as such, had not alarmed Bangkok so long as its ruler showed a measure of deference. Thus, Rama I lent support when Nguyen Anh overthrew the Tay Son regime in 1784 and established the Gia Long dynasty. Until 1802, Nguyen Anh, then Emperor Gia Long, sent annual tribute to Bangkok as a symbol of vassalage. The situation basically changed in the twentieth century, however, when Vietnamese nationalists of all stripes frankly set out to achieve centralized strength and an influential, if not dominant, regional role. The emerging ambitions of the Vietnamese were apparent in the programs of rightist Dai Viet factions as well as the nascent Communist movement. As early as 1947, Kenneth Landon has recalled, even before the Communist victory in China, Thailand could see that Ho Chi Minh would "not become a second Nguyen Anh" and speculated as to whether "it might not be better for Thailand if Vietnam remained divided." When Hanoi enlisted the support of Moscow and Peking, Landon added in a symposium during the war years, this clinched the Thai decision that

> a divided Vietnam would be safer, especially if the South was friendly and an ally. . . . Thailand has joined with the U.S. in a venture to keep Vietnam weak and divided. . . . If China, the U.S. and the U.S.S.R. were out of the Southeast Asian scene, a united Vietnam and Thailand would soon be jockeying for power and influence in the region. A divided Vietnam in such a situation would be no threat. For Thailand, two Vietnams are better than one.[104]

For nearly a decade after the 1954 partition, Thailand had a relatively uncomplicated view of the Vietnam scene, marked by an unabashed preference for the indefinite division of the country not found elsewhere in Asia. In supporting the United States, Thailand was thus doing the right thing, by American standards, but for the wrong reasons, even though Bangkok adorned its policy with a cloak of anticommunist rhetoric. At this stage, Thai encouragement of the American role did not conflict with the traditional Thai propensity for keeping foreign policy options open and avoiding overcommitment to a single foreign power. Later, with the escalation of American involvement in Indochina starting in 1962, Bangkok was torn between its fears of an aggressive Hanoi and its desire to allow for a possible Hanoi victory. For influential elements in the ruling elite, especially in the military, the issue was resolved by a lucrative dollar influx. But a deep uneasiness persisted beneath the surface of Thai political life throughout the war, feeding a growing nationalist mood that contributed to the student-led overthrow of the military regime in 1973.

Former foreign minister Thanat Khoman has left little doubt that the Thai leadership was deeply divided, from the outset, over how far to go in supporting the American role and that the initiative for the introduction of American forces in Thailand came from the United States. When the Kennedy administration asked Thailand to permit the stationing of marines in 1962 to deter Communist moves in Laos, Thanat recalled, he and Prime Minister Sarit Thanarat specifically urged the United States to make clear that "the Thai government had given permission as asked, but the White House spokesman said that we had asked for American troops to protect Thailand, *which was contrary to the reality.*" When Washington negotiated for air bases in northeast Thailand, this was done "secretly, with the Prime Minister as Minister of Defense." The Thai-U.S. agreements for bases at Korat, Takli, Udorn, and Nakorn Phanom were all "secretly done and known only among high-ranking military officers."[105] To some extent, one must reserve judgment on the details of the historical record, given Thanat's strong support of the war during his tenure as foreign minister and the self-serving character of allegations that were made only after his ouster in 1971. In its broad outlines, however, Thanat's picture of a division between military and bureaucratic elements over Vietnam is consistent with other evidence.[106]

Thanat's hard-line approach toward negotiations with the United States on a status of forces agreement, governing jurisdiction over crimes committed by U.S. personnel, was undermined throughout the war by more pliant military leaders who were dealing independently with Washington. The military-bureaucratic division was papered over, in any case, with the Thai elite as a whole intent on making the most of the enormous economic bonanza generated by the construction of U.S. bases, the presence of free-spending U.S. military personnel, and the American subsidies provided for Thai combat troops in South Vietnam and Laos. Most estimates indicate that at least $500 million was spent in Thailand itself for the construction of the bases and that another $400 million went into their operation through 1972. A Senate subcommittee established that some $200 million was paid for the 13,000-man Thai troop contingent in Vietnam between June 1967 and early 1970 alone,[107] not to mention additional, undisclosed sums paid for Thai forces sent covertly to Laos.

There was a significant difference between the qualified criticism of Thai policy voiced within the bureaucracy and the wide-ranging emotional opposition to the war that permeated Thai public opinion as the fighting progressed. Thanat Khoman typified the desire in bureaucratic ranks for a more flexible Thai policy and, above all, a more circumscribed U.S. base presence. Looking back on the war, he has argued that it was "worthwhile for Thailand to have taken the risk" of alignment when Washington was itself firmly committed to intervention in Southeast Asia, but that the Nixon Doctrine made it "too dangerous" to permit the continuance of U.S. bases.[108] Similarly, Bunchana Atthakor, ambassador to Washington from 1967 to 1969, has implied that he favored a more independent diplomacy consistent with "the historic policy of the monarchy in not taking too many steps to the right without some steps to the left." At one point in his memoirs, Bunchana appears to base his preference for a more malleable posture on the belief that China, not Vietnam, posed the real threat to Thailand, and that a nationalist Hanoi "would probably stop China from moving south."[109] For the most part, the bureaucratic critics of Thai policy were arguing in the cold language of realpolitik. Antiwar critics outside the government gave voice to deeper feelings of outrage aroused by the brutality of the war and by the increasingly evident futility of Thai support for an unrepresentative Vietnamese regime.

Despite repressive press controls during the early years of the Vietnam conflict, a leading Thai intellectual journal underlined the nationalist character of Vietnamese communism as early as 1965, declaring that "since the Vietminh was the faction which had led the fight against France, the Vietminh appeared to exercise greater influence over the South Vietnamese than the Government of South Vietnam" during the Diem regime.[110] Even at that stage, there was general recognition that Saigon lacked a nationalist dynamic,[111] but it was only as reports of the destructiveness of the fighting filtered back through censorship that critical appraisals of the war found their way into print. Apart from government press controls, as the editor of the *Social Science Review* complained, Thai intellectuals were "very much bound up in group loyalty, which is more important to them than truth, and were reluctant to voice their opinions in public." This feeling of group solidarity was linked, in turn, with the traditional repugnance for washing dirty Thai linen in public, reflected in the phrase *"saosai hai ga gin"* (literally "to pull out your intestines and let the crows feed on them"). The editor pleaded with Thai intellectuals "to consider the matter a little more deeply than that and to help survey the intestines that some writers have drawn out in order to determine whether they are intestines that work well or are merely some sort of appendix or ductless gland." Intestines "can, after all, become inflamed," the journal warned.[112] By 1967, the *Social Science Review* had questioned the bombing of North Vietnam on the ground that Washington and Hanoi had not declared war on each other. Pointing to Lord Russell's tribunal on U.S. war crimes, the journal speculated on how "Thais who are much younger and much nearer to the place in question feel about this despicable situation."[113] In 1970, a student leader asked whether "the destruction of Vietnamese society is a proper price that moral men can pay for the destruction of Communism" and, in a larger sense, whether "the Vietnam war is a moral war ... the United States is destroying the Vietnamese because she is engulfed in a neurotic fever of anti-Communist fear."[114]

Gradually, antiwar feeling took on a xenophobic character reflected in the Pai Kao (White Danger) student movement.[115] Militant nationalist feeling aimed not only at the United States but also at Japan as a U.S. accomplice[116] was a major stimulus behind the emergence of organized opposition to military rule that culminated in the 1973 overthrow of the Thanom Kittikachorn regime. The coalescence of antigovernment elements produced by the intensification of military control in 1971 was not merely a movement for democratization. It was closely linked with sentiment for an end to Thai involvement in the war and for a more independent foreign policy. Emboldened antiwar elements became increasingly outspoken[117] as the underground struggle against military rule gained momentum, enlisting such prominent figures as Puey Ungphakorn, respected governor of the Bank of Thailand. Later, when the military took power back in 1976, student-led opposition groups continued to base their appeal on nationalism, charging that the coup had been inspired by the United States for the purpose of retaining a base presence in Thailand.

The antiwar protest campaign was directed not only at Thai involvement in Vietnam itself but also at Thai support for the U.S. use of Laos and Cambodia as auxiliary battlegrounds. Thai writers argued that Norodom Sihanouk, not Lon Nol, had the majority support of Cambodians and bemoaned the depradation that engulfed "small and weak countries" such as Laos and Cambodia

> when they become involved in matters involving a big country's face and prestige. . . . How much longer the situation will continue, and how it will end, is as hard to guess as which village will be the next to be destroyed.

Chiang Kwang, Sakul or Techepone may appear to be nothing but shacks with roofs of corrugated iron, thatch or tile; they may not even be towns according to Western standards. But these areas are inhabited by the people who own the country, by Asians. They may be weak, poor and backward, but they are entitled to live in the manner they prefer.[118]

Laos and Cambodia, for their part, had attempted vainly during the early Vietnam period to preserve their fragile national identities by constructing neutralist regimes that would minimize internal political polarization and forestall direct embroilment in the conflict. In the case of Laos, American and Thai policy had been consciously designed from the outset to build a Bangkok-oriented regime in Vientiane, inviting a de facto partition of the country that would "give" Hanoi Communist-controlled tribal areas. The implicit assumption of American and Thai defense strategy was that Laos would have to be divided up, if necessary, in order to assure a Thai buffer against Hanoi along the Mekong.[119] This was rationalized with the arguments that Laotians viewed the Vietnamese as traditional enemies; that the Lao majority lived in the Mekong lowlands; and that historically, in any case, Laos had never achieved more than a nominal unity. In Laotian eyes, however, a Bangkok-oriented Vientiane was not much more palatable than a Pathet Lao regime answerable to Hanoi. An analysis of Lao journals during 1967 showed that the Laotian image of the Vietnam conflict was in substantial part one of cultural and economic penetration by Thailand, under the cover of the war, with the ultimate objective of making Laos a Thai vassal.[120] The neutralist approach identified with Souvanna Phouma, Kong Le, and others was motivated by fear of Thai domination as well as by a recognition, shared with Bangkok, that Hanoi represented a resurgent Vietnamese nationalism.

Premier Souvanna indicated in a 1967 interview that U.S. intervention in Vietnam would have been beneficial to Laos only if the stabilization of the South could have been accomplished without the use of Laotian territory as a battleground and only if Washington "had understood better that we have to keep our unity and maneuverability in order to deal with both of our larger neighbors." Souvanna pointed angrily to the Pentagon proposals then under discussion for an east-west barrier that would have extended across Laos as well as Vietnam. This signified "a monumental insensitivity to our nationalism," he declared, in view of the fact that the greatest obstacle to Laotian unity, historically, had always been the division between the monarchy centered in the north and the Bangkok-oriented Champassak fiefdom in the south.[121] While most of the older generation of Vientiane leaders adjusted with little pain to the financial bonanza represented by the American presence, many

younger Laotians emerged from the war years as militant nationalists. One example of this was the student uprising at Pakse in
February 1974, focused not only on corruption but also on the
American presence and the need for enlarged cooperation with the
Pathet Lao for the sake of a stronger posture against all foreign
influence. In dealing with this little-noticed revolt, Finance Minister
Sisouk na Champassak, an American protégé, was compelled to make
a direct play to nationalist feeling, praising the demonstrators for
"showing the profiteers, and the Laotian and foreign despots, that
true power belongs to the people."122

Like Laos, Cambodia saw the war from the start as a threat to a
precarious national identity that had been subject to Thai and
Vietnamese territorial erosion for centuries. Still, with a stronger
political fabric than Laos and a more clearly defined sense of national identity, Cambodia under Sihanouk was able to maintain a
more effective posture of noninvolvement. Sihanouk saw some
advantages in a divided Vietnam so long as Cambodia could be
insulated from the fighting. And the United States, hopeful of
winning him over, was ambivalent in its response to Cambodian
neutralism, alternating between qualified support of Sihanouk and
occasional harassment reflected in support for Bangkok- and Saigon-
linked Cambodian secessionists seeking to detach the northern and
western provinces from Phnom Penh. Despite persistent Pentagon
pressure, the United States stopped short of carrying the war directly
into Cambodian territory until President Nixon made his controversial volte-face in 1970 following the expanded use of Cambodian
territory in covert support of Communist operations in Vietnam.

Once the war did come to Cambodia, however, it proved to be
even more pervasive in its impact there than it was in Laos. In
contrast to the relative stability of the Souvanna Phouma regime as
the sole focus of noncommunist Laotian leadership, the Lon Nol
regime lacked popular standing and was unable to mobilize a strongly
motivated military force. The Cambodian Communists, relatively few
in number before the fighting started, thus grew rapidly in the face
of a foreign challenge. In Laos, where the Laotians themselves did
relatively little intramural fighting, most of the American bombing
was concentrated in Communist-held areas adjacent to Vietnam. In
Cambodia, the introduction of American firepower set the stage for a
diffuse conflict that could not be contained geographically and
resulted in the indiscriminate destruction of national life. For Cambodians, the war became an unmitigated catastrophe, even though
Sihanouk and his successors had once shared much the same estimate
of the struggle in Vietnam itself, looking with equal apprehension on
the emergence of a unified Vietnam. Against the background of

historically ingrained Cambodian and Laotian enmity toward the Vietnamese, it was the ultimate irony of the war that the devastation suffered by Cambodia, Laos, and the two Vietnams gave them an unprecedented sense of common identity rooted in their shared antagonism toward the United States.

As in the case of Vietnam itself, the carnage in Cambodia cast a dark and heavy pall over already blocked channels of communication between Asia and the West. Not only was empathy difficult at the intellectual level, with the United States largely blind to the nationalist component in communist movements. Even on the plane of elemental human sensibility, Washington appeared to have its own private wavelength. Intellectual confusion led to moral numbness as the enormity of American firepower grew in inverse proportion to the likelihood of realizing American political objectives. In characteristic Asian counterparts of the Western morality play, the mighty are never allowed to prevail over the weak on the basis of superior strength alone, and the victimized underdog is an automatic object of sympathy. Japan, for example, has immortalized the victory of Hangan over his more powerfully armed older brother in the Kabuki classic *Kanjin-chō*. The *hangan-biiki* psychology[123] made it natural for Japan to cheer for North Vietnam and to criticize American demands that Hanoi make the first move in peace negotiations. For Hanoi to accede would have been "contradictory reciprocity," the *Asahi* reasoned,[124] since it was up to Washington, as the stronger party, to find a way out of the conflict. The United States, too, has its tradition of sympathy for the underdog, but this was inoperative during the war years because of a misperception that Saigon and later Phnom Penh were the victims of aggressive power. In the end, when Washington withdrew from direct participation in the war, the United States was deeply divided as to whether it had used too much power or not enough.

General Matthew Ridgway pondered the dilemma resulting from the vast preponderance of American force in the course of a memorable 1967 plea for restraint in Vietnam. The word "victory" loses its meaning, he said, when one side has "a potential for destruction so indescribably vast. . . . It would hardly be counted a 'victory' if one football team were to defeat another through the use of knives."[125] Looking back on his two years as a correspondent in Vietnam, Ward Just struck a similar note, observing that

> a price is paid for the sort of military superiority that we have built in this country, and that price is a certain psychological imbalance. Americans know all about fair play, and this game isn't being played fairly. There is, of course, no other way to play it. A war is not a football game or a tennis match, and points are not given away so that the participants may feel more

evenly matched. But there is a psychological price to pay, and the Americans are paying it.[126]

From an American-centered perspective, the United States has already paid an inordinate price in national self-doubt, tortured as it is by belated guilt for its My Lais in some quarters and puzzled failure, in others, to understand why the war was never carried to its conclusion in the enemy's home terrain. In the larger perspective of American relations with Asia, however, the costs of the American role in Indochina may yet prove to be even greater. Coming so soon after Hiroshima, this new intrusion of American military force has strained the bonds of Asian tolerance perilously close to the breaking point. At best, as I have suggested, the war has seriously aggravated the East-West communication gap. At worst, it may well have left an intangible but nonetheless "real" legacy of Asian alienation, distrust, and incipient racism.

NOTES

1. Walt W. Rostow continues to base his justification of the war on private assurances of support from Asian leaders; see Walt W. Rostow, *Politics and the Stages of Growth* (Cambridge: At the University Press, 1971), p. 310. For a discussion by Selig S. Harrison of the gap between public and private positions presented during the war period see "How Asia Looks at Vietnam" (Paper delivered at the 20th Annual Convention of the Association for Asian Studies Annual Convention, Philadelphia, 23 March 1968).

2. John Foster Dulles, "Laying the Foundation for a Pacific Peace," *U.S. Department of State Bulletin,* 12 Month 1951, p. 403; see also *Documents Related to British Involvement in the Indochina Conflict, 1945–65,* pp. 66–67, cited in Gabriel Kolko, *The Roots of American Involvement* (Boston: Beacon, 1969), pp. 99–100.

3. See the text of Secretary Kissinger's background briefing for editors in Chicago, 16 September 1970, p. 13. For a similar statement by Henry Kissinger see the text of his briefing in San Clemente, 24 August 1970, p. 40. The briefings were not attributable to Kissinger at the time they were conducted but were later attributed to him by White House spokesmen following extensive overseas press speculation, especially in Japan.

4. Iwao Hoshii, "Japan's Stake in Asia," *Orient/West,* 1967, p. 100. Hoshii was formerly rector of Sophia University.

5. *Washington Post,* 17 November 1967, p. 1.

6. "Japan Repeats Endorsement of U.S. Policy in Vietnam," *Baltimore Sun,* 2 December 1967, p. 1. The controversy this provoked in Japan is discussed by Tokuma Utsunomiya, in his account of the January 1969 Japan–United States conference in Santa Barbara, "On Returning from Santa Barbara," *Sekai* (Tokyo), April 1969, p. 20.

7. This comment was made on an NHK television panel discussion, "Nichibei Shunō Kaidan o dō Miruka" [How to look at the U.S.-Japanese summit conference], aired 9 A.M., 9 January 1972.

8. "Betonamu Sensō ho NIHON Keizai eno Keikyō" [Impact of the Vietnam war on the Japanese economy], in *Zaikai Kanosoku* [Financial Prospects] (Tokyo: Security Research Department, Nomura Research Institute, June 1968). This was elaborated in an interview with Hideo Kobayashi of the institute staff.

9. "Betonamu Jōsei Nohenuka to sono Keizai-teki Eikyō" [Changes in the Vietnam situation and their economic impact] (Tokyo: Japan Economic Research Council, December 1968).

10. The Sanwa Bank analyzed the Vietnam impact in the January 1968 issue of its mimeographed, untitled, privately circulated monthly newsletter. *Kangyō Nyuusu* [Kangyō News] published an analysis in its February 1968 issue.

11. In arriving at this estimate, it was assumed that 25 percent ($1.16 billion) of the $4.64 billion in total U.S. military spending for Japanese goods and services was Vietnam related. This assumption is made in Defense Department unclassified dispatch no. 9777, 24 June 1971, provided to me by the Office of Public Information, Commander, U.S. Forces, Japan. The $4.64 billion figure covers the foreign exchange costs resulting from spending by the U.S. forces in Japan and does not cover the total cost of maintaining the U.S. military presence in Japan. The computation of Japanese exports to the United States made possible by war-induced shortages, and of export growth to Asian countries over and above natural export growth, posed technical problems that were resolved differently in each of the expert studies cited and led to a divergence in findings. Median estimates were adopted, with the methods used for the years covered in each of these studies projected to cover the period through 1971 in cases in which the full 1965–1972 period was not covered.

12. The approach of antiwar groups is reflected in Tokuma Utsunomiya, "On Returning from Santa Barbara," pp. 12, 19. A $6.5 billion estimate by the Ministry of International Trade and Industry spanning the period 1965–1972 includes $1.177 billion in direct procurement by the U.S. forces, $2.83 billion in "indirect procurement" by Asian countries, and $1.9 billion in war-related export growth to the United States but appears to understate the Vietnam-related export growth to Southeast Asian countries over and above the natural export growth that might have been projected in the absence of the war. See Jim Stentzel, "Vietnam: Japan's Major Role," *Far Eastern Economic Review*, 12 March 1973, p. 33.

13. *Mainichi* (Tokyo), 20 June 1971, p. 1.

14. Yasuo Takeyama, "Don't Take Japan for Granted," *Foreign Policy*, January 1972, p. 79.

15. Liaison Committee for Cooperation with Vietnam, Keidanren, *Interim Report* (Tokyo: Keidanren, April 1970), pp. 2, 3, 5, 7.

16. Selig S. Harrison, "Japan and Vietnam Policy," *Washington Post*, 14 May 1970, p. A29. This article, which does not name Foreign Minister Aichi,

was based on a dinner meeting held by a group of American correspondents for Aichi at the Hilton Hotel, Tokyo, 9 October 1969.

17. Edwin O. Reischauer, *Beyond Vietnam: The United States and Asia* (New York: Knopf, 1967), p. 127. Japanese disapproval of the bombing was also indicated in a 1965 USIA study of Japanese attitudes, "The Standing of the U.S. in Japanese Public Opinion" (Washington: Research and Reference Service, USIA, December 1965).

18. Afro-Asian Problems Research Group, Liberal Democratic Party, *Declaration* (Tokyo, 11 May 1970), p. 2. For other examples of the analogy between Manchuria and Vietnam see "Tensei Jingo" [Voice of the People], *Asahi Shimbun* (Tokyo), 5 February 1971, p. 4; and Iwao Hoshii, "Japan's Stake in Asia," p. 101.

19. Makoto Matsutani, *Betonamu Sensō no Hansei* [Reflections on the war in Vietnam], supp. and rev. ed., Reading Material 72EO, Foreign-3 (Toyko: National Defense College, 1972), esp. pp. 91-92.

20. Ibid., pp. 108-109.

21. Akitoshi Ota, "Betonamu ni Okeru Minzoku Kaihō Undō no Chishi-teki Yōin; Toku ni Rekishi, Minzoku, Bunka, Seikatsu to Kara no Kōsatsu" [Some topographic factors in the national liberation movement of Vietnam; a study with special attention to history, race, culture, living, etc.], *Kanbu Gakku Kiji* [Organ of the School for Principal Officers], December 1972, p. 31. For other representative military writings on the war see Col. Taguchi Hatsuyuki, "Betonamu Sensō" [The Vietnam war], ibid., March 1973, pp. 21-29; ibid., April 1973, pp. 15-30; ibid., May 1973, pp. 10-19, and Aragata Setsurō, "Betonamu Sensō ni Okeru Beigun no Hairyoku Tōnyū ni Kansuro" [A study of American military power in the Vietnam war], ibid., November 1970, pp. 1-9; ibid., December 1970, pp. 7-16.

22. Oda Makoto, *Gimu to shite no tabi* [My trip as a duty] (Tokyo: Iwanami Shoten, 1967), esp. pp. 156-157, 191.

23. Lawrence Olson, "Vietnam: Notes on the Japanese Reaction," American Universities Field Staff Reports, East Asia Series, vol. 12, no. 2 (New York, June 1965), p. 5.

24. *Sankei Shimbun* (Tokyo), 25 April 1965, cited in Olson, "Vietnam" p. 8.

25. "The Most Primitive Emotion," in *The Pacific Rivals*, by the staff of the *Asahi Shimbun* (New York and Tokyo: Weatherhill and Asahi, 1971), pp. 406-407.

26. Daniel I. Okimoto, *American in Disguise* (New York and Tokyo: Walker/Weatherhill, 1971), pp. 159-160, 162.

27. Matsumoto testified on April 23, 1965. In addition to an unpublished report submitted to the Foreign Ministry, Matsumoto contributed two articles to the *Asahi Shimbun* (Tokyo), 6 and 7 April 1965, which were reported in the *New York Times*, 7 April 1965, p. 1. See also Kan'ichi Fukuda, "Japan's Reaction to the Vietnam Crisis," *Journal of Social and Political Ideas in Japan*, August 1966, pp. 24, 26-27; and Sonnosuke Matsumoto, "Introduction—Selected Articles—1965," ibid., August 1967, pp. 14-15, 19.

28. Omori reviewed the episode in *Ishi ni Kaku* [Writing on stone] (Tokyo: Ushio, July 1971); see also the detailed account of the Omori episode in Selig S. Harrison, "Pentagon Papers Still Cause Debate in Japan," *Washington Post*, 21 September 1971, p. A12. An expression of regret by Ambassador Reischauer with regard to his role may be found in Misao Makino, "Interview with Former Ambassador Reischauer," *Shukan Pōsuto*, Tokyo, 17 September 1971, p. 10.

29. James M. Truitt, "Japan: The Non-Country," *Atlantic*, June 1967, pp. 219–221; see also George R. Packard III, "Living with the Real Japan," *Foreign Affairs*, October 1967, p. 200.

30. Interview, Tokyo, 11 November 1967.

31. For examples of Miki's resistance to the Sato policy see Peter J. Kumpa, "Far East Council Avoids Vietnam," *Baltimore Sun*, 8 July 1967, p. 3.

32. Kinhide Mushakoji, "Still a Preoccupation with Communism," *Japan Times Weekly*, 24 February 1968, p. 2; see also idem, *Kokusaiseiji to Nihon* [International politics and Japan] (Tokyo: University of Tokyo Publishing Association, 1967), esp. pp. 132–134. The "Tuxedo statement" followed a meeting in Tuxedo, New York.

33. Masamichi Inoki, "The Pre-requisites of Government Leadership," *Ushio*, January 1968, cited in *Japan Quarterly*, April–June 1968, p. 254.

34. Daisaku Ikeda, "Press Statement," Mimeographed (Tokyo, 24 August 1967), p. 1.

35. Daisaku Ikeda, *A Proposal on the China Issue* (Tokyo: Sōka Gakkai, September 1968), p. 12.

36. Yukio Mishima, "On the Defense of Culture," *Chūō Kōron*, July 1968, cited in Richard Halloran, "Nationalism Urges Japan to Shed Its Western Trappings," *Washington Post*, 18 August 1968, p. B2.

37. Kazuto Kojima cites this finding in "Public Opinion vis-à-vis the United States in Post-War Japan" (Address presented at the International Press Institute Japanese-American Bilateral Meeting, San Diego, November 26-29, 1972), p. 8.

38. "Tensei Jingo" [Voice of the People], *Asahi Shimbun*, 25 June 1971, p. 6.

39. D. E. Weatherbee, "Vietnam and Indonesian Foreign Policy" (Paper delivered at the Association for Asian Studies Southeast Regional Conference, Duke University, 26–27 January 1968), p. 4.

40. Soedjatmoko, "Indonesia and the World," Dyason Memorial Lectures, lecture no. II (Canberra, Australian National University, 1967), pp. 14, 19.

41. Franklin B. Weinstein, "The Uses of Foreign Policy in Indonesia" (Ph.D. diss., Cornell University, May 1972), pp. 216; see also pp. 228–239 and tables 5.5, 5.6, 5.7.

42. Sunario, "Vietnam, Southeast Asia, and World Peace," *Berita Yudha*, Jakarta, 10 and 11 August 1966, p. 3.

43. Ibid.

44. Suwito Kusumowidagdo, "Indonesia and the War" (Address presented at the Overseas Writers, Washington, 15 September 1967), p. 3.

45. Adam Malik, 28 September 1967. For examples of Indonesian press comment on Vietnam in the initial period after the bombing see A. Laksmy, "The Vietnam Case in the Security Council," *Berita Yudha*, 3 February 1966, p. 2; "U.S. Vice President's Visit," *Merdeka* (Djakarta), 3 November 1967, p. 1; and Al Ichwan, "Vietnam Question in the Spotlight," *Angkatan Baru* (Jakarta), 1 October 1967, p. 3.

46. This is discussed in Weatherbee, "Vietnam," p. 6. However, Weatherbee interprets the Malik posture as an "innocuous" neutralist "balance to Indonesia's growing multilateral and bilateral connections with the U.S. and its friends" (p. 6).

47. "Is It Not Imperative to Review Our Policy on the Vietnam War?" *Angkatan Bersendjata* (Djakarta), 23 October 1967, p. 2.

48. Weinstein, "Uses of Foreign Policy in Indonesia," p. 223.

49. "South Vietnam Army Should Play More Positive Role," *Angkatan Bersendjata*, 6 February 1968, p. 20.

50. "The Tri Ubaya Cakti Programs within the Framework of Implementing the Basic Strategy of the Ampera Cabinet—Secret—I—Plans for the 'Dwi Dharma' Campaign," in *Landasan Idiil Bagi Perdjuangan TNI-AD* [The ideological foundation for the struggle of TNI-AD], Second Indonesian Army Seminar at Army Command Staff School (Bandung, 25–31 August 1966), part I, p. 20; see also the statement by Major General Suwarto, who served as deputy seminar chairman, ibid., pp. 44, 46.

51. Major General Suwarto, "Kearah Koordinasi Diplomacy-Strategy-Prosperity" [Toward coordination of diplomacy-strategy-prosperity], in *Simposium Kebangkitan Semangat '66 Mendjeladjah Tracee Baru* [Emergence of 1966 spirit in exploring new course] (Jakarta: Publication Institute, Economics Faculty, University of Indonesia, 1966), p. 26.

52. White's column linking Indonesia and Vietnam appeared in the *Washington Post*, 18 October 1967, p. A17.

53. "The Visit of the U.S. President," *Kompas* (Jakarta), 3 November 1967, p. 1.

54. S. S. Tasrif, "Indonesia, the Vietnam War, and Regional Cooperation," *Kompas*, 3 July 1967, p. 3.

55. "Welcoming Hubert Humphrey," *Angkatan Bersendjata* (Jakarta), 3 November 1967, p. 1; see also "Repugnant View," *Api Pantjasila* (Jakarta), 28 October 1967, p. 2.

56. For example, see the transcript of Nehru's interview with Paul Niven, "Washington Conversation," ABC Network, 10 November 1971, pp. 13, 16.

57. This is detailed in Selig S. Harrison, "South Asia and U.S. Policy," *New Republic*, 11 December 1961, pp. 13–14.

58. J. J. Singh, "Quo Vadis, America?" mimeographed (New Delhi, 10 August 1967), pp. 6, 8.

59. "Distressed?" *Times of India*, 1 July 1966, p. 8.

60. Bernard D. Nossiter, "Viet War Poses a Dilemma for India," *Washington Post*, 21 October 1967, p. A17.

61. Interview, New Delhi, 20 December 1967; see also D. K. Palit, *War in the Deterrent Age* (London: McDonald, 1966), pp. 136–137.

62. Interview, New Delhi, 19 December 1967.

63. Ibid.

64. Selig S. Harrison, "Mrs. Gandhi: Moderate Signs in China," *Washington Post*, 14 February 1969, p. 2.

65. "Transcript of a Television Interview with the Prime Minister by Four Foreign Correspondents," Television Singapura, 5 November 1967, p. 19-F.

66. "Transcript of a Press Conference with Foreign and Local Press Men," Television Singapura, 5 November 1967, pp. 12–14.

67. "Meet the Press," NBC Network, 22 October 1967, pp. 3, 4, 6, 12.

68. Ibid. For Lee's charges on his return to Singapore that the American press had distorted his views see the transcript cited in note 65 above, p. 19-C.

69. Dennis Bloodworth, "American Bungling in Asia," *Bangkok World*, 8 December 1967, p. 6.

70. Transcript cited in note 63 above, p. 2.

71. Interview with Lee Kuan Yew, Singapore, 28 November 1967.

72. Interview with Lee Kuan Yew, 10 March 1972.

73. Transcript cited in note 66 above, p. 6. See also the transcript of an interview given by Lee Kuan Yew to forty-four journalists representing Scandinavian countries, Television Singapura, 8 November 1967, p. 23.

74. Transcript cited in note 66 above, p. 7.

75. Transcript first cited in note 73 above, p. 20.

76. "The Standing of the U.S. in Philippine Public Opinion," (Washington: Research and Reference Service, USIA, June 1966), p. 3.

77. "The Philippines' Stake in Vietnam" (Text of a television speech delivered by President Ferdinand Marcos, 18 February 1966), p. 3.

78. Ibid., pp. 9-10.

79. Interview with Lt. Gen. James W. Wilson, commander, Thirteenth Air Force, Clark Field, 23 March 1967.

80. Interview with Ferdinand Marcos, Baguio, 26 March 1967.

81. Tom Buckley, "Marcos Sees No Major Effects on Philippines in Vietnam Peace," *New York Times*, 6 April 1968, p. 1.

82. Michael Paul Onorato, "The Philippine Decision to Send Troops to Vietnam" (Paper delivered at the Association for Asian Studies Conference, Washington, March 1971), published in abridged form in *Solidarity* (Manila), November 1971, p. 6.

83. Reported by Associated Press from New Orleans, 1 October 1969.

84. Ward Just, "Our Affair with the Philippines," *Washington Post*, 30 November 1969, p. 15.

85. C. L. Sulzberger, "This Is the War That Was," *Honolulu Star-Bulletin*, 6 April 1973, p. A25. Marcos indicated similar but less explicit distaste for the war in an interview I had with him on March 26, 1972, in Manila.

86. For detailed statistics through 1970 see *United States Security Agreements and Commitments Abroad: Republic of Korea*, Hearings Before the Subcommittee on U.S. Security Agreements and Commitments Abroad of the Senate Committee on Foreign Relations, 91st Cong., 2d sess., 24–26 February 1970, pt. 4:1545, 1571. For 1971 figures see William L. Davis, "Korean Foreign Exchange Earnings from Vietnam," *U.S.A.I.D. Monthly Report*, January 1972, p. 5. For 1972 figures see "Slow Vietnam Economy Hurts Korea Revenue," *Daily Yomiuri* (Tokyo), 15 August 1972, p. 1.

87. Vietnam-related exports were officially listed as $215 million during the period 1965–1972. However, this included barbed wire and galvanized sheets originating in Japan, processed in South Korea, and labeled as South Korean exports. American officials used South Korea as a cover to avoid criticism from U.S. steelmakers resentful of Japanese competition, and South Korean officials welcomed an opportunity to inflate their export statistics.

88. *United States Security Agreements*, pp. 1549-1550, 1633.

89. Ibid., pp. 1568–1572, presents a partial summary of these pay scales.

90. Marquis Childs, "High Cost of Partners in War," *Washington Post*, 2 October 1970, p. 24.

91. "Korea: Can Cold War Ground Thaw?" mimeographed (August 1970, privately circulated), p. 2.

92. "Munoe-mun" [Inside the political scene], *Chosŏn Ilbo* (Seoul), 20 January 1965, p. 4.

93. South Korean National Assembly, *Proceedings*, floor debate, 25–26 January 1965. I am indebted to Yi Yŏng-hŭi for translations of these proceedings.

94. South Korean National Assembly, *Proceedings*, Defense Committee, 8–15 March 1966, pp. 50–51; see also Sŏ In-sŏk, "I Testify on the Additional Troops for Vietnam," *Chosŏn Ilbo*, 9 March 1966.

95. See Kim Hong-ch'ŏl, "The Costs of the Vietnam War," *Sin Tong-a*, Seoul, March 1966; and "The Concept of a Friendly Nation," *Chŏngmaek*, Seoul, March 1966.

96. South Korean National Assembly, "T'ongil paeksŏ" [White paper on unification], mimeographed (Seoul, 1967), chap. 4, pt. 7.

97. Ibid.; see also South Korean National Assembly, *Proceedings*, Special Committee on National Unification, 6 December 1966, pp. 448–449.

98. "It's Time for Us to Seek a Settlement of the Vietnam War," *Chosŏn Ilbo*, 28 April 1970, p. 4.

99. James W. Gould, *The United States and Malaysia* (Cambridge: Harvard University Press, 1969), p. 233.

100. See Inche Mohammed Asri, acting president of the PMIP, "Our Stand" (Excerpt of a speech delivered to a meeting of the PMIP, Kuala Lumpur, 20 April 1965), p. 9. For a sample of criticism from the predominantly Chinese Labor party see Tan Chee-khoon, "Vietnam, Powder Keg of the East" (Address presented at a meeting of the University of Malaya Alumni Society, Kuala Lumpur, 7 May 1966), pp. 4–5.

101. Wang Gung-wu, "Communism in Asia," cited in Gould, *United States and Malaysia*, p. 234.

102. This exchange occurred at the residence of Burmese ambassador Pe Kin, Kuala Lumpur, 24 November 1967.

103. Ghazali Bin Shafie, "Southeast Asia in the Seventies" (Address presented at the Singapore Institute of International Affairs, 16 December 1968), pp. 4, 5.

104. Kenneth P. Landon, "The Effects of the Vietnam War on Thailand" (Paper delivered at the Association for Asian Studies Southeast Regional Conference, Duke University, 26-27 January 1968), pp. 4, 5, 17-18.

105. Thanat Khoman, "Punha Tahan Tang Doa Ni Pratesh Thai Lae Nayobai Tang Pratesh Kong Thai" [The problem of foreign troops in Thailand and Thai foreign policy], *Social Science Review* (Bangkok), May 1973, pp. 27-28.

106. For example, interviews with two former ambassadors to Thailand involved in base negotiations, U. Alexis Johnson (Tokyo, 21 April 1967) and Kenneth Young (Washington, 18 January 1967).

107. *United States Security Agreements and Commitments Abroad: Thailand*, Hearings Before the Subcommittee on U.S. Security Agreements and Commitments Abroad of the Senate Committee on Foreign Relations, 11-17 November 1969.

108. Thanat Khoman, "Punha Tahan Tang Doa Ni Pratesh Thai Lae Nayobai Tang Pratesh Kong Thai," p. 37.

109. Bunchana Atthakor, *Bun Toek Toot Thai* [Memoirs of a Thai ambassador] (Bangkok: Ak-sorn-sum-pun, 1971), esp. pp. 424, 639, 720.

110. Voraupth Jayanama, "American Policy in Southeast Asia," *Social Science Review*, September 1965, pp. 3, 5, 9, 11.

111. This was often acknowledged indirectly in an emphasis on the relative political stability of Thailand and its historic sense of national identity focused in the monarchy. See, for example, Paul Sithi-Amnuai, "Yank, Don't Go Home—Yet," *Life*, New York, p. 32; and Takashi Oka, "Thailand's Foreign Minister on Vietnam," *Christian Science Monitor*, 8 May 1967, p. 9.

112. *Social Science Review* (student ed.), September 1966, pp. 2-4; see also ibid., January 1967, p. 1.

113. "Siam—Vietnam—U.S.A.," *Social Science Review*, June 1967, p. 4. The editor of the *Social Science Review* during this period, Sulak Sivaraksa, deplored the secrecy of the Thai decision to grant bases to the United States in a 1971 Jakarta address. When the owner of the journal barred publication of the reference to the base decision, Sivaraksa resigned. The text of the address was subsequently published by the foreign-owned *Bangkok World*, 28 March 1971, p. 13.

114. Tug Chareomthiaron, "Seeltham Kong Kon Nhoomsao Lae Punha Songkram Vietnam" [The morality of the young and the Vietnam war], *Social Science Review*, September-November 1970, p. 13.

115. The Sapanadowe Student Club at Thammasat University published an underground monthly journal, *Pai Kao*, beginning in 1971, incorporating

selections from this publication in an overtly circulated ninety-one-page volume also entitled *Pai Kao* that was issued in January 1972.

116. The anti-Japanese emphasis of the student nationalist club at Kasetsart University was reflected in a *Pai Kao* contribution by Thanes Apornsuwan, "Pai Kao–Pai Leung: Uppasuk Ni Kan Pattana Pratesh" [The white and the yellow dangers: Obstruction to national development], in *Pai Kao* (Bangkok: March 1972), pp. 44–47. I interviewed the leader of this club, Suparb Pasong, and its faculty adviser, Warin Wangchanchao, on March 10, 1971, and obtained initial copies of *Pai Kao* at the time.

117. For examples of this outpouring of antiwar sentiment see Chanwit Kasetsiri, "Lamdub Hetkarn Songdram Vietnam" [Vietnam war chronology], *Social Science Review*, January 1971, pp. 10–13; Preecha Araya, "Nayobai Tang Pratesh: Tai Din Rue Bon Din?" [Thai foreign policy: Illusion or deception?], ibid., June 1972, pp. 6–12; and Prachit Na Bangchang, "Tang Rawd Kong Thai" [The safe way for Thailand], in Student Club at the University of Chiangmai, "Jodmai Tung Pratesh America Poo Ying Yai" [An open letter to the U.S.A. the Great], (Chiangmai, 1973). See also David Morell, "Thailand," *Asian Survey*, February 1973, esp. pp. 166–168.

118. Kramol Thongthamachat, "Pratesh Thai Kuan Keokong Kub Hetkarn Ni Khmer Rue Mi?" [Should Thailand be involved in the Khmer's situation?], *Social Science Review*, June–August 1970, p. 3; see also Khamsing Srinawk, "Jarakae Ti Puong Kong Plaa" [A Thai view on American policy: A crocodile and a fish], ibid., March–May 1971, p. 18. A full translation of this article was made available by David Morell.

119. Frank C. Darling, "The Role of Laos in the Defense Strategy of Thailand," *Pacific Community*, June 1972, pp. 516–530.

120. See the Vientiane journal *Mittasone*, especially an editorial comment in the July–September 1967 issue, discussing alleged Thai discrimination in railroad rates and transit duties imposed on landlocked Laos (p. 16); and Thao Vapi, "Jokingly Speaking in the Lao Manner," ibid., pp. 4–6, an appeal to the United States not to support advocates of a merger of Thailand and Laos. See also Mme Thong-samount Oudomvilay, "On International Understanding," ibid., pp. 1–4, October–December 1967; and Sulak Sivaraksa, "Laos as Thailand Sees It," *Social Science Review* (Bangkok), September 1966, pp. 6–9.

121. Interview with Premier Souvanna Phouma, Vientiane, 8 December 1967.

122. T. D. Allman, "Lao Students Assert Themselves," *Manchester Guardian Weekly*, 15 February 1974, p. 3.

123. *Nihon a Shiru Jiten* [A dictionary to know Japan] (Tokyo: Shakai Shiso Sha, 1971), pp. 942–943.

124. "Plea for Vietnam Peace," *Asahi Shimbun* (Tokyo), 31 December 1966.

125. Matthew B. Ridgway, "Pull Out, All Out, or Stand Fast in Vietnam?" *Look*, 5 April 1966, p. 81.

126. Ward S. Just, "This War May Be Unwinnable," *Washington Post*, 10 November 1967, p. C3; see also idem, *To What End?* (Boston: Houghton Mifflin, 1968), esp. pp. 28–29.

7. After Korea:
The Stresses of Division

In Korea and Vietnam alike, a common underlying weakness has marked American policies conceived in single-minded containment terms with little or no allowance for the power of nationalism. The issue of unification and national identity was abandoned in both cases to the North. Force was invoked by the Communists not merely for partisan aggrandizement but in the lofty cause of making the nation whole. By contrast, the United States and its allies fell into negative military and political holding actions, committed in effect to the perpetuation of indefinite division.

As we have seen, the Korean partition has endured because nationalism has been temporarily neutralized. While the Vietnamese Communists grabbed the banner of nationalism early, the Communists in Korea were never more than one among many contenders for prewar nationalist leadership. Neither Seoul nor Pyongyang has been able to lay primary claim to nationalist legitimacy since World War II. Even in Korea, however, the stability of the division was gradually eroding long before the change in Sino-U.S. relations led to North-South contacts and the slight thaw in the U.S. approach to the North in 1972.

The aspiration for unification has been a consistently explosive force, progressively building up in strength as the Sino-Soviet split and, above all, the rise of Japanese power have reawakened a sense of common destiny. This has been true not only in Pyongyang, with its officially ordained mission of unifying the country; in South Korea, too, where the very mention of unification was taboo until the Sino-U.S. détente, the issue has nevertheless been a powerful, ever present undercurrent continually churning beneath the surface of public life. The defensive psychology toward the North born of the

Korean War has gone side by side with a deep distress over the prospect of indefinite division. This chapter will seek to explain attitudes toward unification in both the North and the South and show why they constitute an explosive and unpredictable factor calling for a new American approach to the peninsula as a whole.

NATIONALISM GOES UNDERGROUND

In order to appreciate the continuing volatility of the unification issue, it is necessary to recognize clearly how very artificial and unstable the division of Korea has been from the start. Thus, Rhee Syngman, for all of his failures as a political leader in other spheres, was acutely sensitive to the potential of the unification issue, seeking to preempt it with his "March North" slogan and deliberately appeasing nationalist emotions through unyielding anti-Japanese policies. As his prime minister has recalled, Rhee not only "sincerely believed that we could not afford to fall into the Japanese lap economically or politically without perpetuating the division, without driving another big wedge into the already existing national cleavage." Rhee also warned the United States that

> the Communists would call us Japanese stooges, and would say they would liberate us from Japanese domination. . . . The coming over of the Japanese into Korea . . . would develop into a situation where the Southern Koreans would be driven by this force of circumstances toward the Communists. . . . Our national survival requires that we do not get mixed up with the Japanese so long as we are partitioned.[1]

However, even Rhee was unable to contain the unification issue completely. His only significant challenger, Progressive party leader Cho Pong-am, chose "peaceful unification" as his principal battle cry and eventually was executed on treason charges. After the ouster of Rhee, the unification demand grew continually more explosive in the absence of comparable political antennae on the part of Park Chonghui. Seeking to wish away the issue with repression alone, Park merely drove it underground, creating a deceptive facade of consensus belying the actual state of mind in the South.

For a brief period following the departure of Rhee, the South enjoyed a revealing interlude of free speech in which attitudes toward unification received a rare public airing. In July 1960, the first free elections ever held in Korea opened a flood of pent up debate between newly emboldened reformist forces in the anti-Rhee coalition and militant anticommunist elements. The pro-unification cause received a major shot in the arm when Sen. Mike Mansfield made his proposal for unification "in terms of neutralization on the Austrian pattern."2 Largely unnoticed in the American press, the Mansfield plan touched off a major campaign in South Korea under the leadership of Kim Sam-gyu, a former editor of the influential *Tong-a Ilbo* newspaper who had spent the Rhee years in political exile. Neutralization became the intellectual fashion overnight. With unification rallies and torchlight parades gaining in momentum, alarmed conservatives in the government thought they saw the hand of North Korean manipulators and enacted a potent anticommunist law, provoking a wave of new demonstrations during the climactic early months of 1961 leading up to the May 16 military coup.

In a broad sense, the South Korean movement did come partially in response to a mid-1960 Pyongyang unification overture and was thus inherently suspect in conservative eyes. This is not the same as saying that it was Communist engineered, however, and cumulative evidence indicates that the 1960-1961 upsurge primarily reflected spontaneous impulses in the South. In their careful treatise on the history of Korean communism, Robert Scalapino and Lee Chong-sik find "no evidence" that it was directed by Pyongyang.3 Out of the six major elements vying for leadership of the unification cause, only one relatively marginal organization echoed the Pyongyang line and had significant links with North Korean-oriented groups in Tokyo.4 The driving force in the movement was a federation of seventeen campus chapters with a strongly independent flavor. To the extent that political professionals were behind the other groups, they were mostly unionists and leaders of radical fringe groups with explicitly noncommunist credentials. In addition to their major proposal for a meeting with North Korean students at Panmunjŏm on May 20, 1961, the unification advocates called for postal, athletic, journalistic, and trade exchanges with Pyongyang, pointedly stopping short of the confederation proposal put forward by Kim Il-sung in his 1960 message.

The climactic stage of the campaign in May coincided with increasing domestic factionalism in the embattled regime of Premier Chang Myŏn and provoked a strong government crackdown against the students in response to conservative pressures. When North Korea accepted the bid for a student meeting and representatives of the seventeen participating colleges met to map plans for the event, the education minister warned on May 12 that students going to Panmunjŏm would receive the "severest possible punishments" notwithstanding their "burning patriotism and love of nation" since "some aspects of the recent movement are irrational and irresponsible, and we emphatically point out that the North Korean slogan of peaceful unification is a strategy designed for Communist unification."5 On

May 14, a mass rally in Seoul called on the government to endorse
the May 20 meeting, and on May 16, four days before the scheduled
Panmunjŏm encounter, Park Chong-hui and his allies staged their
military coup.

Army leaders have declared that the unification uproar was the
critical factor precipitating their decision to act. In the immediate
aftermath of the coup, officers of the First Airborne Special Forces
Combat Group, which had played a key role in carrying out the
takeover, told interviewers that "the Chang regime was almost help-
less before the emergence of pro-Communist forces and those sympathizers of Communism who disguised themselves as reformists.
Theories of unification through neutralization were gaining force."6
Later, the official Foreign Ministry white paper on the coup indicated that dissatisfaction with political incursions into military personnel affairs had been mounting since the last days of Rhee but that
the spark finally igniting the coup was the unification campaign. For
veterans of Korean War combat less than a decade earlier, the mere
idea of the Panmunjŏm meeting was anathema.

Despite their suspicion of the unification slogan, some of the key
coup leaders recognized the force of the popular upheaval set in
motion by the student movement and made a long, ultimately
unsuccessful effort to give the new regime an offsetting nationalist
rationale divorced from the unification issue. The fact that the coup
had taken place in seeming defiance of U.S. desires helped the regime
initially to establish its patriotic bona fides but still left the new
leaders on the defensive. Asked how the military government differed from its predecessors if it had no apparent answer to the
unification problem, Kim Chong-p'il, architect of the coup and its
principal ideologian in the early years, stressed that "the most
important difference" lay in its independent spirit, "its earnest effort
not to rely on foreign power or to permit the entry of too much
foreign influence into the country." This difference, he said, reflected a long-term perspective addressed "completely, passionately
and in every way" to unification.7

Kim, who was later to emerge as the chief negotiator of the
normalization treaty with Japan and eventually as prime minister,
made clear from the outset that by "foreign power" he meant
American power, calling for efforts "to cleanse the prevailing 'cheap
Yankeeism' from our surroundings"8 and deploring the "corrupt
worship of foreign powers"9 by past regimes. Reunification, he
argued, would logically follow when South Korea had first escaped
from its dependent status and had consolidated its own noncommunist nationalist strength. To those who suggested that this was the
same refrain heard from Rhee and Chang, Kim replied that preceding

regimes had made the mistake of expecting too much from Washington, even though the United States had shared heavily in the blame for the division of the country and thus could not be trusted to help achieve unification. The new government would not make this mistake, recognizing that Seoul would have to take the initiative for unification in the light of Korean interests when the proper moment arrived.

In the immediate aftermath of the coup, Kim and his allies in the new regime gave the impression that they would like to do without U.S. aid altogether and spoke in vaguely leftist terms serving to accent their new posture toward Washington. The first wall posters issued on the day of the coup proclaimed a six-point pledge with a controversial economic plank promising "construction of a planned economy." Three days later this was changed in junta bulletins to "the development of economic plans" and finally, in President Park's official memoir, to "the construction of an independent national economy."[10] The tone of Kim's statements made him suspect in the eyes of some American officials as a secret communist at worst or a demagogue with unworkable socialist ideas at best. As Park's nephew-in-law and the key figure in the coup, he became the organizer of a vast new secret police-intelligence machine, first chairman of the Democratic Republican party, political vehicle of the new regime, and was widely regarded as an eventual Nasser to Park's Neguib who had to be taken seriously. His frankly declared concept of an authoritarian ruling party strong enough to face the North on equal terms in future unification initiatives directly collided with American efforts to establish meaningful democratic institutions.

Kim insisted that he recognized the need for American aid and was not anti-American.[11] Nevertheless, most American officials looked with clearly evident satisfaction on his setbacks in party factional struggles.[12] Partly because he became too great a liability in aid dealings with the United States, partly as a result of corruption charges arising out of his role in negotiating the normalization treaty with Japan, and partly because he simply overreached himself, making a premature bid to succeed Park as president, Kim gradually found his wings clipped. Anxious to challenge Park but never strong enough to do so, he has alternated between long periods of political oblivion and intermittent efforts to test the possibilities for an anti-Park move. Initially, he opposed Park's third-term bid, finally surrendering in 1971 and returning to the government as a figurehead prime minister hewing closely to the Park line in dealings with Washington. By 1976, he had grown restive and once again sought to organize his forces for a possible challenge to Park, only to find himself promptly removed from office.

What makes Kim noteworthy in this analysis is the contrast between his conscious identification with nationalist sentiment and Park's more prosaic political style. While Kim has limitations as a leader in other respects that have undermined his effectiveness, his nationalist aura has given him a certain popularity among many South Koreans, especially during the early years of the military regime. By the same token, it is the lack of sensitivity to nationalist feeling that has been Park's principal political weakness.

The key role played by Kim in negotiating the 1965 normalization treaty made him a lightning rod for anti-Japanese attacks on the Park regime that were largely offset by the nationalist reputation that he had acquired in tilting against the United States. Kim was eclipsed soon thereafter, however, and the regime no longer had even this limited defense against its critics, who could now charge that it was subservient to both Washington and Tokyo and had completely abandoned even its nominal commitment to unification. In Kim's perspective, the normalization with Japan not only was an economic necessity but also was politically valid, in its own right, so long as it went hand in hand with a more freewheeling stance in relations with the United States. The key to making the Tokyo-Seoul tie defensible in Korea lay in presenting it to the country as an offset to American power and in linking it to a pan-Asian nationalist appeal. Kim consistently emphasized Korea's Asian identity, declaring that "we must first be definite Koreans and then become definite Asians in recovering our national spirit. Only then can we think of becoming world citizens."[13] He invariably focused Korean grievances on the United States rather than Japan and even indirectly blamed the United States for Japanese colonialism, arguing that the Taft-Katsura treaty of 1905 implicitly sanctioned the Japanese occupation of Korea in return for unimpeded U.S. rule in the Philippines. The basic responsibility for Korea's present "divided and paralyzed state" rests with Washington, he contended, since it was "American self-interest and convenience that dictated our twin national disasters, the 38th parallel and the 1953 armistice line," although admittedly past Korean regimes had shared in the responsibility.[14]

When it comes right down to it, Kim observed in a 1967 interview, while he felt "a little bit of concern" over the extent of Japanese economic penetration, "it is easier for us to do business with Japan than with the United States. We are together in this part of the world. We understand each other instinctively despite our differences."[15] In early 1971, while still out of office, he revealed an overall nationalist emphasis considerably at variance with the approach of the Park regime, arguing that ties with Japan would not be inconsistent with progress toward unification if South Korean policy on the issue was itself more "positive." When the time is right, he confided, Japan

> may assume a greater role with respect to the unification issue. I hope they will increase their association with the North, since they are the only ones with access to both North and South, the only ones who can liberalize the North and expose them to the air of freedom. In this sense they could be the key. Of course, they should not favor the North or this would make matters more complicated.[16]

As for Park, his saving grace has been a certain insulation from attack by nationalist critics as a man of Spartan probity who has avoided personal corruption. This is what marked him out as the elder statesman of the coup group in 1961. This is what has given him his tepid public acceptance despite the corruption and high living in his regime symbolized by the "Korean Keeler case," a scandal involving the murder of a prosperous call girl that led to the removal of Premier Chung Il-gwŏn in 1970.[17] Park has projected a touch of "messianic, self-styled patriotism,"[18] fueled by a parochial outlook growing out of his humble social origins and his specialized education as a military man. He has a nativistic streak that helps to explain his unbending approach toward Christian dissenters, who represent, in his eyes, a cosmopolitan intrusion on the Korean scene. Nativistic attitudes and nationalism are very different, however, and Park has been largely out of tune with the nationalist urge of younger Koreans, in particular, for a unified identity in world affairs and the strongest possible posture toward Japan. In Park's case, his nationalist bona fides are intrinsically suspect because he served as an officer in the Japanese forces in Manchuria, and this added to his vulnerability as a target for anti-Japanese criticism after Kim's departure.

Yun Po-sŏn, Park's opponent in the 1963 presidential election, addressed Park contemptuously by the name given to him in the Japanese forces. Ridiculing "Lieutenant Masao Takagi, the distinguished graduate of the Emperor's military academy," Yun wondered "how a decent and patriotic Korean could dare to choose military service under the Japanese as his profession? It was a disgrace for a Korean to become a soldier for the Japanese oppressor, shooting his own people."[19] Definitive Japanese[20] and Korean[21] sources attest not only to Park's record but also to that of former premier Chung Il-gwŏn and other leading figures in postwar South Korean regimes. When a number of Korean officers deserted the Japanese in Manchuria and joined the anti-Japanese Korean Liberation Army in Chungking, Park was not among them. Park himself has acknowledged service under the Japanese,[22] but his defenders have denied North Korean charges that he helped to repress Korean Communist forces in Manchuria led by Kim Il-sung. In 1967, a pro-Park writer sought to establish that the president had actually been working within the Japanese forces as a secret agent for the Liberation Army, a contention widely challenged at the time.[23] In general, Park made little effort to counter his pro-Japanese image until the Tokyo-Peking rapprochement, declaring as late as 1971 that he would "not object" to a Japanese military buildup to fill the power vacuum left by the Nixon Doctrine if this were part of an overall Asian security system.[24]

Park has also been attacked for his alleged role as a ringleader of the 1948 Communist rebellion in the army at Yŏsu. Leading U.S. newspapers treated this as common knowledge in accounts of Park's record at the time of the coup, citing both American and Korean official sources, including one of Park's coup allies, Gen. Chang To-yŏng, army chief of staff.[25] The picture emerging from these accounts and subsequent investigation depicts Park as a prominent leader of the Communist apparatus in the Korean army from 1946 until October 1948, when he helped plan but did not take part in the Yŏsu revolt. Facing a military court and possible execution, he turned over a detailed list of Communists in the armed forces and was accordingly spared. General Chang and American officials told the story admiringly, apparently to show that Park had cleared himself of any procommunist taint, and stressed that he had since earned unquestionable anticommunist credentials in the Korean War. When the Yŏsu accusation became a political issue, however, Park himself issued a categorical denial, insisting that he had been unjustly put on trial as the result of army factionalism.[26]

The issue has never completely died and has acquired a significance going far beyond the taint of opportunism or the embarrassment of a former Communist link for the leader of an anticommunist government. The deeper meaning of the Yŏsu episode for nationalists in the South is that it seems to give Park a personal stake in perpetuating the division of the country in order to avoid Northern reprisals. Whether or not he was in fact responsible for the most sweeping purge of Communist elements in the army prior to the Korean War, many Koreans believe that he was and thus see him as peculiarly disqualified to be the executor of unification. It is openly suggested that he is wedded to the status quo,[27] merely paying lip service to the unification goal and going only far enough in contacts with the North to pacify public opinion. This feeling was deliberately exploited in a North Korean unification appeal in 1970 singling out Park as the one South Korean with whom Pyongyang would not negotiate—"Pak Chung Hee, the traitor to the nation, who formerly pledged his loyalty to the Japanese 'Emperor' and who, after the liberation, changed himself to a faithful cat's paw of U.S. imperialism, inflicting all kinds of treacheries upon the Fatherland."[28] When I visited North Korea for five weeks in May and June 1972, the Communist line on Park had softened to fit the needs of a new strategy stressing contact with the South, but I found a distinction in private comments between a contemptuous view of the president and a wait-and-see attitude toward other South Korean leaders.

CONTAINING THE UNIFICATION ISSUE

The underlying weakness of the Park regime from its inception has been its negative posture on the key unification issue. Shunning both Rhee's anti-Japanese salvos and Kim Chong-p'il's thrusts at Washington, Park has been unprotected by nationalist armor of any kind and has remained consistently on the defensive with respect to the unification demand. The first decade of his regime witnessed a continual struggle to resist insistent, recurring nationalist pressures that fluctuated in intensity with every change in the international situation and in the Pyongyang line.

The sweeping anticommunist law enacted by the new regime gave even greater discretion to the police in the arrest of suspected subversives than previous legislation, and the vocal clamor of 1960-1961 quickly subsided in the initial aftermath of the coup, with the exception of a cautious opposition proposal in the 1963 election for athletic, journalistic, and cultural exchanges with the North. In early 1964, however, the French decision to recognize Peking coincided with the climactic stages of government moves then under way to conclude a treaty normalizing relations with Japan. Here was hope for a thaw in relations between China and the West and thus for some form of eventual unification, at the very moment when the division of Korea was being reinforced by the deeply distasteful, American-backed move to align Tokyo with Seoul. An ebullient, student-led popular protest[29] forced the government to defer action on the treaty until June 1965, and even then the ratification bill had to be pushed through the Assembly by the progovernment Assembly majority when the opposition was absent from the chamber. The interval of angry stalemate between the 1964 antitreaty movement and the forcible ratification of 1965 was marked by an extremely unsettled political atmosphere in which the unification issue sporadically resurfaced.

When teams from the North and South were invited to participate in the Tokyo Olympics in October 1964, the South Korean

Central Intelligence Agency sought to engineer the defection of North Korean track star Sim Kŭn-dan by arranging a meeting with her South Korean father. The idea was to arouse sympathy for the daughter in the event that the defection plan failed. Instead, the dramatic meeting, followed by Sim Kŭn-dan's refusal to come South, brought a wave of pathos in the South and demands for measures to facilitate the reunion of divided families. Joined by twenty-six fellow members of the ruling party and nineteen opposition deputies, Yi Man-sŏp, a Democratic Republican member of the National Assembly, introduced his controversial meeting point resolution on October 27, 1964, calling for Red Cross negotiations between North and South and step-by-step procedures for contacts between divided families almost identical with those later discussed in the 1972 North-South talks. The proposal was considered for only two stormy hours in the Foreign Affairs Committee before alarmed conservative forces in the government party maneuvered to have the issue shelved pending a "comprehensive" approach to the unification problem. "We see pictures of Germans embracing in tears at the checkpoints or actually crossing the borders," said Yi Man-sŏp, and "we don't understand how you can oppose our proposal. You say that the West Germans are more advanced economically than we are relative to the North, but in my mind, what is involved is not the difference of economic standards between North and South but the difference in the basic mentality of those in power here." Opposition deputy Kang Mun-bong declared that "this negativism, this implicit reliance on the Americans and the U.N. to solve our problems, can only result in permanent dependence on another nation. We must take care of our own affairs, especially if the caretaker we have is not interested in the same objective we are due to differences of national interest."[30]

Just when the meeting point resolution was introduced in the Assembly, the normally progovernment monthly *Sedae* hit the streets with an article by a member of its editorial board, Hwang Yŏng-ju, president of the Munhwa Broadcasting Company, advocating a neutralist foreign policy shift by Seoul, including North-South contacts in a third country, the admission of both Pyongyang and Seoul to the United Nations, a nonaggression pact, and the withdrawal of all but a "rock-bottom minimum" of U.N. troops, restricted to stations along the cease-fire line. "We must defreeze the current antagonisms between North and South," said Hwang, "in order to force the concerned great powers to find a way to end our territorial division. The 'armistice' we now have has been forced upon us, and we have no reason to be bound by such an artificial situation."[31] Five thousand copies had been sold before the government banned the issue and arrested Hwang.[32] A well-known journalist was jailed a short time afterward for advocating a "two Korea" U.N. policy and "an urgent change of our unification policy" in the first of a series of cases involving the application of the anticommunist law to newsmen. Later, the managing editor responsible for publication of the offending article was also jailed, leading other editors to pull back into their shells.[33]

In the prelude to the 1967 election, Masses party leader Sŏ Min-ho, a controversial opposition figure who shuttled in and out of jail for advocating contacts with the North,[34] became the first South Korean politician to pledge a meeting with Kim Il-sung if elected president. This triggered a temporary shift in government tactics on the unification issue, with President Park pledging overtures toward the North in the "late 1970s" after Southern economic programs had been completed and "some new nationalistic force has emerged in the North."[35] By implication, this suggested that the North was stronger economically than the South. Park found himself more on the defensive than ever, and sought to defuse the issue for the duration of the election campaign by setting up a Special Committee on Reunification in the National Assembly with instructions to hold open hearings and map plans for a "national unification institute" charged with studying possible avenues to national unity. Park's choice as chairman of the nonpartisan committee was Sŏ In-sŏk, a popular, young, ruling party deputy; Sŏ enjoyed credibility with the public as an independent thinker on the unification issue, but was trusted, initially, by party managers as one who would not go too far off the reservation. Shortly after his election as chairman on July 25, 1966, Sŏ set the tone for what was to be a growing tug-of-war with the South Korean Central Intelligence Agency and the party leadership over his conduct of the unification hearings, leading in the end to his political eclipse. In the first of a *Chosŏn Ilbo* series on unification, he spoke of the "suffocating conditions" in which the fatherland had lived for twenty-one years, "its waist bound with the iron strip called the thirty-eighth parallel." Avoiding the officially prescribed term *pukkoe* (Northern puppet), he recalled that

the people in the North once tried to break out of these bonds with a desperate effort, but the result was only to inflict injuries all over the body, leading to further tightening of the yoke and the assignment of a watchman. . . . I don't know when our unification will come, and in what form, but a people endowed with such a high political sense and such a strong national consciousness cannot long be split. The combination to the lock fastening the steel bands around our waist is in our own hands. We will learn to master the combination or we will force the great powers to unlock it for us.[36]

The 190-page transcript of the hearings held intermittently from September through December and the 433-page committee report in early 1967 provide a revealing glimpse into South Korean attitudes showing that the pressures leading to North-South contacts in 1972 were not suddenly generated, full-blown, by the Sino-U.S. détente but had been gradually building up in response to a changing international atmosphere. Even in 1966, the central theme dominating the Unification Committee discussion was the change from a bipolar to a multipolar world and the need for Korea to find a unified national identity in order to avoid becoming a pawn in new big power arrangements. With the world "shaking down into national communities and national interest power relations," declared *Han-guk Ilbo* commentator Sŏl Kuk-hwan, "we have to approach our unification differently." The new situation required a "realistic willingness to bargain" with Peking, Moscow, and Tokyo, especially Peking, since

> the question of our relations with China is the most critical aspect of the unification problem. Historically, it has generally been when we had friendly relations with China that we have enjoyed peace and independence. We must not think of our relations with China only as those with a Communist state but as relations with a neighboring country having its national interests. We have generally had good relations with China except when we had to live under Japanese domination and Japan's relations with China were hostile.[37]

A professor at the National War College, Kim Hong-ch'ŏl, stressed that Japan was beginning to play

> its own independent and unique role in international politics, moving away from its past role of subordination to the United States. Of special significance is the fact that Japan is turning to the manufacture of guided missiles. If we get too close to Japan economically, this will inevitably mean a close relationship militarily, and this will greatly complicate our unification. Japan will henceforth follow its own policies with respect to China, and this may further threaten our unification. History tells us that various regions of the world are bound to have their respective leading nations. As these leading nations get stronger voices, they are favored in the settlement of international disputes affecting their region.[38]

Kim's suggestions that China and Japan might agree to keep Korea divided or that Japan might give China primacy in a unified Korea echoed similar earlier warnings in guarded magazine essays.[39] Now they were accompanied by fervent appeals for "finding an equation, as Koreans, enabling us to decide our own destiny" rather than "clinging to fixed positions while others readjust their policies to suit their interests and convenience." North Korea was changing, he added, since "they are apparently making efforts to establish a political style of their own" as evidenced in their declaration of

Juche from their communist mentors. Sŏl Kuk-hwan, too, pointed to Pyongyang's newly independent line, attributing it to the Sino-Soviet split,[40] and committee chairman Sŏ In-sŏk suggested that North Korea was moving toward economic revisionism in parallel with Eastern Europe.[41]

The first overt interference by ever present CIA representatives attending the hearings came when Kim Hong-ch'ŏl suggested North-South diplomatic exchanges. He drew attention to the Sino-U.S. ambassadorial contacts then being made in Warsaw, maintaining that

> even if we find this intolerable, from the moral point of view, in the practical world of politics it is something that is going on. We cannot understand how the big powers can ask the divided nations to stick to their stereotyped positions, while they themselves adapt to the new realities of co-existence. Indeed, we don't really know whether they are, in fact, asking us to stick to our positions or there are other factors involved. Since the U.S. and China are merely reviving old nineteenth century diplomatic devices by having the Warsaw talks, why aren't we able to do the same, seeking to solve our problems in the light of the realities around us?[42]

Kim was spirited away from the committee session during the recess, he and the chairman later told me,[43] endured several days of interrogation, and never returned to the hearings. His testimony was briefly summarized in the press without mention of the proposal for ambassadorial exchanges. But more than 500 spectators had attended the packed committee session, and the episode became a cause célèbre via the coffee houses.

Proposals for expanded contacts with the North were made frequently during the hearings, leading to sharp clashes between CIA witnesses and opposition leaders pressing for a Red Cross dialogue on divided families.[44] Throughout the proceedings, deputies complained of the sweeping restrictions on discussion concerning unification and North Korean affairs,[45] bringing a semiofficial admission, on one occasion, that West Germans had a less inhibited unification debate than Koreans.[46] By the time Chairman Sŏ presented his report and recommendations to the full National Assembly on January 31, 1967, the Park government had concluded that the effect of the hearings had been to magnify rather than neutralize public interest in the unification issue. Short shrift was therefore given to the committee proposal for autonomous unification institutes in the executive and legislative branches of the government, with the institute in the executive branch to be headed by a minister of state. Recommendations that the institutes "initiate plans for territorial unification," "prepare policies to deal with the problems arising after unification," and "investigate relations between South and North Korea, including contacts and exchanges" were bitterly attacked by progovernment spokesmen on the Assembly floor as tantamount to recognition of the "Northern puppet" regime. By a voice vote, the Assembly shelved the entire committee report.[47] Chairman Sŏ was denied renomination by the party high command and retired to private business until his appointment as principal aide to Premier Kim Chong-p'il in 1971 and his subsequent selection as publisher of the *Korea Herald*. His committee report was issued in mimeographed form by the National Assembly, however, and had a significant impact on South Korean intellectuals.

"The overriding feature of international politics in the 1960's," declared the report, "is the shift from the polarization of two great world powers to polycentrism. . . . But the problem of Korean unification is still treated within the context of the cold war."[48] For Koreans, the most important legacy of the cold war is that

> with U.S. encouragement, Japanese industrial production, triggered by the Korean War, has skyrocketed, and Japan is beginning to tread its way as a strong power in Asia. Whether or not it turns into a "Frankenstein" from the American standpoint, Japan must clearly be reckoned with from now on as one of the big powers most directly influencing the fate of Korea. In the face of this new fact of life, the hunger of the Korean people for unification grows stronger.[49]

In the new context of power politics, the report implied, the greatest barrier to unification would no longer be American-Soviet or American-Chinese tension but rather a U.S.-Soviet desire to prevent a Sino-Japanese combination by keeping Korea divided. "Considering the fact that the reconstruction of Japan was inspired by the new power of China," the report said, "and that the U.S. played such a special role in the normalization of Japan-R.O.K. relations, we cannot but conclude that Korea would be a factor in how America seeks to balance Japanese and Chinese Communist influence as part of its global calculations."[50] Since the big powers "never rest in pursuing their own interest," Chairman Sŏ wrote in his cautious foreword,

> we should also bring our own will to bear on the solution of this question. . . . It is true that people have a fatalistic attitude, and I have encountered many who asked, "is it really possible to unify the country." But I also find them intensely interested. Nobody really wants to live under the existing conditions of division.[51]

Sŏ's attempt to open up greater public discussion on unification came at an unpropitious moment when the South Korean CIA was exercised over signs of accelerated North Korean guerrilla pressures on the South. Foreshadowed in late 1966 by a purge of party leaders identified with a soft line toward the South, the hard-line extreme in Northern policy reached its peak with an abortive raid in January

1968 on the Blue House, Park's official residence, and gradually petered out with an unsuccessful guerrilla landing on the northeast coast seven months later. Soon after the Blue House raid, however, Premier Kim Il-sung declared that South Koreans could achieve liberation "only through their own determined struggle,"[52] marking a basic shift to a moderate policy that was to reach its climax at the Fifth Congress of the Korean Workers party in November 1970. As Northern pressures subsided, so did the intensity of Southern anxieties, and by February 1969 Park had appropriated the National Assembly committee's proposal for a unification institute as his own in a new effort to divert the unification issue into safe channels. His nominee as head of the new National Unification Board was a popular former president of Seoul National University, Sin Tae-wan, founder of the Korean Economic Association and author of Park's first development plan in 1961. Park gave Sin the rank of minister, envisaging the unification portfolio as a symbolic, ceremonial role, only to find that Sin took it more seriously as a vehicle for deliberately provoking public discussion of ways to ease tensions with Pyongyang.

Sin's frequent public references to the need for a more "flexible" approach to the North gradually began to arouse public expectations of serious political initiatives that the Park government had no intention of undertaking before the promised target date for unification negotiations: the late 1970s. After a stormy year in office, Sin was abruptly dismissed after he published a poll disclosing significant support for personnel exchanges with the North. This came in February 1970, just when Chancellor Willy Brandt was about to start his Erfurt discussions with East German leaders, a development keenly watched by politically conscious South Koreans. While President Park had sanctioned holding the poll, aides explained, he expected it to serve as a confidential research guide for government servants and was not consulted before its publication. To make matters worse, following his ouster Sin continued to speak out for more open discussion of unification possibilities. In an interview with me that filtered back into South Korea despite press controls, Sin compared Korea and Germany, declaring that

> we're in the same situation. We're both divided countries, and while we can't go as fast as the Germans are going, we've got to begin turning in the same direction. Without recognizing the existence of the North Koreans as a political force, we will never get anywhere . . . If it is too soon for direct contacts, it is not too soon to begin preparing ground by modifying the Anti-Communist Law so that we can at least discuss developments in the North, such as their increase in consumer goods production. We cannot even admit that they exist. We are risking arrest if we use any phrase other than "Northern puppet."[53]

Sin was interrogated and placed under surveillance after this interview, but his views were vindicated in little more than a year as a rapid sequence of international developments forced Park to modify his ·posture. In addition to the peculiarly sharp impact in Seoul of Brandt's *Ostpolitik*, American troop reductions in Korea inspired mainly by budgetary considerations led to a desire in Washington for a relaxation of tensions to fit in with the new policy. This, in turn, emboldened opposition leaders to use the issue of contacts with the North as a major weapon against Park. Kim Dae-jung, who was to oppose Park in the 1971 elections, reported after a Washington visit that U.S. officials had encouraged postal contacts with the North.[54] Privately, Washington urged Park to assume a "less rigid" posture if only to dull the edge of Northern propaganda. Kim soon launched a major foreign policy offensive, charging that Seoul was "rapidly going under Japanese dominance in the economic, political and military fields."[55] Even when Kim evoked strong popular approval with his election appeal for a new approach to the North, however, Park minimized the issue, responding with a qualified display of flexibility in the form of trade overtures toward "nonhostile" communist countries in Eastern Europe. Given Park's consistently defensive stance, the North-South agreement on Red Cross talks following the initial visit of Henry Kissinger to Peking marked an awkwardly abrupt volte-face on the part of Seoul. Pyongyang, by contrast, had called for Red Cross contacts repeatedly, offsetting the fact that the South was the first to propose talks following the Kissinger bombshell. The very rapidity of Park's footwork after his rigid stance of previous years was responsible for widespread suspicions in the South that he had acted partly in response to private American prompting, suspicions that strongly colored the popular assessment of his later contacts with the North.

"DEVELOPMENT FIRST"

In one significant sphere, economic development, Park has attempted with limited success to give South Korea a positive nationalist symbolism. His proudest boast has been a sustained increase in a growth rate that reached a 13 percent peak in 1969 amid wide acclaim abroad. Despite its undoubted successes in immediate economic terms, however, especially in booming exports and the production of consumer goods, Park's development program has enjoyed only an ephemeral domestic popularity. Higher employment levels and increased output have brought only a marginal payoff because they have come in a psychological vacuum. Nationalist dynamism is inherently missing in a development program insensitive to social inequities, heedless of the political costs incurred through foreign dependency, and unrelated to the overarching ideal of unification.

Taking stock of the prospect facing the South, leading scholars and political figures have periodically questioned the validity of the Park rationale that development should properly precede unification and that only when Seoul has reached an unspecified "sufficient" level of economic strength would it be safe to confront the North in negotiations. The "development first" concept figured prominently in discussions of the special National Assembly Committee on Unification, convened soon after the original enunciation of the Park thesis in 1966. Ch'oe Mun-hwan, president of Seoul National University, testified that "while it is not theoretically sound, the popular belief and wish is clearly that unification should come first. People feel that the real beginning of our development effort will come after we are together."[56] An opposition Assembly member, Cho Yun-hyŏng, responded that he could see nothing theoretically sound about attempting to develop a country in two truncated pieces when "even a brief look at our expanding population and limited space suggest otherwise. We may find international circumstances inhospitable, but the most plausible course for Korea, in economic terms, would clearly be to unite the agricultural potential of the South with the existing industrial base of the North and then to go on from there."[57]

The ultimate issue raised by critics of the "development first" approach is whether the popular élan necessary to mobilize national energies fully can ever be generated in the climate of dependence and uncertainty accompanying partition. Pointing to an ever multiplying external debt burden that had reached $8.4 billion in 1976, the critics ask whether the pursuit of such dependence really represents "progress." This psychological factor did not even occur to American economists David Cole and Princeton Lyman in their lengthy and frankly puzzled search for the possible constraints on South Korean economic progress.[58] To Korean scholars, however, it is the principal factor conditioning the climate in which development takes place. In any developing country, warned Yi Yŏng-hŭi, doyen of political scientists in the South and former president of the Korean Association of International Relations, foreign aid and investment help to build up favored local counterpart groups and thus aggravate the growth of economic disparities. In a partitioned country with a built-in atmosphere of insecurity, "we feel incomplete, as if we are drifting aimlessly, and thus a sense of dependence is peculiarly demoralizing and divisive, breeding debasing, mutually destructive self-seeking." The growth of special privilege and thus "ever-widening gaps" between government and people make it impossible for Korea to develop the type of team spirit underpinning Japanese economic success, Yi contended at a 1968 symposium; yet this inherently accompanies a growth-for-its-own-sake approach, one divorced from a nationalist frame of reference in which the basic aim is "to be completed as a nation-state."[59] In this widely held view, it would be far better to have a slower growth process with greater social equity, less dependence and more of a do-it-yourself component as part of an "urgently unification-oriented policy." Dependence and externally supported privilege could also develop in a unified Korea, it is conceded, but the country would be less readily vulnerable to foreign exploitation.[60]

The corollary to this view is that the Park approach to development actually prolongs and reinforces division by its very nature, leaning excessively on foreign help in its concentration on growth per se and thus adding needlessly to the vested interests with a stake in the status quo. When the military regime first took over, observed the dean of Seoul National University's College of Commerce at a much discussed 1967 symposium, it was motivated partly by a nationalist desire to escape from the overdependence on the United States attacked by Kim Chong-p'il. Washington, however, was seeking to reassign Seoul from one dependency to another and had "actually encouraged the student uprising of 1960 as part of its overall Far Eastern design of linking Korea and Japan, knowing full well that the anti-Japanese Rhee government would stand in the way." In this view, it was not long before the Park government lost its original revolutionary zeal and fell in line with a U.S.-promoted emphasis on modernization through partnership with Tokyo.[61] The result was "sham" development in many areas of the economy in which Korea began to serve mainly as a subcontractor for Japanese and to a lesser extent U.S. industry. In and of itself, the symposium agreed, economic cooperation with Japan would not necessarily be incompatible with Korean interests. But it would have to be put on an equitable basis and counterbalanced with the development of fully Korean-controlled industries, especially in the public sector.[62]

In 1967 and 1968, it was still possible to use the sensitive "Japanese issue" in open academic forums as a basis for criticism of the Park regime, albeit under the watchful eye of government intelligence agents. This became more difficult as the Japanese role grew and as the atmosphere progressively hardened with the shift from authoritarian to virtual totalitarian rule culminating in mid-1972. Using clandestine channels, however, the student government of Korea University circulated an anti-Japanese manifesto in September 1970 charging that Korea had reentered the Japanese sphere through plots between Korean commercial-political gangsters and government-backed Korean zaibatsu. Japan wants us to be dependent and seeks to divide and rule the two Koreas. Let us not repeat the history of 1910–1945. If we think only of comfort, we will produce another ruler who calls himself Korean but is actually like Yi Wan Yong in 1910.[63]

What made the Japanese presence so sensitive politically was not only its ever growing size but also the fact that it was actively encouraged and exploited by the Park regime. South Korean economic technocrats saw Japanese investment as a way of rapidly multiplying employment opportunities, and Park's political managers wanted slush funds from Japanese, American, and other foreign companies to help him consolidate his power. Gradually, Japanese economic involvement in the South has mushroomed under Park's tolerant eye. Japan had a cumulative total of $628.5 million in formal equity investment authorizations in June 1976 as compared to a $258.1 million U.S. figure. Moreover, equity investment was only the tip of the iceberg, given widespread covert financing through dummy partners and the Japanese preference for technical assistance or licensing agreements. All told, enterprises with estimated net assets of $1.7 billion either were directly Japanese-controlled in 1976 or were dependent on Japan for their raw materials, equipment, and spare parts.[64] A nominal 50 percent limit on the foreign share in new joint ventures, enacted in 1974 with Japan in mind, skirted the twin problems of indirect investment and dummy partners. South Korea had a $2.1 billion public and private debt to Japan in 1976, and its dependence on Tokyo has become especially pronounced in a lopsided pattern of two-way trade that reached a two-way volume of $4.9 billion by the end of 1976. The trade imbalance in Japan's favor jumped from $484 million in 1973 to $1.3 billion in 1976. Significantly, even if South Korean exports to Japan were to increase and the $484 million 1973 trade gap were to narrow, this would be of importance mainly in balance of payments terms. It would mean little reduction in Seoul's basic dependence on Tokyo since many South Korean export products are assembled from Japanese components and less than half of their value represents value added in South Korea.[65]

As in other parts of the East Asian culture area, Japan is attracted by an efficient, industrious work force, available, in the case of South Korea, at wages averaging 15 percent of the comparable Japanese level, a differential expected to drop to 10 percent by 1980.[66] The lure of quality low-wage labor held in check by an authoritarian regime prompted a controversial attempt in 1970 by rightist elements in Tokyo to establish a "Japan-Korea Industrial

Coprosperity Zone." Under the plan, proposed secretly by former premier Nobusuke Kishi and his right-hand man, Kazuo Yatsugi, labor and capital would move back and forth freely without national restrictions between southwestern coastal areas of Korea and parts of Japan's Kansai coastal belt embracing southern Honshu and adjacent northern Kyushu.[67] A "Japan-Korea Processing Trade Promotion Corporation" would enable Japanese companies to bypass government investment and tax restrictions in Seoul by operating under a single, nominally binational authority based largely on Japanese capital and clearly designed to be Japanese controlled.[68] Kishi and Yatsugi submitted their draft plan to a closed-door subcommittee of the Japan-Korea Economic Cooperation Committee, a semiofficial group with carefully chosen Korean business and official members regarded as friendly to Tokyo. "In view of the sentiments against foreign capital," said the draft, "the plan should be promoted with caution among the intellectual circles of both countries." But one of the Koreans present leaked a copy to the press, and *Tong-a Ilbo*, the independent newspaper, attacked the Kishi-Yatsugi proposal as "a resurrection of their old dream of a co-prosperity sphere, a plan to make us a permanent processor and subcontractor for Japan. Mr. Kishi dresses it up with talk of an Asian version of the Common Market, but all they want is to keep our labor cheap."[69]

Blacklisted for public office during the U.S. occupation of Japan, Yatsugi operated a strikebreaking "labor discipline" organization for businessmen before World War II. He also directed the ultranationalist lobbying group Kokusaku Kenkyu-kai (National Policy Study Society), which was expanded with influential business support after the war. In a 1974 interview, Yatsugi blamed "procommunists" for the opposition to his plan not only in Korea but also in Japanese labor circles. The plan was altered to "remove misunderstandings," he says, but is "still basically sound, and the substance of our economic relations with Korea is going along the lines I proposed. There can be no other way for them. They can't expect to do what we did overnight. It took us 100 years."[70] In place of the sweeping formal structure originally proposed, more limited arrangements had been quietly made in specific industries, he indicated, with Seoul showing a "cooperative" attitude as part of its overall strategy vis-à-vis Pyongyang. To the consternation of their South Korean friends, however, Kishi and Yatsugi were quick to probe business possibilities in the North after Pyongyang and Tokyo made wary contacts in 1972. Two-way trade between Japan and North Korea soon jumped from a 1972 level of $57 million to $250 million in 1975, with an imbalance of $126 million in Japan's favor in 1975 alone. The total had been expected to reach $400 million by 1977 until the North defaulted on nearly $600 million in debt to Japanese and European creditors in 1976 as a result of excessive foreign purchases based on exaggerated expectations of increased prices for its raw material exports.

The political costs of dependence grew increasingly steep for Park as it became clearer that Japan's objective in Korea is to have it both ways, inching toward a "two Korea" policy with the least possible damage to its economic vested interests in Seoul. Pro-Park elements had not only defended the Japanese presence in economic terms with the argument that Tokyo offered the nearest and cheapest source of imports and capital. Close ties with Japan had also been rationalized on expedient political grounds as a way of heading off contacts between Tokyo and Pyongyang. This was a rationale calculated to please anticommunist diehards. As we have seen, however, it was also certain to outrage unification-minded elements who believe that a Tokyo-Seoul axis directed against Pyongyang only reinforces Korean division. Both groups taunted Park when Tokyo stepped up its North Korean trade, and an upsurge of repressed anti-Japanese sentiment added to the instability of the Park regime resulting from economic inequities and a pervasive unease over the unification issue.

Park made a dramatic attempt to escape from his defensive position on the unification issue in 1972 by entering into talks with the North, setting up a hot line, and joining in the establishment of a permanent North-South Coordinating Committee at Panmunjŏm. Cautiously, South Korean leaders sought to present this in anti-Japanese terms, pointing to the dialogue with Pyongyang as insurance that Tokyo would not be able to play off the two Koreas against each other. When Park later declared martial law, he justified his action by citing the "changes in the security situation" resulting from the visit of Japanese premier Kakuei Tanaka to Peking and warning of the danger that "the interests of smaller countries might be sacrificed for the sake of the relaxation of tensions between big powers." When he put through a revised constitution giving him strengthened personal powers, he emphasized the new focus on unification in the preamble and the creation of a National Conference on Unification, "the first constitutional organ of the nation designed to organize the national forces in the direction of the peaceful unification of the country."[71] For a short time, he was able to improve his image with this sudden accent on nationalism, but the lingering question in the popular mind was whether the North-South talks had been desired by Seoul or whether, in reality, Park had reluctantly adapted to new Pyongyang tactics and to U.S. pressures arising out of the Nixon visit to China.

With his dependence on Japan growing, Park was increasingly unable to project a convincing nationalist image. His critics became more and more skeptical about the motives behind his contacts with the North, suggesting that he was merely using the dialogue with Pyongyang as an excuse for tightening his grip on the South and improving his propaganda posture vis-à-vis Kim Il-sung at the United Nations. Suspicion of Park's motives grew when he spurned Pyongyang's proposals in the North-South Coordinating Committee for talks on a mutual reduction of military forces. Seoul argued that more manageable issues should be settled first; Pyongyang countered that it wanted to test Park's bonafides. If the South had no serious intention of moving toward eventual confederation or unification, the North explained, it would be undesirable to proceed with further talks that would merely serve to legitimize the existence of two Koreas.

The rupture in the North-South talks in 1973 over the issue of force reductions was followed by intensified repression in the South and a resumption of the pre-1972 taboo on public discussion of how to improve relations with Pyongyang. With Kim Dae-jung and other opposition leaders jailed, the anti-Park forces were leaderless, divided and impotent. The mood in the South was increasingly one of cynical resignation and "every man for himself." On the surface, it seemed that the unification issue had been forgotten, but Park's repression covered up a nagging uneasiness over the continued division of the country. Fear of the North was mixed with a hunger for progress toward better relations with Pyongyang and the eventual creation of some form of confederation that would strengthen Korea in its dealings with its larger neighbors. In their explosive "Declaration for Democratic National Salvation" on March 1, 1976, Kim Dae-jung, Yun Pŏ-son and 16 other opposition leaders not only called for more democracy but also strongly implied that Park was deliberately delaying unification in order to preserve his power. This is why Park moved so rapidly to prevent circulation of the statement and to jail its authors. "Depending on the attitudes of politicians, north or south," the manifesto said,

> the opportunity for National Unification can either be brought closer or delayed. Those who truly believe in the nation and our common brotherhood, clearly perceiving the changing international situation, and seizing the chance when it comes, ought to have the wisdom and courage to deal with it resolutely ...
>
> The tragic division of our land for thirty years since liberation has given an excuse for dictatorships in both north and south, and has caused the withering of the spiritual and material resources which should have been mobilized for national prosperity and creative development. For the north

and south to have a combined standing army strength of over a million men, and to maintain these forces with modern weapons, would be beyond the productive capacity and economies of the Korean peninsula without foreign military aid. We cannot bear to see a situation in which the wisdom and originality of our compatriots is destructively wasted in this fashion. Accordingly, National Unification is today the supreme task which must be shouldered by all the Korean people. The barrier dividing north and south must be brought down by the combined strength and wisdom of all 50 million Koreans. If any individual or group uses or obstructs National Unification for its own strategic purpose, it will be impossible to escape the strict judgement of history.[72]

PEACEFUL, YES; COEXISTENCE, NO

The contrast between the psychological vacuum in the South and the climate of lofty nationalism in the North was inescapable to the visitor in 1972. While the Park regime was slipping into its dependence on Japan in the years after 1965, the North, as we have seen in an earlier chapter, was reaching the climax of a long effort to maximize self-reliance and loosen its aid links to Moscow and Peking. The resulting sense of pride in shared economic achievements not only cushioned the impact of the communist-style repression practiced by Pyongyang. It also reinforced the emotional unity rooted in the national myth of an anti-Japanese struggle led by Kim Il-sung and in Korean War memories rekindled nightly on television. This secure self-image as the custodian of Korean nationalism made it relatively easy for Pyongyang to move from a militant unification posture to its new soft line after 1968, confident that the North could more than hold its own in a political and economic competition with the South.

The moderate shift in Pyongyang leading to the 1972 North-South dialogue basically reflected a nationalist reassessment of the changing international environment, a reassessment that had already been in progress for more than five years before the Sino-U.S. détente surfaced in 1971. With the Sino-Soviet dispute growing in intensity, Pyongyang had found itself caught in the cross fire of its two communist near neighbors and had gradually recognized that it could no longer count on massive outside support in any new military conflict with the South. Later, as both Koreas had begun to confront a resurgent Japan, Pyongyang had seen that a policy of indefinite confrontation with the South would only harden the Seoul-Tokyo axis developing in the wake of the 1965 normalization treaty. As early as 1967, it was apparent in conversations with leading pro-Pyongyang Koreans in Tokyo that the Japanese factor and the thaw in the cold war were leading to a reappraisal of policy options. By late 1969, the first cautious approaches looking to eventual visits to North Korea were made to American correspondents in Tokyo. Then came Kim Il-sung's declaration at the Fifth Congress of the Korean Workers party in November 1970, in which he stressed that "the South Korean revolution should, in all circumstances, be carried out by the South Korean people on their own initiative."[73] This was followed by his major policy turnabout on August 6, 1971, soon after the initial Kissinger visit to Peking, indicating that Pyongyang was prepared for direct contacts with the Park government despite the continued presence of U.S. forces in South Korea.[74] It was at this point that I was invited to meet a visiting North Korean Red Cross delegation at a Japanese port in the first such gesture to an American correspondent,[75] a gesture that ultimately foreshadowed invitations to me and to a *New York Times* correspondent to visit the North in May 1972.[76]

The tone of formal interviews and informal conversations in North Korea over a five-week period suggested that Pyongyang found the world an increasingly lonely and topsy-turvy place when an American president could go to Peking and American businessmen could set up shop in Moscow. In this new perspective of shifting alignments, both Japan and the United States were viewed as vehicles for further reducing dependence on China and the Soviet Union. Washington was seen, in addition, as a potential source of leverage against Tokyo in much the same way that it was by the South, an image strengthened, in the communist perspective, by expectations of increasing "contradictions" between Tokyo and Washington. Pyongyang officials were beginning to think that history might not repeat itself, after all, and that the United States might not be destined to play the Japanese game once again as it did in the Taft-Katsura agreement of 1905. In a more immediate tactical sense, North Korean leaders also saw unprecedented opportunities in the newly fluid world environment to undermine the international position of the Park government, and thus to speed up, so they hoped, the end of U.N. and U.S. involvement in the Korean issue. By adopting a softer posture toward the South and opening up contacts with the United States, the North not only sought to undermine U.S. domestic support for a continued American troop presence in the South. Pyongyang also hoped to dissuade the Japanese from maintaining ties exclusively with Seoul by suggesting that Tokyo should take the North into account or risk being caught off guard as it was in the case of the Nixon visit to Peking.

Apart from the changing international situation, powerful economic realities had helped to make a new approach to the South attractive in Pyongyang. [77] A policy of austere economic nationalism places heavy strains on a society under the best of circumstances, and these stresses were multiplied under the special cold war circumstances of a garrison state in a divided country. Between 1967 and 1970, Pyongyang spent an annual average of 20 percent of national income and an estimated 31 percent of its national budget for defense, one of the world's highest levels in proportion to population. [78] Swollen defense budgets seriously aggravated other factors responsible for a critical labor shortage. With the population in the North half as big as that in the South, the impact of military recruitment on the labor supply is inherently greater in the North. In 1976 the North Korean armed forces numbered nearly 500,000 as against 595,000 in the South.

The existence of continuing economic problem areas in the North was implicit in the fact that the Six-Year Economic Plan ending in 1976 lowered the projected target for annual growth in national income from 15.2 percent to 10.3 percent, and the industrial growth target from 18 percent to 14 percent. These were still eminently respectable goals, but there were signs that the defense burden, compounded by bureaucratic inefficiency, had prevented their realization. What makes the impact of defense spending particularly unsettling for North Korean leaders is the competition for limited resources between heavy industry and the light industries needed to expand politically important consumer goods production. North Korean economic strategy had consciously minimized consumer goods during the recovery period after the Korean War and the early stages of the drive for self-reliance. Gradually, as pressures built up, Kim Il-sung recognized that the stability of his regime and of his personal power position would be enhanced by responding to the popular desire for more and better priced consumer goods of higher quality, especially fabrics, shoes, household appliances, and processed foods. The Six-Year Plan pledged doubled production of consumer goods. Even more significantly, the premier acknowledged rising pressure for higher wages. "In the next few years," he told the Fourth Congress of the Workers party, "we should raise the wages of the factory and office workers as a whole, sharply increasing the wages of factory and office workers of the low-wage category in particular."[79]

My impression of a rising popular interest in consumer goods was underlined by numerous signs that the government has quietly accepted the use of monetary incentives to boost production. In six different factories, workers at first responded to questions about their pay by earnestly insisting that they work solely for the love of country and Kim Il-sung. In any case, they added, their salary is supplemented by free medical care, free education, virtually rent-free housing, nominal utility rates, a month's vacation per year, and government-subsidized rice prices. But when asked about incentives, it turned out that the government has started paying substantial bonuses in addition to the higher wages promised at the Fifth Congress. In the rice fields, squads of farmers identified by flags worked in competition, and the unwieldy work teams of sixty originally set up when the collectives were organized have been subdivided into four-worker units in order to pinpoint responsibility. Bonuses are paid to these small units.

North Koreans generally looked well clothed and fed, with any significant discontent tempered by a rigidly enforced equality allowing for few evident disparities in living standards. They compared their present life with the privations of earlier years, and they seemed intensely proud that everything sold in the stores is produced domestically. At the same time, the feeling one receives in the churning shops and department stores is that North Koreans are quietly pressing for more and better things. People linger over their purchases, and lines of jostling, curious buyers form at counters displaying often scarce supplies of electric cooking utensils and other household appliances. Turning on the television one night and expecting to see the usual saga of the Korean War or the life of Kim Il-sung, I found a panel discussion that reminded me of "The Price Is Right": the manager of a local factory explained the virtues of assorted electric cooking gear, vacuum jugs, and glassware newly produced by the plant and members of the local "people's committee" asked questions.

In conversations with North Korean officials, it was clear as early as 1972 that internal economic pressures were forcing Pyongyang to modify its posture not only toward Seoul but toward Tokyo and Washington as well. Given a stabilized relationship with Seoul, economic planners reasoned, the South could purchase the output of Northern mines and heavy industries while offering the North a ready source for some of its consumer goods. More important, they calculated that reduced defense budgets would permit an expansion of their own consumer goods production, including selected imports of Japanese and other foreign machinery needed to upgrade the quality of their consumer goods technology. For all of its dedication to *Juche*, Pyongyang was beginning to realize that self-reliance has its limits and that the South has profited in economic terms through its infusions of foreign technology. This recognition made economic links with Japan increasingly attractive, which in turn made more relaxed ties with Seoul peculiarly desirable in the context of Pyongyang-Tokyo relations. Hesitant to open major trade dealings with

Pyongyang at the cost of its established ties with Seoul, Tokyo wanted a relaxed atmosphere in the peninsula in order to facilitate concurrent dealings with both sides.

From a Pyongyang perspective, Japan is not only the cheapest and closest source for the industrial machinery needed by the North, as it is for the South. It also offers a big new market for iron ore and other North Korean natural resources. Pyongyang seemed confident that state control of the economy offered safeguards against Japanese inroads on Korean sovereignty not available to Seoul. It is one thing to buy equipment for Korean-controlled state enterprises, officials explained, and quite another to permit unrestricted Japanese investment. Still more important, in the North Korean view, Pyongyang would never become as dependent on Japan for spare parts as Seoul had become, balancing Japanese purchases to a greater extent than the South had done with equipment acquired from Europe and, in time, from the United States. As it happened, one should note, Pyongyang did become embarrassingly dependent on the tolerance of Japanese and European creditors in 1976 when it had to seek a rescheduling of debt obligations. But the North Korean people were relatively unaware of the extent of their growing economic involvement with Japan, in any event, since the government propaganda machine could play down the growth in Japanese trade and the Pyongyang Opera could continue to immortalize Kim Il-sung for his guerrilla struggles against the Japanese.

It should be emphasized that the atmosphere in the North was basically one of a highly spirited society with a strong sense of achievement, unity, and confidence in the ability of the government to overcome all shortcomings. Discontent and frustrated economic aspirations have been tempered by a pervasive appeal to work together and sacrifice for survival. After the successive traumas of Japanese colonialism and the Korean War, North Koreans have been living in a semiparanoid state, with American forces in South Korea viewed as a persistent threat and American-South Korean intentions genuinely suspect. This enables Kim to project himself as a nationalist hero, and I sensed that the martial tone of official propaganda has more to do with perpetuating Kim's power than with preparing for an attack on the South. Day in and day out, films, television, and omnipresent radio loudspeakers recalled what the country went through in the guerrilla struggle against Japanese colonialism and in the Korean War years. There were reminders that a new war might be begun at any time by the "American imperialists running amuck in South Korea." But the real point of it all seemed to be that the country owes its existence and its accomplishments to the "iron-willed, genius commander, Kim Il-sung." The emphasis was not on a clear and present threat but rather on a shared national tradition and the consequent legitimacy of a totalitarian Kim regime based on an all-blanketing personality cult.

Kim does not depend on the maintenance of tensions with the South to sustain his regime precisely because he has successfully used this shared tradition to legitimize his rule. He could claim the withdrawal of U.S. forces as a personal triumph and keep up the Korean War movies while acting at the same time to relax tensions with Seoul. By shifting funds from defense to civilian needs, he could minimize economic discontent as a threat to his control. Given his remarkably long tenure, it was not surprising that Kim's monolithic power showed some signs of eroding in 1977 amid reports that his health has been failing and that there has been opposition to his alleged efforts to anoint his son as his successor. Even in the event of Kim's death or his replacement in a power struggle, however, his successors would in all likelihood seek to invoke the same national tradition that Kim has utilized and would continue to enshrine the unification goal as the unifying symbol that holds together the Communist regime. At the same time, they would confront the same economic realities that helped to push Kim toward more moderate policies and might, therefore, be willing to settle for some of confederation as a satisfactory step toward unification in the decades immediately ahead.

At times, after enough ginseng wine at night and enough badgering, my North Korean hosts said things that suggested what they mean and do not mean when they talk of "peaceful coexistence" and of abjuring the use of force. Peaceful, yes, but coexistence, no, if this means placidly accepting the indefinite division of the Korean peninsula. My hosts seemed confident that Seoul depends on anticommunism for its unity and would fall apart politically if a meaningful relaxation in the North-South atmosphere were to take place. Fearful of going too far and yet unable to retreat from a limited détente, Seoul will suffer from a progressively sharpening crisis of identity, they speculated, eventually giving Pyongyang opportunities for cooperative links with disaffected elements in the South. They talked about "the people" ultimately deciding what system would exist in the South and "a Korean consensus" determining the duration of the confederation proposed by Kim Il-sung as the prelude to full unification. The coexistence of differing economic systems under a confederation was implicitly envisaged in the revised constitution promulgated in Pyongyang after the 1972 North-South talks. Article 5 states that the Democratic People's Republic of Korea "strives to achieve the complete victory of socialism in the northern half" while seeking only to "drive out foreign forces on a nation-wide scale."[80]

For both Pyongyang and Seoul, a limited confederation could be an expedient arrangement permitting two absolutist regimes to maintain undisturbed power in their separate domains while moving at the same time to assert a common Korean identity in world affairs. However, while such an arrangement would have domestic advantages for Kim, it could create serious problems for Park. Kim would not have to risk the erosion of his legitimacy that could result from his acceptance of the "two Koreas" principle. A confederation would offer a way to ease his immediate economic problems and accept a de facto division of the peninsula while still remaining nominally wedded to the "one Korea" ideal. Park, by contrast, might find himself squarely on the defensive in a confederation as a result of his Japanese and American dependencies and could be compelled, in time, to redefine his posture toward Tokyo and Washington in order to preserve his domestic position.

THE AMERICAN ROLE AND THE KOREAN IMAGE

An evaluation of the American role in Korea during the first three decades after the Cairo conference points up a complex and potent psychological legacy. From the start, American policies have consciously or otherwise helped to divide the country and then to reinforce the division. Division was initially more feasible in Korea than it was in Vietnam, for reasons already discussed, but the result has been a growing sense of frustration focused against the United States by North and South alike. For the South, in particular, an American dependence married to an American-promoted dependence on Japan has been doubly demoralizing, breeding an incipient xenophobia comparable in kind if not in degree to the legacy of anti-Americanism in the North. Beneath this emotion lies an angry ambivalence, a feeling that a dependence humiliating for Koreans nonetheless reflects what is an obligation on the part of the United States. As one of those responsible for dividing the country, if not the "major" culprit,[81] this view holds, Washington has a responsibility for helping to put the pieces back together and for supporting Seoul until the division can be ended.

The Korean indictment of the United States begins with Cairo, Yalta, and Potsdam, condemning the casual disposition of the peninsula by the wartime allies leading to the division at the thirty-eighth parallel. Since Russian diplomacy traditionally had sought to divide Korea, argued Cho Soon-sŭng in a representative statement of the dominant Korean attitude, the United States either was a gullible fool or must have been more than ready to sacrifice Korean interests for the sake of its own, emerging cold war strategic concerns.[82] Due allowance is made in this view for the confusion marking the last months of the war, especially the fact that the Russians knew of the impending Japanese surrender before the Americans did through a decoded diplomatic cable and were thus able to claim an eleventh-hour role in the war, which gave them their access to North Korea. But it is the very accidental character of the division and the low priority given to Korea by Roosevelt and Truman that has been such a persistent insult. American unconcern regarding Korea and the vagueness of the United States about its occupation plans "amounted to a tacit invitation to the Russians to occupy the peninsula, setting in train the events that led to the division."[83]

Given Soviet complicity in the crime, the American role in the creation of the thirty-eighth parallel might have been canceled out in Korean memories had it not been for the subsequent U.S. approach to Korean domestic politics during the critical 1945-1946 period. Former State Department official Gregory Henderson has sensitively recounted the struggle inside the U.S. government between military leaders with a visceral anticommunist preoccupation and State Department officials seeking to work out a trusteeship arrangement.[84] Faced with the Preparatory People's Republic described in Chapter 5, a representative coalition of noncommunist and Communist nationalist elements, the occupation authorities hurriedly sponsored Rhee Syngman, Kim Ku, and other exiled conservative leaders as a counterforce, thus consolidating an internecine political conflict that led inexorably to the collapse of trusteeship efforts in July 1947.

The fateful and little-known political drama between the proclamation of the People's Republic on August 12, 1945, and the arrival of Rhee under the aegis of the American Military Government on October 16, crystallized the Korean image of the United States as a self-interested interloper insensitive to the traumatic meaning of a divided peninsula in nationalist terms. In Yŏ Un-hyŏng, organizer of the republic, Korea had a noncommunist nationalist leader who had foreseen the possibility of an internationally imposed partition and had laid the groundwork for an independent Korean regime that would head off such an eventuality by setting up the secret Alliance for Korean Independence in 1944. Yŏ was primed to act in the aftermath of V-J Day, when the Japanese colonial authorities, fearful of anti-Japanese riots and searching for a focus of stability, asked him to set up an interim government.[85] The short-lived republic that he led was clearly a broad-based, spontaneous expression of the Korean nationalist impulses that surfaced in the first flush of independence.

The depth and intensity of this phenomenon reflected a radical nationalist mood that went hand in hand, by its nature, with leftist economic attitudes. "During the 36 years of Japanese rule," recalled a leading journalist of the period,

> a dividing line had been established between those who cooperated with the Japanese and acquired personal wealth and those who gladly accepted poverty as the price of upholding the Korean national spirit. For those who chose the latter course, wealth in itself became an evil. Thus it was regarded as a duty or an act of conscience for cultured Koreans to denounce monopoly capitalism and one-sided wealth, and to advocate the nationalization or equal distribution of the wealth left behind by the departing Japanese.[86]

A polarization quickly developed between a militant left and a conservative right led by "Korea's relatively few men of wealth and position, who eyed Japanese property with glinting anticipation."[87] Against this background, it followed as a matter of course that the "dramatic 'Liberation' atmosphere drew most of its political symbolism from the Left"[88] and that Yŏ Un-hyŏng, once a Communist in his youth, attempted to capitalize on the popularity of Communist heroes of the anti-Japanese underground along with other political prisoners released by the Japanese as a condition for his cooperation.

Yŏ set out to create a unifying coalition of diverse nationalist elements, deliberately giving what he saw as a due position of importance to veterans of the underground but assuring representation, at the same time, of leading conservatives and moderates.[89] His nomination of Rhee Syngman as chairman of the September 6 People's Congress, a gathering of more than 1,000 delegates on the eve of the American landing, reflected his desire for a workable nationalist coalition that could head off the impending partition and his recognition that noncommunist Korean nationalist exiles had great popular standing. Yŏ was frustrated in this effort, however, partly by a succession of bad luck[90] but most importantly by the automatic hostility of the American Military Government. The American response was one of uncomplicated hostility to the republic well before the process of Communist penetration got under way. When a moderate delegation representing the republic went to Lt. Gen. John R. Hodge's command ship in Inch'ŏn Harbor, he refused to see the group. His first evaluations of the republic came from a handful of English-speaking Korean advisers, hastily recruited from missionary circles, who were "conservative in instinct" and pinned an undiscriminating Red label on the republic. Yŏ was unable to see Hodge until late October. For three months, the Military Government issued a succession of increasingly strident edicts repudiating the legitimacy of the republic, displacing "people's committees" that often went right on performing local governmental functions until the actual physical arrival of American forces. Hoping for a Korean regime that would function as an arm of the occupation, Washington finally outlawed the assertive republic in December, and South Korean politics splintered into a power struggle between Rhee, Kim Ku, and lesser leaders of more than 400 political parties and social groups. Moderate elements initially attracted to the republic drifted away, not only because the Communists had a beachhead there but primarily because the Military Government refused to give it recognition. Yŏ Un-hyŏng himself left in the face of a U.S. posture that made Communist control of the rump republic machinery inevitable.

The unique position enjoyed by Yŏ Un-hyŏng as a unifying nationalist figure during this period was apparent in the fact that the U.S. State Department called on the Military Government in mid-1946 to encourage a coalition of moderates under Yŏ and Kim Kyu-sik as the first step toward an interim government. Even without Yŏ's assassination in July 1947, the coalition attempt was fore-doomed to failure in a political climate of deepening cynicism provoked by the consolidation of the Kim Il-sung regime in the North as well as the rapidly hardening battle lines between the United States and the USSR in the trusteeship talks.[91] Yŏ's selection, however, underlines the irrelevance of debating whether he should be viewed, on the one hand, as an opportunistic "fellow traveler" and a "dedicated leftist nationalist who did not hesitate to cooperate closely with the Communists and, in so doing, greatly abet their cause"[92] or, rather, as "a dynamic liberal nationalist"[93] who was able to use the Communists for his own ends. Even those who emphasize his early Communist ties concede that if indeed he ever actually belonged to the Communist party, it is "probable" that his membership ended before 1930.[94] What is important for our purposes is that Yŏ became the vehicle for an authentic and powerful nationalist upsurge that the United States was instrumental in suppressing and that he enjoys a special place, accordingly, in the Korean nationalist pantheon.

It was Yŏ who provided the principal symbolism inspiring the nationalist ferment in Seoul during 1960-1961 and 1964-1965, and at one reported Tokyo gathering of pro-Seoul, pro-Pyongyang, and neutralist Koreans,

they agreed that Korea had enjoyed a .fine Korean government right after Liberation Day when the Japanese Governor-General capitulated to Yo Un-hyong and his provisional cabinet of anti-Japanese resisters, but that everything had been spoiled by Korea's false friends, Russia and America, who had insisted on cutting her up and sharing the spoils. Had only the

Koreans' own government been allowed to carry on after the landing of the Americans on September 7, 1945, all would have been well. That was the consensus of opinion and the basis of a National Salvation Front aiming, ultimately, at a "Yo-type" setup.[95]

In South Korea, I have found that the name of Yŏ Un-hyŏng touches a raw nerve of emotion, evoking respectful tributes, a note of distress at the lost opportunity he personified, and a certain embarrassed uneasiness. On my visit to the North, too, I found that Yŏ's name similarly threw people off balance, posing as it does the unsettling question of whether either North or South is really prepared for the compromises that would be necessary to make even a confederation work. Ch'a Il, a commentator on the government organ *Minju Chosŏn*, appeared moved at mention of Yŏ, commenting that he "was not a Communist, but he had a national conscience. If he had lived and had stuck to his original attitude, we could have worked together."

Having alienated those who sought unification through a coalition with the Communists, the United States later found itself on a collision course with Rhee Syngman, whose anticommunism proved to be inseparable from his own brand of nationalism. Rhee's "March North" slogan reflected a grimly serious desire to use American military power for the achievement of unification, a desire much more integral to Rhee's commitment to Washington than has generally been realized. In an unpublished interview with the Dulles Oral History Project, one of Rhee's prime ministers, Paek Tu-jin, recounted the impasse over the unification issue between Washington and Seoul following the Korean War. President Eisenhower, seeking to resolve the issue, invited Rhee to Washington in July 1954, only to find the Korean leader adamant that the passage in the agreed minutes of the talks pledging support for unification read "by all means" rather than by "peaceful means," as a U.S. draft was worded. For six months, Rhee refused to sign the minutes, leading to a virtual paralysis in Seoul-Washington relations and a U.S. cutoff of civilian oil supplies. He finally agreed to give up his language on unification only under pressure from South Korean military leaders anxious to finalize a major arms aid agreement.[96]

The basic conflict between a suppressed Korean aspiration for unification and the negative American containment objective has been reflected in lingering South Korean resentment over the Panmunjŏm armistice. The truce made the United States responsible thereafter for supporting South Korea, argued Hahm Pyong-choon, later to become South Korean ambassador to Washington, and South Koreans looked on American aid as "a form of reimbursement to us for carrying a disproportionate share" in the defense of what were "above all, the interests of the United States in the Western Pacific."[97] When the United States pressed Seoul to send troops to South Vietnam, the ensuing debate was infused with a deep sense of grievance, with a government spokesman justifying the South Korean effort to drive a hard bargain by harking back to the "humiliating truce, in which Korea was sacrificed on the altar of power politics."[98] Escalating economic demands were accompanied by bitter reminders that the "unequal" 1953 mutual security treaty between Seoul and Washington had been "arbitrarily imposed" on the Rhee government, followed by legislative action to revise the treaty "in accordance with Korean sovereignty."[99] The Park government eventually scotched the legislative moves in the face of U.S. resistance, but an officially stimulated campaign continued for the removal of a key provision giving control over South Korean military operations to the U.N. command.[100] The role of the U.N. commander as commander in chief of the South Korean armed forces was all too clearly perceived as a "leash" intended primarily to restrain any "March North" impulses. This and other continuing reminders that South Korea has been a pawn in major power diplomacy have injected a sour note into the gratitude accorded to the United States for its sacrifices in the Korean War, a cynical feeling that American help for Korea has been incidental, in the last analysis, to the pursuit of American interests.[101]

In assessing American motives, Koreans in South and North alike have been powerfully influenced by a persistent American tendency to treat the peninsula as a subsidiary factor in American relations with Japan, insignificant in its own right and expendable when necessary. The Taft-Katsura agreement of 1905 could hardly have been more transparent as a trade-off assuring American hegemony in the Philippines in exchange for U.S. acquiescence in the Japanese annexation of Korea. After this offhand collusion in disposing of Korea, Washington then added insult to injury after 1945, showing little or no awareness of what Japanese colonialism had meant. The tendency to lump Japanese and Koreans together as "the same breed of cat"[102] made it natural for the United States to take the path of least resistance by keeping the colonial bureaucracy and police apparatus intact. Similarly, the United States built its newly created constabulary around Koreans who had served in the Japanese forces, and the twenty Tokyo-trained officers who survived World War II were favored by the United States for the top posts when the armed forces were set up in 1948.[103] In American eyes, a normalization treaty between Tokyo and Seoul was indispensable for South Korean development and for ending a one-sided economic and military dependence that was as insupportable politically in Washington as it was in Seoul. Rhee's intransigence was viewed as irrational emotionalism. In Korean eyes, however, the United States seemed once again to be handing over the peninsula to the Japanese under more dangerous historical circumstances than ever. The North was particularly alarmed because American pressures for the treaty coincided with U.S. efforts to promote Japanese-American-South Korean military collaboration. In the South, there were business and political elements that hoped for a ride on the Japanese gravy train, but there were also widespread fears that Korea would be caught in a squeeze play, once again, with a Japanese-controlled South arrayed this time against Chinese and Soviet interests.

Not only in Seoul but in Tokyo, too, it was sustained and determined American pressure that pushed the two treaty signatories to the negotiating table. Former South Korean foreign minister Lee Tong-hwan has recalled [104] that direct American intervention was necessary to get Japanese foreign minister Shiina to make the eleventh-hour trip to Seoul needed to give at least the appearance of a Japanese apology that was conspicuously missing in the language of the treaty itself. Japan would have preferred a declaration rather than any treaty at all, minimizing both its diplomatic and its economic commitments. While businessmen were eager for access to the South, many Japanese leaders were hesitant about a one-sided involvement in Korea and reluctant to swallow their pride after a decade of Rhee's insults.

Paradoxically, the Tokyo-Seoul treaty served to reinforce the partition at precisely the historical moment when the North was breaking loose from its communist mentors and beginning to grope for a new Korean equation. Seoul has looked to Tokyo since 1965 for support vis-à-vis the North, and Pyongyang has been able to use the anti-Japanese issue in competing with the South for the leadership of Korean nationalism. Inadvertently, the United States handed this potent issue to the North, no more aware of what it was doing in the changing Korean political landscape of the sixties than it had been in the early postwar years. In helping to block a Northern-imposed unification militarily and in successfully sustaining a Southern regime, the United States has been oblivious to the historical factors that have explained communist weakness in the South. Now the United States confronts a radically altered Korean political environment in which the nationalist bonafides of the North have been credibly established and shifting international circumstances have brought a heightened urge for unity transcending the North-South division.

In this new context, the old assumptions underpinning the American presence in Korea have all but disappeared. No longer can

North Korea be characterized accurately as a mere agent of the Soviet Union or China. No longer can the economic support or military defense of the South be equated with the containment of a globally concerted communist threat, and no longer can the South claim support as the sole legitimate champion of self-determination in a civil conflict against another, illegitimate claimant charged with serving alien interests. The issue of legitimacy was never as unambiguously drawn as Seoul contended, in any case, with nationalism neutralized before the division and the Southern conception under American auspices no more immaculate, by Korean standards, than the origins of the Northern regime as a creature of Soviet power. Even as a rationale for supporting the South, however, the issue of legitimacy has worn increasingly thin. Support for Korean self-determination can now be meaningfully expressed only through support for a process of détente and interchange addressed directly to some form of limited confederation and eventual unification.

The fact that U.S. encouragement of a North-South dialogue is largely an offshoot of Sino-American détente has robbed the newly flexible American policy of much of its impact as a gesture to Korean nationalism. In the South Korean perspective, this is typical of an American policy that still slights the importance of Korea in its own right, treating Seoul as a subsidiary factor in relations with other East Asian powers. Linked to this attitude is the belief, discussed earlier, that the United States still fails to acknowledge its guilt with respect to the division of Korea and thus its responsibility to stand by Seoul until unification is achieved. The psychological impact of the long American involvement is pervasive, greatly complicating the problems inherent in a disengagement policy and posing new dangers for the future. Entrenched power groups in the South with a vested interest in the status quo can play on the deep-rooted suspicion of U.S. intentions to resist "self-help" measures. At the same time, even those most urgently committed to unification feel that Washington is obligated to help them get there with a minimum of hardship. History confronts the United States with a "damned if you do, damned if you don't" dilemma. Disengagement could open the way for eventual reconciliation with Korean nationalism, however, while continuance of a one-sided commitment will only prolong the agony, adding to a legacy of bitterness that will be difficult to eradicate under the best of circumstances.

NOTES

1. Transcript of an interview with Pyŏn Yŏng-t'ae, Seoul, 29 September 1964, John Foster Dulles Oral History Project, Princeton University Library, pp. 8, 20.

2. U.S., Congress, Senate, Committee on Foreign Relations, *Report on the Far East*, 86th Cong., 2d sess., 1960, pt. 1:7.

3. Robert A. Scalapino and Lee Chong-sik, *Communism in Korea* (Berkeley: University of California Press, 1973), 1:648; see also Han Sŭng-ju, "The Chang Myŏn Government in South Korea" (Ph.D. diss., University of California at Berkeley, 1970), p. 29.

4. This is the consensus from extensive interviews in Seoul and Tokyo from 1967 through 1972.

5. *Chosŏn Ilbo* (Seoul), 12 May 1961, p. 2.

6. *Tong-a Ilbo* (Seoul), 26 May 1961, p. 4; see also *Chosŏn Ilbo*, 26 April 1962, p. 1, for a summary of the *History of the Korean Revolutionary Trials* (1,040 pages), a detailed account of the circumstances and attitudes leading to the coup.

7. See the text of questions and answers at a discussion sponsored by the Political Science Association, Seoul National University, "Kim Chong-p'il Meets the Students," *Chosŏn Ilbo*, 6 November 1963, pp. 4–5.

8. Ibid.

9. Kim Chong-p'il, "Korea's Modernization," *Chosŏn Ilbo*, 10 November 1963, p. 5; see also ibid., 25 September 1963, p. 2; and an address by Kim Chong-p'il at Korea University, "Korea's Nationalism and Democracy," *Sŏul Sinmun*, 5 November 1963, p. 3.

10. Park Chong-hui, *The Country, the Revolution, and I* (Seoul: Ministry of Information and Broadcasting, 1967), p. 55. The original wall posters used the language "kyehoek kyŏngje," which means "planned economy." This became "kyŏngje kyehoek"—"economic plans"—in the printed bulletins of May 22.

11. For example, see *Korea Herald*, 19 November 1963, p. 1; and Kim Chong-p'il, "Korea's Nationalism and Democracy."

12. One key army G-2 official who dissented from the dominant American estimate took his case to the press in an anonymous article and was reassigned in a revealing episode that I verified. See "Diplomats in Uniform," an anonymous article in the *New Republic*, 2 November 1963, pp. 13–14.

13. *Sŏul Sinmun*, 16 January 1965, p. 2.

14. "Kim Chong-p'il Meets the Students," p. 4.

15. Interview with Kim Chong-p'il, Seoul, 21 October 1967. Kim's defense against pro-Japanese charges is found in "Korea's Nationalism and Democracy"; and "Kim Chong-p'il Meets the Students."

16. Interview with Kim Chong-p'il, Seoul, 29 April 1971.

17. Selig S. Harrison, "Scandal in South Korea," *Washington Post*, 13 February 1971, p. D1.

18. Gregory Henderson, *Korea: Politics of the Vortex* (Cambridge: Harvard University Press, 1968), p. 183.

19. *Chosŏn Ilbo*, 27 September 1963, p. 1. Henderson, *Korea*, p. 180, points out that the Manchurian academy offered channels of social ascent for young men from poor families otherwise closed in Korean society.

20. *Manshū Kokugun* [National Army of Manchuria], comp. Committee for the Publication of the Manshū Kokugun Ransei Kai (Tokyo: Seiko, 1970), p. 194.

21. Kim Se-jin, *Politics of Military Revolution in Korea* (Durham: University of North Carolina Press, 1971), tables IV and V, p. 46.

22. His *Official Biography* (mimeographed, issued by the Ministry of Culture and Information, April 1969), p. 5, notes that Park graduated at the head of his class in the two-year elementary course in the Manchukuo Military Academy in 1942, winning entry to the advanced course in the Japanese Imperial Military Academy and serving as a first lieutenant until the end of World War II.

23. Pak Yŏng-man, *Kwangbokkun* [Restoration Army] (Seoul: Hyŏptong, 1967), 1:371–372, 416–417, 609.

24. See President Park Chong-hui's New Year press conference for 1971, *Decade of Confidence and Achievement* (Seoul: Ministry of Culture and Information, 11 January 1971), p. 11.

25. For example, A. M. Rosenthal, "Rising Power in Korea," *New York Times*, 20 May 1961, p. 3; and Keyes Beech, "How Ex-Communist Directed Takeover of South Korea," *Washington Post*, 20 May 1961, p. 5.

26. *Chosŏn Ilbo*, 8 October 1963, p. 1; see also the text of Park's broadcast over the Korean Broadcasting System Network on September 1, 1963 (mimeographed, issued by the Ministry of Culture and Information); and his interviews in Seoul with the Associated Press on October 8, 1963; and with the United Press on October 13, 1963.

27. Yi Yong-hŭi, "Han'guk minjokchuŭi ŭi chemunje" [The problems facing Korean nationalism], in *Han'guk ŭi minjokchuŭi* [Korean nationalism] (Seoul: Korean Association of International Relations, 1967), p. 13; for a partial English summary of this symposium see Korean National Commission for UNESCO, *Korea Journal*, December 1966.

28. *Korean Daily News* (Tokyo), 8 June 1970, p. 15.

29. For a detailed report on the successful protest movement see "South Korea's 'Other Side,' " *Far Eastern Economic Review*, 18 June 1965, pp. 593–595, including translations of documents of the "National Salvation Resistance," established at eleven universities.

30. South Korean National Assembly, *Proceedings*, Foreign Affairs Committee, 45th sess., 6 November 1964, pp. 11–14. Translated from the Korean by Yi Yong-hŭi.

31. Hwang Yŏng-ju, "Indomitable Will for a Unified Goverment," *Sedae* (Seoul), 26 October 1964, p. 80.

32. Han Nae-bok, "Arrested Debate," *Far Eastern Economic Review*, 26 November 1964, p. 8; see a discussion of Hwang's arrest in a *Chosŏn Ilbo* editorial, "Unhappy Incident," 14 November 1964, p. 3.

33. Yi Yong-hŭi, a political reporter of *Chosŏn Ilbo* and later its foreign news editor, was arrested on October 20, 1964, following his article a day earlier; he served one month of a six-month prison term before being released on parole. Yi's sentence was later suspended after an appeal on July 26, 1967. The managing editor involved was Sŏnu Hwi.

34. For details concerning government measures against Sŏ Min-ho during this period see the "Open Letter" issued by the Masses party on May 12, 1966 in Seoul; the interview with CIA director Kim Hyŏng-uk, *Chosŏn Ilbo*, 5 June 1966, p. 1; and South Korean National Assembly, *Proceedings*, Legislative Committee, 20th sess., 7 June 1966.

35. *Chosŏn Ilbo*, 9 June 1966, p. 1.

36. Sŏ In-sok, "On Unification," *Chosŏn Ilbo*, 1 August 1966, p. 1; this was first in a series of thirteen articles on unification.

37. South Korean National Assembly, *Proceedings*, Special Committee on National Unification, 20th sess., 6 December 1966, in South Korean National Assembly, "T'ongil paeksŏ" [White paper on unification], mimeographed (Seoul, 1967), pp. 448–449.

38. Ibid., p. 463.

39. For example, see Kim Hong-ch'ol, "Concept of a Friendly Nation," *Chŏngmaek*, Seoul, March 1966.

40. *Proceedings*, Special Committee on National Unification, op. cit., p. 481.

41. Ibid., p. 518.

42. Ibid., p. 473.

43. Interview, Seoul, 28 April 1967; interview, Seoul, 21 October 1967.

44. See especially the exchange between Cho Yun-hyŏng and CIA assistant director Yi Pyŏng-du in *Proceedings*, Special Committee on National Unification, 23 November 1966, pp. 438–439.

45. See comments by Yang Ho-min, *Chosŏn Ilbo*, in *Proceedings*, Special Committee on National Unification, 7 December 1966, pp. 530-531.

46. Colloquy between deputy Cho Yun-hyŏng and government expert witness U Pyŏng-gyu of the National Assembly Foreign Affairs Committee staff, in *Proceedings*, Committee on National Unification, op. cit., 2–3 September 1966, p. 434.

47. *T'ongil Paeksŏ*, p. 119, relates this vote on 31 January 1967.

48. Ibid., p. 121.

49. Ibid., p. 25.

50. Ibid., p. 125.

51. Ibid., p. iii.

52. *Korean Daily News* (Tokyo), 7 September 1968, p. 30; see also Peter J. Kumpa, "North Korea's Kim Drops Aim of Unification by Force," *Baltimore Sun*, 9 September 1968, p. 1.

53. Selig S. Harrison, "Two-Germany Talks Spur Similar Ideas in Korea," *Washington Post*, 12 May 1970, p. 4.

54. Kim stated that this suggestion had been made by Deputy Assistant Secretary of State Winthrop Brown, a former ambassador to South Korea, on March 6, 1970.

55. Kim Dae-jung, "My Role in the 1970's" (Address presented at the Seoul Correspondents Club, 12 May 1970), p. 3.

56. *Proceedings*, Special Committee on National Unification, 6 December 1966, p. 452.

57. Ibid., p. 454.

58. David C. Cole and Princeton N. Lyman, *Korean Development: The Interplay of Politics and Economics* (Cambridge: Harvard University Press, 1971), pp. 240-254.

59. Yi Yong-hŭi, "Kijo Nonmum: Han'guk kŭndaehwa ŭi kibon munje" [Keynote address: Fundamental problems in the modernization of Korea], in *Han'guk kŭndaehwa e issŏsŏe kaldŭnggwa chohwa* [Conflict and harmony: Report of conference on Korean modernization] (Seoul: Korean Association of International Relations, 1969), pp. 10-15; see also Ch'a Ki-byŏk, "Han'guk minjokchuŭie ŭi tojŏn kwa siryŏn" [Trials and challenges of Korean nationalism], in *Han'gŭk ŭi minjokchuui*, pp. 33-34.

60. For example, see No Chae-bong, "Han'guk kŭndaehwa e issŏsŏe kaldŭng" [Conflicts in the modernization of Korea], in *Han'guk kŭndaehwa e issŏsŏe kaldŭnggwa chohwa*, pp. 20-30.

61. Pak Hŭi-bŏm, "Kyŏngje kaebalgwa han'guk minjokchuŭi" [Economic development and Korean nationalism], in *Han'guk ŭi minjokchuŭi*, pp. 18-19; see also pp. 34-43; and Pak's comments, pp. 115-139, in the discussion proceedings.

62. Ibid., p. 23 in this volume; see also comments by Yang Ho-min, pp. 183-188, in the discussion proceedings; by Pak Pong-sik, pp. 63-72; and pp. 216-258 for the discussion proceedings on his paper.

63. Student Government, Korea University, *Declaration on the Contemporary Situation of Korea*, issued with the approval of the Contemporary Conference on the "New Order of Korea and Asia," (Seoul, 29 September 1970), p. 3. See also the veiled anti-Japanese allusions in "The Five Thieves," by the South Korean poet Kim Chi-ha, a satirical poem confiscated by the Park regime but available in Japanese translation in Sentarō Shibuya, *Nagai Karayamai no Kanata ni* [Beyond the long night of hatred], (Tokyo: Chūō Kōron-sha, December 1971), pp. 12-13.

64. This information is elaborated in Selig S. Harrison, "Japan's Yen Buys Little Love in Korea," *Washington Post*, 27 February 1973, p. 1.

65. This conclusion is based on interviews with American embassy economic analysts, Bank of Korea officials, and Japanese trading company executives. Estimates of the value added ranged between 38 and 55 percent despite official estimates of 75 percent.

66. *Japan's Economy in 1980 in the Global Context* (Tokyo: Japan Economic Research Center, March 1972), pp. 60-61.

67. Kazuo Yatsugi, "Nikkan Chōki Keizai Kyōryoku Shian" [Long-range economic cooperation between Japan and Korea], mimeo. (Tokyo, 1 April 1970). Privately circulated.

68. Kazuo Yatsugi, "Nikkan Gōben Narabini Kaku Bōeki Shinkō Kōsha Setsuritsu-an" [Tentative plan for the establishment of a Japan-Korea joint venture and processing trade promotion corporation], mimeo. (Tokyo, April 1970). Privately circulated.

69. *Tong-a Ilbo*, Seoul, 24 April 1970; see also Haptong news agency dispatch dated April 25, 1970, and a discussion of the Yatsugi plan in "How to Assess Japanese Capital," *Chosŏn Ilbo*, 29 November 1970, p. 3. For

Japanese discussion of the plan see Yamada Akira, "The Structure of Regional Planning in the 'Smaller East Asia Co-Prosperity Sphere,' " *Asahi Asia Review*, December 1970; and "Japan-Taiwan-Korea Coordinating Committee Maneuvering," *Asahi Journal*, 29 November 1970.

70. Tokyo, 11 November 1974. Similar statements were made in an earlier interview with Yatsugi (Tokyo, 10 April 1971).

71. *The October Revitalizing Reforms of the Republic of Korea* (Seoul: East-West Crosscurrent Center, October 1972), p. 32; see also *Confrontation with Dialogue: R.O.K. Initiates Easing of Korean Tensions*, Policy Series no. 5 (Seoul: Korean Overseas Information Service, 1972). For Northern charges of Southern duplicity in carrying out the 1972 accords see the account of Vice-Premier Pak Sŏng-ch'ŏl's press conference in *Pyongyang Times*, 24 March 1973, p. 4; and Pak Hae-chon, "Easing of Tension in Korea," ibid., 31 March 1973, p. 2.

72. "Declaration for Democratic National Salvation," Seoul, March 1, 1976, mimeo., signed by Hahm Sok-hun, Chung Il-hyung, Kim Kwan-suk, Yun Ban-woong, Ahn Byoung-moo, Suh Nam-dong, Yi Oo-jung, Yun Po-sun, Kim Dae-jung, Eun Myoung-gi, Yi Moon-young, and Moon Dong-whan. This citation is from an authorized English translation made available in Tokyo.

73. Kim Il-sung, *Report on the Work of the Central Committee* (Pyongyang: Fifth Congress of the Korean Workers Party, 2 November 1970), cited in *Korean Daily News* (Tokyo), 5 November 1970, p. 1; see also "President Pak on Unification," *Korean News* (Washington), 16 August 1970, p. 1.

74. *Korean Daily News* (Tokyo), 10 August 1971.

75. See Selig S. Harrison, "Japan is Relaxing Its Pro-Seoul Policy," *Washington Post*, 22 August 1971, p. A20.

76. For the interview with a North Korean spokesman in Tokyo that signaled the invitations to American correspondents in 1972 see Selig S. Harrison, "North Korea Hints at U.S. Ties," *Washington Post*, 6 March 1972, p. 1. For articles written from North Korea see *Washington Post*, May 26, June 6, June 12, June 26, July 3, and July 4, especially an interview with Premier Kim Il-sung, June 26, p. 1.

77. For a detailed statement of this view see Selig S. Harrison, "North Korea: Fewer Guns, More Butter," *Washington Post*, 2 July 1972, p. C3.

78. Chung Joseph Sang-hoon, "The Six-Year Plan (1971–76) of North Korea: Targets, Problems, and Prospects," *Journal of Korean Affairs* (Washington), July 1971, esp. pp. 20–21.

79. Kim Il-sung, *Report on the Work of the Central Committee* (Pyongyang: Fourth Congress of the Korean Workers Party, 16 December 1967), p. 55; see also idem, *On Some Theoretical Problems of the Socialist Economy* (Pyongyang: Foreign Languages Publishing House, 1969), esp. pp. 24–25.

80. "Socialist Constitution of the Democratic People's Republic of Korea," *Korea Today* (Pyongyang), July 1973, p. 24.

81. Cho Sun-sŭng (Cho Soon-sŭng), "Han'guk ŭi yangdan kwa miguk ŭi ch'aegim" [The division of Korea and America's responsibility], *Sasanggye*, Seoul, July 1960, esp. p. 57.

82. Cho Soon-sǔng (Cho Sun-sǔng), *Korea in World Politics, 1940-50: An Evaluation of American Responsibility* (Berkeley: University of California Press, 1967). Pak Pong-sik, "Miguk ǔi oegyo chǒngch'aek kwa han'guk minjokchuǔi" [U.S. foreign policy and Korean nationalism], in *Han'guk ǔi minjokchuǔi*, pp. 55-56; see pp. 224-227 for Pak's exchange with Yi Ki-wǒn. See also the writings of Kim Sam-gyu, particularly *Konnichi no Chōsen* [Korea today] (Tokyo: Kawade Shobō, 1956), pp. 136-137, 141, 156-158.

83. Cho Soon-sǔng, "Han'guk ǔi yangdan gwa miguk ǔi ch'aegim," esp. pp. 60-61; and idem, "Miguk ǔi taehan t'ongil chǒngch'aek" [U.S. policy toward the unification of Korea], *Sasanggye*, February 1960, pp. 262-292; see also idem, *Korea in World Politics*; and Henderson, *Korea*, pp. 121-122.

84. Henderson, *Korea*, pp. 126-129; see also Harold R. Isaacs, *No Peace for Asia* (Cambridge: MIT Press, 1967), esp. pp. 93-94.

85. Yi Yǒng-gǔn, "8/15 Kaihō Zengō no Souru" [Seoul before and after the August 15 liberation], *Tōitsu Chōsen Shimbun*, Tokyo, 15 and 31 August 1970; ibid., 10, 20, and 30 September 1970; ibid., 10 October 1970.

86. O Yǒng-jin, cited in Scalapino and Lee, *Communism in Korea*, p. 240.

87. Isaacs, *No Peace for Asia*, p. 97.

88. Scalapino and Lee, *Communism in Korea*, p. 240.

89. A former associate of Yǒ Un-hyǒng stated that five members of the original seven-man Executive Committee of the Republic of Korea named on August 17, 1945, were conservatives or noncommunists of other hues: Chairman Yǒ, Vice-chairman An Chae-hong, General Affairs Chairman Ch'oe Kǔn-u, Finance Chairman Yi Kyu-gap, and Security Director Kwǒn T'ae-sǒk. Two of these, Ch'oe and Yi, a former Buddhist priest, were outspokenly anticommunist. The two other members, Organization Director Chǒng Paek and Public Relations Director Cho Tong, were described as "moderate Communists." See Yi Yǒng-gǔn, "8/15 Kaihō Zengō no Souru," *Tōitsu Chōsen Shimbun*, 15 August 1970.

90. Henderson, *Korea*, p. 117.

91. In emphasizing the People's Republic, it is not my purpose to establish whether the American nonrecognition policy was in fact a critical factor contributing to the breakdown of the trusteeship effort. Not only would this require consideration of the Soviet role but also, as a variety of observers have pointed out, Korean factionalism was beginning to erupt even during the life span of the republic, and the evidence so far uncovered points to the hand of a rightist rival behind the assassination of Yǒ Un-hyǒng. What concerns us here is rather the enduring psychological and political impact of the nonrecognition policy as part of the continuing pattern of American involvement in Korea.

92. Scalapino and Lee, *Communism in Korea*, pp. 234, 235.

93. Henderson, *Korea*, p. 116.

94. Scalapino and Lee, *Communism in Korea*, p. 234.

95. "South Korea's 'Other Side,' " pp. 594-595.

96. Transcript of an interview with Paek Tu-jin, Seoul, 28 September 1965, John Foster Dulles Oral History Project, Princeton University Library, pp.

11, 15; see also the transcript of an interview with Chŏng Il-gwŏn, Seoul, 29 September 1964, ibid., pp. 29–35; and the interview with Son Wŏn-il, Seoul, 29 September 1964, ibid., esp. pp. 11, 14–15.

97. Hahm Pyong-choon, "Korea's 'Mendicant Mentality'?" *Foreign Affairs*, October 1964, p. 169.

98. Ch'a Chi-ch'ŏl, "Implementation of the 'Brown Memo,'" *Tong-a Ilbo* (Seoul), 20 September 1966, p. 2.

99. South Korean National Assembly, *Proceedings*, Defense Committee, 11–12 March 1966; and ibid., full Assembly session, 6 July 1966.

100. See Ch'a Chi-ch'ŏl, *Uriga sewŏyahal chwap'yo* [The coordinates that we must build] (Seoul: Pommunsa, 1966), pp. 144-152.

101. For example, see Yi Yong-hŭi, "Han'guk sinmun ŭi ubanggwan" [How the Korean press views her ally], *Sinmun p'yŏngnon* [Journalism review] (Seoul), Spring 1968, pp. 13–19.

102. Henderson, *Korea*, n. 29, p. 416.

103. Ibid., pp. 336-337, 342; see also Ko Chŏng-hun, *Kun* [Army] (Seoul: Tongbang Sŏwŏn, 1967).

104. Interview, Seoul, 23 April 1971.

8. Nationalism and the American Military Presence

One central and persistent theme emerges from an analysis of the American military approach to Asia: the diminishing utility of traditional balance of power concepts. The American experience demonstrates the profound political costs of a military presence based on an outdated emphasis on these concepts and insensitive, accordingly, to the intangible but "real" power of nationalism. Military alliances, military aid, and military bases have all been the tools of an indiscriminate effort to balance communist strength by utilizing Asian countries as surrogates and by molding intra-Asian power patterns to suit American purposes. As we shall see, however, the strength of nationalism decisively limits the ability of the United States and other external powers to have more than a transitory impact on intra-Asian power relationships. Where the United States has attempted to play a directly manipulative role, this has fostered artificial imbalances, encouraged other external intervention, and frustrated the evolution of solidly based regional power patterns rooted in local realities. In the process, the United States has seriously compromised its political and psychological relationships with the Asian countries concerned, especially those in which American bases have been established. The cold war obscured the basic fact that nationalism is the ultimate source of "power" in Asia and that the domestic foundations of nationalism ultimately determine the strength of a country. Washington and Moscow both made the mistake of viewing Asian countries as pawns; and this attitude, in turn, led to the fateful assumption that intra-Asian conflicts involved their vital interests. In the aftermath of the cold war, both are more aware that Asia makes a dangerously volcanic chessboard and that intra-Asian conflicts need not jeopardize the larger peace.

ON BALANCING POWER

The waning utility of traditional balance of power concepts was anticipated to some extent even during the cold war years. Thus, in 1960, Walt Rostow spoke of the "diffusion of power" resulting from the technological revolution in communication and transport, the weapons revolution, and the modernization drive of developing countries.[1] In this analysis, however, the new environment of diffused power was simply a more complex and demanding version of the old one, equally subject to American management if the United States would only make the effort. Disregarding both the strength of nationalism and its precedence over ideology, Rostow saw communist parties uniformly as "scavengers" of nationalism without allowance for the fusion of nationalism and communism distinguishing the Chinese and Vietnamese cases. It was this characteristic cold war error that led to the definition of a monolithic threat fundamentally overestimating the identity of interest of Moscow, Peking, Hanoi, and Pyongyang. Gradually, this simplistic imagery was superseded as the meaning of "polycentrism" became more and more apparent, opening the way for the shift to détente in 1972. But the recognition that communism could be an expression of nationalism did not mean that Washington had come to terms with nationalism itself. Power was still measured in military and economic terms alone, and "power vacuums" were still juxtaposed with "power centers" as the bipolar world was succeeded in American thinking by a tripolar world embracing Peking, a "quadrilateral balance"[2] inclusive of Tokyo, and finally a pentagonal "even balance"[3] envisaging the European Economic Community as a unitary power factor.

By continuing to treat "power" too narrowly, multipolar imagery, like bipolar imagery, continued to give the United States a distorted perspective in which its capacity to mold power relationships in Asia was still overestimated. The new imagery was a step in the right direction; yet it continued to gloss over the truism that sovereignty, as such, endows even countries having a relatively small army or GNP with the power to resist external manipulation governed fundamentally by the strength of their identity and internal discipline. It is this "inability of the superpowers to make their will prevail over most nations of the second or third rank"[4] that Hans Morgenthau has properly singled out as the most obvious lesson of the Vietnam conflict. Even before the revolution in communications and the resulting diffusion of expectations, power in this ultimate sense was more diffuse, all along, than it seemed from the vantage point of Washington or Moscow. Now the diffusion of technology has been reinforced by the spread of nationalist consciousness, calling more urgently than ever for a new imagery in which each country is perceived and confronted independently in terms of its separate integrity and identity. In such an imagery, there can be no all-encompassing hierarchies or rank orders since nations are too diverse to be ranked according to a single dimension. Each country, preoccupied as it is with protecting its own identity, pursues its own interests in crisscrossing relationships that make concepts of polarity increasingly meaningless.

Given the "changing essence of power," as Seyom Brown has observed, "those with the most influence are likely to be those which are major constructive participants in the widest variety of coalitions and partnerships . . . of multiple and intersecting webs of interdependence."[5] As interdependence grows, threats of military force will progressively lose credibility, and the economic standard of power will increasingly replace the military standard as the yardstick of international relations. This does not mean, however, that the world has passed "beyond the balance of power";[6] that power rivalries no longer exist; or that military forces are no longer elements in national power. What it does mean is that the power patterns among others are beyond the manipulation of the two superpowers and are largely determined by factors unrelated to the superpower confrontation. Lesser power rivalries, in this perspective, cannot be neatly structured to fit a grand framework defined by the goal of a central nuclear equilibrium, and neither Washington nor Moscow can expect to mold intraregional power relationships on a global scale.

The bedrock determinant of intra-Asian power relationships, as this book seeks to demonstrate, lies in differing domestic foundations of nationalism reflected in differing social structures, differing stages of development, and differing degrees of social equity and social mobilization. This has been largely overlooked, however, in successive attempts to apply European balance of power precedents mechanically to Asia, first in blithe equations between the Soviet encounter with Western Europe and a presumed Chinese threat in Asia,[7] later in analogies between Metternich's entente and the multipolar diplomacy of the Nixon administration. The fact that most Asian countries are still in the early stages of the transition from traditional society to modern state, torn by internal conflicts and revolutionary upheavals natural to this phase of nation-building, sharply distinguishes the Metternich period from the present. Classical balance of power concepts assumed not only an equilibrium of power but also "some shared interest in the status quo and . . . a high degree of control over that status quo by power arrangements and diplomatic contrivances."[8] This common commitment to the status quo was explicitly articulated by Metternich himself, in terms bear-

ing a "striking similarity"9 to the contemporary response of the
affluent world to the poor world. Yet it is hardly a common
denominator in a multipolar conception embracing China; and even
Japan, a status quo country in some respects, is still basically dissatis-
fied with its relative international power position.

The domestic foundations of nationalism are only as strong as
the degree of social équity and social mobilization in a country.
Revolutionary change, therefore, is often the only way to alter a
status quo that renders the nation weak and vulnerable to external
dependence. Where the United States has approached countries
mainly in balance of power terms, this has normally led to economic
and military aid inputs that have altered the internal balance of
forces at the expense of change, frustrating the growth of a vital
nationalism, in particular, by strengthening military elites in their
competition with other elites. In general, where indigenous political
dynamism exists, external aid can give a helpful fillip, as Moscow and
Peking demonstrated in Vietnam; where it does not, external aid
infusions undermine the growth of indigenous strength by dislocating
the nation-building process. This dislocation took its most exaggerated form in divided Vietnam and Korea, but it has been vividly
apparent wherever balance of power objectives have led to the
assumption of varying degrees of U.S. responsibility for economic
development. By reducing the necessity for the domestic mobilization of resources, this assumption of vicarious responsibility has
sapped the strength of nationalism, especially where military forces
have been inflated to levels insupportable by the countries
themselves.

The failure to perceive the integral relationship between nationalism and power has consistently confused American efforts to define
a rationale governing military intervention in Asia. The American
experience in Korea only added to the confusion because in Korea,
where nationalism had been neutralized, the political soil permitted
an American intervention that was a temporary "success" in strictly
military terms but only an illusory success politically. As we have
seen, this intervention was based on a fundamental underestimation
of the long-term nationalist potential in Korea and, as a consequence,
on the questionable premise that a divided peninsula was necessary as
a guarantee of regional stability. This premise has become increasingly vulnerable as nationalism has begun to coalesce and as the
objective of an indefinitely divided Korea has been increasingly
called into question. By contrast, the objective of division proved
unambiguously futile, from the start, in the case of Vietnam, with
the crucial difference resting, as we have argued, in the success of the
Vietnamese Communists in capturing the leadership of nationalism
before the arrival of the United States on the scene.

The depth of American confusion was apparent when defenders of the Vietnam intervention drew a parallel with the failure of the League of Nations to intervene in Manchuria in September 1931, arguing that timely action to stop Japan could have forestalled the chain of events culminating in Pearl Harbor. This analogy totally discounted the fact that the domestic foundations of nationalism in China were still weak when the Japanese performed their surgical amputation. Japan was not stopped, at that point, because a deeply divided China could not and did not resist. As Walter Lippmann pointed out,

> while it is often said that the League of Nations did not stop Japanese aggression, the deeper explanation . . . is that a nation which does not fight for its own unity and sovereignty cannot be endowed with these attributes of nationhood by others. The world can only help those who help themselves, and what we call collective security can only *reinsure* the security of nations and groups of nations.[10]

After China began to search for unity in 1936, Japan accelerated its invasion timetable precisely because of its recognition that time was running out and that a unified China could not be dominated. This posed the elemental challenge to Chinese identity that crystallized the effective nationalist resistance under Communist leadership described in Chapter 3; and it was Chinese resistance that provided the basis for eventual American intervention missing in 1931.

It is not our purpose here to reassess the pros and cons of that intervention or to venture into the "might have beens" suggested by Bruce Russett in his speculative reassessment of the war.[11] Rather, it is to suggest that speculation on whether World War II could or should have been avoided should not be focused on the Manchurian issue but on the same basic bilateral conflicts of interest now dividing Japan and the United States, conflicts over markets, resources, and other issues central to the Japanese-American power relationship in its own right. The Sino-Japanese relationship had a place in the Japanese-American equation, to be sure, but the opportunity for an enduring American impact on the shape and outcome of this intra-Asian conflict came only indirectly, after the test of strength between Japanese nationalism and Chinese nationalism had taken clear indigenous form. Against this background, it is clear why attempts to make the case for intervention in Vietnam on the basis of the "lesson" learned in Manchuria[12] were so misleading. The historical judgment involved was dubious in itself, quite apart from its application to Vietnam. This was linked, in turn, to a warped view of China that ignored the early stage of its nation-building and to a misconception of the Vietnam conflict in which a struggle for national identity was treated as an extension of the cold war. Both aspects of the analogy reflected the same blind spot in confronting the phenomenon of nationalism.

When the United States set out to rebuild Japanese power after World War II, in the name of countering China, Japan not only was at a stage of development far beyond the rest of Asia but also had the built-in advantage of an unusually homogeneous social structure facilitating unusually intensive social mobilization. Peking, by contrast, was just setting forth on the road to development, greatly hampered by its unwieldiness and diversity notwithstanding its totalitarian control system. The American view of a Chinese military threat to the rest of Asia at that stage minimized the importance of the internal problems then preoccupying Peking and the constraints this placed on Chinese expansionism. The assumption of expansionist ambitions rested on two related errors. On the one hand, this view ignored the fact that China had embarked on economic policies consciously designed to maximize the potential for self-sufficiency inherent in its natural resource base and its vast internal market; on the other, it greatly exaggerated the economic advantages for Peking of annexing Southeast Asia. In reality, it was the intrinsically greater dependence of insular Japan on the world economy that led to the most serious expansionist pressures on developing countries in Asia, American-fostered economic pressures that aggravated what would have been significant regional imbalances, in any case, between Japan and its neighbors.

The nature and extent of the distortion in American perspectives was exemplified in an authoritative 1968 study contending that Chinese power had to be balanced by a forward American base presence so that Japan and India could continue to remain "viable, non-Communist states" and the intervening "intermediate areas" would not be consolidated under Chinese control. "The major states of Asia," this study concluded, "cannot or will not assume the roles of counterweights to China."[13] In one compass, this argument embodied the overestimation of China and the underestimation of Japan lying at the heart of American policy in the initial decades after World War II. Even more fundamental, it brushed aside the Japanese and Indian view that the "intermediate areas" were not threatened by direct Chinese aggression and could withstand externally supported insurgency only through internal political and economic vitalization. The Chinese acquisition of a nuclear capability came as a natural reaction to the containment policy, a defensive[14] assertion of the claim to great power status that was greatly accelerated by the sense of American, and later Soviet, encirclement.

The role of counterweights that the United States wanted to assign to Japan and India would have rendered them, in effect,

American surrogates or agents, acting out their parts in an American-authored Asian scenario that bore little relationship to the actual Asian drama as viewed from Tokyo and New Delhi. American ethnocentricity made it seem natural to assign such subordinate roles to Asian countries long regarded, for the most part, as dependents and wards. Historically, the United States had taken pride in an open-door policy toward China nominally dedicated to the principle of China's integrity as a nation and thus saw itself as better prepared to. deal with China on equal terms than the European powers. As Louis Halle has observed, however, "at least part of the reason why we Americans loved the Chinese people was that we were allowed to patronize them."[15] The United States looked with equanimity on the idea of a postwar Asian leadership role by Chiang Kai-shek's China because it was assumed that this would be a role broadly subordinate to American global interests. To argue that postwar American policy toward China reflected opposition to "one-nation dominance" in Asia, as such,[16] falsifies the record. What generated such a strong American reaction in 1949 was not the rise of a strong China, in itself, but of a China "long befriended . . . that kicked its patron in the teeth."[17] In American eyes, this new, freewheeling China seemed at least ten feet tall. Not until the Cultural Revolution did the shock wear off, leading Chalmers Johnson to report, in 1968, a growing realization that the United States had "possibly overreacted rather seriously, and that China is, in fact, beginning to look like a huge, dusty country with some very difficult internal problems."[18]

When Chiang Kai-shek fled from the mainland, Washington looked hopefully, next, to Nehru and India. The whole idea of nonalignment was to avoid the surrogate role, however, and Nehru was quick to rebuff overtures for Indo-American collaboration during his first visit to Washington in October 1949. Reporting on his talks with American officials, Nehru made his pointed statement that he had felt it to be "far more important to have a certain mutual appreciation and respect than merely to do it in a businesslike way of 'making a deal.' There is no question of a deal."[19] This was followed soon thereafter by a military alliance with Pakistan that produced an artificial offset to Indian power and led to a disastrous chain reaction of political and military consequences.

This chapter begins with an analysis of American military policy toward the Indo-Pakistan subcontinent, focusing especially on the impact of American military aid to Pakistan as a classic case history underlining the limited ability of the United States to mold intra-regional power patterns in Asia. Next, Japan is examined in terms of a kindred American effort to find a surrogate, an effort that has yet to be fully abandoned and has led to basic misunderstandings over "burden-sharing." As we shall see, the U.S. image of a Japanese military "free ride" has led to intermittent pressure for greater Japanese armament, greater support of the American nuclear deterrent, and, in some proposals, even for a nuclear Japan, preferably in the form of a "two-key" tactical nuclear capability under the United States-Japan security treaty. Yet the possibility of a nonnuclear Japan is still a real one, in this analysis, and a detached American military posture, especially on the nuclear issue, would maximize the chances for a nonnuclear outcome while minimizing tensions, at the same time, if the nuclear route is chosen.

The American experience in Japan illustrates the special intensity of the affront to nationalism that results from the establishment of U.S. bases in Asian countries. As the most visible symbols of the American presence, American bases have been a natural focus for nationalist attack, often generating political and psychological tensions even more intense and more destructive than the slow-burning conflict arising from incursions on economic sovereignty. The existence of such tensions is widely recognized, to be sure, but they have generally been minimized as the necessary incidental price for the achievement of larger strategic purposes. Both the magnitude and meaning of this price have been consistently underestimated. In most cases, the American military presence has planted the seed of enduring xenophobia and has been a subject of fundamental misunderstanding or calculated dissemblance on both sides. Host governments have accepted American forces as a quid pro quo for American military aid and for other thinly disguised expedient reasons seldom openly acknowledged. The United States, nonetheless, has been reluctant to concede the strength and breadth of antibase feeling, seeking instead to exact a measure of reciprocity or gratitude rarely accorded by the host country. It is this pervasive gap in understanding that has made the American military presence in Asia so vulnerable and explains more than any other factor why the United States should move to the more detached posture suggested in Chapter 9.

THE PAKISTAN ALLIANCE: CASE HISTORY OF A MISTAKE

South Asia and the "Northern Tier"

By the time the United States turned its attention to South Asia in the early years of the cold war, the partition of 1947 had become a settled fact, in American eyes, a dimly perceived historical chapter with little relevance in the grim perspective of the world power struggle then consuming American attention. In Indian and Pakistani eyes, however, the partition had settled nothing. It was only an episode in a continuing Hindu-Moslem rivalry over the terms of a viable regional power pattern.

Harking back to pre-Moghul times, Hindu-majority India wanted unchallenged regional dominance and a common South Asian posture toward the West reflecting Pakistani deference to New Delhi. Despite its inferior size and its division into two widely separated wings, Moslem-majority Pakistan was not yet ready to accept Indian primacy, let alone dominance, in the initial aftermath of independence. This gap between American and South Asian perspectives set the stage for a U.S. military aid policy that subsidized two wars and blocked the evolution of an indigenously rooted power relationship, in the process, leaving behind a damaging legacy of distrust in American relations with India and Pakistan alike.

The territorial settlement of 1947 came after two decades of pulling and hauling in which it was far from clear until the eleventh hour whether there would be one Pakistan, several, or none at all. The geographically dispersed but politically united Pakistan that finally emerged was an improvised, last-minute contrivance. In his 1930 proposal containing the germ of the Pakistan idea, Sir Muhammad Iqbal, the famed poet-president of the Moslem League, had envisaged a "loose federation of all India"[20] giving provincial autonomy not only to Moslem-majority areas but also to the varied linguistic and other subidentities within the larger Hindu society. Even when the idea of a sovereign Pakistan surfaced, it did not initially encompass the Moslem-majority areas of Bengal that became East Pakistan, a fact explicitly recalled by Pakistan president Zulfiqar Ali Bhutto in 1973 after the separation of Bangladesh.[21] When Bengal was later included in the first formal demand for Pakistan in 1940, the Moslem League was still seeking two completely independent Moslem-majority states, one of which would be in the northwest, one in the northeast.

The desire for a single overarching identity in the subcontinent was widespread in Moslem ranks, expressed most passionately by "nationalist Moslem" leaders in the Hindu-dominated Congress party but also by others who eventually shifted to support of the Pakistan concept. The Aga Khan spoke of a "federated Indian Commonwealth of Nations," including Moslem-majority units, and the Punjab Moslem leader Sikander Hyat Khan called for a loose federation in which the Moslem-majority states would have greater bargaining power than Iqbal had envisaged through regional groupings empowered to deal with all matters except foreign affairs, defense, tariffs, and currency. Not until the Moslem League launched its campaign of violent "direct action" in July 1946 was partition a foregone conclusion, and not until June 1947, on the very eve of the transfer of power, was the Mountbatten plan accepted and the outcome sealed.

The dominant Indian attitude toward the creation of Pakistan mingled dismay with a recognition that a loose federation would have carried its own built-in difficulties. Nehru, in particular, felt that economic development required a more unitary state and was regretfully reconciled to partition. Among Hindu conservatives, however, there was a more complicated attitude reflecting humiliating memories of the 700-year Moghul imperium. Nehru had never been able to make secularism more than a thin overlay on the vast Congress organization with its base in orthodox rural India. To Sardar Vallabhai Patel, the Tammany-style wheelhorse who built the Congress machine, Moslems were a necessary evil in the Congress and the country, to be tolerated but not to be given the kid glove treatment accorded, or so he thought, by Gandhi and Nehru. Sardar Patel had been outraged by the threat of a separate Pakistan. Ironically, though, it was Patel who clinched the creation of Pakistan, in the end, by taking the position in Congress councils that the new state would never be viable. It would be good riddance to get at least some of the Moslems off his hands, if only temporarily, and would teach them a lesson. It was deeply exasperating to most Hindus that a Moslem state should be created in part of the motherland envisaged in the ancient Hindu scriptures, and it was deeply frustrating that at the very moment when Hindus were to rule over Moslems for the first time in their history, so many of the Moslems should escape their appointed fate. The saving grace, it was assumed, was that even if the partition endured, a strategically vulnerable Pakistan, divided into two widely separated wings and weak economically in relation to India, would ultimately be compelled to accept Indian regional primacy. India was totally unprepared emotionally, in short, for the cold war intrusion that was to give Pakistan such an inflated power position.

In contrast to the Indian compulsion to pretend that Pakistan was not even there, Pakistan needed the specter of India as an ever present diversionary symbol to hold together a spiritless body politic. Pakistani nationalism rested almost entirely on an anti-Hindu raison d'être and was largely lacking in the underpinnings of a positive economic and social ideology with which Nehru had endowed the Congress movement. This was aggravated by the built-in conflict between a dominant Western wing and a more populous Bengali wing with differing linguistic and cultural patterns. In the Western wing itself, there were stresses among the Punjab, Sind, Baluchistan, and the Pathan areas of the Northwest Frontier comparable to the conflicts among Indian linguistic regions. Above all, cutting across regional divisions was a fundamental controversy over how Islamic or secular Pakistan was to be, a debate that persistently posed the issue of why Pakistan had been formed at all. The nominal raison d'être of the Pakistan movement was not merely the desire to escape Hindu domination. Pakistan was to have been a monument to the Islamic way of life, but it was immediately clear that there was no consensus as to what this meant. Modernists who wanted the commitment to an Islamic state to be nothing more than a statement of values wrangled from the inception of Pakistan with traditionalists pressing for more explicit theological guidelines. This indeterminate character of Pakistani nationalism led inexorably to an India-obsessed foreign policy and a search for ways to restore the glory of the Moghul centuries.

The idea of U.S. military aid to Pakistan was a strange compound of British Tory geopolitical thinking in the immediate aftermath of partition and the emerging cold war collective security concepts of the late Truman and early Eisenhower years. If the idea had any one author, it was Sir Olaf Caroe, a foreign secretary in New Delhi under two viceroys and an authority on Soviet central Asia. After his retirement as the last British governor of the Northwest Frontier Province in 1947, Sir Olaf became a leading proponent of the view that something had to be done to fill the "power vacuum" left by the departure of the raj.

In March 1949, he wrote an article in *Round Table* (still describing itself as "a comprehensive review of imperial politics") which was to mark the birth of the concept of a U.S. military aid role in Pakistan within the framework of the Baghdad Pact.

> The strategic movements of the Allies in Iraq and Persia in the Second War were made possible from the Indian base. . . . In this quarter, as on the Northwest Frontier, Pakistan has succeeded to much of India's responsibility, for the Gulf opens directly on Karachi, in a real sense its terminus. . . . The importance of the Gulf grows greater, not less, as the need for fuel expands, the world contracts, and the shadows lengthen from the north. Its stability can be assured only by the closest accord between the states which surround this Muslim lake, an accord underwritten by the Great Powers whose interests are engaged.[22]

Sir Olaf was not at this point sure what to expect of the new Indian government. "Any concept of defense in this region," he wrote, "must take account . . . of India as the geographical center of Southern Asia." By 1951, however, Sir Olaf had to face the implications of Nehru's by then well-articulated neutralism, and India was left outside his proposal for a defense pact of what he called the "Northern Screen" states along the Soviet border. "India," he wrote in *Wells of Power*, elaborating his earlier article, "is no longer an obvious base for Middle Eastern defense. It stands on the fringe of the defense periphery. Pakistan on the other hand lies well within the grouping of Southwestern Asia, as seen from the air." An elaborate map depicted the area to be encompassed by the new, Karachi-led defense grouping as "a great oval or ellipse." The oil sheikhdoms along the gulf "are so closely associated with the whole surrounding region," Sir Olaf emphasized, "that separate consideration in the sphere of air strategy is impossible. . . . The outer periphery must be held if the lands within the ellipse are to remain secure. . . . A circle which fails to include Pakistan is incomplete."23

In his preoccupation with the oil sheikhdoms, Sir Olaf discounted the natural interdependence of India and Pakistan and made their bad blood an argument for, rather than against, an effort to deal with Pakistan as part of the Middle East. If India's help were to be acceptable in a region "where Pakistan stands in the first line, it will be for India . . . to adjust her differences with the sister state in such a way as to strengthen and not weaken their mutual defenses. Failing a new approach in this matter the pattern will assume a different shape and the Indo-Pakistan frontier will become a permanent limit between two systems."24

Even in Britain, Sir Olaf's topi-and-jodhpurs approach was challenged by pro-Labour elements in a carry-over of the controversy that had surrounded the entire issue of Indian independence. Sir Archibald Nye, United Kingdom high commissioner in New Delhi, was among Sir Olaf's most vocal critics. In Washington, however, the Caroe message came at an impressionable moment and had a powerful impact, providing a clear rationale for advocates of a policy "choosing" between India and Pakistan. Sir Olaf frankly addressed his book to "the Americans," styling it an "attempt to catch and save a way of thought known to many who saw these things from the East, but now in danger of being lost, in the hope that new workers in the vineyard may find in it something worth regard." The British Foreign Office sent him on an American tour, and Sir Olaf later reflected that

> perhaps some of the exchanges I had with State Department officials and others along these lines were not without effect. My Pakistan friends regard me as the inventor of the Baghdad Pact! Indeed, I have more than once ventured to flatter myself that J. F. Dulles' phrase "The Northern Tier" and his association of the U.S. with the "Baghdad" countries in Asia were influenced by the thinking in *Wells of Power*. In that book I called those countries "The Northern Screen"—the same idea really.25

The divergence between an emerging Indian foreign policy of neutralism and Pakistan's eagerness for an alliance had become increasingly clear to American leaders during Nehru's 1949 visit and Pakistani premier Liaquat Ali Khan's American mission in early 1950. India was flushed with a sense of its destiny and identity in this early phase of freedom. By contrast, Pakistani nationalism, as we have seen, was defensive and insecure from the start. The Maginot Line psychology was aggravated by hostile Indian diplomatic tactics, especially in the Middle East, deliberately designed to isolate the Karachi regime. Pakistan embarked on its independent existence in a frank search for dependence on some other power strong enough to shore up its position against India and to forestall the advent of an indigenous power adjustment. Largely devoid of mass political institutions comparable in vitality to the Congress, the new state was under the effective control of a civil service–army hierarchy anxious to bolster its internal power position with a modernized military establishment, especially since Pakistan had come out second best to India in the allocation of defense equipment accompanying partition.

Liaquat was frankly on the make during his 1950 visit, prompting a prescient warning from George Kennan, then a member of the State Department policy planning staff. At a banquet in Liaquat's honor, Kennan cautioned that in dealing with developing countries, the United States should

> think not only about the psychological repercussions of the beginning of any program of special collaboration, but also about the repercussions of its termination. . . . We must observe the utmost care not to enter into relationships which might become the subject of misunderstandings either here or in the partner-country or elsewhere, or which we could not be sure of carrying through to a successful conclusion satisfactory to all concerned.[26]

Pressures for a pro-Pakistan American policy gained momentum, however, after the Korean War started and Indo-American policy differences began to sharpen. India and Pakistan voted alike in the U.N. vote on June 27, 1950, branding North Korea as the aggressor. However, Pakistan abstained on February 1, 1951, when India voted with the Soviet bloc against censuring the Chinese as aggressors, arguing that censure would inevitably lead to Chinese intervention. As the Korean War dragged on, India's vocal role in championing the admission of China to the United Nations intensified American impatience with New Delhi and emboldened advocates of a United States-Pakistan military alliance. General Hoyt Vandenberg, then air force chief of staff, conferring with Ambassador-designate Chester Bowles in September 1951, served notice that "we are going to give you some trouble out there in India because we have our eye on bases in Pakistan."[27]

In Pakistan, itself, the assassination of Liaquat Ali Khan in 1951 had ended the short-lived Moslem League dynasty that began with

Mohammed Ali Jinnah, accelerating the shift of power from political leaders to the civil service–army hierarchy that ultimately took the form of overt military rule. This coincided with the appointment of Henry Byroade as assistant secretary of state for Near East, South Asian, and African affairs in December 1951, replacing George McGhee. Byroade, a West Pointer and a protégé of Gen. George C. Marshall, had served as chief of the international affairs section of the Army General Staff until Marshall brought him to the State Department. He proved more receptive than McGhee to the Caroe line of thought then becoming popular in the Pentagon. Shortly after Byroade took over, the Pentagon was given a green light for discussions with the Pakistanis. It is not clear whether or not Byroade acted with higher clearance. The Korean War was on, and Pakistan was a very peripheral concern to a secretary of state. Dean Acheson remembered that the Pakistanis "were always asking us for arms and I was always holding them off," but he did "not recall" having been called on to decide specifically whether the Pentagon could discuss details of a grant military aid program. By March 1952, in any case, well before the end of the Truman administration, the United States was informally committed to the idea of a grant military assistance program for Karachi and had carried on extensive preliminary negotiations. Pakistani leaders utilized this commitment to force the pace of a formal agreement after the start of the Eisenhower administration.

The antineutralist accent of the nascent Dulles diplomacy and the interest of the new secretary of state in a possible "northern tier" defense pact created a more favorable U.S. climate than ever for the alliance idea after Eisenhower took over. Dulles shrugged off the anxious warnings sounded by Nehru; by retiring ambassador to India Chester Bowles; by a lonely Republican critic, Paul Hoffman; and by an American correspondent who reported from Karachi that "Pakistan is more inclined to build her military strength as a bargaining factor in dealing with India . . . than as a defense against other countries, including the Soviet Union. This is a common admission, privately expressed."28 By November 1953 Pakistani officials were confidently leaking stories of the impending compact to bring matters to a head,29 and Vice-President Richard Nixon returned from an Indo-Pakistan visit ready to put his influence on the Pakistani side in administration councils. In news briefings on his tour that I attended, Nixon made amply clear that he favored the alliance not for its purported defense value against Soviet aggression but "as a counterforce," in the words of one of his authorized early biographers, "to the confirmed neutralism of Jawaharlal Nehru's India."30 The *New York Times* reported from Karachi during Nixon's visit that the military aid decision would "determine whether India, a country often opposed to the U.S. in vital international dealings, is to achieve unquestioned dominance over this entire area . . . whether it is in the best interests of the free world to have India the only strong nation in this part of the world."[31] Similarly, the defense of the impending alliance offered by military analyst Hanson Baldwin had more to do with geopolitical "power vacuums" than with direct military advantages and could have come straight from Caroe's *Wells of Power.*

> The problem which the Pakistan arms aid program is intended to relieve . . . stems chiefly from the decline in power of the British Empire. . . . British power, exercised largely by the British-led Indian Army, once dominated the entire strategic arc from Suez and the Persian Gulf eastward to Burma and Malaya. . . . But the post-war rise of nationalism in the Middle East and Asia, plus the increasing threat of Communism and Nehru's anti-Westernism, altered the entire strategic picture.[32]

Nehru's open protests led to a last-minute quest for a formula to mollify India, but by February 1954 the alliance had been formally concluded. Initially projected as a program of only $25 million, the Pakistan military aid program eventually reached a cumulative total of $1.5 billion in weaponry and in defense-related economic aid.

The alliance decision was made at a time when the developing military crisis in Vietnam had deepened Korea-born fears that the United States would sooner or later face a series of communist military thrusts in Asia. It was in December 1953 that the French retreated to Dien Bien Phu, and the military arguments for a United States–Pakistan pact understandably seemed more important under these circumstances than they now appear in retrospect. The Dulles rationale was essentially that the martial Punjabis and Pathans of Pakistan would be stalwart additions to the local forces needed throughout Asia to deter Moscow and Peking and would cost the U.S. taxpayer much less than equivalent regiments of GIs. Jet airstrips built for the Pakistani air force would be invaluable in a crisis, it was argued, offering an alternate escape route, a "point of return" for U.S. planes after forays into Soviet territory. As later developments were to show, however, the ostensible military rationale revealed only part of the thinking that underlay the alliance. Long after it was generally acknowledged that Pakistan had sought arms for use as a counter to India, rather than the communist powers, the United States nonetheless extended the alliance tie in 1958 in order to get its electronic intelligence installations in Peshawar;[33] five years after the ouster of the Peshawar facility in 1966, the White House was still "tilting" against India in favor of Pakistan during the Bangladesh crisis.

The consistent strand running through the many twists and turns of U.S. South Asian policy has been an implicit view of both India

and Pakistan as pawns in the great power game. In the thinking of
many American officials, it was for the United States to decide
whether and how to utilize them for American purposes or to
checkmate their use by others. Thus, in the Nixon attitude so
widespread in 1954, cold war priorities dictated strengthening Pakistan and weakening India. Later, the objective shifted to strengthening both India and Pakistan against China, preserving an American-
determined balance between them for the sake of their common
confrontation with Peking. Finally, during the Bangladesh crisis, as
we shall see, Pakistan was seen for all practical purposes as China's
pawn and India as the Soviet Union's, with the American interest
limited to making certain that neither Peking nor Moscow had a
"destabilizing" monopoly of influence in the subcontinent. The
power of nationalism in both South Asian countries was consistently
underrated, in this perspective, and the ability of the external powers
to manipulate regional power relationships consistently exaggerated.

In Indian eyes, the Pakistan military aid program was inevitably
viewed as a new variant of British divide-and-rule tactics, the cutting
edge of some deep crypto-imperialism, and the United States soon
became the target for the sublimated feelings toward Pakistan that
had been present since partition. This was true from the Communists
on the left to Hindu chauvinists and anticommunist conservatives on
the right. Nikita Khrushchev made a blatant play to the Hindu
gallery on his 1955 visit, declaring his "absolute conviction" that
"when passions have calmed down and people realize the significance
of this Partition, of such an artificial division of India, they will
regret it."[34] Even Swatantra party leader Chakravarti Rajagopalachari wrote that

> it makes little real difference if we first overspend on defense and then
> depend on American or other foreign assistance for welfare work or whether
> we do it the other way about. . . . And what a curious game it is for America
> to lend or give to each country in the name of making an anti-Communist
> bastion, but really the defense expenditure in each country is for defense or
> offense against the other country as between India and Pakistan—a fact
> known to but winked at by the foreign aid-giving government. . . . It is a
> tragedy how what could have been such a great and prosperous and happy
> nation now stands divided and reduced to so painful a dependence after
> independence.[35]

American indifference to the South Asian perspective was apparent
in recurrent offers of U.S. military aid to India made to establish
U.S. impartiality in the subcontinental rivalry. Since the Indian
objective was a subordinate Pakistan, there was nothing to be gained
from American arms aid if it were paralleled by aid to Pakistan, and
an embargo on arms assistance to both countries would have been

considerably more palatable to New Delhi than a program resulting in increased Pakistani firepower.

From 1956 until 1960, before India had carried out its military counterbuildup in response to the aid pact, the Pakistani army held a four-to-one edge in armor. Although this had been narrowed down to near parity by the 1965 Indo-Pakistan war, partly as the result of Soviet aid, Pakistan nonetheless approached the war with a margin of operational superiority. The U.S. military aid relationship had established a spare parts pipeline, petroleum supplies, and maintenance facilities far surpassing those of the Indian army during years of foreign exchange scarcity, giving Karachi a presumed three-to-one edge in battle-ready "effectives." Beyond this, Pakistan had a prewar edge in the crucial category of heavy armor, with more than 330 Patton M-48s, on top of a smaller number of British-made Centurions, as against India's estimated 225 Centurions. With its Pattons, its self-propelled artillery, and its supersonic aircraft, Pakistan had achieved overall qualitative superiority by 1965. India had a four-to-one margin in the number of planes. This was misleading, though, since the meaningful comparison was between Pakistan's U.S.-supplied F-86 jet fighters and India's Mysteres. The effective margin of Indian superiority in the air was estimated at two to one.[36]

As the 1965 war showed, this command of the air, combined with the Indian army's numerical superiority and Pakistan's inherent strategic vulnerability, canceled out the advantages conferred by U.S. military aid to Pakistan. Moreover, it turned out that the Pentagon had kept Pakistan on a thirty-day supply leash, and in the critical stages of the war American curtailment of petroleum, ammunition, and spares robbed Pakistan of the most important advantages of the aid link. In New Delhi, however, what counted politically was the passionately held conviction that Washington had emboldened Pakistan to thumb its nose at India, in the first place, and was thus responsible for the very fact that a war had occurred at all.

The emotional impact of the Pakistan military aid program in India was heightened in the critical 1960-1965 period by the simultaneous burgeoning of Indo-U.S. economic and military aid relationships designed, in the American conception, to bolster India's power position vis-à-vis China. As India's economic dependence had increased, so had its dismay over the American role in Pakistan. It was bad enough for a proud, newly independent Asian country to become a client seeking ever expanding aid from a rich Western patron. The necessity to acknowledge this status in the face of the persistent affront of a military buildup in Pakistan added to the strains in the Indo-American relationship. At the same time, the fact that Pakistan's developing ties with China and the USSR during this period had not cooled its relations with the United States baffled the many Indians who were unaware of the hush-hush American electronic intelligence installations at Peshawar. Despite the ill-fated adventure of Francis Gary Powers in 1960, resulting in the end of Pakistan-based U-2 overflights, the United States had continued to maintain its highly prized electronic eavesdropping facilities at Peshawar; since these were nominally secret, the United States had never been able to explain the continuance of the alliance in blithe disregard of Pakistan's "normalization" of its relations with Peking and Moscow.

The Search for a Regional Balance

India's modest, $84.5 million program of U.S. military aid after its 1962 border clashes with China involved peculiarly intense stresses. In seeking this aid, India had been no more candid than Pakistan, for a balance of power with China was hardly the only Indian objective. India hoped also to use its military connection with the United States to loosen Washington's tight ties with Pakistan and to build a self-sufficient military base that would indirectly serve to strengthen the Indian position against Pakistan. This veiled difference of approach led to continual friction in the abortive Indo-U.S. negotiations over an enlarged program of American military aid that continued until mid-1964. American planners were seeking to reconcile simultaneous military aid to their two South Asian clients by ordaining, from Washington, what would constitute a stable regional balance of power. Even before the border conflict with China, the United States had implicitly accepted Pakistan's argument that the proper purpose of U.S. arms aid was to promote a military balance with India and Afghanistan. President Kennedy and Marshal Ayub agreed with studied ambiguity in their 1961 communiqué that Pakistan could use U.S. military aid to maintain its "security," omitting any reference to the original anticommunist premises of the alliance.

In marked contrast to the new U.S. approach, the Soviet policy clearly recognized Indian objectives and offered aid without strings. Initially, Soviet military aid was kept in balance with American aid and India hoped to avoid the one-sided dependence that later developed. By the eve of the 1965 war, however, the collapse of the American effort to preside over a regional balance had opened the way for a Soviet-oriented military aid dependence. Columnist Romesh Thapar angrily charged that

> tanks were denied to us because we were told that we were likely to use them against Pakistan. The naval shopping list, so essential for the defense of the Andamans and Nicobars, was also described as likely to make the Pakistanis suspicious. In fact, it was pointed out that the Anglo-American naval concentration in Southeast Asia was adequate protection for the

Indian Ocean. The argument clearly revealed what was intended—an India forever dependent on western protection. It's cheap, they said. And we were encouraged to go West in the hope that we would receive free gifts of equipment. We shall pay in rupees—to the Soviet Union. It's healthier. [37]

Former ambassador Chester Bowles believes that President Kennedy was about to abandon the balancing objective at the time of his death and recalls that Kennedy had scheduled a critical National Security Council meeting for November 26, 1963, just four days after his assassination occurred. Bowles was seeking a $500 million military aid program designed to improve the Indian defense posture vis-à-vis China regardless of how this affected the Indian-Pakistani balance. [38] This would have neutralized, to some extent, the profound hostility engendered by the Pakistan buildup and would have obviated the necessity for a lopsided Soviet arms dependence. Like the earlier, emergency arms aid of 1962, it would have been an expedient Band-Aid useful for plastering over the deep emotional wounds then troubling Indo-American relations. As we will explain in Chapter 10, however, the Bowles program would have embodied the central error of cold war military aid in Pakistan and other countries by making too easily available on a grant or concessional basis arms that would otherwise have had to be justified in internal budgetary battles. Had such a program become self-multiplying and open-ended, like so many other U.S. arms aid programs, it could have had new distorting effects on the evolution of locally rooted power relationships. In strictly military terms, Chinese ambitions with respect to India were generally viewed in exaggerated terms during this period. [39] As the shock of 1962 receded, it became increasingly clear that the China-oriented deterrent value of external arms aid was subsidiary, in Indian eyes, to its impact on the regional balance with Pakistan.

India has consistently attempted to utilize both its modest American military aid and its estimated $1 billion in Soviet arms aid to establish defense industries of its own. One should not go overboard, in any case, when estimating the long-term impact of the Soviet dependence on such a big country with such a strong nationalist commitment. The impact could prove greater in the other South Asian country most sharply affected by the Pakistan aid program, undeveloped Afghanistan, where social mobilization is limited, nationalism has a narrow base, and geography inhibits freedom of action to an unusual degree. Kabul turned to Moscow immediately after the conclusion of the alliance in 1954, and by 1967 the Afghan armed forces were "almost completely dependent" on the Soviet Union not only for equipment but also for logistic support. Soviet economic and military aid then totaled more than $600 million, as against $340 million in U.S. aid.

In Pakistan as in India, the 1965 war marked the climax of a crisis of confidence that had been steadily building up under the stresses of the U.S. effort to stabilize a regional balance. The Kennedy administration had attempted to combine its shift to a newly positive U.S. approach toward India, accepting neutralism, with the retention of the Pakistan alliance. From the Pakistani standpoint, the terms of the regional balance envisaged by the United States under this new approach would have meant Indian "hegemony"[40] even without the straightforward pro-Indian shift sought by Bowles. What was left of the spirit of 1954 quickly vanished when the United States cut off military aid evenhandedly to both sides during the war. Since the United States had complete information on Pakistan's supply position and since Pakistan, unlike India, depended wholly on its U.S. supply line, the cutoff was viewed as a deliberately pro-Indian move.

The depth and violence of Pakistan's reaction to its "betrayal" were basically the result of an ambivalent attitude toward the United States that had festered beneath the surface from the very beginnings of the alliance. Pakistan's politically conscious middle class had a world view differing little from India's. As Keith Callard observed in his sympathetic 1958 study of Pakistani foreign policy, there was a limited consciousness of Middle East and Islamic world ties in the case of West Pakistan that added an extra dimension to its perspective not found in New Delhi. But this was missing in East Pakistan, and in general, Callard found, Pakistan had "no strong convictions about the balance of righteousness between the West and the Communist powers" before 1953 and "shared many of the preconceptions of those areas of Asia and Africa that have recently secured independence," notably a general acceptance of the Leninist theory of imperialism and the sentiment of "Asian, or perhaps non-white solidarity."[41] With their Afro-Asian preconceptions, most of Pakistan's politically conscious elements looked on the alliance with the United States as a distasteful marriage of convenience and would have been more comfortable with a neutralist policy, perhaps less pretentious and less abrasive in tone than the Indian variety often seemed to be but nonetheless a policy unfettered by alignment in the cold war.

Although India was often criticized in the United States for its China policy, Pakistan, too, was one of the first nations to recognize the Peking regime. Madame Sun Yat-sen was received as a state guest in Karachi in 1956, and in June 1957, the prime minister and foreign minister were scheduled to leave for Peking until U.S. pressure forced cancellation of their tour. Former prime minister H. S. Suhrawardy did finally go to China in October 1957, leading to a return visit by Chou En-lai in December. Zulfiqar Ali Bhutto, who was later to initiate close ties with Peking as foreign minister, began to extricate Pakistan from the anti-China assumptions of the alliance as early as November 1962, when he told the National Assembly that Pakistani friendship with Peking was an "independent factor" and that "even if the Kashmir dispute is settled amicably, we will not join India against China." The Western objective of joint defense for the Indian subcontinent presumed a hostile China, he said, but it might be that "the answer for both India and Pakistan lies in finding some sort of equation between ourselves without jeopardizing our friendship with China. If we both pursue a correct policy, the question of joint defense will not become relevant." In an interview soon afterward, Bhutto first set forth the concept of a Pakistani-American identity of interest with respect to China that was to figure significantly in his policies and that he was to elaborate to me frequently in subsequent years. In the short run, he acknowledged, Sino-Pakistani ties would be damaging to Pakistani-American relations, but before long China and the United States would patch up their differences, "probably in the early Seventies." China merited Pakistani friendship, in any case, as "a champion of Asian self-respect and self-reliance widely admired in Pakistan." This rationale not only was compelling in itself, he said, but also would acquire added magnetism if the India-China rivalry were to intensify, leading to an implicit mutuality of security interests between Pakistan and China.[42]

Bhutto was correct in his calculation that the Sino-Indian conflict would intensify, and the Sino-Pakistani relationship soon became essentially an India-focused relationship, culminating in Peking's ultimatum to New Delhi at the height of the 1965 war and in substantial Chinese military aid. Yet the China tie also had the more wide-ranging appeal in Pakistan that he had perceived—to pan-Asian feelings, to ideological doubts about the big business cast of the Ayub Khan regime, and to popular sympathy with China's development struggles. This was apparent in the explosion of neutralist sentiment following the 1965 cease-fire. Bhutto personally capitalized on his identification with the China relationship during his subsequent rise to political power. For somewhat different reasons, the Soviet Union also proved to have greater appeal than had been evident during the alliance years, though a considerably less potent appeal than that of China. Pakistan was immediately responsive when Moscow showed a new readiness for limited ties following Nehru's death in 1964. Important bureaucratic elements, in particular, eyed public sector development aid that had not been available from

Washington. Both China and the Soviet Union were attractive to Pakistani planners as sources of diversified soft loan aid after so many years of a narrow U.S. dependency.

Pakistan had swallowed its pride and had entered the alliance in order to utilize the United States in outflanking India. Thus, when the United States attempted to be India's friend, too, the sacrifice of freedom of action in world affairs necessitated by the alliance became increasingly intolerable. The birth of neutralism came long before the start of military aid to India, often depicted as the sole provocation for the post-1962 neutralist shift. The belief that the alliance could have been maintained if only the United States had refrained from aiding India rested on a very narrow definition of "Pakistan." For a military elite that had fortified its domestic power through external support, and for business-oriented bureaucratic factions concerned primarily with the U.S.-financed flow of imports for private industry, a return to 1954-type normalcy after 1965 might have had its attractions. For public opinion generally, however, the end of the alliance was an opportunity to move simultaneously toward a more self-respecting world role and, it was hoped, toward more broadly based political processes in Pakistan itself. The alliance had never been subjected to the sort of open debate that accompanied the formulation of Indian foreign policy. Popular at first, it had been increasingly identified with unpopular authoritarian ruling groups, especially by Bengali East Pakistan. As the Bengali former premier H. S. Suhrawardy wrote during the early years of the alliance, it had been conceived and negotiated

> as the business of a few ministers sheltered in secrecy. The result has been a set of commitments in the legal sense, yet not sufficiently felt as commitments in the consciousness of the people themselves. . . . The very secrecy with which our engagements have been entered into, the lack of public airing in debate, has left them vulnerable to suspicion that they have somehow rendered us subservient and then drained away our autonomy.[43]

The impact of U.S. military aid grants on the interplay between elite groups in Pakistan not only gave the military an edge over civil service and political factions. In so doing, it also strengthened and hardened the dominant position of West Pakistan over the numerically superior Eastern wing, thus accelerating a breakup of Pakistan that might otherwise have occurred under circumstances more favorably suited to an Indo-Pakistan accommodation. The social base of the Pakistani armed forces has been overwhelmingly West Pakistani. Moreover, as we saw in an earlier chapter, the West Pakistani-dominated military juntas that controlled Pakistan prior to 1972 worked hand in hand with narrowly based business groups that were also similarly centered in the western wing.

American military aid grants helped to give the ruling military-business leadership their entrenched position in the West, and this, in turn, encouraged their unyielding response in the face of an increasingly determined Bengali posture.

It might very well be that military rule would have come to Pakistan in one way or another, whatever the United States had done, and that the eventual collapse of the partition settlement was foreordained by the inherent anomaly of a state so diverse and so geographically truncated. This view is supported by the fact that the creation of Bangladesh marked the precise fulfillment of the original 1940 Moslem League demand for two independent Moslem states in the northwest and northeast of the subcontinent. The inevitability of a total East-West rupture must remain a moot point, however, as W. H. Morris-Jones has argued, [44] and one of the crucial factors to be considered in speculation on this issue is the interaction between autonomy demands in the Eastern and Western wings. Under military-dominated regimes, Bengali autonomy demands posed a direct threat to the ruling power groups since concessions to autonomy in the East would have intensified Pathan and Baluchi demands in the West. By contrast, given a looser, federal pattern in the West, and a more broadly based power structure, Bengali, Pathan, and Baluchi interests would have been mutually reinforcing. The struggle in the West was closely divided in the fifties between advocates of federalism, on the one hand, and the "one-unit" setup finally adopted. In the absence of U.S. arms aid, some form of accommodation might well have evolved between a less cocky military hierarchy and other West Pakistani elite groups. Even after a decade of the Ayub Khan regime, there was a powerful surge of unified action among Bengali, Pathan, and Baluchi groups during the stormy interval of relative political freedom spanning the last months of Ayub and the Yahya Khan coup.

My own conversations with Nehru revealed that at the time of his death, he was seeking to move toward an overall South Asian confederation plan that would have retained an altered Pakistan, at least transitionally trading a newly autonomous status for the Eastern wing within Pakistan for comparable autonomy to Kashmir within the Indian framework. Nehru felt that West Pakistan would be more likely to accept the Indian primacy implicit in a confederation if it continued to retain a reassuring special link with East Pakistan. By the same token, he reasoned, full sovereignty for the East would breed paranoia in the West and complicate Indo-Pakistan accommodation. [45] Even after the start of the Bangladesh hostilities, many Indian leaders would still have preferred to see a loosely confederated Pakistan. This would have been much less costly for India, economically, than the sequence of events that ensued, while still assuring a greatly weakened Pakistan. It would have denied the symbolism of Bangladesh to separatist elements in the south Indian state of Tamilnad and to Bengali regionalists in Indian West Bengal. After the carnage in Dacca on March 25, however, the Bangladesh movement acquired a momentum of its own. Each passing month made the possibility of a confederation compromise that much more remote and increased the internal Indian political pressures for a military move that would annul the partition settlement once and for all. A Bengali Moslem identity that had been sharpening for years under the repression of the West rapidly crystallized into a full-blown nationalism after the Dacca massacre.

American efforts to salvage a confederated Pakistan in late 1971 failed to take into account the strong bargaining position of the pro-independence forces in the Bangladesh movement resulting from this birth of nationalism. Saddled firmly to West Pakistan, the United States rationalized Yahya Khan's unwillingness to release Sheikh Mujibur Rahman and suggested terms for a confederation bargain that basically reflected the West Pakistani stand.[46] Despite the destructive role played by the United States in the long chain of events leading up to this spectacular climax, Washington piously lectured from the sidelines until the very eve of the Indian invasion. To Henry Kissinger, the United States had engaged in a "love affair" with India reflected in American economic aid and admiration for a demanding development effort under democratic auspices. It was thus a source of "enormous pain," he said, to watch "military action taken without adequate cause . . . to dismember a sovereign state and a member of the U.N."[47] To India, however, the United States had consistently shown hostility on the one issue closest to Indian hearts by seeking to freeze the 1947 settlement.

In defense of the Nixon policy, many have argued that the close White House collaboration with Yahya in the 1971 China break-through left no alternative to a pro-Pakistan "tilt" during the Bangla-desh crisis. This implies that the Bangladesh policy was a temporary tactical aberration, but in reality it was merely one facet of Nixon's approach to South Asia as an arena of multipolar diplomacy. Disenchanted with their development problems and their internecine strife, the United States had consciously backed away from India and Pakistan after 1968, confident that Soviet and Chinese influence would balance each other and thus compensate for the termination of a direct U.S. balancing role. It was this approach to the subcontinent that accounted for the intensity of his reaction when the president reached his highly questionable conclusion that India sought to destroy West Pakistan. Nixon's dismay was occasioned not by any dedication to the Pakistani cause, as such, but by his fear that the

Sino-Soviet balance in the subcontinent would be upset by the removal of China's pawn from the game.[48] It was an image of the crisis as mainly a Soviet gambit that also explained the quixotic dispatch of the *Enterprise*. After the Indian victory, the United States sought to rectify what it saw as a new imbalance by siding with China and Pakistan on the Kashmir issue in the 1972 Shanghai communiqué and by cautiously loosening up the restraints on arms to Pakistan imposed after the 1965 war. Returning full circle to the Caroe approach of 1949, Washington proceeded to build up Iranian power, not only as a counter to the Soviet presence in the Middle East and the Persian Gulf but also to offset India's Soviet-supported naval ambitions in the Indian Ocean.

BURDEN-SHARING AND A NUCLEAR JAPAN

The Tacit Trade-Off

The American-Japanese security relationship has been molded by a basic underestimation of Japanese nationalism and has been a focus of continuing friction and controversy. Viewing a vanquished rival through superpower lenses, the United States saw only physical devastation and economic prostration. American policy minimized the psychological and social strength that gives Japan its powerful inner dynamism. Not only did this lead to a remarkably wanton approach to the economic reconstruction of Japan as a cold war bastion—billions in reconstruction aid, indiscriminate infusions of the best in American technology, and American-aided access to markets and raw materials in Asia under artificial, optimum conditions. Militarily, too, the cold war objective of a stronger Japan reflected a profoundly patronizing assessment of Japanese ambitions and of the Japanese potential. As we shall see, recurring American pressures for Japanese rearmament have betrayed an implicit long-term view of Japan as an American surrogate or, at the very least, as a dependent junior partner sharing a predestined mutuality of interest.

Not surprisingly, this patronizing image of Japan has gone together with a correspondingly benign American self-image that made a clash of perspectives concerning the security relationship inevitable. As many Americans see it, the United States showed a rare benevolence in helping a defeated enemy to its feet, and the affluent Japan of the seventies should feel indebted for past assistance as well as for its continuing military "free ride."[49] Without American loan capital and technical help, this view holds, not to mention the Japanese earnings from the Korean and Vietnamese wars, Japan could never have achieved its "economic miracle." The return of Okinawa is perceived in this light as the crowning instance of a consistently generous American attitude that now calls for a spirit of reciprocity at a time when the United States faces balance of payments deficits. This concept of a "debt" is flatly rejected by Japan, however, reflecting as it does widely divergent perspectives on the nature of American motives and on the real meaning of the security connection.

In Japanese eyes, the idea of a debt is completely inconsistent with the fact that the United States rebuilt Japan for its own strategic reasons as an industrial bulwark against the Soviet Union and China. Most Japanese acknowledge that the cold war was a bonanza, greatly speeding their recovery, but this is seen as an incidental by-product of American policies conceived with American purposes uppermost. The postwar "miracle" is viewed as a natural outgrowth of the progress Japan had achieved on its own before the war. This progress is attributed to many of the same factors typically cited by foreign observers—a unified social structure unique in Asia, a driving nationalism, and a disciplinarian work ethic—all-important qualities that basically explain, in the Japanese self-image, why they were able to make more effective use of the cold war dollars flowing their way than most other Asian countries. During the Korean War, it is argued, Japanese technical know-how made Japan an indispensable logistical base for U.S. forces, and the rebirth of Japanese industry generated by Korea-related contracts was the product not of U.S. magnanimity but of sheer necessity. In any case, a sharp distinction is made in Japanese thinking between the economic stimulus provided by the Korean War at a critical moment in the recovery process and what is seen as the more marginal impact of Vietnam at a time when the postwar growth spiral had already acquired its own momentum. As for Okinawa, the United States decided to give the island back, in the Japanese view, only when this was deemed the best way to neutralize growing anti-Americanism and thereby to prolong the U.S. base presence there. President Nixon completely robbed the gesture of even the appearance of magnanimity, in the Japanese image, when he linked reversion with a Japanese promise to limit textile exports.

Far from feeling indebted for the U.S. military presence, Japanese spokesmen cite the market value of the real estate used for bases, contending that this has easily outweighed U.S. foreign exchange outlays for the operation of facilities in Japan.[50] Indeed, American bases have been a continual affront to nationalist feeling not only because they serve as a reminder of Japan's defeat in the war but also because they have been used for American military purposes in Asia that were deeply repugnant to most Japanese. The contrast between the Japanese perception of the American presence and the sanguine American self-image in Japan has been documented in a significant unpublished case study of the interaction between two adjacent U.S. Army posts and the surrounding communities in the Kantō Plain near Kamagaya. The late William L. Caudill and Mieko Imagi Caudill, assisted by Japanese researchers and a psychological testing team from the Walter Reed Army Medical Service Graduate School, found that nearly 70 percent of the American military personnel interviewed regarded Japanese attitudes toward the U.S. base presence as favorable. Interviews with Japanese produced estimates of Japanese attitudes that were almost the precise reverse of the American results, with the contrast between U.S. enlisted men and ordinary, nonofficial Japanese especially pronounced. The prevailing sentiment among the Japanese was that it was "not natural" for the United States to defend Japan and that "the Americans were guarding Japan out of self-interest, rather than out of any particular concern for Japan itself." As one Japanese official noted, "some businessmen who profit from the bases don't mind them," but the "decent people" were distressed by the mass influx of camp followers and the ugly, new shantytown of bars and brothels that had suddenly sprung up amid previously placid rice paddies.[51]

For the most part, the United States has tended to dismiss expressions of antibase sentiment as the manipulations of unrepresentative, vocal minorities or as the product of isolated local grievances resulting from the concentration of key bases near expanding urban centers. But opposition to the American base presence persists even though Washington moved to scale down and relocate U.S. installations in 1970, reflecting the deeper psychological factors underlying the popular attitude. Most Japanese feel that they are doing the United States a favor by granting bases and that the United States, rather than Japan, is the indebted party in the relationship.

Even with respect to the nuclear umbrella, as we shall elaborate later, the Japanese approach has been ambivalent, clashing directly with the underlying assumption of the "total force" defense strategy that allies have an obligation to help the United States in maintaining its defense shield. The dominant but seldom stated Japanese attitude was expressed in a 1970 government think tank study dwelling at length on the debt issue and contending, in particular, that "the protection given to Japan under the U.S. nuclear umbrella does not increase the cost for America, since Japan or no Japan, the U.S.

would have its Polaris and Poseidon missiles in the Pacific. The Security Treaty enables America to maintain an effective deterrent against China and the U.S.S.R. at a lower cost than would otherwise be possible."[52] Kazushige Hirasawa, former editor of the *Japan Times*, has argued that in view of the Soviet-American nuclear monopoly "the offer of nuclear protection is not a favor but rather an obligation which the U.S. must discharge in response to Japan's commitment to oppose nuclear proliferation. . . . Japan is entitled to ask for the protection of the American nuclear umbrella."[53]

The motive is supremely important in the traditional Japanese code of honor. One incurs a *giri*, or generalized sense of obligation, to another only if the giver gives in a selfless, forthright spirit, never suggesting that a deal has been struck or that reciprocity is expected. Once incurred, however, a *giri* weighs heavily, requiring multiple repayment. It is therefore best to avoid this burden if at all possible, handling most of life's transactions on a one-shot, businesslike, tit-for-tat basis. Japanese are compelled by their social norms to take obligations very, very seriously. Precisely for this reason they have unusually definite notions about just what does or does not constitute indebtedness, and they are extremely chary of acknowledging indebtedness where there is as much ambiguity as one finds manifest in most aspects of the American postwar role. Herbert Glazer has observed, in a similar vein, that since "the Western morality of helping a man when he's down does not exist in Japan . . . the man who is helped up does not feel grateful. Rather, he feels ashamed at having received help and resentful at the man who helped him and who, by helping him, made him feel ashamed and embarrassed."[54]

Fundamental differences over the gravity of the threat posed by the Soviet Union and China underlay the emotional confusion surrounding the debt issue from the start. Rejecting George Kennan's proposal for a neutral Japan,[55] Secretary of State Dulles saw the communist threat as a clear and present one, and as early as 1950, Dulles launched what was to become a continual U.S. campaign for Japanese rearmament and for a regional Japanese defense role. The late Premier Yoshida recalled his bitter arguments with Dulles over rearmament as well as his determined efforts to negotiate an acceptable security relationship with the United States.[56] As Martin Weinstein showed in his study of the origins of the Japan-United States security treaty, Yoshida wanted the American alliance mainly for Japanese-centered, geopolitical reasons transcending the cold war, not because he shared the Dulles perspective of a rigid dichotomy between a righteous United States and an expansionist communism with unlimited ambitions. Given the developing Moscow-Washington confrontation, it was a matter of deciding which side could best be utilized for promoting Japanese interests. For many Japanese leaders of the Yoshida generation, it was conventional wisdom that Japan stood to profit from division between Russia and America and would suffer, conversely, if the two ever joined forces. The alliance was also viewed as a way of assuring the early end of the occupation and the restoration of Japanese sovereignty. To the extent that Yoshida saw a clear and present Soviet threat, this was limited to the uncertain first years following V-J Day. Thereafter, the communist threat was viewed largely as an internal one, part of a broader domestic leftist challenge that conservative leaders undertook to handle themselves as a quid pro quo for the security treaty. In general, as Weinstein concluded, while Yoshida was "quick to see that for Japan, a bit of cold war might not be such a bad thing," it also "seemed terrifyingly possible . . . that the United States was overreacting to the Communist victory in China and the war in Korea . . . that the Americans might provoke an avoidable showdown with the Russians in northeast Asia." Once the U.S. base presence was established under the treaty, therefore, "the Japanese leaders concentrated their efforts from that time on to gaining a veto over the use of those forces and having them reduced to a symbol of the American guarantee."[57]

For all practical purposes, successive Japanese conservative regimes have regarded their "special relationship" with the United States as a tacitly understood trade-off in which Tokyo has provided military privileges and foreign policy support in exchange for U.S. solicitude in economic matters. Tokyo has valued its military alliance with Washington primarily as a means of helping to assure access to the American market as well as to stable supplies of foodgrains and to a variety of natural resources, notably oil, enriched uranium and coking coal. Thus, Makoto Momoi, calling for "de-Americanization in strategic concepts" in a 1973 work, declared that a vanquished Japan "had no other option" in the 1950s but complete military reliance on the United States and had continued this reliance in the 1960s "as a matter of political and economic expediency, at a time when Japan was simply too busy with its economic activities to pay attention to military affairs."[58] Similarly, Kei Wakaizumi, writing in 1975, has also explained Japanese support for the treaty largely in terms of bilateral political and economic relations with the United States. "In reality," he said,

> it is probably the uncertainty of what the American reaction would be in the Treaty's absence that generates support for it, rather than the fear of destroying the existing international balance. The Japanese are unwilling to second-guess whether the United States would retain active and friendly relations without the Security Treaty.[59]

The Japanese attitude was clearly understood by American business leaders with interests in Japan, one of whom complained during the early months of the Nixon administration that the United States has directed its relationship with Japan primarily toward political and military objectives. While Japanese leaders have negotiated on political and military subjects, the prime focus of the Japanese has been on economic gain. U.S. officials have failed to grasp the subtle policy concepts underlying the Japanese economic thrusts and have consistently bartered economic advantages for political and military concessions of little consequence.[60]

It was also instinctively recognized by the Japanese public, which explains in part why the conservatives continued to win elections[61] despite widespread fears of involvement in an "American war" in Korea and consistently strong antibase sentiment focused on the use of American installations, especially in Okinawa, for storing nuclear weapons and servicing nuclear-equipped planes and ships. To the extent that the security treaty had its rationale in the protection of Japan itself, it enjoyed a measure of positive support in its own right from a conservative minority. Increasingly, however, it was openly interpreted by U.S. spokesmen as an element in the larger American Far Eastern defense scheme, with Japan assigned the task of its own conventional defense. By and large, the alliance was politically tolerable in Japan only on the strength of its economic rewards; as a consequence, periodic efforts to push Japan into directly or indirectly "sharing the burden" of its defense have been politely parried.

When Washington tried to drive a hard economic bargain, Tokyo's ultimate defense during the early years of the alliance was the unspoken threat of a rupture in the security link. This defense was no longer reliable, however, once the Nixon administration started taking a tougher economic stance toward Tokyo, and the 1972 "Nixon shocks" produced unprecedented strains in the special relationship. What made the impact of the Nixon moves so traumatic and so enduring was not the change in America's China policy, as such, for this was consistent with the widespread pro-Peking feeling in Japan. The severity of the impact came primarily from the fact that a simultaneous shift to a hard-line economic policy accompanied the unilateral execution of the China initiative. To be sure, the trauma was heightened by the sense of betrayal resulting from a sudden, unilateral American initiative, coming after so many years of reluctant Japanese acquiescence in cold war policies that were widely rejected elsewhere in Asia. But beneath the sense of betrayal lay the deeply unsettling realization that Nixon had called into question the entire postwar pattern of Japanese-American relations. In effect, the White House had served notice that military and political factors would thereafter be subordinate to, or at best coequal with, economic factors. The president's desire to change the bidding in the

Japanese-American relationship was explicitly spelled out in 1973 when he offered his own conception of the trade-off between economic and security factors in terms that were the complete reverse of the Japanese image. "Without conscious effort of political will," Nixon warned in his State of the World message, "our economic disputes could tear the fabric of our alliance."[62]

From the Japanese perspective, it was difficult to know what to make of an American policy that blithely attempted to preserve the alliance bereft of its economic payoff. The security treaty was clearly destined to become a liability if the United States treated it as a lever for extracting economic concessions. At the same time, the central Japanese objective in the American relationship continued to be access to the American market, and abrogation of the treaty was viewed as a needless irritant to American sentiment. In the wake of the Nixon and Tanaka visits to Peking the Japanese public tended to favor a policy of benign neglect, with a progressively skeletonized alliance retained for such symbolic value as it still had until both sides were equally prepared to write it off. Opponents of military expansion saw the symbolism of the treaty as a temporary brake on Japanese defense budgets. Even proponents of a bigger defense capability felt that the alliance might be milked to the Japanese advantage a bit longer, especially for the acquisition of specialized military technology, and they were in no hurry to force the issue.

From the dominant American perspective, however, benign neglect was more difficult to accept. Under the "total force" strategic concept initiated by former defense secretary Laird, the United States could reduce its worldwide commitments only if there were allies ready to play a compensating role at their own expense, if possible under overall U.S. control. The new doctrine led to an intensification of U.S. "burden-sharing" pressures at the very time when the hard-line Nixon economic approach made the foundations of the alliance weaker than ever before in Japan.

The burden-sharing emphasis of the Nixon administration was not a mere expedient response to the balance of payments deficits that began to develop in 1971 and 1972. Behind the economic pressures resulting from the balance of payments issue lay deeper emotional compulsions that led total force advocates to press for an expanded Japanese defense role as the most appropriate way for Japan to repay its debt to the United States. In its application to Japan, the total force concept rested on the nagging feeling that the United States had been played for a sucker; that Uncle Sap had been "overly generous"[63] with Japan and "had been robbed."[64] The exaggerated image of Japanese sins in the trade field, discussed in an earlier chapter, strengthened the determination to make Japan pay for its military free ride. Increasingly, the burden-sharing approach carried with it a readiness to call Japan's bluff: if Tokyo was not prepared to help pay for the U.S. deterrent, the United States should not be afraid to see Japan go it alone militarily, even to the extent of nuclear weaponry. Given the preponderance of American power and Japanese dependence on the world economy, this approach assumed, Tokyo would have no choice but to remain on the U.S. side in the power balance with the Soviet Union and would probably agree, in the end, to a two-key arrangement retaining partial U.S. control. By 1971, as we shall see, Tokyo had been assigned an even larger role as part of a pentagonal global balancing scheme in which a nuclear Japan was viewed with frankly expressed equanimity.

The Nuclear Issue in Japan-U.S. Relations

The full implications of the burden-sharing issue can be understood only in the context of the powerful, subsurface controversy in Japan over whether, when, and how to acquire nuclear weapons. As economic recovery has progressed and national confidence has grown, an influential pronuclear minority centered in the governing Liberal Democratic party has become increasingly assertive. Chinese nuclear progress has provided the strategic rationale for this minority, but resurgent nationalism has been its most salable stock-in-trade. On the defensive in their own country, Japanese hawks have looked to the Pentagon for help, first in overcoming the "nuclear allergy" in Japan, later in obtaining nuclear technology without having to wage politically awkward domestic budget battles. Ironically, even when Japanese-American relations have been rocky in the economic and political spheres, a transpacific dialogue has persisted between like-minded elements on both sides persuaded that some form of Japanese nuclear capability would best serve the common interest.

My first awareness of the existence of serious proposals for possible two-key nuclear cooperation between Japan and the United States came in conversations in the mid-sixties with leading U.S. Navy planners.[65] By 1967, the antiballistic missile debate in Washington had spawned a subsidiary mini-debate in Tokyo, in which one leading Japanese strategist had proposed a sea-based ABM system that would initially be U.S. controlled but could be jointly manned "if the situation so requires."[66] The U.S. Navy had just unveiled its plan for a U.S.-controlled Seabased Antiballistic Missile Intercept System (SABMIS), specifically proclaiming the protection of Japan and India against Chinese nuclear blackmail as one of the proposed system's objectives, [67] and a Council on Foreign Relations study had suggested a "naval bilateral nuclear force." [68] The naval bilateral nuclear force (BLF) idea came at a time when U.S. military planners, anticipating the return of Okinawa, were seeking ways to compensate for the possible denuclearization of the island. In Japan, however, with its post-Hiroshima nuclear allergy still severe, the public was deeply fearful of involvement in an "American war" that seemed sure to involve nuclear weapons. The *Pueblo* seizure and the subsequent deployment of the aircraft carrier *Enterprise* from a Japanese port reawakened these ever present anxieties, forcing Prime Minister Sato to make a Diet pledge that Japan "will not possess nuclear weapons or allow their introduction into this country." By March 1969, mounting domestic pressures had forced Sato to declare that Japan would accept the return of Okinawa only after the U.S. nuclear weapons there were removed. The Pentagon gradually abandoned its efforts to obtain nuclear storage facilities or two-key nuclear arrangements as part of the Okinawa reversion package but did seek to obtain private assurances from Japanese leaders that they would seek to prepare public opinion for the possible reintroduction of U.S. nuclear weapons to the island in an emergency or, ideally, for the development of a Japanese-American defensive nuclear capability. Six weeks before the Okinawa agreement was signed, Gen. Earle G. Wheeler, chairman of the Joint Chiefs of Staff, stopped off in Tokyo for talks with Sato, explaining to journalists that he had been "satisfied" by his assurances on the nuclear issue. "We will have to take a hard look at our needs on Okinawa," General Wheeler said,

> and they will have to take a look at their attitudes. If you're willing to have a nuclear-powered merchant ship, and a nuclear reactor, you have to look at the question of nuclear weapons also. . . . Whether we like it or not, we live in the nuclear age. Whether we like it or not, the Chicoms are developing a nuclear force. Do we want to extend our nuclear umbrella forever over Japan, India and other countries? On balance, I'm against their having nuclear weapons, though. There are other ways.[69]

The Sato-Nixon communiqué, pledging the return of Okinawa, carefully left the door open for a change in the Diet pronouncement of January 1968, barring the introduction of nuclear weapons. The president expressed his "deep understanding" of the "particular sentiment of the Japanese people against nuclear weapons and the policy of the Japanese government reflecting such sentiment."[70] But the keyword "policy" gently underlined the fact that the nuclear prohibition in Japan did not reflect a binding law or treaty. Less than three weeks later, Sato underlined his own ambivalent attitude on the nuclear issue, sarcastically observing in an address before top leaders of the Keidanren business federation that

> we seem to be unable to possess a complete system of armament in our country, since we were the ones who were "nuclear-baptized" and the

Japanese people have a special sentiment against nuclear weapons. It's regrettable, indeed, but that's where we stand just now.... While I do not regard it as a complete system of defense if we cannot possess nuclear weapons in the era of nuclear weapons, I will, nevertheless, adhere faithfully to the pledge I have made to the people. We will not possess, manufacture or permit the introduction of nuclear weapons; but this being so, it is inevitable, then, that we must seek our security under the U.S. nuclear umbrella.[71]

The continuing strength of pronuclear feeling in Japan following the Okinawa agreement was apparent in the cold reception given to the nuclear nonproliferation treaty (NPT) then pending. It was galling to the pronuclear elements that Washington should press them to keep the Japanese nuclear option open while urging them, at the same time, to sign the NPT and trust in the U.S. nuclear shield. When Japan did sign the treaty in February 1970, the Foreign Ministry expressed open doubts that foreshadowed the ensuing six-year delay in ratification. In a striking departure from the cautious understatement marking most official Japanese pronouncements, the eleven-point Foreign Ministry manifesto called for "maximum use" of national self-inspection procedures under International Atomic Energy Agency agreements governing peaceful nuclear programs and suggested that Japan should be treated on a par with Euratom. Charging that the treaty "permits only the present nuclear-weapon states to possess nuclear weapons," the manifesto said that "this discrimination should ultimately be made to disappear through the elimination of nuclear weapons by all the nuclear-weapon states from their national arsenals." The sharp tenor of this jibe at the very concept of the treaty was nothing new. Vice Foreign Minister Takeso Shimoda had greeted initial proposals for the treaty in 1966 with the quick retort that "Japan cannot agree to such a big power-centered approach, implying as it does a treaty that would bar the nonnuclear states from having nuclear capabilities without requiring the nuclear powers to reduce their nuclear capabilities or stockpile."[72]

The inspection procedures envisaged under the treaty were genuinely worrisome to Japanese business leaders, with their ambitions for world leadership in the nuclear field. Moreover, in addition to fears that technical secrets would leak, Japan, like India, had been outraged by the fact that the treaty not only barred the manufacture of nuclear weapons but also explicitly prohibited the development of nuclear explosive devices for peaceful nuclear explosions. It would have been one thing to subscribe to an international ban on the manufacture of nuclear weapons that could have been violated only at the high cost of damaging economic and other relations with fellow signatories. It was quite another matter to foreclose the national option of acquiring even a capability for the manufacture of nuclear weapons. Japan, like India, found this a galling reminder of the place it still occupied in a "big power-centered" world.[73] In the final analysis, however, Tokyo concluded that signing the treaty would not fully foreclose efforts to move toward an independent nuclear capability, since the key to nuclear independence did not lie in the right to conduct peaceful nuclear explosions but rather in the right to develop an independent uranium enrichment capability and thus an autonomous fuel cycle. By signing the treaty in 1970, Japan avoided an immediate confrontation with the United States. But at the same time Tokyo set the stage for later conflict by quietly going ahead with its program to develop an autonomous fuel cycle as part of its civilian nuclear program.

The nuclear issue came to a head in late 1970 when the Defense Agency issued an unprecedented white paper consciously designed to feel the public pulse. While declaring that Japan would be a "non-nuclear, medium rank" power, the white paper simultaneously echoed the theme suggested by Sato in 1967, pointedly observing that "small-yield, tactical, purely defensive" nuclear weapons would not be legally barred by the "no-war" clause of the constitution. The outcry was sharp and swift, and it was clear that popular sentiment against a Japanese nuclear capability was hardening. Even more important, from the Pentagon perspective, the Japanese public remained just as nuclear-allergic as ever to each and every nuclear-powered U.S. ship or submarine entering Japanese harbors, not to mention the nuclear-armed aircraft and naval vessels that were generally suspected to be transiting in and out of Japanese ports without public knowledge. The U.S. Navy, in particular, found it exasperating to be treated with undisguised suspicion by an ally and had never forgiven Japan for the uproar over alleged nuclear leakage in a 1968 incident at Sasebo involving a U.S. nuclear submarine.[74] Tensions grew in Washington between the Pentagon, on the one hand, and the State Department, allied with the Atomic Energy Commission, over how far to push the Japanese for more thoroughgoing military cooperation with the United States, particularly with respect to access by nuclear-powered vessels.

The issue of nuclear access to Japan had assumed a special importance in the eyes of Pentagon planners seeking to implement the total force strategy. In his annual defense report to Congress in March 1971, Defense Secretary Laird had given increased emphasis to the concept of "theatre nuclear deterrence" as the key to compensating for the limitations on the U.S. military posture imposed by the new "one and one-half war" strategy and the Nixon Doctrine. Both Laird and the president emphasized that the administration's policy of "truly flexible response" permitted the use of a "full range of options" without regard to the level of conflict selected by possible enemies. In effect, Laird proposed to compensate for the reduction of conventional capabilities in Asia with a more credible threat to use tactical nuclear weapons. But this presupposed, in turn, that the total force idea could really be put into practice through "a new basis of cooperation between us and our allies which takes into account their growing capabilities."[75]

In Japanese eyes, the report left little doubt that even in their hypothetical war games, Pentagon planners were no longer thinking seriously in terms of an ICBM exchange in defense of allies.[76] The underlying objective of theater deterrence was clearly to limit the U.S. nuclear defense of allies to tactical nuclear weapons and to confine any nuclear damage to the territory of U.S. allies or their enemies.

Moreover, in addition to its new note of ambiguity on ICBM protection, the Laird strategy raised questions in Tokyo by sketching an ideal model of theater deterrence in which allies were depicted as having their own tactical nuclear capabilities. There was no direct mention of Japan in this connection, either pointing toward nuclear weaponry for Tokyo or specifically ruling this out. However, the inability of Japan to play a tactical nuclear role à la West Germany was treated, by implication, as an unfortunate anomaly. Summarizing the principles underlying the total force concept, Laird drew a pointed distinction. In deterring strategic nuclear war, he said, "primary reliance will continue to be placed in U.S. strategic deterrent forces." By contrast, he declared, with an approving nod toward the NATO nuclear partnership, "in deterring theater nuclear war, the U.S. also has primary responsibility, but certain of our allies are able to share this responsibility by virtue of their own nuclear capabilities."[77]

The Laird report contained another passage that was to assume added significance when the nuclear issue arose during his controversial July visit to Japan. While U.S. nuclear superiority could "contribute significantly" to deterring aggression by Peking, Laird observed, the American deterrent would be "strengthened further with an area ballistic missile defense effective against small attacks."[78] This was an allusion to the U.S. Navy's four-year-old proposal for SABMIS as a complement to the Safeguard ABM program. The $2 billion plan envisaged a fleet of up to forty armored ships equipped with Spartan nuclear antimissile missiles and a miniaturized Nike-X radar and computer apparatus. The proponents of SABMIS were only too aware in early 1971 that the SALT I talks then under way were expected to rule out sea-based as well as land-based American

ABM systems. A future SABMIS in Asia would have to be Japanese, possibly based on American technological help purchased from American defense industries.

Pentagon critics made no secret of their view that the SALT agreement could threaten the efficacy of the U.S. military posture in the Far East in ways even more important than its proposed restriction on sea-based ABM systems. Moscow had been pushing the idea that all nuclear deployments capable of reaching the Soviet Union should be classified as strategic weapons—specifically pointing to U.S. tactical nuclear weapons in Europe. Logically, once accepted in the case of Europe, the concept of "forward-based systems" (FBS) could also be applied to nuclear-equipped U.S. aircraft based in South Korea or on Seventh Fleet carriers. The issue was set aside in May 1971 to permit progress in other areas of the SALT negotiations. Like the impending ABM agreement, however, the FBS issue cast a long shadow over Japan in the thinking of military planners in Tokyo and Washington. Advocates of a hard line in dealing with Moscow on the FBS issue could warn that retreat would mean eventual U.S. nuclear withdrawal from the Far East and thus a nuclear Japan. On the other hand, those who saw some advantages in a nuclear Japan, including burden-sharing enthusiasts in the Pentagon, had new reason to feel that things were going their way and were increasingly anxious to speed up the process. As we shall see, this helps to explain why the Laird visit became the occasion for a studied effort to bring the nuclear issue into the open.

On July 5, 1971, the second day of his Tokyo visit, Laird outlined the case for a nuclear Japan at a meeting with six ranking American embassy officials, conducting what several of those present described as a "Socratic dialogue." His personal position was not flatly stated, as such, but the clear impression left was that he had been testing his own views. Embassy officials were anxious but not surprised, therefore, when Laird's spokesman, Jerry Friedheim, then deputy assistant secretary for defense for information and later to become assistant secretary, floated some of the same ideas at a background briefing for American and British journalists on July 7. Under the customary ground rules of such briefings, journalists attending were asked to attribute statements to "U.S. officials" authorized to explain Laird's thinking but not directly to members of the Laird entourage.

The implicit thrust of Friedheim's initial comments was that budgetary pressures would sooner or later force cutbacks in the American presence in Asia, calling for a compensatory Japanese military buildup. Secretary Laird "feels very strongly," Friedheim said, that some other nations in the world have simply got to come to grips with the realities that we face at home, particularly in the Congress. . . . We are not going to be able to do everything. We will be asking other nations to contribute more. Now how they can do that becomes a case by case basis. . . . It was news to us who came from Washington that there was great bandying about here of the idea of Japanese militarism. In Washington the pressures would seem to be in the other direction.[79]

Asked what Japan could do, Friedheim referred to the fact that Japan spent less than 1 percent of its GNP on defense and pointed to the pending Japanese Fourth Five-Year Defense Plan, observing that "the question is whether that still turns out to be one percent of G.N.P. or, hopefully, greater than that." After Vietnam, he said, the Seventh Fleet would have to be reduced for budgetary reasons, and Japan "might develop more naval capability. They build the best ships in the world, and they've got the capability to build aircraft."[80] What Japan did in developing its own forces was not for the United States to dictate, he declared, but the maintenance of the U.S. nuclear deterrent was of more direct concern to the United States. In providing the deterrent, Friedheim said,

We have to hope that other nations will understand that as we provide this shield, we do have ships that go places and do things, airplanes that go places. . . . We don't talk about where we have or don't have nuclear weapons. We simply say that we have to have some someplace, and anybody that wants to benefit from being under our nuclear umbrella, we would hope would understand that.[81]

With the Soviet-U.S. strategic balance "becoming more and more a situation of parity" and with Soviet missile-firing submarines operating in the Pacific, on station, the need for nuclear access to Japan would become increasingly important. Moreover, the SALT talks might also "change the U.S. strategic deterrent force in some respects in relation to the Soviet Union."[82] This would have an indirect impact on Asia since

the S.A.L.T. talks do not include mainland China. It's just us and the Soviets. . . . As we look at mainland China we see a capability for M.R.B.M.'s, with some beginning of deployment, and we still predict an I.C.B.M. capability in the next two years or less. This missile capability is not a capability that will trouble the U.S. strategically but it's a thing that Asia will have to watch closely.[83]

What Friedheim had in mind did not become fully clear until the tape recorder was off, the initial portion of the briefing had ended, and a group of interested correspondents pursued the discussion further. The FBS issue and the possibility of a reduced U.S. nuclear posture in the Pacific resulting from the SALT talks could have important implications for Japan, he emphasized, since Peking would still be free to develop its missile strength unchecked. This would pose a growing threat to Japan at a time when the ICBM threat to the United States from Peking would still be "decades" away and when the United States would feel less directly endangered than ever before by Moscow. No longer could Japan take it for granted that it would be the indirect beneficiary of an anti-Soviet strategic posture maintained by the United States basically for American reasons. In this changed strategic setting, Tokyo could choose to acknowledge its new position as the immediate beneficiary of the deterrent and actively help the United States to maintain it, partly by abandoning its inhibitions with respect to nuclear access, partly by direct financial support, and partly by building auxiliary conventional naval forces of its own. Conceivably, however, Japan might begin to worry about U.S. reliability and decide to develop its own defensive nuclear weapons either as a two-key supplement to the U.S. umbrella or under independent control. "They might want to go for A.B.M.'s on ships," Friedheim said, apparently alluding to the SABMIS idea.

The point of it all was not so much that the United States should directly encourage Japan to go nuclear but rather that the Japanese should begin to pay a greater price for U.S. nuclear protection. Only by suggesting that the U.S. nuclear shield could no longer be taken for granted and that the United States is not afraid to see Japan go nuclear, this rationale implied, could the United States genuinely change the bidding in the overall bargaining relationship between the two countries. Laird reflected this same approach in his farewell press conference. When a hawkish Japanese reporter asked how the United States would react if Japan developed tactical nuclear weapons, Laird replied that Japanese defense planners should give "higher priority" to upgrading conventional military capabilities, adding that "President Nixon and our government will continue to provide the nuclear umbrella. . . . I do not foresee a role for Japan as far as the nuclear deterrent is concerned during the period of the 1970's and beyond." He spoke of the issue as one of "priorities" four times in the course of his reply, and the inference drawn by most Japanese observers was that he did not necessarily rule out the future desirability or inevitability of nuclear arms after the conventional buildup then programmed had ended in 1980.[84]

Neither my report nor those of other correspondents present[85] had stated that Laird directly called on Japan to share a tactical nuclear defense role, though Japanese press reports attributed an exploratory suggestion in this vein to Armistead Selden, Jr., principal deputy assistant secretary of defense for international security affairs, in a meeting with Takuya Kubo, Defense Agency counsellor, during the Laird visit. 86 The mere fact that American officials were floating trial balloons concerning a nuclear Japan had an explosive impact in Washington, however, coming as it did at a time when Kissinger was already secretly in Peking. When the State Department issued an angry disclaimer stating that "no responsible body of opinion" in the United States favored nuclear weapons for Japan, Friedheim said confidently, at first, that "they have their version, and we have ours." When the summer White House at San Clemente joined in with a sharp disavowal of its own, the Laird party knew that something was seriously wrong, but what it was did not become clear until the announcement of the Kissinger visit. Thereafter, Laird made strenuous efforts to cover up his tracks. The Pentagon circulated incomplete transcripts of the Friedheim briefing, and the Senate Republican Policy Committee attributed the Tokyo reports to Japanese defense officials who were afraid to face their own public opinion, it was said, and had used U.S. journalists as sounding boards. 87 In Washington, the issue was effectively confused for a short time by these tactics; in Tokyo, however, the Japanese public was generally persuaded, as the *Asahi* observed editorially, that "smoke does not arise where there is no fire whatsoever." 88

The emergence of a new American attitude on the nuclear issue was soon confirmed when a White House official told *Nihon Keizai* editor Yasuo Takeyama in November 1971 that "if Japan wishes, the U.S. is prepared to provide Japan nuclear warheads or the know-how to manufacture nuclear warheads." 89 The Takeyama report was paralleled by a proposal in a Foreign Ministry-subsidized journal for an American-aided "multilateral nuclear force" to compensate for the fact that Chinese missiles "would deter the U.S. and Soviet use of strategic nuclear weapons in the neighborhood of Japan." 90 Changing American attitudes with respect to a nuclear Japan were most forcefully suggested when President Nixon made his controversial statement in January 1972 that "I think it will be a safer world and a better world if we have a strong, healthy United States, Europe, Soviet Union, China, Japan, each balancing the other, not playing one against the other, an even balance." 91 This marked a change from the careful reference in his Kansas City speech, six months earlier, to "five great economic superpowers." 92 This time, the economic qualifier was missing, and the inference was clearly drawn in Tokyo that the balance could not be "even" unless both Japan and Europe were nuclear.

The Nixon statement had not come out of the blue; it reflected a frankly Soviet-preoccupied line of thought in conservative intellectual circles that was becoming more and more explicit. William Kintner of the Foreign Policy Research Institute of the University of

Pennsylvania had spelled out this view in its most coherent form at a conference in November 1971, calling for a "pentagonal power system" in which a nuclear-armed Japan would "work with the U.S. to build up a regional balance of power in the western Pacific."[93] The Kintner message had reverberated loudly in Japan, and I first received a copy of his paper from a professor at the National Defense College. As the Soviet deployment of Polaris-type submarines grows, he warned, the credibility of the U.S. deterrent in Asia and Europe alike would diminish, leading to "increasing instability." A tripolar world embracing Peking would still be "transitory and unstable" since "ideological considerations" could not be ignored and two of the states involved would, after all, be "Communist states which appear committed to the ultimate reduction of U.S. influence and power."[94] If the Soviet strategic buildup continues, Kintner declared, "it would seem evident that the Soviet Union is developing its nuclear capabilities for a *toutes horizons* strategy. In response, the United States should advocate a British-French nuclear consortium for a politically-integrated Western Europe, including Germany, and the movement of Japan toward the acquisition of nuclear weapons."[95] A world "organized around a five nuclear power nucleus" would be a "complicated" one, but it constitutes

> one method of preventing the Soviet Union from becoming the dominant world center. . . . Efforts to move in this direction are implicit in the Nixon Doctrine. . . . If a de facto five-power world emerges, the U.S. will find that its interests will be quite compatible with those of Western Europe and Japan. Consequently, the problem of nuclear collaboration is perhaps soluble if the will exists between the U.S. and its European and Japanese associates to coordinate their foreign and military policies and create practical arrangements for planning and coordinating the systems under which nuclear weapons might be employed.[96]

It was "quite possible," Kintner conceded, that Japan would choose to have an independent nuclear capability. But in any case,

> the United States would find the conditions of a five-power world more attractive, in general, than an endeavor to keep up the competition with the U.S.S.R. by sustaining or recreating the conditions of a bipolar world. . . . There is much to suggest that the Soviet Union is more adverse to sharing power than the United States.[97]

The Kintner approach assumed that Japan would remain basically oriented toward the United States in the Soviet-American balance since Washington would be more hospitable to "sharing power" than Moscow. From the Japanese vantage point, however, the distinction between U.S. and Soviet virtue was not obvious. The nationalist image of the two superpowers had been vividly drawn in a revealing analysis by Yasuhiro Nakasone during his tenure as director of the Defense Agency.

> American-Soviet relations are indeed curious, to say the least, in that their ideologies are poles apart, but their mutual national interests coincide in many respects. Whether their interests will coincide with Japan's is extremely doubtful. . . . Japan should always remember that a mutual agreement—tacit, if not overt—exists between the U.S. and the Soviet Union on how to share the trophies of World War II. . . . The two superpowers seem determined to maintain their dominance in nuclear technology in general and its military application in particular. It is difficult to contradict the contention that both the 1963 partial nuclear test ban treaty and the current nuclear non-proliferation pact are primarily designed—even if covertly—to preempt, or rather deter, both Japan and West Germany from acquiring nuclear arms and thereby undermining the basis of U.S.-Soviet nuclear hegemony.[98]

Nominally, the even balance idea implied an end to the duopoly, but would the balance really be even? Pronuclear advocates in Tokyo suspected that the Kintner approach would add up to a two-key arrangement in which Japan would be a junior partner under built-in pressure to play the U.S. game in matters involving the Soviet Union.

Détente and the Security Treaty

Psychologically, the climate in Japan for such an intimate relationship with the United States was growing more unfavorable than ever in the tempestuous aftermath of intermingled economic and political Nixon shocks. The Nixon visit to China crystallized a mood of nationalist introspection and assertiveness that was to linger long after Japan had normalized its own relations with Peking. Burden-sharing was more repugnant than ever in the light of a changing U.S. Far Eastern policy. "They ask us to build up our defense strength," said *Sankei*, an organ of pro-Sato business groups, "but they want us to play the role of a balancer against China under this pretext of sharing the burden fairly."[99] "While the U.S. is trying to bring the 'Total Force' concept into practice," said Hajime Doba, a respected military expert, "it is also talking with Peking. This 'self-contradictory' policy suggests to me that they want to see Japan and China set up in opposition to each other, without favoring one or the other."[100] The depth of the new nationalist mood was apparent in the popular response greeting Fumihiko Kono, board chairman of Mitsubishi Heavy Industries, who sought to protect Japanese defense industries and fend off pressures for U.S. weapons purchases by suggesting that Japan should "pay" for the U.S. nuclear umbrella through the purchase of American Treasury bonds or

greater foreign aid.[101] Public opinion reacted sharply to the suggestion that Japan was in debt, with *Asahi* mirroring the prevailing view
that "both superpowers intend to use their nuclear power to impose
a nuclear order they desire on lesser powers rather than for protection of their allies. There is no ground to pay for the nuclear
umbrella, which is not reliable, in any case, and is intended only to
enhance the interests of big powers."[102] Critics of the Kono proposal cited Nixon's 1972 State of the World message, which declared
that "our alliances are no longer addressed primarily to the containment of the Soviet Union and China behind an American shield.
They are, instead, addressed to the creation with those powers of a
stable world peace."

On the eve of the Nixon visit to Peking, the political-military
counselor of the American embassy in Tokyo told a group of
Japanese defense writers that the prevention of a nuclear Japan was a
"concomitant" element in the security treaty.

> An effect of the Security Treaty, as long as it's regarded by Japan as a
> meaningful commitment, is to undercut or remove the desire or necessity
> for the development of Japanese nuclear weapons. That's not the purpose of
> the treaty.... But an element in the picture is the degree to which other
> major countries, and I mean specifically in this case China and the Soviet
> Union, see the defense relationship with the U.S. as providing an element of
> stability in relationships among the four major powers—Japan, the U.S.S.R.,
> the P.R.C. and the U.S.—in this area.[103]

"This is indeed a very important statement," editorialized the
Mainichi,

> in that the U.S. has now admitted that the Security Treaty has changed in
> nature. Such a statement can only accelerate our defense debates in Japan
> from now on. We wish to refute the concept that the Treaty serves even in
> part to check Japan's development of its own nuclear weapons. The Japa-
> nese people find this suggestion arrogant and extremely unpleasant to
> contemplate. Japanese nuclear policy should be determined by Japan itself,
> independently.[104]

Gradually, the security treaty became doubly suspect after 1972, not
only as an American instrument for dividing Japan from China but
also, in a larger sense, as a collective instrument for the containment
of Japanese power. In earlier years, there had been guarded statements from both Japanese and American sources that the Soviet
Union took a benign view of the security treaty as a way of keeping
Japan nonnuclear. Now it was all out in the open, with pretense
thrown to the winds. China, too, had a common interest with the
United States in keeping Japan nonnuclear, and it also suited Chinese

purposes, at least temporarily, for an American naval presence to remain in Japan as an offset to Soviet power.

For most Japanese, American policy increasingly appeared to pose an implicit long-term choice between two equally distasteful alternatives: a role as an anti-Soviet surrogate within the two-key concept, or indefinite continuance under the shadow of a tripolar "nuclear order." Both were equally repugnant, in nationalist terms, and there was powerful support in Japan for other options based on policies independent of the United States. It would not be easy to chart an independent course, however, after so many years of habituation to the U.S. link. As Hisao Iwashima of the National Defense College observed, Japanese foreign policy formation was still "flexible, some might say vulnerable enough to move in any direction in response to internal and external pressures. In the final analysis, whether or not Japan becomes 'militaristic' will depend upon the interaction of these internal and external forces. Japan is traversing a narrow ridge, and her balance is somewhat unstable."[105] Among other things, Iwashima and other opponents of nuclear weaponry were fearful that two-key advocates in both countries might forge a winning transpacific combination. The debate in the United States over defense policy toward Japan had become part and parcel of the policy struggle in Japan itself, with Japanese pronuclear elements banking heavily on support from Washington.

On one side in the U.S. debate were those who either favored a nuclear Japan or felt that Japan was moving inevitably toward a nuclear capability, in any event, and that the United States should anticipate this development by integrating Japanese tactical nuclear forces into U.S. defense efforts. Nuclear depth charges dropped from destroyers or unmanned helicopters would have a range ten times greater than that of conventional homing torpedoes and could be a powerful factor in coping with the Soviet submarine fleet. Dual-capable delivery systems could be installed not only for depth charges but also for antisubmarine rockets, air-to-air missiles, and ground-to-air missiles; all that would be required, under a minimal two-key program, would be the training of specialists to use the nuclear warheads provided in time of emergency. Already, this argument ran, Mitsubishi and other Japanese firms were making nuclear-capable missiles and rockets for the Self-Defense Forces under license to U.S. firms, notably the Nike-Hercules anti-aircraft missile and the ASROC launcher, a U.S. Navy antisubmarine weapon used for firing nuclear depth charges. Already, in its satellite program, Japan had launched a rocket with a thrust and payload capacity comparable to those of the U.S. Minuteman missile,[106] and an even bigger rocket of the Thor-Delta class was under development in the satellite program with U.S. help. At any rate, inevitable or not, some argued, if Japan did seem on the verge of going nuclear, the United States should be ready to join in a two-key arrangement in order to forestall an independent Japanese capability. This point of view surfaced in a study by Zbigniew Brzezinski concluding that Japan would be likely to go nuclear only "in the event of a major shift in world affairs," in which case "it actually may then be in the U.S. interest to assist the Japanese nuclear program, through direct technical assistance and perhaps also—as a transitional stage, prior to Japan's effective acquisition of nuclear weapons—through the so-called 'two-key' system."[107]

Echoing Kintner, Jay B. Sorensen, a consultant to the Los Alamos Weapons Laboratory, argued in late 1975 that when the United States had strategic superiority, nuclear proliferation was undesirable, but "in a situation of parity, the United States could use allies more than ever, and proliferation could be advantageous."[108] While the United States should not encourage Japanese nuclear ambitions, Sorensen wrote, Washington should be prepared for "a new form of nuclear sharing" in the event that Japan should decide independently to go nuclear.[109]

> Under the conditions of a Japanese decision to become the ninth or tenth nuclear power, it might actually be in the interest of the United States to offer all assistance possible within the framework of the Non-Proliferation Treaty. . . . An independent Japanese decision to produce nuclear weapons while maintaining the alliance with the United States would change the entire picture and open all sorts of new possibilities. . . . Very advanced warhead designs for the equivalent of the Skybolt and Polaris airlaunched and submarine-launched ballistic missiles might not be possible under the Non-Proliferation Treaty, nor perhaps would the sale of Polaris missiles; but the associated equipment might be.[110]

Other analysts contended that "Japan's acquisition of a nuclear deterrent . . . need not end the U.S.-Japanese security partnership" and that even if it did, "cooperation and coordination" might still be possible.[111] One writer implied guardedly that such cooperation could extend to "cruise missile technology, which is relatively inexpensive and increasingly attractive."[112] In 1976, a Pentagon analyst publicly outlined a plan for Japanese cooperation in antisubmarine warfare in which a prominent role was assigned to a new nuclear-capable torpedo mine being developed by the U.S. Navy, known as CAPTOR.[113]

Just as advocates of a two-key approach stressed the inevitability of a nuclear Japan, so opponents argued that a nuclear outcome was far from inevitable. Strategically, a densely populated island nation located so closely to most of its conceivable enemies would be highly vulnerable, and it would be extremely expensive to develop an independent nuclear force capable of surviving an attack by a nuclear superpower.[114] To be meaningful, even a sea-based ABM force would have to be equal in size and technological sophistication to the MIRV potential permitted under the SALT I agreement. For all of Japan's scientific progress, there were still important gaps that would be difficult to overcome quickly, especially in guidance and reentry technology. It would be quite a big leap, therefore, from possessing the reactor capacity to produce ninety 20-kiloton nuclear warheads annually [115] to actually mobilizing a military nuclear program on a scale rivaling that of the superpowers. Given the costs involved in a full-scale nuclear effort, the threat would have to be a clear and present one to overcome the deep antinuclear feeling in Japan; despite Kintner's conviction that a tripolar nuclear balance in Asia would be unstable, the consensus in Japan was more sanguine.[116] American opponents of the two-key approach found their strongest argument against the inevitability thesis in the fact that most Japanese do not feel directly threatened by Soviet and Chinese military power and believe that the diplomatic liabilities of a nuclear program could well outweigh the military advantages. Even on the right, where pronuclear sentiment is strongest, many business leaders fear that nuclearization would make Japan too controversial abroad and would jeopardize access to foreign markets.

In the American debate over defense policy toward Japan, it was assumed that the security treaty would continue and, conversely, that an independent nuclear force would follow if the treaty came to an end. This not only underrated the persistent strength of antinuclear sentiment in Japan but also obscured the real outlines of the security controversy there at a time when the political foundations of the alliance structure were decaying. In the Japanese nuclear debate, the treaty was a relatively peripheral factor. The essential strength of the antinuclear forces lay in the widely held belief that détente had made the need for expanded defense forces problematical—treaty or no treaty. Even the appeal that nuclear weapons did have was not strategic but political. As former foreign minister Kiichi Miyazawa once declared, looking toward Washington as well as Moscow and Peking, popular support for nuclear weapons was largely a matter of emotional nationalism, of whether "the major nations of the world, who have nuclear capabilities, try to be too assertive and push Japan around too much and too far."[117] The security treaty was measured in economic rather than military terms, as we have seen, and such deterrent value as it might have had during the early cold war years was no longer a substantial factor in Japanese calculations. Five years before Laird presented his theater deterrence concept, a representative Japanese expert panel had concluded in 1966 that it would be "highly unthinkable" for the United States to use military pressure to protect Japan from nuclear blackmail. The communist powers could use Japan as a hostage to deter an American attack, and there would be "little practical meaning" in the destruction of communist cities after "Tokyo and Osaka had been turned into a second Hiroshima and Nagasaki."[118]

Cautiously eyeing the shifting international scene, Japan searched during the seventies for an alternative to an either-or choice between the indefinite continuance of a close treaty relationship, on the one hand, and nuclear independence in its stead. The middle course most widely acceptable, as we have noted, was a policy of benign neglect toward the treaty, gently nudging along the transition to a looser, skeletonized arrangement. But as the climate of détente grew, so did pressures to speed up the transition by blending a looser alliance with a more independent diplomacy, including intensified arms control negotiations with Moscow, Peking, and Pyongyang. Leading strategists promoted the idea of a "crisis cooperation mobile strategy"[119] based on a completely rewritten treaty. Fixed U.S. bases would gradually be replaced in this approach by military and civilian Japanese facilities geared for "emergency intervention,"[120] an idea long promoted by moderate opposition elements who saw no pressing military threat to Japan but wanted to retain the symbolism of the treaty as a brake on Japanese militarism. The Seventh Fleet could retain the right to call for repairs at Japanese ports under contracts with the Japanese Maritime Self-Defense Force or Japanese civilian shipyards. The removal of fixed bases was explicitly proposed by Democratic Socialist leader Ikko Kasuga in a much publicized exchange with Deputy Defense Secretary David Packard in late 1971. "If the Japanese government should come to feel that Japan did not need our protection," Packard replied, "and wished to assume total responsibility for Japan's security, including defense against the nuclear threat, we should have no forces in Japan. But then, would we need the treaty?"[121] As this retort showed, the idea of a looser alliance posed the free ride issue in aggravated form since the United States would still be nominally obligated to defend Japan without retaining the use of Japanese bases in return.

For its own budgetary reasons, the United States was increasingly prepared for substantial base cutbacks in Japan, and the more conspicuous elements of the army, air force, and marine presence were progressively reduced in populous urban areas where antibase sentiment was especially acute. The future of the U.S. naval presence posed a potentially more difficult issue, however, given the increase in Soviet naval power at a time when budgetary constraints were forcing reductions in U.S. naval strength, including a drop in the number of aircraft carriers. To offset this imbalance, the Pentagon wanted a forward presence assuring maximum visibility and maneuverability. "Homeporting" ships in Japan, with dependents of the crews housed there, would make it unnecessary for these vessels to go back to San Diego for six months after every nine in the Pacific, increasing their time on duty despite the reduction in numbers. It would also be cheaper to homeport ships in Japan than to ply back and forth as in the past, using Japanese bases only for repairs. This cost factor would grow in importance if the number of nuclear-powered carriers rose to four by the end of the seventies.[122]

The Japanese reaction to U.S. pressures for "homeporting" on a permanent basis was cool, given the scarcity of land and housing facilities and a continuing undercurrent of anti-base sentiment, especially in the areas surrounding the Yokosuka and Sasebo installations. Overt opposition to the storage of nuclear weapons in U.S. bases and the presence of nuclear-equipped aircraft aboard U.S. carriers grew less vocal as the seventies progressed, but the continuing sensitivity of the nuclear issue made Japanese officials reluctant to accept the idea of permanent homeporting. The Japanese Maritime Self-Defense Forces and civilian Japanese shipyard interests both coveted the elaborate Yokosuka repair docks. At the same time, Japan became increasingly aware of its vulnerable position as a raw material importer during the seventies and had no desire to disturb its economic links with the United States so long as Washington was prepared to keep the "trade-off" operative. With the Vietnam war over and Sino-U.S. tensions greatly reduced, the security treaty was less controversial than it had been during the sixties. Tokyo did not make a major issue of the U.S. base presence but sought to forestall any major expansion of U.S. naval facilities.

Until his departure as Defense Secretary in early 1973, Laird repeatedly urged that Japan increase its own naval capability, helping the United States to protect the Indian Ocean supply lines used by Japanese oil tankers.[123] The United States spoke in discordant voices on this issue,[124] and in Japan itself, the feasibility and wisdom of attempting to patrol such an extended lifeline was a subject of intermittent controversy. The first phase of the debate over whether to build a navy capable of reaching beyond the Malacca Straits raged from 1966 to 1970, with Osamu Kaihara, former chairman of the National Defense Council, successfully championing the view that

> our supply lines are safe today simply because the world is peaceful, and this safety has nothing to do with anybody's efforts to secure our sea routes. What would happen to these routes in time of war? It is ridiculous,

wishful thinking to believe that we could protect their security if we were ever to get into a conflict with a big power such as the Soviet Union or China.[125]

Kaihara analyzed a variety of "big navy" proposals, some calling for a fleet big enough to protect Japanese shipping as far as Saipan, others suggesting a reach as far as Malacca. If a "vital interest" were really involved, he argued, halfway efforts would have little meaning and Japan would logically have to extend its reach to the Persian Gulf, not only with ships but also with submarines and antisubmarine aircraft. This, in turn, would involve Japanese bases along the way, he warned, which is "utterly impossible for the Japan of today to do, politically."[126] Another influential critic of the big navy view wrote that "Japan simply cannot protect all of its merchant ships around the world. It is cheaper to charter foreign flag vessels, as we do to quite an extent, to put Japanese ships under foreign registry, or in time of war, to keep ships and freighters waiting in neutral ports until the crisis is over."[127] A persistent navy and shipbuilding lobby notwithstanding, the dominant mood in the seventies was that Japan should try to avoid getting involved in a costly naval competition in the Pacific, keeping a wary eye on the Moscow-Peking-Washington triangle and encouraging a general reduction of tensions. Above all, in this view, Japan should avoid embroilment in the Sino-Soviet rivalry.

In the context of détente, the case for a big navy with a long reach, or for an enlarged army, was less defensible both politically and strategically than the case for a bigger and better defensively oriented air force. The immediate Japanese defense controversy in the seventies centered, accordingly, on what constituted defensive aircraft and missilery. Looking ahead, however, Japan was disturbed by the continuing tension in Sino-Soviet relations and the military implications of a growing Moscow-Peking conflict, especially on the naval balance in the Pacific. To remain a medium-range naval power made sense in the face of a standoff between the U.S. and Soviet fleets. But what if China embarked on a major naval buildup in order to counter Moscow? This development not only would add new uncertainty to the military equation but also would introduce unsettling political and psychological factors into the Japanese debate. The affront to Japanese nationalism inherent in a Soviet-American naval condominium in the Pacific was bad enough, a necessary evil justified, at least temporarily, by the inordinate costs of seeking to rival the superpowers. To remain a medium-range naval power outclassed by China would be more difficult to swallow, politically, and in military terms, a Chinese naval reach would be more menacing in Japanese eyes than a nuclear capability viewed mainly in terms of the

Chinese equation with the superpowers. The big navy option thus remained wide open. It was here, in particular, that the nuclear option also remained open, for as we have seen, the most serious advocacy of a nuclear component in Japanese strategy has focused on antisubmarine warfare and a sea-based ABM system.

The alternatives in the Pacific were outlined by Makoto Momoi of the National Defense College, writing under a pseudonym on the eve of the Nixon visits to China and the USSR in 1972. Peking, Moscow, and Washington should not forget, he warned, that while Japan could accept the role of a bystander in the tripolar nuclear balancing game,

> a trinational game of deterrence not directly affecting us, we could not remain unperturbed in the event of a destabilized naval balance of power in the Pacific, where nations are made neighbors by bodies of water. . . . The Soviet Union does not seem to put a pause to its naval expansion. China can hardly ignore that. Neither can the U.S. if it is to remain a Pacific power.[128]

One way of seeking to achieve a balance, he reasoned, would be for the U.S. Navy to keep pace with both Soviet and Chinese deployments; another would be a "de facto Sino-U.S. naval alliance"; still another, a Japanese-American naval combination. These were all likely to be financially or politically exorbitant options, he implied, and the time appeared ripe, instead, for a serious arms control initiative before China and Japan plunged into the race. Unlike the Washington naval conference of 1921-1922, a new naval limitation conference attuned to the seventies, eighties, and nineties would regulate the number rather than the tonnage of vessels. Submarines, aircraft carriers, and helicopter carriers would not be covered, in the case of the superpowers, and the coastal defenses of China, Japan, and other Asian countries would also be unaffected. The agreement would be restricted to oceangoing surface ships deployed in the Pacific. Its purposes, in short, would be limited to preventing dominance of the Pacific by any one power and reducing the need for non-Asian intervention in local conflicts. The superpowers would be free to maintain their strategic forces in the region. When fixing the ratio of surface ships permitted, one major objective would be to prevent either China or Japan from challenging the United States or the USSR. At the same time, China, Japan, and lesser Asian powers would be jointly enabled to deter either the United States or the USSR "from taking actions against the interests of Asia."[129]

In the absence of such meaningful arms control, Momoi concluded, Japan might well begin to explore its own naval options "in the second half of the Seventies." This was really a more substantial issue than the nuclear issue per se since Japan could have an impact on the Pacific naval balance, including its nuclear dimension, much more significant than its impact on the global strategic balance. China has justified its nuclear weapons as necessary to force super-power disarmament. Japan, for its part, has little hope of restraining the superpowers and knows that threats to go nuclear, made to curb the strategic arms race, "would be interpreted as an empty bluff of the weak and the nuclear impotent." Political constraints severely limit Japanese use of the nuclear option, but "a naval option is quite another matter. This is not the bluff of the weak and the impotent. This will be the bluff of one who is desperate and competent."[130]

NOTES

1. Walt W. Rostow, *The United States in the World Arena* (New York: Harper, 1960), pp. 411-442.

2. For example, see A. Doak Barnett, "The New Multipolar Balance in East Asia: Implications for U.S. Policy," *Annals of the American Academy of Political and Social Sciences*, July 1970, pp. 21-27.

3. President Richard M. Nixon suggested this concept in an interview published in *Time*, 3 January 1972, p. 11.

4. Hans J. Morgenthau, "Nixon and the World," *New Republic*, 6 January 1973, p. 20.

5. Seyom Brown, "The Changing Essence of Power," *Foreign Affairs*, January 1973, p. 279.

6. This is the title of a forthcoming book by Earl C. Ravenal reflecting a line of analysis foreshadowed in "The Strategic Balance in Asia," *Pacific Community*, July 1972, pp. 613-620.

7. For example, see Bernard K. Gordon, *Toward Disengagement in Asia* (Englewood Cliffs: Prentice-Hall, 1969), esp. p. 79; and a rejoinder by Selig S. Harrison, "After Vietnam," *New Republic*, 29 November 1969, pp.. 30-31.

8. Zbigniew Brzezinski, "The Balance of Power Delusion," *Foreign Policy*, Summer 1972, p. 55.

9. Rupert Emerson, *From Empire to Nation* (Cambridge: Harvard University Press, 1960), pp. 192-194.

10. Walter Lippmann, *U.S. War Aims* (Boston: Little, Brown, 1944), p. 21. This view is also ably developed in Louis J. Halle, *Dream and Reality* (New York: Harper, 1958), pp. 218-220.

11. Bruce M. Russett, *No Clear and Present Danger* (New York: Harper & Row, 1972).

12. The *Washington Post* drew this analogy in an extensive Pearl Harbor Day editorial, "1931 and 1966," 7 December 1966, p. 23.

13. Fred Greene, *U.S. Policy and the Security of Asia* (New York: McGraw-Hill, 1968), p. 356; see also pp. 62, 66, 197, 356.

14. An early appraisal emphasizing the desire to avoid nuclear blackmail by the United States as a basic motivation behind the Chinese nuclear program is found in Morton H. Halperin and Dwight H. Perkins, *Communist China and Arms Control* (Cambridge: Center for International Affairs, Harvard University, 1965), esp. pp. 63–66. For other substantive samples of a wide-ranging body of analysis supporting this interpretation see John Gittings, *The Role of the Chinese Army* (New York: Oxford University Press, 1967); Arthur Huck, *The Security of China* (London: Chatto & Windus, 1970), pp. 221–240; and William W. Whitson, *The Chinese High Command: A History of Communist Military Politics, 1927–71* (New York: Praeger, 1973), esp. pp. 489–490.

15. Louis J. Halle, *The Cold War as History* (New York: Harper, 1962), p. 193; see also idem, *Dream and Reality*, p. 218.

16. Gordon, *Toward Disengagement*, esp. p. 42.

17. John K. Fairbank, *China: The People's Middle Kingdom and the U.S.A.* (Cambridge: Harvard University Press, Belknap, 1967), p. 96; see also p. 51.

18. Chalmers Johnson, "Changing U.S. Attitudes toward China," *Bulletin of the International House of Japan*, October 1968, p. 49.

19. Selig S. Harrison, *India, Pakistan, and the United States*, a reprint of three articles published in the *New Republic*, August 10, August 24, and September 7, 1959, p. 4.

20 Cited in Sir Reginald Coupland, *India: A Re-Statement* (London: Oxford University Press, 1945), p. 189.

21. Zulfikar Ali Bhutto, "Pakistan Builds Anew," *Foreign Affairs*, April 1973, p. 545.

22. Sir Olaf Caroe, "The Persian Gulf—A Romance," *Round Table* (London), March 1949, pp. 133–138.

23. Ibid., pp. 136–137.

24. Sir Olaf Caroe, *Wells of Power: The Oilfields of Southwest Asia* (London: Macmillan, 1951), pp. 168–169.

25. Sir Olaf Caroe to Selig S. Harrison, 10 July 1959. Sir Olaf also recalled the impact of *Wells of Power* on U.S. policy in "The Foreign Policies of Pakistan," *Pakistan Quarterly*, Summer 1958, pp. 30–35. His six-week U.S. visit in 1952 was from May 5 through June 20.

26. Cited in Harrison, *India, Pakistan, and the United States*, p. 4.

27. Harrison, *India, Pakistan, and the United States*, p. 4, based on an interview with Bowles.

28. John P. Callahan, *New York Times*, 21 November 1953; p. 1.

29. For example, see the *New York Times*, 12 November 1953, p. 3, for an account of Governor General Ghulam Mohammed's visits to President Eisenhower and Secretary Dulles; and a subsequent Karachi dispatch by John P. Callahan, ibid., 1 December 1953, p. 4.

30. Ralph de Toledano, *Nixon* (New York: Duell, Sloan & Pearce, 1956), p. 164.

31. Robert Trumbull, "U.S. Faces Decision on Major Asia Ties," *New York Times*, 9 December 1953, p. 3; see also Walter Waggoner, "Nixon Due to Urge Pakistan Arms Aid," 10 December 1953, p. 1; and Robert Trumbull, "Pakistan Eyed as Balance," ibid., p. 2.

32. Hanson W. Baldwin, *New York Times*, 22 December 1953, p. 6.

33. A detailed analysis of the Peshawar installations as a factor in U.S. South Asian policy prior to 1966 may be found in Selig S. Harrison, "America, India, and Pakistan: A Chance for a Fresh Start," *Harper's*, July 1966, pp. 56–68.

34. Welcome address, Srinagar, 10 December 1955.

35. Chakravarti Rajagopalachari, "A Confederation of India and Pakistan," *Times of India*, 29 January 1959, p. 5.

36. Selig S. Harrison, "U.S. at Crossroads in India-Pakistan Policy," *Washington Post*, 29 August 1965, p. E4.

37. Romesh Thapar, "Impending Battles," *Economic Weekly* (Bombay), 10 July 1965, p. 1089.

38. Chester Bowles, *Promises to Keep* (New York: Harper & Row, 1971), pp. 481–484.

39. See especially Neville Maxwell, *India's China War* (London: Cape, 1970); and John Kenneth Galbraith, *A China Passage* (Boston: Houghton Mifflin, 1973), pp. 71–73.

40. Zulfikar Ali Bhutto, *The Myth of Independence* (London: Oxford University Press, 1969), pp. 79–93.

41. Keith Callard, *Pakistan's Foreign Policy* (Hong Kong: Hong Kong University Press, 1959), pp. 2–3, 9.

42. Interview, Rawalpindi, 10 December 1962. Bhutto reaffirmed his expectation of a Sino-U.S. détente in an interview at Larkana on December 20, 1967, and later in *Myth of Independence*, p. 21.

43. H. S. Suhrawardy, "Political Stability and Democracy in Pakistan," *Foreign Affairs*, April 1957, p. 431.

44. W. H. Morris-Jones, "Pakistan Post-mortem and the Roots of Bangladesh," *Political Quarterly* (London), April–June 1972, pp. 187–200.

45. Selig S. Harrison, "Nehru's Plan for Peace," *New Republic*, 19 June 1971, pp. 17–22; for an earlier Nehru discussion of the confederation idea see his interview with C. L. Sulzberger, *New York Times*, 2 March 1957, p. 23.

46. Henry Kissinger's White House briefing of December 7, 1971, and Assistant Secretary of State Joseph Sisco's briefing of December 4, 1971.

47. Henry A. Kissinger, White House briefing, 7 December 1971.

48. This interpretation is reflected in William J. Barnds, "India, Pakistan, and American Realpolitik," *Christianity and Crisis*, 12 June 1972, pp. 143–149; see also President Richard M. Nixon's State of the World message to Congress, White House Press Office, 25 February 1972; and an interview with Nixon in *Time*, 3 January 1972, p. 10.

49. The "debt" issue is discussed in Selig S. Harrison, "Japan: A Question of Gratitude," *Washington Post*, 26 September 1971, p. 1; see also President Nixon's State of the World message to Congress, White House Press Office, 25 February 1972, pp. 21–22; and Hiroshi Kitamura, *Psychological Dimensions of U.S.-Japanese Relations*, Occasional Papers in International Affairs no. 28 (Cambridge: Center for International Affairs, Harvard University, August 1971), pp. 16–17.

50. As an example of this rationale see Y. Suenaga, "Japan-U.S. Relations—1," *Daily Yomiuri* (Tokyo), 23 January 1972, p. 5. Suenaga is a pseudonym for Makoto Momoi, international affairs director of the National Defense College.

51. William L. Caudill, "American Soldiers in a Japanese Community" (May 1968), based on a report to the U.S. surgeon general under Contract DA-49-007-MD-685, esp. pp. 8, 13, 26, 30, 43–44, 61–65. Privately circulated.

52. Chikara Makino, Planning Office, Minister's Secretariat, Ministry of International Trade and Industry, "Japan-U.S. Relations: Analysis of the Present Situation and Experimental Discussions on Future Prospects," *Tsusan Journal*, May 1970, p. 19.

53. Kazushige Hirasawa, "Changing Japanese-American Relations in the 1970's," Dillingham Lecture (East-West Center, 17 May 1972), p. 4.

54. Herbert Glazer, *The International Businessman in Japan: The Japanese Image* (Tokyo: Sophia University Press, 1968), p. 9.

55. George F. Kennan, *Memoirs: 1925-50* (Boston: Little, Brown, 1967), pp. 368–393.

56. Interview with Shigeru Yoshida, Tokyo, 30 September 1964, John Foster Dulles Oral History Project, Princeton University Library, pp. 3–5, 22.

57. Martin E. Weinstein, *Japan's Postwar Defense Policy, 1947-68* (New York: Columbia University Press, 1971), pp. 12–43; see also pp. 13–43 and 130–132.

58. Makoto Momoi and Masataka Kosaka, *Takyoku-jidai no senryaku* [Strategy in the multipolar era] (Tokyo: Nihon Kokusai Mondai Kenkyujo, 1973), vol. 2, pp. 463–464.

59. Kei Wakaizumi, "Japan's 'Grand Experiment' and the Japanese-American Alliance," Woodrow Wilson International Center for Scholars, 9 October 1975, p. 20, mimeo.

60. Raymond Kathe, vice-president for Asia and the Pacific, First National City Bank of New York, in a dissent to the panel report on U.S.-Japanese political relations, *Critical Issues Affecting Asia's Future* (Washington: Center for Strategic Studies, Georgetown University, 1969), p. 19.

61. A revealing statement of the political rationale offered in behalf of the security treaty is found in "Need for Firm Maintenance of Japan-U.S. Security Setup," an analysis issued by the Security Policy Study Committee of the Liberal Democratic party (Tokyo, 28 August 1967).

62. Richard M. Nixon, *U.S. Foreign Policy for the 1970's* (Washington: Government Printing Office, 1973), p. 102.

63. George W. Ball discussed this feeling in *United States Foreign Economic Policy toward Japan*, Hearings Before the Subcommittee on Foreign Economic Policy of the House Committee on Foreign Affairs, 92nd Cong., 2nd sess., 2–4 and 8 November 1971, p. 4.

64. Hiroshi Kitamura, *Psychological Dimensions of U.S.-Japanese Relations*, p. 18.

65. As a participant in the annual U.S. Military Academy Faculty Conference, "U.S. Security Policy and Asia, 1966–1976," West Point, 20–25 June 1966.

66. M. Makoto, "Wanted: A Seaborne ABM System to Meet China's Missile Threat," *Daily Yomiuri*, 27 January 1967, p. 5.

67. George Wilson, "Navy Proposes Floating Defense against Missiles off Russia, China," *Washington Post*, 23 July 1967, p. 1. The initial SABMIS plan also was discussed in Paul C. Davis, "Sentinel and the Future of SABMIS," *Military Review*, March 1968, pp. 20–22, and Hanson W. Baldwin, *Strategy for Tomorrow* (New York: Harper & Row, 1970), pp. 100–101, 223–224.

68. Greene, *U.S. Policy and Security of Asia*, p. 296.

69. American embassy briefing, Tokyo, 8 October 1969.

70. "Sato-Nixon Communiqué," *New York Times*, 22 November 1969, p. 14.

71. This is based on access to the tape recording of Sato's informal comments at Keidanren headquarters in Tokyo on December 8, 1969; see Selig S. Harrison, "Japanese Wary of Nuclear Treaty," *Washington Post*, 15 December 1969, p. 3.

72. Press conference, Foreign Ministry, Tokyo, 17 February 1966.

73. Ibid.

74. *See Naval Nuclear Propulsion Program*, Hearings before the Joint Committee on Atomic Energy, 92d Cong., 1st sess., 10 March 1971, pp. 82-83.

75. *Defense Report*, Statement of Secretary of Defense Melvin R. Laird before the Senate Armed Services Committee on the FY 1972-76 Defense Program and the 1972 Defense Budget, 92d Cong., 1st sess., 15 March, 1971, pp. 15, 75-77.

76. See the statement by Gen. Bruce K. Holloway on March 23, 1971, in *Department of Defense Appropriations for 1972*, Hearings before the Subcommittee on Appropriations of the House Committee on Appropriations, 92d Cong., 1st sess., 1971, pt. 2: 274–275. Samples of the Japanese response may be found in "What Shocking Surgical Operation Is Nixon Going to Perform on Japan Next?" *Gendai*, October 1971; and M. Yasuda, "U.S. Nuclear Umbrella No Longer Credible," *Daily Yomiuri*, 18 August 1971, p. 3.

77. *Defense Report* (for 1972), p. 22; this same phraseology was frequently used by Laird in discussing the 1973 budget, p. 23.

78. *Defense Report* (for 1972), p. 19.

79. Friedheim's comments are presented as they appear in the text of his July 7 briefing, Department of State, Unclassified Tokyo Dispatch 6709, 7 July

1971, addressed to the Secretary of Defense and signed by Friedheim, p. 4, and are in accord with my own less complete notes.

80. This phraseology is based on my own notes and those of others present but is in general accord with the edited transcript in ibid., p. 11.

81. Ibid., p. 12.

82. Ibid., p. 13.

83. Ibid. This is supplemented by my own notes and those of others present.

84. Selig S. Harrison, "Laird Confuses Japan on A-Arms Issue," *Washington Post*, 14 July 1971, p. 1.

85. For example, see Takashi Oka, "Laird Advises Japan to Spur Defense," *New York Times*, 8 July 1971, p. 3; and Elizabeth Pond, "Will Japan Assume a Stronger Defense Role?" *Christian Science Monitor*, 12 July 1971, p. 5.

86. For example, see *Yomiuri*, 11 July 1971, p. 2.

87. "The Tokyo Bomb Caper," *Republican Report*, 29 July 1971, full issue.

88. *Asahi* (Tokyo), 12 July 1971, p. 4; see also an editorial in *Yomiuri*, 12 July 1971, p. 5, and "Shocks a Nuclear Dispatch Has Given," *Asahi Journal*, 23 July 1971, p. 8.

89. "Japanese-American Bilateral Meeting" (Transcript of the Third Annual Conference sponsored by the International Press Institute, San Diego, 26-29 November 1972), p. 76; see also Yasuo Takeyama, "Bei no Shin-sekai Senryaku to Nihon—II" [The new U.S. world strategy and Japan, Part 2], *Nihon Keizai*, 30 November 1971, p. 1.

90. Hideo Sekino, "U.S.-Japan Military Relations at a Turning Point," *Kokusai Mondai* (organ of the Japan Institute of International Affairs), November 1971, pp. 15-16.

91. *Time*, 3 January 1972, p. 11.

92. See the analysis of Nixon's address in Kansas City on July 6, 1971, and the *Time* interview in Graham T. Allison, "American Foreign Policy and Japan," *Discord in the Pacific*, ed. Henry Rosovsky (Washington: Columbia Books, 1973), pp. 35-38.

93. W. R. Kintner, "Arms Control for a Five-Power World" (address prepared for the Fifth International Arms Control Symposium, Philadelphia, 15 October 1971), pp. 15-16; see also idem, "Japan and the U.S.—New Directions," *Freedom at Issue*, September-October 1971, pp. 5-6.

94. Kintner, "Arms Control," p. 26.

95. Ibid., pp. 34-35.

96. Ibid., p. 40.

97. Ibid., p. 32.

98. Yasuhiro Nakasone, "International Environment and Defense of Japan in the 1970's" (address presented at the Harvard Club of Japan, Tokyo, 30 June 1970), p. 6; see also pp. 4, 8.

99. "Limits of U.S. 'Diplomacy of Balance,'" *Sankei Shimbun* (Tokyo), 11 February 1972, p. 4; see also "Nixon Diplomacy," *Nihon Keizai*, 10 February 1972; and Nixon's Realism," *Yomiuri*, 12 February 1972.

100. Hajime Doba, a member of the Yomiuri International Affairs Research Council, in an interview in *Kokubō* [National defense], Tokyo, September 1971, p. 5.

101. "Kono Says 'Pay for N-Umbrella'," *Mainichi Daily News*, Tokyo, 14 January 1972, p. 6.

102. "Nuclear Umbrella," *Asahi Shimbun*, 16 January 1972, p. 4.

103. From the American embassy transcript of a briefing for Japanese defense correspondents by Howard Meyers, political-military counselor, Tokyo, 13 January 1972, p. 3.

104. "Careless Arguments on 'Japan Going Nuclear'," *Mainichi Daily News*, 14 January 1972, p. 3.

105. Hisao Iwashima, "Trends of Peace Research and Military Studies in Japan," paper presented at fifth annual convention of the International Studies Association, Dallas, 14-18 March 1972, p. 9.

106. See Selig S. Harrison, "Japan Puts Satellite into Orbit," *Washington Post*, 29 September 1971, p. 2.

107. Zbigniew Brzezinski, *The Fragile Blossom* (New York: Harper & Row, 1972), p. 137; a similar view is expressed by Kenneth Hunt, deputy director of the International Institute for Strategic Studies, in "Security Systems in East Asia" (paper delivered at the "Peace in Asia" conference, Kyoto, 7 June 1972), p. 7.

108. Jay B. Sorenson, *Japanese Policy and Nuclear Arms*, Monograph Series No. 12, American-Asian Educational Exchange (New York: National Strategy Information Center, 1975), pp. 59-60.

109. Ibid., p. 18.

110. Ibid., p. 58.

111. William R. Van Cleave and S. T. Cohen, "Nuclear Aspects of Future U.S. Security Policy in Asia," *Orbis*, Fall 1975, p. 1167.

112. Robert L. Pfaltzgraff, Jr., and Jacquelyn Davis, *Japanese-American Relations In a Changing Security Environment*, The Foreign Policy Papers, vol. 1 (Beverly Hills: Sage Publications, 1975), p. 31. The authors do not advocate nuclear sharing. Under present circumstances, they urge a strong U.S. defense posture in the Pacific and a strong Japan-U.S. alliance that would make it unnecessary for Japan to go nuclear, warning against U.S. concessions in a SALT II agreement that would "erode the credibility of the U.S. nuclear guarantee" (p. 32).

113. David Shilling, "A Reassessment of Japan's Naval Defense Needs," *Asian Survey*, March 1976, p. 229. Shilling was identified as an analyst in the Asia Division of the Office of the Assistant Secretary of Defense (Program Analysis and Evaluation).

114. The cost issue is discussed in Albert Wohlstetter, "Security Policies of Japan as a Non-nuclear State" (paper delivered at the "Peace in Asia" conference, Kyoto, June 1972), pp. 8-9.

115. Hisao Iwashima, "Trends of Peace Research," p. 7.

116. For example, see Yasuhiro Nakasone, "International Environment and

Defense of Japan," p. 10; see also Selig S. Harrison, "Japan's Defense Minister Drops Advocacy of Nuclear Force," *Washington Post*, 5 March 1970, p. 2.

117. "Miyazawa on Nuclearism," *Far Eastern Economic Review*, 18 December 1971, pp. 21-22.

118. Kobayashi Yosaji, ed., *1970: An Approach to Revisions of the Security Treaty* (Tokyo: Yomiuri, 1966), pt. II, chap. 2, pp. 109-110.

119. "Post-Pullout Crisis Aid Plan Proposed," *Mainichi Daily News*, 31 December 1970, p. 1.

120. See *Views on the Theory of Emergency Deployment* (Tokyo: Foreign Ministry, 20 April 1966), a compendium of proposals for an emergency intervention approach, with a government rebuttal. For responses by the Democratic Socialist party see *Decisions* of the *Ninth National Convention* (Tokyo, 1967), pp. 75-79; and a critique by DSP defense specialist Eichi Nagasue in *Kaikakusha* [Reformer], July 1966, pp. 30-35. See also a subsequent discussion of this issue in *Nippon no Anzenhōsho o Kangaeru* [Some thoughts on the security of Japan] (Tokyo: Foreign Ministry, 1969), esp. chap. 9, sec. 2.

121. This version of the Packard response is attributed to secret minutes of the meeting by Jack Anderson in *Mainichi Daily News*, 29 January 1972, p. 2. Substantially similar accounts appeared in dispatches from B. Takahama in the *Daily Yomiuri*, 3 December 1971, p. 1, following the December 1 meeting; and from R. Kamisue in *Nihon Keizai*, 5 December 1971, p. 3. According to the minutes provided by the Democratic Socialist party, however, Packard said that "one question that would arise from the removal of U.S. forces would be what is going to be done with respect to Japan's nuclear armament."

122. *Defense Report*, statement of Secretary of Defense Elliot L. Richardson before the Senate Armed Services Committee on the FY 1974 Defense Budget, 94th Cong., 1st sess., 10 April 1973, pp. 13, 82-83.

123. For example, see Laird's interview, "Why Soviet Arms Worry U.S.," *U.S. News and World Report*, 27 March 1972, p. 44.

124. In a news conference in Tokyo on June 12, 1972, Kissinger was asked about Laird's view and said that there would be "no American pressure" for Japan to expand its defense role beyond the home islands.

125. Osamu Kaihara, *Senshi ni manabu* [To learn from the history of wars] (Tokyo: Asagumo, 1970), pt. 2, no. 1, scenario 7.

126. Ibid., scenario 3; see also idem, *Waga kuni no bōei ni tsuite* [On the defense of this country] (Tokyo: Bōei Konwakai, 1967).

127. Y. Suenaga, "Japan Wants a Voice in Pacific Naval Balance," *Daily Yomiuri*, 31 January 1972, p. 6.

128. Ibid.

129. Y. Suenaga, "Wanted: Disarm Conference to Freeze Navies in the Pacific," *Daily Yomiuri*, 28 January 1972, p. 6; see also idem, "Japan Wants a Voice in Pacific Naval Balance."

130. Y. Suenaga, "Japan Wants a Voice in Pacific Naval Balance," p. 6.

9. Nationalism and the American Economic Presence

The transformation of the American role in the world economy is predicted in strikingly similar terms by messiahs preaching the virtues of foreign enterprise and prophets of doom warning against the onrush of a rapacious capitalism in vulnerable developing countries. Both see the United States inescapably cast as a headquarters or "service" economy drawing its primary balance of payments sustenance not from direct exports but from American or American-controlled multinational corporations[1] with manufacturing activities based increasingly in low-wage areas.

By 1985, argues an executive of a leading Pacific-based multinational, college graduates will outnumber non–high school graduates in the U.S. labor force, and

> in an American society steadily more crowded, steadily more educated, competing for steadily diminishing natural resources . . . we can expect the exportation of those jobs that people with greater expectations find dull, repetitive, physically unpleasant or dangerous, and the continued conversion of the U.S. to a center of high technology. . . . The domestic profit squeeze will accelerate the search for increased productivity and most assuredly accelerate the growth of multinational manufacturing, with corporations seeking areas of lowest material and labor costs. The multinational firm has been the normal outgrowth from the new awareness of the total, interrelated nature of our world and its economy. . . . We are in a *period of necessary and inevitable integration and synthesis in all things!*[2]

In the "oligopolistic equilibrium" and "hierarchical division of labor between regions" resulting from American, Japanese, and West European business expansion, echoes a scholar gloomily,

> high-level decision-making occupations will be centralized in a few key cities in the advanced countries, surrounded by a number of regional sub-capitals,

311

with the rest of the world confined to lower levels of activity and income, i.e., to the status of towns and villages in a new imperial system. Income, status, authority and consumption patterns would radiate out from these centers along a declining curve, and the existing patterns of inequality and dependence would be perpetuated.[3]

For the executive and the scholar alike, the common denominator underlying expectations of an ever spreading expansion of the power of multinational corporations is the assumption that nationalism must sooner or later yield not only to economic imperatives but also to the progressively tightening "transnational" linkages of transportation, communication, and technology now girdling the globe. This assumption has been implicitly accepted even by the most sensitive and conscientious analyst of the problems attendant on the spread of the multinationals, Raymond Vernon, who stresses their economic contribution and focuses on ways to achieve "more tolerable levels of tension"[4] between foreign investors and host governments through international accountability and regulation. The assumption has also been widely questioned by economists as well as others, however, even by an unusually ardent defender of the comparative advantage concept, Paul Samuelson, who foresees some shift of manufacturing industry abroad but warns against letting it go too far. Pleading for floating exchange rates and a free trade policy maximizing American competitiveness, Samuelson has observed that

economics, alas, cannot be divorced from politics and from trends of ideologies hostile to absentee ownership. Suppose that economic equilibrium did dictate our becoming a service economy, living like any rentier on investment earnings from abroad. Let us grant that such an equilibrium, if permanent, could be optimal for the United States. But would it be safe for us to succumb to this natural pattern of specialization in a world of rising nationalism? Can one really believe that in the last three decades of the twentieth century the rest of the world can be confidently counted on to permit the continuing flow of dividends, repatriation of earnings and royalties to large corporations owned here?[5]

NATIONALISM AND FOREIGN INVESTMENT

In Asia, where American direct investment totaled $9.07 billion out of a worldwide total of $133.2 billion in 1975,[6] growing business interest has been stimulated by rich natural resources, low labor costs, and average annual profits running substantially higher (23.5 percent) than those in Latin America (14.2 percent) and Europe (16 percent).[7] Ironically, however, this developing shift of interest has come at the very time when nationalism is on the upsurge in Asia as never before, foreshadowing a political climate increasingly hostile to foreign investment. It is my contention in this chapter that nationalism would progressively inhibit an American economic strategy based on "natural" specialization in a comparative advantage framework and that American political relations with Asia would become more and more poisoned if equity investment, as against trade and aid, should ever dominate the American economic presence. By its nature, nationalism rejects the plea that foreign enterprise "should be judged by how it operates rather than for what it is."[8] It defies the assumption of many a Western observer that if "the children live better than the parents, this matters more than the closing of some abstract and statistically ambiguous gap between rich and poor nations."[9] The nationalist compulsion is not simply for economic growth as an end in itself, even when the country concerned is relatively low on the global economic ladder. As we have stated earlier, it is for growth achieved with a maximum of national control, leading to as much nationally controlled economic power as a particular national bargaining position permits.

This climate of economic nationalism reflects something more than the narrowly based "defensive reactions" of local elite groups seeking to protect their own power, of local business elements with their own ambitions, or of intellectuals animated by a doctrinaire hostility toward capitalism.[10] It is not just a matter of clashing cultures or a "Trojan horse" syndrome,[11] in which the foreign enterprise is seen as an agent of American diplomatic interests. The continually shifting rationalizations[12] advanced in resisting investment betray a visceral and deeply embedded revulsion. The emotional roots of this resistance lie in the elemental hunger for a basic change in world power relationships, a change that in the nationalist perspective can come about only if the expansion of existing economic power centers is slowed down and Asian countries are substantially insulated from foreign equity investment while their own power is built up. In this perspective, slower growth is preferable to growth as an extension of Western power; foreign-owned enterprise is not regarded as growth at all; and decentralized, labor-intensive small industry, maximizing self-reliance, is often seen as a sounder foundation for development than big factories with the latest foreign machinery.

The character and intensity of economic nationalism in Asia was underlined by the restrained Asian reaction to the oil price increases initiated by OPEC in 1973. For India, Bangladesh, and other countries already caught in a balance of payments squeeze, these price increases had a devastating impact. In Asian eyes, however, the new power of OPEC was seen as a long-term breakthrough for the non-Western world as a whole. OPEC was viewed not only as an economic instrumentality but also as an organization profoundly political in its purposes, comparable to the European Coal and Steel Community, in its own way, rather than to an old-style cartel. With Arab per capita income less than half that of the United States and the Indonesian per capita level still near $80, it was sophistry, in this perspective, to equate the OPEC new rich and the old rich of the West; OPEC aid efforts were measured, accordingly, by a more lenient yardstick than Western aid programs. The "energy crisis" was perceived in Asia as part of a broader international economic malaise rooted in disproportionate consumption on the part of the industrially advanced countries, especially those in the West; in inflationary trends that predated the OPEC increases; and in high prices for food and other imports from the West that were applied, like oil prices, without regard for the developmental level of consuming countries or their ability to pay. Moreover, Western oil companies— above all, the majors—were blamed for passing on price increases to consuming countries and maintaining what have long been regarded in Asia as extortionate profit levels. China alone, with its emphasis on maximizing self-reliance, was largely beyond the reach of the majors and emerged with enhanced prestige. To the extent that other Asian countries have emphasized self-reliance in the petroleum field at the expense of maximum production, as in the case of India, they have felt vindicated by a changing economic climate in which the power of the multinationals was no longer unchallenged. Spurred by OPEC successes, Asian countries were more anxious than ever to exploit their own natural resources fully but more determined than ever to retain national control over their petroleum development as part of an overall posture of increasing resistance to foreign economic penetration.

To say that nationalism promises growing hostility toward foreign investment is not to say that Asian countries eager for technology and capital will necessarily reject any and all American investment or all forms of American business and government participation in Asian development. On the contrary, given the extent of the economic need in Asia and the aggressive thrust of the multinationals, selective American investment arrangements are likely to continue as part of a more and more diversified economic landscape in which other, preferred forms of American business involvement will be actively invited. Experience to date suggests that joint ventures in the private sector with varying degrees of local ownership will generally be the preferred form for these selective investment relationships. But even joint ventures are likely to have a tenuous coexistence with growing local private enterprise, often patronized by local governments, and with steadily expanding public industrial enterprises in search of foreign cooperation.

The precise role of foreign business will vary in accordance with the economic and political bargaining power of Asian countries, especially their natural resources, and with the nature of their leadership at any particular point in time. Where authoritarian governments or oligarchic elites ignore popular attitudes and utilize outside strength to shore up their domestic power, the foreign investor will often find an artificially warm welcome dependent on the survival of a particular regime. This element of artificiality will be enhanced where corruption and galloping inequities sow the seeds of future upheaval or where transitional political entities seek to buy time by giving foreign investors a stake in the status quo, as in South Korea, Taiwan, and pre-1975 South Vietnam. Where a large country has a sense of its own potential, as in India, foreign investment is automatically suspect; where a tiny entrepôt lacks a clear rationale for national identity, as in Singapore, foreign hostages strengthen the odds for survival. In all of these cases and others, the immediate benefits that can be offered by the foreign investor in the form of jobs and otherwise unavailable technology are balanced against nationalist values that will be more strongly defended under one set of economic and political circumstances than another. Broadly speaking, however, the overall long-term trend is likely to be increasing antagonism to conventional patterns of foreign equity investment. By the same token, nationally controlled public sector industry is likely to grow, and this chapter will focus, accordingly, on the deep-rooted social and political factors that make public industrial enterprise an integral expression of nationalism in Asia. Public enterprise is often deliberately used to shield key areas of industry from foreign investment and has thus become a major focus of tension in American relations with many Asian countries. It is in this context that the troubled American experience in relating to Asian industrialization will be compared with the more successful record of a rapidly expanding Japan.

The relationship between the United States and Asian countries seeking modernization of their economies is inherently abrasive because the United States is solidly identified with the legacy of Western economic colonialism. Simply because it is so big and so rich, the United States is automatically regarded as a latter-day imperialist, and the American economic record in the Philippines lends substance to Asian suspicions. As the world's principal industrial power, the United States is measured even more searchingly than others in terms of the central Leninist premise that the industrialized powers would like to keep undeveloped Asian countries in the perpetual status of an agricultural suburbia. This basic psychological conditioning indelibly marks all Asian attitudes toward American investment and tends to obscure the fact that American aid programs have in many cases provided the indispensable underpinnings for industrialization in the fields of power, transportation, and education, not to mention the constructive U.S. role in strengthening Asian agriculture.

There is no escape from the damaging fact that American bona fides on the issue of independent industrialization are most profoundly suspect in the very country in which the American presence has been longest and most intensive. As Frank Golay has observed, the economy inherited by the independent Philippines "conformed to the stereotype of the colonial-type economy."[13] Tariff-free American manufactured goods flooded the islands during the colonial years and discouraged local efforts to industrialize. At the same time, the United States tied Manila to a trade dependence by stimulating the production of sugar, copra, and hemp for the American market. Even in granting independence, Washington took its pound of flesh by insisting on a privileged position for American business as a condition of self-rule, and the Philippines now has the largest concentration of American capital in Asia. An interagency government survey of a cross-section of 1,383 leading firms showed that American capital constituted 79.2 percent of the foreign investment in these enterprises; 30 percent of all investment, foreign and non-foreign; and a "very significant" 32 percent of manufacturing investment.[14] American investment had increased from $149 million in 1950 to $415 million in 1963 and to $975 million by the time of the Marcos takeover in 1972, in the official American estimate,[15] with some estimates ranging as high as $2 billion.[16] This disproportionate American presence has become a target of nationalist discontent focused not only on the United States, as such, but also on a repressive Manila regime viewed as an American client.

In the view of many Filipinos, the Marcos coup was directly inspired by pressures from American business leaders who feared the rising power demonstrated by economic nationalist forces at the constitutional convention that was being held in late 1971 and early 1972. There is considerable support for this view in the fact that the convention had profoundly alarmed the American business community[17] in Manila, with its detailed and deadly serious discussion of proposals for expropriation and restrictions on new investment.[18] At the time of the coup, the American business lobby was fighting vigorously against such proposals; immediately afterward, Marcos moved to scotch them, opening the way for further expansion of U.S. and foreign investment. It would be difficult to make a precise assessment of the relative importance of the investment issue as against other factors in precipitating the takeover or to determine the extent to which Marcos utilized the investment controversy as one among many justifications for action that might have occurred for other reasons. But there can be little doubt that many, if not most, politically conscious Filipinos put much of the blame for the coup on the United States and are now more suspicious of American bonafides than ever.

The challenge to nationalism is unusually formidable in the Philippines, where the economic carry-over of colonialism in the industrial field has been so much greater, relative to the indigenous private sector, than in the erstwhile British, French, and Dutch colonies.[19] This entrenchment of foreign influence has been largely made possible, in turn, by the disparate character of nationalist resistance in a diverse archipelago where geographic, social, and linguistic obstacles to a sense of national identity have been reinforced by the unusual circumstance of two successive colonial regimes followed by a military occupation and the relatively painless acquisition of independence without the necessity of a bitter struggle. As we observed in an earlier chapter, the manner in which freedom was achieved and the legacy of a common Filipino-American struggle against Japan tended to vitiate the emotional intensity of subsequent opposition to the American military and economic presence during the early years of independence. Clearly, the Philippines cannot be considered a representative case in an analysis of economic nationalism in Asia; yet it is instructive that even where national identity is still so inchoate, and a "late-blooming"[20] nationalism so formless, the specter of foreign economic power has provided such an important rallying point.

Where national identities are sharper and the anticolonial animus deeper, the intensity and breadth of nationalist resistance to foreign investment have generally been correspondingly greater. Throughout Asia, however, the rationale for economic nationalism rests on substantially the same assumptions as it does in the Philippines: the West wants to see as little independent Asian industrialization as possible; it wants to keep Asia as a preserve for Western investment, especailly for the extraction of natural resources needed in the home countries; and the alleged benefits of such investment to Asian countries are far outweighed by the costs even in strictly economic terms.

Far from diminishing with time, as we shall see, the image of the West as opposed to independent Asian industrial growth has been intensified by the pro-agriculture bias of American aid ideology and the growing emphasis on population control. For Asian leaders who

see industrialization as an essential element in keeping pace with
population pressures, appeals for population control unaccompanied
by an equal emphasis on industrial growth are automatically suspect.
Indeed, warnings against overpopulation, pollution, and the deple-
tion of resources are often perceived as manifestations of Western
hostility toward industry. Thus, Tarzie Vittachi, former director of
the Press Foundation of Asia and author of an anticommunist
critique of the Sukarno regime, voiced a characteristic attitude cutting across political creeds and national boundaries in Asia when he
angrily charged in 1972 that

> the general idea, it seems, is for the poor world to stop having babies so that
> the rich can stay rich. The second remedy suggested is that the poor world
> should not make the mistakes that the rich world has made, such as taking
> to industry. Look at what industry has done to the West, says the West. All
> that foul air, all that garbage, all those beer cans in the rivers. Nasty. So why
> shouldn't the poor world stay agricultural and spiritual in its traditional
> ways and thus avoid industrial pollution? It would be one thing for Asia to
> remain the world's village if only the rich world would stick to industry and
> not meddle with agriculture. But why is the Asian farmer still poor? Because
> there are no markets for his produce. Why not? Because America, Japan,
> Russia and the European Common Market are overproducing agricultural
> goods. . . . The acquisitive society is scared of environmental pollution
> because it fears that there will be no more raw materials to be taken out of
> the poor world to enable the wheels of industry to keep turning round in
> the West. . . . The real problem is not that the earth has insufficient
> resources, nor that the world is getting dirtier, nor even that there is bad
> resource planning, but that the riches of the world are owned by a few
> countries and by a few people within those few countries.[21]

Rhetorical overstatement aside, this passage suggests the depth of the
controlled rage that lies behind the Asian side of the running controversy over whether or not foreign investment benefits developing
countries. Since Western motives are fundamentally suspect, the
burden of proof rests entirely with the defender of investment who
gives assurance of, let us say, the local reinvestment of profits. This is
especially so at a time when multinational corporations appear to be
talking out of both sides of the mouth by promising local reinvestment to Asian countries while simultaneously pledging maximum
remittances to their home countries as an aid to the balance of
payments. In the nationalist perspective, it is not really necessary to
await a comprehensive, final verdict when the circumstantial evidence is so strong. Asian economists such as Gerardo Sicat, who
support the investment cause, are either dismissed as sycophants or
condemned for their failure to see the forest for the trees, a failure
attributed to an intellectual and cultural alienation resulting from
overexposure to American development economics.[22]

The classic statement of the view that foreign investment is the most expensive form of foreign capital was made as early as 1950 by Hans Singer [23] and has since been the focus of a continuing expert debate. Studies by Asian and Western economists alike have offered voluminous evidence seeking to demonstrate that foreign equity capital imposes a greater balance of payments strain than loan capital [24] and stressing, at the same time, both the high cost of the technology acquired through foreign investment as well as the perils of dependence on foreign partners who hold their know-how closely. [25] Raymond Vernon has presented the most competent rebuttal to the nationalist case, emphasizing the stake acquired by investors in the economic fate of the countries in which they operate and their consequent vulnerability to the renegotiation of the original terms of their entry in favor of the host country. [26] By and large, as Matthew Kust has observed with reference to India, [27] there is a consensus in most Asian countries that foreign investment carries exorbitant costs. Where it is invited nonetheless, the determining reason most often lies in a deliberate decision to bear the costs involved for the sake of critically desired technology not otherwise available and in a grudging recognition that this technology is likely to be transmitted most effectively, under present circumstances, if the investor has an equity stake in the undertaking.

NATIONALISM AND PUBLIC ENTERPRISE

As new statistical evidence accumulates, the technical economic debate over foreign investment rages unabated, but economic issues are subordinate to political questions where there is endemic hostility toward foreign economic power as such. The effort to insulate key areas of the national economy from foreign control has a momentum of its own and leads to a variety of defensive reflexes. It does not necessarily find its primary expression, as in the Philippines, in government support of indigenous private business. In many cases, the private sector offers a less satisfactory answer to the foreign investment challenge than the public sector in nationalist terms; the reasons for this are stubborn ones rooted in intractable social, political, and economic factors that we will now explore.

For the most part, the persistence of a significant public sector commitment in so many Asian countries has been explained in terms of economic necessity or ideological bias. It is thus generally recognized that certain areas of industrial development require a capacity for large-scale economic risk that only governments are generally ready to assume. Similarly, the neo-Marxist and Fabian influences in the thinking of many Asian leaders have been widely noted. What is often missing in these explanations, however, is the all-important nationalist dimension. Measured by nationalist standards, public sector industrial development often takes clear preference, despite a record of relative inefficiency, because it lends itself to a greater degree of national control than private sector development as well as a greater eventual payoff in the state power needed for national security. It symbolizes national progress, equally shared, as against unbalanced development in which disparities in wealth multiply. It is seen as a pillar of self-reliance and independence. This identification of the public sector with the national interest is heightened when foreign investment pressures are directly targeted on public sector industry as an obstacle to investment objectives.

The nationalist motivation behind public sector industry acquires special strength from the fact that control of the indigenous private sector in Asia normally rests with certain tightly knit social minorities or family groups who got a head start in the economic race during colonial rule. Since these groups are beyond the competitive reach of newly rising social forces within a private enterprise framework, the public sector is utilized to offset multiplying concentration of economic power. Moreover, since their minority status makes such groups feel insecure, they often turn to foreign business as a prop to their domestic power position, provoking nationalist reliance on the public sector to safeguard national control of key areas of the economy. In the case of the Chinese and Indian business communities in Southeast Asia, the social minorities involved are regarded to one degree or another as alien to the nationalist cause irrespective of the citizenship factor. But even minorities with a place in the indigenous social structure are often controversial and embattled, resented not only for their disproportionate power as such but also because they symbolize mercantile values traditionally held in low esteem. The public sector thus has greater meaning as a generalized symbol of national progress than private enterprises that are frequently viewed as Trojan horses or as symbols of social injustice. This overarching meaning is present in varying degrees even when the immediate motivation behind public enterprise in a given case might be ideology, social vendetta, or the pure and simple thirst of a strategically situated bureaucratic or military clique for patronage, power, and graft.

Use of the public sector for the purpose of countering Chinese influence has been most pronounced in Cambodia, Malaysia, and Thailand, albeit with wide variations in the political and ideological factors defining the character of public sector enterprise. Indonesia presents a much more complex picture in which the anti-Chinese motive operates side by side with other factors, social and ideological, explaining a long-standing public sector commitment that has spanned the Sukarno and Suharto regimes. Herbert Feith has described the distinctive indigenous trading groups, largely from Sumatra and Sulawesi, who combined with orthodox *santri* Moslem landed elements in Java to form the Masjumi party.[28] President Sukarno's ambitious public sector enterprises reflected not only his socialist expression of nationalism but also his orientation in the deep-seated *santri-abangan* conflict, elaborated in Chapter 2, and the problem of containing Chinese power common to both the Sukarno and Suharto regimes. These basic social factors have continued to operate in the post-Sukarno period despite the diminished importance of ideology and the enhanced power of Masjumi-oriented elements. Even Masjumi partisans support a limited public sector, in any case, for nationalist reasons.[29] Under new policies designed to make public sector enterprises pay their way, the more efficient public enterprises were retained and in some cases expanded under Suharto as part of an increasing commitment to heavy industrialization. The new order, while less doctrinaire than the old in its attitude toward foreign investment, nonetheless has been anxious to limit foreign control over the expansion of key industries by strengthening the public sector.

To the extent that control over public enterprise fortifies the power of a corrupt authoritarianism, it becomes a focus of popular opposition not because the public sector is under attack as such but because it has fallen into suspect hands and has been diverted from its nationalist purposes. Thus, in the case of Indonesia under Suharto, there was undiminished national pride in the efficient performance of certain public enterprises established under Sukarno that remained relatively free of political interference, especially fertilizer and cement enterprises that will be examined later in another context. In addition to these manufacturing enterprises, however, the new government also organized a network of graft-ridden semiofficial conglomerates, partly mercantile in character, controlled by leading military figures or units and organized in most cases with the help of Chinese capital. The Suharto regime contended that the "Tju-kong" (literally "Chinese influence behind the military") conglomerates forced the local Chinese business community to serve Indonesian purposes, but nationalist critics responded that the Chinese and their foreign business allies wield disproportionate power. The emergence of the government oil monopoly Pertamina as a vast, integrated financial empire in its own right provided an even more visible target, prompting allegations of graft on a colossal scale as well as nationalist criticism that expansion had become an objective in itself, without reference to overall Indonesian development goals. Pertamina's defenders argued that it has to be big enough—and autonomous enough—to compete effectively with the Western majors and other state oil companies in Asia and elsewhere. But growing revelations of corruption and financial mismanagement in 1977 led to demands for closer regulation by the central government along with a reappraisal of the role of oil exports in the development process.[30] On balance, Pertamina's achievements were still widely respected, and its growing technical competence was a strong source of national self-confidence.

The interwoven factors of nationalism, ideology, and social conflict rarely turn up in quite the same mix from one country to another, but there is a significant public sector component of some kind in every Asian economy that seems likely to grow rather than diminish in importance, with the possible exception of the Philippines,[31] in the formative decades of development lying ahead. Thus, while Burma's move to socialism had a Marxist impetus, it basically reflected a desire to remove British, Chinese, and Indian economic power. A visitor in 1972 pointed to the mismanagement of many public sector enterprises resulting from the sweeping and precipitate fashion in which Burma displaced its entire entrepreneurial and management framework. But he also emphasized the egalitarian, nationalist tenor of Burmese socialism and found corruption in public enterprises "limited, by Asian standards."[32] In Sri Lanka, a strong public sector was not necessary in strictly economic terms, but public enterprise has been promoted rapidly, nonetheless, as a means of supplanting British power in the economy and of preventing the minority, non-Sinhalese Tamil business community from enhancing its already disproportionate power by moving into the resulting vacuum.

As embattled segments of divided countries, Taiwan, the defunct Republic of South Vietnam, and South Korea have consistently viewed public sector industry as a factor in their rivalry with their communist counterparts, not only their power rivalry in industrial and military terms but also, more fundamentally, their overall competition for the psychological leadership of nationalism. In Taiwan, public enterprise has also served as an instrument for preserving dictatorial rule by a social minority. While giving free scope, on the one hand, to private entrepreneurs drawn from the Taiwan-born majority, the mainlander-dominated Kuomintang regime has carefully balanced the power of the Taiwanese business community with a powerful public sector controlled by the ruling party. From the start, industrialization has been central to the nationalist dream in Vietnam, and even one of the leading non-Marxist nationalist parties active in Saigon politics before 1975, the Vietnam Quoc Dan Dang (VNQDD), has long envisaged a mixed economy with a strong state sector pacing the development of industries "too vital to the economic life of Vietnam, and too important, to be governed only by private capital."[33] The influence of French Marxist and socialist thought and a desire on the part of successive Saigon regimes to check the power of the Cholon Chinese merchants reinforced this identification of the public sector with nationalism. The Vietnamese economists, bureaucrats, and politicians encountered by the United States in the post-1954 period strongly resisted the American emphasis on the promotion of domestic private enterprise. My own experience with Vietnamese diplomats in Washington and with Vietnamese officials in Saigon amply confirms Robert Scigliano's observation that the American policy of "opposition to publicly controlled industrial development . . . was the cause of considerable strain in Vietnamese-American relations."[34]

In South Korea, the conscious use of the public sector as a symbol of nationalist competition with the North has been more explicit than in the case of war-torn South Vietnam, especially since the advent of the Park regime. As we saw in an earlier chapter, the economic program initially promulgated after the 1961 coup pledged a "planned economy." Park was more moderate in his economic views than Kim Chong-p'il but directly linked his ideal of an "independent national economy" with the goal of "fostering the national strength necessary to overthrow the North,"[35] hailing the U.S.-backed state enterprises then existing as "the only mainstay of our key industries" after a decade of American aid excessively oriented toward consumer goods. Once in power, Park expanded the public sector with Japanese backing, but this was offset, in nationalist eyes, by his promotion of a nouveau riche class of politically allied private entrepreneurs, also largely tied to Japanese credit sources. The growth of the government-controlled steel complex at P'ohang and other heavy industries beyond the reach of the private sector, mainly with Japanese credits, was initially popular as a bow to the goal of self-sufficiency. Later, this became a focus of anxiety as a new weapon in the hands of a dictatorial regime and an addition to an already excessive dependence on Tokyo.[36]

In a seeming parallel to the Park case, the Ayub Khan dictatorship in Pakistan also patronized favored business interests that became the target for a successful opposition reform drive calling for, among other things, a greater public sector emphasis designed to curtail the concentration of economic power. In the case of homogeneous South Korea, however, the concentration of economic power has not been of limited benefit to particular social minorities; whereas Pakistan has followed more closely the characteristic Asian pattern already mentioned. Three-fourths of the industrial assets owned by Moslem firms were in the hands of members of seven small, clearly identifiable trading "quasi-castes" in 1959. One of these, the Halai Memoms, claimed 26.5 percent alone, and two, the Memoms and Chiniotis, controlled more than half of the cotton textile assets.[37] The concentration issue thus became the common property of left and right alike during the struggle against Ayub, with the orthodox Moslem Jamaat-e-Islami railing against "five small communities of traders, totalling one-half percent of the population, who control more than half of our industry"[38] and Zulfiqar Ali Bhutto dedicating his new People's party in 1967 to the goal of ending "this monstrous system of loot and plunder" by nationalizing key industries.[39]

The emergence of the public sector as an integral expression of nationalism was delayed, in the case of Pakistan, by the conservative ideology of the Moslem League and of postindependence elites drawn narrowly from the same feudal social base. Anti-Indian slogans were successfully used to divert popular attention from issues of internal social justice until the explosion of the late Ayub years. Also, Pakistan lacked significant iron and coal resources, a built-in restraint on its ambitions for the heavy industries that call most urgently for public sector initiatives. India, by contrast, had a nationalist movement with a broadly diversified social base and a quasi-socialist credo that deliberately made social justice the touchstone for judging independent Indian governments. Moreover, with iron, steel, and other resources not found in Pakistan and with its vast internal market, India had a powerful economic rationale supporting its nationalist ambitions for a strong state-controlled industrial sector within a mixed economy framework.

In order to appreciate the strength of the Indian public sector commitment, it is necessary to recognize that nationalism rather than economics has been determinative, principally in the form of the nationalist drive to maximize self-sufficiency but also in a preoccupation with the internal social equities necessary for a coherent national identity. The public sector is in significant measure a response to the concentrated economic power of certain entrenched *bania*, or merchant castes, especially the Marwaris, who epitomize the avaricious robber baron in Indian political symbolism. Although the term "Marwari" can be used broadly to denote all 4.2 million speakers of the Marwari dialect of Rajasthani, it is popularly applied to members of three specific trading castes native to the Marwar area of Rajasthan, the Oswals, Agarwals, and Maheshwaris.[40] Like the Memoms in Pakistan and the Chinese moneylenders in rural Malaysia, these closely knit castes offer a ready target for popular grievances in a setting of poverty. The precise extent of concentration has yet to be definitively established in terms of social groupings, but one study found that eight Marwari families, some of them related by marriage, held 565 directorships in Indian industry, banking, and insurance.[41] Other studies have suggested that seventy-five "groups,"[42] centered in thirteen business "complexes," controlled 36 percent and 50 percent of the total assets of all companies in the Indian private sector in 1958 and 1964, respectively. In addition to the large-scale industrial power of well-known Marwari tycoons such as G. D. Birla, Marwari moneylenders hold widely diffused power in far-flung villages and provincial towns. Their cosmopolitan, supraregional social and economic position sets them sharply apart from the largely regionalized structure of Indian society. Indian "socialism" might have had its birth in the Fabianism learned by Nehru and others at Cambridge or the London School of Economics, but it is continually reactivated by the anti-Marwari bias of the backcountry nouveaux riches. Significantly, the dominant Indian view in the early postindependence decades was that the best way to limit economic concentration was not through the nationalization of existing enterprises but through the development of a counterbalancing public sector. For the most part, the public and private sectors have operated in a complementary way, with public enterprise helping private business expansion.

Viewed in terms of the concentration problem alone, the long-term future of the public sector might be regarded as problematical in India, given the increasing vitality of the medium and small business sector, the leverage afforded by licensing, and the mixed performance record of public enterprises. At this point, however, we are brought back to the overarching nationalist significance of the public sector. As regional political power has grown in the post-Nehru years, the central government has found it increasingly difficult to arbitrate between states in the allocation of investment licenses, with some states even demanding the decentralization of licensing. Centrally controlled public sector enterprises serve as the strong arm of New Delhi in preserving national economic coordination, as well as in dealing with powerful monopolies; above all, as we have pointed out, they serve as the shield of economic independence for the country as a whole in the face of foreign political and investment pressures.

The public sector has not grown as much or as rapidly as some of its more ardent advocates have desired,[43] but as an OECD study has pointed out, its growth has nonetheless been "phenomenal," representing an overall share of developmental investment "quite large and intended to be steadily increased," especially in strategic heavy and chemical industries.[44] In 1977, the Indian government operated 149 industrial companies with a capital investment of more than $10 billion. To most politically conscious Indians, this record of expansion is a critical measure of the national effort to maximize self-sufficiency, and American hostility toward the public sector has thus had a divisive impact out of all proportion to its intrinsic importance, nullifying, to some extent, the favorable political impact of aid programs in agriculture and industry alike that have contributed greatly to Indian progress toward economic independence. In light of the economic factors reinforcing the commitment to public sector industry in India, the record of Indo-American conflict in this sphere, which we will now examine, reveals a recurring pattern of American myopia and dogmatism. More than in authoritarian Asian countries, where the public sector has been in part merely one more instrument of control and official corruption, public enterprise in India has been an authentic expression of broad-based nationalist aspirations. The Indian case thus points up American insensitivity to nationalism with unusual clarity and suggests, accordingly, unusually unambiguous lessons with respect to future policy.

HAS INDIA FAILED?

By the standards of many economic observers, Indian and foreign alike, India has pursued wastefully inefficient economic policies marked by an excessive emphasis on import-substituting industrialization at the expense of priority needs in agriculture.[45] Even supporters of an industry-oriented development strategy who emphasize the progress achieved believe that the economy has been "over-controlled"[46] and that a turning point has been reached[47] requiring a harmonization of import-substituting and export-oriented policies. It is not my intent here to render a judgment on the Indian record in economic terms or to challenge the expert consensus that India has paid a high economic price for what it has accomplished. Rather, it is my contention that the Indian development experience cannot be meaningfully judged in a narrowly economic context. For the implicit rationale underlying Indian policies has been a nationalist rationale, a readiness to bear inordinate costs, if necessary, to maximize the independent character of the industrialization achieved.

In terms of nationalist objectives, India has clearly made significant industrial progress during the early decades of independence, securing a degree of national control over its economic destiny that contrasts sharply with the more dependent patterns of industrialization in many neighboring countries. Pakistan, in particular, appears to Indian observers as a sorry case, with little to show for its industrial development efforts but a consumer-oriented sector heavily dependent on imports financed through foreign aid.[48] In some areas, notably petroleum, steel, aluminum, cement, railway equipment, industrial machinery, chemicals, mining, motor vehicles, and machine tools, Indian industrial progress has been striking,[49] and India has managed to acquire a substantial amount of its foreign technology without submitting to foreign control. The compound annual rate of growth has averaged 27.3 percent in the output of petroleum products, 21.1 percent in aluminum ingots, 18.6 percent in diesel engines, and 8.7 percent in finished steel and cement. India can make its own machinery for steel plants, fertilizer plants, and refineries. It is virtually self-sufficient in the manufacture of railway equipment, with the exception of certain components for diesel electric locomotives. Motor vehicles are 90 percent locally produced, including components made by more than 200 ancillary industries, aided by marginal imports of foreign parts. Other developing countries have begun to look to India for help in their own industrialization, and Indian firms were involved in 128 industrial joint ventures in 25 countries in 1976,[50] in addition to the technical advisory role played by leading public sector enterprises abroad. The Indian record does not fully match that of China,[51] properly hailed by ECAFE as the Asian model of self-reliance,[52] but it nonetheless ranks as a creditable achievement in the light of Indian adherence to a relatively undisciplined parliamentary framework. As we shall see, the degree of success achieved has been greatly facilitated in such pivotal areas as oil and steel by the Soviet role in assisting the public sector; in the case of the lagging fertilizer industry, however, Moscow lacked the technology required to help and Washington sought, largely in vain, to gain entry for American private investment.

The case of petroleum sharply illustrates the trials and tribulations that India has faced in its continuing effort to maximize its economic sovereignty, with an expanding public sector oil industry utilized to balance an unavoidable measure of dependence on the international companies. Fear that a one-sided dependence on the Western majors would invite high crude oil import prices, which would in turn eat into scarce foreign exchange reserves, led to extensive arrangements with the Soviet bloc in developing a government drilling and refining program. This fear proved fully justified, and the Soviet link has made India's relationship with the majors a stormy one, but the net result from the nationalist vantage point has been the acquisition of extensive petroleum technology without payment of the price of Western dominance of the economy. The annual production of crude oil in India increased from 259,000 tons in 1950 to 3 million tons in 1965 to 9.5 million tons in 1976, an impressive record although India cannot keep pace with expanding needs. In refining, India has increased its output from 251,000 tons in 1950 to 9.7 million tons in 1965 to 28 million tons in 1976. By 1980, crude output is scheduled to reach 14 million tons and refinery capacity 37 million tons, almost all of the latter in the public sector. India has paid an economic price, however, in order to acquire a public sector refining capacity that could have been acquired at a lower cost by permitting the Western majors to expand their facilities.

At the time of independence, India was almost wholly dependent on imported petroleum products. The British government made little effort to search for oil during the colonial period, stressing negative geological evidence on exploration prospects, and British oil interests developed only one small field at Digboi in Assam. With an eye to minimizing the foreign exchange drain, the government of independent India placed its first priority on developing an indigenous refining capacity, turning to the foreign oil companies for assistance. But the companies were prepared to set up refineries only through wholly owned Indian subsidiaries, flying in the face of the newly declared Indian policy providing that "the major interest in ownership and effective control" of enterprises involving foreign collaboration "should, as a rule, be in Indian hands."[53] Moreover, the foreign companies insisted from the outset on freedom to import their own crude oil at world market prices in their own tankers, unanimously stipulating that these imports of crude be free from import duty unless and until this were required for the protection of indigenous crude oil.

Despite its distaste for these terms, India had little bargaining power in dealing with the majors at this point, especially after the nationalization of the Abadan refinery by Iran sent international prices upward. In its anxiety to forestall the foreign exchange outlays resulting from the lack of domestic refining capacity, New Delhi made a series of hasty agreements in the 1951-1953 period with Standard Vacuum, Burmah-Shell, Esso, and Caltex that were destined to become a focus of bitter controversy in later years. The 1951-1953 refinery agreements were severely criticized for what amounted to extraterritorial provisions exempting the Western companies from certain taxes and customs duties. But the most rankling fact was that the foreign-controlled refineries could not be relied upon to use domestic crude oil in the event that India found oil in significant quantities. In addition, criticism focused on provisions safeguarding the refineries from nationalization for a twenty-five-year period and giving them freedom to use their own tankers to bring in crude.

Although the government "smarted under the memory of the Agreements," Michael Kidron has related, "it could not do much to alter them; neither persuade the companies to reduce prices nor, in the absence of alternative supplies, force them to. It had tried to interest other Western companies in prospecting in India but with no success."[54] Finally, in 1955, India turned to the Soviet Union, and by May 1956 Soviet and Eastern European experts had returned from prospecting surveys in the Indian countryside with favorable estimates in widely scattered parts of the country. In 1957, India began what was to become a protracted pressure campaign to force the Western companies to modify crude oil prices that have been attacked by a former Socony Mobil official as "incredibly bloated." Most of India's oil came from Kuwait in 1960 and was produced at a cost of less than $0.07 a barrel, according to this indictment, but despite this low production cost and transport costs of $0.20 a barrel or less, India was paying as much as $2.00 per barrel for its oil in that year, with a posted price of $1.59 and $0.40 for transportation, primarily as the result of a cozy arrangement between the majors at the expense of India.[55]

The Indian price offensive went into high gear in tandem with a Soviet offer to sell 2.5 million tons of crude oil at 20 percent less than the price then prevailing on a basis of local currency and commodity repayment that did not strain foreign exchange reserves. Timed to hit the majors when they were suffering from surplus capacity, the Soviet squeeze play forced the majors to make a 12.5 percent price cut and emboldened the Indian government to make its first formal bid for the revision of the 1951-1953 agreements by setting up a high-level Oil Price Inquiry Committee empowered to carry on an extended probe into the operations of the majors. India also pressed the majors to refine the incoming Soviet crude, but had no more success than the Castro regime in Cuba in moving the companies. It was this that finally hardened Indian determination to give priority to government refineries rather than to the expansion of its existing private facilities.

The United States, other Western donor countries, and the World Bank were openly hostile to the Indian oil policy during this critical period, with a Bank mission suggesting in mid-1960 that "a change in this policy could free significant amounts of foreign exchange for other uses during the Third Plan by attracting additional foreign capital into the oil industry."[56] Western pressures for greater Indian receptivity to the expansion of foreign-owned refineries and to foreign oil exploration led to intensive negotiations with the majors that foundered in the face of Indian efforts to set up public sector partnerships on terms viewed as stiff by then prevailing international standards. India wanted "undivided control of any oil found"[57] as part of a policy frankly focused on expansion of the public sector and on preferential treatment for public sector refineries designed to protect them from foreign competition. Thus, the construction of a Soviet-built oil refinery in Gujarat, drawing on Soviet-assisted oil discoveries at nearby Cambay and Ankleshwar, meant that Burmah-Shell was denied permission to expand its refinery near Bombay on the argument that the new Soviet-aided refinery would meet all needs in that part of India.

Although the majors rejected the Oil Price Inquiry Committee's 1963 demand for price reductions of 8-10 percent, and India was in no position to press its case during the years of economic stringency following the 1965 conflict, New Delhi induced the companies, step by step, to share, if only in a modest degree, the local market for crude and products; to invest some of their profits within India; and to give up much of the extraterritoriality embodied in the refinery agreements. More important, India won new refinery agreements in 1963-1966 with Phillips Petroleum and American International carrying significant price concessions as well as unprecedented acceptance of ultimate public sector control. The companies accepted a majority government equity position in return for an assured outlet for crude and effective management control for a ten-year period. This greatly stiffened the government stand on the price issue and set the stage for the gradual takeover of foreign refining facilities following the OPEC price increases initiated in 1973.

As Dilip Mukerji observed, the only leverage in Indian hands in showdowns with the major and the producers has been the existence of a "very substantial" public sector refining capacity that offered a backstop in the event of a sudden punitive reduction in petroleum supplies.[58] By the same token, in the case of exploration and production, it was the existence of significant public sector technical capabilities that enabled New Delhi to enlist foreign technical help in the offshore field in 1974 on relatively favorable terms. For the most part, the Oil and Natural Gas Commission has kept direct control of offshore exploration and production operations, utilizing service contracts only to fill specific technical gaps and insisting on a more stringent variant of Indonesian production-sharing in its carefully limited exploration arrangements with foreign partners. Ironically, India's overall industrial progress has complicated its oil strategy, and by 1976, the need for petroleum was growing at a much faster rate than the development of indigenous crude sources despite some encouraging offshore discoveries. This led to a sharply upgraded Oil and Natural Gas Commission budget of $1.6 billion for the five-year period ending in 1980, twice the amount allotted during the previous five years.

The history of Indian relations with the oil companies has been closely tied to a parallel Indian struggle to establish a strong public sector in the fertilizer industry. More and more, U.S. fertilizer firms have been coming under the corporate control of the majors, and two of the key raw materials used in fertilizer manufacturing, naphtha and ammonia, are by-products of different stages of oil refining operations. This natural link between the petroleum and fertilizer industries has led to a continuing interest on the part of the oil companies in the fertilizer needs of developing countries, including, at times, unabashed efforts to use the bait of urgently required fertilizer plants as a means of promoting crude oil sales and breaking down nationalist resistance to the establishment of foreign-controlled refineries. In the case of India, with its unusually large and expanding fertilizer market, the oil companies have waged a peculiarly unremitting psychological warfare against the public sector, pointing to the specter of famine and the growing importance of fertilizer as an argument for abandoning nationalist reservations.

The urgency of increased fertilizer production in India at a time of recurring food scarcity and rapid population growth has been repeatedly elaborated. Thus, one authoritative twenty-year projection in 1967 estimated that the demand for nitrogenous fertilizer would reach 3.8 million tons in 1976, 5.24 million tons in 1981, and 6.3 million tons in 1986. As against this, the estimate pointed to a projected 1.7 million-ton capacity in 1976 and 2.037 million-ton capacity in 1981 as "reasonably firm" probabilities on the basis of plants in operation, under construction, or then contemplated. [59] By 1976, India was already producing 1.8 million tons of nitrogen, including output from nine public sector plants with an 812,000-ton capacity, but only after a bitter, unresolved tug-of-war over the public sector issue with the World Bank, American aid officials, and Western investors.

Initially, India assigned fertilizer development entirely to the public sector, primarily in recognition of the domestic political sensitivity of fertilizer prices and through fear of possible profiteering by foreign enterprises at the expense of the Indian farmer. When India outlined its plans to the Bank in 1952, requesting loans to build public sector plants, the Bank responded with firm strictures against the very concept of public enterprise. One rebuff after another, coupled with the monsoon crisis of 1957 and growing food scarcity, led to a new policy opening the fertilizer industry to private participation side by side with the public sector. This resulted only in a continuing stalemate, however, with the Indian government battling a concerted phalanx of foreign firms, the United States government, and the World Bank, all of them pressing New Delhi to build its fertilizer policy around the private sector and to liberalize its investment terms.

By the end of the Eisenhower administration, only one private American fertilizer project had materialized, an International Minerals and Chemicals venture at Coromandel financed largely with American aid and Export-Import Bank loans on the basis of a debt-equity ratio of 4.26 percent. Like International Minerals, most of the nine other foreign firms licensed by India for fertilizer investment at that time served notice that they would be interested in going ahead only if American aid agencies took the lion's share of the risk. This confronted Indian planners with a dilemma, foreshadowing, as it did, diversion of a major share of the American aid then under discussion to finance foreign private investment that was acceptable, in their eyes, only if it offered a way of obtaining otherwise unavailable investment capital. In the Coromandel case, a compromise formula was devised providing for a companion public sector loan to build the Trombay plant at Bombay. But this was a one-shot concession, in the U.S. view, and the two sides settled down for a long confrontation over investment terms that was aggravated by tensions over the expansion of American food aid during the Johnson administration. President Johnson became personally identified with a policy making food aid conditional on an increased Indian emphasis on agriculture reflected in a new hospitality to foreign fertilizer investment and a larger allocation of aid funds for imports of U.S. fertilizer. Both the United States and the World Bank applied heavyhanded pressures attributable, in good measure, to the White House interest in the issue, provoking angry demands in India for a firm government stand.

What India really wanted was foreign participation restricted to turnkey projects or management contracts within a joint venture framework assuring government control. At the very least, where private sector Indo-American partnerships were to be permitted, India wanted the foreign investor to risk enough capital to assure his best efforts in the execution of the venture. In addition to the equity issue, however, another persistent controversy over pricing and distribution mirrored the uneasiness of American investors confronted with a strong public sector fertilizer capability. Just as India feared that private foreign firms would charge excessively high prices, so the foreign firms feared that they would be undersold by a privileged public sector. Some foreign companies wanted fertilizer prices decontrolled, and India reluctantly agreed to do this in December 1965, after a virtual U.S. ultimatum in which a $50 million fertilizer import loan was conditioned on decontrol. [60] Other foreign investors, however, were not prepared to take any risks in a mixed economy environment. The fertilizer investment controversy was epitomized in the abortive bid by a consortium sponsored by the Bechtel

Corporation to build five factories with a dollar equity investment of $155 million. Initially encouraged by the U.S. government, the Bechtel negotiations proved to be a red flag to nationalist sentiment in every respect and left a lingering legacy of ill feeling. First, the consortium sought a guaranteed price for the fertilizer produced, fixed at a level that would assure the repatriation of all of its invested capital within five years; to add insult to injury, the Bechtel group sought a guarantee that the Indian government would buy at the proposed fixed price whatever the companies were unable to sell on their own in the free market. Second, and even more important, the consortium was unwilling to accept the Indian demand for a joint venture in which the government would have at least nominal majority control. The Indian stand on the issue of national control was greatly reinforced by the Indian discovery that leading oil companies were behind the consortium. Not until a relatively advanced stage of the discussions did the Bechtel negotiators tip their hand and make clear that their proposition hinged on Indian agreement to buy a stipulated amount of crude for refineries then being sought and to give the firms involved the right to supply the fertilizer plants crude oil and naphtha from their own sources.

The Bechtel rupture was followed by another oil company initiative designed to promote the sale of liquid ammonia from nearby Middle East installations. In place of their existing practice of "flaring" natural gas, the oil companies saw a chance for added profits through the manufacture of liquid ammonia as part of their Middle East operations and its export to India and other neighboring countries. This was presented as a way for India to reduce the cost of fertilizer production, but New Delhi reacted sharply in nationalist terms, pointing to the availability of naphtha produced by Indian refineries. Not only could India make its own ammonia from naphtha at a lower cost than the imported ammonia, officials argued; suppose unexpected oil reserves were discovered as a result of Indian exploration efforts, resulting in a greater supply of naphtha than anticipated? "These lobbies," explained a *Hindu* correspondent, "do not seem to understand that India cannot afford to have part of its fertilizer complex situated outside in countries whose political fidelity India cannot take for granted."[61] The Bechtel bid and the ammonia proposal convinced Indians for years to come of American and World Bank complicity with the oil companies.

At the same time that the United States and the World Bank were pushing, with limited success, foreign investment as the solution to the fertilizer impasse, White House science adviser Roger Revelle,[62] Iowa agricultural economist Jonathan Garst,[63] and Ford Foundation fertilizer consultant Raymond Ewell were pressing for a

U.S. program of public sector fertilizer loans. Ewell pointed to the inadequacy of the investment influx in the face of a mounting need, proposing that the United States loan at least $200 million in foreign exchange loans and an equal amount in rupees for the construction of 1.6 million tons of new nitrogen capacity by U.S. firms in cooperation with the Indian government.[64] Responding to continuing criticism, the United States suspended its hostility toward the public sector for a brief period in 1967 by sending a team of TVA experts to advise the Fertilizer Corporation of India on ways to increase the efficiency of its five plants, and in July 1968, in a more significant departure, a $37 million U.S. aid loan was granted to quadruple the capacity of the public sector Trombay plant built with U.S. aid help under the Eisenhower administration. With these exceptions, however, Washington continued to pursue its objective of a modified Indian policy toward foreign investment, and India, though financially constrained, sought to expand the public sector with Japanese, Italian, and British technology. By 1973, India's own fertilizer engineering firms at Alwaye and Durgapur were able to design and equip fertilizer plants on their own, making 75 percent of the necessary machinery domestically.[65] But India recognized that fertilizer could be manufactured most efficiently with the help of ever changing technological innovations still in foreign hands, notably the centrifugal compressor, and continued to seek foreign collaboration on politically acceptable terms.

In retrospect, while India has acted effectively in pursuit of its nationalist goals, this obviously carried with it important short-run liabilities. Fertilizer production capacity has not, in the end, been increased rapidly enough, and foreign investors with an equity stake might well have built more efficient plants than some of those constructed, achieving much faster results at a time when expanding fertilizer output was badly needed. At the same time, Western aid policy was also self-defeating since one of its major objectives, bolstering Indian agriculture, was undermined for more than two decades by resistance to public sector loans. "Blame" cannot be clearly fixed in a struggle between two sides guided by basically differing values.

In the case of fertilizer, the Soviet Union has not been able to give India significant help, dependent as it has been on Western fertilizer imports for its own agricultural needs. Steel, however, is a very different story. The leverage afforded by the cold war enabled India to achieve a steel production level of 8.2 million ingot tons by 1976 (6.5 million tons of finished steel) and a projected capacity of 18.8 million tons. This was an impressive record, albeit one marred by incomplete utilization of capacity and one far short of

China's 23 million ton production level during the same year. Moscow has made aid for public sector steel plants the centerpiece of its psychological offensive in New Delhi, while Washington has maintained alternating postures of apathy and hostility, with the notable exception of the abortive plan for American aid to build the Bokaro steel plant.

Before turning to the Soviet Union, India made a series of efforts to develop its steel industry with American assistance, only to experience consistent frustration and failure. In 1948, soon after independence, J. C. Ghosh, director of industries in the Production Ministry, came to the United States in an attempt to attract American private investment in Indian steel development. The Tata steel mill at Jamshedpur had been built at the turn of the century with the assistance of American expertise, and Indian officials thought of the United States as the undisputed leader in world steel technology. But Ghosh found no interest either in Washington or in the steel companies in the expansion of Tata or the other private mill then existing. Indian officials recall resentfully that the very idea of American investment in Indian steel development was airily laughed off both in 1948 and later in 1951, when others took their case again to Washington and Pittsburgh. Finally, Bonn broke the ice in 1953, when the West German combine Krupp-Demag agreed to build India's first public sector steel mill at Rourkela. The Soviet Union offered to support a second public sector mill at Bhilai in January 1955, and Britain followed with support for a third at Durgapur. But even after West German, Soviet, and British identification with public sector steel development had become an accomplished fact, the United States continued to plead the case for private rather than public control of any further capacity developed and, in general, to accentuate the negative with respect to the Indian steel potential.

The Bokaro fiasco dramatized more than any other single episode the inability of the United States to contribute to public sector development. Initially, the United States pushed for a mill completely in the private sector, albeit to be financed by aid credits. This gave way to a more flexible approach when the Kennedy administration proposed a $512 million loan for a plant that was to be nominally controlled by the Indian government but would have a built-in management role for U.S. companies. The Kennedy plan soon became a political football in both New Delhi and Washington, with Indian critics alarmed by the anticipated degree of American control and the U.S. steel industry even more disturbed by the very idea of U.S. government support for a public enterprise. U.S. Steel experts sought to demonstrate that India would not have enough demand to sustain both public and private operations,[66] an argument contested vigorously both by Indian experts [67] and by U.S. ambassador John Kenneth Galbraith.[68] At the instance of one of its more influential members, former World Bank president Eugene Black who had previously blocked public sector fertilizer loans to India, a White House study committee on foreign aid headed by Gen. Lucius D. Clay concluded that the United States "should not aid a foreign government in projects establishing government-owned industrial and commercial enterprises which compete with existing private endeavors."[69] In a news briefing on the report, General Clay left no doubt that the committee had the Bokaro project in mind in making this recommendation. President Kennedy made a personal appeal for Bokaro at his press conference on May 8, 1963, stressing that this was not a case of nationalizing private companies but of "building something new that the economy of India requires." Nevertheless, congressional sentiment progressively hardened, with support for Bokaro from the United Steel Workers and others progressively drowned out. On August 23, 1963, Congress decisively struck it from the aid bill, and within sixteen months India had signed an agreement with the Soviet Union for public sector assistance.

Coming on top of a widely hailed Soviet record of success at Bhilai, blunt American rejection of public sector aspirations gave Moscow an unusually enduring political payoff for its aid ventures in the industrial field. It was Soviet identification with public enterprise quite as much as its pro-Indian posture on issues involving Pakistan that established the psychological basis for the increasingly intimate military aid ties between Moscow and New Delhi after 1962. Sudhir Ghosh, a key figure in the Indian steel development program, sang the praises of Soviet aid in his memoirs, contrasting American insistence on a U.S.-conducted feasibility study at Bokaro with Soviet acceptance of Indian expertise at Bhilai. Ghosh stressed Soviet willingness to share know-how "without any reservation" through on-the-job training in Soviet mills. He recalled his difficulties in getting American agreement for a comparable training program and the more limited access to concrete experience in American mills granted to the 591 Indian steel men who finally went to the United States between 1957 and 1961.[70] As it happened, Soviet tactics changed during the construction of Bokaro, resulting in recurring tensions over Indian technical involvement, but the basic "partnership" stereotype had already crystallized.

"Unhappily for the American image in India," as former U.S. aid director John P. Lewis wrote,

> the agriculture-first critique of the country's heavy industrial undertakings came, in the late 1950s, to be regarded as a peculiarly American complaint. The Indian government suspected that many leading Americans, official and

otherwise, who adopted a pro-agriculture, anti-heavy industry posture were motivated by such comparatively extraneous considerations as, first, distaste for the public enterprise form in which the Indians choose to organize most of their new heavy industries and, second, fear of eventual Indian competition with American industrial exports.[71]

Lewis rejected the second suspicion but concurred in the first, acknowledging that "because of the public-versus-private enterprise issue, the U.S. aid program tended to shy away from heavy industrial projects, other than those in the electrical power field."[72]

In many cases, American distaste for inefficient public sector management in India has been understandable, but there have been success stories, too, notably Hindustan Machine Tools, hailed by *Newsweek* as "one of the largest and most efficient machine tool manufacturers in the world," a potential "Indian Renault,"[73] which became a regular supplier of radial drills and engine lathes to American Tool in 1971.[74] Management experts have also pointed to Hindustan Antibiotics, the Integral Coach Factory at Madras and, above all, Bharat Heavy Electricals as examples of efficiently managed and highly successful public sector industrial enterprises.[75] A complex of seven separate plants, Bharat Heavy Electricals had a $390 million gross turnover in 1974-1975, a $63 million profit and $51 million in export orders for a wide range of products from transformers and switchgear to turbine components and onshore oil rigs.[76] "The improved performance of public sector enterprises has been a marked feature of the economy," reported the World Bank in May 1976. Citing "higher levels of efficiency" in public sector enterprises as a whole, the Bank stressed the fact that steel output rose by 1.2 million tons in 1975-1976 (24 percent) and that India had not only become a net exporter of steel but was also helping other developing countries to set up steel enterprises.[77]

Beginning with John Kenneth Galbraith's jibe at India's "highly uneven" public enterprises as "post office socialism,"[78] the standard prescription for the improvement of the public sector has been stricter profitability standards and greater managerial autonomy. The profitability test was clearly accepted, in principle, by the Fourth Five-Year Plan,[79] and Indian leaders have shown an increasing awareness of the need to apply this test in practice.[80] Gradually, public impatience has forced increasing efforts to attract private sector managers into the public sector, including one plan for partially restructuring the public sector by incorporating private capital participation and managerial expertise into "joint sector" ventures.[81]

What well-disposed foreign critics of Indian policy have advocated is a "mixed but free economy"[82] retaining a more efficiently managed public industrial sector while reducing an array of licensing and import controls regarded as destructive of economic growth in public and private sectors alike. This distinction between the "public sector issue," as involving a central expression of nationalism, and the more diffuse, multifaceted "decontrol issue," has been conspicuously missing in American policy in most Asian countries. In bracketing the two issues together under a socialist label, the United States not only has undermined its own diplomatic and political posture but also has often generated a defensive response that has impeded the natural processes of internal self-criticism and reform in the countries concerned.

JAPAN, CHINA, AND THE UNITED STATES

To the extent that the United States is unable to reach agreement with Asian countries on the terms for collaboration in economic development, others will soon step into the breach, as Western European countries and the Soviet Union have already done in the case of the Indian oil and steel industries. In ideological terms, the Soviet Union can relate more easily than the United States to countries with public sector ambitions, and Moscow has also begun to pursue its interests through private banking and trading activities. In technological terms, however, the Soviet Union offers less competition than West Germany, France, and Japan, with Japan, in particular, already far stronger as an economic force in Asia than the United States.

By a monumental quirk of history, the rapid rise of Japan to a position of regional economic primacy has come about in large part as a consequence of American sponsorship and support. While Japan would eventually have achieved powerful regional influence, in any case, the speed, scope, and thrust of Japanese economic expansion in Asia have been the direct result of American policies conceived in a narrow cold war framework. The United States was equally blind to the depth of Japan's own nationalist dynamism and the lack of a comparable dynamic in other Asian countries still in the nation-building process. As a consequence, American policy inadvertently contributed to an erosion of the economic sovereignty of these countries before their defenses were strong enough to withstand the Japanese assault. Under certain circumstances, this could lead in future decades to a Tokyo-dominated Asian economic order largely closed off to the United States, conceivably with the blessing or collaboration of China. One key variable in this equation will be whether American and European protectionism impels Japan to fall back on Asian-centered economic policies. But another equally determinative factor, as our analysis already suggests, will be whether the United States offers an attractive alternative to reliance on Japan by providing technology, capital, and markets to developing Asian countries on terms compatible with their nationalist objectives.

American sponsorship of Japanese expansion in Asia was a natural corollary to the central American objective of building up Japan as a bulwark against an assumed threat of Soviet and Chinese aggression. By encouraging Japanese access to neighboring countries, the United States saw an opportunity in one stroke to preclude communist inroads in noncommunist Asia, reduce the chances of a Sino-Japanese combination, and help Japan to rebuild economically. The United States ran interference for Japan in working out reparation agreements with South Korea and Southeast Asian countries that permitted Japan to atone for its wartime sins not through direct financial obligations but through more than $1.7 billion in machinery and other exports. Apart from the widespread corruption this entailed, especially in the Philippines and Indonesia, the reparations program was a key factor in helping Japan to familiarize other Asian countries with Japanese products and to open up new markets. When the Vietnam war came, bringing an enormous temporary upsurge in the purchasing power of countries economically or militarily linked to the U.S. effort, Japan was in a position to cash in, as Chapter 6 elaborated, preempting key market areas in a relatively short span of years. American aid and procurement dollars enabled Japan to make its breakthrough in Asian markets under artificial optimum conditions since Asian governments could finance their trade deficits with their U.S. subsidies. It was during this period that the United States also exhorted Japan more insistently than ever to "play a greater role in Asia" not only in the aid field but politically and, in limited ways, even militarily.

The implicit American assumption in pressing for a larger Japanese role in Asia was that this would serve American interests by reducing American "burdens" and giving stability to the area through infusions of economic strength. But Tokyo, for its part, never having shared the premises of American involvement, felt that Washington's self-imposed burdens were its own problem. The Japanese export offensive was based largely on short-term credit commitments that progressively added to the American aid load, and it was not offset by compensating Japanese aid except, in most cases, aid linked to Japanese exports or investment not otherwise supportable. By the early seventies, it was generally recognized that Japan had its own fish to fry and that the ever proliferating Japanese economic power in Asia might well prove adverse to American interests in a number of ways. American companies operating in Asia were the first to call for a new approach frankly treating Japan as a competitor. Gradually, as country after country fell into one-way trade dependencies on Japan, with Japanese imports centered mainly in natural resources, it grew increasingly apparent that Japan might become a focus of instability, generating nationalist tensions and straining the still tenuous economic fabrics of developing countries in its orbit.[83]

The emotional response of countries with heavy dependencies on Japan has more of an ambivalent, love-hate quality than is readily apparent in nationalist rhetoric. As an economically successful Asian power, Japan provides a source of self-esteem for other Asian nations; yet exploitation is still exploitation, whether from Marunouchi or Wall Street. The nationalist response has thus combined resistance with simultaneous attempts to remind Japan of its Asian identity and to win recognition of a basic Japanese stake in Asia ruling out the abrasive role of "Yellow Yankees." In recurring discussions with strategically placed Asian economic bureaucrats and political leaders playing a role in relations with Japan, I found this ambivalence repeatedly echoed. Thus, Emil Salim, chairman of the Indonesian Planning Board, Bappenas, spoke of how

> now, for the first time, we have an Asian developed country, and this is bound to have a special impact on the Asian area. When Germany grows, it has its main impact in Europe. This time it's an Asian country in an area of poor countries. . . . When I negotiate with the Japanese, it's more than what you say, you feel your way. With an American, X is simply X. We want the Japanese to treat us as Asians. It's when they act non-Asian, that's when there is the danger of a clash, that's what hurts most.[84]

In the Philippines, Benigno Aquino, the Liberal party presidential aspirant later imprisoned by President Marcos, was an outspoken critic of Japanese business tactics but concluded hopefully, after a 1972 Tokyo visit, that

> the Nixon Shocks have brought home the realities to Japan—that the U.S. is not the be-all and end-all of its existence. They realize now that they're in Asia, of Asia and that they must give more thought to cultivating their interests in Asia. The world will be split into blocs, and we will need each other. It won't be the same as the Co-Prosperity Sphere, it will be more of a partnership. They're the giant among us, to be sure—they'll be the senior partner—but they will have to give us handicaps, preferential tariffs and the rest, especially for our agricultural products.[85]

Bunchana Atthakor, former Thai commerce minister and the leading Thai critic of "Ugly Japanese" methods, urged Japan to make "a permanent commitment to Thailand," calling Tokyo

> our most logical supplier of technology and capital, for geographical as well as economic reasons. . . . The U.S., as Japan is learning, is no longer an easily

accessible market, and Europe is turning more and more into an economic bloc. It would appear, therefore, that Japan's destiny still lies with Asia and she must come to terms with this continent. As a start she must follow more enlightened and committed economic policies and not erode the countries in this region with policies dominated by thoughts of quick gain.[86]

At a time when the challenge of foreign investment increasingly preoccupies Asian countries, admiration for Japan as the pace-setting Asian modernizer focuses most sharply on the fact that Japan was able to keep out foreign equity inroads during the Meiji years and that even after the turn of the century there were only "small amounts"[87] of foreign equity, constituting a "small fraction"[88] of overall investment, in a controlled process of foreign economic interchange restricted largely to floating bonds and hiring technicians on restricted short-term assignments. From a Filipino vantage point, Alejandro Lichauco points to Japan as the prime example of do-it-yourself industrialization:

> It was an arduous process, no doubt, and one recalls how the Filipinos before the War looked with derision and contempt at the inferior quality of Japanese goods. We laughed at Japanese technology. But what we did not realize was that the awkward Japanese products then were reflecting the grim and heroic determination of an Asian people to educate themselves in the processes of industrialization. And, as we were laughing at the Japanese, they were laying the base and foundation for their country's greatness. They are laughing at us now.[89]

Similarly, a Thai commentary cited Japanese resistance to foreign investment as an answer to Western economists who

> are severely critical of developing countries whose governments discourage or restrict the flow of private investment from abroad. India, for example, has been hauled over the coals for keeping the American chemical firms out of the fertilizer manufacturing business in India at a time when the country is calling for every ton of fertilizer it can get. . . . Yet the Meiji reformers of Japan in the comparable years of Japanese economic development sternly refused to build on foreign loans or investment. They suspected that foreign ownership would bring unwelcome foreign interference . . . and to this day Japanese industry is remarkably home-owned (much to the envy of the Americans).[90]

There is no ready Filipino or Thai answer to those who point to the special historical factors affecting the Japanese record or who argue that the emulation of the Japanese model requires that "unusual capacity for the mobilization of domestic savings"[91] reflected in the postal savings and insurance funds used to support so many Japanese development finance institutions.[92] Admiration for Japan on the part of less disciplined countries is blended with envy and, in addition, with angry dismay when Tokyo single-mindedly pushes its own interests in the rest of Asia at the expense of local nationalist objectives. The anti-Japanese reaction in South Korea, Indonesia, Thailand, and the Philippines has carried unusual force precisely because it is rooted in a love-hate ambivalence. In assessing this backlash, it is necessary to bear in mind the residual attractive power of Japan for other Asian countries, a factor that could quickly assume enhanced importance if Japan were to make a more effective effort to get in tune with local nationalisms.

Ironically, despite its patronizing attitude toward other Asian countries and its insensitivity to their nationalist aspirations, Tokyo has adopted modes of operation in Asia for reasons of simple business pragmatism that have inadvertently served to make the Japanese economic presence less offensive to nationalism than the American presence. Except for extractive industries, direct investment has played a relatively small role in Japanese expansion in Asia. Official Japanese figures listing $720 million in Japanese direct investment in South Korea, Taiwan, South Asia, and Southeast Asia in 1972 showed only the tip of the iceberg. In a detailed survey of twelve Asian capitals during 1971-1972, I found that the figure easily exceeded $2.5 billion if one added in two other key elements. The most important of these is what has been variously defined by Asian governments as "nonequity investment" (the Philippines), "loan investment" (Taiwan), or "indirect investment." In place of stock holdings, the Japanese often prefer to provide export credits for raw materials, equipment, and components, tying the local businessmen to Tokyo without risking an equity stake. As an ECAFE study emphasized, while export credits do not promote the transfer of technology and managerial know-how to the same degree as investments, "export credits, like portfolio investments, are free from the foreign control which is associated with direct investment, with the result that allocation and management are in the host country's hands."[93]

In addition to aboveboard export credit relationships, the Japanese have often converted their credit position into disguised equity shares held under local names to circumvent requirements for local control, usually after a company has proved itself. It is this practice that has been the principal target of anti-Japanese feeling, together with the clannishness of overseas Japanese business communities, the reluctance of Japanese firms to hire local personnel, and Japanese unwillingness, in most cases, to go from assembly operations to "value-added" manufacturing or, in the case of natural resources, from exclusively extractive operations to more mutually beneficial arrangements including local processing. Significantly, however, while they are hard bargainers, the Japanese are also agile bargainers who know when to make eleventh-hour concessions to nationalism if this is the best way to get business. A 1971 Philippine government survey in seven Southeast Asian countries, supported by the U.N. Development Program and the World Bank, found that Japanese investors were "more amenable to setting up joint ventures than those of other nationalities" and "quicker to sense the acceptance of projects in the host country if local partners are involved."[94] On the public sector issue, too, the Japanese have shown greater flexibility than others, with the export credit format suited equally to public sector or private sector sales. When the Indonesian government nickel enterprise first set out to build the state-owned Pomalaa nickel refinery in 1971, paying for the project out of the profits of the ore, Mitsubishi's Pacific Metals, anxious to corner as much of the nickel output at Pomalaa as possible, agreed to cooperate despite the projected public ownership. By March 1976, Japanese investment authorizations in Asia had soared to $4.2 billion, an increase of $1.1 billion over the previous year, and steady increases in nonequity investment had pushed the figure still higher. This was still smaller than the $9.07 billion level for the United States cited earlier, but it was nearly as large as the nonpetroleum component ($4.99 billion) of the U.S. figure.

Apart from other, loftier considerations, the case for an American business posture more sensitive to nationalism in developing areas can be made solely in terms of the worldwide competitive challenge posed by Japan. American technological assets alone would not be enough to overcome Japan's cost advantage in the absence of a new measure of adaptability; yet given this adaptability, the United States is still in a strong position. Even in Asia, as we will elaborate in Chapter 10, the United States could compete effectively despite Japan's geographical head start. For proximity cuts two ways. Confronted with a malleable American approach on the investment issue, along with a share in the growth of the American market, most Asian countries would choose to offset excessive dependence on a Japanese colossus too close for comfort. By helping to strengthen the economic independence of Japan's Asian neighbors, a politically sensitive American economic policy could do much to reduce the dangerous regional imbalance resulting from the special circumstances prevailing in Asia after World War II. Against the background of the postwar Japanese advance, however, a regional consolidation under Japanese leadership could also develop if the overall world economic environment should lead Japan to resort to Asian-centered economic policies. Protectionism in the West has steadily strengthened this possibility, and a continuing deterioration in the Japanese-American economic relationship, in particular, could have a decisive impact on the Japanese approach toward Asia not only in strictly economic terms but in psychological terms as well.

American economic policy toward Japan has reflected the same basic disregard for nationalism shown toward other Asian countries. Pressures for investment access, involving a direct collision with nationalism, have been applied in indiscriminate combination with pressures for liberalized trade, a sphere in which mutual accommodation is possible for Japan without the sacrifice of basic nationalist priorities. The resistance to foreign investment is, if anything, more deeply rooted in Japan than in other Asian countries, embracing as it does special factors going beyond those noted in these other cases. In the case of Japan, foreign investment has been viewed as a frontal attack on an elaborate structure of business-government linkages reflecting a business role as the standard-bearer of nationalism dating back to the Meiji period. This mutually supportive relationship of government and business is the shield of their economic independence, in the eyes of most Japanese, and the real secret of their economic success.

The American-Japanese collision over the slow pace of investment liberalization—and over nominal concessions so often frustrated in practice—has been at the heart of the continuing tensions between the two countries. At a time when Japanese investment is invited in the United States, many Americans have argued, how can Japan justify its failure to reciprocate? The Japanese respond that meaningful economic reciprocity would logically imply a welcome for Japanese labor along with Japanese capital that is conspicuously missing in the American attitude.[95] American readiness to accept Japanese investment corresponds with American interests at this stage of U.S. economic history, in this view, and Japanese reluctance to return the favor reflects the Japanese interest at a stage of growth when Japanese economic power is still no match for American might. For both sides, as most Japanese see it, foreign investment involves infringements on sovereignty in the form of ownership and control that are not present in the case of trade. It is thus the sovereign prerogative of each to decide how much of what kind of investment it can absorb at a given stage of development. In agreeing to trade liberalization, the Japanese argument runs, Tokyo would still retain the defensive armor of tariffs and other regulatory devices that are readily adjustable, by their nature, in the face of changing circumstances. Foreign investment, by contrast, could be securely controlled only by antitrust laws[96] that would undermine a domestic edifice of cartels and monopolies, a carry-over of the prewar *zaibatsu*, which has been consciously perpetuated for the very purpose of standing up to the American-controlled multinationals. Where there is no way to get desired technology except through equity investment, Japan increasingly gives ground, but not out of deference to an American definition of "reciprocity" that Tokyo does not share.

When American critics taunt Japan for "poor-mouthing" and contend that Japanese business is strong enough now to compete on an equal footing, Tokyo responds by contrasting the debt-equity ratio of even the biggest Japanese firms with the financial and technological strength of American-controlled multinationals and points to the American economic penetration of Western Europe as a fate that Japan hopes to avoid. Beyond this, Tokyo scoffs at the very idea of reciprocity in the investment sphere between two such unevenly matched rivals. In 1976, the American GNP of $1.69 trillion was triple the Japanese level of $550.2 billion. More important, in the Japanese perspective, Washington still commands a much greater degree of control over raw materials and resources than Tokyo does, and Japanese-American economic relations thus reflect a Japanese dependence that more than offsets the bilateral trade surpluses registered by Japan. If Washington wants reciprocity in economic relations, Tokyo believes, this would be meaningful only in terms of a "balance of equity" going beyond the balance of trade and embracing the entire range of Japanese-American economic relations.

The main thrust of this argument is that the United States has been seeking to have it both ways by continuing the unchecked expansion of its multinational enterprise while asking Japan, at the same time, to maintain strictly balanced bilateral trade. If the U.S. Commerce Department is correct in its contention that the multinationals make a net contribution to the U.S. balance of payments, this argument holds, then some recognition should be given to the fact that Japan, as one of their major customers, "had a place in these positive statistics."[97] If, on the other hand, as most Japanese believe, it is the multinationals, combined with overseas military expenditure, that account for the bulk of American payments deficits, then Japan is being used as a scapegoat for the failure of the United States to take self-corrective measures. Pointing to the estimate of a probable overseas investment outlay in 1973 of more than $13 billion, the Mitsubishi Bank declared that the basic causes of U.S. unemployment, inflation, and payments deficits

> are to be found in the lack of sufficient capital outlays in basic U.S. industries. . . . To step up capital spending in U.S. domestic manufacturing industries, a shift would have to be made to drastic measures centered in the moving of industries into new fields, restraints on overseas investment, and preferential treatment for domestic investment.[98]

In contrast to the note of injured innocence marking the Japanese reaction to U.S. investment pressures, the protracted struggle over the Japan-United States trade imbalance has been a more complex affair. The bitterness that has developed since 1969 has not reflected fundamental differences of perception. Rather, the issues at stake and the serious conflicts of interest involved have been all too clearly perceived by both sides in broadly similar terms, leading to an inherently difficult bargaining confrontation.

Both sides have been guilty of insensitive tactics in handling delicate trade issues. As Commerce Secretary, Maurice Stans outraged Japan with his table-pounding style. President Nixon was also asking for trouble when he made restraints on Japanese textile exports a quid pro quo for the reversion of Okinawa, and Premier Eisaku Sato made matters worse by giving an implied promise of textile curbs that he later attempted to slough off. The 1969-1971 textile controversy not only placed the United States in an undisguised protectionist posture at the very time when Washington was seeking to break down Japanese import restrictions. It also implanted the firm belief that the United States has singled out Japan as a special target in the trade area. Despite continuing tension over trade issues, however, Japan has viewed the principle of reciprocity in much the same way that the United States has and has simply been playing for time, recognizing that tariffs, nontariff barriers, and internal distribution restraints will all have to be reduced over time as part of a stable reciprocal trade relationship. The United States, for its part, has continued to charge Japan with one-sided policies that violate the principle of reciprocity. But there has been increasing American recognition that the gap between Japanese and U.S. restrictions has been steadily narrowing as Japan has liberalized and as the once liberal United States has grown steadily more protectionist. As Hugh Patrick observed, the American complaint "has been a case of the pot calling the kettle black"[99] in view of "voluntary export quotas" and other American nontariff barriers.

One of the major deterrents to improved Japan-United States trade relations is a Japanese conviction that U.S. protectionism is basically rooted in domestic factors and will continue to grow without any necessary relation to the extent of Japanese liberalization. Japanese liberalization moves have therefore been viewed largely as public relations exercises and have often stopped short of substantive concessions that would indirectly result in opening up imports from Europe and developing areas to an undesired degree. Here one can see the critical interdependence between the American-Japanese relationship and the interplay of the United States and Japan in the rest of Asia. For if the U.S. protectionist drift were to be firmly checked and the United States were to make its industry more competitive, adopting a serious export promotion policy and abandoning the rentier mentality, Japan, in turn, would be increasingly vulnerable to American liberalization pressures and would see a more credible reward for continuing liberalization in the form of a greater share in the growth of the American market. Indirectly, liberalization would serve to open Japanese markets to imports from newly industrializing Asian countries, offsetting the pressure on the U.S. market from these countries.

Given continuing American investment pressures on Japan and a growing protectionist drift in the United States and the EEC, Japan would be encouraged to increase its economic stake in Asia. For Asian countries, this could have beneficial effects in the form of economic stimuli and more liberal Japanese aid and trade policies. For the West, however, a growing Japanese emphasis on Asian economic links could have pan-Asian overtones of an unsettling character in the context of economic rivalry between Japan, on the one hand, and the United States and the European Economic Community, on the other. The key barometer of Japanese intentions is likely to be whether Tokyo pursues the long simmering idea of a yen settlement bloc anchored in Asia or a more directly Asia-centered preferential trade area going beyond a settlement union. In 1973, Finance Minister Kiichi Aichi spoke of a Japanese role as "Asia's nucleus in currency transactions."[100] A leading American banker in Japan speculated that a yen settlement bloc

> doesn't necessarily have to be limited to Asia, but probably it will be because it looks like the European bloc will get tighter, and the U.S. will not be easing up on import restrictions, so that Japan is kind of forced into its back yard . . . Probably what all this boils down to is that a yen trade bloc in Asia is not imminent, it depends on the strength of the dollar, depends on to what extent Japan is shut out in the U.S. and European markets, and thereby, relating to that, to what extent Southeast Asian nations are shut out or disadvantaged competitively and might look more to Japan for trade.[101]

A cautious Sanwa Bank analysis stressed the existing dependence of both Japan and the rest of Asia on the dollar but noted that "the Southeast Asian peoples are racially closer to the Japanese" and urged cooperative long-term economic ties with other Asian countries that would pave the way for a regional bloc.[102] Japan reacted coolly to an ECAFE proposal for an Asian reserve bank[103] that would obviate the need for a yen bloc and place Japanese aid for Asian development within a broadly controlled regional framework. Speculating on the reasons for this cold reception, one of the authors of the plan suggested directly that "Japan may even be thinking about the possibility of forming a yen bloc in Asia as an alternative to the E.C.A.F.E. proposal."[104]

The great imponderable in the Asian equation is whether China
and Japan will move toward rivalry, partnership, or something in
between. Chapter 11 suggests that a limited partnership is most likely
for elemental cultural and psychological reasons that have been
reinforced by a sense of common historic destiny in relation to the
West. Moreover, as I have argued in detail elsewhere,[105] for all of the
haggling on a wide range of disputes, the pattern of Sino-Japanese
economic relations emerging since 1972 has pointed to a much
greater degree of interdependence than had been generally anticipated. China sees economic collaboration with Japan as the surest
way to prevent Japanese economic ties with the Soviet Union from
developing into a political combination. Lingering Chinese mistrust
of Japan rooted in memories of World War II is offset by the Soviet
factor, by the economic advantages of proximity, and by Chinese
expectations of a growing clash of Japanese and American interests
that would give Peking a secure bargaining position in relations with
Tokyo. Japan, for its part, seeks a harmonized expansion of its
economic relations with China and the Soviet Union alike but has
found this complicated by the pro-Chinese undertow that has recurrently enveloped Japanese politics. While both countries have promising natural resources, there is much more oil close at hand in China
than in the Soviet Union, and China, given its present stage of
development, has a greater market growth potential than the USSR.

A key factor is that Japan sees a critical connection between its
economic relationship with China and its interests in the rest of Asia.
In Japanese calculations, the quid pro quo for helping China economically is likely to come not only in future rewards in China itself
but also in Chinese tolerance of Japanese trade and investment
throughout Asia. In their bargaining with Chinese officials, Japanese
businessmen have been notably quicker to adapt to nationalist sensi-
tivities over the terms of foreign economic involvement than they
have been in dealing with Southeast Asians. "It's not just that they
think they have a lot to gain from China," explained Indonesian
investment chief Mohammad Sadli. "The point is that they don't
look down on the Chinese as they do on most other Asians. The
Japanese and Chinese have deep feelings of cultural affinity, and they
are natural allies."[106]

Shingo Moriyama of the powerful Japan External Trade Organization (JETRO) warned that a confrontation could conceivably
occur if Japan were to divert exports to Southeast Asia from the
United States and Europe without regard for what China does. In the
Thai market, he declared, there has been a "phenomenal" improvement in the quality of Chinese products. Many of these are smuggled
goods with a marked competitive price edge over Japanese products,

he stated, among them clocks, textiles, medical supplies, transistors, tape recorders, electric bulbs, lamps, and electric toys.

> There is a possibility of a confrontation, but there is no need for one if we are at all realistic, and this is now increasingly recognized in Japan. China needs an outlet for certain items. We can move out of these into higher-technology fields to give them a chance. They don't invest, and the obvious thing for us to do is to shift somewhat from exports, where the two countries conflict, to investment in fields where we don't conflict. . . . We in Japan used to think of China as a threat to our interests overseas. We even thought of a naval buildup to protect our access to the Malacca Straits. But we have a better understanding of China now, and it is increasingly clear to both of us that the international economy is drifting apart, more or less along regional lines. It is necessary and possible for China and Japan to adopt coordinated policies and create a bloc of our own in Asia. Of course, we will still go where we can in other parts of the world.[107]

"There is room enough for both of us," says Jirō Fukushi, managing director of the giant Marubeni-Iida trading combine. "China will have to expand its trade with its Asian neighbors eventually, but we can avoid damaging competition. We are not competing for natural resources. There is no reason why we should have serious conflict politically if we are able to harmonize our economic interests. We will phase out our light industrial exports to make room for them and concentrate on high-technology heavy industry."[108]

To be sure, one should make allowances for the depth of the bitterness left by the World War II Japanese invasion of China and for possible conflict over the offshore oil and gas resources of the East China Sea, especially in the Senkaku Islands (Tiao-yü t'ai) area. Another danger is that Japan's economic dynamic will sooner or later seek an outlet in a level of military spending that will alarm China or that Soviet-oriented Chinese military preparations will arouse Japanese fears, setting in motion an escalating Sino-Japanese military rivalry. As Chapter 10 shows, however, this danger is generally exaggerated in the West. The more serious issue, in Asian minds, is how close the Sino-Japanese partnership will be, and this, in turn, is viewed in relation to the growth of Western protectionism and the evolving global power equation among Moscow, Peking, Washington, and Tokyo.

The central question most often heard in all parts of Asia is whether the United States and the newly enlarged European Economic Community will retreat into prosperous economic isolation or adopt new global trade and aid policies designed to check the steady increase in the gap between rich and poor countries. If protectionism were to shut off Asian exports, many Asian observers warn, Japan, China, and the less powerful Asian countries would eventually find themselves in the same boat. The investment stake of American multilateral corporations in Europe could, in this view, lead the United States and the EEC into a common posture toward Japan. Japan would then be drawn, willy-nilly, into an Asian-centered role in collaboration with China, while other Asian countries would seek to strengthen their position vis-à-vis the West by giving Tokyo and Peking first priority in their external relationships. India alone would stand apart from this constellation, slowly building its own industrial strength and balancing its Japanese economic ties with more substantial Soviet links than those of any other Asian capital. Japan would still have worldwide economic involvements to the maximum extent possible and would carefully regulate its Asian trade and investment to minimize conflict with China. But the combined importance of its economic interests in China, Taiwan, North and South Korea, and Southeast Asia would loom much larger relative to the West than it does today.

In 1976, the dominant impulse in Japan was to seek acceptance on its own as a global economic and political coequal of the present superpowers, avoiding an overcommitment to its impoverished Asian neighbors and a one-sided involvement in the Sino-Soviet rivalry. Faced with political resistance in Asia, Japan drew back; yet at the same time protectionism in the West, coupled with a growing awareness of its vulnerable position as a raw material importer, brought an increasingly defensive inwardness and a reappraisal of options. More and more influential Japanese began to toy with pan-Asianism as a way to strengthen their competitive posture in relation to the West and the Middle East oil producers. The polarization between right and left in the Diet since 1973 has reflected not only domestic grievances but also a growing sense of national insecurity and a search for new international moorings. The new legitimacy given to the left by the Tokyo-Peking détente brought partially to the surface widespread but hitherto repressed popular feelings, and as Henry Rosovsky has properly warned,

> these feelings of insecurity could destroy the centrist consensus of Japan and lead to greater right or left-wing extremism combined with nuclear rearmament. In the economic sphere, these feelings could easily lead to greater emphasis on creating "spheres of influence," and since these are likely to be in Asia, we are in danger of sharpening the divisions between the white and non-white peoples of the world.[109]

NOTES

1. This analysis brackets together American firms with operations abroad, American-controlled multinationals, and more fully multinationalized

"international" corporations. For a discussion of the criteria distinguishing these categories see Charles Kindleberger, *American Business Abroad* (New Haven: Yale University Press, 1969), pp. 179–210.

2. John R. Jensen, group vice-president, Dillingham Corporation, "The Multinational Corporation in Pacific Area Development" (Address presented at the Annual Installation Dinner of the Hawaii Economics Association, Honolulu, 30 November 1972), pp. 5–6. Italics added.

3. Stephen Hymer, "The Multinational Corporation and the Law of Uneven Development," Center Paper no. 181 (New Haven: Economic Growth Center, Yale University, 1971), p. 113; see also pp. 128–129.

4. Raymond Vernon, *Sovereignty at Bay* (New York: Basic Books, 1971), p. 271.

5. Paul A. Samuelson, *International Trade for a Rich Country* (Stockholm: Federation of Swedish Industries, 1972), p. 26.

6. U.S. Department of Commerce, *Survey of Current Business*, August 1976, vol. 56, no. 8, table 14, p. 49; this estimate includes Japan ($3.32 billion). Nearly half of the total ($4.08 billion) represents petroleum or petroleum-related investment. As Vernon points out in *Sovereignty at Bay*, p. 18, the book value of long-term equity and debt held abroad does not show the dimensions of the overseas assets controlled through these investments.

7. *Business Asia* (Hong Kong), 24 January 1975, pp. 25–26. This is based on 1973 figures, derived partly from U.S. Commerce Department studies and partly from independent sources. The worldwide average for 1973 was 15.9 percent. "Asia" in these statistics ranges from East Asia, including Japan, to Southeast and South Asia, including India and Pakistan, but does not cover Australia and New Zealand. See also "Organizing for Asia-Pacific Operations," *Business International Asia/Pacific* (Hong Kong), December 1972, p. 6.

8. Kindleberger, *American Business Abroad*, p. 6.

9. W. W. Rostow, *Politics and the Stages of Growth* (Cambridge: At the University Press, 1970), p. 316.

10. Vernon, *Sovereignty at Bay*, pp. 196, 201, 249.

11. Raymond Vernon, "Multinational Enterprise and National Security," *Adelphi Papers* (London: International Institute of Strategic Studies, March 1971), pp. 19–25.

12. Vernon, *Sovereignty at Bay*, pp. 170–171.

13. Frank H. Golay, "Economic Collaboration: The Role of American Investment," in Golay, ed., *The United States and the Philippines* (Englewood Cliffs: Prentice-Hall, 1966), p. 95.

14. *Inter-Agency Survey of Direct Investment* (Manila: Board of Investment, 1972), pp. 2–9.

15. This is the American embassy estimate given to me and to other journalists. See, for example, Henry Kamm, "Americans in Philippines See Marcos as a Friend," *New York Times*, 3 November 1972, p. 1. Based on Commerce Department statistics, this estimate represents a cumulative total of the value of equity investments at the time of their acquisition.

16. This estimate is cited in "A New Relationship," *U.S. News and World Report*, 16 October 1972, p. 34; and Robert B. Stauffer, "The Political Economy of a Coup: Transnational Linkages and Philippine Political Response," mimeographed, p. 25. Privately circulated.

17. See U.S. Embassy, "Current Economic Situation and Trends" (Manila, 1 March 1972), p. 6; and an aide-mémoire to members of the Philippine-American Chamber of Commerce, Tristan E. Beplat, "Problems Facing Foreign Investors in the Philippines," Philippine-American Relations Series, no. 14 (Manila: USIS, January 1971).

18. See *Constitutional Reforms on Socio-economic Policies*, Background Studies no. 6 (Manila: Araneta University Research Foundation, 14 December 1971), p. 41; Frances Starner, "Looking Past Laurel-Langley—I" *Far Eastern Economic Review*, 4 March 1972, p. 77; and idem, "Looking Past Laurel-Langley—II," ibid., 11 March 1972, p. 57.

19. In Malaysia, Sri Lanka, Cambodia, and South Vietnam, the only other countries in which the economic carry-over of the former colonial ruler relative to indigenous economic power is on a comparable scale, British and French influence has been centered in the plantation sector.

20. David Wurfel, "Problems of Decolonization," in *United States and the Philippines*, p. 167.

21. Tarzie Vittachi, "Polluting the Truth," *Insight* (Hong Kong), July 1972, p. 54.

22. Alejandro Lichauco, *Imperialism and the Security of the State*, a memorandum to fellow delegates at the Constitutional Convention, Manila, 19 April 1972, p. 39; see also pp. 40–44 and idem, *Nationalism, Economic Development, and Social Justice* (Manila: Economic Society of the Ateneo de Manila, 1967), pp. 39–44.

23. Hans W. Singer, "The Distribution of Gains between Investing and Borrowing Countries," *American Economic Review*, May, 1950, pp. 35–60.

24. For example, see K. N. Raj, *Indian Economic Growth: Performance and Prospects* (New Delhi: Allied, 1965), pp. 23–24.

25. Michael Kidron, *Foreign Investment in India* (London: Oxford University Press, 1965), pp. 308–312.

26. Raymond Vernon, "Foreign Owned Enterprise in the Developing Countries," in *Public Policy*, ed. J. D. Montgomery and Arthur Smithies (Cambridge: Harvard University Press, 1966), pp. 374–377; see also Vernon, *Sovereignty at Bay*, pp. 180–186; and Kindleberger, *American Business Abroad*, pp. 172–173.

27. Matthew J. Kust, *Foreign Enterprise in India* (Durham: University of North Carolina Press, 1964), pp. 55–56.

28. Herbert Feith, *The Decline of Constitutional Democracy in Indonesia* (Ithaca: Cornell University Press, 1962), esp. pp. 3, 138, 219; see also Leslie Palmier, "Sukarno the Nationalist," *Pacific Affairs*, June 1957, p. 115; and D.H. Burger, *Structural Changes in Javanese Society*, Translation Series (Ithaca: Cornell Modern Indonesia Project, 1956), p. 22.

29. Sjafruddin Prawiranegara, *Membangun Kembali Ekonomi Indonesia* [Economic rehabilitation of Indonesia] (Jakarta: Al-Ma'arif and idem, *Islam*

dalam Pergolakan Dunia [Islam and the turmoil of the world], 2d ed. (Bandung: Al-Ma'arif, 1947).

30. The regulatory problems associated with the rise of Pertamina are discussed in Rudhi Prasetya and Neil Hamilton, "The Regulation of Indonesian State Enterprises," and idem, "Pertamina: A National Oil Company," International Legal Center, *Law and Public Enterprise in Asia* (New York: Praeger, 1976), pp. 147-182 and 194-233.

31. The reasons for the marginal position given to public enterprise in the Philippines are discussed in A. H. Hanson, *Public Enterprise and Economic Development* (London: Routledge & Kegan Paul, 1959); and Golay, "Economic Collaboration," pp. 105-106. The unusually severe problem of corruption in Filipino state enterprises is discussed in Selig S. Harrison, "Japan's Penetration of the Philippines," *Washington Post*, 28 February 1973, p. A20.

32. Lee Lescaze, "Burma Seeks Equality in a Dwindling Economy," *Washington Post*, 28 June 1972, p. A17.

33. Milton Sacks, "Political Alignments of Vietnamese Nationalist," Report no. 3708 (Washington: Office of Intelligence and Research, U.S. Department of State, 1 October 1949), p. 114; see also Phan Quang Dan, *Volonté vietnamienne* (Dornach: Hutter, 1951), p. 20.

34. Robert G. Scigliano, *South Vietnam: Nation under Stress* (Boston: Houghton Mifflin, 1963), p. 200. Student support for a militant "nationalist socialism" was expressed in an interview with Tran Quang Tri, president, and the Executive Committee of the Saigon Students Union, Saigon, 10 April 1967. See also Vu Quoc Thuc, *L'Economie communaliste de Viêtnam* [The communal structure of the Vietnamese economy] (Paris: Faculty of Law, University of Paris, 1950).

35. Park Chong-hui, *The Country, the Revolution, and I*, trans. Leon Sinder (Seoul: Leon Sinder, 1963), pp. 41, 46, 78-79.

36. See the keynote address by Yi Hyo-jae, professor of sociology, Seoul Women's University, in *Han'gug in kwa sahoe chŏngŭi* [Koreans and social justice], Report no. 29 in a series of round table discussions sponsored by the Congress for Cultural Freedom, Seoul, 12 April 1967; see also Chu Yo-han, "The People Must Fight for It," *Taehan Ilbo* (Seoul), 1 June 1967, p. 4; Y. H. Shin, "The Formation of Monopoly and the Situation of Middle and Small Industry," *Chŏnggyŏng Yŏn'gu* [Political and economic research] (Seoul), June 1966, pp. 10-13; special issues of *Chŏnggyŏng* on "Monopoly and the Social Economy" (November 1966) and "Plutocracy in Our Growth" (October 1967); and "Chaebol (Zaibatsu)," *Taehan Ilbo* (Seoul), 19 August 1965, p. 4.

37. Gustav F. Papanek, *Pakistan's Development: Social Goals and Private Incentives* (Cambridge: Harvard University Press, 1967), pp. 40-42, 69.

38. Abul Ala Maudoodi, "A Myth Exploded: Jamaat-e-Islami's Report on the Pakistan Economy," mimeographed (Karachi, December 1964), p. 25.

39. Pakistan People's Party, *Foundation and Policy*, Foundation Meeting Document no. 1 (Karachi, December 1967), pp. 5-6. On the eve of Ayub's overthrow, the chief economist of the Planning Commission reported that

66 percent of the nation's industrial assets and 80 percent of the banking assets were controlled by twenty-two families (see Planning Commission, Government of Pakistan, *Socio-economic Objectives of the Fourth Five Year Plan* [Islamabad: Khursheed, November 1968], pp. 3, 17, 21).

40. For historical and sociological analyses of the Marwaris see Selig S. Harrison, *India: The Most Dangerous Decades* (Princeton: Princeton University Press, 1960), pp. 114-122; see also Harry A. Millman, "The Marwari: A Study of a Group of the Trading Castes of India" (M.A. thesis, University of California at Berkeley, 1955), p. 4; and R. K. Hazari, *The Structure of the Corporate Private Sector* (Bombay: Asia, 1968).

41. Kodia Bhimsen, *The Marwari Community in India*, cited in D. R. Gadgil, "Notes on the Rise of the Business Communities in India," mimeographed, p. 18.

42. *Report of the Monopolies Inquiry Commission* (New Delhi: Government of India Press, 1965), pp. 35, 122-124; and Hazari, *Structure of the Corporate Private Sector*, table 2.2, pp. 37, 322.

43. Planning Commission, Government of India, *Notes on Perspective of Development, India: 1960-61 to 1975-76* (New Delhi: Perspective Planning Division, Planning Commission, April 1964), pp. 8-9, 23; see also K. D. Malaviya, "Declaration of Northern India Congress Workers' Convention" (New Delhi, 6-7 September 1964).

44. Jagdish N. Bhagwat and Padma Desai, *India: Planning for Industrialization* (London: Oxford University Press, 1970), pp. 135-140.

45. Ibid.

46. John P. Lewis, *Wanted in India: A Relevant Radicalism*, Policy Memorandum no. 36 (Princeton: Center for International Studies, Princeton University, December 1969), p. 10.

47. Anne O. Krueger, "Import Substitution in India: A Case Study" (Study prepared for the Agency for International Development, New Delhi, July 1970), esp. p. 79.

48. K. N. Raj, *India, Pakistan, and China* (Bombay: Allied, 1967), esp. pp. 12-14, 51-52.

49. See Jagdish Bhagwat and Padma Desai, *India*, tables 5.1, 5.2.

50. "List of Indian Joint Ventures Abroad," *Journal of Industry and Trade*, Bombay, July 1976, pp. 64-67.

51. *People's Republic of China: An Economic Assessment*, A Compendium of Papers submitted to the Joint Economic Committee, U.S. Congress, 92d Cong., 2d sess., 18 May 1972, esp. pp. 72-73; see also K. N. Raj, "Role of the 'Machine-Tools Sector' in Economic Growth: A Comment on Indian and Chinese Experience," *in Socialism, Capitalism, and Economic Growth*, ed. C. H. Feinstein (Cambridge: At the University Press, 1967).

52. U.N. Information Center, Tokyo, Press Release no. 72/18, 14 February 1972, reporting a statement by U Nyun, ECAFE executive secretary, at a meeting of the ECAFE Committee on Industry and Natural Resources.

53. Government of India, *Policy Statement on Foreign Capital* (New Delhi: Press Information Bureau, Government of India, 6 April 1949), p. 3.

54. Kidron, *Foreign Investment in India*, p. 168; see also an excellent case study of Indian oil policy by Michael Tanzer, *The Political Economy of International Oil and the Underdeveloped Countries* (Boston: Beacon, 1969), pp. 163-165; see also pp. 166-256.

55. Bushrod Howard, Jr., "India's Oil Problem," *Washington Post*, 1 October 1960, p. 10; see also idem, "Russian Oil for the Lamps of Fidel Castro's Cuba," 16 October 1960, p. E7.

56. Cited in an editorial in *Capital* (Calcutta), 8 September 1960, p. 353.

57. *Petroleum Press Service Newsletter*, Geneva, June 1961, p. 217.

58. Dilip Mukerji, "War of the Crude," *Far Eastern Economic Review*, 19 February 1970, p. 73.

59. Science Advisory Committee, Office of the President, *The World Food Problem*, Report of the Panel on the World's Food Supply (Washington, May 1967), table A1-4, 2:707; see also 2:380-381.

60. See the exchange of letters between John P. Lewis, director, USAID, 18 December 1965, and S. Bhootalingam, Indian economic affairs secretary, 20 December 1965 (New Delhi: Press Information Bureau, Government of India, 28 December 1965).

61. Easwar Sagar, "Fertilizer Plants," *Hindu Weekly Review* (Madras), 17 October 1966, p. 3.

62. Cited in *The Involvement of U.S. Private Enterprise in Developing Countries*, Hearings Before the Subcommittee on Foreign Economic Policy of the House Committee on Foreign Affairs, 90th Cong., 1st sess., 10 October 1967, p. 173.

63. Marquis W. Childs, "Plan to Build Fertilizer Plants in India Stirs Interest," *St. Louis Post-Dispatch*, 16 March 1966, p. 1-B.

64. Raymond Ewell, "Increasing Fertilizer Production in India," mimeographed (December 1965), p. 7. Privately circulated. Ewell made his proposal in a State Department meeting of experts called to discuss the population-food crisis on November 19, 1966, and in a letter to President Johnson.

65. Indian progress in the design and manufacture of fertilizer plants is discussed in *The Fourth Five Year Plan: A Draft Outline* (New Delhi: Government of India Press, 1973), p. 271; and Paul Pothen, "The Cochin Fertilizer Plant: A Case Study," *Economic Times* (Bombay), 13 April 1967, p. 4.

66. Agency for International Development Steel Mission, *Summary of Report on Proposed Bokaro Steel Mill* (New Delhi: USIS, 27 April 1963), p. 15; see also William A. Johnson, *The Steel Industry of India* (Cambridge: Harvard University Press, 1966), pp. 141-145.

67. M. N. Dastur and Company, "Preliminary Report to Hindustan Steel Limited on the Establishment of an Integrated Steelworks at Bokaro" (Calcutta, 24 December 1959), pp. 6-7.

68. USIS, New Delhi, press release, 9 May 1963.

69. *Washington Star*, 29 March 1963, p. 2.

70. Sudhir Ghosh, *Gandhi's Emissary* (Boston: Houghton Mifflin, 1967), pp. 277–292; see also a description of the Ford Foundation—sponsored training program in the *New York Times*, 22 April 1957, p. 10; and a formal report, *Steel in India: Report on "Program Instep"* (New York: American Iron and Steel Institute, February 1960).

71. John P. Lewis, *Quiet Crisis in India* (Washington: Brookings Institution, 1962), pp. 48–49; see also pp. 231 and 256.

72. Lewis, *Quiet Crisis in India*, p. 256.

73. "An Indian Renault?" *Newsweek*, 26 October 1970, p. 100.

74. "Pioneering in India," *Fortune*, February 1971, p. 40.

75. Leland Hazard, former president of Pittsburgh Plate Glass, "Journey to India," *Pittsburgh Post-Gazette*, 14 October 1963, p. 16; see also Kust, *Foreign Enterprise in India*, p. 73.

76. *BHEL 1975*, Bharat Heavy Electricals Ltd. (New Delhi: Mehta Printers, March 1975), pp. 2–3.

77. *India: A Background Note on the Economy* (Washington: International Bank for Reconstruction and Development, Information and Public Affairs Department, May 1976), p. 5; see also p. 3.

78. J. K. Galbraith, "Some Notes on the Rationale of Indian Economic Organization," mimeographed (New Delhi, 29 April 1958), p. 8.

79. *Weekend Review* (New Delhi), 29 April 1967, p. 25.

80. See an interview with former Prime Minister Indira Gandhi, "Not Only in Name but in Fact Also," in "The Public Sector," a special issue of *Citizen* (New Delhi), 24 January 1970, p. 57.

81. See A. Hariharan, "Joint Sector Syndrome," *Far Eastern Economic Review*, 16 February 1972, p. 43.

82. Leland Hazard, "Strong Medicine for India," *Atlantic*, May 1965, p. 46.

83. For a detailed analysis of the Japanese impact on Asian economies see Selig S. Harrison's eight-part series in the *Washington Post*, 25 February to 4 March 1973.

84. Interview, Jakarta, 15 March 1971. For other Indonesian views of Japan see Koentjaraningrat, "Indonesian Image of Japan," *International House Bulletin* (Tokyo), July 1970, full issue; and Lie Tek-tjeng and Yoshida Teigo, "Some Remarks on the Problems and Difficulties Besetting Present-Day Indonesian-Japanese Relations," Lembaga Research Kebudajaan Nasional, Bagian Asia Timur no. IX/11, Jakarta, 13 March 1968.

85. Interview, Tokyo, 30 March 1972.

86. Interview with Bunchana Atthakor, *Asahi Shimbun* (Tokyo), 14 December 1970, p. 3.

87. William W. Lockwood, *Economic Development in Japan* (Princeton: Princeton University Press, 1954), p. 322.

88. David S. Landes, "Japan and Europe," in *The State and Economic Enterprise in Japan*, ed. William W. Lockwood (Princeton: Princeton University Press, 1965), pp. 94–96.

89. Alejandro Lichauco, *Nationalism, Economic Development, and Social Justice*, p. 10.

90. "Japan's Takeoff Owes Little to Foreign Capital," *Bangkok Post*, 3 December 1967, p. 6; for an Indian view see D. R. Gadgil, "Analysis of Policies of India and Japan," *Daily Yomiuri* (Toyko), 23 June 1971, p. 8.

91. Vernon, "Foreign Owned Enterprise in Developing Countries," p. 377.

92. William W. Lockwood, "The Socialistic Society: India and Japan," *Foreign Affairs*, October 1958, p. 122.

93. ECAFE, *Economic Survey of Asia and the Far East, 1970* (Bangkok: ECAFE, 1971), p. I-130.

94. Philippine Board of Investment, *Direct Investment of Japanese Enterprises in Southeast Asia,* cited in Juan L. Mercado, "Fund-Pinched Southeast Asia Looks over Tokyo's Cash," *Depth News* (Kuala Lumpur), 5 May 1973, p. 3.

95. Chikara Makino, Planning Office, Minister's Secretariat, Ministry of International Trade and Industry, "Japan-U.S. Relations: Analysis of the Present Situation and Experimental Discussions on Future Prospects," *Tsusan Journal* (Tokyo), May 1970, p. 15. For a similar view see an analysis by Mahbub ul Haq, World Bank director of policy planning, "Development and Independence," *Development Dialogue* (Uppsala: Dag Hammarskjöld Foundation), February 1974, p. 11.

96. This view is found in Kiichi Miyazawa, "Shihon jiyuka to Nihon no taidō" [Capital liberalization and our view], *Chuō kōrōn* [Management essays] (Tokyo), Spring 1967, pp. 68–69.

97. Nobuhiko Ushiba, "The U.S. and Japan in World Development: Competitors or Partners?" (Address presented at a San Francisco Civic Luncheon, 16 February 1973), p. 13.

98. *Mitsubishi Bank Review* (Tokyo), February 1972, p. 102; see also ibid., September 1971, p. 84.

99. Hugh Patrick, Testimony before the Subcommittee on Foreign Economic Policy of the House Committee on Foreign Affairs, 92d Cong., 2d sess., 4 November 1971, p. 9; see also John C. Renner, director, Office of International Trade, U.S. Department of State, "American-Japanese Trade Pattern: Is It Different" (Address presented at the American Management Associations, New York City, 23 March 1971), esp. tables on p. 14.

100. "Yen Bloc Concept under Study in Bold Attempt to Raise Status," *Business Japan* (Tokyo), July 1973, p. 30; see also a report of Aichi's testimony on the yen bloc before the Finance Committee of the lower house of the Diet in *Nihon Keizai* (Tokyo), 19 April 1972, p. 3.

101. Interview with Cushman May, vice-president for Asia of the Chase Manhattan Bank, *Business Japan*, July 1973, pp. 30–31.

102. A. Tanaka, *Yen keizaiken kōsō ni tsuite* [About the yen economy bloc scheme] (Tokyo: Sanwa Bank, 14 June 1973), pp. 15–16; earlier discussion of the yen bloc concept may be found in Toshio Watanabe, "Yen and Dollar in Southeast Asia," *Asahi-Asia Review* (Tokyo), Summer 1972, pp. 5–7.

103. This proposal is summarized in "Feasibility Study on the Establishment of an Asian Reserve Bank: A Summary," Intergovernmental Committee on

Establishment of an Asian Reserve Bank, Report Trade/TLP/ARB(1), ECAFE, Bangkok, 27 June 1972.

104. Youngil Lim, "Japan and E.C.A.F.E. in Economic Cooperation for Trade and Development in Asia" (Paper delivered at the Twenty-ninth International Congress of Orientalists, Paris, 16–22 July 1973), p. 11; see also idem, "Reserve Bank Plan Would Not Put a 'Heavy Load' on Japan," *Asian* (Hong Kong), 10–16 September 1972, p. 7.

105. Selig S. Harrison, "China and Japan: The New Asian Partnership?" *Washington Post*, 4 March 1973, p. B5; see also idem, *China, Oil, and Asia: Conflict Ahead?* (New York: Columbia University Press, 1977), chap. 7.

106. Interview, Djakarta, 14 March 1971.

107. This passage is derived from an address by Shingo Moriyama at a JETRO Tokyo conference on November 11, 1971, a press conference on that date, and a subsequent transcribed interview with *Mainichi* trade specialist Tokuji Nimura made available to me in full. An abridged version of Moriyama's comments appeared in "J.E.T.R.O. to Reexamine Southeast Asian Policy toward Economic Cooperation with China," *Mainichi* (Tokyo), 18 December 1971, p. 3.

108. "Japan in Asia," *Japan Times Weekly*, 10 December 1971, p. 4; see also Teiichirō Morinaga, *Asia Toyushi Chōsadan chūkan hōkoku* [Interim report by the Survey Mission on Investment and Financing in Asia] (Tokyo: Asia Toyushi Chosadan, April 1971), p. 5; see also a discussion of Japanese relations with the overseas Chinese by Morinaga and other business leaders in "Joint Ventures Cannot Raise Funds Locally," *Keidanren Review* (Tokyo), Spring 1971, p. 5.

109. *United States Foreign Economic Policy toward Japan*, Hearings Before the Subcommittee on Foreign Economic Policy of the House Committee on Foreign Affairs, 92d Cong., 2d sess., 2–4 and 8 November 1971, p. 82.

IV

NATIONALISM AND AMERICAN POLICY

10. The Future of U.S. Military Policy in Asia

In attempting to suggest new guidelines for American military and economic policy in Asia, this analysis proceeds from the pivotal assumption that nationalism sharply circumscribes the American role. American policy options are defined, in this approach, by the limits inherent in the situation rather than by an a priori definition of American interests as viewed in a global perspective from the vantage point of Washington. Thus, the United States must differentiate between a variety of distinctive regional and national environments, each struggling for its own place in the sun, each with its unique world view, and each with an identity worthy of American recognition in its own right.

American interests in this racially divided, multipolar world are in the deepest sense indivisible. In a long-term perspective, there is only one, generalized American interest in an open world moving with all deliberate speed toward the reduction of the inequities discussed most extensively in Chapter 9. The test of a successful American policy in such a setting becomes the ability of the United States to maintain broadly diversified worldwide relationships transcending the rivalries of others. For as the pursuit of equity intensifies, so does the danger of economic and military collision, and the mainsprings of this multiplying conflict are beyond the effective manipulation of the superpowers. Nationalism sets the ground rules of shifting struggles in which a beleaguered superpower, commanding a disproportionate share of the world's resources, is best able to roll with the punches by minimizing its entanglements.

The diffusion of power accompanying the spread of nationalist consciousness greatly reduces the danger of one-nation dominance that has provided the rationale for the past application of balance of power logic to Asia. In a geopolitical landscape that becomes more and more kaleidoscopic, the enduring American interest does not lie in any particular transitory balance of power but rather in compatible relationships with countries big and small cutting across the multipolar spectrum. The accelerating struggle for equity progressively erodes the obsolete liberal ideal of world order. Stability comes, if it comes, not through some new global "architecture" but through the evolution of regionally rooted power patterns that reflect indigenous power realities. This appraisal of the international environment leaves great scope, in the economic field, for an outgoing policy of responsive cooperation on a basis consistent with nationalism. In the military arena, however, it calls for a cautious posture marked by reserve and detachment.

THE CASE FOR AN INDIGENOUS BALANCE OF POWER

The task of defining an appropriate American military policy in Asia is facilitated by making a clear distinction between two separable objectives that have been consistently merged in cold war perspectives. One is the maintenance of a global American military capability, encompassing Asia, designed primarily to assure a stable bilateral power equation with the Soviet Union. The other is the promotion of regional power balances within Asia, buttressed by the continuing interposition of American forces and American military aid. The first objective can be pursued in ways that avoid a direct collision with nationalism in Asia; the second, by its nature, places the United States on a collision course with nationalism and can only be self-defeating. This analysis makes no attempt to discuss the future of the bilateral American-Soviet encounter in its global dimensions. Instead, our focus will be on the Asian environment as it restricts and shapes the American pursuit of global and regional objectives alike.

Broadly defined, the basic task of the United States is to distinguish between international aggression, as in the Japanese invasion of China, and the military aspects of internecine struggles to decide the leadership of nationalism or the shape of national identity, as in Korea, Vietnam, Cambodia, Laos, Thailand, Taiwan, and the Indo-Pakistan conflicts of 1948, 1965, and 1971. Where such internecine struggles are involved, the long-term impact of external intervention is likely to be marginal and its political costs colossal. By contrast, where a national identity has crystallized and an external challenge to this identity takes the form of military aggression, the opportunity for effective intervention exists and the United States must then assess whether possible benefits justify probable costs. Thus, by 1936, as we argued earlier, China had begun to mount its own unified response to Japan and the political preconditions for effective American intervention were present. This discussion does not rule out the hypothetical need for comparable military intervention again and focuses in particular on the technological breakthroughs in strategic mobility that would permit the United States, without retaining fixed bases there, to act in the event of international aggression in Asia. In the larger global context, this analysis concludes, the maintenance of a bilateral Soviet-U.S. power equation encompassing Asia is also possible without a politically self-defeating base presence.

As a first step in illustrating what these guidelines imply, let us examine the case of Korea, a critical problem area in Asia, where the crystallization of a national identity and the evolution of intraregional power patterns rooted in local realities have been delayed, in part, by a unilateral American force presence and a vicious circle of military aid inputs on both sides of the thirty-eighth parallel.

In North and South Korea alike, external support freezes a posture of confrontation and thus impedes unification by lifting the burden of inflated military establishments, in varying measure, from the shoulders of those directly concerned. This is particularly so in the South, where American military aid and American troops have made possible a defense outlay smaller in proportion to the national budget than that in the North.[1] With more of the burden on their own shoulders, Southern leaders would be compelled to weigh the risks of moving toward unification against the costs of division more seriously than in the past. Thus, the military aid "modernization" commitments made by the United States in 1970 and 1977 to cushion reductions in American force levels have helped to freeze the North-South confrontation and to stimulate new military aid inputs to the North, thus nullifying, to a great extent, the value of U.S. force reductions as a means of promoting a relaxation of tensions in the peninsula.

The long-term American interest in Korea lies in a phased disengagement from involvements that frustrate the growth of an indigenous North-South balance and, in the process, delay the emergence of a coherent nationalism capable of serving as a balance wheel in East Asia. This calls for more than the mere stabilization of the existing division at a lower level of tension for the limited purpose of minimizing the risk of conflict.[2] It points to an eventual withdrawal of the American military presence whether or not, as Morton Abramowitz has proposed,[3] this can be linked to the pace of North-South accommodation. In the United Nations, it presupposes not only the end of one-sided U.N. involvement in Korea, facilitating North Korean participation in the world body, but also American identification with a membership formula giving Korea a single personality in the international setting. An American policy in tune with Korean nationalism would consciously seek to extricate the United States from a one-sided commitment to Seoul in all spheres, including the critical areas of military and economic aid, moving toward a symmetrical relationship with Pyongyang and Seoul designed to promote a similar detachment on the part of Moscow, Peking, and Tokyo. Trade, aid, and diplomacy would all reflect this new symmetry. The continuance of the U.S.- South Korean security treaty following the withdrawal of U.S. forces and the closing of U.S. bases would be necessary insurance, initially, to offset the risks of renewed external intervention inherent in such an approach. But the treaty would no longer be sacrosanct and would be reassessed and renegotiated at short-term intervals to encourage a corresponding reappraisal of North Korean treaty ties with Moscow and Peking. In effect, such a policy would seek a de facto neutralization of the peninsula as an arena of major power conflict without necessarily waiting for the conclusion of the formal four-power arrangements often advocated. It would be a vote of confidence in Korean nationalism and in the potential of a unified Korea as a buffer state, implying a rejection, at the same time, of proposed policies posing the indefinite division of the peninsula as the price of stability in the triangular.Soviet-Chinese-Japanese encounter.

In a characteristic statement of the case for a continued American presence, Robert Osgood has argued that an American withdrawal would be "unsettling" in the absence of an agreement that would stabilize the relationship of "the two Koreas" to the satisfaction of the major powers. Such a withdrawal would leave a "vacuum of influence," he has contended, opening the way for "Chinese or Soviet paramountcy, or Japan's assumption of America's security role." History is invoked to show that Moscow, Peking, and Tokyo would "each be afraid to stay out of this tripolar game at the risk of ceding paramountcy to either of the other two players."[4] Yet in drawing this historical parallel, Osgood has ignored the contrast between the relative political quiescence of Korea prior to the turn of the century and the subsequent birth of a modern nationalist consciousness. Four decades of Japanese colonialism and three postwar decades of partition have created a powerful spirit of Korean nationalism, introducing a new and potentially decisive factor into the historic equation. This pent-up nationalism cuts across the North-South barrier, as Chapter 7 showed, and has grown in intensity and vitality despite the artificial constraints of the cold war period. The very continuance of two Koreas has become increasingly subject to this imponderable and pervasive challenge. Pyongyang, for its part, not only has made nationalism the basis of its legitimacy in the North but also has gradually emerged as a bona fide contender for nationalist leadership in the country as a whole. Consequently, whether it be Southern-dominated, Northern-dominated, or some new amalgam, the leadership of a unified or confederated Korea would be likely to act as a jealous guardian of national sovereignty. Even in the cold war context, Pyongyang has progressively broken loose from satellite status and was never the "puppet" of Korean War imagery, in any case, as Charles Bohlen has reminded us.[5] In a more fluid Asian environment, a Northern-dominated regime would have more options than ever permitting a freewheeling nationalist role that encompasses noncommunist as well as communist relationships. The "vacuum of influence" left by an American withdrawal would eventually be filled, in short, by Korea itself.

To say that the aspiration for unification is a powerful one is not to predict the early achievement of a formal union or to suggest that the two Korean states are likely to leap overnight from their present confrontation to confederate harmony. On the contrary, any movement toward confederation or unification by peaceful means would no doubt have to come in very gradual stages and would have to be preceded, in all likelihood, by the emergence of more compatible regimes in North and South that would be willing to take the risks involved in cultural and political interchange. The most that can be realistically expected in the foreseeable future is a reduction of military tensions and a tortuous movement toward *de facto* coexistence. In dwelling upon the strength of nationalist feeling, our intent is to point up the critical difference between a *de facto* coexistence that would leave the door open for moves toward confederation or unification and *de jure* "Two Korea" arrangements that would appear to freeze the division in its present form indefinitely. So long as there is no sense of movement toward confederation or unification, there will be a serious danger of a military explosion in Korea, whether triggered by a frustrated North or, over time, by an increasingly well-armed South. At best, even if military tensions can be reduced, it will not be easy for external powers to promote "Two Korea" arrangements after the German model unless these are clearly linked to projected steps in the direction of confederation or unification.

In contrast to the German case, the prospect of Korean unification would not be viewed as a threat to the outside powers concerned and would thus not be likely to invite preemptive action.

Germany united was expansionist, but Korea before its division was the victim of Japanese colonialism. The argument that Japan would seek to assume a quasi-military role in the South following an American withdrawal has a superficial plausibility in view of the extensive Japanese presence established in the South under the U.S. aegis. Japan's one-sided commitment to the South has been predicated largely on a protective American presence, however, and an American withdrawal would intensify latent pressures for a more symmetrical policy balancing Japanese interests in Seoul and Pyongyang. Already, Japan has been moving fitfully and hesitantly toward a more balanced Korean policy but has keyed this movement to its shifting assessment of U.S. plans and desires.

Japanese attitudes toward the American military role in Korea are much more complicated than is often suggested by advocates of a continued U.S. presence in the South. To the extent that the U.S. presence keeps the South "safe for Japanese investment" without involving Japan militarily, it is welcome to pro-Seoul conservatives and tolerable to centrist public opinion as one of the necessary costs of the security treaty. To the extent that the danger of fighting in Korea appears real, however, support for the American presence is offset by fears of Japanese involvement. While most Japanese would not like to see a communist triumph in Korea, it is not the communist danger, as such, that worries them most. Rather, it is the possibility of impulsive American intervention that could embroil Japan militarily or, alternatively, equally precipitate American disengagement from Korea that would not allow time for Japan to readjust its policy and protect its interests. Kei Wakaizumi, explaining why Japan is fearful of a Korean conflict, put his emphasis not on the danger to Japan from the North but on the "profound apprehension that such a conflict may draw Japan into a conflict with China or the Soviet Union, or that it may damage her relations with the United States."[6] Similarly, when pressed to define the nature of the security threats that would result from a Pyongyang victory, Foreign Minister Miyazawa did not point to the danger of Northern aggression against Japan. Instead, his concern was addressed to the immediate spillover effects of a Korean civil conflict, principally the flood of refugees or "routed troops" who might seek shelter in Japan as a consequence of Japan's current ties to Seoul.[7] Even many pro-Seoul conservatives who hope that the United States will do whatever can be done to perpetuate a non-Communist South would probably be ready to swallow a Communist victory rather than pay the price of Japanese military involvement. Edward Seidensticker, analyzing these conservative attitudes, observed that "to such Japanese, it does not seem fair that Tokyo should be asked now to repair the damage wrought by Washington thirty years ago" when it took over Korea, displaced Japanese colonial rule and joined with the Soviet Union in dividing the peninsula.[8]

A more symmetrical policy in Korea would be essential to sustain the central Japanese objective of a collaborative relationship with China discussed in the concluding chapter. Thus, for this reason alone, the concept of a triangular Sino-Soviet-Japanese competition for paramountcy suggested by Osgood is likely to have little practical meaning. If there is a competition for paramountcy in Korea, it exists in the more limited context of the Sino-Soviet rivalry. As near neighbors with a strategic stake there, both Moscow and Peking are anxious that the other not gain the upper hand in Korea; yet by the same token their very proximity inspires redoubled Korean nationalist vigilance, as Pyongyang has demonstrated in its skillful balancing of Soviet and Chinese aid. The ability of Korea to offset Soviet and Chinese influence with other ties would be enhanced in a continuing climate of détente and would be fundamentally improved if a unified Korea could deal with all of the major powers from a position of concerted strength. Conversely, in the absence of unification, the opportunity for Soviet and Chinese inroads would continue to be significant, especially if Moscow and Peking could keep alive the specter of American intervention in the North-South struggle for ascendancy by pointing to American bases in Japan. Far from insuring stability, as the Osgood view contends, division perpetuates a dangerous instability. The intensification of the Japanese presence in the South under American protection could stimulate Chinese interest in the North that would add not only to Sino-Japanese tensions but also to Sino-Soviet tensions. An American withdrawal, on the other hand, would set in motion forces enabling the North-South balance to find its own level, politically and militarily, opening the way for an eventual resolution of the present impasse and a more authentic stability reflecting Korean realities.

The attitude of China and the Soviet Union toward Korea in the event of an American withdrawal hinges not only on what Japan does in its own right, as part of a tripolar competition, but also on whether Japan continues to maintain its security links with the United States. American forces poised in Japan for a possible return to Korea would make the competition quadrilateral in the eyes of the Soviets and Chinese, increasing their military stake in Pyongyang. The difficulty of neutralizing Korea without also neutralizing Japan has been sharply underlined in proposals over the years for the neutralization of northeast Asia by George Kennan,[9] Ambassador Mike Mansfield,[10] and leading Japanese foreign policy thinkers.[11] In Kennan's case, however, Korea has been implicitly treated as a mere pawn in an American-Soviet bargaining game. The game could have been played in 1948, he has suggested, but the United States lost the opportunity to do so by concluding a military alliance with Japan before it had tested Soviet readiness for neutralization. In later proposals, Kennan has continued to urge an American-Soviet understanding with respect to the neutralization of Japan[12] but has disregarded the critical Korean factor in the northeast Asian equation, declaring that "a curious balance of power does already exist in east Asia, as between the Russians, the Chinese and the Japanese."[13] Since this balance exists at the cost of a divided Korea, a cost less and less acceptable to the Koreans themselves, it is likely to prove a most precarious arrangement, subject to profound and sudden dislocation by Korean-initiated moves to force a change in the status quo.

Should the United States follow a withdrawal from Korea with a gradual lowering of its posture in Japan, this would enhance the prospects for a neutral Korea while promoting an indigenous East Asian balance of power in a broader sense. It would set the stage for meaningful arms control efforts in the area, as we shall elaborate later, and it would encourage a positive Japanese role in such efforts by underlining the costs of an expanded defense buildup. In Japan, as in Korea, the American military relationship has postponed the necessity for a defense debate based on regional realities. It is often argued, in defense of the American presence, that a U.S. withdrawal would lead to compensating security efforts by Japan itself posing a threat to regional stability. Yet, as our earlier analysis indicated, this assumption rests on a misreading of how most Japanese assess the threats facing them.

In some areas of the Japanese defense program, an American withdrawal might lead to increased Japanese defense expenditures. In others, the American security relationship has enabled Japan to make use of sophisticated technology at bargain basement prices that would not necessarily be available in the absence of a special relationship. The development and deployment of nuclear weapons, in particular, would entail huge costs for Japan in an autonomous national program that would be difficult to sustain politically barring a radically altered international environment. Under the Japan-United States partnership, by contrast, a two-key arrangement could conceivably be used to appease or circumvent Japanese domestic opinion. The net effect of an American withdrawal would be to sharpen a domestic battle over the budget in which growing welfare demands would tend to restrain the pace of military expansion. Hard choices between welfare and defense priorities would compel Japan to reevaluate its regional relationships in a new light. The specifically Japanese interests that would then govern bilateral relationships with the Soviet Union, with China, and with North Korea would have to be distinguished, in this reassessment, from the derivative Japanese interest in cold war American policies toward these countries, policies that were economically rewarding for Japan but were nonetheless American in conception. This is a process of reappraisal that appears destined to gain momentum, in any event, whether or not the United States disengages, and its ultimate outcome depends on factors beyond American control. To the extent that an American disengagement would affect the scope of the Japanese defense build-up, however, this could well strengthen antimilitarist forces in Japan by helping to improve Japanese relations with the communist powers.

As we indicated earlier, Japanese opposition to the security treaty with the United States has declined in intensity as a result of the post-1972 improvement in Sino-U.S. relations and the growing sense of economic vulnerability felt by Tokyo following the rise of OPEC. There is a reluctance to make an issue of the treaty for fear that the United States would react by being less solicitous to Japan in economic matters. Increasingly, however, Japan has been seeking to redefine the meaning of the treaty in economic and political rather than military terms. The implicit trade-off discussed in Chapter 8 has been more and more explicitly acknowledged; [14] but at the same time, the calculus of the trade-off has been gradually changing. The economic benefits resulting from the American connection, while still substantial, are tapering off in some areas and slowly declining in others. Protectionism in Washington is sharply limiting the growth of Japanese exports to the American market. Tokyo no longer sees its dependence on the Western oil companies as advantageous and is cautiously moving toward direct deals with producer countries. In the critical area of enriched uranium supplies, Tokyo is unsure whether it can rely on the United States. Meanwhile, Japanese and American interests have begun to clash in the worldwide scramble for markets and resources; and in the military sphere, Tokyo still politely but firmly sidesteps Pentagon efforts to promote burden-sharing in antisubmarine warfare and other areas. As time passes, the United States will gradually be forced to reconsider whether it really wants to perpetuate the "special relationship" and pay the economic price expected by Japan for a continuance of the security commitment. Three meaningful options will be open to the United States: to retain a symbolic treaty but let it fade away in practical terms, gradually reducing the remaining American base presence; to replace it with an explicitly nonmilitary friendship treaty; or to phase it out entirely by mutual agreement with Japan.

The Korean and Japanese cases both highlight the need to disentangle the goal of an indigenous regional balance from the overlapping objective of a global balance with the Soviet Union. In

Korea, the Sino-Soviet rivalry gives Moscow a stake in the North that would lend a minor international dimension to renewed North-South hostilities. Barring the unlikely eventuality of direct intervention in Korea by Soviet forces, however, the global Soviet-American balance would not be critically affected by the outcome of a new Korean war. The Soviet objective in Korea is the limited one of preempting Chinese dominance, and the hypersensitivity of the Sino-Soviet rivalry would lead a unified Korea to avoid overcommitment to either superpower. A continuation of the American presence in Korea would therefore sacrifice the advantages of an indigenous East Asian balance for what would be marginal or nonexistent gains in the global equation. Similarly, in the Japanese case, American burden-sharing proposals have been formulated in terms of a presumed Soviet naval threat without reference to the impact that expanded Japanese defense forces would have on regional power patterns. The United States would continue to play its own preeminent role in the Pacific and Indian oceans, with Japan assigned to a role of secondary importance in the American context but of potentially grave import to neighboring countries.

The danger of an overlap between global and regional objectives is accentuated by the Sino-Soviet rivalry and the resulting temptation to strengthen China as part of the overall U.S. effort to balance Soviet power. Direct assistance to Peking was first advocated by Zbigniew Brzezinski in a 1973 proposal for "some form of aid designed to create greater stability in the Sino-Soviet nuclear stand-off (such as the transfer to China of sophisticated communications systems)."[15] Even weapons and aircraft have since been suggested obliquely by others so long as these are defensive. The immediate purpose of such assistance would be to promote a Sino-Soviet equilibrium, but it would also have a disproportionate and profound impact on Asian regional power patterns. The existing military imbalance between China and both Japan and India would be aggravated by American efforts to bolster Peking technologically vis-à-vis Moscow. In particular, American encouragement of a Chinese "blue water" naval capability could arouse a competitive nationalist response in Japan, as we discussed earlier, touching off a disruptive naval race in the Pacific.

Apart from direct assistance, the continuance of an American presence in other Asian countries has been increasingly defended as an indirect contribution to the Sino-Soviet balance made with Chinese approval and encouragement. Two successive defense secretaries have justified the American presence in Korea by citing Chinese fears that a premature U.S. withdrawal would have an adverse impact on China's power position vis-à-vis the Soviet

Union.[16] China itself has muted its opposition to U.S. bases in Japan and even to a nonnuclear Japanese defense buildup in the name of a growing Soviet threat. The changing Chinese attitude toward the American presence was sweepingly described after his 1972 China visit by former president Gerald Ford, then House Republican leader. Ford declared flatly that "they don't want the United States to withdraw from the Pacific or the world at any point."[17] This was an overstatement of the Chinese attitude, however, as other accounts[18] by Ford himself indicated. What Premier Chou En-lai had said reflected a preoccupation with the overall Soviet-American balance, especially the strategic balance, but did not necessarily imply a carte blanche for U.S. bases in Asia. Chou had pointed with alarm to the defense budget cuts advocated by Democratic presidential candidate George McGovern, Ford related, and had warned that cuts of such magnitude would upset a global nuclear balance in which China had a stake. Ford drew the "impression"[19] from this that Peking wanted a continued American presence in the Pacific, but his companion on the China visit, the late House Democratic leader Hale Boggs, pointedly avoided this linkage when asked at a news conference whether Peking looked on Thai and Okinawan bases more charitably than on U.S. bases in Vietnam. "As they put it," Boggs replied,

> there are two superpowers, the United States and Russia, and if Russia becomes a greater superpower then much of the world could well be in difficulty. But where that means people would be located physically or what kind of weapons are required is something else.[20]

Formally, China continued to make occasional demands for the "progressive evacuation"[21] of U.S. forces from Asia following the Ford-Boggs visit but gradually softened this stand. Informally, some Chinese officials implied that even the change in tone was a matter of cosmetics rather than substance, part of an overall effort to defuse Sino-U.S. and Sino-Japanese tensions for anti-Soviet reasons. By dropping the issue of American bases, these officials stated, China did not mean to signify that it approved the presence of foreign forces in Asia. China would applaud a withdrawal of the American presence so long as it did not mean a lessening of U.S. interest in Sino-U.S. relations. In particular, China would welcome the removal of U.S. forces from the Asian mainland. At the same time, it was suggested, this need not and should not mean the withdrawal of the Seventh Fleet from the Pacific, nor would China like to see abrupt dislocations that might be exploited by Moscow. The Chinese attitude toward the American presence has been ambivalent, as these statements make clear, and Peking's military anxieties are focused not on Asia as such but on the global strategic equation.

Sino-U.S. détente would not necessarily be impaired by a detached approach to Asia that distinguishes between the objectives of a global and a regional balance. Indeed, in the long run, a detached approach might well help to stabilize Sino-U.S. relations. One should not forget Peking's staunch insistence on a general withdrawal of foreign bases from Asia prior to the Shanghai communiqué. China has its own ambitions as a great power not only in relation to other Asian countries but as the vanguard of the Asian response to the West. Sooner or later, a continuing American military presence in Asia is likely to conflict with these Chinese ambitions. The "Asian" component of Chinese nationalism leads Peking to view Soviet and American influence in Asia with equal distaste, even though it is temporarily expedient to utilize one relatively distant barbarian to offset another closer at hand. The United States has often oversimplified the Chinese world view and has exaggerated Chinese readiness to subordinate its other interests to its desire for an American balancing role vis-à-vis the Soviet Union. This has been particularly apparent with respect to the American approach to the Taiwan issue. Given its anti-Soviet preoccupations, some observers have argued, Peking can be induced to accept a normalization of relations with Washington even if the United States retains its security treaty with Taiwan or, at a minimum, continues to sell government-subsidized military equipment to Taipei following the cessation of diplomatic relations with the island. In Peking's eyes, however, the Taiwan issue has an overriding importance in its own right because it involves national identity. While showing tactical flexibility with regard to timing and other matters, Peking is most unlikely to tolerate official military links of any type between Taipei and Washington following a normalization of Peking-Washington relations, including military aid credits underwritten directly or indirectly by the U.S. government.

THE CASE FOR A DETACHED U.S. POSTURE

Apart from what Peking wants, the future of American bases should ultimately be decided in the context of the bilateral U.S. political and psychological relationships with each of the Asian countries concerned. After subordinating these relationships to an anti-China policy for two decades, it would be a bitter irony if the United States were now to sacrifice them on the altar of a pro-China policy. The case for a detached U.S. posture can be made in technical military terms, as we shall see, but it rests at bottom on a recognition of the political costs of American bases. The mere presence of foreign forces in a country engenders political tensions, and in Asia this problem is aggravated by racial and cultural differences between American troops and Asians. In every Asian country in which the United States has had bases, there have been bitter periodic controversies concerning status of forces agreements governing jurisdiction over crimes committed by U.S. servicemen. These have not been mere legalistic arguments, as it has often seemed, but basic conflicts over the sovereignty of the host country in which there has been little scope for compromise. Where circumstances have permitted, as in Thailand, the United States has tried to avoid a status of forces agreement altogether. Where authoritarian regimes hold sway, in particular, American military personnel have been understandably fearful of arbitrary judicial processes, and their reluctance to accommodate to nationalist feeling has been reinforced by the belief that the host country owes American forces extraterritorial privileges. In Asian eyes, however, nothing less than national self-respect has been at stake. To the extent that local leaders have been regarded as "selling out" under American pressure, the country concerned has felt debauched and the United States has been viewed in neocolonial colors. Even in the Philippines, where the U.S. presence is particularly helpful to the local economy, American bases have become increasingly unpopular. The Marcos regime has consciously exploited this unpopularity in its effort to extract greatly stepped-up U.S. military aid as the price for extending base rights.

In contrast to the United States, the Soviet Union has not generally established overseas bases, a policy reflecting in part, at least, a recognition of the high political costs involved. The Soviet navy boasts that it "does not threaten the sovereignty and freedom of any state" and that Soviet seamen go to foreign ports only as "welcome guests" who are "brought up to have respect for other nations, their customs and traditions."[22] Soviet claims concerning the ideological discipline of Soviet seamen are echoed by Western reports that "hawkers and whores are dismayed by the Spartan conduct and serious demeanor of the Russian sailors . . . unlike their Western counterparts."[23] As the Soviet naval presence has grown in the Pacific and Indian oceans, Moscow has made use of a variety of facilities in friendly ports that have often been loosely and incorrectly characterized as bases. India has permitted visits for recreation and repairs but on a case-by-case basis no different from that applicable to the noncombatant vessels of other countries.[24] The U.S. Navy specifically denied one report that a Soviet facility had been established on the Persian Gulf island of Socotra and another, concerning Singapore, in which permission for the repair of merchant ships and trawlers was treated as the acquisition of a base.[25] A Soviet shipping and civil aviation agreement with Mauritius has been viewed as a base by some observers, but most evidence suggests a carefully proscribed civilian access that has not altered the exclusive British military use of the island.[26] Noting the Soviet Union's "reluctance to make use of bases overseas," Barry Blechman observed that

> whether for ideological reasons, because of Soviet observation of problems that the United States faces connected with its bases, or because of lack of opportunities, the Soviet Navy's support infrastructure in foreign countries is relatively limited. Although much has been made of Soviet arrangements with various states for the use of ports and airfields for the support of merchant, fishing and, in some cases, naval vessels, such arrangements are quite different from the attainment of less transitory and more exclusive naval "bases." The use of foreign facilities is helpful in maintaining a standing peacetime presence in distant areas; such facilities are, however, unlikely to be helpful in conflict situations, or at least Soviet decision-makers cannot count on their availability.[27]

The most extensive Soviet repair facilities and visiting rights in areas militarily related to Asia have been in ports in Iraq, Aden, Yemen and Somalia where Moscow has given construction aid. In practical terms, the use of Somali ports, in particular, has proved to be of operational importance, providing communications, logistic and tactical air support that would not otherwise be available at such a great distance from Soviet territory. So far as can be determined, however, Moscow has had ad hoc arrangements in Somalia that cannot properly be described as base rights. The crucial political distinction between the Soviet arrangements and the American base structure lies in the fact that sovereignty is not formally infringed, in the Soviet case, by the acquisition of legal prerogatives conferring either de facto or de jure extraterritoriality. As T. B. Millar noted in a comparison of the Soviet presence in Yemen, Aden, and Somalia with earlier British access to bases in the Persian Gulf area, the Soviet presence is "more precarious. They are invited guests, resident or nonresident protectors, moneylenders; they have no constitutional authority or power. This makes them less an object of nationalist antagonism, but equally makes their tenure less secure."[28]

As of 1977, Moscow appeared to have limited objectives in Asia that did not require a formal base presence. Soviet naval forces "are seeking to familiarize themselves with operational conditions in the area," argued Maj. Gen. D. Som Dutt, a leading Indian defense ideologian, not to prepare directly for a hypothetical conflict by staging a "massive buildup."[29] In any case, even if one were to quarrel over what is "limited," the fact that Soviet objectives have related primarily to the global strategic balance with the United States is of special relevance in this analysis. It is widely agreed that the major Soviet concern in the Indian Ocean has been the possible deployment there of MIRV-armed U.S. nuclear submarines targeted on the Soviet Union.[30] While Moscow has its regional balance of power objectives, too, largely in the context of the Sino-Soviet rivalry, it has pursued these objectives very selectively. More important, it has done so through military aid to regimes with a solid nationalist base, as exemplified by the case of Vietnam. Direct Soviet force deployments have related to the Sino-Soviet balance only in a secondary, contingent, long-term sense as part of a policy that distinguishes implicitly between global and regional goals. By applying such a distinction to its own force deployments, that is, by phasing out its base presence in Asia, the United States not only would serve its political objectives but also would discourage any future Soviet moves to establish a forward presence, thus improving the chances for regional arms control arrangements.

Even in a narrowly military perspective, the United States would not need a forward presence in Asia in order to maintain a global balance with the Soviet Union in either strategic or conventional deployments. The strategic balance rests mainly on missile-firing submarines that do not require the use of forward bases. Guam gives the United States proximity to both Soviet and Chinese targets, and even Guam is not essential to an effective sea-based deterrent, though Guam-based submarines, by virtue of their location, would have 10–15 percent greater operating efficiency than submarines based in Hawaii.[31] More complex issues arise with respect to the extra wallop that would be added to the deterrent by land-based strategic missiles or tactical nuclear weapons deployed from forward bases and by tactical nuclear weapons deployed from aircraft carriers. However, the vulnerability of land-based missiles overseas has long been recognized, and the overwhelming weight of expert opinion also minimizes the importance of forward-based tactical nuclear weapons as an auxiliary to the strategic deterrent, so long as the United States maintains an adequate carrier force capable of playing both a second-strike and a poststrike role. In its emphasis on theater deterrence, as we noted in an earlier chapter, the Nixon administration underlined its belief in the auxiliary role of tactical nuclear weapons as part of the strategic deterrent. But the concept of theater deterrence rests primarily on carrier-based aircraft armed with nuclear weapons, not on battlefield nuclear weapons such as those long maintained in South Korea.

With respect to the strategic and conventional balance alike, the critical issue would appear to be whether an adequate carrier force can be maintained at an acceptable economic cost in the absence of forward bases. This involves value judgments concerning the relative

importance of political and economic factors that lie beyond the
scope of this book; however, in general, it is clear that the United
States, like the Soviet Union, could afford to manage without a
forward presence if it chose to do so. World War II carriers operated
from Hawaii, it should be remembered, in the same areas now
covered from the Subic Bay naval base in the Philippines. Even now,
two carriers could be based in Hawaii without major alterations in
docking facilities.[32] Like Subic, the Yokosuka naval base in Japan is
a valuable facility that makes it much easier to operate the Seventh
Fleet. It is "obviously a convenience and obviously a saving" to be
able to utilize Yokosuka, as former undersecretary of state Alexis
Johnson testified, but it is "not essential" and "there are lots of
things we could do"[33] to get along without Yokosuka if this were
deemed desirable for political reasons. The costs of compensating for
a forward presence would be minimized if the United States built
contemplated naval and air installations in Micronesia and obtains
access to the new Australian naval base at Cockburn Sound. Nevertheless, even with only Guam available, the United States would not
need forward bases in Asia to maintain a global balance with
Moscow.

Many advocates of a forward presence base their case not on the
needs of a regional or strategic balance but rather on the danger of
Soviet adventurism in Asia arising from the Sino-Soviet rivalry.
Others point to the hypothetical dangers of Soviet-focused Chinese
adventurism or of expansionist regional ambitions on the part of
China, Japan, Indonesia, India, or other Asian countries. To improve
American capabilities for intervention in cases of international aggression, it is argued, the United States should retain a forward
presence wherever the resulting political damage would be least
severe. This argument poses the fundamental issue of when U.S.
intervention would be prudent or necessary, an issue not specific to
Asia; still, one can rebut the case for a forward presence, without
reference to this broader issue, by considering the technical factors
that will govern future U.S. military capabilities in Asia. As we shall
see, effective American military intervention in Asia would be possible even without a forward presence. The parameters of this issue are
continually changing, almost from year to year, as technological
breakthroughs are made in strategic mobility. Even in 1977, however, the United States already had operational capabilities in its
C-141 and C-5A transport planes that underlined the rapidly declining importance of forward bases.

A systematic attempt to assess potential U.S. strategic mobility
capabilities for the purposes of this analysis was made for me by
Charles Stevenson with the support of the Brookings Institution. In

cooperation with concerned Pentagon officials,[34] who prepared unclassified replies to detailed questionnaires, Stevenson developed a series of estimates indicating how long it would take differing numbers of C-141s and C-5As to airlift differing quantities of troops and equipment to various potential crisis areas in Asia. Differing assumptions were posited as to what bases in Asia and the Pacific, if any, would be available and whether there would be companion naval help in the form of commercial cargo vessels or the futuristic "fast deployment logistics" (FDL) ships that were then projected by the navy. The methodology and technical assumptions followed were submitted to the cooperating Pentagon officials and were analyzed both in writing and in discussions in which I participated.[35] This analysis took account of the numerous technical variables involved, among them airfield saturation and turnaround time, refueling problems, local transportation at the destination, and maintenance capabilities in each locale. In general, the assumptions we used understated U.S. capabilities;[36] in any case, technical advances have been made since the study was conducted. The results were not endorsed or validated by the Pentagon, nor was this endorsement sought, and the purpose was not to produce a definitive study honed finely enough for use by military practitioners. At the same time, the findings do represent a reasonably close, conservative approximation of the time factors that would govern U.S. intervention in the cases indicated without the use of forward bases in Asia. These cases were chosen solely to illustrate mobility capabilities without reference to political considerations.

To illustrate partially the spectrum[37] of findings with respect to Thailand, a logistically difficult case, let us begin by assuming a need to intervene with troops and equipment deployed from Guam and the continental United States, utilizing half of a worldwide force of ninety-six C-5As and twelve out of a worldwide total of thirty FDL ships or a comparable number of requisitioned commercial vessels. Under a "worst case" hypothesis, with no refueling locally available and no bases in Australia, the United States could move an entire airborne division to Thailand in 3.6 days, an infantry division in 5.9 days, and two infantry divisions in 7.8 days if both were based in Guam. Given Darwin and in-theater refueling, the time would be reduced to 1.9 days for an airborne division, 4.2 days for an infantry division, and 5.6 days for two Guam- and Darwin-based infantry divisions. If only an airborne brigade and its equipment were involved, given in-theater refueling, the time would be 1.1 days from Guam; if only a battalion, 10 hours. Ten hours, in short, is all that would be needed for the first arrivals in deployments of any size. A more favorable case would assume both in-theater refueling and prepositioned equipment in Thailand despite the closure of U.S. bases. In this scenario, an airborne division could be deployed entirely from the continental United States in 3.9 days and from Hawaii in 3.3 days. As it happens, the actual U.S. capability as of 1977 did not include FDL ships. Should one wish to take this factor into account and consider in addition the element of uncertainty involved in requisitioning commercial vessels, the time required for the deployment of troops and equipment could significantly increase, perhaps doubling if no commercial shipping at all could be found in time and air transport alone were available.

Turning to South Korea and assuming a combination of air and ship transport on the limited scale indicated in the Thai case, the greater proximity of Guam to the target area produces more striking examples of high-speed mobility. An airborne division and its equipment could be deployed from Guam and continental U.S. bases in 1.4 days; two Guam-based infantry divisions, in 3.7 days. With prepositioned equipment, an infantry brigade could be deployed in 24 hours and an airborne brigade in 17 hours. All of these cases assume in-theater refueling, but even in the absence of this, refueling problems are less formidable in Korea than in Thailand. Given both in-theater refueling and prepositioned equipment, an airborne division could be moved from the continental United States in 2.5 days. South Korea was used as the site for a U.S. demonstration of airlift capabilities even before the C-5A had come into service. In this 1969 exercise, 1,320 men of the Eighty-second Airborne Division were flown from North Bragg to Seoul in 31 hours, utilizing C-141s and C-130s without a naval "marry up."

The time factors cited in both the Thai and South Korean cases would be radically improved if the number of C-5As were assumed to be greater or if their capabilities were upgraded through the application of technical improvements already available. In any case, even the examples presented show that the United States could respond to crises with great rapidity despite the absence of forward bases in Asia itself. How fast is fast enough? This would depend on strategic warning time; the availability of tactical air support from aircraft carriers at the moment of crisis; the speed of any other foreign intervention; and, above all, the effectiveness of local forces prior to the arrival of foreign support. Reliance on strategic mobility is undeniably linked with the strength of nationalism in the country under attack. A nationalist will to resist would be the essential precondition for intervention, as we have observed, and the proximity of forward-based U.S. forces would no longer serve as a substitute for this will, propping up regimes and states that lack a legitimate popular foundation.

The termination of the U.S. base presence in Asia would not be predicated on exaggerated faith in mobility as a source of miracles. Rather, it would reflect a new perspective on Asia viewing the diffusion of nationalism as a constraint on both external intervention and intraregional expansionism. Equally important, it would reflect a new perspective on the Soviet-American rivalry giving arms control efforts a growing emphasis. The cold war premise of a clear, present, and continuing danger to the United States in Asia would give way, in this overall perspective, to a case-by-case appraisal of incipient changes in regional power relationships. The United States would not seek to police the Asian power landscape but would, on the contrary, consciously stand aside to facilitate the emergence of indigenous power patterns providing an improved environment for regional arms control initiatives. The Seventh Fleet would be retained in Asian waters for the separate and distinct purpose of bolstering the global U.S. power position vis-à-vis Moscow, a circumscribed goal rendering bases unnecessary. Thus, carriers would not be homeported in Asian bases, despite the added costs this would entail,[38] and any role carriers might play in hypothetical Asian crises would be incidental to their basic, Soviet-focused mission. Mobility would not be a sine qua non for such a posture of detachment but would clearly make it much less risky by preserving the option of effective intervention. While forces now deployed in fixed bases would be disengaged in this approach, "detachment" differs significantly from "disengagement," with its connotation of irrevocable withdrawal.

Some proposals for a detached posture would permit the retention of a reduced number of bases in Asia by distinguishing between the political impact of bases on the mainland, where Chinese interests are directly involved, and others offshore; between bases in a relatively stable and developed country such as Japan and those in less developed countries such as the Philippines and Thailand, where the U.S. military presence has been used to shore up local regimes.[39] A similar distinction could be made between bases that affront national sovereignty in countries with a clear sense of identity and bases on an isolated island such as Diego Garcia, where few people are affected by an American presence. In themselves, these are all valid distinctions, and they could be utilized to establish an order of political priorities governing the location of bases. Such distinctions have their value, however, only in the immediate context of the bilateral American relationships with each of the peoples concerned. In the larger framework of a policy based on the interplay of indigenous power realities and directed in the long run to regional arms control efforts, a more comprehensive elimination of the American presence would appear desirable.

The case of Diego Garcia is to the point. In establishing a base there, the United States did not directly incur significant political costs because the uprooted local population of imported laborers was relatively small and did not have a strong sense of identity or sovereignty. To India, however, as the principal Indian Ocean littoral country, the American move has come as a direct nationalist challenge. India has been building its own navy with Soviet assistance after unsuccessfully seeking British and American help for more than two decades. The United States has discounted Indian ambitions for a powerful naval role in the Indian Ocean and has treated India as a mere extension of Soviet power, encouraging China, Pakistan, and Iran, in turn, to look on the American naval presence in the area as a counterforce serving their interests. This has been a continuation of the long-standing American effort to block Indian regional primacy discussed earlier. As a result, the United States not only has reinforced the Indian hostility produced by earlier support for Pakistan but also has caused concern in Sri Lanka, Bangladesh, Burma, and Indonesia, as well as in India, by fueling a naval race with Moscow that could ultimately generate Soviet pressures on littoral countries for bases.

Much of the Soviet interest in the Indian Ocean has been attributable, as we have seen, to fears that the United States plans to deploy missile-firing submarines there. The Diego Garcia base has been defended in part with the argument that it would be readily convertible for the use of Polaris-Poseidon submarines, if necessary, indicating that these anxieties are not without foundation. Yet as advocates of an Indian Ocean naval limitation agreement have argued, missile deployments there have not been necessary for an effective U.S. global strategic posture and would only become essential in the event of giant Soviet strides in antisubmarine warfare requiring greater dispersion of the Polaris-Poseidon fleet.[40] Even then, a base at Diego Garcia, though helpful, would not be necessary. President Carter's 1977 proposal for a "demilitarization" of the Indian Ocean was vague regarding the future of Diego Garcia, but it opened up the possibility of an understanding in which the United States would give up the base in exchange for the Soviet Union's withdrawal from some of its Indian Ocean facilities, notably the Berbera facility in Somalia. In the event that Moscow should ever violate the terms of an Indian Ocean agreement and threaten oil tanker routes, the United States could rapidly reestablish its presence there by earmarking fast support ships and nuclear-powered carriers for the area. Temporary mid-ocean bases could even be established on floating prestressed concrete platforms, one of the more significant advances in military-related ocean technology now on the drawing boards.

BASES, MILITARY AID, AND ARMS CONTROL

To a great extent, the Indian explosion of a nuclear device in May 1974, can be explained in terms of the American-Soviet rivalry in the Indian Ocean and the establishment of a permanent American base presence. Domestic political considerations were also a factor, and in a broader sense the explosion was a generalized assertion of Indian sovereignty in the face of an inherently unequal nonproliferation treaty. Given the central importance of Indian ambitions for regional primacy, however, the explosion was essentially a way of responding to the prospect of a superpower arms race in India's immediate neighborhood, above all to an American nuclear presence serving to strengthen the power position of Pakistan, China, and Iran in relation to India. New Delhi has consistently sought to discourage American naval interest in the Indian Ocean since 1963,[41] warning that this would provoke a Soviet response. Since 1974, India's insistence on the peaceful purpose of its nuclear program has left open the continuing option of an arms control agreement to keep the Indian Ocean a nuclear-free zone. But such an agreement would clearly require a recognition by the superpowers that they cannot have it both ways, deploying their own nuclear weapons freely in all parts of the world while expecting others to abjure a nuclear role and accept permanent second-class military citizenship. Even if Diego Garcia is kept for nonnuclear uses, the United States should be prepared to forswear its use as a base for missile-firing submarines, in return for comparable Soviet concessions with respect to Indian Ocean facilities.

The possibility of regional arms control efforts in northeast Asia is similarly linked to the withdrawal of American bases in South Korea and Japan. This is especially true with respect to proposals for a nuclear-free zone in northeast Asia[42] embracing China, Japan, and the two Koreas. In return for the "no first use" pledge expected from China as a part of such proposals, however, it would not be enough for Japan and Korea to forswear nuclear weapons in their own armed forces. At the very least, the United States would also have to give up the use of its bases in Japan for nuclear-equipped carriers and to remove its tactical nuclear weapons from South Korea. A decision to remove tactical nuclear weapons, in turn, would greatly reduce the pressures for maintaining nonnuclear forces in South Korea since one of the crucial arguments for retaining a minimal U.S. force presence in the South has been the need to guard the nuclear weapons there.

The critical issue likely to affect the prospects for a nuclear-free zone in northeast Asia is whether China, Japan and the two Koreas would be willing to conclude a regional agreement of their own that did not encompass the full range of Soviet and U.S. nuclear deployments in the area. To pursue the nuclear-free zone idea seriously, Washington would not only have to relinquish the use of Japanese bases for nuclear-equipped carriers but might also have to give up its sea-based tactical nuclear capabilities in northeast Asia as part of a global arms control equation with Moscow. In Europe and Asia alike, limitations on the use of cruise missiles with nuclear warheads would have to be considered, and means would have to be devised for verifying any limitations agreed upon. In its initial SALT II proposals in 1977, the Carter Administration reserved the right for the U.S. to deploy cruise missiles with a range up to 1,500 miles, just enough for strikes at Soviet Siberian bases from Seventh Fleet carriers. Moscow has argued, in turn, that U.S. tactical nuclear weapons in Europe and Asia capable of striking at Soviet territory—"Forward-Based Systems" (FBS)—should be classified as strategic weapons. The willingness of the United States to include the sensitive FBS issue on the SALT agenda could well determine the success or failure of the entire Soviet-U.S. arms control effort. In meaningful arms control negotiations, the U.S. would eventually have to acknowledge the impact of tactical nuclear weapons on the strategic equation and would have to be prepared to treat reductions in its carrier-based nuclear forces in the Pacific as part of the overall SALT bargaining equation with Moscow.

Assuming a readiness to remove all bases from Asia, would a policy sensitive to nationalism necessarily extend to the concomitant termination of all treaty relationships? Here a flexible, case-by-case approach would appear feasible and desirable. As we have already argued, continuation of the South Korean– United States security treaty following a U.S. base withdrawal would be appropriate insurance against possible external intervention, though this could lead to involvement in a strictly Korean conflict unless the treaty were redefined. The United States should not relinquish its treaty tie with Seoul until Moscow and Peking are prepared to relinquish their links with the North. By contrast, the danger of external intervention is minimal in Taiwan, and the United States can extricate itself from the civil conflict between Taipei and Peking with greater ease, writing off its security treaty with Taipei as necessary to the normalization of relations with Peking. In the case of Japan, the security treaty with the United States could remain in effect for some years without seriously damaging political consequences if the U.S. does not use it as a pretext for burden-sharing pressures. The continuation of the treaty for an interim period following the closure of U.S. bases would smooth the transition to a new Tokyo-Washington relationship by facilitating contractual links for the U.S. military use of Japanese docks and airfields. It would improve the chances for speedy access when needed in any military emergency, and it would permit the possible retention of U.S. intelligence installations and intelligence ties with Japan not requiring the deployment of U.S. combat personnel in bases. In deciding on its tactics in Japan, the United States should be sensitive to public opinion there, neither actively seeking retention of the treaty in the face of substantial opposition nor hastening its demise in the event that a consensus continues to exist in support of a loose treaty tie.

Perhaps the most difficult questions involved in defining a detached U.S. posture concern the criteria that should govern military assistance, military sales, trade in defense-related industrial products, and cooperation in defense production. Even without treaty ties and pressures to use military aid as rent for bases, the United States may frequently be asked to make its military technology and equipment available as an earnest of its friendship. In such cases the American response should be extremely cautious and should be limited to sales, as against grants, generally on a straight commercial basis.[44] By insisting on sales, as I have long urged,[45] the United States would seek to discourage casual military spending, consciously forcing budgetary battles within the countries concerned over the extent of arms purchases politically and economically supportable in domestic terms. Grant military aid was often designed to buy the loyalty of military elites or to improve their domestic position vis-à-vis that of other elites as part of broader cold war objectives. A detached posture would allow domestic power relationships to find their own level. This would make it more difficult for national military forces to expand beyond domestically supportable levels and would thus incidentally help regional power relationships to find their own level as well.

In implementing a cautious sales policy, the United States should avoid becoming the sole or even the principal military supplier of those countries to which it chooses to sell equipment. Where a regime enjoys broad-based nationalist support, overidentification with the United States would undermine this position; where a regime uses repressive methods to compensate for the lack of domestic support, the United States would be held responsible for this repression to the extent that Washington becomes the major arms source for the regime in question. In general, the United States should exercise special caution in cases where arms are sought for internal law and order purposes rather than for national defense. In many cases of this character, Asian governments want weaponry to suppress regional or tribal minorities, and the United States could easily become embroiled in civil struggles over national identity. An American policy designed to stay clear of such struggles would be a complete reversal of past policies designed to promote stability by building up local constabularies and intelligence agencies.

The most clear-cut occasion for large-scale military sales would arise when external aggression or externally supported insurgency threatens a regime with bona fide nationalist roots. In such cases, emergency credit arrangements would not be ruled out. More often than not, however, insurgencies are likely to be borderline cases marked by confusion over the degree of external support involved and the meaning of the insurgent challenge in domestic terms. Burma, for example, has yet to evolve a workable federal structure bringing the Karens, Kachins, and Shans into an accepted nationalist consensus. Unless the insurgency there should lose its essentially intra-Burmese significance, therefore, military credits to Rangoon would constitute intervention in an internecine struggle to shape a national identity. Chinese use of the insurgency to annex border territory would pose the type of extreme and clearly defined challenge calling for concessional military credits. Other degrees of Chinese support for insurgent operations would present more complex dilemmas in which the more detached approach of straight commercial sales would generally be prudent. In South and Southeast Asia, especially, the degree of external involvement often is likely to be moot in socially heterogeneous border areas where ethnic and national boundaries overlap.

Where an insurgency has strong enough domestic roots, it is likely to succeed with or without external support, and in many cases a more stable government would result if the insurgency were to displace or broaden a weak regime. In such cases, the United States should seek to avoid becoming positioned against the insurgents, even if they are receiving aid from another power. Thus, the United States would refuse to extend concessional credits to the embattled regimes in question, though it might make selective cash sales to governments that had previously obtained their arms from Washington, such as sales of spare parts and ammunition. By the same token, a detached American approach would rule out efforts to condition bilateral or multilateral economic aid on specific military spending decisions by sovereign governments as the United States has intermittently sought to do. Where the need for economic aid arises from consistently profligate military expenditure, the credit rating of the government concerned will be affected. But a detached approach would recognize that economic aid inevitably releases funds for military spending and that military capabilities are by their nature a matter for sovereign national judgment. What the aid donor can properly judge is not the military "need" of a country but whether the military spending in question has broad-based national support or serves the domestic power interests of a narrow elite.

The interdependence of economic aid and military power has a special significance for American policymakers where endemic intra-regional rivalries exist, as in the complex interplay among India, Pakistan, and Bangladesh. In such cases, the United States should sell little or no military hardware to any of the contending parties unless it is able to sell to all of them and, even then, should avoid becoming the principal military supplier to any of them. At the same time, however, the United States should continue to play an active role in multilateral and bilateral economic aid programs designed to strengthen the countries concerned within the limits imposed by their respective size and natural endowments. Unavoidably, American economic aid will contribute to military purchases from countries other than the United States, but the responsibility for the level and character of such purchases will rest with each of the countries concerned. In the case of India, the United States has already had to face the fact that its economic aid has helped to underwrite rupee arms purchases from Moscow; in Pakistan, U.S. aid has subsidized arms purchases from China and France. Distasteful as this situation is, it is the price that must be paid for the ill-fated U.S. policies described in Chapter 8. The alternative of a total withdrawal of all aid would lead to even more undesirable consequences and would make a mockery of the enormous expenditure of U.S. resources already devoted to South Asian countries. In Pakistan and India alike, the cold war has left a legacy of one-sided military dependence that poses awkward transitional problems for the United States. American policy should now be designed to further a process by which both governments increasingly diversify their external sources of military supply. Thus, while Pakistan, with its U.S.-modeled military machine, should be permitted to buy spare parts for the equipment already in its armories, the United States should exercise great caution in making any sales of new items to Islamabad, gauging the level and character of such sales with an eye to those by other suppliers and to those made by the United States in New Delhi and Dacca.

To distinguish between military aid and "commercial" transfers of military technology is not to minimize the need for careful, politically sensitized licensing controls over all such transfers. For example, the partial relaxation of U.S. controls on trade with Peking since 1972 has permitted the sale of important defense-related items, especially in the electronics and computer field. The U.S. balance of trade with Japan has been systematically bolstered through the sale of surface-to-air missiles, radar systems, military aircraft, and much of the production technology needed for the domestic manufacture of these items. American firms have also sold the technology for the manufacture of the Thor-Delta rocket to Japan, including carefully screened increments of the relevant guidance and control technology up to the level needed for civilian uses of this rocket. The controversial Thor-Delta deal was nominally intended to aid the Japanese communication satellite program but was approved with a clear U.S. awareness of the convertibility of the rocket for military purposes.

As a contribution to burden-sharing, the encouragement of U.S.-linked Japanese defense production has a simple logic, and in balance of payment terms, close Japanese-American defense manufacturing linkages are also attractive. But the Japanese case clearly illustrates the dangers of an approach to military sales devoid of political restraints. For as the bitter 1972 defense debate in the Japanese Diet showed, defense production partnerships, actively promoted by the United States, have made possible an expanded defense buildup in certain areas that would otherwise have involved prohibitive costs in independent research and development and might therefore have been politically insupportable in Japan. The power relationship between Japan and China is critically affected by such preferential defense production ties, and one of the frankly stated objectives of the Chinese in their 1972 change of posture toward the United States was to slow down American help for Japanese defense industries, a matter of more direct long-term concern to Peking than American bases in Japan. Preferential ties may prove unavoidable so long as the Japan– United States security treaty lasts, but they would no longer be encouraged in a detached posture toward Asia. In time, Japan would be treated no differently in the defense production field from China or others. Peking, for its part, as we have already indicated, would likewise be denied preferential U.S. military treatment despite the advantages such treatment might appear to offer with respect to the global Soviet-U.S. balance. For the Sino-Japanese relationship has its inflammable aspects and merits careful, continuing American attention in its own right.

One aspect of the Sino-Japanese military balance in particular deserves repeated emphasis as a possible flash point in the long-term Asian scene. This is the danger of a naval race discussed in a previous chapter. It is one thing for Japan to accept the role of a bystander in a tripolar nuclear balancing game in which Chinese missile capabilities can be viewed mainly in terms of Peking's power equation with Moscow and Washington. It would be another thing, however, for Japan to remain a medium-range naval power should China ever embark on a major naval buildup as a counter to the Soviet Pacific fleet. A Chinese blue water navy in the Pacific would be a challenge to Japanese nationalism far more disturbing than Soviet and American navies, which are not regarded as part of the intra-Asian power equation. Such a development, an eminently possible one in coming decades, could provide the psychological catalyst for a big navy movement that was missing in Japan during the early postwar decades. A detached U.S. posture would scrupulously avoid pushing either China or Japan in the direction of naval expansion and would limit transfers of military technology to both Peking and Tokyo. Detachment on the part of the United States would be an essential precondition for the proposed Pacific naval limitation agreement outlined earlier. American and Soviet surface vessels would also be limited, but one of the central purposes animating the Japanese architects of the proposed agreement has been to head off a Peking-Tokyo naval race. The agreement would exempt submarines and would not affect the global Soviet-U.S. missile balance. It would thus be most significant in intra-Asian terms. Technological progress would complicate such an agreement in many ways, with the new variety in ship sizes making it necessary to limit the number of vessels rather than the tonnage, as envisaged in the Washington conference of 1921-1922. New weaponry, combined with the new disparity in sizes, would call for inventive arms control formulas balancing off, let us say, the missile power of a PT boat and the conventional gunnery of a destroyer. Still, these are not insoluble problems, and even the appearance of a stable Sino-Japanese balance in surface ships would have great political and psychological importance.

Detachment would be the most valuable contribution that the United States could make to the evolution of an intra-Asian balance reinforced by a structure of arms control agreements. The capacity of the United States to affect the indigenous momentum of Asian events is relatively limited, as we have seen, but its capacity for distortion through artificial power inputs is infinite. This point is of critical relevance in the nuclear field. The United States could help to propel Japan into nuclear weaponry, for example, by offering cutrate tactical nuclear weapons for balance of payments reasons or by pursuing the burden-sharing concept to its logical conclusion. In 1977 the United States was still toying with the idea of joint Japanese-American antisubmarine warfare (ASW) efforts extending as far south as the Philippine Sea. The U.S. Navy's separate antisubmarine force was abolished in part at least because the total force doctrine led to exaggerated hopes for allied burden-sharing.[46] Would cooperation in antisubmarine warfare stop with joint detection or would an expanded, U.S.-aided Japanese ASW force in 1986 or 1996 be equipped with U.S.-supplied nuclear depth charges?[47] The American rationale for nuclear cooperation would be to forestall Japanese nuclear independence. If Japan goes nuclear, however, as we have argued, it would be for political and psychological reasons that would presuppose independent control. The United States is much more likely to expedite a nuclear Japan than to prevent it through the transfer of nuclear know-how.

A detached American role would be meticulously sensitive to the limits of American power in the delicate nuclear sphere. The United States would neither promote nuclear weapons nor seek to block their proliferation. It would not suddenly flip-flop from one extreme to the other, replacing the surrogate concept implicit in burden-sharing with Robert Tucker's view that proliferation offers "perhaps the one prospect for creating an indigenous Asian balance of power."[48] Neither would it pass judgment on the nuclear decisions made by Japan, India, or others while continuing to proliferate its own nuclear weapons. A concept of power in which nationalism is emphasized would look on military strength, nuclear or otherwise, as only one of many factors in an indigenous balance. Thus, Japan may gain compensating economic strength by eschewing nuclear weapons; "China opted for 'going nuclear without pants,' " as Yasuhiro Nakasone put it, while "Japan has remained non-nuclear, preferring to be decently dressed."[49] India asserted its option to go nuclear in 1974, but it withheld what would be a domestically controversial decision to make large-scale allocations of funds for a nuclear weapons program. In both cases, a decision to go nuclear would be an expression of defensive nationalism dictated less by military considerations per se than by the symbolic importance that nuclear weapons have acquired as an emblem of sovereignty and national pride. American efforts to block proliferation would thus have the opposite effect, especially against the background of a continuing American military presence in Asia.

In Japan, the suspicion that the Japan–United States security treaty is used to "watch" Tokyo and to keep it from going nuclear is itself a potent source of pronuclear nationalist sentiment. The inherently unequal assumptions of the nuclear nonproliferation treaty (NPT) foreordained a cool reception in both India and Japan despite the positive role long played by both of these countries in arms control and disarmament efforts. In particular, as we observed earlier, the attempt to proscribe peaceful nuclear explosions made the treaty completely incompatible with nationalism. The original draft had the more limited objective of restraining the actual manufacture of nuclear weapons. As in the earlier nuclear test ban, violations of such a limited but valuable accord would have been detectable and would have carried a high cost in relations with fellow signatories. By contrast, the ban on peaceful explosions marked a frank attempt to foreclose the nuclear option itself, "indefinitely freezing the international power structure and the present international hierarchy."[50] As such, it was a red flag to nationalist sentiment and contributed to the anti-NPT backlash that delayed Japanese ratification for five years after the signing of the treaty and led to the 1974 Indian explosion.[51] The Carter administration made matters considerably worse in the case of Japan by seeking to condition the sale of enriched uranium on Japan's abandonment of programs designed to develop an autonomous fuel cycle. Washington saw nothing amiss in asking Tokyo to give up its efforts to achieve an autonomous fuel cycle while the United States itself continued to have nuclear autonomy. Even if Tokyo should accept such a position of dependence in the short run, the net result would not be likely to serve the cause of nonproliferation, for the resentment thus engendered would help to fan Japanese sentiment in favor of a nuclear weapons buildup that might otherwise lie dormant.

The manner in which Washington and Moscow have sought to freeze the existing nuclear power structure has epitomized the insensitivity of both superpowers to the strength of nationalism in other countries. Washington, however, has been the most vocal of the two and is likely to pay the highest political price for its policies. Sanctimonious in its dedication to the nonproliferation ideal, the United States, with few dissenters,[52] has pursued its own national goal of an airtight treaty and a static nuclear power structure with little regard for the interests or attitudes of others. In the absence of the peaceful explosions clause, it was argued, the treaty would be meaningless; India and Japan, each economically beholden to the United States in different ways, would not dare to defy Washington whether or not they signed up. Within eight years, the naivete of this egocentric world view had been dramatically demonstrated in the Indian explosion; Japan, too, while maintaining a lower posture, was systematically developing a sophisticated civilian nuclear capability that had enormous military potential, especially in the field of rocketry for communications satellites. In the short run, the superpowers can frustrate the nuclear ambitions of a dependent regime in Seoul or Taipei or Islamabad. But in the final analysis, the ideal of nonproliferation is indivisible, and the prospects for arms control in Asia are inseparable from the larger question of whether Washington and Moscow set the pace with substantial reductions in their own nuclear stockpiles.

NOTES

1. According to the U.S. Arms Control and Disarmament Agency (ACDA), the North received only $922 million in military aid from its allies between

1963 and 1973, as against $2.7 billion received by the South (*World Military Expenditures and Arms Trade, 1963-73*, ACDA Publication no. 74 [Washington: Government Printing Office, 1975], table V, p. 99). In an address before the American Chamber of Commerce in Seoul on 6 August 1970, pp. 5-6, U.S. ambassador William J. Porter cited detailed statistics showing that South Korea's defense expenditures were low by comparison with other Asian countries in relation to its GNP.

2. This thesis is advocated by Robert A. Scalapino, "The United States and Asia," in *U.S. Foreign Policy: Perspectives and Proposals for the 1970's*, ed. Paul Seabury and Aaron Wildavsky (New York: McGraw-Hill, 1969), pp. 128-129.

3. Morton Abramowitz, *Moving the Glacier: The Two Koreas and the Powers*, Adelphi Paper no. 80 (London: International Institute of Strategic Studies, September 1971), esp. pp. 19-24.

4. Robert E. Osgood, *The Weary and the Wary* (Baltimore: Johns Hopkins Press, 1972), pp. 70-71, 73, 79.

5. Charles E. Bohlen, *Witness to History* (New York: Norton, 1973), pp. 294-295, recalls a statement by Nikita Khrushchev that the initiative for the North Korean attack had come from Kim Il-sung.

6. "Japan's 'Grand Experiment' and the Japanese-American Alliance," Woodrow Wilson International Center for Scholars, 9 October 1975, p. 33, mimeographed.

7. "Foreign Minister Refers to Inflow of Refugees and Routed Troops as Effect of 'War in R.O.K.' upon Japan's Security," *Yomiuri*, 23 August 1975, p. 1.

8. Edward Seidensticker, "Japan after Vietnam," *Commentary*, September 1975, p. 56.

9. George D. Kennan, *Memoirs: 1925-1950* (Boston: Little, Brown, 1967), esp. pp. 394-396.

10. U.S., Congress, Senate, Committee on Foreign Relations, *Report on the Far East*, 86th Cong., 2d sess., 21 October 1960, pt. 1:9.

11. For example, see Shigeharu Matsumoto, "Japan and China: Domestic and Foreign Influences on Japan's Policy," in *Policies toward China*, ed. A. M. Halpern (New York: McGraw-Hill, 1965), p. 156.

12. George F. Kennan, "Japanese Security and American Policy," *Foreign Affairs*, October 1964, p. 27.

13. "X plus 25: Interview with George Kennan," *Foreign Policy*, Summer 1973, p. 18.

14. For example, see Kei Wakaizumi, "Japan's 'Grand Experiment' and the Japanese-American Alliance" (Washington: Woodrow Wilson International Center for Scholars, Smithsonian Institution, 9 October 1975), esp. pp. 14, 16, 25.

15. Zbigniew Brzezinski, "U.S. Foreign Policy: The Search for Focus," *Foreign Affairs*, July 1973, p. 721.

16. See accounts of Elliot L. Richardson's briefing with American correspondents on the Korea troop issue in the *Washington Post*, 31 March 1973,

p. 2; and the *Chicago Tribune*, 9 April 1973, p. 10. James R. Schlesinger's testimony on Korea before the House Appropriations Subcommittee on Defense is reported in the *Washington Post*, 2 April 1974, p. 3.

17. *Transcript of Ford-Boggs Press Conference* (Washington: USIA, 8 July 1972), p. 5.

18. I interviewed Ford in Peking on June 29, 1972, and later interviewed U.S. officials in Hong Kong after their debriefing session with Ford immediately following his departure from China. See a critique of the Ford-Boggs visit in Selig S. Harrison, "China Hits Taiwan-U.S. Ties," *Washington Post*, 12 July 1972, p. A24.

19. *Transcript of Ford-Boggs Press Conference*.

20. Ibid., p. 6.

21. "China Opposes Continued U.S. Stay in Far East," *Mainichi Daily News* (Tokyo), 19 July 1972, p. 2.

22. *Soviet Navy* (Moscow: Novosti, 1971), p. 16.

23. "Power Play on the Oceans," *Time*, 23 February 1968, p. 27.

24. This is based on conversations with U.S. and Indian officials as of mid-1976. American naval vessels paid goodwill visits to Indian ports on numerous occasions prior to direct U.S. intervention in the Vietnam war but were thereafter subjected to a strict noncombatant test that discouraged U.S. interest. Meanwhile, Soviet aid to the Indian navy and assistance in port improvement at Vizagapatnam have facilitated regular Soviet access on a case-by-case basis.

25. "Soviet Naval Forces in the Pacific," a summary provided to me by the commander in chief of the Pacific Fleet (Honolulu: Public-Legislative Affairs Office, 4 September 1973), p. 4.

26. Australian defense specialist Geoffrey Jukes analyzed the Soviet-Mauritius agreement with this issue in mind in *The Soviet Union in Asia* (Berkeley and Los Angeles: University of California Press, 1973), pp. 81-82.

27. Barry Blechman, *The Changing Soviet Navy* (Washington: Brookings Institution, 1973), p. 3.

28. T. B. Millar, "Soviet Policies South and East of Suez," *Foreign Affairs*, October 1970, p. 71.

29. D. Som Dutt, "Indian Ocean," in "A Symposium on India: 1972," *Seminar* (New Delhi), January 1973, p. 61.

30. See especially Jukes, *Soviet Union in Asia*, p. 89; Blechman, pp. 36-37; and William Barnds, "Arms Race or Arms Control in the Indian Ocean," *America*, 14 October 1972, pp. 280-281. For a differing view stressing the danger of a massive Soviet buildup see *Soviet Sea Power*, Special Report Series no. 10 (Washington: Center for Strategic and International Studies, Georgetown University, June 1969), esp. pp. 62-65.

31. This estimate was made during a series of interviews in Honolulu, August 20-27, 1973, with Vice Adm. E. P. Aurand, former commander of U.S. Navy Anti-Submarine Forces in the Pacific. I have also drawn heavily in this chapter from interviews with ranking military authorities at the head-

quarters of the commander in chief, Pacific, Honolulu, July–August 1973; interviews with numerous Pentagon officials in 1967–1968 and 1973–1974; and continuing interchange with American military authorities at all levels and in all services in Tokyo, Seoul, Taipei, Manila, Bangkok, and Saigon from 1968 through 1972.

32. Interviews with Vice Admiral Aurand.

33. *U.S. Security Agreements and Commitments Abroad: Japan and Okinawa*, Hearings Before the Subcommittee on U.S. Security Agreements and Commitments Abroad of the Senate Committee on Foreign Relations, 91st Cong., 2d sess., 26–29 January 1970, pt. 5: 1261–1262.

34. Gen. A. S. Low, assistant for logistics planning, U.S. Air Force; his associates Col. Dana Stewart and Lt. Col. Marvin T. Ross; Lawrence Lynn, deputy assistant secretary of defense for systems analysis (Economics and Mobility Forces); and David C. Dellinger, director, Strategic Mobility and Transportation Division, Systems Analysis. I am indebted also to Gen. John Cary, Institute for Defense Analysis, for guidance based on his air force experience.

35. The first of three exploratory meetings with Lynn and Dellinger took place on August 31, 1967. Subsequently, a preliminary statement of technical capabilities addressed to our written questions and accompanying scenarios was provided by the Office of the Assistant Secretary of Defense for Systems Analysis in "Deployment Times," 1 February 1968 (sixteen pages, seven tables). This led to meetings with David Dellinger on February 26, April 2, and June 7, 1968; a memorandum from Dellinger on aerial refueling dated May 3, 1968; a meeting with General Low, followed by a letter outlining our revised methodology and seeking direct air force comment on June 18, 1968; and a critique in response by Lt. Col. Ross dated July 12, 1968.

36. The critique by Lt. Col. Ross already cited states that "the study understates the capabilities of airlift forces as well as air power."

37. The spectrum covers 14 differing scenarios with respect to the mix of forces moved and 16 differing assumptions as to base availabilities; i.e., data for 224 cases. These were developed for Thailand, South Korea, and India and are available for examination, together with accompanying explanatory memoranda on saturation and turnaround time, refueling factors, and other technical assumptions. Calculations were based on the Military Airlift Command's definition of a squadron as 16 planes and standardized treatment of an infantry division as 18,000 men with a total weight of 40,800 tons and of an airborne division as 11,500 men with fully equipped weight of 14,500 tons.

    The projections made in 1968 were reviewed in 1971 and 1974 in the light of the controversy surrounding the development of the C-5A and the marginal impact of this controversy on the plane's capabilities. However, renewed consultation with the Pentagon was not feasible, adding to the likelihood that the projections understate U.S. capabilities by failing to incorporate research and development advances in other areas.

38. In the absence of homeporting, carriers would be rotated as in the pre-1973 period between forward deployment and home base in the continental

United States, Hawaii, or Micronesia, with only one out of three normally forward at a time. This would suggest the need for a total Pacific-Indian Ocean carrier force of six attack carriers in order to permit the forward deployment of two carriers simultaneously. The precise number of carriers needed would be dependent, however, on the progress of arms control efforts, especially in the Indian Ocean.

39. Edwin O. Reischauer, "Trans-Pacific Relations," in *Agenda for the Nation*, Kermit Gordon, ed. (Washington: Brookings Institution, 1968), p. 430.

40. Barnds, "Arms Race or Arms Control."

41. Plans for a U.S. Indian Ocean task force were first reported by Selig S. Harrison in "U.S. Plans Navy Patrol off South Asia," *Washington Post*, 9 December 1963, p. 6. Indian opposition to this move and the formal Indian government posture toward port calls by U.S. vessels were reported in idem, "Patrol in Indian Ocean Stirs New Delhi Outcry," ibid., 17 December 1963; idem, "Nehru Declines to Attack Plan," ibid., 18 December 1963; and idem, "U.S. Expects Pakistan to Accept Navy Move," ibid., 20 December 1963. In an unpublished interview in New Delhi on December 19, 1967, the Indian army chief of staff, Gen. M. S. Kumaramangalam, urged that "the American presence not be felt physically in the Indian Ocean area. What we want is for you to maintain your power; your Poseidons, your submarines, in the world generally. But you don't need bases."

42. For example, see Allen S. Whiting's proposal in testimony before the Senate Foreign Relations Committee on June 28, 1971; Hisashi Maeda, "A Nuclear-Free Zone?" (Tokyo) *Asahi Journal*, 24 December 1971, p. 20; idem, *Arms Control for East Asia*, Research Papers, Series A-2 (Tokyo: Institute of International Relations, Sophia University, June 1970); Ralph N. Clough, "China as a Nuclear Power" (Background paper prepared for the Arms Control Study Group of the Carnegie Endowment for International Peace, New York City, 9 January 1973), esp. p. 12; and William J. Cunningham, *Arms Control in Northeast Asia*, U.S. Department of State, 14th sess., Senior Seminar in Foreign Policy, 1971–1972, May 1972, esp. pp. 12, 14–19.

43. However, carrier-based aircraft in the Pacific and forward-based nuclear weapons in South Korea were both recognized as "complicating factors" in the SALT I talks in Andrew J. Pierre, "Can Europe's Security Be 'Decoupled' from America?" *Foreign Affairs*, December 1973, p. 765.

44. This approach, phasing out grant aid in four years, was embodied in the military aid legislation unsuccessfully advocated by Sen. J. W. Fulbright in 1974. See U.S., Congress, Senate, Committee on Foreign Relations *Report on S. 1443*, 93d Cong., 1st sess., 4 June 1973, esp. pp. 7–10.

45. See Selig S. Harrison, "Undoing a Mistake," *New Republic*, 7 September 1959, pp. 10–14; idem, "South Asia and U.S. Policy," ibid., 11 December 1961, esp. p. 16; and idem, "Troubled India and Her Neighbors," *Foreign Affairs*, January 1965, pp. 327–328. Norman D. Palmer endorsed this approach in *South Asia and United States Policy* (Boston: Houghton Mifflin, 1966), p. 210.

46. As an example of such hopes see the annual posture statement by Adm. Elmo R. Zumwalt, Jr., chief of naval operations, from 1971 to 1973,

especially in U.S. Congress, Senate, Committee on Armed Services, Hearings on Authorization for Military Procurement, Research and Development, March 15–May 7, 1971, 92d Congress, 1st sess., on S. 939 (H.R. 8687), pp. 894–914.

47. For a discussion of proposals outlining two-key naval cooperation in tactical nuclear weapons see James E. Auer, *The Postwar Rearmament of Japanese Maritime Forces, 1945–71* (New York: Praeger, 1973), pp. 139–143; see also the comment by Hideo Sekino in *Soviet Sea Power*, pp. 127–128. The view that detection is the key factor in antisubmarine warfare and that nonnuclear depth charges and homing torpedoes will be adequate in the context of expected improvements in detection is gaining in support in the U.S. Navy.

48. Robert Tucker, *Nation or Empire?* (Baltimore: Johns Hopkins Press, 1968), p. 153.

49. Yasuhiro Nakasone, "International Environment and the Defense of Japan in the 1970's" (Address presented at the Harvard Club of Japan, Tokyo, 30 June 1970), p. 6.

50. Tucker, *Nation or Empire*, p. 153.

51. The "peaceful bomb" issue in India is discussed in George H. Quester, *The Politics of Nuclear Proliferation* (Baltimore: Johns Hopkins Press, 1973), pp. 72–75; see also Shelton L. Williams, *The U.S., India, and the Bomb*, Studies in International Affairs no. 12 (Baltimore: Johns Hopkins Press, 1969); and idem, *Nuclear Proliferation in International Politics: The Japanese Case*, University of Denver Monograph Series in World Affairs, vol. 9, no. 3 (Denver: University of Denver, World Affairs Program, 1972), esp. pp. 36–40.

52. A series of editorials in the *Washington Post* by Selig S. Harrison was among these dissenting voices ("Non-Proliferation in Focus," 3 November 1966, p. 21; "The Proliferation Debate," 10 February 1967, p. 23; and "Nuclear Breakthrough," 17 February 1967, p. 21). The strength of pronuclear nationalist feeling in India also was emphasized in idem, "Troubled India and Her Neighbors," *Foreign Affairs*, January 1965, p. 328.

11. The Future of U.S.
Economic Policy in Asia

In its post-World War II response to the Asian economic scene, the United States has given primary attention to the problems of agricultural development, reasoning that predominantly agricultural countries should improve their food production before seeking to catch up with the West industrially. Where industrialization is feasible, in this approach, it should be accomplished largely through foreign investment. The United States has taken understandable pride in its constructive contributions to agricultural progress in Asia; yet as Chapter 9 has shown, the Asian image of the American role has been ambivalent at best and for the most part frankly suspicious. The American motive in emphasizing agricultural development has been widely viewed as one of keeping Asian countries in permanent subordination to an already industrialized West. This chapter will focus, accordingly, on guidelines for an American policy more sensitive to the Asian desire for rapid, Asian-controlled industrialization. Such a focus is appropriate in an analysis of the interaction between Asian nationalism and American policy. Moreover, it reflects the fact that the problems besetting U.S.-Asian relations in the agricultural field, though not negligible, are much less serious than those in the industrial field.

On the one hand, as we have seen, U.S. investment pressures in Asia are growing; on the other, Asian determination to build nationally controlled economic strength is also increasing. This determination is typically expressed in the creation of the public sector industrial enterprise, and the United States has all too often opposed expansion of the public sector. Despite its overall record of hostility to public sector industry, however, the United States did make notable exceptions in a handful of cases, and it is in these experiences that one can find the guidelines for a long-term policy enabling American business and government to play a politically digestible role in Asian development. Together with new forms of support for nationally controlled development banks, oriented primarily to small-scale private enterprise, new forms of cooperation in developing more efficient public enterprise would do much to further a constructive coexistence with rising nationalism. Only a policy newly sensitive to nationalism in this fashion can open the way, politically, for the expanding reciprocal trade that should increasingly constitute a central American objective in Asia. While governmental development aid will still be needed as part of such a policy, it will be relevant only to the extent that it takes nationalism into greater account. This implies not only greater hospitality to public sector development but also more genuinely internationalized multilateral aid institutions and a new recognition that outside capital is no substitute for internal nation-building vitality.

THE CHALLENGE OF PUBLIC ENTERPRISE

During the Sukarno years, the United States made two successful public sector loans in Indonesia, one for the $33 million PUSRI fertilizer plant, another for the $22 million Gresik cement plant, both of which have been expanded under the Suharto regime with multilateral aid assistance. American firms designed and built both plants with Export-Import Bank backing. Since the promotion of American exports was its acknowledged mandate, the Bank had a more single-minded focus than the U.S. aid program, and the hostility of some of its officials toward the public sector was neutralized, in these and several other instances, by the lure of assured equipment and construction contracts for American companies that were actively lobbying in behalf of loans. As a Japanese government study team observed in 1969, the principal reason for the success of the two plants amid a welter of failures on the Indonesian aid scene was the fact that the American contractors involved had designed, constructed, and installed the plants as straightforward turnkey projects. At the same time, they had trained enough Indonesians in the United States well enough that the factories had a solid technological foundation.[1] This differed conspicuously from the many Japanese and Soviet aid ventures in which equipment was sold and left without any assumption of follow-up responsibility. Originally made to produce 100,000 tons of urea per year, the PUSRI plant has been expanded to a 400,000-ton capacity by another American contractor, and another public sector fertilizer plant has been constructed at Tjirebon. In 1976, the Suharto regime had embarked on further expansion of the public sector, with five new government cement plants under construction by Japanese firms in addition to twelve spinning mills.

Despite widespread mismanagement of public enterprise under Sukarno, the Indonesian experience does not confirm the view that the public sector is by its nature doomed to inefficiency. The World Bank, in its report on the proposed PUSRI expansion, declared that the initial 1963 plant has been "satisfactorily operated and maintained . . . it is generally considered as one of the few industrial enterprises in Indonesia that is well-managed."[2] While its profits had been overstated, the Bank said, reflecting inadequate depreciation charges, its profitability was difficult to estimate meaningfully, in any case, as a result of government policies deliberately fixing prices below those of imports to stimulate the use of fertilizer and to help farmers. The Japanese study team, pointing to the good managerial record at the factory, found an added factor confusing the profit picture in a wide range of welfare activities operated by an inflated administrative staff, including wharves, schools, hospitals, temples, and housing facilities. When the team visited the AID mission in Djakarta, the director deplored the politically governed pricing policies at PUSRI but stressed that it had generally operated above 95 percent of capacity. He also praised Gresik for its "good managers."[3] In 1970, as one of the conditions for its expansion loans from the World Bank, the Asian Development Bank, and the Japanese Overseas Economic Cooperation Fund, the PUSRI plant revised its pricing policy and agreed to operate on a "commercial basis, with its management having more clear-cut lines of authority and a large degree of autonomy in its operations" in relation to government ministries.[4] Private participation in the ownership of the company also was to be permitted on a limited basis within the framework of government control. In general, the Suharto regime has attempted to make public enterprises meet commercially defined tests of profitability or face a possible transfer to private hands.

The importance of a less doctrinaire approach to public enterprise will become increasingly obvious in U.S. dealings with China, North Korea, and Vietnam. But even in noncommunist countries, the conventional American image of public enterprise as inherently inefficient finds little acceptance in Asia and is directly contradicted by many specific cases in such differing countries as Taiwan,[5] South Korea,[6] Burma,[7] Ceylon,[8] and, as we have seen, India and Indonesia. As the Pakistan Planning Commission pointed out, the private sector is often far from a model of efficiency,[9] and in many Asian countries the same cultural and social factors undermining the management of public enterprise affect private enterprise as well. The basic Asian attitude on this issue was clearly stated by a respected Pakistani economist:

> There is nothing inherent in the public sector that makes it inefficient, and if it can be run with reasonable efficiency we will have great social advantages, such as limiting the concentration of wealth, as well as other, economic advantages . . . not the least of which is the fact that private enterprise, guided by the consideration of private profit, will invariably go for a capital intensity higher than socially desirable in labor-surplus countries. . . . Private enterprises, on the other hand, however efficiently run and managed, cannot give us these advantages.[10]

Significantly, the pragmatic approach followed by Indian, Indonesian, and other Asian planners in seeking to combine public control of industrial enterprises with minority private participation in management and ownership has been paralleled by a decline of dogmatism in the Soviet approach to Asia. Soviet ideologians have warned the "progressive forces . . . not to fall prey to leftist deviations by calling for nationalization and socialist reforms for which the time is not yet come."[11] In a memorandum to the Indian government, Moscow gently urged the completion of already started public sector projects before undertaking new ones and warned that confidence in state enterprise might be "discredited as much by its indifferent performance as by its sworn enemies."[12] In Indonesia, Soviet observers threw up their hands at the corruption in the public sector under Sukarno, suggesting that little else could be expected in a country run by the "bureaucratic bourgeoisie."[13] Soviet state trading corporations are doing a growing business with private enterprises in India, Sri Lanka, Malaysia, and other Asian countries, just as in the Soviet Union itself, American and West European enterprise is now given a carefully proscribed new role. On balance, the Soviet Union is still ideologically handcuffed in its approach to Asia, but the dogma gap between Moscow and Washington is slowly narrowing as both capitals search for new ways to adapt to Asian realities.

For the most part, American thinking has been focused narrowly on how to conduct a more effective holding operation, perpetuating the present direct investment approach, rather than on devising entirely new forms of genuinely welcomed American business involvement in Asian development. Instead of striving for an authentic compromise with nationalism likely to survive over time, the United States has searched for means of neutralizing and deflating nationalism. This has not necessarily reflected malice aforethought, given the widespread American conviction that "the more private investment is pumped into the less developed countries, the better off everyone will be."[14] Investment guarantees and loan programs subsidizing investment in developing countries have assumed a need and a desire for American private capital and have stimulated, accordingly, the search for ways to make a continuing investment flow acceptable.

Faced with nationalist resistance, the more adaptable businessman has been ready to accept joint ventures with local private partners in place of wholly owned subsidiaries, with the argument centering on whether or not the foreign partner gets a majority position. Even this concession has been avoided as much as possible by most investors, however, except in mining and extractive ventures, where an unusually "strong case can be made . . . since natural resources are often all that a small nation has to offer, and it is justified in having a voice in deciding how those resources are to be exploited."[15] In manufacturing industries, the built-in tensions in joint ventures are especially acute, and a U.N. panel on investment in the developing countries reported in 1971 that "the feasibility of joint ventures depended on the technological complexity of the industry, with the successful ones more likely to be found in the technologically simpler and traditional industries."[16] Multinational corporations, in particular, have found that joint ventures conflict with their freedom to behave as part of global entities. Raymond Vernon and others have consequently minimized the future importance of the joint venture, emphasizing instead the need for new ways to subject multinational enterprise to international accountability and regulation, especially in the sphere of taxes, with "substantially better disclosure" of their operations.[17] But even these reforms, Vernon has conceded, are more likely to be acceptable to American business in "the comparative safety and security of the advanced countries" than in developing countries in Asia and elsewhere.[18]

In addition to their intrinsically limited appeal to Asian countries that regard equity investment as a necessary evil, at best, the unpopularity of joint ventures with most American and foreign investors has given birth to a new school of thought advocating the conversion of American-controlled multinationals into genuinely internationalized structures with a broadened financial as well as managerial base. Like the joint venture, this concept, too, is likely to have only selective applicability as a pattern for enduring American business relationships in Asia primarily because the possibility of authentic internationalization is so deeply distrusted: it is taken for granted that a facade of "Asianized" corporations would conceal what would still be Western control. A more promising direction may be indicated by proposals to build mechanisms for eventual divestment into new investments, setting a specified term of years[19] at the end of which foreign ownership would lapse. Albert O. Hirschman, who has spelled out this idea with reference to Latin America, suggests tax incentives for investors accepting this approach. In addition, he proposes a regional divestment corporation within the Inter-American Development Bank, linked with new public agencies in host countries, able to acquire foreign-owned assets of existing as well as new foreign enterprises and to hold them until such time as they can be placed with local investors. Preferably, in his view, these foreign assets would be sold on the installment plan to small investors, broadening the base of local industrial ownership.[20] The proposed application of this constructive concept to Asia, utilizing the Asian Development Bank,[21] would offer a useful means of psychologically defusing the explosive potential of new investments and could be applied where necessary, in the case of existing investments, to forestall expropriation. All of these approaches and others of a similar nature share the same basic weakness, however, in that they assume the continuance of equity investment in one form or another. In the short run, such a holding action may succeed to a limited extent, but in the long run the unbridled growth of investment is likely to breed profound tensions and increasing expropriation.

As Dwight Perkins has observed, the investment issue must go "a long way" in Asia before it acquires the importance that it has in the relations between the United States and Latin America,[22] if only because American business has concentrated until relatively recently on Europe, Canada, and the Latin countries. Asia presents a peculiarly appropriate arena for a new approach to the American business role precisely because it is still a relatively clean slate, in most cases, offering an opportunity to avoid the mistakes exemplified in the "Cuban syndrome." Nevertheless, the American record in Indonesia during the early Suharto years offers little encouragement, and the pell-mell influx of American and Japanese investment during this period, often on politically abrasive terms, has left a legacy of festering economic nationalism that could explode at any time.

In the immediate aftermath of Sukarno, the new Indonesian regime faced a seemingly hopeless economic morass and was so eager to attract foreign support, public and private, that foreign businessmen were in an extremely advantageous bargaining position. Mohammed Sadli, the Indonesian investment czar from the advent of the Suharto regime until 1972, told me in 1967 that "we made many of the agreements we did because our backs were to the wall. We felt that we had to regain foreign confidence, at any cost, and the American companies were very aggressive."[23] One such instance mentioned by Sadli was an agreement giving Freeport Sulphur exemption from any Indonesian taxation, other than explicitly agreed levels of income tax, for the full thirty-year period of its commitment. To the company, this was a reasonable provision, given the uncertainties of the Indonesian political scene and the high costs of copper mining in the undeveloped Indonesian interior; to Indonesians, it was a symbol of their national weakness, especially since Freeport obtained a three-year tax holiday on all taxation during the first three years of mining activity and concessional tax rates during the first ten years after that. The idea of a tax holiday proved so controversial in Jakarta that the company later agreed to reduce it from three years to one. Jakarta was also disturbed by the fact that Freeport kept its status as a U.S. corporation under the agreement for reasons relating to its U.S. tax treatment. In strictly economic terms, Freeport felt that these concessions were necessary, and the company could point to other cases elsewhere, at that time, in which similar terms had been granted. Politically, however, the 1967 agreement and others like it contributed to a mood of repressed nationalism that has continued to feed on itself ever since. A realistic American business approach would seek maximum staying power and political security over time, recognizing that the bedrock Indonesian attitude, spanning the Sukarno and Suharto years, is one of deep suspicion of investment and of foreign economic designs.

In formally defining "the enemy," the secret report of a high-level seminar held at the Army Command Staff School soon after the Suharto takeover listed Communist subversion first and second, "the subversion and infiltration of the United States and other nations of the Western bloc in general, especially in the economic sector."[24] One of the key leaders of the Islamic student movement that helped overthrow Sukarno has campaigned strenuously against the "craven attitude" of the Suharto regime, planting "poorly-negotiated investment time bombs that will eventually explode," and has warned other Asians not to "become little duplicates of the Philippines, as we are on the way to becoming."[25] "Foreign investment has been pouring in since we changed our policy in 1967," warned the government's planning chief, Emil Salim,

> but it is important to realize that the continuation of this policy depends very much on how both of us are doing it. Both of us, Indonesia and the foreign investor, should see that foreign investment is not merely a repetition of the past, producing wealth for them but poverty and backwardness for Indonesia. Foreign investment should not degrade itself into a political tool to transform the country into a "banana republic."[26]

Indonesia, with its rich natural resources, presents a prime example of the need for new approaches replacing direct investment with other formats geared in particular to cooperation with public sector enterprise. Apart from the cases of the fertilizer and cement plants already cited as instances of the Indonesian use of the public sector, the entire field of natural resource development is one that Jakarta would like to keep under government control to the greatest extent possible. Given its weak bargaining position and the attitude of most foreign firms possessing desired technology, Indonesia, like other Asian countries, has accepted foreign private investment on a widespread scale even in the resource field. This has masked a continuing effort to assert national control, however, with Timah, the state tin venture, and Aneka Tambang, in nickel and bauxite, typifying the eagerness of government enterprises for as big a role as foreign firms can be made to accept. In the case of Timah, "the degree of control from mining to marketing exceeds that of any non-socialist tin-producing nation," and it is being steadily extended.[27] In the case of bauxite, the government is seeking to control the smelting of most of the alumina for the aluminum refinery to be operated by Japanese companies as part of the $830 million Asahan River hydroelectric complex. The government expects to finance a state-run smelter on Bintan Island with $360 million in Soviet credits and technical aid. In nickel, massive foreign-controlled processing ventures at Saroako and Gag Island will be balanced by the state-run Pomalaa plant launched in 1976.

The most serious struggle over resources between the Indonesian government and foreign companies has concerned petroleum, with Jakarta progressively stiffening its terms but seeking to do so in a way that will not drive the companies out. In 1967, the aggressive state oil enterprise Pertamina won a production-sharing formula despite the resistance of the Western companies, rejecting the concession pattern then accepted in most oil-producing countries and displacing the previous managerial control of the Western oil firms then operating in Indonesia. Caltex and Stanvac were permitted to operate under their existing contracts until they expired, but new agreements were on a production-sharing basis, which greatly strengthened Pertamina's bargaining position by giving the state enterprise a marketing role that assured its control over prices. The companies were disturbed, in particular, by a management clause giving Pertamina nominal operational authority. As a practical matter, management remained largely in the hands of the foreign contractors during the first decade of production-sharing, and an uneasy truce developed between Pertamina and the foreign oil companies. The state oil enterprise has gradually expanded its own operations, however, in some cases buying out existing foreign facilities. As it gains in technical competence, Pertamina is likely to assert its management prerogatives and to seek radical changes in the nature of its arrangements with foreign oil companies. An American lawyer with a close knowledge of Indonesia has cautioned that the very purpose of the management clause is to "institutionalize dialogue between Pertamina and the contractors, thereby triggering an educational and operational process which lays the ground work for the eventual transfer of the industry from foreigners to Indonesians." [28] Over the years, foreign companies are likely to confront a choice between withdrawal in the face of growing nationalist pressures or adaptation to a progressively reduced status. In effect, the foreign companies willing to stay are likely to be cast in the role of service contractors, helping Indonesia to fill technological gaps that are likely to continue for decades to come. The rewards for playing this role could be considerable; conversely, the costs of intransigent efforts to perpetuate the advantageous terms of the past could take damaging political as well as economic form. Even if the companies were able to exact artificially generous terms by capitalizing on corruption or political weakness in Jakarta, this could easily boomerang later, generating nationalist pressures for punitive policies on the part of Pertamina.

Initially regarded as a victory at a time when world oil prices were going down, the Indonesian production-sharing formula has increasingly been subject to nationalist attack as unsuited to getting Pertamina a share of world price increases comparable to those enjoyed by Middle East producers. The original formula gave the foreign companies a 40 percent share of their production to cover operating costs, regardless of the price level, together with a share of the remaining 60 percent, which added up, all told, to the lion's share of total production. Thus, when the price rose to $12.60 per barrel in 1974, most foreign companies in Indonesia grossed about $6.17, or $5.13 more than in 1970. Pertamina acknowledged the validity of this criticism in 1975 by negotiating a partial linkage between prices and the production allocation formula. Then, in 1976, faced with a financial crisis as a result of Pertamina's corruption and overspending, Jakarta used the occasion to demand an overall revision of the production-sharing formula, which was regarded as long overdue by many Indonesians. Under the new arrangement, the government will get a flat 85 percent of the profits; yet even so, nationalist critics were quick to point out, the companies will still make a profit of at least $1.30 per barrel on Indonesian crude, as against 50 cents in the Arab countries, and the exploration incentives offered in 1977 added another 50 cents for "new oil."

Despite continuing controversy over some other Pertamina policies, the production-sharing concept itself has been widely accepted both in Indonesia and elsewhere in Asia. Significantly, though, in adapting the Indonesian concept, other Asian countries have come up with widely divergent formulas reflecting the degree of economic nationalism governing their policies at a given time. India, for example, enforced more stringent terms than Pertamina in its 1974 offshore exploration agreements, while the Marcos regime in the Philippines was more lenient. The cautious Indian use of production-sharing was carefully balanced with a service contract arrangement in New Delhi's most promising offshore area, the "Bombay High" in the Gulf of Cambay, where the government Oil and Gas Commission sought to operate its own production platforms. Pernas, the Malaysian government oil company, more or less followed the Indonesian example in its 1976 agreement with Shell and Exxon, but insisted on more extensive taxes and bonuses as well as royalty arrangements over and above production-sharing. The Communist regime in Vietnam surprised many foreign observers by alluding to the production-sharing principle in its 1977 foreign investment guidelines, although it was not clear what this would mean in practice. As the most determined champion of economic nationalism in Asia, China had resisted anything smacking of the production-sharing principle up to 1977 and appeared determined to minimize foreign involvement in its rapidly growing oil industry even if this meant a slower rate of development than would otherwise be possible. The Chinese approach was to buy, copy, and adapt prototypes of Western technology, supplementing this where necessary with selective partial service contract arrangements. Typically, American companies were less flexible in seeking ways to meet nationalism halfway in China than were Japanese and European companies.[29]

NEW APPROACHES TO ASIAN INDUSTRIALIZATION

By and large, the posture adopted by American business in Asia has offered little cause for hope that the mistakes of the past will be avoided. The Asian-Pacific Council of the American Chambers of Commerce has pressed for an American policy in Asia oriented to investment promotion, urging in a characteristic declaration that

all loans, grants and other funds expended as aid and assistance to less-developed countries shall be channeled through existing private American business organizations and financial institutions on an incentive basis, such as low-interest rate loans and guarantees against certain risks. The United States government, acting with American business interests, should foster and promote the growth of multi-national corporations originated and oriented toward American business corporations ... recognizing the vital role of private enterprise in "economic diplomacy."[30]

This approach has been largely accepted in the creation of the Overseas Private Investment Corporation as a major arm of the aid program equipped not only to give guarantees but also to make its own loans. *Fortune*, only reluctantly conceding the need for joint ventures at all, has specifically frowned on joint ventures with governments.[31] Scattered voices in the business world have been more farseeing, however, notably former Treasury undersecretary Robert Roosa of Brown Brothers, Harriman, who has warned that

> the international corporations that in so many instances represent the United States are going to have to find much more scope for imaginative techniques. . . . The concept of the nineteenth century of the direct ownership of the land and what lies beneath it, and of all of the resources engaged in local production, is going to have to give way to techniques which may very well prove at least equally profitable, at least equally rewarding to those who carry them out. We are going to have to rely on the methods of licensing, of management contracts, of workouts on the basis of initial commitment of resources. . . . In capital movements, we are going to see much less proportionally in the way of direct investment and certainly much less over the long pull proportionately in portfolio investment crossing the frontiers of one nation or another . . . largely because of the many nationalist patterns of emphasis which have to be recognized and dealt with in such a way that they do not discourage business intercourse. The transnational or multinational corporations will have to reveal adaptations of much greater variety and ingenuity in order to meet the nationalist aspirations of nations who still need, increasingly need, the organizing and the technology that a transnational corporation can provide.[32]

In a pioneering analysis of " 'management contracts,' 'coproduction agreements,' 'contractual joint ventures' and the like," Peter Gabriel of McKinsey and Company observed that all of these have three salient features in common: ownership remains "in whole or in controlling part, in national hands"; the duration of the foreign company's presence is limited; and explicit provision is made for the renegotiation of terms at specified intervals. Generally speaking, as Gabriel pointed out, joint ventures involving foreign ownership pose problems and are likely to decline in their importance. Nevertheless, there is a major difference, politically, between private joint ventures and joint ventures in which foreign companies join hands as junior partners with governments. Governments often see an advantage in a joint venture with a minority foreign partner since this arrangement gives the foreign enterprise a stake in optimal performance and smoothes the transfer of technology. In nationalist terms, a minority foreign ownership position under public sector control, and in furtherance of a successful public sector, is quite different from foreign ownership inroads via private joint ventures. From the foreign company's point of view, however, contractual arrangements with governments may well be more desirable than joint ventures with them involving equity investment because where the local partner is a government agency, critical management decisions may be made with even less sensitivity to the foreign investor's interests than in a private partnership. Gabriel thus predicted a clear trend away from investment in any format, but he warned that contractual devices would prove a mutually acceptable basis for the operations of American business in developing countries only if two conditions were met. First and most important, in the absence of an investment stake, the foreign company should not be expected to risk its capital in other ways. This implies national and multilateral aid loans to the government or private entrepreneur in Asia that would engage the foreign contractor. Second, Gabriel urged, the host country must honor its contract obligations, and this, in his view, is more likely to occur than it is in the case of investments because "the host government's self-interest will be the multinational corporation's protection."[33] Vernon similarly has anticipated a growing role for management contracts and licensing agreements but distinguishes between firms "that do little international cross-hauling" and larger multinational enterprises that are more likely to resist new modes of operation serving to weaken their centralized global control networks.[34] The U.S. Steel official who, during the Bokaro negotiations in India, remarked disdainfully to me that "we're not in the business of selling technology" would likely have increasing difficulty sustaining this approach in the complex world of the seventies and eighties.

The case for a reorientation of American business thinking has often been advanced in terms of the growing opportunities for business dealings with the USSR, Eastern Europe, and China. Thus, Roosa referred to 140-odd contractual and joint venture arrangements in 1969 alone between Western European firms and Moscow, alluding to "the surging requirements and needs of vast populations" that will be reflected sooner and "much more effectively" in the case of China than they will be in that of other less developed countries.[35] In order to make the most of such big potential markets under such "effective" control, it is implied, compromises will be necessary that might not always be required in dealing with weaker, noncommunist developing countries at earlier stages of growth where the immediate rewards are not so substantial and where greater dependence gives the foreign company a stronger bargaining position. This is an understandable short-range attitude, in business terms, but it could have serious long-range political implications. For the application of one set of standards to China, Vietnam, and North Korea and other, more exacting standards to countries with mixed economies would rub salt in already tender nationalist wounds, penalizing, in effect, the very countries that have attempted to harmonize the values of an open society with developmental goals while also defending their economic sovereignty. In the long run, both business objectives and the liberal values embodied in the mixed economy concept would be better served by a more consistent American posture reflecting greater recognition of an American stake throughout Asia and greater confidence in the eventual ability of all Asian countries to modernize their economies.

Despite their reluctance to join hands with state enterprises, American and West European companies have entered into numerous joint ventures in Yugoslavia and Rumania on a minority equity basis, and in the Soviet Union a new pattern of licensing agreements, management contracts, and "coproduction" ventures is emerging that contrasts markedly with the modus operandi of American business in the past. China, as an Asian country nursing memories of quasi-colonial exploitation, is likely to rule out direct investment in the Yugoslav-Rumanian mold; however, other forms of cooperation with American business are fast developing in Peking. In contrast to the case of India discussed earlier, where U.S. firms have pressed for direct investment access with little regard for nationalist desires, M. W. Kellogg, a leader in fertilizer manufacturing technology, was helping China to build eight late-model ammonia plants in 1977. If such a technological partnership is acceptable in the Communist capitals, it might well be asked why American business should be so reluctant to depart from the objective of direct investment in New Delhi, Rangoon or Jakarta.

The answer rests partly, at least, in an implicit respect for the self-reliant nationalist discipline of the spartan Communist regimes and a corresponding lack of confidence in the economic prospects and credit standing of many noncommunist developing countries with deeper internal social problems and less self-discipline. To the extent that this explains the American business attitude, one of the keys to an effective American policy in support of Asian development would appear to lie, as Peter Gabriel suggests,[36] in a broadened role for national and multilateral aid agencies capable of underwriting the credit risks involved in contracts and joint ventures with Asian governments. In some cases, tied loans on newly soft terms could be made by the Export-Import Bank or the Overseas Private Investment Corporation to governments planning to utilize the services of American firms. These would roughly follow the pattern of loans to the Indonesian PUSRI and Gresik plants, except for the proposed liberalization of terms. Such tied loans would be acceptable, however, only where the American price proved competitive or the technology concerned could best be obtained from the United States. Moreover, such turnkey projects, in which the foreign firm is responsible for the construction work, would not be desirable in countries whose technological capabilities are already significant and in which there is a will to learn through trial and error. Flexibility would therefore be necessary, and this, in turn, would enhance the role of U.S.-backed multilateral aid institutions free to make untied loans for ventures that could utilize local technology alongside needed foreign management and consulting services.

Such an aid approach has been employed in isolated cases but has been frustrated, in the main, by hostility toward the public sector on the part not only of U.S. aid agencies but of U.S.-oriented multilateral institutions as well. The attitude of the World Bank, already cited, prompted an appeal by leaders of the U.N. Conference on Trade and Development in the 1967 Charter of Algiers that "there should be no discrimination by international lending institutions against the public sector, in particular, in industry."[37] Escott Reid, upon retirement as South Asian operations director of the Bank, wrote that "the Bank's ideological bias against public ownership of manufacturing industry has until recently been so strong that to most West Europeans it . . . has been a demonstration of the domination of the Bank by the predilections and prejudices of the United States."[38] The Asian Development Bank has been used largely to support the private sector, and at the founding session of the Bank the Soviet delegation, declining an invitation to join, explained that the tone of the draft agreement suggested that

> a situation could arise in which the Bank's resources would be predominantly used for financing the private sector at the expense of the public sector. We believe that this could have a most unfavorable effect on the economy of those countries of the region which regard development of the public sector as the best means of overcoming backwardness and speeding up economic and social progress.[39]

By contrast, agencies of the United Nations, such as ECAFE, the U.N. Development Program, and the U.N. Industrial Development Organization, have shown a less doctrinaire approach, reflecting their broader base of membership, but have received only marginal U.S. backing.

The bias of the Western-oriented aid agencies has even included opposition to government control of development banks intended to stimulate local private enterprise. Louis Walinsky, former chief economic adviser to the Burmese government, has recalled that the World Bank refused a loan for a proposed development bank because Burma insisted on a government equity interest of at least 50 percent. The Burmese concern was to channel loans to Burmese as against Indian, Pakistani, or Chinese businessmen, but the World Bank argued that only private management could assure efficiency.[40] While this attitude has softened over the years, the U.S. aid program and the international agencies have continued to treat the role of development banks largely in conventionally defined economic terms at the expense of political and social factors. This has strengthened local forces tending to make such banks instruments for extending the power of existing business elites rather than broadening the social base of industrial ownership. Increasingly, however, it has been recognized that one of the basic obstacles to nation-building and development in poor countries is the existence of "dual societies" dominated by elites reluctant to trust in grass-roots initiatives. One of the principal elements of this dualism is a lopsided growth pattern in which the development of large, centralized, capital-intensive industrial units is not adequately complemented by the smaller, decentralized, labor-intensive enterprises, at times claiming fifty workers or fewer, which have provided such a powerful economic stimulus in Taiwan and China. Development along such decentralized lines is not likely to be sponsored by existing business elites in many instances. By its nature, it presupposes broadly based local initiatives, whether private as in Taiwan or publicly organized as in China, linked to the search for "intermediate technologies" suited to local needs and local self-reliance. Foreign investment, too, only tends to accentuate the dual society pattern, as Soedjatmoko, the former Indonesian ambassador to Washington, has pointed out, for

> the operations of foreign business in the less developed countries, especially those of the highly efficient and powerful multinational corporations, may make it very difficult, if not impossible, for "intermediate technologies"— understandably less efficient, at least in its early stages—to take root. Self-sufficiency may not always be compatible with optimal efficiency, yet it may be unavoidable in certain fields for socio-political reasons, primarily in order to create employment opportunities. Furthermore, the presence of a large foreign business and professional community may give rise to consumption levels and patterns among the elite that are too costly for the country as a whole and therefore disfunctional.[41]

What is needed, in short, are more national development banks like the Philippine Development Bank, the Medium Industry Bank in South Korea and the Indonesian Bapindo. Such institutions can be restructured in ways that would help to break down the dual society dichotomy,[42] and foreign support would enable them to escape from the influence of local vested interests in the large-scale industrial sector. American governmental and private flows should most often be directed to such restructured national development banks rather than to local private interests over the heads of governments. These flows would supplement the continued public and private financing of needed large-scale development projects, including high-technology industrial ventures requiring foreign collaboration, as already discussed. However, in an approach emphasizing labor-intensive enterprises, the role of the foreign private sector would be much smaller than that of donor governments and multilateral agencies. Some foreign firms may be able to adapt to the need for labor-intensive production processes, as Robert Shaw and Donald Sherk have advocated,[43] but this is likely to be a peripheral factor in Asian development. More frequently, the capital-intensive character of foreign enterprise will increase the likelihood that it will be a target of nationalist attack.

A new emphasis on small industry would be a major contribution to solving the persistent problems of rural development in the poor countries. Despite the widespread tendency to treat agricultural and industrial development as involving a basic conflict of priorities, these are more and more recognized to be interlocking tasks. The most penetrating studies of agricultural development, linking economic, social, and political considerations—notably the work of Kusum Nair[44]—has consistently stressed the need for complementary agro-industrial economic patterns in the Asian countryside capable of meeting employment needs that defy absorption solely in the large-scale industrial sector. Such agro-industrial development is necessary to meet rural demands not only for simple, low-cost consumer goods but also for more directly farming-related inputs. Agro-business should thus be developed at two levels, both of them central to the life of the countryside: at the decentralized, local level and, in the case of specialized products such as fertilizer, at the level of larger and more centralized manufacturing enterprises. In both cases, nationalism offers little scope for foreign investment.

As a strategic factor in the economy, close to the daily lives of the rural millions, agro-business will be jealously guarded by national governments if these regimes have roots in their own soil. It has thus not been surprising that so much of the fertilizer industry has been kept under state control in India, Pakistan, Indonesia, and other countries. By the same token, it would be a fundamental error to seek to make foreign investment the basic channel for the transfer of agro-business technology. Instead of expecting the poor countries to "try to 'denationalize' the subject of agro-business investment," as Lester Brown has urged,[45] the United States should approach this crucial aspect of its relationship with Asia through diversified support for public enterprise, on the one hand, and development banks oriented to decentralized private enterprise, on the other.

In general, it would not be enough for Washington to adopt a noncommittal posture, avoiding positive identification with investment pressures but standing aside disinterestedly while private American businessmen make as much hay as they can on their own. Just as the United States has encouraged investment in the past, actively opposing public enterprise, so it would be desirable now to go beyond the mere removal of existing tax incentives for investors[46] by offering new inducements in their place, not available to the private investor, for management contracts, turnkey projects, and other nonequity links with public and private enterprise. The urgency of a change in the U.S. posture is particularly great in extractive industries, where the danger of nationalization is most widespread. Rather than wait for the inevitable, making as few concessions to nationalist sentiment as possible and devising ever new techniques for frustrating nationalist desires,[47] American business should seek to roll with the punch, shifting the form of its operations to avoid a confrontation with nationalism. American investment is destined to remain a much more compelling target than European or even Japanese investment for many years because it is by far the most powerful symbol of an unequal world. British investment, by contrast, as the symbol of a waning economic empire, has actually increased in some countries [48] without incurring nationalist wrath. The saving grace for American investors, in some cases, has been the desire to offset Japanese power or the local power of the overseas Chinese, as in Malaysia, but the long-term force of nationalism is likely to affect American and Japanese investors alike.

By reducing its reliance on investment remittances as a source of balance of payments support, the United States would be deliberately and confidently staking its future in Asia on its capacity to develop growing reciprocal trade relationships. This raises many issues that have been widely discussed elsewhere and will not be examined here. The present analysis accepts the more optimistic cstimates of American adaptability and of future prospects in world trade. It should be emphasized, however, that balanced trade patterns could be developed only in the context of a progressive narrowing of the gap in living standards between Asia and the West. The United States would have to make its trade posture more competitive by reshaping its cost-price structure, while wages in Asian countries would have to rise as part of a gradual process of economic development. As Paul Samuelson has pointed out, this would presuppose tax reforms and other new ways of making U.S. income distribution more equitable, cushioning the impact of stabilized wage levels on labor.[49] Moreover, in addition to the short-term sacrifices required on the part of various interest groups in the United States, such a policy would involve a protracted transition period in which large Asian surpluses in trade with the United States would be normal, especially if American agricultural exports were curtailed for domestic reasons. How long such a transition would last would depend ultimately upon how rapidly Asian countries were able to develop and increase their purchasing power.

Should the United States shrink from the sacrifices required to evolve balanced trade relationships with Asian countries, the Asian response would necessarily be to turn inward, building exclusive trade patterns either within Asia itself or within the larger realm of developing countries as a whole. Similarly, a failure on the part of the United States to take into account the special problems of developing countries, especially in the early transition period, would make large-scale trade links impossible. The United States should not only grant UNCTAD trade preferences to open up Asian exports to the American market but also make its own exports to Asia more palatable, at least initially, through government-subsidized credits at low interest rates. It was thus a step in the wrong direction when Washington, Tokyo, and four West European capitals signed a gentlemen's agreement in 1975 designed to keep interest rates high. The signatories fixed a minimum rate of 7.5 percent on export credits of five years or more to countries with a per capita income of $3,000 or less. The United States should withdraw from this agreement and seek instead to outbid Japan and Western Europe in trade with the developing countries. This sort of trade war would be healthy as part of an overall global movement toward greater economic equity. The best hope for the stable evolution of economically independent Asian countries lies in their ability to play off the United States and Japan against each other, and Washington and Tokyo have much more to gain from a hospitable economic climate in Asia than from one of deepening tensions. In the long run, both Japan and the United States should direct more and more of their exports to developing countries rather than to each other, building for this eventuality through expanded aid programs.

The continuing importance of development loans and technical assistance in American foreign economic policy would be undiminished in an approach more cognizant of nationalism. In its broad impact, a more generous American aid approach, placing the United States once again in the forefront of donor nations as it was until the cutbacks of the sixties, would do much to temper the feeling that the West wants to keep Asia in an inferior position. In its specific application, however, such an aid posture would properly channel more of the available development capital to U.N. aid agencies or to other multilateral institutions as they become more internationalized, embracing communist countries, largely phasing out bilateral aid unless this becomes an excuse for ending all aid. A transfer of resources on this disinterested basis would help to signify empathetic understanding of the nationalist aspirations of all Asian countries, while bilateral aid, as many have written, linked as it is with transitory American political objectives, leaves a more ambivalent psychological legacy. The allocation of aid under multilateral auspices would also be the best way to avoid the tension-breeding social distortions and imbalances within and between countries that result from bilateral aid programs. With less need to answer to national legislatures for specific allocative decisions, multilateral institutions could take a relatively evenhanded view of the development challenge, channeling resources not only on the basis of where the short-term economic payoff will be greatest but also on the basis of where the challenge is greatest.

The underlying paradox confronting aid planners is that the countries with the greatest self-reliant nationalist momentum of their own in development—and thus the maximum ability to utilize aid effectively—should not necessarily be the countries that get the most aid in a balanced multilateral scheme designed to help the laggards to catch up. Aid should properly be viewed as a tool used by the international community to compensate for the wide variations in nationalist dynamism as among Asian countries resulting in part from differing historical experience. This approach has its limitations, to be sure, and past experience amply demonstrates that even the most disproportionate infusion of outside resources can have little enduring economic impact if a political leadership is locally regarded as the custodian of factional or private interest rather than of nationalist aspirations. In most Asian countries, however, the issue was not that clearly drawn during the sixties and seventies. At one extreme, Peking, Hanoi, and Pyongyang opted for austere self-reliance and maximum equity; at the other, Seoul, pre-1975 Saigon, and the Ayub regime in Islamabad consciously sacrificed equity on the alter of growth, with such economic progress as they achieved primarily an extension of external dependencies. In between these extremes, governments with varying degrees of nationalist vitality wrestled with the deep-rooted problems of dual societies. The task of the aid planner is to find the pockets of authentic local initiative in these societies and support them on as broad a field as possible, mindful of economic criteria but carefully weighing economic tests against the claims of equity both within and between different parts of Asia. For in rectifying the larger imbalance in the world as a whole, it would indeed be self-defeating to foster new intraregional imbalances and distortions that could also prove threatening to a stable world order.

NOTES

1. *Indonesia Keizai Kyoryoku Chōsadan Chosa Hokoku* [Investigation report of the Economic Cooperation Investigation Team to Indonesia] (Tokyo: Foreign Ministry of Japan, 1969), p. 37.

2. *Appraisal of the PUSRI Fertilizer Plant Expansion*, Report no. PI-3a (Washington: International Development Association, International Bank for Reconstruction and Development, 20 April 1970), pp. ii, 10.

3. Ibid., p. 16; see also the discussion of the impact of Gresik as the first major industrial success in Indonesia in Herbert Feith, *The Decline of Constitutional Democracy in Indonesia* (Ithaca: Cornell University Press, 1962), p. 558.

4. *Appraisal of the PUSRI Fertilizer Plant*, p. ii.

5. The profitability of the public sector is discussed in Melvin Gurtov, *Recent Developments on Taiwan* (Santa Monica: Rand Corporation, February 1967), p. 46.

6. Park Chong-hui, *The Country, the Revolution, and I*, trans. Leon Sinder (Seoul: Leon Sinder, October 1963), pp. 42, 82.

7. Louis J. Walinsky, *Economic Development in Burma, 1951-60* (New York: Twentieth Century Fund, 1962), pp. 299-317, 448-464.

8. A World Bank team pointed to "impressive" production increases in a generally favorable judgment of public sector enterprises in Ceylon, terming many of the problems "teething troubles." See International Development Association, *Review of the Economic Situation and Foreign Exchange Problem of Ceylon*, Report no. AS-118a (Washington: International Bank for Reconstruction and Development, 1 December 1966), p. 33. For a later, more negative view see B. H. S. Jayewardene, "Mistaken Emphasis?" *Far Eastern Economic Review*, 16 January 1971, p. 54.

9. This is cited in Planning Commission, Government of Pakistan, *Reports of the Advisory Panel for the Fourth Five Year Plan, 1970-75* (Islamabad: Government of Pakistan, July 1970), 1:57.

10. Azizur Rahman Khan, former research director, Pakistan Institute of Development Economics, in *Forum* (Dacca), 16 May 1970, p. 11.

11. "When Ideology Is a Burden," *The Asian* (Hong Kong), 15 September 1972, p. 6.

12. *Times of India*, 10 March 1966, p. 7.

13. See I. O. Farizov, *Sovetsko-Indoneziiskoe ekonomicheskoe sotrudnichestvo* [Soviet-Indonesian economic cooperation] (Moscow: Institute of Far Eastern Studies, 1964), p. 50; and the writings of V. Andreev.

14. Robert E. Asher, *Development Assistance in the Seventies* (Washington: Brookings Institution, 1970), pp. 196-197.

15. "The Challenge of Multinational Business," *Fortune*, 15 August 1969, p. 74.

16. "Agreed Statement," Third Meeting of the U.N. Panel of Experts on Private Foreign Investment in the Developing Countries, International Development Association, Tokyo, 1 December 1971, p. 6.

17. Raymond Vernon, *Sovereignty at Bay* (New York: Basic Books, 1971), pp. 188-201.

18. Ibid., p. 235.

19. In one of the few Asian cases in which a time limit has been built into a foreign investment, the Thai Oil Company's Sriracha refinery, a ten-year

limit was stipulated, after which the venture was to revert to the Thai government (Derek Davies, "Refining with Thais," *Far Eastern Economic Review*, 7 January 1965, pp. 21-23). Vernon, *Sovereignty at Bay*, p. 191, argues that most investors will demand "on the order of 12 to 15 years" of undisturbed ownership as the condition of a prearranged divestiture. In an earlier proposal for a time limit on American investments Aaron Scheinfeld proposed twenty-five years (*A Plan for Accelerating Private Investment in Developing Countries* [Santa Barbara: Center for the Study of Democratic Institutions, September 1965], esp. p. 7).

20. Albert O. Hirschman, *How to Divest in Latin America, and Why*, Essays in International Finance no. 76 (Princeton: Department of Economics, Princeton University, November 1969, esp. pp. 13-17. A precursor of the tax incentive proposal is found in Harry G. Johnson, *Economic Policies toward Less Developed Countries* (Washington: Brookings Institution, 1967), p. 128.

21. Dwight Perkins, "The United States and Japan in Asia," in *Discord in the Pacific*, ed. Henry Rosovsky (Washington: Columbia, 1973), p. 70.

22. Ibid.

23. Interview, Jakarta, 3 April 1967.

24. *Doktrin Perdjuangan TNI-AD "TRI UBAYA CAKTI"* [The struggle doctrine of TNI-AD "TRI UBAYA CAKTI"], Master Book, Volume I, "Doktrin Dasar TRI UBAYA CAKTI" [The basic doctrine of TRI UBAYA CAKTI], Product of the Second Army Seminar, 25-31 August 1966, at the SESKOAD (Army Command Staff School), Bandung, Appendix 1: "TRI UBAYA CAKTI Programs in Context of the Implementation of the Basic Strategy of the AMPERA Cabinet," p. 1.

25. Nono Makarim, in an extemporaneous address at "The Press and the Generation Gap," a seminar sponsored by the Press Foundation of Asia (Tokyo, 27 March 1970). See also recurring editorials on investment in Makarim's *Harian Kami*, e.g., January 8, January 30, February 8 and March 3, 1971, Mochtar Lubis' *Indonesia Raya* and Rosihan Anwar's *Pedoman*.

26. Emil Salim, *Oil and Indonesian Development*, Bappenas, Publication no. D-II-1971-150 (Jakarta, 3 February 1971), pp. 4-5.

27. "Tin: Indonesia's Brighter Side" (unsigned), *Far Eastern Economic Review*, 10 March 1971, p. 37; see also Ismail and Suratman (sic), "Activities of the Indonesian State Tin Enterprise (P. N. Timah), 1968-72," in Committee for Coordination of Joint Prospecting for Mineral Resources in Asian Offshore Areas (CCOP), *Report of the Ninth Session* (Bangkok, 1973), pt. 2:158-165.

28. Robert Fabrikant, "Production-Sharing Contracts in the Indonesian Industry," in *Asia, Oil Politics, and the Energy Crisis*, IDOC International Documentation nos. 60-61 (New York: IDOC/International Documentation Center, 1974), p. 158. For comparisons of Indonesian and Indian production-sharing terms see *Petroleum Intelligence Weekly*, 3 June 1974, pp. 9-10, and D. B. Mahatme, "India's Search for Offshore Oil," *Petroleum News-Southeast Asia*, February 1975, pp. 11-13.

29. See Selig S. Harrison, *China, Oil, and Asia: Conflict Ahead?* (New York: Columbia University Press, 1977).

30. "A New Economic Diplomacy for the 1970's" (Tokyo: Asian-Pacific Council, American Chambers of Commerce, February 1970), pp. 8-9.

31. "Challenge of Multinational Business."

32. Robert V. Roosa, "World Trade in 1990: Particularly with the U.S.S.R. and China" (Edited transcript of extemporaneous comments at the White House Conference on the Industrial World Ahead, Washington, 9 February 1972), pp. 4-5.

33. Peter P. Gabriel, "MNC's in the Third World: Is Conflict Unavoidable?" *Harvard Business Review*, July-August 1972, esp. pp. 98-101.

34. Vernon, *Sovereignty at Bay*, p. 122.

35. Roosa, "World Trade," p. 10.

36. Gabriel, "MNC's in the Third World," p. 103.

37. Finance Committee, UNCTAD Preparatory Conference, *Trends and Problems in World Trade and Development* (Algiers, 24 October 1967), p. 14.

38. Escott Reid, *The Future of the World Bank* (Washington: International Bank for Reconstruction and Development, September 1965), p. 21; see also a discussion of the Bank and the public sector in Alec Cairncross, *The International Bank for Reconstruction and Development*, Essays in International Finance no. 33 (Princeton: International Finance Section, Department of Economics and Sociology, Princeton University, March 1959), p. 22.

39. "Statement by the Delegation of the Soviet Union," in ECAFE, *Report of the Preparatory Committee on the Asian Development Bank* (Bangkok, 21 October-1 November 1965), pp. 46, 48.

40. Walinsky, *Economic Development in Burma*, p. 317.

41. Soedjatmoko, *Technology, Development, and Culture* (Memorandum prepared for a colloquium conducted by the Institute for Religion and Social Change at Santa Barbara, 10-12 April 1972), pp. 4-5.

42. Recommendations for redesigned agricultural extension services with credit facilities linked to national and regional development banks were made by a seminar on small industry sponsored by the U.N. Industrial Development program and ECAFE, New Delhi, 5-9 April 1971.

43. Robert Shaw and Donald R. Sherk, *The International Utilization of Labor and the Multinational Corporation in the Pacific Basin* (Washington: Overseas Development Council, 1972), esp. pp. 9, 13-14, 21-22. For an analysis of the capital-intensive character of foreign investment in Indonesia see Alan Chalkley, "Indonesia," *Insight* (Hong Kong), August 1972, esp. p. 66.

44. Kusum Nair, *The Lonely Furrow* (East Lansing: Michigan State University Press, 1971), esp. chap. 29; see also idem, "The Green Revolution in South Asia," in *Change and the Persistence of Tradition in India*, ed. R. L. Park (Ann Arbor: Center for South and Southeast Asian Studies, University of Michigan, 1971); idem, "Inducing Change and Mass Participation in Devel-

opment," in *Development and Change in Traditional Agriculture* (East Lansing: Asian Studies Center, Michigan State University, November 1968), pp. 52–61; and idem, "Technology, Growth, and Income Distribution" (July 1973). Privately circulated.

45. Lester R. Brown, *Seeds of Change: The Green Revolution and Development in the 1970's* (New York: Praeger, 1970), p. 65.

46. Jack N. Behrman, "U.S. Private Investment in the Developing World," in *The United States and the Developing World: Agenda for Action* (Washington: Overseas Development Council, 1973), p. 44, argues that the elimination of tax credits and deferrals would be "quite effective" in discouraging investment; see also the Overseas Development Council's recommendation that the United States "reconsider its policies of promoting foreign investments abroad" in its *Summary of Agenda for Action*, no. 4, September 1973, p. 3.

47. In "New Deal or Raw Deal in Raw Materials," *Foreign Policy*, Winter 1971–1972, esp. pp. 125–127, Theodore H. Moran perceptively analyzes the factors of interdependence that can be exploited at the expense of economic nationalists.

48. Prakash Anand estimates the annual increase in British investments in India from 1964 to 1967 at $25 million, including plantation interests, in *The Sourcebook of Business Opportunities and Prospects for Foreign Collaboration in India* (Bombay: Shilton, Smith, Hammond, 1968), p. 716.

49. Paul A. Samuelson, *International Trade for a Rich Country* (Stockholm: Federation of Swedish Industries, 1972), pp. 25–27.

V

NATIONALISM, "ASIANISM," AND THE COLOR LINE

12. The Meaning of Regionalism

The foundation stone of this book lies in the distinction between the "old," European-model nationalism, generally equated with self-determination, and the "new" nationalism animating societies with a non-Western self-image in their drive for equity vis-à-vis the North American- European- Soviet "West." As I suggested in Chapter 1, nationalism in Asia is something much more than the assertion of linguistic, cultural, or ethnic identity as such. It is a search for foci of identity and self-respect that can temper the inferiority feelings generated by white, Western dominance. In the initial phase of this quest, the parameters of identity are defined by language, culture, or ethnicity, but these boundaries may well expand as transnational influences make themselves felt. Technological change has drastically compressed the historical processes of social awakening, fusing local and global horizons in overlapping dimensions of nationalist consciousness. The resulting hunger for strength and adequacy puts a premium on size, and a multilingual or multiethnic entity may well offer greater psychological support in the world setting than a more vulnerable, smaller unit.

Nationalism becomes a comprehensible concept in the Asian context only when viewed as a multidimensional search for the most appropriate and workable vehicles for the Asian response to Western dominance. Subnationalism and nationalism are two sides of the same coin, in this perspective, just as nationalism and regionalism are companion expressions of the same hunger for greater world stature. A multidimensional view of nationalism explains why the diversity of social identities in Asia does not necessarily presage political fragmentation. More important, as I shall now seek to demonstrate, it shows why the assertion of national identity is compatible with the parallel emergence of regional or subregional groupings. Both are

421

ultimately addressed to the goal of a stronger posture toward the West despite the immediate focus of nationalism in so many cases on internecine rivalries within Asia.

NATIONALISM WRIT LARGE

The characteristic American approach to Asia has identified nationalism and regionalism as the opposite poles of a historical cycle, and Asia has been urged, in effect, to leapfrog directly into regionalism, profiting from the lessons of the European past by omitting the nationalist stage entirely.[1] A more meaningful approach, however, would depict Asia as inescapably straddling historical epochs, confronted by the simultaneous demands of the nation-building process and the search for larger identities. To say that the emergence of nationalism has been telescoped by modern technology is not to suggest that the process can be eliminated or abbreviated. The dynamism of the nationalist awakening in Asia has only been intensified by its compression from centuries into generations. Where technological change may well have its impact, nonetheless, is in the elasticity of the political forms assured by nationalism.

The anachronistic aspects of narrowly conceived national sovereignty are increasingly apparent at a moment of history when science offers ever new solutions to problems that transcend political boundaries. In differing respects, the United States, the Soviet Union, and the European Economic Community each exemplify the advantages enjoyed by large-scale, socially heterogeneous political entities in making the most of technological advances. The challenge posed by such agglomerations of Western power strengthens the multilingual or multiethnic state in its struggle against separatism and stimulates intermittent Asian efforts to find valid spheres of regional and subregional cooperation, especially in the economic field. Technological change cuts two ways: it makes the world "smaller" and more interdependent, in a superficial sense, but it also acts divisively by magnifying the disparities between stronger and weaker regions. In the case of Asia, the impact of technological change is essentially divisive, and this is what gives rise to regionalism. The further growth of regionalism would represent a defensive response to the continuing subordination of Asia rather than a step toward universal community. It would mark a collective effort to shield Asian nation-building rather than the homogenization of Asia as part of a Western-dominated global power structure. Regionalism in Asia would not follow, supersede, or dilute nationalism, in short, but would merely be nationalism "writ large."[2]

Much of the confusion in the American approach to Asia would be cleared away by the recognition that Asia is not living "between two ages"[3] but is compelled to live psychologically in two ages at once. It would then be easier to see nationalism as a multidimensional phenomenon and thus to apply the concept of regionalism to Asia with greater realism than in the past. The misconceived American effort during the sixties to promote regional groupings in Asia epitomized in particularly sharp fashion the consequences of a failure to comprehend the elastic dimensions of nationalism. Given its cold war objectives, the United States was easily entrapped in the belief that the only satisfactory alternative to total American involvement in the world would be devolution of responsibility to regional centers of power broadly serving American purposes. "Regional groupings will have to take over major responsibility for their areas," wrote Henry Kissinger as late as 1968, "with the United States being concerned with the overall framework of order rather than with the management of every regional enterprise."[4]

To its advocates, especially during the Johnson years, American support for regionalism offered a "halfway house"[5] between untempered nationalism and excessive American involvement, but to most observers abroad, the American ideal of regionalism concealed what was in fact an effort to perpetuate elements of American hegemony, albeit in a looser, federalized structure.[6] As a sympathetic student of Asian regionalism later concluded, the very existence of the Association of Southeast Asia (ASA), the Southeast Asian Ministerial Conferences on Transport and Education, and most of the other flimsy regional groupings spawned during this period would have been "altogether unlikely"[7] without financial and other encouragement from the United States. Only the Association of Southeast Asian Nations (ASEAN), formed in 1967, was primarily indigenous in its inspiration, though it received important American support—initially as a means of reconciling ASA with the lingering Maphilindo concept and subsequently as an offset to China. To the extent that it was inspired by an Indonesian desire for regional leadership, even ASEAN has suffered from built-in limitations. A collision between the leadership ambitions of Indonesia and Thailand has been prevented largely by the common stake of ASEAN members in containing Japan. This is not what the United States had in mind, however, when it helped to promote the new grouping.

The United States regarded ASEAN as part of an Asia-wide pattern of regional cooperation led by a Japan tied closely to the United States and directed primarily to balancing Peking, not Tokyo. In this respect, American support of ASEAN has been self-defeating, reflecting the same misperception of Asian realities that led to overrating other, Japanese-sponsored regional enterprises that were artificial from the start.

Significantly, ASEAN, for its part, has been unable to surmount its internal divisions by relying on an anti-Japanese appeal alone. Its declaration against foreign bases[8] and its later accent on neutralization proposals support the contention that viable regional identities in Asia are likely to depend, in the long run, on successful appeals to the underlying Asian desire for a stronger posture toward the West. A multidimensional view of nationalism would underline this fundamental emotional requirement while recognizing, at the same time, that the precise boundaries of durable regional identities would have to coincide with meaningful horizons of social consciousness. As one example, the Indonesian desire for a position of regional primacy might be accommodated more gracefully in a grouping of relatively kindred neighbors, reminiscent of Maphilindo, than in an ASEAN framework including Thailand. A regional grouping based on Malay identity could be more specifically addressed to the containment of the economically powerful overseas Chinese within member countries than a heterogeneous organization in which a greater diversity of attitudes toward local Chinese elements would be likely. Such an approach was foreshadowed when the military leaders who took power in 1966 privately proclaimed the destiny of Djakarta to sponsor the eventual formation of "Maphilindo or Maphilindo-at-Large . . . building the forms and character of an Organization of Unity of the Nations of East and Southeast Asia on the basis of the economic interests of the Large Family of Malays."[9] Similarly, in the case of Japan, as we shall see, the boundaries of a larger identity are more likely to coincide with northeast Asian cultural and ethnic affinities than with a more heterogeneous, all-embracing "Asia."

BEYOND THE BALANCE OF POWER?

Like regionalism, the concept of "spheres of influence" can be applied most sensitively to Asia with the help of a multidimensional view of nationalism. By its nature, rooted as it is in conventional balance of power theory, this concept is blind to the character and strength of nationalism as the critical factor shaping intra-Asian power patterns and setting the political boundaries of identity. It draws a uniform, universal dichotomy between dominant big powers and dominated smaller powers without regard for the historical and other variables that differentiate one part of the world from another. Even in relatively streamlined form, spheres of influence thinking ignores, in one stroke, both the common perspective toward the West shared by all Asian countries, big and small, and the special determination of countries in the formative anguish of nation-building to limit external influences from near and far alike. Thus, Ronald Steel, in his advocacy of a "mature spheres of influence policy," envisages Chinese- and Japanese-dominated spheres, by implication in Southeast and Northeast Asia, respectively. These would be "relatively equal" to parallel regional spheres of influence dominated by the United States, the Soviet Union, and the European Economic Community, producing a world balance that would reduce the danger of superpower confrontation.[10] In Steel's view, it was "lack of respect for a Chinese sphere of influence in southeast Asia (that is, the recognition that China was not yet a superpower, and that Indochina was thus still a 'contested' area)" that led the United States to intervene in Vietnam.[11] It was possible for the United States to "deny" China its sphere in Southeast Asia "only because China was relatively weak."[12] Steel's version of a spheres of influence policy would be "mature . . . in that while it recognizes the dominant interest of great powers in areas they deem essential to their security, it does not give them carte blanche to treat those areas as colonies."[13] However, if smaller countries escape satellite status, this would be attributable to self-imposed restraints on the part of the great powers, which would "grant" to each other "certain rights in areas they deem essential to their own security."[14] Vietnam and other smaller countries in Southeast Asia emerge in this and similar analyses as "contested" pawns irrelevant in their own right as power factors and significant in American terms only as potential focal points of conflict with China.

In sharp contrast to this approach, a multidimensional view of nationalism rests on a basic faith in the capacity of smaller countries with a solid sense of identity to defend their position, over time, in the interplay of Asian power patterns. Big or small, as we saw in Chapter 1, it is the strength of their identity that determines their staying power in protecting national sovereignty. Such a view allows for possible future power groupings in response to Western dominance led by China, Japan, or both in concert, while recognizing, nonetheless, the decentralized character that such groupings are likely to have at a time when nation-building efforts coexist with the search for larger identities. Vietnam emerges, accordingly, not as a contested pawn but as a country that has been seeking all along to realize its own interlocking hierarchy of objectives: first, the achievement of national identity; next, subregional primacy, leading to a common Indochinese front against Chinese incursions; and in tandem with these aims, the expulsion of Western influence, a goal made acute and urgent by the special circumstances of the war. The Steel argument ignores the fact that American intervention was ultimately frustrated by the power of Vietnamese nationalism even in the absence of Chinese intervention. It is Vietnamese nationalism that has obstructed Chinese hegemony in the past and is likely to prevent the establishment of a Chinese sphere in the future.

If anything, American intervention in the war helped Peking to make its inroads in Indochina by obstructing the consolidation of a Vietnamese identity capable of checkmating Chinese influence in Cambodia and Laos as well as in Vietnam itself. As a near neighbor and a communist power, China might well have closer relations with a communist Vietnam than other powers would have, and Peking might well seek to use the overseas Chinese more aggressively than in the early postwar decades to expand Chinese influence throughout Southeast Asia.[15] But the position of Vietnam and other peripheral countries in their relationships with China is not likely to fit the concept of a Chinese sphere of influence. The intra-Asian regional balances discussed in an earlier chapter are likely to reflect a more complex process of adjustment. It will not often be necessary for the great powers to "constrain one another" from establishing regional spheres, as James Chace put it;[16] in most cases, Asian countries are likely to take conscious initiatives of their own to diversify their external dependencies as much as possible. This would require close ties with the West in a variety of ways; yet the very growth in Western contacts could produce an accompanying urge for a stronger Asian bargaining posture, accelerating the search for regional combinations side by side with the defense of national integrity. The power groupings of the future in Asia are likely to be new departures in their political format, much less monolithic than the concept of spheres of influence would connote but much more closely coordinated than past regional groupings insofar as relations with the West are concerned.

The desire for a stronger posture toward the West makes it unlikely that Asia will be the diffuse and undisciplined mélange of freewheeling countries envisaged in a provocative essay by Earl Ravenal. In a world that has gone "beyond the balance of power," Ravenal prophesied, the United States will confront a "pluralism of unaligned states," a "quasi-anarchy" among nations best described as "general unalignment." [17] The basic fallacy in this projection is that the world has not gone "beyond" the balance of power but has rather entered a new phase in which the meaning of this concept has changed. Traditional balance of power thinking has been rendered obsolete by the upsurge of nationalism and its relentless spread, limiting as this does the ability of superpowers to mold regional and subregional balances in most parts of the world. Indigenous regional balances and imbalances do exist, however, as Ravenal has acknowledged elsewhere,[18] if only because the power of nationalism varies from country to country and gives differing degrees of impact to other forms of power. Since we have ruled out spheres of influence, does this merely foreshadow ever shifting struggles for vantage in which changing economic and political fortunes favor first one country, then another? With respect to Asia, at least, the evolution of regional power patterns is likely to be a more ordered process governed by a unifying urge for a stable accommodation of interests. Cutting across the many differences that divide Asian countries is the pervasive aspiration, already emphasized, for a stronger collective posture toward the West. It is the desire for a new global balance of power that explains, at bottom, why the growth of organized regional or subregional power groupings in some form would appear more probable than the drift to formless general unalignment.

As Chapter 9 concludes, one of the most powerful stimuli leading to the growth of Asian regionalism would be a climate of continuing economic inequity between Asia and the West. Already, one existing regional grouping, ESCAP, has become the champion of Asian industrialization in the face of recurring Western pressures for priority to agriculture.[19] The growth of protectionism in the United States and Western Europe, in particular, possibly resulting in trade blocs, could create a sense of common cause transcending the many variations in stages of economic growth among Asian countries. Another factor pushing Asian countries together would be a continuance of the disproportionate Western consumption of the world's limited natural resources, accompanied by undiminished attempts to preserve preferential Western access to or direct control of these resources, especially in Asia itself, on terms that would perpetuate existing patterns of inequity. The fact that some Asian countries have greater natural riches than others gives the more fortunate ones a temporary palliative but does not automatically eradicate their deep-seated poverty or alter the staggering global arithmetic of power confronting the entire region. More important, it does not remove the strong sense of racial victimization that coincides directly with Asian feelings of economic subordination.

HIROSHIMA, VIETNAM, AND THE TAINT OF RACISM

By far the strongest potential source of Asian solidarity is also the most difficult to discuss in "provable" and quantifiable terms.

Color, as such, is not necessarily a governing factor in intergroup relations, especially where there are other overlapping social divisions. However, where a sense of subordination exists, and where color is the only or principal basis of differentiation between those in dominant and subordinate roles, color readily becomes an invisible common denominator.[20] The color line dividing Asia and the West has a profound psychological importance that is no less authentic because it is intangible, and the white-hot embers of racial consciousness have been kindled and rekindled in Asia by one exacerbating reminder of Western ethnocentricity after another. The Canton famine of 1850 resulted in the first wave of large-scale Asian immigration to the United States, which soon elicited a blatantly racial response in the form of increasingly sweeping discriminatory legislation, starting with the Chinese Exclusion Act of 1882 and climaxed by the Japanese Exclusion Act of 1924. An enduring image of an American racial animus was seared into Asian minds by the reception given to the early Chinese, Japanese, and Korean immigrants to California, as well as by American behavior in the Philippines, where frankly stated theories of Anglo-Saxon racial superiority were reflected in all-white clubs, a taboo in intermarriage at marked variance with Spanish practice, and an earthy army song to the tune of "Tramp, Tramp, Tramp":

> Damn, damn, damn, the Filipino,
> Pock-marked Khakiac ladron [copper-colored thief]
> Underneath the starry flag
> Civilize him with a Krag [rifle]
> And return us to our own beloved home.[21]

The racist reputation of the United States in Asia, already well established, was reinforced during World War II when Japanese-Americans, unlike Germans and Italians, were singled out for confinement in detention centers and deprived of their property. As late as 1952, Congress upheld the principle of an "Asian-Pacific" immigration quota in legislation that avoided the references to specific countries in earlier laws but clearly aimed at excluding all Asians. The quota was set at 100 per year, and not until 1969 were the gates opened to Asians on a nondiscriminatory basis.

It would be difficult to exaggerate the depth of the subsurface racial bitterness induced by the atom bombings of Hiroshima and Nagasaki. Whatever others might argue, the dominant conviction in Asia is that nuclear weapons would not have been dropped on Germany or Italy. In the West, the nuclear threat made by the United States to end the Korean War has been of interest largely in the context of historical disputation over what was most decisive in bringing about the Panmunjōm truce. For many Asians, by contrast, this was a racially tinged reminder of Hiroshima. The general tone of American postwar policy often has betrayed the underlying color consciousness exemplified by Gen. Douglas MacArthur's reference to the Pacific as an "Anglo-Saxon lake."[22] This attitude has been damaging enough in itself, but it has been sharpened and multiplied in its impact by an implicit U.S. devaluation of the importance of Asian lives that has continued to aggravate the emotional wounds left by the 1945 trauma. President Eisenhower's campaign slogan, "Let Asians Fight Asians," boldly expressed the more carefully stated rationale running through congressional military aid presentations for the two decades thereafter. In Asian eyes, the wanton abandon marking the U.S. military role in Vietnam was only a gross and overt expression of attitudes that were already taken for granted. The fact that American lives had been lost in the war was easily blotted out, psychologically, especially when the withdrawal of American forces was followed by relatively undiminished U.S. aid for Saigon and a readiness to see continued fighting so long as the "color of the corpses" had been changed. To the "slopeys," "Wogs," and "gooks" of Asia who had felt the presence of American GIs in World War II, Korea, and Vietnam, Mylai was not as incredible as it was to many Americans, and the army's characterization of Lt. William Calley's victims as "70 Oriental human beings"[23] readily fit their prevailing perception of the American approach to Asia as essentially racist. By a more objective test, as James Thomson observed in a discussion of the Vietnam experience, the ingredient of "crypto-racism" in American attitudes toward Asia does not necessarily imply "any conscious contempt for Asian loss of life" and has aspects of cultural condescension that do not have a specifically racial imprint.[24] But from an Asian perspective, American behavior has been besmirched by a recurring racial arrogance demonstrated most dramatically at Hiroshima and displayed vividly during the Vietnam years.

Chapter 6 demonstrated the basic similarity in the attitudes of major Asian countries toward the Vietnam war despite their widely divergent economic and political circumstances. The common denominator that cut across so many variations of ideology and special interest was a sense of impotence and racial anger in the face of the largely unrestrained application of white, Western power. For all of their ethnic differentiation, Japanese, Indians, and Filipinos shared an Asian racial identity in their response to the bombing of the North and other manifestations of American might. Senator Daniel Inouye, a Hawaiian of Japanese ancestry, echoed this Asian sentiment when he said that the bombing amounted to "the big bully of the Western world telling the little brown men of Asia, 'you go

our way or else.' "25 The success achieved by the North in stale-
mating the United States did little to relieve the feelings of frustration and inadequacy engendered by such devastation wrought with
such conspicuous impunity. Deep currents of resentment were set in
motion by the war, adding to the festering emotions left over from
the colonial past and the postindependence nationalist reaction generated by Western political and economic pressures. The resulting
malaise remains suppressed to a great extent but could lead to a
xenophobic backlash expressed in a variety of possible ways, ranging
from terrorism and prestige nuclear explosions to the nuclear "wars
of redistribution" envisaged by Robert Heilbroner.26

Edwin Reischauer posed a question of transcendent relevance
when he asked in his postmortem on the war whether Asia would be
oriented in future years toward world cooperation or would be
"driven by deep inner tensions and desires for revenge."27 The
balance between these alternatives has become a perilous one, indeed, in the wake of the cold war military incursions epitomized by
Vietnam. The seeming quiescence of Asian opposition to the American military role following the 1972 truce has led to the widespread
belief that antiwar emotions were transitory. Warning against such a
myopic assumption with respect to China, John Fairbank, supported
by Reischauer, pointed in a 1967 symposium to the

> Chinese doctrine of requital, that you must always pay back, good or ill,
> whatever you get, forever keep it in mind and pay it back. It seems to me
> that the war in Vietnam has loaded us with a degree of Chinese hatred that
> we do not now realize that will come up against us at sometime in the
> future as a problem.... For us to bomb on their frontier can only produce
> feelings that they don't dare express but which begin with fear and then go
> on to humiliation and then get to rage and hatred against us.... I think the
> Chinese attitude is underground in their hearts and minds.28

The "doctrine of requital" cited by Fairbank is the concept of *pao*,
emphasizing strict reciprocity as a basis for social relations. As a verb,
pao literally means "to retaliate, retribute, or repay" in addition to
its more generalized connotation of "response." "The Chinese believe that reciprocity of actions (favor and hatred, reward and pun-
ishment) between man and man, and indeed between man and
supernatural beings, should be as certain as a cause and effect
relationship," wrote Yang Lien-sheng in his definitive study of *pao*.
Significantly, the invocation of *pao* to justify the retributive principle of "recompensing injury with injury" came only after a controversy among Confucian scholars, Yang pointed out, signaling the
triumph of the "realistic" school represented by Hsün-tzu over the
"idealistic" school identified with Mencius.29 This was an intellectual victory of far-reaching significance in other Asian societies

influenced by Confucian thought and has been reflected in kindred concepts of social relations suggestive of *pao*, notably *on* and *giri* in Japan. In general, retribution is treated with less ambiguity in Asian ethical codes than in Christian teachings, though with more subtlety than the Old Testament injunction of "an eye for an eye, a tooth for a tooth." Thus, Japan has its own special style of requital summed up in the samurai saying *"Edo no kataki o Nagasaki de toru,"* loosely translated as "When insulted in Tokyo, bide your time and take your revenge later, in Nagasaki." The Nixon shocks of 1971 first brought this familiar couplet into contemporary political currency,[30] but it has a wider application, aptly conveying the way Japan approaches its overall future relationship with the West. There are many scores to be settled, in Japanese eyes, not the least of which is the insensate use made of Western military power at the expense of Asian lives. Japan's own guilt feelings with respect to World War II have been largely focused on China,[31] with the United States blamed not only for the economic discrimination that allegedly provoked the war but also for cold war policies that served to divide Tokyo from Peking.

The temporary sublimation of Japan's Asian identity was an inescapable consequence of its military defeat by the United States and the expedient policy of support for the American role in Asia discussed in earlier chapters. Despite surface appearances, however, Japan continued to have a "victim-type racial consciousness"[32] rooted in Hiroshima and in memories of the U.S. exclusion acts that still remain vivid.[33] The strong Japanese sense of kinship with North Vietnam underlined in Chapter 6 was one of the more visible symptoms of this psychological framework. In the rich-poor dichotomy, Japan has only a qualified identity with the "north" as against the "south"; its self-image is rather "eastern" or perhaps an ambivalent "northeastern." Modernization is not necessarily westernization, and even the economic progress achieved during the postwar years has not made Japan feel Western. On the contrary, Western resistance to Japanese economic expansion has only sharpened feelings of "Asianness," evoking a resentful response fundamentally different from the Japanese reaction to "Ugly Japanese" charges made by Indonesians or Thais. Most Japanese believe that their limited economic success has been achieved in the face of Western opposition, a conviction not altered by the record of postwar U.S. help given, as they see it, for self-interested American reasons. Accordingly, the pride generated by their progress is pride in an Asian success story, and criticism from fellow Asians arouses more confused emotions than Western resistance viewed as unabashedly racial in its motivation. Tristan Beplat, senior vice-president of the

Manufacturers Hanover Trust Company, recounted the complaint of a leading Japanese banker who asked,

> "Why is it every time we get someplace in the world, the big powers push us down?" And I said, "Oh, I don't think so." He said: "Well, this is the way we feel." He said: "We have just made this remarkable recovery since the end of the war. We have just reached a place where we are establishing ourselves and you are now pushing our heads down again."[34]

A Japanese scholar has suggested more pointedly that Americans have

> not yet completely overcome the psychological aftermath of the "Yellow Peril" theory.... Some of us have noticed that although European countries impose almost the same restrictions on imports, the Americans rebuke only Japan and demand that Japan alone should control its exports "voluntarily." ... If there is even the slightest suggestion of a double standard, the Japanese will feel discriminated against.[35]

When protectionism began to grow acute in 1970, the *Asahi's* most widely read columnist wrote that "at the bottom of the movements to shut out Japanese products, there is the racial discrimination of whites toward 'Japanese with yellow faces who are upstarts.' "[36] Japanese feelings of racial victimization were accentuated during the Nixon years by indications of a specific anti-Japanese animus on the part of the president and other administration leaders that made Tokyo a special target of hardened U.S. policies on trade and other economic issues. The most telling episode in this regard was an imitation of a Japanese bowing and hissing, performed by the president himself at a meeting of his Commission on Trade and Investment Policy on September 13, 1971, shortly before the publication of its final report. One of those present said that Nixon was delivering an exasperated recital of Japanese obstinacy in the textile negotiations and had imitated Premier Eisaku Sato in the course of this. Another commission member said that the imitation was not of any particular Japanese but was rather a description of "the way they are."[37] Both agreed that the ethnic slur was unmistakable.

Emphasis on the nature and strength of racial consciousness in Japan is necessitated by the widespread tendency to equate modernization with westernization and by a Western debate over the future of Japanese nationalism generally formulated without adequate reference to the Asian component of Japanese identity. For the most part, Japanese nationalism has been equated with the militarism and emperor worship of the thirties. In Japanese terms, this is *kokka-shugi*, the exaltation of the national state above all else, as distinct from *minzoku-shugi*, or racial consciousness, which does not require expression through militarism or imperialism and is not necessarily limited in its horizons to an exclusively Japanese racial identity.[38] As we have observed in discussing their sense of kinship with North Vietnam, many Japanese applied the latter definition of nationalism to the North Vietnamese struggle against the United States, with a leading conservative newspaper urging Americans to recognize that "*minzoku-shugi* in Asia is racialism full of resistance."[39] In conflicts within Asia, this "racialism" can be narrowly chauvinist, but it may also be expansible to a regional or subregional identity in the face of a common non-Asian challenge. To consider the future of Japanese nationalism solely in terms of the chances for revival of *kokka-shugi*, therefore, is to miss a considerably more pertinent issue, namely, whether *minzoku-shugi* will gain momentum and will seek its outlet in a regional combination linking Japan, China, and eventually Korea.

"THE EASTERN THREE"

In Chapter 8 we examined the economic factors affecting both the Japan-China relationship and the larger possibility of a pan-Asian response to protectionism and economic aggrandizement on the part of the West. Economic considerations alone are not likely to determine the form of Asian regional identities, however, and it is only when economic advantage coincides with a sense of political and psychological community that regionalism is likely to become a serious possibility. In the case of Japan, the search for a larger identity no longer extends to the pan-Asian horizons encompassed in the prewar dream of a greater East Asia coprosperity zone. The rise of nationalist resistance to Japan in Southeast Asia has strengthened the natural differentiation in Japanese imagery between culturally and ethnically kindred near neighbors and other Asian countries. Jōji Watanuki, who conducted a revealing study in 1972 of Japanese perceptions of the outside world, found evidence of an "increasing identity crisis." As an industrialized society, Japan was conscious of greater similarity with the West than with Asia but felt drawn to Asian countries, nonetheless, as "most familiar" and "most trusted."[40] When his respondents were then asked to indicate what countries were covered in their minds by the phrase "Asian nation," China, Japan, Korea, and Taiwan proved to be the ones named by an overwhelming majority.[41] More specifically, China emerged as the single country in the world most trusted by Japanese. If forced to make a choice among future reliance on the United States, China, and the Soviet Union, Japanese at all educational levels replied that they would select China, with those at the highest educational levels favoring Peking by a two-to-one margin.[42]

The nominal objective of Japanese foreign policy has been to maintain a careful equidistance between Peking and Moscow, avoiding embroilment in the Sino-Soviet rivalry. In actuality, Japan has been caught up in a slow but steady drift toward a relationship with China that may well become closer than any it enjoys with other powers. This is basically explained by the atavistic pull of common ethnic and cultural roots summed up in the Japanese *dōbun dōsyu* ("same race, same letters"). Despite the linguistic divergence that has developed over the centuries, the common usage of Chinese ideographic characters confers a feeling of filial closeness and visceral understanding. *Haragei*, the subtle, indirect, often unspoken communication of mood and meaning so difficult for Japanese to achieve with blunt-spoken Russians or Americans, comes more naturally in dealings with Chinese than with any other non-Japanese people. Prime Minister Tanaka's 1972 visit to Peking had an aura of easy empathy suggestive of this common ancient heritage: Chou En-lai depositing food on Tanaka's plate with deftly handled chopsticks, "a pleasant reminder," said *Asahi*, "that 900 million people in the east Asian cultural area eat in a similar fashion";[43] Tanaka presenting a personally composed poem to Chou, inscribed in Chinese characters and written in Kanshi style, a Japanese imitation of old Chinese court verse; a folk dance for Tanaka played by a Chinese orchestra at ease with Japanese musical forms; a gracious gesture to the Shinto tradition in a song about Kompira shrine, a venerable landmark in Foreign Minister Ohira's hometown.

Reinforcing the ties of culture and ethnicity is a Japanese sense of shared destiny with China in the face of the West that dates back to the fall of the Tokugawa shogunate in the mid-nineteenth century. "Japan and China," declared Shinkichi Eto, the doyen of Japanese sinologists,

> are considered to be to each other as lips are to teeth and the mandibula is to the maxilla. . . . The notion of a state of close interdependency and complementarity of interests grew out of a Japanese awareness of the probable consequences of Western expansionist pressures and a realization that, in order to repel these forces, the development of Japan alone was inadequate. The Meiji leaders grew ever more anxious for a parallel strengthening of China.[44]

In the confused, uncertain debate that enveloped Japan for fifty years after Meiji, both imperialists and anti-imperialists alike saw an indispensable role for China in a pan-Asian front against the West. The imperialists clinched their case by arguing that China needed a guiding Japanese hand to cope with Western pressures. The early Chinese nationalists, for their part, also thought initially in terms of a common Sino-Japanese destiny. Sun Yat-sen's concept of pan-Asianism centered around a detailed program for a Sino-Japanese bank, compatibility in military equipment, and prior consultation before either concluded "important agreements with a third power on matters relating to Asia."[45] "Without Japan," declared Sun, "there would be no China; without China, there would be no Japan. . . . Japan, because of her similarity in language and race with China, can be of even greater assistance to China than America."[46] Chiang Kai-shek echoed Sun's hopes for a collaborative relationship with Japan even after the Mukden incident. In 1934, writing under a pseudonym, Chiang made a long since forgotten appeal to Japan to reconsider its aggressive course that makes interesting reading today. Chiang himself had the essay republished in Chinese in Taiwan in 1952, acknowledging his authorship, and wrote an introduction suggesting that his message "might still be helpful to the peoples of east Asia."[47] Utilizing the same metaphor that Eto was to employ three decades later, Chiang wrote that

> no matter how one looks at the history, geography and racial character of China and Japan, it is clear that their relations should be on a level of intimacy even higher than the interdependence of lips and teeth, or cheek and jawbone. Their peoples truly live or perish together. Only if there exists an independent China able to enter into mutual nourishment with an advanced Japan can Japan properly exercise her special position and interests in east Asia, and only then can China also carry out her mission in east Asia.[48]

Japan's subsequent attempt to establish military dominion over China took the inordinately rapacious form detailed in Chapter 3 and left a legacy of bitterness that aggravated the ideological differences dividing Peking and Tokyo after the Communist takeover. By the time the two countries had reestablished top-level contacts in 1972, however, they were both ready to wipe the slate clean and make the emotionally demanding effort to restructure their relationship. In effect, they decided to go back to the turn of the century and to start all over again. China was able to submerge its war-born bitterness toward Japan in its fears of the Soviet Union, and Japan was anxiously searching for new moorings in a period of growing international economic and political uncertainty. At the same time, Tokyo was compelled to come to terms with the reality of a strong, centralized China that was no longer vulnerable to external domination and had its own claims to a position of regional primacy in which Japan would be subordinate or at best coequal.

China poses a unique psychological dilemma for Japan. Conscious as it is of hierarchy in its domestic social life, Japan assigns a status to other countries reflecting their global military and economic rank, a status that must be either higher or lower than that of

Japan. The concept of sovereign equality among nations runs against the grain. The United States thus enjoyed a special brand of respect during the initial decades after V-J Day, while Asian poor relations were treated with particular disdain. China alone, as Japan's cultural mentor, has defied easy categorization. Economically, Japan set a faster pace, but a profound feeling of cultural debt makes it difficult for Japan to look on China as a junior, quite apart from the inherent endowments of size and natural resources that give Peking long-term economic prospects equal to or more promising than those of Tokyo.

To some extent, Japan appears to be burdened with an inferiority complex rooted in its ingrained sense of cultural subordination to China. This would suggest an explanation of past Japanese behavior toward China as a subconscious effort to remove inferiority feelings by demonstrating military and economic dominance.[49] In the contemporary context, by contrast, the same psychological conditioning could explain what has been a very different response under very different historical circumstances. Faced with the settled reality of a strong China, Japan appears to be sliding into a progressively more adaptive stance. Japanese leaders, responding to popular moods, have repeatedly bowed to Chinese wishes since 1972 in order to keep the wheels of normalization turning. A close and compatible relationship with China appears to have a special importance for many Japanese, satisfying, in some measure, their hunger for a feeling of anchorage and emotional security amid shifting international currents. As China grows in strength, Japan could well "abdicate"[50] almost without realizing it, implicitly accepting second place in Chinese-centered regional arrangements.

Some observers who concede the Japanese desire for close ties with China nonetheless discount the prospect for such a relationship by pointing to Chinese attitudes. "The Chinese would dearly love to manipulate the Japanese," Edwin Reischauer has contended, "but not to have a special relationship with them on terms that the Japanese would find acceptable."[51] This analysis is valid as far as it goes, stressing the patronizing Chinese image of the Japanese, but it ignores the Japanese response to Chinese condescension. Precisely because they are aware of how China regards them, Japanese appear unable to escape from their inferiority feelings and are driven into their compliant posture toward Peking on many issues. The terms that China might seek to impose in a close collaboration could well prove digestible, therefore, especially since China has its own reasons for desiring a firmly anchored Japan and might well moderate its own expectations should this prove necessary.

The most immediate motivations pushing China toward Japan are a desire to head off close Japanese relations with Moscow and a need for expanded economic ties at the relatively favorable prices made possible by Japanese geographical proximity. But behind these tangible factors, in addition, lies a subtle emotional bond as Asian powers facing a common challenge of Western dominance. Reischauer attributes Japan's sense of affinity with China primarily to "anxieties over strategic or cultural domination by the West." At the same time, he gives no attention to the possibility that China's even more pronounced and more explicit anxieties with respect to the West could lead to reciprocal feelings of affinity with Japan. My own conclusion after a number of sharply focused discussions in 1972 with Chinese officials, students, and scholars [52] is that Japan, as an Asian near neighbor, has a much more important place in the Chinese scheme of things than the United States. The central historic thrust of Chinese foreign policy has not been altered by the Shanghai communiqué. Peking is still dedicated to the interlocking goals of a stronger China and Asian parity with the West as part of a broader restructuring of the global balance of power. Japan is perceived as a valuable potential partner in achieving these basic objectives, while the United States is assigned to an expedient and limited role.

New Chinese tactics toward Washington had become necessary in 1972 if only as a temporary response to tensions with Moscow. But the Soviet problem is only one facet of the larger problem of coping with an assortment of Western powers, in Chinese eyes, and the use of one of these powers to offset another does not in itself signify a basic change in direction. Peking also sees other possible dividends in a softened approach to the United States, principally the diversification of its sources of foreign technology and the accession of Taiwan. With respect to these objectives, as in the deterrence of the Soviet Union, the Chinese rapprochement with Tokyo has served immediate tactical purposes similar to those served by the new approach to Washington. Over and above this, however, the Japanese link has a place in long-term Chinese plans automatically ruled out in the case of the United States at the present stage of the relationship between Asia and the West.

While bitter wartime memories persist, China no longer fears Japan as much as it did during the early postwar decades. A sea change has occurred in Peking's attitude as its own power has grown and as its bargaining position in dealings with Tokyo has become more and more secure. The growth of tensions in the Japanese-American relationship, in particular, has reinforced Chinese confidence. "Contradictions" between Japan and the United States are likely to grow, China reasons, and Japan is too dependent on the world economy to threaten China in the absence of American sponsorship. Japan, for its part, has grown correspondingly conscious of its economic vulnerability since oil prices were raised in 1973. Confidence in Peking has been paralleled by despond and insecurity in Tokyo. Despite its heightened urge for an independent posture in world affairs, Japan has been conspicuously reluctant to take the risks involved in striking out on its own. A combination with China would offer an outlet for *minzoku-shugi* nationalism without such risks and could thus become increasingly attractive, especially if protectionism were to grow in the West as projected earlier.

The participation of Korea in a regional grouping together with Japan and China would appear to be a distinct possibility but would not be likely to materialize until a unified Korea confronts Peking and Tokyo from a position of enhanced strength. While the Japanese and Chinese would both welcome Korean participation irrespective of unification, the Koreans themselves have a more conditional attitude. The Korean role is likely to be a potent and imponderable variable in the future of northeast Asian regionalism, and a Sino-Japanese combination without Korean involvement would be much less cohesive than a tripartite grouping.

Many Japanese are strongly attracted to the idea of such a tripartite grouping, often spoken of as the "Eastern Three," especially those Japanese most drawn to China. Thus, political scientist Michio Rōyama, rejecting Western proposals for regional cooperation among Japan, Australia, India, and Indonesia, observed in 1967 that "if there is an ideal regional cooperation which Japan could dream of, it should be the one that includes both China and Korea, which are more natural partners in terms of geographical propinquity and special historical relations." Rōyama saw the division of Korea as unnatural and believed that a tripartite grouping would necessarily await not only the full normalization of Sino-Japanese relations but Korean unification as well.[53] However, another leading Japanese advocate of regionalism known for a more cautious approach to China, economist Kiyoshi Kojima, has proposed a northeast Asian free trade area embracing initially Japan, North and South Korea, Taiwan, and Hong Kong. Even before unification, he argued in a 1973 Seoul conference, North and South would profit from "economic integration" and could take part in a larger grouping as a single economic unit, avoiding the wasteful duplication of economic effort resulting from their division. With regard to the United States, the Soviet Union, and China, Kojima declared, northeast Asian countries "are all in the same boat and share the same fate. And including China, they are all of the same Mongolian race."[54] While equidistant policies toward the Big Three are desirable, he added,

> within these equal distance policies various subtleties will naturally develop. The close links with America are obvious and will be strengthened further.

It is a common concern that, while not jeopardizing friendship with Russia, peace and economic interdependence between China and northeast Asian countries including Japan be pursued and promoted. It is in this respect that Japan and northeast Asian countries are "in the same boat" and may be expected to confirm their common solidarity. And it is to be hoped that China will come to share this solidarity. The move for unification of North and South Korea will give an important fillip to this confirmation.[55]

Toward Japan and China alike, the Korean posture is viscerally defensive and suspicious, but especially toward Japan. From a Korean perspective, Kojima's approach smacks of a mini-Coprosperity Sphere similar to that of the Yatsugi plan outlined in Chapter 7. It is only with the inclusion of China that the regional idea would become attractive, and only then after unification. A unified Korea, though still dwarfed by Tokyo and Peking, would be sizable enough to defend its major interests by playing off one capital against the other.

The case of Korea as a divided country illustrates in aggravated form the general dilemma of Asian countries seeking both to find their national identity and to reach out for larger identities suited to a technologically shrinking world. Yi Yong-hŭi, a leading South Korean political scientist, pleads that

partitioned as we are, we must give first and urgent priority to the completion of our national self. A divided Korea will become more and more of an anachronism as the world goes beyond nationalism in search of multinational patterns. But we can only play a part in this larger quest for unity when we have caught up with the rest and can stand firm on our own national identity. How ironic it is that before we can move in the cosmopolitan main current of history we must struggle to vindicate a principle already on the way to obsolescence.[56]

Even after unification, Korea, as a smaller power, would tend to distinguish its attitude toward the West from that of Japan and China. As viewed by a representative South Korean, "the basic mentalities and interests of Japan and Communist China would be to determine and reduce, to the maximum possible extent, the presence and existing vested interests of the two 'alien' forces in Asia . . . the United States and Russia." Koreans, by contrast, would like to see an American presence in the Pacific in some form to check "the two indigenous giants."[57] Korean emotions toward the United States are nonetheless ambivalent, as we demonstrated earlier, and there is a latent dimension of Asian identity in the Korean emotional framework that cannot be lightly dismissed. This has been effectively manipulated by Pyongyang in its articulation of nationalist feeling; in the South, Kim Chong-p'il's early nationalist phase, discussed in Chapter 7, was notable for important nuances in outlook as between

Asia and the West. Noting that "instinctive understanding" in communication between Koreans and Japanese,[58] notwithstanding their feelings of mutual distaste, Kim declared that "we must first be definite Koreans and then become definite Asians in recovering our national spirit. Only then can we think of becoming world citizens."[59] Given a protectionist trend in the West and a concerted response by China and Japan, the Asian component in Korean identity could well be magnified and accentuated. Noncooperation in the fulfillment of regional ambitions could invite Sino-Japanese retaliation; conversely, Tokyo and Peking could make it much more profitable for Korea to join their club than to play the difficult game of a freewheeling loner.

Korea and Vietnam are often bracketed together as countries historically subject to Chinese pressure and thus intent now on avoiding any hint of a return to Chinese suzerainty. The two cases are clearly differentiated, however, by the contrasting geographical factors involved. Vietnam is in a position to build its own subregional grouping, while Korea, trapped as it is by its location, has more limited options. China, for its part, would no doubt prefer continued division as against a unified Korea under Southern domination. Chinese attitudes toward Korea are complex and difficult to gauge but appear to be strongly colored by the Sino-Soviet rivalry. By all indications, a regional grouping that would help to insulate a unified Korea from Soviet influence would be extremely attractive to Peking, not to mention the strength that Korea would add to such a grouping in its dealings with Western powers.

THE IMPACT OF U.S. POLICY

In the more extravagant expressions of Japanese enthusiasm for pan-Asianism, a Sino-Japanese combination has been depicted as the hub of a larger regional grouping encompassing not only Korea but Southeast Asia as well. The leader of Japan's powerful Sōka Gakkai movement, Daisaku Ikeda, declared in a characteristic oratorical climax that "it is only when all Asians, with the Japanese and Chinese as the center, come to befriend and protect one another that the dark clouds of cruel war and poverty now blanketing Asia will be dispelled." [60] Lee Kuan Yew, reflecting an overseas Chinese perspective, spoke in similar terms on his return from an acrimonious encounter with President Lyndon Johnson in November 1967, recounted in Chapter 6, angrily warning that "there is as much arrogance in the Asian as in the American," and that

... one day, and not too far ahead, some Asians are going to prove that they can more than equal American industrial and military capability ...

[When the Chinese] send in cadres of technicians to tap this wealth, I think even the Japanese will begin to think that it is worthwhile joining or, at least, taking a more neutral stand. . . . I think you are going to have a greater co-prosperity sphere for the whole of East Asia, eventually the whole of South Asia right up to Iran. Half of mankind in one solid block.[61]

This is strikingly reminiscent of George Orwell's world of three vast superstates, a Soviet-dominated "Eurasia," an American-dominated "Oceania," and an "Eastasia" consisting of China "and the countries to the south of it," plus Japan and Mongolia.[62] In Orwell's grim flight of fancy, the only forces of consequence in the late twentieth century were totalitarianism, technocracy, and militarism; but in the real world, where nationalism is also a significant force, superstates are vulnerable to overpowering centrifugal stress. At one extreme of prophecy, the imagery of a hopelessly Balkanized Asia misses the elasticity and multidimensional character of nationalism. At the other, the superstate image underrates the primary dimensions of identity on which nationalism ultimately rests. The power patterns discussed in Chapter 10 appear most likely to take the intermediate form of subregional identities—self-centered, for the most part, but capable of a loose pan-Asian linkage in the face of severe challenges from the non-Asian world.

Predictions of a Sino-Japanese hegemony in Southeast Asia over-estimate the degree of integration likely to develop between China and Japan while underestimating, at the same time, the capacity of Southeast Asian countries to resist absorption into external power constellations. As an extension of their cooperation in northeast Asia, China and Japan would no doubt seek to avoid a serious trade rivalry elsewhere and to this extent might present a united front to their southern neighbors. In the political field, however, Chinese and Japanese interests could well diverge on local issues, offering opportunities for maneuver by weaker Southeast Asian countries. Even in the economic field, a northeast Asian grouping would be likely to accelerate the growth of an ASEAN or a Maphilindo as a counter-force. Considering the economic head start already enjoyed by northeast Asia, especially Japan, Southeast Asian countries would be on guard against a division of labor consigning them to the roles of subcontractor and raw materials source. Nevertheless, both northeast and Southeast Asian groupings would share a raison d'être in relation to the West and would have an expanding community of interest if Western protectionism grows. The degree of solidarity between these two parts of Asia would be greatest in the context of a global fragmentation into regional economic blocs and would be determined, in particular, by the nature of Western economic policies toward Asia.

Under certain circumstances,[63] as we noted in Chapter 9, Japan might relax its rigid foreign exchange controls and encourage the development of a yen-based trade and financial bloc centered in Asia. This is one way in which a pattern of institutionalized linkages between northeast and Southeast Asia might conceivably evolve. A yen bloc could take a variety of forms and would not necessarily represent neo-imperialism on the part of Japan. In a climate of conflict with the West, Japan could well make the terms for participation in such arrangements more flexible than its past policies toward Southeast Asia would suggest. In dealing with resource-rich Asian countries, especially, Tokyo was under increasing pressure for a more flexible posture even in the early seventies. The course of Japanese relations with Southeast Asia would appear to be closely linked with the future of the Sino-Japanese relationship and the overall opportunities open to Tokyo. Close cooperation with China would help to absorb Japanese economic energies that might otherwise be focused more intensively on Southeast Asia and could help to restrain possible Japanese political ambitions resulting from economic involvements. Conversely, should a Sino-Japanese rivalry develop, neighboring countries would be buffeted by conflicting pressure to take sides.

As we noted at the outset of this book, there is a supreme irony in the fact that the United States, historically dedicated to a balance of power in Asia, seriously aggravated existing power imbalances by basing its postwar policies almost exclusively on cold war objectives for more than two decades. If a monolithic pan-Asianism is unlikely, this is in spite of the distortions fostered by the American role. Not only did the United States enhance the danger of Japanese economic dominance and delay the emergence of China as an offset to Japan. In addition, American policies reinforced other factors blocking Indian involvement in Southeast Asia. For a brief initial period, Washington encouraged New Delhi to increase its interests in Southeast Asia as a counter to China, just as it urged Japanese involvement for the same reason. Once the American stake in Vietnam began to grow, however, Indian opposition to the American role led the United States to reverse its attitude and to look on New Delhi as an uncooperative nuisance with no place in Vietnam-centered regional activities. An unusually explicit expression of the official American perception of India during this period came in a 1967 academic forum on Asian images of the Vietnam war. When I observed that the United States had pressed for Indian support on Vietnam without really asking how New Delhi felt about the war, State Department official Philip Habib, later to become assistant secretary of state for East Asian affairs, replied that India was not really a "part of Asia" because it had declined to play the Vietnam peacekeeping role desired by the United States. "I've heard an awful lot about what India thinks," Habib said, "and I think it's irrelevant in many respects because they've read themselves out of Asia. I am concerned, however, about what Japan thinks and what Indonesia thinks. . . ."64

Washington gave its blessing when Tokyo maneuvered the exclusion of India from Japanese-sponsored regional ventures 65 and when Prime Minister Sato specifically omitted India from his concept of a "Pacific Asia" ending at Burma.66 India, for its part, while historically closer to Southeast Asia than Japan, had a patronizing approach to the area during the Nehru years that neutralized this advantage, facilitating Japanese maneuvers. In the future evolution of Asian power relationships, Indian trade and economic involvement in Southeast Asia might yet provide an eventual counterweight to Japanese and Chinese influence. But Tokyo is entrenched in Southeast Asian markets as a result of the Vietnam period, and its lead over New Delhi in economic development, already enormous, has been multiplied by the damaging impact of oil price increases on Indian industrial expansion.

In summary, Asia appears to be slowly drifting toward four or more subregional identities loosely linked by the shared legacies of colonialism and the Vietnam years and the common sense of historical destiny in relation to the West emphasized throughout this work. In South Asia, heterogeneous India is a subregional identity unto itself and appears likely to remain unified despite serious unresolved problems of internal adjustment among its differing linguistic components. Pakistan, Bangladesh, Sri Lanka, and Nepal appear strong enough to retain separate identities and to prevent the establishment of an Indian sphere of influence but not strong enough to challenge Indian primacy directly, for very long, in the fashion exemplified by Pakistan in its pre-1972 behavior. In Southeast Asia, Indonesian-centered and Vietnam-centered identities could well emerge side by side, coalescing into a single Southeast Asian grouping only in the unlikely event of concerted Sino-Japanese pressure. In northeastern Asia, some form of special relationship would appear likely between China and Japan, possibly embracing Korea at a later, postunification stage. The cohesion of each of these subregional identities and the extent of the linkage among them will be contingent on more than indigenous factors: the political, economic, and military policies pursued by the West will have a crucial impact, as earlier chapters elaborated, and policies insensitive to nationalism in its many dimensions will strengthen the forces of pan-Asian consolidation. Divisive Western tactics would risk a long-term backlash, whether they be tactics designed directly to obstruct a drift to consolidation or indirectly divisive as a by-product of anti-Soviet policies in the military field such as those discussed in Chapter 8 with respect to Japan and China. In the economic sphere, especially, Western efforts to perpetuate the existing global edifice of inequity would be likely to stimulate intra-Asian economic patterns coordinated in some cases with the economic strategies of other less developed regions. For example, protectionist Western trade policies would stimulate intra-Asian trade, a trend already foreshadowed by the shift in the focus of Southeast Asian exports from the United States to Japan.

In itself, the growth of intra-Asian trade patterns would not necessarily be adverse to the interests of the United States and might even be a natural part of a phased transition to a more equitable world.[67] If these patterns are forced upon Asia by Western protectionism, however, they are likely to develop with an artificial intensity, leading to the growth of hostile economic blocs in Asia and the West perennially on the verge of political and even military collision. It would thus be self-defeating in the extreme to retreat to a Fortress America psychology in the economic sphere, as implicitly suggested by Robert Tucker,[68] restricting imports along with a cutback of foreign investments in an indiscriminate search for economic self-sufficiency.

A policy alert to the meaning and character of nationalism would seek to discourage American equity investment in Asia but would promote economic collaboration on equitable terms and, above all, would facilitate American imports from less developed Asian countries as part of broader preferential policies toward developing countries on the UNCTAD pattern. This in turn would presuppose more serious efforts to increase the competitiveness of U.S.-based manufacturing industry, together with a graceful adaptation to changing cost-price structures reflecting higher raw material prices. The gradual evolution of a world in which the U.S. living standard were more or less the same as that of other nations would mean difficult adjustments for Americans, but this outcome would appear inescapable. Moreover, in a racially divided world, Western efforts to prevent such an evolution could provoke ugly, irrational conflict on a scale hitherto unimagined.

Over time, policies sensitive to nationalism would make for a more stable international order, while insensitive, die-hard policies would push nationalism in destructive directions. Given the racial factor, in particular, David Calleo's plea with respect to transatlantic relationships applies with special force to the Pacific:

> The American failure to retrench voluntarily ... may very well lead us not only to a world of blocs, which is probably inevitable, but to a world of

hostile blocs, where the prolonged disintegration of American hegemony will have embittered . . . relations for a generation. . . . Chaos and conflict normally come at precisely those moments in history when an old order is decaying but will not die, and when the forces for change are not quite strong enough to impose a new system.[69]

NOTES

1. For example, see the text of comments by Eugene Black (Foreign Correspondents Club of Japan, Tokyo, 25 November 1966), p. 4, voicing the hope that "the nations of Free Asia will not be as backward as Europe was in seeing where their national interests lie." See also idem, *Alternative in Asia* (New York: Praeger, 1968), esp. pp. 30–65; and a report on President Lyndon Johnson's 1966 Asian tour, *The Promise of a New Asia*, U.S. Department of State Publication no. 8166 (Washington: U.S. Government Printing Office, 1967).

2. This metaphor is used with respect to the EEC in Max Kohnstamm and Wolfgang Hager, eds., *A Nation Writ Large? Foreign Policy Problems before the European Community* (London: Macmillan, 1973). Carl J. Friedrich suggests that "we must broaden our concept of the nation, giving it a more general connotation than it has had in the European past. . . . Are not the men who are unifying and integrating Europe engaged in the task of 'nation-building' just as much as is Nehru or those who try to weld tribes into nations?" ("Nation-Building?" in *Nation-Building*, ed. Karl W. Deutsch and William J. Foltz [New York: Atherton, 1963], pp. 31–32).

3. Zbigniew Brzezinski, *Between Two Ages: America's Role in the Technetronic Era* (New York: Viking, 1970).

4. Henry A. Kissinger, "Central Issues of American Foreign Policy," in *Agenda for the Nation*, Kermit Gordon, ed. (Washington: Brookings Institution, 1968), p. 614.

5. W. W. Rostow, *Politics and the Stages of Growth* (Cambridge: At the University Press, 1970), p. 324.

6. Robert E. Osgood noted this in "Wars Don't Fix Foreign Policy," *Washington Post*, 25 January 1970, p. B5, an excerpt from *America and the World* (Baltimore: Johns Hopkins Press, 1970). An example of this view as expressed by the American-oriented *Japan Times* may be found in "Asia after Vietnam," an editorial analysis of a plea for a stronger Japanese regional role by Richard Nixon, *Japan Times Weekly*, 21 September 1968, p. 7. The editorial criticizes the American goal of "a regionalism on which a solid foothold can be secured for the American presence."

7. Bernard K. Gordon, *Toward Disengagement in Asia* (Englewood Cliffs: Prentice-Hall, 1969), p. 120. The ineffectuality of the ASA is discussed at length in idem, "Regional Cooperation in Southeast Asia," *Current History*, February 1965, pp. 103–108.

8. V. K. Pollard, "A.S.A. and A.S.E.A.N., 1961–67," *Asian Survey*, March 1970, p. 254.

9. Major General Suwarto, "Aspek-Aspek Pertahanan Indonesia dalam Perkembangan Dunia Sakarang" [Aspects of Indonesian defense in the present world developments], in *Landasan Idiil bagi Perdjuangan TNI-AD* [The ideological foundation for the struggle of TNI-AD], Product of the Second Indonesian Army Seminar, at the Army Command Staff School, Bandung, 25–31 August 1966, p. 45.

10. Ronald Steel, "A Spheres of Influence Policy," *Foreign Policy*, Winter 1971–1972, p. 114.

11. Ronald Steel, in "Spheres of What? An Exchange," *Foreign Policy*, Spring 1972, p. 151.

12. Steel, "Spheres of Influence Policy," p. 112.

13. Ibid., p. 114.

14. Ibid., p. 111.

15. This view is ably argued by C. P. Fitzgerald in "The Emergence of China: Internal Dynamics" (Paper delivered at the Fourteenth Annual Conference of the International Institute of Strategic Studies, Montreal, 15 September 1972), p. 11; see also idem, *China and Southeast Asia since 1945* (London: Longmans, Green, 1974), esp. pp. 92, 100.

16. James Chace, "Nixon Is Tackling a Changing World," *New York Times Magazine*, 20 February 1972, p. 7.

17. Earl C. Ravenal, "The Case for Strategic Disengagement," *Foreign Affairs*, April 1973, p. 506.

18. Earl C. Ravenal, "The Strategic Balance in Asia," *Pacific Community*, July 1972, p. 613.

19. See especially David Wightman, *Toward Economic Cooperation in Asia* (New Haven: Yale University Press, 1963), pp. 50, 112–123.

20. Donald L. Horowitz draws this distinction effectively in "Three Dimensions of Ethnic Politics," *World Politics*, January 1971, p. 233; and idem, "Multiracial Politics in the New States: Toward a Theory of Conflict," in *Issues in Comparative Politics*, R. J. Jackson and Michael Stein, eds. (New York: St. Martin's, 1971).

21. Moorfield Storey and Marcial P. Lichauco, *The Conquest of the Philippines by the United States* (New York: Putnam, 1926), p. 122.

22. *New York Times*, 2 March 1949, cited in Allen S. Whiting, *China Crosses the Yalu* (Stanford: Stanford University Press, 1968), p. 39.

23. George R. Packard cites the army charges against Lieutenant Calley in *A Crisis in Understanding* (Paper delivered at the Third Japanese-American Assembly, Shimoda, 8 June 1970), p. 28.

24. See commentary by James C. Thomson in *No More Vietnams?* Richard M. Pfeffer (New York: Harper & Row, 1968), pp. 48, 261.

25. William M. Ringle, "Inouye Calls U.S. Bully," *Honolulu Star-Bulletin*, 5 January 1973, p. 1.

26. Robert L. Heilbroner, *An Inquiry into the Human Prospect* (New York: Norton, 1974), pp. 39–43.

27. Edwin O. Reischauer, *Beyond Vietnam: The United States and Asia* (New York: Knopf, 1967), p. 56.

28. "Discussion of Senate Committee Hearings," Transcript of a panel discussion on WNDT-TV, New York City, 11 March 1968, p. 27, prepared by Radio-TV Reports, Inc.

29. Yang Lien-sheng, "The Concept of *Pao* as a Basis for Social Relations in China," in *Chinese Thought and Institutions,* ed. John K. Fairbank (Chicago: University of Chicago Press, 1957), esp. pp. 291–294, 298, 305.

30. This usage is discussed in Selig S. Harrison, "Japanese Nurse Injuries by U.S.: Nixon, Sato at Summit," *Washington Post,* 6 January 1972, p. 1.

31. Kyozō Mori, "The Shift in Nixon Diplomacy," *Sekai* (Tokyo), September 1971, pp. 22–23, and idem, "Recollections from the Future: A Vision of Japanese Diplomacy," a series of six articles in the *Asahi Shimbun* (Tokyo), January 1972; see also idem, "Two Ends of a Telescope," *Japan Quarterly,* January–March 1968, pp. 13–18.

32. Shigeyoshi Urushiyama, "Security and Mass Communication in the 1970's," *Sogo Journalism Kenkyū,* Summer 1970, p. 6.

33. The exclusion acts are cited in ibid; Richard Halloran, *Images and Realities* (Tokyo: Weatherhill, 1969), p. 58; and Hiroshi Kitamura, *Psychological Dimensions of U.S.-Japanese Relations,* Occasional Papers in International Affairs no. 28 (Cambridge: Center for International Affairs, Harvard University, August 1971), pp. 32–33.

34. *United States Foreign Economic Policy toward Japan,* Hearings Before the Subcommittee on Foreign Economic Policy of the House Committee on Foreign Affairs, 92d Cong., 2d sess., 2, 3, 4, and 8 November 1971, p. 124.

35. Hiroshi Kitamura, *Psychological Dimensions,* pp. 6, 32–33.

36. "Tensei Jingo (Voice of people)," *Asahi Shimbun,* 6 November 1970, p. 8.

37. This characterization and the date of the commission meeting in question were provided by a commission member who asked to remain anonymous. Another commission member who also asked to remain anonymous confirmed the episode and added his impression that Sato was the object of the imitation. Joseph Kraft referred obliquely to the incident in his column in the *Washington Post,* 31 August 1972, p. 21, and word-of-mouth reports also traveled widely in high places in Tokyo.

38. *Minzoku-shugi* and *kokka-shugi* are discussed in Kyozō Mori, "Two Ends of a Telescope," pp. 14–15, together with *kokumin-shugi,* a concept of nationalism as the embodiment of the popular will as distinct from the state, irrespective of racial identity. See also Lawrence Olson, *Vietnam: Notes on the Japanese Reaction,* East Asia Series, vol. 12, no. 2 (New York: American Universities Field Staff Report Service, June 1965), pp. 5–6.

39. *Sankei* (Tokyo), 25 April 1964, cited in Olson, Vietnam, p. 8.

40. Jōji Watanuki, *Contemporary Japanese Perceptions of International Society* (Honolulu: East-West Center, 1973), pt. 2:7; see also tables 31, 32, pt. 2:22; and idem, *Contemporary Japanese Perceptions of International Society,* Preliminary Report, Series A-13 (Tokyo: Sophia University, 1973), table Q-27, p. 10.

41. Jōji Watanuki, *Contemporary Japanese Perceptions,* Preliminary Report, p. 20.

42. Jōji Watanuki, *Contemporary Japanese Perceptions*, pt. 2:9; see also table 44, pt. 2:31, and table 44, p. 31.

43. *Asahi Shimbun*, 27 September 1972, p. 1.

44. Shinkichi Eto, "Japan and China—A New Stage?" *Problems of Communism*, November–December 1972, p. 5.

45. This is spelled out in Marius Jansen, *The Japanese and Sun Yat-sen* (Cambridge: Harvard University Press, 1954), esp. pp. 192-193.

46. Ibid., p. 208; see also pp. 1-6, 68-73, 204-213.

47. "Ti-hu? yu-hu?" [Friends or enemies?], in Ko-ming shih-chien yen-chiu-yuan [Research Institute of Revolutionary Practices], *Tsung-ts'ai yen-lun hsüanchi: III-cheng-chih* [Collection of speeches and essays by Generalissimo Chiang Kai-shek] (Taipei: Chung-yang kai-tsao wei-yuan-hui [Central Reconstruction Committee], 1952), p. 364. The original essay bore the pseudonym Hsü Tao-ling.

48. Ibid., p. 366.

49. Chang Hsin-hai, *America and China: A New Approach to Asia* (New York: Simon & Schuster, 1965), p. 206, offers this interpretation.

50. This apt characterization of a Japanese acceptance of second place in relations with China is found in Johan Galtung, "Japan and Future World Politics" (Paper delivered at the Conference on Modern Japan, Oxford University, 10-12 April 1973), pp. 33-35.

51. Edwin O. Reischauer, "The Sinic World in Perspective," *Foreign Affairs*, January 1974, p. 346.

52. At my request, groups conversant with foreign policy issues in general and Sino-Japanese relations in particular were assembled at Peking University, Futan University in Shanghai, and Canton Teachers College, in addition to less systematic discussion with Foreign Ministry officials, commune and factory committees, and secondary school teachers encountered during a three-week visit from June 15 to July 10, 1972. My principal account of these discussions appears in "China Notebook," *Washington Post*, 13 August 1972, p. D4.

53. Michio Rōyama, *The Asian Balance of Power: A Japanese View*, Adelphi Papers no. 42 (London: International Institute of Strategic Studies, November 1967), p. 15.

54. Kiyoshi Kojima, "Korean Unification in the Wider International Economic Context" (Paper delivered at the Sixth International Conference of the Korean Institute of International Studies, Seoul, 10-13 July 1973), p. 3.

55. Ibid., p. 4.

56. Yi Yong-hui, "Kijo nonmun: Han'guk kundaehwa ŭi kibon munje [Keynote address: Fundamental problems in the modernization of Korea]," in *Han'guk kŭndaehwa e issŏsŏ-ŭi kaltŭng kwa chohwa* [Conflict and harmony: Report of the conference on modernization], Publication no. 8 (Seoul: Korean Association of International Relations, 1969), pp. 10-15.

57. Byung Kyu Kang, "The Asian and Pacific Peace System in the 1970's," (Paper delivered at the Fourteenth Annual Conference of the International Institute of Strategic Studies, Montreal, 13 September 1972), p. 4.

58. Interview, Seoul, 21 October 1967.

59. *Sŏul Sinmun*, 16 January 1965, p. 2; see also "Kim Chong-p'il Meets the Students" (Text of questions and answers at a discussion sponsored by the Political Science Association, Seoul National University), in *Chŏson Ilbo*, 6 November 1963, pp. 4–5; and Kim Chong-p'il, "Korea's Modernization," *Chosŏn Ilbo* (Seoul), 10 November 1963, p. 5.

60. Daisaku Ikeda, "A Proposal on the China Issue" (Address presented at the Eleventh General Meeting of the Student Division, Soka Gakkai, Tokyo, 8 September 1968), in *Sōkagakkai* (Tokyo), September 1968, p. 19.

61. See Lee Kuan Yew, "Prime Minister's Address to the American Association" (Singapore, 10 November 1967), p. 8; and "Transcript of a Television Interview with the Prime Minister by Four Foreign Correspondents," Television Singapura, 5 November 1967, pp. K–L.

62. George Orwell, *1984* (New York: New American Library, 1949), esp. pp. 152–153.

63. Ernest H. Preeg suggests these circumstances in *Economic Blocs and U.S. Foreign Policy*, Report no. 135 (Washington: National Planning Association, January 1974), p. 128.

64. This exchange occurred during a panel discussion entitled "Asia Looks at Vietnam" at the Association for Asian Studies Convention in Philadelphia, March 23, 1968. The discussion was taped by J.W. Alverson and was transcribed by Selig S. Harrison at the convention and again, in 1973, with the assistance of Patricia Loui at the East-West Center in Honolulu.

65. The Japanese effort to exclude India is discussed in "Indo-Japanese Relations," *Asahi Evening News* (Tokyo), 23 June 1969, p. 4; see also the transcript of a press conference by Foreign Minister Kiichi Aichi with Indian journalists accompanying Prime Minister Indira Gandhi to Japan, Tokyo, Foreign Ministry of Japan, 27 June 1969, esp. pp. 5–6; and Tarō Senba, "Why Does Japan Try to Shut India Out of Asia," *Daily Yomiuri* (Tokyo), 18 April 1970, p. 5. A perceptive analysis of the overall record of Indo-Japanese relations may be found in K. V. Narain, "Lapses in Indo-Japanese Relations," *The Hindu* (Madras), 15 April 1967, p. 1.

66. "Address by H. E. Prime Minister Eisaku Sato at the opening Session of the Fourth Ministerial meeting of A.S.P.A.C.," (Ito) 9 June 1969, p. 4.

67. This is argued by David P. Calleo and Benjamin Rowland in *America and the World Political Economy* (Bloomington: Indiana University Press, 1973), esp. pp. 258–259.

68. Robert Tucker, "The National Interests of the United States" (Address presented at the Pacem in Terris Convocation sponsored by the Center for the Study of Democratic Institutions, Washington, 10 September 1973), pp. 10–11.

69. David P. Calleo, "The Dollar's Political Problems," *New York Times*, 6 July 1973, p. 23.

Bibliography

NATIONALISM IN ASIA

Books

General

Deutsch, Karl W. *Nationalism and Social Communication.* 2d ed. Cambridge: M.I.T. Press, 1966.

Emerson, Rupert. *From Empire to Nation.* Cambridge: Harvard University Press, 1960.

Harrison, Selig S. *The Most Dangerous Decades: An Introduction to the Comparative Study of Language Policy in Multilingual States.* New York: Columbia University, 1957.

Hay, Stephen N. *Asian Ideas of East and West: Tagore and His Critics in Japan, China, and India.* Cambridge: Harvard University Press, 1970.

Isaacs, Harold R. *Idols of the Tribe.* New York: Harper and Row, 1975.

——. *No Peace for Asia.* Cambridge: M.I.T. Press, 1967.

Kautsky, John H., ed. *Political Change in Underdeveloped Countries: Nationalism and Communism.* New York: John Wiley & Sons, 1962.

Tagore, Rabindranath. *Nationalism.* New York: Macmillan Co., 1917.

South Asia

Binder, Leonard. *Religion and Politics in Pakistan.* Berkeley: University of California Press, 1961.

Brecher, Michael. *Nehru: A Political Biography.* London: Oxford University Press, 1959.

Gankovsky, Y.V. *Narodny Pakistan* (The peoples of Pakistan). Moscow: Nauka Publishing House, 1964.

Harrison, Selig S. *India: The Most Dangerous Decades.* Princeton: Princeton University Press, 1960.

Jahan, Rounaq. *Pakistan: Failure in National Integration.* New York: Columbia University Press, 1972.

Kautsky, John H. *Moscow and the Communist Party of India.* Cambridge, Mass.: Technology Press; New York: John Wiley & Sons, 1956.

Wriggins, W. Howard. *Ceylon: Dilemmas of a New Nation.* Princeton: Princeton University Press, 1960.

Southeast Asia

Buttinger, Joseph. *The Smaller Dragon: A Political History of Vietnam.* New York: Praeger, 1958.

——. *Vietnam: A Dragon Embattled.* 2 vols. New York: Praeger, 1967.

Dan, Phan Quang. *Volonté vietnamienne* (The will of Vietnam). Dornach, Switzerland: Hutter & Co., 1951.

Dao, Hoang Van. *Vietnam Quoc Dan Dang, 1927–54.* Saigon: Khai-Tri Book Store, 1970.

Doktrin Perdjuangan Tentara Nasional Indonesia/Angkatan Daurat: "Tri Ubaya Cakti" (The struggle doctrine of the Indonesian Armed Forces/Army: "The three-pronged power") Report of the Second Army Seminar, 25–31 August 1966, at the SESKOAD (Army Command Staff School), Bandung. Limited circulation.

Du, Nguyen. *Kim Van Kieu.* Translated by Le Xuan Thuy. 2d ed. Saigon: Khai-tri, 1965.

Geertz, Clifford. *The Religion of Java.* New York: Free Press, 1960.

Jay, Robert R. *Religion and Politics in Rural Central Java.* New Haven: Yale University Press, 1965.

Kebangkitan Semangat '66: Mendjeladjah Tracee Bara (Emergence of 1966 spirit in exploring new course). Symposium sponsored by the University of Indonesia, Bandung, May 1966. Jakarta: University of Indonesia Publication Institute, 1966.

Kerkvliet, Benedict. "Peasant Rebellion in the Philippines: The Origins and Growth of the H.M.B." Ph.D. dissertation, University of Wisconsin, 1972.

Mus, Paul. *Vietnam: Sociologie d'une guerre* (Vietnam: sociology of a war). Paris: Editions du Seuil, 1952.

Pomeroy, William J. *Guerrilla Warfare: Liberation and Suppression in the Present Period.* New York: International Publishers, 1964.

Pye, Lucian W. *Politics, Personality and Nation-Building: Burma's Search for Identity.* New Haven: Yale University Press, 1962.

Race, Jeffrey. *War Comes to Long An: Revolutionary Conflict in a Vietnamese Province.* Berkeley: University of California Press, 1972.

Sacks, I. Milton. "Communism and Nationalism in Vietnam: 1918–1946." Ph.D. dissertation, Yale University, 1960.

Steinberg, David J. *Philippine Collaboration in World War II.* Ann Arbor: University of Michigan Press, 1967.

Trai, Tang Thi Thanh. "American Policy and the Vietnamese Revolution from 1940 to 1963." Ph.D. dissertation, University of Chicago, 1967.

Weinstein, Franklin B. *Indonesian Foreign Policy and the Dilemma of Dependence.* Ithaca: Cornell University Press, 1976.

Northeast Asia

Doi, Takeo. *Amae no Kōzō* (The structure of amae). Tokyo: Kobundo, 1971. For an adaptation of this work in English see Doi, Takeo. *The Anatomy of Dependence.* Translated by John Bester. Tokyo: Kodansha International, 1973.

Fitzgerald, C. P. *The Chinese View of Their Place in the World.* London: Oxford University Press, 1964.

Henderson, Gregory. *Korea: The Politics of the Vortex.* Cambridge: Harvard University Press, 1968.

Hsu, Francis L. K. *Iemoto: The Heart of Japan.* Cambridge, Mass.: Schenkman Publishing Co., 1973.

Israel, John. *Student Nationalism in China, 1927–1937.* Stanford: Hoover Institution Press, 1966.

Jansen, Marius. *The Japanese and Sun Yat-sen.* Cambridge: Harvard University Press, 1954.

Johnson, Chalmers. *Peasant Nationalism and Communist Power.* Stanford: Stanford University Press, 1962.

Kataoka, Tetsuya. *Resistance and Revolution in China.* Berkeley: University of California Press, 1974.

Lee Chong-sik. *The Politics of Korean Nationalism.* Berkeley: University of California Press, 1963.

Levenson, Joseph R. *Liang Ch'i-ch'ao and the Mind of Modern China.* Cambridge: Harvard University Press, 1953.

Nakane, Chie. *Japanese Society.* London: Weidenfeld and Nicolson, 1970.

Scalapino, Robert A. *The Japanese Communist Movement, 1920–1966.* Berkeley: University of California Press, 1967.

Scalapino, Robert A., and Lee Chong-sik. *Communism in Korea.* Berkeley: University of California Press, 1972.

Selden, Mark. *The Yenan Way in Revolutionary China.* Cambridge: Harvard University Press, 1973.

Self-Reliance and the Building of an Independent Economy. Pyongyang: Foreign Languages Publishing House, 1965.

Suh, Dae-sook. *The Korean Communist Movement, 1918–1948.* Princeton: Princeton University Press, 1967.

Teng, S. Y., and Fairbank, John K. *China's Response to the West.* Cambridge: Harvard University Press, 1954.

Van Slyke, Lyman. *Enemies and Friends: The United Front in Chinese Communist History.* Stanford: Stanford: Stanford University Press, 1967.

Articles, Papers, and Documents

Berlin, Isaiah. "The Bent Twig: A Note on Nationalism." *Foreign Affairs,* October 1972.

Congress for Cultural Freedom. *Han'gug in kwa sahoe chŏngŭi* (Koreans and social justice). Report no. 29 in a series of roundtable discussions sponsored by the South Korean branch of the congress. Seoul, 12 April 1967.

Emerson, Rupert. "Post-Independence Nationalism in South and Southeast Asia: A Reconsideration." *Pacific Affairs*, Summer 1971.

Harrison, Selig S. "Nehru's Plan for Peace." *New Republic*, 19 June 1971.

Hoan, Nguyen Ton. "Le Dai-Viet Quoc-Dan Dang et son idéologie." Paris, 1963. Mimeographed.

Huy, Nguyen Ngoc (Hung Nguyen). "Chu-Nghia Dan-Toc Sinh-Ton" (Doctrine of national survival). Saigon, 1964. Mimeographed.

Kim Chi-ha. "The Five Thieves." In Shibuya, Sentaro, ed. *Nagai Karayamai no Kanata ni* [Beyond the long night of hatred]. Tokyo: Chūō Kōron-sha. December 1971.

Kim Dae-jung. "My Role in the 1970s." Address to the Seoul Correspondents Club. Seoul, 12 May 1970.

Korean Association of International Relations. *Han'guk kǔndaehwa e issǒsǒ-ǔi kaltǔng kwa chohwa* (Conflict and harmony). Report of Conference on Modernization, 20 April 1968. Publication no. 8. Seoul, 1969.

Korea University Student Government. "Declaration on the Contemporary Situation of Korea." Issued with the approval of the Contemporary Conference on the "New Order of Korea and Asia." Seoul, 29 September 1970. Limited circulation.

Lambert, Richard D. "Comment: Comparativists and Uniquists." In *Approaches to Asian Civilizations*. Edited by William de Bary and Ainslee Embree. New York: Columbia University Press, 1964.

Levy, Marion J. "Contrasting Factors in the Modernization of China and Japan." In *Economic Growth: Brazil, India, Japan*. Edited by Simon Kuznets, W. E. Moore, and J.J. Spengler. Durham: Duke University Press, 1955.

———. "Some Social Obstacles to 'Capital Formation' in Underdeveloped Areas." In *Capital Formation and Economic Growth*. Edited by National Bureau Committee for Economic Research. Princeton: Princeton University Press, 1955.

McAlister, John T., Jr. "Mountain Minorities and the Viet Minh: A Key to the Indochina War." In *Southeast Asian Tribes, Minorities, and Nations*. 2 vols. Edited by Peter Kunstadter. Princeton: Princeton University Press, 1967.

Nagai, Michio. "Westernization and Japanization." In *Tradition and Modernization in Japanese Culture*. Edited by Donald Shively. Princeton: Princeton University Press, 1971.

Persatuan Islam Sa-tanahmelayu Islamic Party. "Our Stand." Kuala Lumpur, April 1965.

"Ti-hu? Yu-hu?" [Friends or enemies?]. In *Tsung-ts'ai yen-lun hsüan-chi: III-cheng-chih* (Collection of speeches and essays by Generalissimo Chiang Kai-shek). Edited by Ko-ming shih-chien yen-chiu-yuan (Research institute of revolutionary practices). Taipei: Chung-yang kai-tsao wei-yuan-hui (Central reconstruction committee), 1952.

U.S. Department of State. "Nationalist Politics in Vietnam." Prepared by the Senior Liaison Office, U.S. Embassy. Saigon, May 1968. Limited circulation.

U.S. Department of State. "Political Alignments of Vietnamese Nationalists." Office of Intelligence Research, OIR Report no. 3708. Washington: Department of State, 1 October 1949. Mimeographed.

NATIONALISM AND DEVELOPMENT

Books

Bhagwati, Jagdish N., and Desai, Padma. *India: Planning for Industrialization.* Organization of Economic Cooperation and Development. London: Oxford University Press, 1970.

Farizov, I. O. *Sovietsko-Indoneziiskoe ekonomicheskoe sotrudnichestvo* (Soviet-Indonesian economic cooperation). Moscow: Nauka Publishing House, 1964.

Frankel, Francine R. *India's Green Revolution: Economic Gains and Political Costs.* Princeton: Princeton University Press, 1971.

Golay, Frank H., Anspach, Ralph, Pfanner, M. Ruth, and Ayal, E. B. *Underdevelopment and Economic Nationalism in Southeast Asia.* Ithaca: Cornell University Press, 1969.

Hazari, R. K. *The Structure of the Corporate Private Sector.* Bombay: Asia Publishing House, 1968.

Hoshii, Iwao. *The Dynamics of Japan's Business Evolution.* Tokyo and Philadelphia: Orient/West, 1964.

International Legal Center. *Law and Public Enterprise in Asia.* New York: Praeger, 1976.

Kidron, Michael. *Foreign Investment in India.* London: Oxford University Press, 1965.

Kust, Matthew J. *Taxation for Economic Development: A Study within the Constitutional and Institutional Framework of India.* Center for International Legal Studies. Cambridge: Harvard Law School, 1956.

Lockwood, William W. *The State and Economic Enterprise in Japan.* Princeton: Princeton University Press, 1965.

Raj, K. N. *India, Pakistan and China.* Bombay: Allied Publishers, 1967.

Tanzer, Michael. *The Political Economy of International Oil and the Underdeveloped Countries.* Boston: Beacon Press, 1969.

Vernon, Raymond. *Sovereignty at Bay.* New York: Basic Books, 1971.

Wightman, David. *Toward Economic Cooperation in Asia.* Carnegie Endowment for International Peace. New Haven: Yale University Press, 1963.

Articles, Papers, and Documents

Araneta, Salvador. *Economic Nationalism and Capitalism for All in a Directed Economy.* Rizal: Araneta University Press, 1965.

Araneta University Research Foundation. *Constitutional Reforms on Socio-Economic Policies.* Background Studies, no. 6. Prepared for the 1971 Constitutional Convention. Manila, 14 December 1971.

Chŏnggyŏng yŏn'gu (Political and economic research), Seoul. Special issues on "Monopoly and the Social Economy" (November 1966) and "Plutocracy in Our Growth" (October 1967).

Institute of Economic Studies and Social Action. *The Challenge of Communist China and the Example of Japan.* Report no. 17. Rizal: Araneta University, June 1966.

Intergovernmental Committee on Establishment of an Asian Reserve Bank. "Feasibility Study on the Establishment of an Asian Reserve Bank: A Summary." ECAFE Report, Trade/TLP/ARB/(1). Bangkok: 27 June 1972.

Japan Economic Research Center. *Japan's Economy in 1980 in the Global Context.* Tokyo, March 1972.

Japan, Foreign Ministry. *Indonesia Keizai Kyoryoku Chōsadan Chosa Hokoku* (Investigation report of the economic cooperation investigation team to Indonesia). Tokyo, 1969.

Krueger, Anne O. "Import Substitution in India: A Case Study." Prepared for the Agency for International Development. New Delhi, July 1970.

Lewis, John P. *Wanted in India: A Relevant Radicalism.* Center of International Studies, Policy Memorandum no. 36. Princeton: Princeton University, December 1969.

Lichauco, Alejandro. *Nationalism, Economic Development, and Social Justice.* Manila: Economic Society of the Ateneo de Manila, January 1967.

Lie Tek-tjeng and Teigo, Yoshida. *Some Remarks on the Problems and Difficulties Besetting Present-Day Indonesian-Japanese Relations.* Bagian Asia Timur, no. IX/11. Jakarta: Lembaga Research Kebudajaan Nasional, 13 March 1968.

Morinaga, Teiichirō. *Asia Toyushi Chōsadan Chūkan Hōkoku* (Interim report by the survey mission on investment and financing in Asia). Tokyo: Asia Toyushi Chosadan, April 1971.

Pearl, Allan R. *Liberalization of Capital in Japan.* Studies in Japanese Law, no. 1. Cambridge: Harvard Law School, 1974.

Prawiranegara, Sjafruddin. *Membangun Kembali Ekonomi Indonesia* (Economic rehabilitation of Indonesia). Jakarta, 1947.

Reid, Escott. *The Future of the World Bank.* Washington: International Bank for Reconstruction and Development, September 1965.

Salim, Emil. *Aid and Development.* Jakarta: Bappenas, 3 February 1971.

———. *Oil and Indonesian Development.* Jakarta: Bappenas, 3 February 1971.

Samuelson, Paul A. *International Trade for a Rich Country.* Stockholm: Federation of Swedish Industries, 1972.

Tanaka, A. *Yen Keizaiken Kōsō ni Tsuite* (About the yen economy bloc scheme). Tokyo: Sanwa Bank, 14 June 1973.

U.S. Department of State. *The Impact of Economic Nationalism on Key Mineral Resource Industries.* Report of a conference sponsored by the Bureau of Intelligence and Research, Washington, 17 December 1971. Washington, 1972.

Yatsugi, Kazuo. "Nikkan Chōki Keizai Kyōryoku Shian" (Long-range economic cooperation between Japan and Korea). Tokyo, April 1970. Limited circulation.

NATIONALISM AND AMERICAN POLICY

Books

Asahi Shimbun Staff. *The Pacific Rivals.* New York and Tokyo: Weatherhill/Asahi, 1971.

Barnds, William. *India, Pakistan and the Great Powers.* New York: McGraw-Hill, 1967.

Bhutto, Zulfikar Ali. *The Myth of Independence.* London: Oxford University Press, 1969.

Bowles, Chester. *Promises to Keep.* New York: Harper & Row, 1971.

Calleo, David P., and Rowland, Benjamin. *America and the World Political Economy.* Bloomington: Indiana University Press, 1973.

Ch'a Chi-ch'ŏl. *Uriga sewŏyahal chwap'yo* (The coordinates that we must build). Seoul: Pŏmmunsa Publishers, 1966.

Chang Hsin-hai. *America and China: A New Approach to Asia.* New York: Simon and Schuster, 1965.

Cho Soon-sung. *Korea in World Politics, 1940-1950: An Evaluation of American Responsibility.* Berkely: University of California Press, 1967.

Constantine, Renato, ed. *The Recto Reader: Excerpts from the Speeches of Claro M. Recto.* Manila: Recto Memorial Foundation, 1965.

Golay, Frank H., ed. *The United States and the Philippines.* American Assembly. Englewood Cliffs, N.J.: Prentice-Hall, 1966.

Gould, James W. *The United States and Malaysia.* Cambridge: Harvard University Press, 1969.

Ikeda, Daisaku. *A Proposal on the China Issue.* Tokyo: Sōka Gakkai, September 1968.

Isaacs, Harold R. *Scratches on Our Minds.* New York: John Day and Co., 1958.

Jukes, Geoffrey. *The Soviet Union in Asia.* Berkeley: University of California Press, 1973.

Kaihara, Osamu. *Senshi ni Manabu* (To learn from the history of wars). Tokyo: Asagumo Shimbun-sha, 1970.

Kasetsiri, Chanwit, Samutuanit, Chaisiri, Boonsue, Pridi, and Yova, Suthichai. *Khmer Kub Songkram Indochina* (Cambodia and the Indochina war). Bangkok: Pikanes Press, August 1973.

Kim Sam-gyu. *Konnichi no Chōsen* (Korea today). Tokyo: Kawade Shobō, 1956.

———. *Modern History of Korea.* Tokyo: Chikuma Shobō, 1963.

Ko Chŏng-hun. *Kun* (The army). Seoul: Tongbang Sŏwŏn, 1967.

Luan, Cao Van. *Ben Giong Lich Su* (Beside the stream of history). Saigon: Tri Dung, 1972.

Makoto, Oda. *Gimu to Shite no Tabi* (My trip as a duty). Tokyo: Iwanami Shoten, 1967.

Matsutani, Makoto. *Betonamu Sensō no Hansei* (Reflections on the war in Vietnam). Supp. and rev. ed. Reading Material 72EO, Foreign-3. Tokyo: Bōei Kenshujo (National Defense College), 1972.

Mitchell, Edward J. "Land Tenure and Rebellion: A Statistical Analysis of Factors Affecting Government Control in South Vietnam." Rand Corporation, Memorandum no. RM-5181-ARPA (abridged). Santa Monica, June 1967.

Mushakoji, Kinhide. *Kokusaiseiji to Nihon* (International politics and Japan). Tokyo: University of Tokyo Publishing Association, 1967.

Olson, Lawrence. "Vietnam: Notes on the Japanese Reaction." American Universities Field Staff Reports, East Asia Series 12:2. New York, June 1965.

Osgood, Robert E. *The Weary and the Wary.* Baltimore: Johns Hopkins University Press, 1972.

Palmer, Norman D. *South Asia and United States Policy.* Boston: Houghton Mifflin Co., 1966.

Park Chung Hee. *The Country, the Revolution and I.* Translated by Leon Sinder. Seoul: Ministry of Information and Broadcasting, 1967.

The Pentagon Papers. Senator Gravel Edition. Boston: Beacon Press, 1971.

Quester, George H. *The Politics of Nuclear Proliferation.* Baltimore: Johns Hopkins University Press, 1973.

Reischauer, Edwin O. *Beyond Vietnam: The United States and Asia.* New York: Alfred A. Knopf, 1967.

Russett, Bruce. *No Clear and Present Danger.* New York: Harper & Row, 1972.

South Korea, Taehan Minguk Kuk-hoe (National assembly). *T'ongil paeksŏ* (White paper on unification). Including proceedings of the Special Committee on National Unification. Seoul, 1967.

Taylor, George E. *The Philippines and the United States: Problems of Partnership.* Council on Foreign Relations. New York: Praeger, 1964.

Thi, Nguyen Chanh. *Vietnam Tu-Do: Di Ve Dau?* (What future for free Vietnam?). Saigon, 1964.

Tsou, Tang. *America's Failure in China, 1941-1950.* Chicago: University of Chicago Press, 1963.

Weinstein, Martin E. *Japan's Postwar Defense Policy, 1947-1968.* New York: Columbia University Press, 1971.

Williams, Shelton L. *The U.S., India and the Bomb.* Studies in International Affairs, no. 12. Baltimore: Johns Hopkins University Press, 1969.

Yosaji, Kobayashi, ed. *1970: An Approach to Revisions of the Security Treaty.* International Policy Research Council. Tokyo: Yomiuri Publishing Co., 1966.

Articles, Papers, and Documents

Abramowitz, Morton. *Moving the Glacier: The Two Koreas and the Powers.* Adelphi Papers, no. 80. London: International Institute for Strategic Studies, 1971.

Araya, Preecha. "Nayobai Tang Pratesh: Tai Din Rue Bon Din" (Thai foreign policy: Illusion or deception?). *Social Science Review*, Bangkok, June 1972.

Atthakor, Bunchana. *Bun Toek Toot Thai* (Memoirs of a Thai ambassador). Bangkok: Ak-sorn-sum-pun, 1971.

Barnds, William. "Arms Race or Arms Control in the Indian Ocean?" *America.* 14 October 1972.

Chi, Hoang Van. "Why No Peace in Vietnam." In *Vietnam Seen from East and West.* Edited by S. N. Ray. New York: Praeger, 1966.

Cunningham, William J. *Arms Control in Northeast Asia.* Senior Seminar in Foreign Policy, 1971-72, 14th session, Department of State. May 1972.

Fall, Bernard B. "Sociological and Psychological Aspects of Vietnam's Partition." *Journal of World Affairs,* no. 2, 1964.

Hao, Tran Van. "Nhung Ao Tuong Cua Dan Anh" (The illusions of the older generation). *Sinh Vien* (Student), organ of the Saigon University Student Union, 1 August 1967.

Harrison, Selig S. "America, India and Pakistan: A Chance for A Fresh Start." *Harper's,* July 1966.

Japan, Foreign Ministry. *Views on the Theory of Emergency Deployment.* Tokyo, 20 April 1966.

Kasetsiri, Chanwit. "Lamdub Hetkarn Songkram Vietnam" (Vietnam war chronology). *Social Science Review,* supp. no. 4, Bangkok, January 1971.

Khoman, Thanat. "Punha Tahan Tang Doa Ni Pratesh Thai Lae Nayobai Tang Pratesh Kong Thai" (The problem of foreign troops in Thailand and Thai foreign policy). *Social Science Review,* Bangkok, May 1973.

Kintner, W. R. "Arms Control for a Five-Power World." Address to the Fifth International Arms Control Symposium, Philadelphia, October 1971.

Kitamura, Hiroshi. *Psychological Dimensions of U.S.-Japanese Relations.* Occasional Papers in International Affairs, no. 28. Cambridge: Harvard University, August 1971.

Korean Association of International Relations. *Han'guk ŭi minjokchuŭi* (Korean nationalism). Report of a seminar sponsored by the Association. Seoul, 1967.

Maeda, Hisashi. *Arms Control for East Asia.* Institute of International Relations, Research Papers, series A-2. Tokyo: Sophia University, June 1970.

Makino, Chikara. "Japan-U.S. Relations: Analysis of the Present Situation and Experimental Discussions on Future Prospects." *Tsusan Journal* 3-5, Tokyo, 1970.

Nakasone, Yasuhiro. "International Environment and Defense of Japan in the 1970s." Address to the Harvard Club of Japan, Tokyo, June 1970.

Oka, Takashi. "Buddhism as a Political Force." Tokyo: Institute of Current World Affairs, July 1966. Mimeographed.

Pak Chun-gyu. "Han'guk, miguk, ilbon" (Korea, the U.S., and Japan). *Sasanggye* 102, Seoul, December 1961.

Sapanodowe Student Club, Thammasat University. *Pai Kao* (White danger). Bangkok, January 1972.

Sekino, Hideo. "U.S.-Japan Military Relations at a Turning Point." *Kokusai Mondai,* organ of the Japan Institute of International Affairs, Tokyo: November 1971.

Shafie, Ghazali Bin. "Southeast Asia in the Seventies." Address to the Singapore Institute of International Affairs, December 1968.

Soedjatmoko. "Indonesia and the World." Dyason Memorial Lectures II, Canberra, 1967.

Trung, Nguyen Van. "Nhan Dinh va Tim Hieu Thoi Cuoc Hieu Tai a Mien Nam Vietnam" (Researches and views on the present situation in South Vietnam). *Tim Hieu* (Research), Faculty of Saigon University, 1 November 1964.

Vapi, Thao. "Jokingly Speaking in the Lao Manner." *Mittasone*, Vientiane, July- September 1967.

Williams, Shelton L. *Nuclear Proliferation in International Politics: The Japanese Case*. Monograph Series in World Affairs 9:3. Denver: University of Denver, 1972.

Index

Abdul Rahman, Tungku, 52, 190, 191
Abramowitz, Morton, 363
Acheson, Dean, 266
Aden, 374
Afghanistan, 271
Aggression from the North: The Record of North Vietnam's Campaign to Conquer South Vietnam (U.S. Department of State), 114-115
Agriculture, 316-318, 395, 410
  fertilizer industry, 327, 331-334, 396-397, 410
Agro-business, 410
Aichi, Kiichi, 164-165, 347
Aidit, D. N., 58
American International Corporation, 330
Andhra, 50, 51, 52, 61
Anh, Truong Tu, 94
Annam, 15, 112
Antiballistic missile (ABM) systems, 284, 288-289, 302
Anti-Fascist People's Freedom League (AFPFL), 54
Aquino, Benigno, 340
Arms control, 286-290, 382, 387-389
Army of the Republic of Vietnam (ARVN), 118-120
Asian Development Bank, 397, 400, 408
Association of Southeast Asia (ASA), 423
Association of Southeast Asian Nations (ASEAN), 423-424, 441
Atomic Energy Commission (AEC), 287
Ayub Khan, 28, 270, 323, 324
Aung San, 54

Baghdad Pact, 263
Bagong Hukbo Ng Bayan (New People's Army), Philippines, 62
Balance of payments issue, 283, 318, 319, 411
Balance of power concepts, 253-256, 362-372, 424, 426-427
Baldwin, Hanson, 267
Balkanization, 4, 12

Bangladesh, 11, 12, 14, 28, 33, 261, 267, 268, 275-276, 313, 443
Bao Dai, Emperor, 15, 96, 97, 99, 101, 105, 116
Bases, U.S., 278-279, 289, 299-303, 372-383, 424
Bechtel Corporation, 332-333
Belden, Jack, 75
Ben-Dasan, Isaiah, 23
Bengal, 50, 51, 52, 261
Beplat, Tristan, 431-432
Berlin, Isaiah, 24
Bharat Heavy Electricals, 337
Bhutto, Zulfiqar Ali, 27, 261, 273, 324
Binh, Nguyen, 97, 98
Bipolar imagery, 254
Birla, G. D., 325
Black, Eugene, 336
Blechman, Barry, 374
Bloodworth, Dennis, 181
Boggs, Hale, 371
Bohlen, Charles, 365
Bokaro steel plant, India, 335, 336
Bowles, Chester, 265, 266, 271, 272
Brandt, Willy, 223, 224
Brown, Lester, 410
Brown, Seyom, 255
Brown, Winthrop G., 185
Brzezinski, Zbigniew, 3, 295, 370
Buddhism, 53, 105-107
Bunchana Atthakor, 194, 340-341
Burma, 384, 408
  communism in, 46, 54-55
  economy, 30
  subnational identities, 11, 12
  public enterprise, 322
Burma-Shell, 328, 330
Buttinger, Joseph, 99, 123
Byroade, Henry, 266

C-5A transport planes, 376-378
C-141 transport planes, 376-377
Callard, Keith, 272
Calleo, David, 444

Calley, William, 429
Caltex Petroleum Corporation, 328, 402
Cam Ranh Bay, Vietnam, 88, 116-117
Cambodia, 188
  communism in, 55
  public enterprise, 320
  on U.S. in Vietnam, 189-190, 197-198
Cao Dai sect, 107
Caroe, Sir Olaf, 263-264, 266, 267
Carter, Jimmy, 380
Catholicism, 105-107
Caudill, Mieko Imagi, 279
Caudill, William L., 23, 279
Central Intelligence Agency (CIA), 103
Ceylon, 55, 443
Cha Il, 241
Chace, James, 426
Chang, John, 211
Chang Do Young, 216
Chang Keun-kim, 189
Charter of Algiers (1967), 408
Chau, Phan Boi, 95
Chi, Hoang Van, 98-99, 122
Chiang Kai-shek, 69-72, 80, 259, 435
Chieu, Pham Xuan, 103
Childs, Marquis, 185
China: see People's Republic of China; Taiwan
Chinese Exclusion Act of 1882, 428
Chinese Soviet Republic, Kiangsi, 71, 73
Chinh, Truong, 92
Chiniotis, 324
Cho Chung-hun, 185
Cho Pong-am, 210
Cho Soon-sung, 144, 237
Cho Yun-hyong, 225
Choe Mun-whan, 225
Choik Suk-chae, 189
Chondogyo (Teaching of the Way of Heaven) movement, Korea, 132, 134
Chou En-lai, 273, 371, 434
Chu Nom script, 15
Chung Il-kwon, 215
Civil service
  in North Korea, 137
  in Vietnam, 102-104, 111
Clay, Lucius D., 336
Clifford, Clark M., 120
Club of Rome, 27
Cochin China, 15, 16, 98, 101, 111-114
Cockburn Sound naval base, Australia, 376
Cole, David, 225
Collaboration, 100-104
Colombo Plan, 27
Colonialism, 6, 8, 9
Comintern, 54, 134
Commerce, U.S. Department of, 345
Communism
  in Burma, 46, 54-55
  in Cambodia, 55
  in China, 47, 61, 69-84, 89, 90, 121
  in India, 46, 48-51, 61
  in Indonesia, 46, 56-60
  in Japan, 63-65
  in Malaysia, 52-53
  in North Korea, 132, 136-150
  in Philippines, 61-63
  in South Korea, 135, 148-150

  in Thailand, 53-54
  in Vietnam, 47, 61, 87-89, 108-109, 114-124, 149-151
Comparative advantage concept, 312, 313
Confucianism, 80, 431
Coproduction ventures, 405, 407
Corruption, 28, 29, 321-322
Council for Mutual Economic Assistance (COMECON), 145
Cuba, 329
  missile crisis, 147
Cultural Revolution, China, 32, 83

Dai Viet (Greater Vietnam) party, 88, 93-94, 103, 106, 122
Dan, Phan Quang, 102-103
Dao Duy Anh, 90, 91
d'Argenlieu, Thierry, 98
December 9 movement, China, 71
Diego Garcia, 379, 380
Diem, Ngo Dinh, 88, 100-106, 109, 116-117, 176, 180
Dien Bien Phu, battle of, 104, 116, 267
Doan Quoc Sy, 110
Doba, Hajime, 294
Dong, Pham Van, 114, 150
Dravidian movement, 61
Dual societies, 409, 413
Duan, Le, 114
Dulles, John Foster, 74-75, 181, 266, 267, 280
Dutt, D. Som, 374

East Germany, 150, 223
East Pakistan: see Pakistan
ECAFE, 327, 342, 347, 408
Economy, 26-31
  in Burma, 30
  in China, 30, 80
  foreign investment, 312-319, 332-334, 395, 398-401, 404, 409
  in India, 315, 324-338
  in Indonesia, 396-397, 398, 400-403
  in Japan, 30, 162-163, 277-278, 338-350, 431-432
  multinational corporations, 5, 311, 312, 314, 318, 345, 399, 405-406
  in North Korea, 31, 145-147, 232-234
  in Pakistan, 27
  in Philippines, 315-317
  public enterprise, 315, 319-327, 329-332, 335-337, 395-404, 408, 410-411
  in South Korea, 31, 224-227, 323
  in Thailand, 30
  in Vietnam, 322-323
Eisenhower, Dwight D., 241, 429
Energy crisis, 314
Erikson, Erik H., 20-21
ESCAP, 427
Esso, 328
Eto, Shinkichi, 434, 435
European Atomic Energy Commission (Euratom), 286
European Economic Community (EEC), 347, 349, 350
European nationalism, 4, 5, 11, 12
Ewell, Raymond, 333, 334

Export credits, 342, 343, 412
Export-Import Bank, 396, 407

Fabianism, 325
Fairbank, John, 6, 430
Fall, Bernard B., 25
Fast deployment logistics (FDL) ships, 377, 378
Feith, Herbert, 58, 321
Fertilizer Corporation of India, 334
Fertilizer industry, 327, 331-334, 396-397, 410
Fitzgerald, C. P., 75, 79
FitzGerald, Frances, 114
Floating exchange rates, 312
Ford, Gerald, 371
Foreign investment, 312-319, 332-334, 395, 398-401, 404, 409-411
Fortress America psychology, 444
Forward-based systems (FBS), 289, 375-379, 382
Fosdick, Raymond B., 74
France, in Vietnam, 16, 93, 95, 97-103, 106, 111, 115, 116, 123-124
Free trade policy, 312
Freeport Sulphur Company, 400-401
Freud, Sigmund, 20
Friedheim, Jerry, 289-292
Fromm, Erich, 20
Fukushi, Jiro, 349
Galbraith, John Kenneth, 336, 337
Gandhi, Indira, 28-29, 176-179
Gandhi, Mahatma, 51
Garst, Jonathan, 333
Ghazali Bin Shafie, 191
Ghosh, J. C., 335
Ghosh, Sudhir, 336
Gia Long, Emperor, 15, 192
Giap, Vo Nguyen, 91
Giau, Tran Van, 97
Gillin, Donald G., 76-77
Glazer, Herbert, 280
Golay, Frank, 316
Gould, James, 190
Green revolution, 27
Gresik cement plant, Indonesia, 396, 397
Group identity, 20-25
Guam, 375-378
Gullion, Edmund A., 102

Ha Long Bay, Vietnam, 124
Habib, Philip, 442-443
Hahm Pyong-choon, 241
Halle, Louis, 259
Hammer, Ellen, 109
Harkins, Paul D., 118
Hatta, Mohammed, 56-59
Hawaii, 375, 376
Heilbroner, Robert, 430
Henderson, Gregory, 186, 238
Hindley, Donald, 60
Hindus, 13, 261-263, 268
Hindustan Antibiotics, 337
Hindustan Machine Tools, 337
Hirasawa, Kazushige, 280
Hiroshima, 428, 429, 431
Hirschman, Albert O., 400
Ho Chi Minh, 47, 90, 91, 93, 95-99, 101, 105, 109, 123

Ho Kai, 137
Hoa Hao sect, 107
Hoan, Nguyen Ton, 103
Hoc, Nguyen Thai, 93
Hodge, John R., 239
Hoffmann, Paul, 266
Hsu, Francis L., 22, 23
Hsung-tzu, 430
Huk movement, Philippines, 61-63
Humphrey, Hubert, 175
Huntington, Samuel P., 107
Huong, Tran Van, 112, 113
Hwang Yong-ju, 218-219

Identity, 20-25, 79, 421, 425
Iemoto principle, 22-23
Ikeda, Daisaku, 170, 440
Immigration quota, 428
India, 7
  China, relations with, 50, 51, 178-179, 273
  communism in, 46, 48-51, 61
  economy, 315, 324-338
  Gandhi, Indira, 28-29
  industry, 326-337, 404, 410
  navy, 380
  neutralism, 32-33, 263, 264, 266, 272
  nuclear weapons, 381, 388, 389
  Pakistan, relations with, 261-262, 264-269, 275-276
  public enterprise, 324-327
  social structure, 22
  subnational identities, 11, 12
  U.S., relations with, 32-34, 176, 258, 259, 265-272, 274, 326, 332, 385
  on U.S. in Vietnam, 171, 176-179, 442-443
  U.S.S.R., relations with, 48-51, 268-271, 327, 329-330, 334-336, 350
Individual identity, 20-25
Indonesia
  communism in, 46, 56-60
  economy, 396-397, 398, 400-403
  independence, 172
  industry, 396-397, 402-403, 410
  Japan, relations with, 342
  natural resource development, 402-403
  public enterprise, 320-322, 396-397, 398, 401-402
  subnational identities, 11, 12
  Suharto regime, 174-175, 401
  Sukarno regime, 173, 174
  U.S., relations with, 58, 174-175, 396-397, 400-401
  on U.S. in Vietnam, 171-176
  U.S.S.R., relations with, 56-57
Indo-Pakistan war (1965), 33, 269, 272
Industry, 316, 318
  in India, 326-327, 404, 410
  in Indonesia, 396-397, 402-403, 410
  in Malaysia, 404
  in Pakistan, 326-327, 410
  private enterprise, 319, 320, 325, 397-398, 408, 410
  public enterprise, 315, 319-327, 329-332, 335-337, 395-404, 408, 410-411

Inoki, Masamichi, 169
Inouye, Daniel, 429
Integral Coach Factory, 337
Inter-American Development Bank, 400
Intercontinental ballistic missile (ICBM) systems, 288, 290, 291
International Atomic Energy Agency, 286
International Control Commission (ICC), 176
International monetary crisis, 163
Iqbal, Sir Muhammad, 261
Iran, 277
Iraq, 374
Isaacs, Harold R., 21
Ismail Bin Abdul Rahman, 191
Israel, John, 71
Iwashima, Hisao, 296

Jacoby, Annalee, 75
Jamaat-e-Islami, 324
Japan
    burden-sharing issue, 282-284, 294, 369, 382, 387, 388
    China, relations with, 69-78, 81, 83, 84, 164, 165, 257, 348-350, 386-387, 433-438, 440-443
    communism in, 63-65
    debt issue, 277-280
    economy, 30, 162-163, 277-278, 338-350, 431-432
    export credits, 342, 343
    foreign investment in, 341, 344
    Hiroshima, 428, 429, 431
    identity, 22-23
    Indonesia, relations with, 342
    Korea, relations with (pre-1945), 9, 18, 133, 138-139, 141-142
    Manchuria, relations with, 70, 71, 160, 164, 165, 257
    military sales, 385-386
    modernization, 8, 63
    navy, 300-303
    Nixon moves, 278, 282-283, 431
    North Korea, relations with, 228-229, 231-232, 234-235
    nuclear issue, 260, 284-299, 302-303, 368, 381, 387-389
    nuclear umbrella of U.S. and, 279-280, 290-291
    Okinawa issue, 16-17, 161-162, 278, 282, 285, 346
    pan-Asianism, 350
    Philippines, relations with, 340-342
    primogeniture in, 22
    public enterprise, 343
    racism and, 427-433
    reparations program, 339
    requital, doctrine of, 431
    Russo-Japanese War, 10
    security treaty with U.S., 64, 280-283, 295, 298-300, 369, 382-383, 386, 388, 389
    social mobilization, 258
    social structure, 22-23
    South Korea, relations with, 152, 212, 214-217, 220, 222, 226-230, 238-239, 242-243, 342, 366-367
    Taiwan, relations with, 17-19

Thailand, relations with, 340-342
total force concept, 283, 287-288, 294, 387
U.S. bases and, 278-279, 299-303, 381, 382
Vietnam, relations with, 164, 170-171, 431, 433
    on U.S. in Vietnam, 160-171, 198
    withdrawal issue, 368-369
    yen settlement bloc, 347, 442
Japanese-Americans, 428
Japanese Exclusion Act of 1924, 428
Japanese Overseas Economic Cooperation Fund, 397
Java, 56, 58, 60
Johnson, Chalmers, 72-78, 121, 259
Johnson, Lyndon B., 179, 181, 332, 440
Joint ventures, 399, 405-407
Juche policy, North Korea, 142-145
Just, Ward, 184, 198-199

Kahlin, George McT., 57
Kaihara, Osamu, 300-301
Kan Mung Bong, 218
Kang Mun-dong, 186-187
Kashmir, 277
Kasuga, Ikko, 299
Kautsky, John H., 6
Kennan, George, 265, 280, 367-368
Kennedy, John F., 116, 176, 270, 271
Kerala, 50, 51, 52
Khanh, Nguyen, 112, 117
Khmer ethnic minority, 107
Khrushchev, Nikita, 144, 268
Kidron, Michael, 328-329
Kim Chong-p'il, 212-215, 226, 323, 439-440
Kim Dae-jung, 187, 224, 230
Kim Hong-ch'ol, 188, 220
Kim Il-sung, 132, 136-150, 152, 211, 219, 223, 231-237
Kim Ku, 238, 240
Kim Kyu-sik, 240
Kim Sam-kyu, 211
Kim Sung-eun, 187
Kim Tu-bong, 137, 139
Kim Van Kieu, 15
Kintner, William, 292-294, 298
Kishi, Nobusuke, 228
Kissinger, Henry A., 10-11, 160-161, 224, 276, 292, 423
Kokka-shugi, 432, 433
Kong Le, 196
Kono, Fumihiko, 294
Korea: see also North Korea; South Korea
    Japan, relations with (pre-1945), 9, 18, 133, 138-139, 141-142
Korean Fatherland Restoration Association, 138, 141
Korean Independence League, 139
Korean Liberation Army, 215
Korean Revolutionary Army, 139, 141
Korean War, 147-149, 265
Kubo, Takuya, 291
Kumaramangalam, K. S., 178
Kuomintang, 17, 19, 69-75, 77, 79-82
Kuril islands, 64
Kust, Matthew, 319

Kusumowidagdo, Suwito, 173
Ky, Nguyen Cao, 112

Laird, Melvin, 283, 287-289, 291, 292, 300
Lambert, Richard, 34
Land reform
    in China, 76, 77
    in Vietnam, 91-92, 104
Landon, Kenneth, 192
Lansdale, Edward G., 119
Lao Dong party, 114
Laos
    student movement, 197
    subnational identities, 11, 12
    on U.S. in Vietnam, 189-190, 196-197
Laswell, Harold D., 24
League of Nations, 257
Lee Chong-sik, 139, 211
Lee Dong-whan, 243
Lee Kuan Yew, 30, 179-182, 440
Lee Man Sup, 218
Lee Seung-hwa, 137
Lenin, V. I., 48
Leninism, 8
Levenson, Joseph R., 80
Lewis, John P., 336-337
Li Sung-gi, 146
Liaquat Ali Khan, 265
Licensing agreements, 405, 406, 407
Lichauco, Alejandro, 341
Lin Piao, 89
Lippmann, Walter, 257
Lon Nol, 195
"Long Live the Victory of the People's
    War" (Lin Piao), 89
López, Salvador P., 184
Luan, Father Cao Van, 116-117
Lyman, Princeton, 225

Macapagal, Diosdado, 182
MacArthur, Douglas, 429
Madiun revolt of 1948, Indonesia, 57-59
Magsaysay, Ramón, 62
Makoto, Oda, 167
Malaysia, 9
    communism in, 52-53
    oil industry, 404
    public enterprise, 320
    on U.S. in Vietnam, 189, 190-192
Malik, Adam, 174
Management contracts, 405, 406, 407
Manchuria, 70, 71, 160, 164, 165, 257
Mansfield, Mike, 210-211, 367
Mao Tse-tung, 32, 47, 70, 80, 81, 83
Maoism, 79, 80, 90
Maphilindo, 14, 424, 441
Marcos, Ferdinand, 28, 62, 182-184,
    316-317
Marshall, George C., 266
Marwaris, 324-325
Marxism-Leninism, 47, 91
Matsumoto, Shunichi, 168
Matsutani, Makoto, 165-166
Mauritius, 373-374
McAlister, John T., Jr., 78, 120
McGhee, George, 266
McGovern, George, 371
McNamara, Robert, 117

Memons, 324
Mencius, 430
Metternich, Klemens von, 255
Michael, Franz, 75
Miki, Takeo, 169
Military sales, 383-386
Millar, T. B., 374
Minh, Duong Van, 104, 112, 117
Minzoku-shugi, 432, 433, 438
Mishima, Yukio, 170
Miyazawa, Kiichi, 298, 366
Modernization, 8, 63, 431
Modjopahit dynasty, Java, 60
Mohammed Ali Jinnah, 266
Momoi, Makoto, 281, 302-303
Montagnard peoples, 107, 151
Morgenthau, Hans, 254
Moriyama, Shingo, 348-349
Morris-Jones, W. H., 275
Moslem League, 27, 49, 50, 51, 261, 275,
    324
Moslems, 12, 13, 56-60, 261-263, 323-324
Mountbatten plan, 262
Mukerji, Dilip, 330
Multinational corporations, 5, 311, 312,
    314, 318, 345, 399, 405-406
Multipolar imagery, 254
Mushakoji, Kinhide, 169
Musso, 57
Mylai, 429

Nagasaki, 428
Nair, Kusum, 410
Nakasone, Yasuhiro, 162, 294, 388
Narayan, Jayaprakash, 29
Nation-building, 4, 9, 111, 255
National Liberation Front (NLF), Vietnam,
    112-115, 149
National Salvation movement, China, 71
National Union Front, Vietnam, 97
Nativism, 8
Naval bilateral nuclear force (BLF), 284-285
Naval capability, 284-285, 289, 296, 297,
    299-302, 369, 370, 375, 376, 379,
    380, 382, 387
Nehru, Jawaharlal, 32-33, 46, 48-51, 87,
    176, 259, 266, 267, 275, 325
Nepal, 55, 443
Neutralism, 32-33, 263, 264, 266, 272
New Vietnam Revolutionary party, 91, 93,
    95
Nguyen An Ninh association, 91
Nixon, Richard M., 46, 143, 164, 170, 179,
    188, 197, 266, 268, 276, 278,
    282-283, 291, 292, 295, 346, 432
North Korea
    China, relations with, 82, 138-139,
        142-145, 364, 367, 370, 438-440
    communism in, 132, 136-150
    economy, 31, 145-147, 232-234
    Japan, relations with, 228-229, 231-232,
        234-235, 438-440
    Juche policy, 142-145
    Kim Il-sung regime, 132, 136-150
    Korean War, 147-148, 265
    military self-reliance, 147
    Pueblo incident, 148, 285
    unification issue, 209-213, 216-226,

229-232, 236-237, 241, 243-244, 363-365, 367, 438-440
united front strategy, 149-150
U.S., relations with, 148, 209, 232, 364, 367, 368, 370
U.S.S.R., relations with, 132, 136-137, 139, 142-145, 147, 237-238, 367
North Vietnam: see Vietnam
Northeastern People's Revolutionary Army (NPRA), China, 138, 139
Nuclear nonproliferation treaty (NPT), 286-287, 388-389
Nuclear weapons, 258, 260, 279-280, 284-291, 293-294, 302-303, 368, 375, 380-382, 387-389
Nye, Sir Archibald, 264

O Yŏng Jin, 140
Oh Ki-sup, 135, 137
Oil policy, 313-314, 327-330, 404
Oka, Takashi, 99-100, 122
Okimoto, Daniel I., 167
Okinawa, 16-17, 161-162, 278, 282, 285, 346
Olson, Lawrence, 167
Omori, Minoru, 168
Onorato, Michael, 184
Organization of Petroleum Exporting Countries (OPEC), 10, 313-314, 369
Orwell, George, 441
Osgood, Robert, 364, 367
Ostpolitik, 224
Overseas Private Investment Corporation (OPIC), 404-405, 407

Pacification, 121-122
Packard, David, 299
Pai Kao (White Danger) student movement, Thailand, 195
Paik Too-chin, 241
Pak Hon-yong, 135, 136-137, 150
Pakistan, 11-14, 49, 50, 51, 443
Ayub Khan regime, 323, 324
Bangladesh, 11, 12, 14, 28, 33, 261, 267, 268, 275-276, 313, 443
China, relations with, 269, 270, 272-274
creation of, 261-263
economy, 27
India, relations with, 261-262, 264-269, 275-276
industry, 326-327, 410
private enterprise, 397-398
public enterprise, 323-324, 397-398
U.S., relations with, 34, 176, 177, 259, 263-277, 385
U.S.S.R., relations with, 269, 270, 273, 274
Pan-Asianism, 82, 350, 433-435
Pan-Malayan Islamic party, 53
Pang Hak-se, 137
Park Chong-hui, 28, 210, 213-217, 219, 223-227, 229, 230, 237
Passin, Herbert, 23-24
Patel, Sardar Vallabhai, 262
Pathet Lao, 55, 196, 197
Patrick, Hugh, 346
Pearl Harbor, 257

Peasant nationalism debate, China, 72-79
Pentagon Papers, 117, 167, 171
People's Republic of China, 7
communism in, 47, 61, 69-84, 89, 90, 121
Cultural Revolution, 32, 83
economy, 30, 80
growth-with-equity, 29
India, relations with, 50, 51, 178-179, 273
Japan, relations with, 69-78, 81, 83, 84, 164, 165, 257, 348-350, 386-387, 433-438, 440-443
land reform, 76, 77
Maoism, 79, 80, 90
North Korea, relations with, 82, 138-139, 142-145, 364, 367, 370, 438-440
nuclear weapons, 258, 284, 290-291, 303
Pakistan, relations with, 269, 270, 272-274
peasant nationalism debate, 72-79
requital, doctrine of, 430
revolution of 1911, 17-18
social structure, 22
South Korea, relations with, 220
spheres of influence policy and, 425, 426
student movement in, 71, 72
subnational identities, 11
Taiwan issue, 17-20, 372
U.S. relations with, 82, 83, 170, 209, 221, 231, 244, 258-259, 294, 370-372, 386, 407, 427
U.S.S.R., relations with, 45, 50, 82-83 143, 144, 231, 375, 434, 440
Vietnam, relations with, 15, 425-426
People's Revolutionary party (PRP), Vietnam, 114, 115
People's war strategy, 80, 89
Perkins, Dwight, 400
Pertamina, 321-322, 402
Peshawar installations, Pakistan, 267, 270
Petroleum: see Oil policy
Phat, Huynh Than, 114
Philippines, 9
communism in, 61-63
economy, 315-317
Huk movement, 61-63
Japan, relations with, 340-342
racism, 428
subnational identities, 11
U.S. relations with, 62, 63, 182-184, 315-317, 373, 376
Vietnam, involvement in, 182-184
Phillips Petroleum Company, 320
Phu, Pham Van, 104
Pike, Douglas, 97, 111
Pleiku, Vietnam, 104
Pleime-Chu Prong struggle, 118-119
Pochonbo, battle of, 138, 139, 141
Pomeroy, William, 62
Pope, Allan, 58
Popular Front, 48, 49
Population control, 317, 318
Powers, Francis Gary, 270
Prasad, Rajendra, 13

Primogeniture, in Japan, 22
Private enterprise, 319, 320, 325, 397-398, 408, 410
Protectionism, 343, 346, 347, 349, 350, 369, 427, 432, 438, 441, 443
Public enterprise, 315, 319-327, 329-332, 335-337, 395-404, 408, 410-411
Pueblo incident, 148, 285
Puey Ungphakorn, 195
PUSRI fertilizer plant, Indonesia, 396, 397
Pye, Lucian W., 21

Quang, Thich Tri, 109

Race, Jeffrey, 78
Racism, 428-433
Rahman, Ziaur, 28
Rajagopalachari, C. R., 177, 268
Rama I, 192
Ravenal, Earl, 426, 427
Razak, Tun, 52, 191
Recto, Claro, 30
Regionalism, 4, 5, 421-424, 427, 433, 438
Reid, Escott, 408
Reischauer, Edwin O., 46, 165, 430, 436, 437
Reparations program, Japan, 339
Requital, doctrine of, 430-431
Revelle, Roger, 333
Revolutionary Development program, Vietnam, 122
Rhee Syngman, 131, 133, 135, 137, 149, 210, 238-241, 243
Ridgway, Matthew B., 131, 198
Romulo, Carlos P., 184
Roosa, Robert, 405, 406
Roosevelt, Franklin D., 238
Rosovsky, Henry, 350
Rostow, Walt W., 26, 179, 254
Royama, Michio, 438
Rusk, Dean, 181
Russett, Bruce, 257
Russo-Japanese War, 10

Sacks, Milton, 90, 98
Sadli, Mohammed, 348, 400
Sainteny, Jean, 98
Sakhalin Island, 65
Salim, Emil, 340, 401
Samuelson, Paul, 312, 411
Santri-abangan conflict, Indonesia, 56-60, 321
Sarekat Islam organization, 56
Sarit Thanarat, 193
Sato, Eisaku, 12, 161, 169, 285-286, 287, 346, 432, 443
Scalapino, Robert A., 63, 211
Schram, Stuart, 75
Schwartz, Benjamin I., 75
Scigliano, Robert, 323
Scorched earth tactics, 74
Seabased Antiballistic Missile Intercept System (SABMIS), 284, 288-289, 291
Search and destroy strategy, 118
Seidensticker, Edward, 8, 366
Selden, Armistead, Jr., 291
Selden, Mark, 76-78

Senkaku Islands, 349
Shaplen, Robert, 124
Shaw, Robert, 410
Sheehan, Neil, 119
Shiina, 243
Shim Keun Dan, 218
Shimoda, Takeso, 161, 286
Shin Tae-wan, 223-224
Sihanouk, Norodom, 195, 197
Sikander Hyat Khan, 261
Singapore, 373
    foreign investment, 315
    on U.S. in Vietnam, 179-182
Singer, Hans, 319
Singh, J. J., 177
Sisouk na Champassak, 197
Sjahrir, Sutan, 57
Snow, Edgar, 81
Slote, Walter, 21
So Min Ho, 219
Social mobilization, 5, 9, 255, 256
Socotra, island of, 373
Soedjatmoko, 172, 409
Somalia, 374
Sorensen, Jay B., 297
Souphanouvong, Prince, 55
South Korea
    Chang regime, 211, 212
    China, relations with, 220
    communism in, 135, 148-150
    "development first" approach, 224-227
    economy, 31, 224-227, 323
    foreign investment in, 315
    Japan, relations with, 152, 212, 214-217, 220, 222, 226-230, 238-239, 242-243, 342, 366-367, 438-440
    Korean War, 147, 149
    military coup (1961), 211, 212-213
    nuclear weapons, 381
    Park regime, 27, 28, 212-217, 224-227, 323
    public enterprise, 322, 323
    student movement, 211-212
    unification issue, 209-213, 216-226, 229-232, 236-237, 241, 243-244, 363-365, 367, 438-440
    U.S., relations with, 30, 131, 135, 147-148, 151-152, 185-189, 212-214, 224, 226, 237-244, 256, 363-368, 370, 378, 381
    Vietnam, involvement in, 185-189
    Yosu revolt, 216
South Vietnam: see Vietnam
Southeast Asian Ministerial Conferences on Transport and Education, 423
Souvanna Phouma, 196
Spheres of influence, concept of, 424-427
Sri Lanka
    public enterprise, 322
    subnational identities, 11, 12
Stalin, Joseph, 48, 50
Standard Vacuum, 328, 402
Stans, Maurice, 346
State, U.S. Department of, 114-115, 118
Steel, Ronald, 425
Stevenson, Charles, 376-377
Strategic Arms Limitation Talks (SALT I

and II), 288-290, 298, 382
Strategic balance, 374-380
Student movement
    in Laos, 197
    in South Korea, 211-212
    in Thailand, 195
    in China, 71, 72
Study of the Vietnamese Revolution (Dao
    Duy Anh), 90
Subic Bay naval base, Philippines, 376
Subnationalism, 4, 5, 11-20, 48-51, 89, 111,
    421
Suh Dae-sook, 138
Suh In-suk, 186, 187, 219, 221, 222
Suharto, 28, 59
Suhrawardy, H. S., 272, 274
Sukarno, Achmed, 46, 56-60, 87, 321
Sul Kuk-hwan, 188, 220, 221
Sun Yat-sen, 7, 17, 70, 79-81, 84, 93, 434
Sun Yat-sen, Madame, 81, 272
Sunario, 173
Sung, Dang van, 94, 132
Suwarto, 174

Taft-Katsura treaty of 1905, 214, 232, 242
Tagore, Rabindranath, 7
Taiwan, 372, 382, 437
    China, relations with, 17-20, 372
    foreign investment in, 315
    Japan, relations with, 17-19
    public enterprise, 322
    U.S., relations with, 30
Takeyama, Yasuo, 292
Tamil Communists, 61
Tan Chee Khoon, 52
Tanaka, Kakuei, 170, 229, 434
Tasrif, S. S., 175
Tay Son revolt, Vietnam, 15
Taylor, George E., 74
Terrorism, 121
Thailand, 9
    communism in, 53-54
    economy, 30
    Japan and, 340-342
    public enterprise, 320
    student movement, 195
    subnational identities, 11
    U.S., relations with, 373, 377-378
    on U.S. in Vietnam, 189, 192-196
Thakin Soe, 54
Than Tun, 54
Thanat Khoman, 193, 194
Thang, Nguyen Duc, 119
Thanh, Au Truong, 113
Thanom Kittikachorn, 195
Thao, Trinh Dinh, 114
Thapar, Romesh, 270
Theatre nuclear deterrence, concept of,
    287-288, 375
Thi, Nguyen Chanh, 104, 118
Thieu, Nguyen Van, 103, 113-114, 118
Tho, Nguyen Huu, 114
Thomson, James, 429
Thor-Delta rocket, 386
Tied loans, 407
Tonghak movement, Korea, 132
Tonkin Gulf incident, 116
Total force strategic concept, 283, 287-288,

294, 387
Trager, Frank N., 109
Trai, Tang Thi Thanh, 123
Truman, Harry S., 238
Trung, Nguyen Van, 122-123
Truong, Thao, 110
Tucker, Robert, 388, 444

Ung Uy, Prince, 96
Union of Soviet Socialist Republics
    China, relations with, 45, 50, 82-83,
        143, 144, 231, 375, 434, 440
    India, relations with, 48-51, 268-271,
        327, 329-330, 334-336, 350
    Indonesia, relations with, 56-57
    North Korea, relations with, 132,
        136-137, 139, 142-145, 147,
        237-238, 367
    nuclear weapons, 289-291, 293-294
    overseas bases, 373-374
    Pakistan, relations with, 269, 270, 273,
        274
    public enterprise, 398
    U.S., relations with, 289-291, 293-294,
        299, 301
    Zhdanov line, 48, 54-55
United front strategy, 90, 133-134, 149-150
United Malay National Organization (UM-
    NO), 53
United Nations, 218, 219, 364
United Nations Conference on Trade and
    Development (UNCTAD), 412, 444
United Nations Development Program, 408
United Nations Economic Commission for
    Asia and the Far East, 27
United Nations Industrial Development
    Organization, 408

Van, Tran Van, 113
van der Kroef, Justus, 59
Van Slyke, Lyman, 79
Vandenberg, Hoyt, 265
Vernon, Raymond, 312, 319, 399, 406
Vientiane, 196
Viet Cong, 118
Viet Minh, 96-97, 99-101, 124, 149, 194
Vietnam
    army, 102, 118-120
    bombing of, 165, 167-168, 173-174,
        177, 180, 429
    Cambodia on U.S. in, 189-190, 197-198
    China, relations with, 15, 425-426
    civil service, 102-104, 111
    collaboration, 100-104
    communism in, 47, 61, 87-89, 108-109,
        114-124, 149-151
    Diem regime, 100-104, 108, 111, 116
    economy, 322-323
    French in, 16, 93, 95, 97-103, 106, 111,
        115, 116, 123-124
    Geneva partition, 88, 111
    India on U.S. in, 171, 176-179, 442-443
    Indonesia on U.S. in, 171-176
    Japan, relations with, 164, 170-171,
        431, 433
    Japan on U.S. in, 160-171, 198
    Ky regime, 109, 112, 113
    land reform, 91-92, 104

Vietnam (*cont.*)
   Laos on U.S. in, 189-190, 196-197
   Malaysia on U.S. in, 189, 190-192
   pacification, 121-122
   Philippines on U.S. in, 182-184
   Pleime-Chu Prong struggle, 118-119
   racism and, 429-430
   religion, 105-107
   search and destroy strategy, 118
   Singapore on U.S. in, 179-182
   social structure, 22
   South Korea on U.S. in, 185-189
   southern solution, 111-115
   subnationalism, 89, 111
   terrorism, 121
   Thailand on U.S. in, 189, 192-196
   Thieu regime, 109, 113-114
   unification issue, 107-111
   united front strategy, 90
Vietnam Nationalist party (VNQDD), 93, 94, 122, 322
Vittachi, Tarzie, 318
Vy, Nguyen, 110

Wakaizumi, Kei, 281, 366
Walinsky, Louis, 408
Wang Gung-wu, 190
Watanuki, Joji, 433
Weinstein, Franklin, 172, 174

Weinstein, Martin, 280, 281
West Germany, 223, 335
West Irian, 58
West Pakistan: *see* Pakistan
Wheeler, Earle G., 285
White, Theodore, 75, 82
White, William S., 175
Whiting, Allen S., 82
Wilson, David, 53
World Bank, 329, 331, 332, 333, 337, 397, 408

Yahya Khan, 275, 276
Yang Lien-sheng, 430
Yatsugi, Kazuo, 228
Yemen, 374
Yen Hsi-shan, 73, 76-77
Yenan faction, 137, 139
Yi Hyo-sun, 150
Yi Yong-hùi, 225, 439
Yŏ Un-hyŏng, 134, 135, 238-241
Yokosuka naval base, 376
Yoshida, Shigeru, 280, 281
Yosu revolt (1948), Korea, 216
Yun Po-sun, 186, 187, 215, 230

Zagoria, Donald, 61